The Golden Age of RADIO

An Illustrated Companion

Denis Gifford

B.T. Batsford Ltd · London

For Big, Stinker,
Mrs Bagwash, Ernie, Nausea,
Lewis the Goat, Basil and Lucy,
Mr Walker, and all at
Top Flat, Broadcasting House

Also by Denis Gifford:

The Illustrated Who's Who in British Films
The British Film Catalogue
The Pictorial History of Horror Movies
Karloff: The Man, The Monster, The Movies
Chaplin
British Cinema
Science Fiction Film
The Great Cartoon Stars
Run Adolf Run
Test Your N.Q. (Nostalgia Quotient)
The International Book of Comics
The British Comic Catalogue
Victorian Comics
Happy Days: 100 Years of Comics

ISBN 0 7134 4234 4

Photoset by Servis Filmsetting Ltd, Manchester
Printed in Great Britain by
Butler & Tanner Ltd, Frome, Somerset
for the Publisher
B.T. Batsford Ltd
4 Fitzhardinge Street
London W1H 0AH

STATION CHART

BERGEN 352·9

OSLO 1154

MOTALA 1389

GÖTEBORG 318·8

HÖRBY 265·3

KALUNDBORG 1261

COPENHAGEN 255·1

HAMBURG 331·9

HUIZEN 1875

HILVERSUM 301·5

BERLIN 356·7

POZNAN 345·6

COLOGNE 455·9

ANTWERP 204·8

LEIPZIG 382·2

BRESLAU 315·8

LE 247·3

BRUSSELS 483·9 & 321·9

FRANKFURT 251

LUXEMBOURG 1304

NÜRNBERG 236·8

PRAGUE 470·2

VIENNA 506·8

STRASBOURG 349·2

STUTTGART 522·6

The
Golden Age of
RADIO

Foreword by Richard Murdoch

It would be difficult to overpraise Denis Gifford's painstaking efforts in compiling this huge history of Radio. What hours he must have spent rummaging in the archives.

Most of the programmes mentioned would have been broadcast by the Variety Department of the BBC, now superseded by the Department of Drama and Light Entertainment. Indeed, what is now called Radio was known in my early days as The Wireless. I recall a letter from my young niece in Ceylon: 'We heard Uncle Dick on the wiles.'

This volume is of particular interest to me as I have taken part in so many of the programmes mentioned, not only those of the BBC but also Radio Luxembourg. Here it must be admitted that one worked for Radio Luxembourg mostly to earn a little money. The content of those old variety shows on Luxembourg was never quite up to BBC standards.

On reading through the book I lost count of the number of shows I had appeared in. When one is in a successful series one is constantly appearing as guest in other people's shows.

Having been in three long-running, successful BBC variety shows – *Band Waggon*, *Much-Binding-in-the-Marsh* and *The Men From the Ministry* – I have probably taken part in more programmes than anyone. I was, in fact, co-scriptwriter of the first two mentioned. I recall with pleasure 'Puzzle Corner' in *Monday Night at Eight*, *Friday Roundabout*, *Workers' Playtime*, and *Variety Bandbox*; and I greatly enjoyed *Housewives' Choice*, especially in the early days when we could take home the postcards and compile our own programmes. One could have filled a whole hour of requests for Gracie Fields singing 'Bless This House'. Two requests I well remember: 'Will you please play some barrel-organ music so that we can tape it as we need some for our school play', and 'Please play "Island in the Sun" sung by Arabella Fontaine'.

I consider Denis Gifford's title thoroughly appropriate as the early days of the wireless were so wonderful! I hope others will get as much pleasure out of browsing through this excellent volume as I have done.

Richard Murdoch
4 February 1985

Denis Gifford with Bobby Jaye (producer)
announcing his nostalgic radio series *Sounds
Familiar*

Picture acknowledgements
The author and publisher make grateful ac-
knowledgement to the following (numerals
represent page numbers): The Amalgamated
Press Ltd. 21, 93, 105; The Argus Press Ltd.
177; Ernest Benn Ltd. 49; The BBC 24, 25, 38,
66, 99, 115, 142, 169, 178, 205, 231, 250, 255,
299; Robert Hale Ltd. 220; Insignia Books 282;
The Marconi Company 40, 165; Denny Miller
197; The Thames Publishing Co. Ltd. 204;
Thames Television 120; Dennis Yates 221. The
majority of the pictures are from the author's
own collection of radio memorabilia. The radio
set photographed for the jacket was kindly lent
by Morgans (vintage radio shop), London.

Preface: 'Pin Back Your Lug'oles'*

Only one magazine ever came to our house, *Radio Times*, a thick lump on the doormat every Friday, price twopence. In the thirties going to the pictures was a rare treat, almost on a par with pantomimes, so listening to the wireless was my – our – only entertainment. You had to work at it too, in those days. And not just turning knobs to change wavelengths and tune in: there were batteries to be bought and accumulators to be topped up. This meant a lug round to Old Hooky's shop, and a lug back in due course. You can always tell a radio child by the acid scars on his hand.

What are the perimeters of the Golden Age of Radio? Easy: they are defined exactly by my own life as a listener. I can remember jumping about whenever Jack Payne played the exciting novelty number, 'Fire! Fire!', and imitating his 'Sez you! Sez me!' in the comedy duet about Sergeant Flagg and Sergeant Quirt. And as, by quickly referring to the entry for the BBC Dance Orchestra, I see that Jack Paynes' tenure of it terminated on 11 March 1932, when I was four, I can pinpoint my awakening interest in the wireless with reasonable accuracy. It is more easy to recall the end of the Golden Age. One by one favourite shows faded from the air, some transferring to television: *Hancock's Half Hour* is a classic case in point. The BBC themselves marked the grave for good when the Home Service and the Light and Third Programmes, became Radios 4, 2 and 1, and 3, on 30 September 1967. The first real sign of decline came in the week of 15 February 1957, when *Radio Times* moved all the television programmes, which had been tucked behind each day's radio, up to the front pages. Then on 6 October 1960 *Radio Times* changed the running order of the week away from Lord Reith's traditional Sunday to Saturday, to ITV's weekend-oriented Saturday to Friday: the end of the wireless world as we knew it.

This book, therefore, takes its main span as the thirties to the fifties, but not too strictly. It looks forward to the mid-sixties (after all, what book on radio entertainment could possible exclude *I'm Sorry I'll Read That Again?*), and tunes back to the twenties. Indeed, the earliest years of broadcasting became so fascinating as I dug deeper into these unrecorded radio times, that I decided to extend the original scope of this book to include as many 'firsts' in broadcasting and programmes as I could find. So, programmes and personalities apart, you will also find entries herewith for more general subjects. These include the BBC itself, both as Company and as Corporation, the many prewar commercial stations now narrowed down to Radio Luxembourg alone (and, by the way, the hardest to research – having no public duty, the commercial companies kept no archives), and topics like Comedy, Quizzes, Serials, and even the Six Pips!

Compiling this book has been an exhausting pleasure, but one which will, I trust, bring you pleasure without the exhaust. I hope it will also place on convenient record the facts, as well as the achievements, of British popular broadcasting in its heyday. Until now these have lived only in the memories of we, the radio generation. The regret is that they cannot all be revived in their full glory of words and music.

DENNIS GIFFORD
Sydenham 1985

---

*Cyril Fletcher, 1939

Using this Companion

The arrangement of entries is basically alphabetical; personalities are listed by surname, while fictional characters are arranged by their first name. Titles of programmes and series are arranged by the first word in the title (ignoring any article). In other words, you will find Richard Murdoch under M for Murdoch, but Nausea Bagwash under N for Nausea. Nausea's mother, Mrs Bagwash, having no known Christian name, is under M for Mrs. *The Will Hay Programme* is under W, *The Man in Black* under M. Entries based on initials come at the start of each letter group; thus BBC is at the start of the Bs, and not following the Ba of *Band Waggon*. There are many cross-references, and these appear in the body of the entries as capitals and small capitals. Thus, in the *Band Waggon* entry, both ARTHUR ASKEY and RICHARD MURDOCH are in capitals and small capitals, and so you should look under their own main name entries for further information.

This Companion concentrates on shows and performers as far as main entry titles go. Producers and script-writers are given within show and series entries wherever possible, but only have main entries under their own names when they are also performers (as with Bob Monkhouse and Denis Goodwin). Such teams, by the way, are entered under the surname of the first member.

Most of the programmes given in the book were transmitted by the BBC, although the early commercial stations broadcasting in English from the Continent are covered in some detail. Where no information is given to the contrary, programmes can be taken as BBC transmissions. Where a date is given for the appearance of a performer or a character, it can be taken as that of the first appearance; the character may have carried on for a long time subsequently.

AEF Programme

Radio service for the Allied Expeditionary Forces which opened up on 285 metres the day after D-Day, on 7 June 1944. The signature tune, 'Oranges and Lemons', was followed by *Rise and Shine*, an ad-lib disc-jockey show co-hosted by Sergeant Dick Dudley from the USA and AC2 Ronnie Waldman from the BBC. Programmes were split between British and Canadian forces and the Americans, who brought in their own popular series, *Amos and Andy*, COMMAND PERFORMANCE, and the BOB HOPE SHOW. Major Glenn Miller and his American Band of the AEF broadcast frequently despite the obstructiveness of BBC policy under Maurice Gorham (see *Star Spangled Radio* by Kirby and Harris, published in 1948). There were also regular Wednesday-night broadcasts by the British Band of the AEF conducted by Regimental Sergeant-Major George Melachrino, often backing such guest stars as Bing Crosby, Marlene Dietrich, Jessie Matthews and Webster Booth. The AEF announcers included Jean Metcalfe and Margaret Hubble, who closed down the service on D-Day plus 417 (28 July 1945).

AFN

Compulsive late-night listening in the post-war forties, and Britain's only experience of 100 per cent American radio. This was the American Forces Network, which moved into Europe with the advancing Yankees, bringing the sounds of home to GIs dissatisfied with the Anglo-American programmes of the AEF service. The BBC lost the right to transmit the de-sponsored JACK BENNY, FRED ALLEN, BOB HOPE, CHARLIE McCARTHY shows, and deprived English ears needed to tune to the fading AFN on 547 metres medium wave, Munich and Stuttgart. Late-night reception was best, which was fine for record fans who were able to

enjoy the ad lib humours of DUFFLE BAG, MIDNIGHT IN MUNICH, and Ralph 'Muff-it' Moffatt.

Accent on Rhythm

Pleasant musical series starring the Bachelor Girls (Maria Perilli, Rita Williams, Donna la Bourdais) and Peter Akister. Produced by James Moody; first heard 4 August 1944.

Accent on Youth

Michael Miles presented this revue series by professional artistes under 21 years of age from 10 January 1952. The alphabetically arranged cast was Jean Brown, John Charlesworth, Leslie Crowther, Max Devine, Ann Hart, Peter Keaton, Dilys Laye, Shani Wallis, plus the Ilford Girls' Choir and the Revue Orchestra conducted by Robert Busby. Script by Peter Jeffries, producer Frederick Piffard.

Ack-Ack Beer-Beer

Morse code words for the initials of the Anti-Aircraft and Balloon Barrage Commands, used as the title of a twice-weekly series broadcast especially for them every Monday and Thursday on the FORCES PROGRAMME from 1 July 1940. The first programme included SANDY MACPHERSON at the BBC THEATRE ORGAN, an Ack-Ack sketch by Tommy Thompson, and a Topical Talk. Programme Two introduced 'Up to the Bell', a boxing serial written by Jack Jones, records presented by DORIS ARNOLD, and a General Knowledge Test. Later came 'Rough and Ready' (two willing lads) and 'All For a Tanner', a paperback book revue by John Watt. By December 1942 the features included 'Artists in Uniform', 'Comedy Quiz' and 'Jack Henry and His Friends'. Music came from the Royal Artillery Theatre Orchestra directed by Captain Geary. The series ended on 27 February 1944 with programme No. 324. Featured was the Dance Orchestra of No. 1 Balloon Centre (The Skyrockets) directed by Corporal Paul Fenoulhet. Alfred Dunning produced, and the series signature tune was 'On Target'.

Adolphus

Lauri Lupino Lane played MR MUDDLE-COMBE's irritating office boy in the series OFFICE HOURS (1941). Catchphrase: 'You shouldn't 'ave done that!'

Adolphus Spriggs

Probable brother of Jim Spriggs, although was known to work under the name of Jim Pills. Failed STROLLING VAGABOND whose nasal rendition of Cavan O'Connor's signature song seldom succeeded. Played by SPIKE MILLIGAN in THE GOON SHOW (1955).

Adventure Unlimited (1)

Daily serial replacement for DICK BARTON, commencing 5 April 1948. Episode 1, 'Death in the Jungle', introduced the new hero, Jackson, played by Philip Cunningham. John Sharp played his comedy sidekick, Sam Steed. Written by Basil Dawson, produced by Cameron McClure, with music by Kenneth Pakeman and the old Dick Barton announcer, Hamilton Humphreys.

Adventure Unlimited (2)

'Introducing the many voices of Stephen Jack', this children's serial was sponsored by the Boy Scouts' Association and broadcast on Radio Luxembourg in 1950. One of several stories serialized was *The Red Patrol* by Robert Leighton.

The Air-Do-Wells

Radio concert party (a pun on 'ne'er-do-wells') featuring Eve Becke, Jean Colin, Claud Gardiner, Effie Atherton, Ronnie Hill, Betty Astell and the Three Rhythm Aces, first broadcast 26 July 1934. Later shows added Wilfrid Thomas to sing baritone, Marjorie Stedeford, and BRYAN MICHIE, one of the devisers. The other was Max Kester, and between them they produced.

Air Express From Hollywood

'A thrilling programme of music and glamour from the film city' presented by Max Factor Make-up on RADIO LYONS from 19 December 1937.

Air Raids

The first weekly entertainment series with a title (preceded by CHARLOT'S HOUR): 'Light entertainment in a series of rapid flights planned and landed by Albert de Courville, the well-known theatrical producer, assisted by Jack Padbury's Cosmo Club Six'. It took off on 9 October 1928 for six successive Tuesdays; on board were Ethel Levey, Roma June, Midgie Bradfield, Eric Worsley and Lindie Jeune.

Ajello, Wynne

Soprano who will always be remembered as radio's Snow White: she played the part in the oft-repeated John Watt production of Walt Disney's feature-length cartoon, *Snow White and the Seven Dwarfs*. After making her first broadcast as a coloratura in 1925, she became so popular with listeners and producers that she had clocked up 400 broadcasts by 1935.

Wynne **Ajello**: radio's 'Snow White'

The Al Read Show

'Such is life, life is what you make it', sang Al Read at the start of his occasional series of looks at the lighter side of life, first broadcast 18 September 1951 following his many successful solo spots in variety bills. Producer Ronnie Taylor gave him guest stars JIMMY EDWARDS and Pat Kirkwood, plus music from the Kordites and the Northern Variety Orchestra, but multi-voiced Al only needed himself to converse with. Catchphrases: 'You'll be lucky!' and 'Right, monkey!' The series won the 1953 NATIONAL RADIO AWARD for the most promising new programme, prompting a monthly series from 8 October. Items included 'A Famous Guest', 'A Highlight in Music' and 'The Lifetimers'. The first weekly series started 2 December 1956: 'Al takes life as he finds it and shares the fun with some friends from the world of music.' These were the Kordites and the

NVO conducted by Alyn Ainsworth. The next series started 29 September 1958 with songs by the Allegros.

Al's next series was entitled *Al Read 64* and began 27 September 1964 with Al 'taking the lid off life'. Alan Wheatley was the first guest star, with songs from the Morgan James Duo. Ronnie Taylor scripted and Bill Worsley produced. It was back to the regular title for the 12 December 1965 series, which was stronger musically: the Raindrops, Rawicz and Landauer the pianists, and Woolf Phillips and his Orchestra. In 1976 Read made a comeback with *Al Read Classics*.

A.J. Alan

The first Mystery Man of radio. 'A.J. Alan' was the nom-de-air of a well-spoken gentleman who read his own quirky short stories on the National Programme from 31 January 1924. The first was entitled 'My Adventure in Jermyn Street'. The mystery surrounding his real identity had much to do with his continuing popularity, and he broadcast from Radio Luxembourg from 9 July 1939 for a 15-minute series called *Story Telling*. When he died in 1941 there was some little disappointment to learn that he was really Captain (rtd) Leslie Harrison Lambert, a civil servant. His catchphrase 'Good evening, everyone!' became the title of his book of collected stories (1928).

Album Leaf

Evelyn Laye 'bringing you words and music in retrospect' with Mark Hambourg and Frank Titterton, the BBC Chorus and Revue Orchestra. Written by Aubrey Danvers-Walker, producer Michael North; weekly from 30 September 1941.

Alexander and Mose

Blackface comedy crosstalk act in the style of the American 'Two Black Crows', devised by variety star Billy Bennett when his contract banned him from broadcasting as himself. The names were taken from the songs, 'Alexander's Ragtime Band' and 'Mumbling Mose', and disguised Bennett and the American actor James Carew, who played Alexander, the straight-man of the act. Carew was later replaced by comedian Albert Whelan. Typical phrase: 'Decarbonize yo'self, brudder, decarbonize yo'self!'

Alf 'Awkins

Cockney character created by comedian Leon Cortez in 'APPY 'ARF 'OUR (1939) and *Alf and His Coster Pals* (1942).

The Alfred Marks Show

Series for the comedian, shared with his wife, impressionist Paddie O'Neil. Also appearing were Peter Reeves, Patricia Gilbert, Michael Deacon, and Burt Rhodes and his Orchestra. Script by George Evans, Derek Collyer and Dick Vosburgh; producer Alastair Scott Johnston. First broadcast 1 May 1964.

Alhambra of the Air

Ambitious, 90-minute Sunday night variety series broadcast to celebrate the BBC Silver Jubilee, commencing 12 October 1947. Stars in the first show: ELSIE AND DORIS WATERS, Binnie and Sonnie Hale, Anna Neagle and Michael Wilding, GILLIE POTTER, TED RAY, Beatrice Lillie, Tessie O'Shea, REGINALD FOORT at the organ, Gladys Ripley, Trefor Jones and the Alexandra Choir. Leslie Mitchell was Master of Ceremonies, and the two producers were Tom Ronald and Michael North. A second series started on 6 October 1948: slightly less ambitious, it ran only 60 minutes. Franklin Engelmann was the new MC and the stars were

Alexander and Mose: blackface broadcasters Billy Bennett and Albert Whelan

REVNELL AND WEST, Terry-Thomas and Max Wall for comedy; Norman Woolland, Sarah Churchill and Cyril Cusack for drama; Peter Dawson and the Variety Orchestra conducted by Rae Jenkins for music. Michael North produced.

Ali Oop

Saucy seaside postcard salesman at Foaming-at-the-Mouth: 'Excuse please, meester – you buy nice postcard? Very grimy – oh blimey!' Played by Horace Percival in IT's THAT MAN AGAIN (1941), with the regular exit line: 'I go – I coom back!'

Alka Seltzer Boys

Duettists Browning and Starr, introduced by Bob Danvers-Walker in their sponsored series on RADIO LUXEMBOURG (1938). Signature song: 'Hang On to Happiness', not too difficult when Alka Seltzer provided 'Inner Cleanliness'.

Alka Seltzer Movie Parade

Home-grown successor to the American pro-duced *Alka Seltzer Show* (Curt Massey, Martha Tilton, and Country Washburne and his Band) which had been running on Radio Luxem-bourg from 1952. Desmond Carrington intro-duced music and scenes from the latest films and interviews with future stars. The first programme (2 October 1955) included Doris Day and James Cagney in *Love Me or Leave Me*.

All at Sea

'A laugh on the ocean wave' with Northern comic Ken Platt ('I won't take me coat off, I'm not stoppin'!'), Sydney Tafler as Sid Sharp, Herbert Smith as Signor Goldini, plus the Singing Stewards and the Northern Variety Orchestra conducted by Alyn Ainsworth. Written by Frank Roscoe, produced by Johnny Ammonds. Set sail 21 May 1956.

All Hale

Rare radio series for the famous brother and sister of musical comedy and revue. They played all the parts, and signed off as 'Binnie Hale and Sonnie Hale and Sonnie Hale and Binnie Hale and . . .' (fade out). Supported by Frank Cantell with the Revue Orchestra, producer Michael North, and scripts by Loftus

Wigram and C. Gordon Glover. Most memor-able weekly moment: Sonnie singing 'Picture a country vicarage with ivy on the wall, see the reverend gentleman . . .' always to be inter-rupted by Binnie with: 'Sidney! Stop that filth!' First broadcast 19 May 1946. One of the items was 'Cad's Guide to Radio'. The Hales clocked up a grand total of 131 different characters in the first run of seven programmes. A second series started 27 October and they returned again somewhat belatedly on 7 November 1951, and again on 10 July 1952.

All My Eye

'And Kitty Bluett', to quote the full title. Comedy series for the Australian comedienne, ex-wife to Ted Ray in RAY's A LAUGH, in which she was supported by new Scottish comedian Stanley Baxter, Terry Scott and Patricia Hayes. 'Dispensing the Music is Hutch' (Leslie A. Hutchinson) with Paul Fenoulhet and the Variety Orchestra. Producer Alistair Scott-Johnston; script by Terry Nation and Dick Barry. First broadcast 7 June 1955.

All Star Bill

Major series 'presenting the musical stars of show business in Britain' supported by Stanley Black and the Dance Orchestra. A different comedian compèred each week, the first being Terry-Thomas (8 August 1951), the second PETER SELLERS. The musical stars were Bill Hanson, Vanessa Lee, the Beverley Sisters, Rawicz and Landauer, and the George Mitch-ell Glee Club. The feature item, 'Meet Britain's Composers', began with Harry Parr Davis. The return series began 29 September 1952 with BERNARD BRADEN as compère interrupted by Graham Stark as Ex-Lieutenant Bowser Smythe and the eight-year-old pest, Sylvester. The stars were Donald Peers, Larry Adler with his harmonica, Julie Andrews, and the Malcom Mitchell Trio, with support from the George Mitchell Glee Club and Stanley Black with the Dance Orchestra. Script by Ray Galton and Alan Simpson; producer Dennis Main Wilson.

Allen, Les

Canadian crooner, the first BBC 'staff' crooner with HENRY HALL's Dance Orchestra, and the first of his kind to attract overwhelming adula-tion of lady fans, as demonstrated on the first public appearance of the Band and Les at

RADIOLYMPIA 1933. A former choirboy, he toured Canada singing with the 28th High-landers Band and came to London in 1923 as a saxophonist. Hit songs on record include 'Let's All Sing Like the Birdies Sing', 'Have You Ever Been Lonely' and 'Little Man You've Had a Busy Day'.

All Join In

Sing-song show: 'Tune time for the Forces, when you are invited to sing, hum or whistle your favourite tunes'. Started 30 December 1944 with Denny Dennis, Edna Kaye, Vincent Tildsley's Mastersingers, and Stanley Black with the Dance Orchestra. The first guest star was Jack Buchanan, and the second, Bobby Howes.

Allison, George

Greatest of the pre-war football commentators who made his first broadcast describing the cup-tie between the Corinthians and New-castle United from Crystal Palace on 29 January 1927: the second football commentary ever transmitted. Famous for his well-spoken clar-ity, but with a tendency to clear his throat during moments of Cup Final excitement. Born at Hurworth-on-Tees in County Durham, he rose from sporting journalist in Plymouth to manager of the Arsenal football team, and may be seen playing himself in the film, *The Arsenal Stadium Mystery* (1939).

George **Allison**: 'soccer master of the microphone'

Les **Allen**: 'radio's ace crooner'

Almost an Academy
Comedy quiz: musical spelling bee run by Professor Billy Bennett (Almost a Gentleman) assisted by his music master, SANDY MACPHERSON at the organ. Began 20 January 1939.

Alonzo MacTavish
Private detective played by Nicholas Hannen in two series (1939; 1940) written by novelist Peter Cheyney. Ronald Kerr played Detective Inspector Gringall. *The Adventures of Alonzo MacTavish* was produced by Howard Rose.

The Alpine Hut
'Unparalleled views and music at an altitude of 6000 feet' with proprietor Fabre Fatscher, Augustus Fazil's Schamel Quintet, Reserl the landlord's daugher and Ernst the Singing Guide. Among the guests of 13 February 1939: Lorna Stuart the singer, Larry Adamson the yodeller and Jacques Brown 'who can do anything'. Producer Anthony Hill.

Alternative Programmes
In the early years of broadcasting the only alternative to the official BBC radio station in the area was whatever could be picked up by twiddling the knob. The first BBC alternative programme came via DAVENTRY on 21 August 1927, the choice of station 5XX (1604 metres) or 5GB (491 metres). Listeners could choose between *Military Band Concert* (the Wireless Military Band conducted by Walter O'Donnell, with Edith Furmedge contralto) or *Recital of Organ Music* (Rev Cyril Jackson, with Kate Winter soprano). The first really difficult choice came two days later: *Dance Music* from the Hotel Cecil, or *Variety* with HARRY HEMSLEY. Fully alternative programmes were introduced with the NATIONAL and REGIONAL on 9 March 1930, via the new twin transmitters at Brookman's Park.

Ambrose
King of Saturday late-night dance music before the war, from 10.30 to midnight when he would fade out with his signature tune, 'When Day Is Done'. Elegant, sophisticated, immaculate Ambrose, society's favourite band leader, seldom revealed that his Christian name was Bert. He first broadcast from the May Fair Hotel in 1927, a venue he reigned at for nearly eight years. Vocalists included LES ALLEN, Sam Browne, Leslie Sarony, Elsie Carlisle, the Three Ginx, Evelyn Dall, Anne Shelton, Leslie Carew, VERA LYNN, and the comedy drummer Max Bacon. Novelty numbers, especially musical melodramas like 'Home James and Don't Spare the Horses', were always part of his programmes.

Ambrose and his May Fair Hotel Orchestra

America Calling

Irregular series devised and compèred by Eddie Pola, burlesquing commercial broadcasting as heard in the United States. The first show (24 July 1933) featured Al Bowlly, Mary Lee, Reilly and Comfort, C. Denier Warren, Ben Welden, the Southern Sisters, CARROLL GIBBONS and the Savoy Orpheans, and Pola himself. The cast of the 30 March 1936 show was completely different: Ann Lenner, Gordon Little, Beryl Orde the impressionist, Gerry Fitzgerald the crooner, and the Radio Three. Pola mounted the programme as a stage production and presented it at the London Palladium.

Among Your Treasures

RADIO LUXEMBOURG's poetry series introduced by ROY PLOMLEY. Valentine Dyall and Jill Balcon read listeners' favourite verses, sponsored by Reckitt's Bathjoys. Produced by Edgar Blatt (1950).

Andy Mann

Character played by comedian KEN DODD in his several radio series, lovingly based on the late Robb Wilton.

Angus Prune

Sole prop of Radio Prune and sponsor of Full Frontal Radio on I'M SORRY I'LL READ THAT AGAIN (1964 onwards). Sang, with the voice of Bill Oddie, his own Angus Prune Tune:

> My name is Angus Prune
> And I always listen to
> I'm Sorry I'll Read That Again
> My name is Angus Prune
> And I never miss
> I'm Sorry I'll Read That Again.
> I sit in my bath
> And I have a good laugh
> Cos the sig-tune is named after me! (etc.)

Announcers

Radio announcers, being the first voices regularly heard in the home, were the first personalities created by radio. The earliest included announcing as part of their other duties, thus the early 2LO staff all took turns at the microphone: ARTHUR BURROWS, Rex Palmer, Cecil Lewis. John Dodgson was the first full-time announcer, including acting as host to broadcasters and paying them before they went home. STUART HIBBERD joined the BBC in 1924 and was made Chief Announcer in 1928. Then came JOHN SNAGGE, Derek McCulloch (before he became UNCLE MAC), David Tarrant, Ajax Farrar, ALVAR LIDELL, and the first to be dubbed 'the Golden Voice of Radio', ERIC DUNSTAN. Later the BBC decreed that announcers must remain anonymous, although MRS BORRETT was given great publicity when she was made the first Lady Announcer. Announcers were identified again when they became Newsreaders during the War: Bruce Belfrage, Frank Phillips, Frederick Allen and Joseph Macleod became known so that listeners should not be fooled by Fifth Column substitutes. Other announcers became known through joining-in comedy shows as super straight-men: Norman Woodland in MUSIC HALL, LIONEL GAMLIN in OLD MOTHER RILEY TAKES THE AIR, David Dunhill in TAKE IT FROM HERE, Wallace Greenslade in THE GOON SHOW. The BBC allowed them to reveal their personalities a little in ANNOUNCERS' CHOICE, a record programme beginning on 22 July 1944 with Alvar Lidell's personal selection. The public affection for announcers was crystallized in FLOTSAM AND JETSAM's popular song, 'Little Betty Bouncer loved an Announcer down at the BBC'.

The first staff announcer in commercial broadcasting was Major Max Staniforth who joined RADIO NORMANDY in 1931. Stephen Williams followed in 1932, later moving to RADIO LUXEMBOURG. Well remembered voices from Normandy: Bernard 'Benjy' McNabb and Bob Danvers-Walker (later the voice of *Pathé News*). From 1932 John Sullivan and Faith Shipway announced for RADIO PARIS, Alexander Wright for RADIO ROME while RADIO SAN SEBASTIAN had H. Gordon Box and RADIO LYONS Tony Melrose. The post-war Luxembourg opened with Stephen Williams again, followed by Geoffrey Everitt and Teddy Johnson.

Another Spot of Bother

Fifteen minutes of fun from cross-talk comedians CLAPHAM AND DWYER, sponsored by Ex-Lax Chocolate Laxative, and featuring Harry Bidgood and his Buccaneers. RADIO LUXEMBOURG from 1936.

The Announcers: Stuart Hibberd, Freddy Grisewood, John Snagge and colleagues of the thirties

The Answer Man

'Write to him if there is anything you want to know'. Sustaining series on RADIO LUXEMBOURG from 1950.

Any Answers

FREDDY GRISEWOOD compèred this Radio Correspondence Column of the Air, which was instituted for listeners to comment upon the answers given by the team in the week's broadcast of ANY QUESTIONS. First heard on 6 October 1954, the 400th programme was broadcast on 13 May 1965. Producer, Michael Bowen. The programme continues to this day. Later presenters have included David Jacobs and, most recently, John Timpson.

Any Minute Now

'Disappointing Cabaret' with Ivor Moreton and Dave Kaye (the Tiger Ragamuffins), Warden and West (Biddy and Fanny), Hugh Morton, Denny Dennis, the Cavendish Three, and Billy Ternent and the Dance Orchestra.

From April 1940; by Ronnie Hill and Peter Dion Titherage.

Any More?

Or, 'Who's For a Sail?' Weekly series starring top Northern comedian Frank Randle in his famous Old Boatman role. Malcolm Graeme played the Harbourmaster, with Jack McCormick and his Troubadours as the Longshoremen. Produced and devised by Richard North; from 7 September 1940.

Any Questions (1)

'Things worth knowing presented in a way worth hearing': the first intellectual radio series to attain the popularity of a variety series. Started 1 January 1941: 'Questions set by men and women serving in the forces, answers given by a panel of five great personalities of our time.' They were question-master D.H. (Donald) McCullough, Professor Julian S. Huxley, Dr C.E.M. Joad, Commander A.B. Campbell, and a guest. Presented by Howard Thomas and Douglas Cleverdon, the title was changed to THE BRAINS TRUST from 4 January 1942.

Any Questions (2)

'Questions of the moment are put by members of the audience and answered spontaneously' in this popular series which began in the West Region on 12 October 1948, moving to the HOME SERVICE on 13 June 1950. The first Travelling Question Master was FREDDY GRISEWOOD, who served for 18 years before giving up his seat to David Jacobs – who also served for 18 years. The original panel was Ralph Wightman, Graham Hutton, Monica Dickens and John Summerson, and the programme came from the Guild Hall, St Ives. The 10th anniversary programme, broadcast 10 October 1958, featured A.G. Street, Lord Boothby, Anthony Wedgwood Benn and Lady Violet Bonham Carter.

Anything Goes (1)

West Region comedy series which came to the Light Programme from 21 February 1952. Benny Hill starred and scripted, supported by Cherry Lind, Jack Watson, Johnny Morris and the Ivor Raymonde Seven. Produced by Duncan Wood.

Anything Goes (2)

Luxembourg's singing sweethearts, Teddy Johnson and Pearl Carr, sang hit songs to the accompaniment of Norrie Paramor and his Orchestra in this series broadcast from 6 August 1954. John Witty compèred, Philip Jones produced, and Horace Batchelor sponsored with his Infra-Draw Method for success on the football pools.

Appointment With Fear

Weekly half-hour of Mystery and Suspense broadcast at 10.30 at night from 11 September 1943. The plays, originally written for American radio by John Dickson Carr, were produced by Val Gielgud and Martyn C. Webster, and narrated by the sinister storyteller, the MAN IN BLACK (Valentine Dyall). The first play, 'Cabin B13', starred Constance Cummings. The second series began on 6 January 1944 with 'Vex Not His Ghost', and a new story-teller, Valentine's father, Franklin Dyall. The son was back for the third series, which began on 13 March 1944 with 'The Speaking Clock' (Esme Percy and Belle Chrystal). The fourth series started 5 October 1944 with 'I Never Suspected', starring Linden Travers and

Eric Portman. The fifth series consisted of repeats and ran from 11 September 1945, quickly followed by a new series commencing 23 October with 'He Wasn't Superstitious'. The seventh series started on 26 March 1946 with 'The Nutcracker Suite', by Eliot Crawshay Williams. The eighth series began 25 February 1947, and the ninth on 14 January 1948 with 'The Clock Strikes Eight' featuring Laidman Browne as John Dickson Carr's famous fictional detective, Dr Fell.

The series returned on 26 July 1955, by which time the sinister mysteries were considered suitable for an 8.45 slot. The first play was Carr's 'The Man Who Wouldn't Be Photographed', produced by David H. Godfrey.

'Appy 'Arf 'Our

Leon Cortez and his Coster Pals (conducted by Alan Paul) provided the cheerful music and banter in this 1939 series. 'Osts were the 'Awkins Family, Alf, Liz and Judy. Alf reappeared in *Alf and his Coster Pals* (20 October 1942) with Doreen Harris as wife Fanny, Sidney Broughton as son Alfie, and Billy Ternent with the BBC Dance Orchestra. The series was revived from 23 February 1952 with Cortez and spiv comedian ARTHUR ENGLISH as his resident guest. Songs from Doreen Harris, Nat Gonella and the Four Barrow Boys, with a newly formed Coster Pals Band. Produced by George Inns.

The Archers

This serialized 'everyday story of country folk' started as a one-week trial in the Midland Region on Whit Monday, 1950. It moved to the Light Programme on New Years Day 1951; here it made such an impact that it moved from 11.45 am into the DICK BARTON slot (6.45 pm) in March, perhaps helped by the fact that it was written by the Barton team of Geoffrey Webb and Edward J. Mason. Realism was the keynote here, however, and the original cast was Harry Oakes (Daniel Archer), Gwen Berryman (Doris Archer), Norman Painting (young son Philip), Pamela Mant (daughter Christine), Denis Folwell (older son Jack), June Spencer (his wife Peggy), Monica Grey (Grace Fairbrother), Eddie Robinson (Simon the farm-hand), and Robert Mawdesley (crusty old neighbour Walter Gabriel). The Archers' address was Brookfield Farm,

'Appy 'Arf 'Our: Leon Cortez, Doreen Harris and their Coster pals

Ambridge, and their signature tune 'Barwick Green'. By their third year (1954) the authors calculated they had written 3,500,000 words between them. The series originated in Birmingham with Godfrey Baseley, who produced farming programmes and acted as editor, and Tony Shryane, producer. Monte Crick, formerly accompanist for comedian Ronald Frankau, took over as Dan Archer, and was later replaced by Edgar Harrison, who died in harness after 13 years. Frank Middlemass has played Dan since 1982. Gwen Berryman played Doris for 30 years, retired in 1980 and was awarded an MBE. Norman Painting (Philip) received an OBE on the 25th anniversary, became one of the series' scriptwriters, and wrote the book, *Forever Ambridge*. The power of the serial was demonstrated on the night of 22 September 1955, when the BBC stole all the attention from ITV's opening night by 'killing' Grace Archer in a fire.

The Archers won two NATIONAL RADIO AWARDS for the Most Entertaining Programme of 1954 and 1955. The serial maintains a loyal following in the 1980s, albeit with considerable character and cast changes, and no longer in the 6.45 pm slot.

Archie Andrews

Most famous ventriloquist's dummy on the air. Peter Brough, who had previously worked with one 'Jimmy', introduced Archie Andrews (named by writer TED KAVANAGH) in a series called 'Archie Takes the Helm', a sub-series of NAVY MIXTURE, on 4 May 1944. His own series, EDUCATING ARCHIE, followed on 6 June 1950, rapidly becoming the most popular series on British radio. An attempt to make Archie grow up failed (ARCHIE'S THE BOY, 1954), and he returned to being a saucy young limb. An offbeat one-off was *Archie in Goonland* (11 June 1954), a mixture of styles which failed to jell. Archie was the first dummy to be made into a dummy – by Madame Tussaud's!

The Archers: stage version of 'radio's greatest serial'

Archie Andrews: first book appearance of the radio dummy (MacMillan & Co. Ltd.)

Archie's the Boy

Basically EDUCATING ARCHIE grown up, this series sought to establish ARCHIE ANDREWS as a graduated teenager no longer needing instruction. Curiously, then, his main partner-in-crime was schoolgirl MONICA ('she's my best friend and I hate her!') played by Beryl Reid. She also impersonated the Brummy sexpot, Marlene ('Good evening, each!'). Benny Hill added comedy quality, as did Graham Stark as Nigel Bowser-Smythe. Shirley Eaton added glamour, and the Coronets sang to Harry Rabinowitz and the Revue Orchestra. Script by Eddie Maguire, Ronald Wolfe and Rex Dawe; produced by Roy Speer; first broadcast 11 November 1954.

The Armchair Detective

Ernest Dudley, crime writer and critic, who reviewed detective fiction with dramatized excerpts from 10 December 1942 in *For the Armchair Detective*. His soothing tones counterpointed the 'murder, mystery and mayhem' he described. He starred as himself in a film version, *The Armchair Detective*, produced in 1951.

Armour's Quality Variety

Eddie Carroll and his Band with singer Don Carlos, plus impersonator Michael Moore, comedian LEONARD HENRY, and impressioniste Beryl Orde, broadcast in this series from RADIO LUXEMBOURG starting 11 May 1939. Sponsored by Armour's Corned Beef.

The Armstrongs

Radio family devised as an educational experiment for schools programmes, and developed into a wartime series for adults. *The Armstrongs* was first broadcast 6 August 1940, created by playwrights Ronald Gow and Walter Greenwood, and scripted by E. Arnot Robertson. Joe Armstrong (Philip Wade), Mrs Armstrong

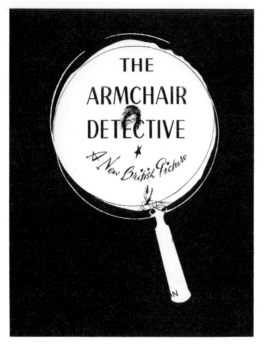

The Armchair Detective: film version of Ernest Dudley's popular series

Doris **Arnold**: one of the first lady disc-jockeys

(Gladys Young), Frank (Tony Halfpenny), Ted (Clive Baxter), Thelma (Audrey Cameron), Pat (Jane Barrett), Walter (George Dixon), and Mrs Drummond, neighbour (Vivienne Chatterton). Producer George Dixon.

Arnold, Doris
One of the first lady disc-jockeys, although she would never have approved of today's term: she devised and presented the semi-classical, somewhat sentimental series THESE YOU HAVE LOVED. Earlier she was a pianist, earlier still a BBC secretary from Wimbledon. Her break came when she deputized at a moment's notice for an absentee accompanist in CHILDREN'S HOUR. Often heard in double-piano harmony with Harry S. Pepper, she attained extra fame by arranging the choral numbers for the Kentucky Choir in THE KENTUCKY MIN-STRELS; best-remembered arrangement, 'Bless This House'.

Around the World With Sandy Powell
First radio series for the Yorkshire comedian with the catchphrase, 'Can you hear me, mother?' Sponsored by Atora Shredded Beef Suet and broadcast on RADIO LUXEMBOURG from 5 January 1939, the programmes featured Joe (Adrian Thomas), Sandy's pal, and Miss Pontefract II, Sandy's second-hand aeroplane. Producer Andrew Allan.

The Arrow
Stephen Arrow, 'an entirely new radio detective', was described as 'a humorous cynic with a not always happy penchant for whistling a certain tune'. Created by Ernest Dudley for CRIME MAGAZINE (1940) and played by Billy Milton. 'Meet him by night or meet him by day, the Arrow goes whistling on his way'.

The Arthur Askey Show
Comedy series reuniting the BAND WAGGON team of ARTHUR ASKEY and RICHARD MURDOCH, written by and including BOB MONKHOUSE AND DENIS GOODWIN, with cute Diana Decker and comical Pat Coombs. Paul Fenoulhet conducted the Variety Orchestra and Leslie Bridgmont produced. Started 30 September 1958.

Arthur Fallowfield

Farmer and rustic philosopher of BEYOND OUR KEN (1958) whose answer to every Searching Question was 'The answer lies in the soil!'. Played by Kenneth Williams in a clever takeoff of Ralph Wightman.

The Arthur Haynes Show

The former stalwart of CHARLIE CHESTER's Crazy Gang, having become a television star, came back to radio in his own series from 22 October 1962, Nicholas Parsons, his TV straight-man, came with him, as did the sketches by Johnny Speight. Haynes played his established character, the artful tramp, the cockney loudmouth, and music was supplied by the Temperance Seven with Whispering Paul McDowall. The second series (23 June 1963) had more formal music from Janie Marden with the Revue Orchestra, conducted by Malcolm Lockyer. Producer Richard Dingley. The third series (15 July 1965) gave Arthur a new feed in Tony Fayne, currently sundered from his former partner, David Evans. There were also Warren Mitchell, Patricia Hayes, and Mr Acker Bilk and his Paramount Jazz Band.

Arthur's Inn

Comedy series built around ARTHUR ASKEY with Brian Reece (PC49) as his straight man. They shared the comedy with two bright girls, Sally Ann Howes and Diana Decker, with music from the Revue Orchestra conducted by Robert Busby. Script by Alan Melville, Bob Block and Bill Harding. Started 17 June 1952.

Askey, Arthur

'Big Hearted Arthur', the immortal 'silly little man' of BAND WAGGON (1938), the first great comedy series on the BBC. Shot to instant fame as a chirpy, spontaneous funmaker in crosstalks with RICHARD MURDOCH, and as purveyor of Silly Songs ('The Bee', 'The Worm', 'The Seagull') written by Kenneth Blain and a legacy from the seaside concert parties where he served his apprenticeship. Big's catchphrases included 'Ay thang yow!' (inspired by a London bus conductor), 'Oh don't be filthy!', 'Doesn't it make you want to spit!', 'Here and now, before your very eyes!' and references to Nausea Bagwash, Dagenham and Dogsbody's, and the Junction Cocoa Rooms. Broadcasts

Arthur **Askey**: 'The Band Waggon Song Book', 1939

from 1930 included MUSIC HALL and the role of Nobby Clarke in EIGHT BELLS. After the war broke the Askey–Murdoch team, he did several series with KENNETH HORNE, David Nixon, and his daughter, Anthea Askey. There were also several nostalgic reunions with Dickie on *Sounds Familiar* and other programmes, and many ad lib appearances as a panellist on DOES THE TEAM THINK.

Askey Galore

Arthur, of course, with magician David Nixon as his partner, daughter Anthea Askey, and his television discovery, the well-upholstered Sabrina. Vanessa Lee sang to the music of Billy

Ternent and his Orchestra. Script by Dick Vosburgh and Brad Ashton, producer Dennis Main Wilson. First broadcast 30 January 1957.

Assignment Scotland Yard
'Records the exploits of a cop from Brooklyn and Inspector Henley of Scotland Yard, who are working together temporarily as a team. Orthodox police procedure improbably tangles with the more bizarre methods of the Brooklyn boy.' RADIO LUXEMBOURG from 12 April 1957. One of the 'World's Greatest Mysteries' series hosted by Basil Rathbone, produced by HARRY ALAN TOWERS.

At Home With the Hulberts
Claude Hulbert and Enid Trevor, comedy act and real-life husband and wife, starred in this weekly RADIO NORMANDY series for Cow & Gate Milk. Beginning 13 January 1937, it interspersed domestic situations with comedy songs such as 'Why Has a Cow Got Four Legs?'.

At the Billet-Doux
'Alf Perkins says It's a Bit of All Right!' was how this early war series was announced. Cast: MAURICE DENHAM, Betty Huntley-Wright, Horace Percival, Winifred Doran, Sidney Burchall and the Male Voice Quartet. From 14 September 1939, produced by Bill MacClurg.

At the Black Dog
'Mr Wilkes at Home in His Own Bar Parlour' described this lunchtime series which began on the EMPIRE SERVICE in October 1937, and proved so popular that it moved onto the NATONAL PROGRAMME from 23 December. William Wilkes, landlord, of the Black Dog pub, somewhere in the West End, and his good lady Aggie, were played by Cyril Nash and Sunday Wilshin. Howard Marshall was well promoted as their regular customer. Visiting personalities included Jean Batten (Queen of the Air), Billy Bennett (Almost a Gentleman), Patsy Hendren (Lord of the Willow), and Primo Carnera. The producer, making good use of clinking-glass sound effects, was Pascoe Thornton. The 100th show was broadcast on 31 May 1940, and the writer was S.E. Reynolds.

Atlas
Wheezy weakling in IT'S THAT MAN AGAIN (1948) played by hearty Fred Yule. Catchphrase: 'What me, in my state of health?'

Aunt Sally
Tommy Handley was her nephew, and she called him 'Tommy Wommy', much to the embarrassment of IT'S THAT MAN AGAIN (1944). Played by Diana Morrison.

Auntie Rides Again
Situation comedies starring Athene Seyler as Miss Amelia Grimly-Bracewell, managing director of G-B Motor Works, with Hubert Gregg as Charles Todmarsh, Mary Mackenzie as Pamela Scott, Leslie Dwyer as Bert Crocker, and Patrick Cargill as Harry Perkins. Episode 1, 'Send For the Manager', was broadcast on 11 May 1955, written by Len Fincham and Lawrie Wyman; produced by Vernon Harris.

B

14 November when ARTHUR BURROWS read the news at 6 pm. (Earlier broadcasts from 2LO were by the MARCONI Co.). The first Chairman was Lord Gainford, a former Postmaster General, and the General Manager was Mr J.C.W. Reith; Director of Programmes was ARTHUR BURROWS with Cecil Lewis as his Deputy. Music Controller was Percy Pitt, with L. Stanton Jeffries as Music Director. Chief Engineer was P.P. ECKERSLEY, and Director of the London Station, REX PALMER. The first office was in Magnet House, Kingsway, moving to No. 2 Savoy Hill on 2 February 1923. The British Broadcasting Corporation was constituted under Royal Charter as from 1 January 1927 with a ten-year licence to 'carry on a broadcasting service as a public utility service'. The first Chairman was Lord Clarendon, and the first Director General John Charles Walsham Reith, who was knighted in 1927. To quote from *Who's Who in Broadcasting* (1933), 'the high tone of British broadcasting owes much to his resolute character and practical idealism'. The BBC's motto is 'Nation Shall Speak Peace Unto Nation'.

BBC Birthday

The first birthday of the BBC was celebrated with a special programme broadcast on 14 November 1923. Mr J.C.W. Reith spoke on 'The Year's Work', Sir Patrick McGrath described how he was the first journalist to report the success of MARCONI's experiments in wireless telegraphy, and the rest was described as 'an emergency programme by a distracted staff'. L. Stanton Jeffries conducted the Wireless Orchestra. It was the first of many anniversary programmes to come.

BBC Concert Party

Following the great success of CONCERT PARTIES on the air, the BBC formed its own official concert party, *Entre Nous*, which gave its first broadcast on 6 August 1927. Described as a 'Radio Revuette' the entertainment included 'W.O.W – Whosit's Omnipotent Whatnots', and the team consisted of John Armstrong, Vivienne Chatterton, Harold Clemence, Esther Coleman, Rex Evans (later a Hollywood character actor), Florence Oldham, Foster Richardson and 'Yvette'. The series was written, arranged and directed by Gordon McConnell and Stanford Robinson.

BBC: *All About the BBC*, 1924

BBC

The British Broadcasting Company Ltd was formed of some 300 wireless manufacturers and shareholders at a meeting on 18 October 1922. It was registered on 15 December and received its licence to broadcast from the Postmaster General on 18 January 1923. But the BBC had already been broadcasting daily from Tuesday

BBC: the official coat of arms

BBC Dance Orchestra (1)

JACK PAYNE, director of the Hotel Cecil Dance Band (first broadcast 26 December 1925), was invited to form the original BBC Dance Orchestra, and they made their debut on 12 March 1928 complete with signature tune,

BBC Dance Orchestra (no. 1): directed by Jack Payne

'Say It With Music'. There were ten musicians including Harry Mills, Jesse Fuller, Frank Wilson and Bob Busby, and the staff arranger was Ray Noble. Their big success was with novelty numbers such as 'Fire! Fire!', comedy numbers like 'Sez You – Sez Me!', and special arrangements of 'Trees'. By the time Payne left four years later (11 March 1932) the band was receiving 10,000 fan letters a week. They had made over 4000 broadcasts, representing 6000 hours of rehearsal and 2600 hours on the air. Their first record was 'Sunny Skies' on Columbia 4932 (July 1928).

BBC Dance Orchestra (2)

The New BBC Dance Orchestra under the direction of HENRY HALL made their radio debut on 15 March 1932, celebrating the opening of the new HQ, BROADCASTING HOUSE. The first programme opened with 'It's Just the Time For Dancing' and closed with the soon-to-be-classic 'Here's to the Next Time'. Between the two signature tunes they played 'Songs That Are Old Live For Ever', 'Gettin' Sentimental' (their first record for Columbia, on CB431), 'Now's the Time to Fall in Love', 'Speak to Me of Love', 'Home', 'Rio de Janeiro', 'By the Sycamore Tree' and 'Where the Blue of the Night'. Personnel included Frank Wilson, Freddy Williams, Burton Gillis, Harry Robbins and Cyril Stapleton (who would years later form the BBC SHOW BAND). Val Rosing was vocalist, who gained fame for his 'Teddy Bear's Picnic'. Later vocalists included Dan Donovan, Kitty Masters, LES ALLEN ('Little Man You've Had a Busy Day'), Phyllis Robins ('I Took My Harp to a Party'), Len Bermon ('Leave the Pretty Girls Alone'), George Elrick ('The Music Goes Round and Round'), Elizabeth Scott ('It's a Sin to Tell a Lie'), Bob Mallin ('Horsey Horsey'), and Molly, Marie and Mary. Perhaps the Band's most popular slot was 5.15, thus depriving many youngsters of CHILDREN'S HOUR. The Band shifted studios to a warehouse by Waterloo Bridge in 1934, and in late 1935 moved to a purpose-built studio in Maida Vale. The last performance was broadcast on Saturday 25 September 1937, after which Henry Hall took the Orchestra on tour under his own name.

BBC Dance Orchestra (3)

The third BBC Dance Orchestra was formed in the second week of World War II under Billy

BBC Dance Orchestra (no. 2): directed by Henry Hall

BBC Dance Orchestra (no. 3): directed by Stanley Black

Ternent, a Tynesider who had become ace arranger and deputy conductor for JACK HYLTON. Billy's signature tune was 'She's My Lovely' and his Geordie accent soon became popular through his stooging for comedians, most notably with FRANKIE HOWERD in VARIETY BANDBOX. After backing all the radio variety shows, Billy resigned in 1944. He was replaced with pianist Stanley Black and the new signature tune, 'That Old Black Magic'.

BBC Dancing Club
Long-running mixture of dance instruction and strict-tempo dance music by VICTOR SILVESTER and his Orchestra, presented by David Miller. Lesson one, given on 30 July 1941, was for the quickstep, and the famous instruction – 'Slow-slow-quick-quick-slow' – became virtually a catchphrase. The signature tune was Silvester's own, 'You're Dancing On My Heart'.

BBC Fortieth Anniversary
The BBC began celebrating early with a week of star presenters on HOUSEWIVES' CHOICE, beginning with Frankie Vaughan on 12 November. The same day KENNETH HORNE

hosted *Forty Laughing Years* with records of comedians past and present. *Scrapbook for 1922* (14 November) included radio pioneers P.P. ECKERSLEY, ARTHUR BURROWS, Percy Edgar, L. Stanton Jeffries and REX PALMER. *Ted Ray and the Cat's Whisker* and David Jacobs hosting *The Twenties to the Twist* were on the 15 November, and Ken Sykora surveyed 40 years of Pop Music in *Forty Years On* (16 November). BBC TV showed a documentary, *World of Sound* (13 November), narrated by Edward Ward and featuring FRANK MUIR, DENIS NORDEN, and ROY PLOMLEY.

The BBC Presents the ABC
Saturday night variety series billed as 'An Alphabetical Miscellany', in which all the items began with a single letter each week, running from A to Z. Devised by Alan Keith, producer A.W. Hanson, signature tune by REGINALD FOORT. Began 10 March 1937.

BBC Show Band
The last of the great house dance bands, the Show Band was organized by conductor Cyril Stapleton and made its debut on 2 October 1952. The 17 instrumentalists included Bill McGuffie at the piano, Tommy McQuater on trumpet, and Tommy Whittle, saxophone. The first vocalists were Lee Lawrence, Jean Campbell, Johnny Johnston and the Johnston Singers, and Louise Traill, with Harold Smart at the Organ. The first resident comedian was Stan Stennett, and the producer was Johnnie Stewart. For their most popular series see THE SHOW BAND SHOW. Signature tune:

> Just for you,
> Words and music we're blending,
> From the Show Band we're sending
> Our greetings with this melody.

BBC Silver Jubilee
The 25th Anniversary of the BBC was celebrated with a week of special programmes. On 9 November 1947 Robert Donat narrated *The Mirror of Our Times*, written and produced by D.G. Bridson. On the 10th, Jubilee editions of STAND EASY and IGNORANCE IS BLISS. On the 11th, *This BBC* illustrated 24 hours in the life of the corporation, produced by Peter Eton. There was also *Arthur's Big-Hearted Jubilee*, produced by Harry Pepper. On the 12th the *Theatre Programme* put on a pageant of plays and

players introduced by Alec Guinness, produced by Archie Campbell. CRISTOPHER STONE introduced a *Dance Parade* on gramophone records. On the 13th Terry-Thomas was the guest star in *The* CARROLL LEVIS SHOW *Jubilee Edition*, which included four Discoveries, and there was the Jubilee Revival of BAND WAGGON with Askey and Murdoch. On the 14th, *Do You Remember* was a reminiscence by MABEL CONSTANDUROS, TED KAVANAGH, STUART HIBBERD, Harold Nicholson, Wynford Vaughan Thomas and JOHN SNAGGE, produced by Francis Worsley and Michael Barsley. On the 15th *Jubilee* MUSIC HALL produced by John Sharman starred Peter Bernard, NORMAN LONG, CLAPHAM AND DWYER, Elsie Carlisle, G.H. Elliott, TOMMY HANDLEY, ELSIE AND DORIS WATERS, and the Variety Orchestra conducted by Rae Jenkins. Lionel Marson announced. The Third Programme joined in with *How To Listen*, by and with Joyce Grenfell and Stephen Potter. On the 16th *Jubilee Variety Gala* closed the celebration with a two-hour show live from His Majesty's Theatre: CHARLIE CHESTER and his Gang, the Radio Revellers, VERA LYNN, ERIC BARKER, Pearl Hackney, the Luton Girls Choir, VIC OLIVER, TOMMY HANDLEY and Company, Rawicz and Landauer, MURDOCH AND HORNE, Anne Ziegler and Webster Booth, TWENTY QUESTIONS, ELSIE AND DORIS WATERS, Julie Andrews and the BBC Variety Orchestra, conductor Rae Jenkins. Producers Harry S. Pepper and Ronnie Waldman.

BBC Tenth Anniversary
The first major milestone to be celebrated on the air and with a special edition of RADIO TIMES. The cover illustrated the growth in number of licences from 18,000 (1922) to 5,000,000 (1932). Special programmes included *A Tour of Broadcasting House* (14 November 1932) personally conducted by John Watt; *Birthday Week Variety* (15 November) 'specially chosen for the Prince of Wales', with HENRY HALL and the BBC DANCE ORCHESTRA, Jeanne De Casalis (MRS FEATHER), GILLIE POTTER, CLAPHAM AND DWYER, CICELY COURTNEIDGE, Leslie 'Hutch' Hutchinson, Florence Desmond, Jack and Claude Hulbert; MUSIC HALL (16 November) with Horace Kenney in 'The Trial Turn', JACK PAYNE and his Band, FLOTSAM AND JETSAM, Billy Bennett ('Almost a Gentleman'), Hetty King and Gretl Vernon

'The Viennese Nightingale'; an all-star edition of *Songs From The Shows* (17 November) with Nelson Keys, Florence Smithson, Hayden Coffin, Renee Mayer and Harry Welchman; *British and American Dance Bands* (19 November) with Paul Whiteman and his Band from New York, the BBC DANCE ORCHESTRA, AMBROSE and his May Fair Hotel Orchestra, Lew Stone and his Monseigneur Dance Band, JACK PAYNE and his Band, and the debut of Roy Fox and his Café Anglais Band.

BBC Theatre Organ

The opening broadcast of the new Theatre Organ was given from St George's Hall on 20 October 1936. John Watt compèred, Harry S. Pepper produced, and four organists participated: Quentin Maclean, Harold Ramsey, Reginald Porter-Browne, and the man who became the first BBC resident organist, REGINALD FOORT. The mighty organ was accompanied by the BBC Theatre Orchestra conducted by Mark Lubbock, and the BBC DANCE ORCHESTRA conducted by HENRY HALL. Foort was succeeded in 1938 by SANDY MACPHERSON. The organ was blitzed in 1941 and replaced by Foort's own, which the BBC purchased and installed in Jubilee Hall, East Road, in 1946.

BBC Variety Orchestra

Formed in 1934 to provide suitable musical accompaniment to MUSIC HALL and other radio variety shows. Kneale Kelley was the original director, the most famous being CHARLES SHADWELL. There were sixteen players.

Back With Braden

Comedy series with BERNARD BRADEN (but without Barbara), in which singers Annie Ross, Franklyn Boyd and Group One were backed by old friends Benny Lee and Nat Temple with his Orchestra, plus announcer Ronald Fletcher. First broadcast 24 April 1956, with script by Ray Galton and Alan Simpson, producer Pat Dixon.

Backstage Wife

'The drama of Mary Noble, a little provincial girl, who married Brian Noble, London's most handsome and popular star, dream sweetheart of a million other women. Hers is the story of struggle to hold the love of her famous husband; of what it means to be the wife of a famous star; of the intrigues, the joys and sorrows that face one in the complicated life Backstage.' Presented by the makers of Dr Lyons' Tooth Powder, daily on RADIO LUXEMBOURG from 3 October 1938.

Backyard Follies

Rare series for 'Wee' Georgie Wood, the veteran variety comedian who always played the small boy, Georgie Robinson. As ever, Dolly Harmer played his mum, Emma Robinson, supported by Charles Harrison as Henry Townsend, Gwen Lewis as Ada, Joe Moss as Joe, Tom Moss as Foreman Tom Leatherbarrow, Arthur Tolcher as Arthur Dudley, and variety star Karina as Annie McLeod. Music by Dustbin Charlie and his Ragamuffins; 'concocted' by Georgie Wood, with additional dialogue by Bert Lee. Commenced 31 December 1941.

Band Call

First British radio series to feature the current best-selling tunes: 'Songs and music from sweet to swing in the Hit Parade of 1944.' Began on 21 January 1944 with Philip Green and his Dance Orchestra, JACK JACKSON, Fred Emney, Paula Green, Sam Browne and the Aristocrats. Produced by Henry Reed.

Band Parade

'45 minutes of the best in dance music played in contrasting styles.' The first show, broadcast 8 January 1950, spotlighted Eric Winstone and his Orchestra and the Hermanos Deniz Cuban Rhythm Band as guests, with GERALDO and his Orchestra as residents. JACK JACKSON, himself an ex-danceband leader, introduced, and Petula Clark guest-starred. Feature items included 'Comedians Sometimes Sing' (No. 1: SAM COSTA), and 'Musical Portrait of a Lady'. John Foreman and John Simmonds co-produced.

Band Waggon

The radio series which established a new formula: a regular weekly show with 'resident comedians' at a fixed time and day (7.15 pm on Wednesdays from 5 January 1938). Originally planned as a danceband show (Phil Cardew and the Band Waggoners, singers Bettie Bucknelle and Miff Ferrie and the Jakdauz) with organ interludes (REGINALD FOORT at the

Band Waggon: Richard Murdoch and Arthur Askey at the microphone

BBC THEATRE ORGAN) plus feature items ('What Do You Think', a radio problem by Hans W. Priwin, and 'NEW VOICES') with a lacing of comedy linkage: ARTHUR ASKEY ('Big Hearted Arthur, that's me!') and his straight-man RICHARD 'Stinker' MURDOCH quickly came to dominate the content thanks to their spontaneous fooling and the creation of a highly believable setting, the Top Floor Flat at Broadcasting House. This was peopled with pets (Basil and Lucy the pigeons, Lewis the goat) and characters (MRS BAGWASH and her daughter, NAUSEA), and peppered with catchphrases ('Ay thang you!'; 'Ah! Happy days!'; 'Light the blue touchpaper and retire immediately!'; 'Askitoff will take it off!': 'Pretty isn't it? Yes, everso!'). The second series began on 5 October 1938, introducing SYD WALKER in 'Mr Walker Wants to Know', and concluded 15 March 1939.

The third series started on 7 October 1939 with 'Your Old Chum Syd Walker in 'Syd Sees It Through', and 'I Want to Be an Actor' presented by Vernon Harris. Billy Ternent conducted the New Waggoners. The last broadcast on 2 December 1939 with the realistic departure of Big and Stinker from their famous flat left listeners in tears. Scripts were by Vernon Harris, Gordon Crier, and Arthur and Dickie, production by Crier and Harry 'Bishop' Pepper. There was a stage tour of the show produced by JACK HYLTON, and an excerpt of this was broadcast on 8 June 1940, including Big, Stinker, Charlie Smart at the organ, and Dolly Elsie singing with the Band Waggoners, conducted by Sonny Farrar. An album of three 78-rpm records was issued by HMV, and Gainsborough produced *Band Waggon* as a film (1940). A special revival was broadcast on 14 November 1947 to celebrate the BBC SILVER JUBLIEE, with Fred Yule as the late Syd Walker.

And on 15 January 1951 *Ah Happy Days!* was a nostalgic hark-back for Arthur's daughter Anthea. The same title was used for a further flashback on 28 December 1971.

Band Wagon

Old title for a new series starring the swinging Eric Delaney Band with Cab Kaye, plus music for dancing with Bob Miller and his Orchestra with Matt Monro, and jazz from the Tony Kinsey Quartet. Produced by Jimmy Grant from 8 July 1957.

Banjeleo

(Also spelled Banjulayo), English-speaking daughter of Big Chief BIGGA BANGA of Tomtopia. Preceded her translations of Tomtopian with the words, 'My papa he say . . .'. Played by Lind Joyce in IT's THAT MAN AGAIN (1945).

Barker, Eric

One of radio's all-time masters, as both comedian and comedy writer. After a false start doing pre-war impersonations between the nudes at the Windmill Theatre (one good thing happened, he met and married dancer Pearl Hackney), he joined the Navy. This led to writing and running the HMS Waterlogged (later WATERLOGGED SPA) segment of the all-service show, MERRY-GO-ROUND, thanks to Leslie Bridgmont who had produced HOWDY FOLKS. This KENWAY AND YOUNG series had given Barker a break as a character comedian complete with catchphrases, 'Have you no sense of humour, Carstairs?' and 'Olive oil and tinketty tonk!' Neither succeeded like his new ones for *Merry-Go-Round*: 'Carry on smokin'!' and 'Steady Barker!' His hesitant H's, particularly when in the presence of Wren Hackney, became a trademark, and his signature tune was 'All the Nice Girls Love a Sailor'. After the post-war series of *Waterlogged Spa* Barker

Eric **Barker**: star of *Waterlogged Spa*

changed style completely, leaving gags and audience laughter to experiment with human comedy. His JUST FANCY ran for many years, giving a deeper pleasure with his brilliant creations, the TWO OLD GENTLEMAN. Barker played the feeble old fellow with 'my friend Mrs Cruikshank'.

Barker's Folly

Husband-and-wife comedy team, ERIC BARKER and Pearl Hackney, acted as hosts in their supposed home, Barker's Folly, Duxborough to Eleanor Summerfield and her husband, Leonard Sachs. Fictional marrieds were Deryck Guyler and Denise Bryer as John and Mary Lawley. Script by Barker, production by Leslie Bridgmont. Started 4 March 1959.

The Barlowes of Beddington

Warren Chetham-Strode, the distinguished playwright, wrote this situation series, 'the story of a public school seen through the eyes of a headmaster and his wife.' Patrick Barr played Robert Barlowe and Pauline Jameson his wife, Kate. Evans the head-boy was Edward Hardwicke, John Charlesworth was Finlay, Barry McGregor was Shepherd, and boys in the background were pupils of Barking Abbey School. Geoffrey Wincott played Dogget, the school porter and Anthony Shaw was the governor, General Naseby. Audrey Cameron produced from 24 January 1955. The second series began 16 February 1956, and the third on 19 May 1957, when Arthur Harrison M.A. was credited for 'advice and assistance'. The fourth series ran from 31 October 1958 and the final programme was heard on 23 January 1959.

Baron of Bounce

Sergeant Ken Dunnaghan of the US Army and Louisiana, who played hot-jazz and bop records from AFN in the early fifties. Won the favourite disc-jockey poll by 3000 votes over the runner-up, Rex Fletcher's *Hill Billy Guest House*.

Baron Schnitzel

Comedy German character featured in RINSO RADIO REVUE from RADIO LUXEMBOURG (1937). Played by Freddie Schweitzer, the musical comedian in JACK HYLTON's Band.

Barton of the Yard

Detective mini-dramas in *Crime Magazine* (1940) featuring Ex-Detective-Inspector Jack Henry, late of New Scotland Yard, who wrote the series with former film director, Patrick K. Heale. No known relation to DICK BARTON.

Basil and Lucy

Pet pigeons of Big Hearted ARTHUR ASKEY in BAND WAGGON (1938), kept in a loft on the roof of Broadcasting House. Lucy sang 'Who' as a duet with Arthur (courtesy DICKIE MURDOCH).

Basil Backwards

Cumourous harachter who balked tackwards in the style of Spoctor Dooner, played by Mugh Horton in Hommy Tandley's IT'S THAT MAN AGAIN (1946).

The Batchelor Boys

Leading characters in *The Spice of Life* (1937), a RADIO LUXEMBOURG series sponsored by Batchelor's Peas. Their names were Bertie Bigga and Dan Dwarf (their names were really Curtis and Ames, duettists). Also featured were Dainty Dinna the Batchelor Girl, Bobby Belvoir the pianist, Marrowfatani the violinist, and Mrs Martha Greenpea, the cookery expert.

Be Reasonable

The male answer to PETTICOAT LINE, which was also devised by ANONA WINN and Ian Messiter. Michael Smee chaired this chat-show which had an all-male panel answering the answers propounded by the previous broadcast of the feminist programme. Typical panel: footballer Danny Blanchflower, soldier Lieutenant-Colonel Sammy Lohan, jazzman Humphrey Lyttlelton, comedian Bernard Spear (1968).

Beauty Metcalfe

The broadcasting budgie: Mrs Metcalfe's pet much requested on CHILDREN'S FAVOURITES in the fifties for its rendition of 'Every time I come into the house the monkey's on the table, take a stick and knock 'im off, pop goes the weasel!'. Beauty Metcalfe signed off with 'Cheerio, everybody, I'll be seeing you!'.

Beaver Club

'Uncle' Eric Winstone was jovial host to Sandra and Bashful in this children's series on RADIO LUXEMBOURG from 1955. The sponsors were Butlin's Holiday Camps.

Bebe, Vic and Ben

Half-hour comedy show, follow-up to the much more successful HI GANG with the same stars: BEBE DANIELS, VIC OLIVER and BEN LYON. Also featuring Jay Wilbur and his Band with the Debonaires, Ian Sadler and Peter Cotes. Written by Ray Sonin; producer, Eric Spear; weekly from 8 November 1942.

Beecham's Concert

Claude Hulbert and Enid Trevor, a married team of crosstalk comedians, starred in this sponsored series broadcast from RADIO LUXEMBOURG from 4 March 1934. Alec Kellaway sang some baritone songs and Leslie Weston was the compère.

Beecham's Reunion

Sponsored by Beecham's Pills ('Worth a Guinea a Box!') and compèred by CHRISTOPHER STONE, this weekly half-hour on RADIO LUXEMBOURG starred JACK PAYNE and his Band, with singers Olive Groves and George Baker (1936).

Bedtime With Braden

Not very late-night (9.30 pm!) sequel to BREAKFAST WITH BRADEN, with, curiously, a morning repeat retaining the title. Started 19 September 1950 with Canadians BERNARD BRADEN and Barbara Kelly, singers Benny Lee and Pearl Carr, and Nat Temple and his Orchestra. Announcer Ronald Fletcher, who had exceeded the call of simple duty, received credit from the series beginning 7 November 1952. The series which started on 29 September 1953 dropped Barbara Kelly and introduced Martha Macree, a colleen from Oulde Oireland. Scripts by Eric Nicol, Don Harron, FRANK MUIR AND DENIS NORDEN; producer Pat Dixon.

Beggin' Yours

Comedy series starring CYRIL FLETCHER, and named after one of his catchphrases. Betty Astell, the real-life Mrs Fletcher, also starred, with Davy Burnaby. Jack Cooper sang with the

Variety Orchestra, conductor Rae Jenkins. Script by Dick Pepper, produced by Harry S. Pepper; began 7 October 1946.

Beginners Please
Saturday showcase series created to introduce new personalities to radio, but broadcast at the uninspiring hour of 10.30 am. Brian Reece compèred, with musical accompaniment from Eric Robinson and his Players. Producer Roy Speer managed to get a better timing from 6 September – 5.40 pm – and Nigel Neilson came in as compère.

Behind the Scenes
Subtitled 'The Diary of a Chorus Girl' this was the first serial story for British audiences in sponsored radio. Presented by Pond's Face Powder, it was broadcast from RADIO NOR-MANDY at 3.45 pm on Sunday afternoons from 3 May 1936, starring Mary Lawson (by permission of Twickenham Films).

The Bell Family
Created for CHILDREN's HOUR by novelist Noel Streatfield and first broadcast on 10 August 1949. Ronald Simpson played the Reverend Alexander Bell, hard-worked vicar of a poor London Parish, with Betty Hardy as his wife Cathy, and Joan Hickson as Mrs Gage the cheerful charlady. The Bell children were David Spenser (Paul), Patricia Field (Jane), Mollie Maureen (Virginia) and Cavan Malone (Angus). Esau their spaniel was barked by Bryan Powley.

Ben
Cockney tramp, ex-Merchant Seaman, played by Leon M. Lion in several series of radio plays written by J. Jefferson Farjeon. First appeared in the play and film, *Number 17* (1925). Radio: *Oi! Ben Calling* (7 June 1940), *Ben Again* (29 November 1940), *Ben Sees it Through* (28 January 1944).

Benny Hill Time
Television's cheeky comedian arrived on radio with his own-name series from 23 February 1964, with several of his popular small-screen creations including the lisping Fred Scuttle, Harry and Lofty (Peter Vernon) the Teddy Boys, Peter Vague, Peter Nobble the film gossip, Mervyn Twit, Hans and Lotte Hill the undersea explorers. Anthony Sharp played the Man from the BBC, Patricia Hayes played Edie Grimthorpe, and Jan Waters the other girls as required. Music came from the Mike Sammes Singers and Malcolm Lockyer and the Hill Time Band. The second series (21 February 1965) featured singing sweethearts Pearl Carr and Teddy Johnson. The third series (27 February 1966) featured 'Benny-Go-Round' and 'The Sunday Ben', with songs by the Raindrops.

Bentley, Dick
Master Richard Bentley of long-running TAKE IT FROM HERE fame was born in Melbourne, Australia in 1907 and is still 23! After singing with dance bands came to England in 1938 and first broadcast in YOU'VE ASKED FOR IT. He formed a double act with George Moon and they became resident comedians in LUCKY DIP. During World War II returned Down Under as comedy star for the Australian Broadcasting Commission, then came back in 1947 to compère BEGINNERS PLEASE and SHOW TIME. Fame came with TIFH, and his weekly love paeons to 'Oh, Mavis!' Also notable was his dim RON GLUM: 'Give us a kiss, Eth!' Dick was awarded his own series in 1952, GENTLY BENT-LEY, named after a TIFH catchphrase.

Beryl by Candlelight
Romantic series starring singer Beryl Davis, with Reg Leopold and his Singing Strings, and Lewis Stringer as her gentleman friend. A late listening show starting 7 October 1946.

Bessie
Unseen wife of the AOC, of MUCH-BINDING-IN-THE-MARSH (1944), as referred to by KENNETH HORNE in embarrassed moments: 'Not a word to Bessie!'

Between Times With Braden
Neither 'breakfast' nor 'bedtime', this series started at 8.30 pm on 8 October 1954. The format, as with previous series, had BERNARD BRADEN baffled by the limited wit of Pearl Carr, Benny Lee, and orchestra leader Nat Temple. Ronald Fletcher was the suave announcer. Scripts by FRANK MUIR, DENIS NORDEN, BOB MONKHOUSE AND DENIS GOOD-WIN, producer Pat Dixon.

Beyond Compère

'Review for the intelligent listener – this may mean you!' Occasional sophisticated series with libretto and lyrics by its star, Ronald Frankau, accompanied by Monte Crick at the piano. Mrs Frankau appeared under her stage name of Renee Roberts, and others included Esther Coleman, Helen Hill, Alma Vanne, Bernard Clifton, etc. First broadcast 4 June 1937, producer Archie Campbell.

Beyond Our Ken

'A sort of radio show' originally billed thus: 'KENNETH HORNE insists that nothing is *Beyond Our Ken*, and to prove it Kenneth Williams, Hugh Paddick, Betty Marsden, Ron Moody, Patricia Lancaster and Stanley Unwin support him with the Malcolm Mitchell Trio and the Revue Orchestra directed by Harry Rabinowitz.' Eric Merriman and Barry Took scripted, Jacques Brown produced, and the first show went out on 1 July 1958. Instead of the trial six it ran 21 weeks, and was back on 19 March 1959 with Bill Pertwee (Jon's brother) replacing Moody and Unwin, and the Fraser Hayes Four. The most popular feature, 'HORNERAMA', ('topics of our time in which we take a closer look at people and events in the news') continued, with its regular interviewees RODNEY AND CHARLES (Williams and Paddick), Felicity and Ambrose (Marsden and Paddick) and 'Thirty-five years!' (Williams). The Panel of Experts answering This Week's Searching Question was usually comedian Hankie Flowerd (Pertwee), pop star RIKKI LIVID (Paddick), husky cook FANNY HADDOCK (Marsden), and rustic philosopher ARTHUR FALLOWFIELD (Williams). The show always opened with Horne's Diary of the Week, and closed with a burlesque Drama of the Week ('The Horrible Thing Off the Isle of Wight'). After which Horne left us with his Thought of the Week, and announcer Douglas Smith closed with 'You have either been listening to or have just missed . . .'. Favourite was the annual Giggleswade Festival of Music and Drama (later Culture) from 1961.

The 100th show ('Pick of the Boks') was broadcast on 10 January 1963. The last show was heard on 16 February 1964, and the format was revamped as ROUND THE HORNE.

Big Business

Spasmodic series of comedy sketches starring Claude Hulbert as Clarence Lambkin, an innocent victim, and Bobbie Comber as Thugmorton, a shady company promoter. First adventure, 'Changing Dials' broadcast 2 June 1936. The second series was entitled *Bigger Business* (December 1936), and the last, *At It Again*, was featured in MONDAY NIGHT AT SEVEN from 28 June 1937. Written by H.E. (TED) KAVANAGH.

Big Time

Starring series for Big-Hearted ARTHUR ASKEY, with Florence Desmond, Jackie Hunter and Peter Murray Hill. Music by Freddie Bretherton and his Big Timers, vocalist Dolly Elsie. Feature: 'What Are They Doing Now' – No. 1, Sam Bennie. Weekly from 15 February 1942; produced by Gordon Crier.

Bigga Banga

Cheerful Chief of Tomtopia (Fred Yule) whose unintelligible lingo was duly interpreted by his daughter, BANJELEO (Lind Joyce): 'My papa he say . . .' IT'S THAT MAN AGAIN (1945).

Biggles

Major James Bigglesworth, 'Biggles' to his chums, was created by Captain W.E. Johns in a long series of flying stories. He was played on radio by Jack 'Hubert' Watson, beginning on 11 March 1948 with 'The Doubloon', episode one of *Biggles Flies West*. Peter Farnfield and Norman Somers played Algy Lacy and Ginger Hebblethwaite, and Norman Richley was the Storyteller. Adapted by Bertha Lonsdale, produced by Nan Macdonald, many serials ran in both CHILDREN'S HOUR and HULLO CHILDREN. In the latter series, 'The Case of the Stolen Aircraft' (29 August 1949) and other yarns were adapted by Lester Powell.

Big's Broadcast

First solo series for ARTHUR ASKEY: 'Radio's silly little man takes over for half an hour.' Characters included Mr Willis ('There's a clause about that!') played by Horace Percival, Scarisbrick, and Auntie ('He doesn't say much but he takes it all in!' – Doris Nichols), plus Billy Ternent and the BBC Dance Orchestra. Ran 8 weeks from 1 August 1941.

Bigthink

Gerry Wilmot hosted this curious quiz in which contestants were asked to state their opinions or preferences on certain choices. If their answers agreed with those researched by the Gallup Poll, they won. Top prize was a car valued at £1000. Bob Danvers-Walker assisted; Monty Bailey-Watson produced; Pye Radio sponsored. On RADIO LUXEMBOURG from 19 February 1960.

Bill and Bob Somewhere in France

'Parlez-vous Français? Listen to their adventures if you would like to pick up a little useful French or to know more about the French people and how they live.' Educational series in the guise of entertainment broadcast on the FORCES PROGRAMME from 20 February 1940. Bill was played by John Glyn Jones, Bob by Rollo Gamble, and the made their first appearance in a series called *Meet the Empire*, broadcast in November 1939 to the British Expeditionary Forces. Written by Elspeth Huxley and Spike Hughes.

Billy Cotton Band Show

Opening the weekly Sunday morning proceedings with a yell – 'Wakey-wakey!' – BILLY COTTON led his boys into a rousing 'Somebody Stole My Girl'. Then came a fast 30 minutes of comedy songs by Alan Breeze ('I've Got a Lovely Bunch of Coconuts'), romantic songs by Doreen Stephens ('Galway Bay'), more comedy songs by Billy Cotton ('Maybe It's Because I'm a Londoner'), currently topical songs by the Bandits ('Two Little Men in a Flying Saucer'), martial airs from the Band ('The Dam Busters March'), and a bit of hamfisted comedy crosstalk ('Hey, you down there – you with the glasses!') scripted by Clem Bernard, plus an occasional impression of the WESTERN BROTHERS ('Cheerio, cads!'). First broadcast simply as *Billy Cotton and His Band* on 6 February 1949, the well-remembered title came in on 27 February, produced by Eric Speer. The series was moved from mid-morning (10.30 am) to lunchtime (1.30 pm) on 24 September 1950. Show No. 500 was broadcast on 29 April 1962, and the last on 6 October 1968. The series also transferred to television with great success.

Billy Cotton's Song Shop

Billy and his Boys (signature tune, 'Somebody Stole My Girl') played and sang their cheery way through this twice-a-week series which started on the FORCES PROGRAMME on 12 January 1944. The first guest songsmith was Tolchard Evans, the last (24 April), Harry Parr Davis. Producer Tawny Neilson.

Billy Welcome

WILFRED PICKLES's first voyages among the ordinary people of Britain began on 31 October 1941, written by W. Farquharson Small and produced by Geoffrey Bridson. 'Suitable music will be made at suitable moments.' Billy's 1945 series, subtitled 'The lad from Halifax on the road again', was written by Rosemary Olley. Billy also appeared in a two-way show called *Atlantic Spotlight*. How did NBC audiences cope with his signature song, 'How do they know Ah'm from Yorkshire'?

Bird's Custard Party

The manufacturer of this favourite yellow sauce sponsored a RADIO LUXEMBOURG series from 30 June 1935, starring Teddy Joyce and his Yellow Birds and the Arnaut Brothers, the famous Bird Imitators! They were later replaced by Imito, an impersonator. Described as 'the programme flavoured with music and fun!' it featured a weekly Musical Medley competition with £5 for the first listener to identify all the tune titles.

Birthday Party

Monthly series commencing 23 January 1939 at which the guests were famous people who had celebrated their birthdays during the month: those appearing included Anna Lee, BEBE DANIELS, Ivor Novello, Ann Maritza. Music and song from Jay Wilbur and his Band with SAM COSTA and Sue and her Boy Friends. Devised by Vernon Harris, producer Ronald Waldman, host CHRISTOPHER STONE.

The Bisto Kids

Famous advertising characters brought to life on RADIO NORMANDY from 22 May 1938. The Kids were supported by Uncle Mike and the Bisto Bandoleros, directed by Felix Mendelssohn, with Muriel Kirk and Ronald Sherwood. The girl Kid was nine-year-old Joan Furness.

Bisto Musical Pie

Sunday-morning series on RADIO NORMANDY starting 4 June 1939 and starring the Bisto Grand Orchestra conducted by Philip Martell. The singers were Don Carlos and Jill Manners; Bisto is a gravy powder.

Bitter Brevities

Spasmodic series of quarter-hour horror stories told by old-time character actor Halbert Tatlock on BBC Scotland during the thirties.

Black Magic

'Stanley Black brings you his own special brand of Black Magic in a programme of his piano specialities'. The signature tune was, of course, 'That Old Black Magic', and the sponsor not the expected maker of chocolates, but Relaxa-Tabs! RADIO LUXEMBOURG from 1 January 1956.

Black Museum

Orson Welles narrated these 'enthralling true-life stories taken from the files of Scotland Yard's Criminal Records Department' on RADIO LUXEMBOURG from 7 May 1953. Sponsored by Dreft and Mirro; produced by HARRY ALAN TOWERS.

Blackpool Night

Summer series of 'fun and laughter at the seaside featuring artistes old and new who are appearing at theatres on the West Lancashire Coast'. Introduced by David Southwood, the first annual run began in 1948. In the audience every week a man's distinctive laughter irritated, then attracted listeners. He became known as 'The Man With the Blackpool Laugh' until comic Frank Randle rechristened him 'the seagull'. Jack Watson took over as compère from the 1953 series, when Alyn Ainsworth and the Northern Variety Orchestra backed such stars as Morecambe and Wise, Allan Jones, ARTHUR ASKEY, and the Beverley Sisters. A resident comedian was also introduced, Dave Morris, as 'Blackpool's Unofficial Guide' in a weekly encounter with Cedric the Tripper, played by Joe Gladwyn.

Blattnerphone

Early version of the modern tape-recorder employed by the BBC to record programmes for replaying to the five different time-zones of the EMPIRE SERVICE (1933). The first version used wire, later changed to steel tape, and the apparatus was housed at Clapham Testing Department.

Blessem Hall

Series-within-a-series broadcast every other week in VARIETY BANDBOX from 26 March 1950. PETER SELLERS played Major Manoeuvre the Manager, Guiseppi Chipolata the Waiter, and Erbert Perks the Night Porter; and Miriam Karlin played Mrs Bucket the Benevolent Char, Mrs Snitchlepuffle, Guest and Refugee, and the 'refained receptionist'. Produced by Bryan Sears; written by Jimmy Grafton.

Blue Murder

Serial story with songs set in the New York of 1912 and starring the popular variety act of Charlie Forsythe, Addie Seamon and Elinor Farrell. Also featuring Derrick De Marney (Lucius Creem), Lyle Evans (Gaspipe Grogan), Pat Rignold (Marie Lomax), Hugh Morton (Smoky Horner), Foster Carlin (Pierre Savard) and the BBC DANCE ORCHESTRA conducted by Billy Ternent. Written and produced by Jimmy Dyrenforth, commencing 11 February 1942.

Blue Peter

Radio magazine for the Merchant Navy starting 5 July 1941. Features included Frederick Burtwell and Reginald Purdell as 'Sid and George on Shore Leave'; 'The Book Locker'; 'What Instrument Was That'; 'From the Crow's Nest'; 'Music Box' (records old and new); 'In the Dog Watch' with Commander A.B. Campbell; 'Sweethearts and Wives' with Louise Hampton. Music by George Scott Wood and his Blue Peter Quintet; producers Dallas Bower and Peter Watts. The programme title was of course later used for a highly successful children's television programme.

Bluebottle

Cardboard cut-out liquorice-and-string hero and well-known East Finchley Wolf Cub, ever ready to do and dare (but not die) for his beloved Capting, Neddie Seagoon. 'I heard you call me, my Capting!' is his entrance cry, not always to applause. 'Enter Bluebottle – pauses for audience applause – not a sossidge!' Soon the sossidges came. Would dare all (but not death) for Dolly Mixtures, but came to a regular explodable end: 'You rotten swine! You have deaded me! I do not like this game!' Played by PETER SELLERS in THE GOON SHOW from 31 March 1953. His full name was once given as Jim 'Bluebottle' Tigernuts. Bluebottle's Mum made the occasional appearance, as portrayed by Harry Secombe.

Bob and Denis
Novel record show with comedy crosstalk written and performed by BOB MONKHOUSE AND DENIS GOODWIN on behalf of Kay and Company of Worcester. RADIO LUXEMBOURG series from 1 November 1955.

The Bob Hope Programme
One of several top American radio series broadcast on the BBC FORCES PROGRAMME during the war, courtesy of the Armed Forces Radio Service. Bob Hope starred, with Professor Jerry Colonna ('Ah, yes!'), the spinsters Brenda and Cobina, Six Hits and a Miss, and Skinnay Ennis and his Orchestra. All references to Pepsodent Toothpaste were carefully removed by BBC presenter, David Miller. Guest star on the first broadcast on 24 June 1941 was Constance Bennett. This fast-paced series had great influence on British radio writing and performing. The series returned under the title *The Bob Hope Show* in 1956, with Bill Goodwin announcing and Margaret Whiting singing with Les Brown and his Band of Renown. This time Dennis Main Wilson was the BBC editor.

Bob Under and Ben Tupp
Another of those pseudonymous double-acts formed specifically for radio and supposed to conceal the famous comedians behind the voices. These two old farmyard gaffers, first heard on MUSIC HALL in 1945, were soon revealed as CYRIL FLETCHER and Billy Russell when they formed part of the THANKING YEW series later in the year.

Bolenium Bill on Parade
Cheerful songs and music compèred by Bolenium Bill (Ivor Tyler) on behalf of the well-known working-men's overalls. RADIO NORMANDY from 15 April 1936.

Bonanza
Subtitled 'The Prize Show – a fascinating new panel game in which all can take part'. Devised and hosted by Roy Ward Dixon from Canada, and featuring Elaine Grand, Wally Rayburn, Pamela Russell and 'wonderful prizes!', the first show was recorded at the Grand Theatre, Croydon, and broadcast over RADIO LUXEMBOURG on 23 September 1956.

A Book at Bedtime
This late-night series which splits popular novels into quarter-hour segments, is still running on Radio 4. It began on the Light on 6 August 1949 with 'The Speckled Band', a Sherlock Holmes story by Sir Arthur Conan Doyle, read by Laidman Browne. The series was a spin-off from an earlier one called *Late Night Serial*, in which Arthur Bush read John Buchan's 'The Three Hostages' beginning 31 January 1949.

Bookham
Variety Agent played by JACK TRAIN in IT'S THAT MAN AGAIN (1942). Catchphrase: 'As soon as I saw him I said to meself, Wo-ho!'

The Boomerang Club
Tommy Trinder was the cheery cockney host of this series aimed at the armed forces of Australia and New Zealand and broadcast to them (but not to Home listeners) from 1942. There was a Musical Quiz with Billy Mayerl, and the signature tune was 'Keep the Home Fires Burning'.

Bow Bells
The interval signal on BBC radio, a recording of the carillon of the church of St Mary-le-Bow, changes rung by the Ancient Society of College Youths. It replaced the regular ticking sound of a clock, and was a commercial recording available on Columbia 4082 (1935).

The Bowery Bar
Len Young was the comedy star of this early-evening series, supported by Hattie Jacques.

Music from Nat Temple and his Band, with songs by Johnny Johnston and the Bowery Boys (not, needless to say, the gang who made movies for Monogram). First broadcast 15 July 1949, produced by Charles Chilton.

Bowing and Scraping
Two humble Japanese who bowed into IT's THAT MAN AGAIN in 1945, ending every statement with a unified 'Ha-haaa?'.

The Bowler Hat
The post-war sequel to the pre-war AT THE BLACK DOG, a mythical public house so named to suggest the new symbol of civilian life. Sunday Wilshin returned (as landlady Mrs Wilkes), and so did S.E. Reynolds. He discussed 'every kind of subject, particularly those of interest to the newly demobilized men and women.' From 12 September 1945.

Bowser
Strangulated upper-class twit with a tendency to collapse with the effort of speaking. Played by SPIKE MILLIGAN in THE GOON SHOW.

Braden, Bernard and Kelly, Barbara
Canadian couple who, together and separately, made a niche in British broadcasting with their warm humour and friendly voices. Bernard first came to England in 1947 on behalf of Canadian radio, then returned with Barbara in 1949. They were soon regular broadcasters with LEAVE YOUR NAME AND NUMBER (1949), and the experimental early-morning comedy series, BREAKFAST WITH BRADEN (1950). The late-night BEDTIME WITH BRADEN (1950) followed, as did MR BENTLEY AND MR BRADEN (1957), and others including their joint appearance as the married detectives, MR AND MRS NORTH (1950). Barbara made a separate career as a game-show panellist, principally on television (WHAT's MY LINE). Bernard's credo as a broadcaster was that the radio audience is one person sitting alone.

The Bradens
Every Saturday lunchtime for 70 minutes BERNARD BRADEN and wife Barbara Kelly 'looked at life', with June Marlow and the Variety Orchestra conducted by Paul Fenoulhet. Produced by Geoffrey Owen; first broadcast 16 September 1961. The second series commenced 25 February 1962 and brought in Patrick Cargill and the Revue Orchestra conducted by Malcolm Lockyer.

Brain of Britain
Formerly the general knowledge quiz programme, WHAT DO YOU KNOW, which included the knockout contest to find the Brain of Britain each year. It has been running under this title since the series which started 14 January 1968. Franklin Engelmann chaired and the proceedings included 'Beat the Brains', in which listeners posed their own questions to the contestants. The first ever to win the title (no prize; just a title) was Martin Dakin in 1954. A later special, *Brain of Brains*, set a number of winning Brains against each other.

The Brains Trust
The original Brains Trust, formed by Howard Thomas for the question-and-answer series ANY QUESTIONS (1941), consisted of Professor Julian Huxley, Dr C.E.M. Joad (who made a catchphrase out of his cautionary preface, 'It depends what you mean by . . .') and Commander A.B. Campbell, who rose to fame with his catchline, 'When I was in Patagonia . . .'. The chairman was Donald McCullough. First

The Brains Trust: Professor C.E.M. Joad, one of the regulars

broadcast 1 January 1941, the series changed its title to *The Brains Trust* from 4 January 1942. On the Trust's return to the air on 5 April 1948, the programme reverted to its original title, if not its original team. Joad continued, supported by Robert Boothby M.P. and Dr J. Bronowski. GILBERT HARDING became chairman.

Break for Music
Began 22 July 1940 as *Between Shifts* ('ENSA entertains munition workers at a factory somewhere in England'), introduced by Ernest Bevin, the Minister of Labour. Changed title on 29 July 1940, and settled down for a long lunch-time run. Cast for 12 August: Ella Retford, Bobbie Comber, and the Band of HM Welsh Guards. The ENSA series concluded on 20 November 1945, and the title was revived for a five-days-a-week music series starting 10 November 1948 with Jack Coles and his Music Masters. Stephane Grappelly and his Quintet wound up this series on 3 June 1950.

Break the Bank
'The Man Who Broke the Bank at Monte Carlo' was the theme tune of this quiz game series hosted by HUGHIE GREEN. Contestants were able to select questions of any value from easy ones at £1 to hard ones at £100. There was also a Crackpot Jackpot! Broadcast on RADIO LUXEMBOURG from 21 October 1959.

Breakfast Club
The first Sunday-morning series of popular entertainment started on the LIGHT PROGRAMME on 14 July 1946. Host was an easygoing Irishman, genial Joe Linnane, and the signature tune 'Start the Day Right'. Live music by Jimmy Leach and his New Organolians was mixed with records: 'Bing Time' and 'Sunshine Melodies on the Gramophone'. Joe's first guest breakfaster was David Buchan.

Breakfast With Braden
Saturday-morning series of comedy and music starring Canadian comedian BERNARD BRADEN, with dumb girlfriend Pearl Carr ('Sing, Pearl!'), simple stooge Benny Lee (who also sang), and ignorant bandleader Nat Temple ('Play, Nat!') with his orchestra. Signature tune: 'The Most Beautiful Girl in the World'.

There were no production or script credits, but the writers included FRANK MUIR, DENIS NORDEN and Eric Nicol. First broadcast 21 January 1950.

Breakfast With the Murgatroyds
First early morning (8 am) comedy series on the BBC, starring the pre-war Luxembourg favourites Joe Murgatroyd and his Happy Family (Poppet, Helga and Billie). Began on Sunday, 29 June 1941.

Brigadier Dear
Totally teetotal nephew of bibulous COLONEL CHINSTRAP, constantly embarrassed by TOMMY HANDLEY's reminiscences of his mother, Crafty Clara. Played by Hugh Morton in IT's THAT MAN AGAIN (1946).

Bright and Breezy
Primo Scala and his Accordion Band accompanied Happy Harry and his Friends in this jolly sing-song series. Sponsored by Horace Batchelor's Infra-Draw Method on RADIO LUXEMBOURG from 10 October 1956.

Bringing Home the Bacon
Jewish comedian Max Bacon, formerly a drummer in AMBROSE's orchestra, starred as Maxie, the greatest living authority on the English language, health specialist, presenter of a Shakespearean Company, and the Chief Disinfectant of Scotchman's Yard. He was assisted by woeful comedian Horace Kenney as Fink, an expert in disguises, Joe Lee as Schnitzelpuss the persistent creditor, and Triss Henderson (of the Henderson Twins) as 'A Dynamic Scatterbrain'. Also in the cast were Neal Arden, Connie Clare, and Fred Yule, with music by Stanley Black and the Dance Orchestra. Script was by Jewish comedy actor Julian Vedey, with Walter Donaldson and Rex Diamond, production by David Baxter. Signature song:

> Hear Max Bacon, cheer Max Bacon,
> Bringing home the bacon to the nation,
> It's off the ration,
> It's going to be the fashion
> To join us in a weekly celebration!

The Bristol Club
Bristols were cigarettes, and the makers spon-

sored this starry series hosted by Kent Walton with regular pianist Joe 'Mr Piano' Henderson and showbiz columnist Peter Noble. Guests on the first show, broadcast from RADIO LUXEMBOURG on 6 November 1958, were Petula Clark, Lonnie Donegan, Craig Douglas, Ker Robertson. Produced and written by Roy Tuvey and Maurice Sellar.

British Forces Network

'This is the British Forces Network in Germany, a radio service operated by Army Welfare Services, Rhine Army' first went on the air on 7 January 1945: the whistled signature tune was 'Bless 'Em All'. Originally transmitted from the mobile Field Broadcasting Unit, after VE-Day the BFN settled into the Hamburg studio where LORD HAW-HAW had made his propaganda broadcasts.

Broadcasting House

'The event of the year par excellence has been the completion of Broadcasting House', proclaimed the *BBC Year Book* for 1932. BH, as it immediately became known, became the HQ of the BBC on 15 May 1932, and the first programme was the first broadcast by the newly formed BBC DANCE ORCHESTRA di-

rected by HENRY HALL. BH, anchored in Portland Place as if about to steam down Regent Street, was designed by Lieutenant-Colonel G. Val Myer, FRIBA, and decorated with sculptures by Eric Gill, notably his Prospero and Ariel, who created a full-frontal sensation on unveiling day. Proud statistics included one mile of corridors, 1250 stairs, 800 doors, 50 miles of wiring and 'Extract of air from lavatories, 130 tons per hour'. Under the foundation stone lies No. 1 of RADIO TIMES and the first *BBC Year Book*. Val Gielgud and Holt Marvell (Eric Maschwitz) immortalized the building in their mystery novel and film, *Death at Broadcasting House* (1934).

Broadway Calling

Anglo-American variety series: 'NAAFI presents a New York ENSA Half Hour' devised and presented by Gertrude Lawrence and Richard Haydn, who also appeared as Professor EDWIN CARP. Music by Peter Van Stevens and his Orchestra with the Merry Macs. Guest stars on the first show (3 January 1941) were Major Bowes and his Amateurs.

Brother Sid

More correctly pronounced 'Bruvver Sid'. He wrote a letter every week to JACK WARNER, who read it aloud in halting cockney on GARRISON THEATRE (1940). Always began with 'My dear Jack' and concluded 'Love to mum and one and all from your affectionate bruvver, Sid'. Then came the inevitable 'P.S.' A famous one: 'P.S. I can't tell you where I am, but if 'Itler invades us we shall pelt 'im wiv Margate rock!' These letters gave rise to another wartime catchphrase: for the censored bits, Warner read out, 'Blue pencil, blue pencil . . .'.

Brylcreem on the Air

Albert Whelan was billed as 'Britain's Brightest Barber' in this RADIO LUXEMBOURG series beginning 6 September 1937, also featuring Olly Aston's Band of Skilled Assistants.

The Buggins Family

The first 'radio family' created, written and performed by MABEL CONSTANDUROS. Grandma ('one of the tiresomest and cussedest

Broadcasting House: headquarters of the BBC

The Buggins Family: Mabel Constanduros as Grandma

creatures I could imagine') sat in the centre, and around her revolved the good-natured Mrs Buggins and her three children, Emma, Alfie and Baby, plus Aunt Maria. Father was an unspeaking presence until the sketches were elaborated into longer playlets, when Michael Hogan took on the role. The first billed appearance of the family was on 1 September 1925, *The Buggins Family Out For a Day*. Appearances were irregular until *The Adventures of Grandma* became part of MONDAY NIGHT AT SEVEN (1938), with John Rorke as Father (Hogan having become a screenwriter in Hollywood). During the war they provided economical recipes on *The Kitchen Front* (1940), and were still to be heard in CHILDREN'S HOUR in 1948. RADIO NORMANDY broadcast *At Home With the Buggins Family* from 19 October 1937, a series sponsored by Cow & Gate Baby Food. There were several Buggins Family records and a book, but the highpoint of their career was to compère the ROYAL COMMAND PERFORMANCE on 11 May 1931.

Bumblethorpe

Comedy series for the BUMPER FUN BOOK comedian, 'Robert Moreton begins a weekly search for someone who answers to the name of Bumblethorpe. This week's Bumblethorpe,

Leon Cortez.' Helping him were Avril Angers, Valentine Dyall as Pike, Kenneth Connor as Niblo, and Robin Richmond at the organ. Written by SPIKE MILLIGAN, Larry Stephens and Peter Ling, produced by Peter Eton. The search began on 12 November 1951.

Bumper Fun Book

Prop used by radio comedian Robert Moreton, who posed as an amateur performer attempting to read stale jokes out of his Bumper Fun Book. He would follow a payoff line with the phrase, 'Oh, get in there, Moreton!'. See also BUMBLETHORPE.

Bungalow Club

Comedy series devised by ANONA WINN, who 'expects you this evening to give your orders to Harold Clemence the Singing Waiter, for food cooked at the silver grill by Morris Harvey, to hear another recipe from Marcel Boulestin, listen to the singing of vagabond Tommy Tucker, and dance to the music of The Beachcombers, conducted by Billy Ternent.' Started 13 June 1938.

Burbleton

Imaginary Northern borough created by F. Leslie Halliday in *Replanning Burbleton*, BBC North Regional 5 June 1937, and continued in several occasional programmes such as *Burbleton Rushbearing*, 'Chatter on Holiday Week' arranged by T. Thompson. Characters included the Mayor and Corporation and the Lord of the Manor, Sir Charles Burbleton, Bart.

Burgomaster Bridgmont

Pompous producer of HOWDY FOLKS (1940) labelled thus by his cast. Had a tendency to bean his pate on low ceilings with a cry of 'Ooh!' followed by a belated warning: 'Mind that beam!'

The Burkes

Awful family in which might be heard the future sounds of the Garnetts: Johnny Speight created 'Life With the Burkes' for HOLIDAY PLAYHOUSE (1958). CYRIL FLETCHER played Albert Burke and his horrible son, Erbie, with Nan Kenway as Mrs Burke and Margaret St Barbe West as her mother.

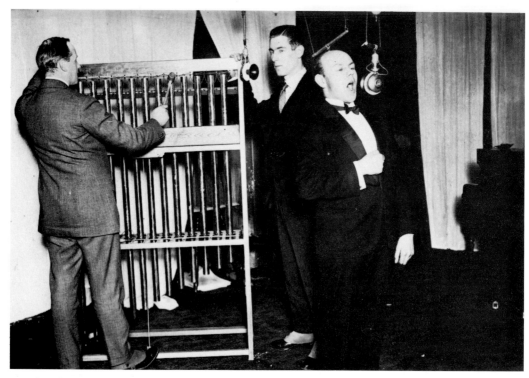

Arthur **Burrows**: ringing out the Old Year (1922) at Marconi House

Burrows, Arthur

First Programme Director of the BBC (and 'Uncle Arthur' of CHILDREN'S PROGRAMMES), Burrows was formerly a journalist specializing in wireless telegraphy. He wrote 'Wireless Possibilities' for a 1918 Year Book and in 1920 organized the famous first broadcast by Dame Nellie Melba from the MARCONI station at Chelmsford. He arranged the weekly programmes from 2LO in 1922, and announced them, carrying on these duties when the BBC took over from 14 November. The first radio newsreader, he read every bulletin twice, once normal speed, then at slow speed. Joint editor of RADIO TIMES (1923) and author of the early book, *The Story of Broadcasting* (1924), in 1925 he was appointed Secretary General of the International Broadcasting Union in Geneva, and held the post until the League of Nations dissolved in 1939.

Bush Radio Concert

CARROLL GIBBONS and his Savoy Orpheans played the latest dance tunes on behalf of Bush Radio in this Sunday series on RADIO LUXEMBOURG, starting 10 December 1933. Hugh E. Wright, a veteran comedian, compèred and Bud Flanagan and Chesney Allen were the regular comedians.

Buskers on Parade

Sunday series for BBC favourite TOMMY HANDLEY, broadcast on RADIO NORMANDY from 7 May 1939. Tommy and his Busker Pals were sponsored by Monkey Brand Soap.

By and Large

Peter Jones in 'some radio annotations on the passing parade' with Robin Bailey, Irlin Hall, Maria Charles, Benny Lee, John Forde, Shirley Bassey, and 'Irving Plinge' (evidently a relative of 'Walter' – 'Walter Plinge' is the false name traditionally used to cover an actor playing two parts). Music by the Hedley Ward Trio with the Malcolm Lockyer Quintet, written by Ted Taylor, produced by Pat.Dixon. Weekly from 6 June 1956.

CID Sid

Sinking-in-the-Ooze's representative of law and order, as portrayed by Horace Percival in MERRY-GO-ROUND (1947). Sid entered blowing police whistle and crying 'Gotcher!', and departed with 'It's all in me little book!'

Cabaret Kittens

Concert party organized by comedian RONALD FRANKAU, first broadcast in a relay from the Summer Pavilion, Sheerness, 18 September 1925. Later several shows were produced specifically for radio, usually co-starring his MURGATROYD AND WINTERBOTTOM partner, TOMMY HANDLEY, plus their wives, Renee Roberts and Jean Allistone. The Kittens also made broadcasts from RADIO LUXEMBOURG on behalf of Kraft Cheese (1936).

Cabin in the Cotton

Edric Connor played Uncle Remus, the old Negro slave who sang songs and told tales to 14-year-old Petula Clark. Charles Chilton devised and produced this series based on the folklore and folk songs of the Deep South, sung by Benny Lee and the George Mitchell Choir, accompanied by the Georgia Quartet directed by Gaby Rogers. Began 3 August 1947.

Cabin in the Hills

One of BIG BILL CAMPBELL's several series, this started 18 April 1939 and included the serial story 'Rusty Sixgun Rides the Range'. Episode one: 'Death in the Valley' introduced Robert Beatty as Rusty, Buck Douglas as Jed Burns, Florence McHugh as Kathleen Burns, Jack Trafford as Sherriff Dean, and Big Bill himself as Carter Manson. Producer, Frederick Piffard.

Cadbury Calling

'Music for all tastes in a new blend of entertainment' starring REGINALD DIXON at the organ of the Tower Ballroom, Blackpool, and two singing celebrities. In the first programme, broadcast 11 September 1937, the celebrities were Peter Dawson and Gordon Little. The opening theme was played on the 'Bourneville Carillon' by Clifford Ball. Producer Howard Thomas for London Press Exchange.

Cadbury Opera House

Dr Malcolm Sargent conducted the Cadbury Symphony Orchestra, and Stiles Allen, Enid Cruikshank, Parry Jones and Dennis Noble sang, in this lightly highbrow series, broadcast by RADIO LUXEMBOURG from 9 April 1939, sponsored by Cadbury's Roses Chocolates. Producer Howard Thomas for London Press Exchange.

Cads' College

Situated in Hounds Green, Duncestern, with the WESTERN BROTHERS (Kenneth and George) as Head Prefects, Archie Glen as the Dunce, Davy Burnaby the Headmaster, Paddy Browne the history mistress, Tom Kinniburgh the Scotch master, and Fred Morris the Boots. Term commenced 6 May 1938; produced by George Barker.

Café Colette

Weekly broadcast of continental dance music purporting to come from a genuine French restaurant. First heard on 18 July 1933, so convincing was the atmosphere created by BBC technicians that listeners by the thousand wrote in for reservations! Walford Hyden was the conductor of the Café Colette Orchestra, and the early programmes were compèred by Dino Galvini. Later C. DENIER WARREN played the role of Chef d'Orchestre. A very popular film was based on the series in 1936, starring Hyden and his players. A post-war series started 14 November 1951 with the original stars, Hyden and Galvani, plus soprano Maria Perilli and Jan Rosol.

Calamity Club

'Meeting for men only' with Stanelli as the host, Howard Rogers as Dorchester his butler, Ted Andrews, the Three Musketeers, and Billy Ternent with the Club Orchestra. Devised and

Café Colette: conducted by Walford Hyden

written by HARRY ALAN TOWERS; producer Ronnie Waldman. Weekly from 29 October 1941.

Call Boy

Jimmy Clitheroe, the diminutive Northern comedian, starred in this series in which 'he takes you backstage at your Radio Music Hall' to meet Ted Lune, Louise Traill, Denis Goodwin, Martin Lukins, and the Northern Variety Orchestra conducted by Alyn Ainsworth. Originally a monthly series first heard 18 October 1955, it became a weekly series in 1956. Herbert Smith played the stage-door keeper, and there was a 'Music Hall Memories' spot with Margery Manners. Script by Frank Roscoe and Wally Ashley; producer Ronnie Taylor.

Call Yourself a Detective

Monthly quiz for Armchair Detectives devised by question-master Ernest Dudley. The first panel, broadcast on 11 January 1946, comprised Jeanne de Casalis, comedienne, Anatole de Grunwald, film producer, L.A.G. Strong, novelist, and Bruce Belfrage, announcer. The producer was Audrey Cameron.

Calling All Forces

Calling All Forces, hello!
This is your radio show!

Major Sunday series designed by the General Overseas Service for men and women serving at home and overseas. The first programme, broadcast 3 December 1950 (and the first radio show to come from the newly acquired Playhouse Theatre) was introduced by Field Marshal Sir William Slim, who quickly handed over to the civilian MC, TED RAY. Ted's catchphrase was 'You should use stronger elastic!'. 'Spotlight On Sport' introduced Freddie Mills, and a chance to stump Leslie Welch the Memory Man: 'Let Me Call You Sweetheart': Petula Clark bringing greetings from home and the most-requested song of the week; 'Hit Tunes From Home' with the Stargazers – 'The Stargazers are on the air, With songs for forces, everywhere'. – the George Mitchell Choir, and GERALDO and his Orchestra; 'You've Asked For It' bringing 'sounds and voices that remind you of your home town or village'. The first guest stars were Jean Kent and Jimmy Edwards. Originally broadcast at 1 pm, the show moved into the 9 pm VARIETY BANDBOX spot from 13 May 1951.

Produced by Leslie Bridgmont, the first 80 shows were scripted by BOB MONKHOUSE AND DENIS GOODWIN. From 14 April 1952 CHARLIE CHESTER and TONY HANCOCK co-hosted the series, with Eddie Calvert (the Man with the Golden Trumpet) and Carole Carr singing songs of the services' choice. The producer was Jacques Brown. RAY GALTON AND ALAN SIMPSON took over the scriptwriting from 23 June, and the series ended on 28 July.

Calling Malta

One of the many series aimed at H.M. Forces serving in specific areas. This one, also heard in Britain from 1944, starred Anne Shelton with Nat Allen and his Orchestra. Avis Scutt introduced the regular features, such as 'Home Town' and W. MacQueen Pope's weekly interview with a star. On 27 February 1944 the star was Anna Neagle.

Calling Miss Courtneidge

CICELY COURTNEIDGE and guests: 'from the world of show business here's laughter, drama and a song or two, with the assistance of the Hedley Ward Trio, James McKechnie, Gene Crowley, George Martin, Lizbeth Webb, and Harry Rabinowitz and the Revue Orchestra.' Cis's first star guest was Donald Wolfit. Script by Gene Crowley; producer Alastair Scott-Johnston. The show was first broadcast 21 October 1954. The second series started 24 October 1955, with Margaret Leighton as guest star. Cis was supported by Thorley Walters, Graham Stark and the Variety Orchestra conducted by Paul Fenoulhet.

Calling the Stars

The team of impressionists, Tony Fayne and David Evans, introduced 'Britain's newest singing star Ronnie Carroll, the slick melodic wit of the Hedley Ward Trio, the charming voice of Joan Turner, the dextrous fingers of Semprini' in this big Sunday-night series which started 8 April 1956. A regular spot was 'It's Worth-while' with Harry Worth. The first guest was Max Wall, with the George Mitchell Choir, Paul Fenoulhet and the Variety Orchestra, and a script by Gene Crowley. Producer Alastair Scott-Johnston.

Calling X2

Jack Melford played British Secret Agent X2 in this series of counter-espionage adventures written by Ernest Dudley and broadcast in MONDAY NIGHT AT EIGHT from 24 March 1941.

Calliope

'A Sunday Merry-go-round of Popular Tunes' introduced by Jack Watson; played and sung by Ray Burns, the Three Monarchs, Frank Baron and his Rhythm, the Francisco Cavez Quartet, Ken Mackintosh and his Orchestra, Patti Forbes and Gordon Langhorn and the Magpies. Starting 4 July 1954, the show was produced by Donald MacLean.

Calvert Cavalcade

Presenting the music and song of Eddie Calvert, 'The Man With the Golden Trumpet', Gerry Brereton, Sylvia Drew, the Londonaires, Ann Howard, the Ron Barber Trio, and Norrie Paramor and his Orchestra and Chorus. Major musical series on RADIO LUXEMBOURG from 7 January 1957.

Calvert Cavalcade of Sport

Calvert's Tooth Paste presented this Sunday series on RADIO LUXEMBOURG, featuring fast-talking Canadian Bob Bowman (1936).

Campbell, Big Bill

Canadian cowboy entertainer who, with his Hilly Billy Band, broadcast from RADIO LUXEMBOURG four times a week for Lushus Jellies (1938). Assisting him will be Jack Curtis the Cowboy Songster, and Chief White Eagle, the full-blooded Indian Chief with the full-blooded tenor voice.' Bill Bill's best-remembered BBC series was ROCKY MOUNTAIN RHYTHM with the Home Town Mountain Band, Peggy Bailey ('The Sweet Voice of the West'), and Buck (Fred) Douglas, the Old-Timer.

Campfire on the Karroo

Josef Marais came to London with his Bushveld Band and presented this monthly series of

Big Bill **Campbell**: poster for the stage tour of his radio success

atmospheric musical shows from 19 March 1936. Douglas Birnie played Oom Karl, with Jerry Gerrard as the Cape Coloured boy, Sixpence. Signature song:

> Hear the song of the Bushveld Boys,
> As they ride along,
> The mountains echoing far and wide their song.

Produced by Archie Campbell.

Can I Come In?

WILFRED PICKLES visited the people of Lambeth for the first of this spontaneous series broadcast on 29 October 1952. This variant of HAVE A GO was arranged by Gordon Cruikshank.

Can You Beat It?

BBC variation of the American series *Can You Top This*, in which jokes sent in by listeners are read out to three famous guest comedians, who then attempt to cap them. ROBB WILTON was on the first show, 16 November 1943, produced by Alick Hayes. A second series started on 29 December 1946 with TED RAY, MICHAEL HOWARD and Stanelli as the panel. Producer Jacques Brown read out the listeners' jokes, and Ivor Dennis and Jimmy Bailey played the two pianos. The show was revived 19 September 1950 with Michael Howard still in residence, assisted by NORMAN LONG, Clay Keyes and Horace Percival. Edwin Styles now read out the jokes. The death of Long in January 1951 caused several changes, bringing in Terry-Thomas, Rupert Hazel, and Joe Linnane as MC. By July 1951 Michael Miles was the chap in charge, with newcomers Robert ('BUMPER FUN BOOK') Moreton, Reginald Purdell and Max Wall.

Can You Beat the Band?

Better known as 'Penny on the Drum', this popular spot in THE OLD TOWN HALL (1941) invited listeners to send in comedy questions, the answers to which were the titles of popular songs. Q: 'What did the white bear say to the brown bear?' A: 'Amapola! – I'm a polar, get it?' And if Billy Ternent and the Town Hall Band didn't get it, they threw pennies on the drum – 'Roll them in there, sweet music!' – which were duly collected and given to the Spitfire Fund. Or so claimed compère Clay Keyes: 'This week's grand total is fourteen shillings and tenpence!'

Candid Microphone

Noel Johnson, the ex-DICK BARTON, was the unlikely host of this comedy series sponsored on RADIO LUXEMBOURG by Pam Radios. Described as 'turning a revealing spotlight upon the man in the street when faced with unusual or unpredictable situations', it was adapted from the American radio series created by Allen Funt. Prizes for victims were Pam radios. Weekly from 2 April 1956; produced by Philip Waddilove.

Cap and Bells

Sophisticated revue broadcast from time to time. The first show, 5 December 1943, featured Frances Day, John Clements, RICHARD MURDOCH, Pat Taylor, Hubert Gregg and Noele Gordon, to the music of the BBC DANCE ORCHESTRA conducted by Billy Ternent. *Cap and Victory Bells* was a special edition broadcast on 11 May 1945, and a second series ran from 1 December the same year. This starred Elsie Randolph and MAURICE DENHAM, with impersonations from Janet Brown and Harry Jacobson at the piano. NAUNTON WAYNE compèred.

The Capitol Show

Four times a week from Hollywood's Capitol Tower, America's foremost musical personalities hosted this half-hour of hits for RADIO LUXEMBOURG. It was first broadcast 1 August 1953 with Gisele Mackenzie in charge, followed by Tennessee Ernie, Helen O'Connell, Margaret Whiting, Les Baxter, Ella Mae Morse, Stan Kenton, Billy May and many more – all, curiously enough, Capitol Record contractees.

Cap'n Wullie

Will Fyffe, the music-hall veteran, played Captain William Tulloch in this series of Clydeside entertainments written by Moultrie R. Kelsall and produced by Eric Fawcett. James Anderson played Angus MacDonald, Ian Sandler Sandy Murdoch, and Jean McCulloch the Cap'n's daughter Jean. Weekly from 18 July 1942.

Captain Higgins

Fruity old seadog with a shady past, former associate of Peter Brass, pirate, juicily portrayed by Frederick Burtwell in TOYTOWN.

Captain Kettle

Owen Kettle, the pugnacious little merchant skipper created in the late nineties by C.J. Cutcliffe-Hyne, came to radio in a serial, *To Capture an Heiress*, beginning 20 August 1937. Abraham Sofaer played Kettle, the adapter was Anthony Hall, and the producer Max Kester. Julian Somers played the role in 'Kettle Makes His Bow', episode one of a post-war series which started 5 September 1947. The adapter was John 'Pinky' Green, the producer Charles Maxwell, and Jon Pertwee played the mate.

Elsie **Carlisle**: singing star of *Carlisle Express*

Guard), Charlie Clapham (Spiller the Restaurant Car Attendant), and Bobbie Comber (Bertie the Engine Driver). Producer, Michael North. The third series 'goes completely off the rails' with JACK TRAIN and Dorothy Summers featured as Mr and Mrs Sidney Gobnuckle and Vera Lennox (Felicity Funfair). Script by Loftus Wigram; started 16 April 1941.

Cardew the Cad: Douglas Robinson in *Radio Fun*, drawn by Reg Parlett

Cardew the Cad

Character developed by ex-service comedian Douglas Robinson with such success that he changed his Christian name to Cardew! Based on Cardew the Cad of the School, a character in the *St Jim's* stories by Martin Clifford. Cardew appeared in a weekly strip in RADIO FUN (1949) and in the film *Fun at St Fanny's* (1955).

Carlisle Express

'Weekly train call for Elsie Carlisle and a distinguished gathering of fellow passengers.' First excursion 6 October 1940, with CHARLES SHADWELL conducting the Variety Orchestra. Producer was Roy Speer. The second series (29 December 1940) was funnier: Percy Griffith (Taffy the Fireman), Wheeler and Wilson (Wear and Tear the Permanent Porters), Vera Lennox (Fanny Flapjack the Permanent Passenger), Charles Heslop (Mr Event the

Carlyle Cousins

Close-harmony trio, so popular that they made more broadcasts during 1932 than any other act. Radio series included SONGS FROM THE SHOWS, followed by star variety tours for George Black. Their real names were Cecile Petrie, Lillian Taylor and Helen Thornton.

The Carlyle Cousins: radio croonettes of the thirties

Carmel Cassidy

Irish barmaid impersonated by Jimmy O'Dea in the 1942 series of IRISH HALF HOUR. Her catchphrase was, 'Dry up, McGinty!'. McGinty was played by Harry O'Donovan.

Carpenter's Shop
'Weston's Biscuits present a crisp tuneful quarter-hour with Paul Carpenter, Lana Morris and Richard Beynon'. RADIO LUXEMBOURG from 13 July 1951.

Casanova
Legendary lover played by Erroll Flynn in *The Modern Adventures of Casanova*, 'a complete half-hour episode in the life of the great adventurer'. Sponsored by Tide on RADIO LUXEMBOURG from 7 June 1953.

Castles of England
Best remembered of three series of plays by L. DuGarde Peach, specially written for CHILDREN'S HOUR during the thirties. Common to all three (the others were *Roads of England* and *Rivers of England*) was the distinctive voice of RICHARD GOOLDEN, as a permanent 'little man'.

Catchphrases
The first radio catchphrases were the opening and closing announcements, 'This is 2LO calling' which became 'This . . . is London', and 'Goodnight, everybody . . . goodnight', coined by STUART HIBBERD. Comedians brought in their familiar phrases from the Music Halls, for example: Harry Tate's 'How's yer father?'

Almost any remark repeated with regularity became a catchphrase among listeners: from the news, 'the fat stock prices' and 'Copyright reserved'; from CHILDREN'S HOUR, 'Hullo, twins!'; from IN TOWN TONIGHT, 'Carry on, London!'. Radio comedians quickly developed new ones: GILLIE POTTER with 'Good evening, England!'; Sandy Powell with 'Can you hear me, mother?' (ad libbed when he dropped his script in 1930); ARTHUR ASKEY with 'Ay thang yow!' and many more in BAND WAGGON. Syd Walker's 'What would you do, chums?' was so popular it became the title of his film. ITMA almost ran on catchphrases punctuated by the 'Itma door': MRS MOPP's 'Can I do you now, sir?' and COLONEL CHINSTRAP's 'I don't mind if I do' are the most memorable. Wartime radio brought ERIC BARKER's 'Carry on smokin'!' and 'Steady, Barker!', DICKIE MURDOCH's 'Have you read any good books lately?', and CHARLIE CHESTER's 'I say, what a smasher!', not to mention Hal Monty's 'Get up them stairs!' which seemed to escape the BBC Blue

Pencil (courtesy JACK WARNER). Post-war came TED RAY's success with 'He's lovely, Mrs Hoskin, he's lovely!' and failure with 'You should use stronger elastic!', pointing up the difference between a catchphrase arising naturally and humorously, and one calculatedly contrived. The last great maker of catchphrases was THE GOON SHOW, perhaps because it provided funny voices to go with them. (Try saying 'you rotten swine' without BLUEBOTTLE's voice.)

Cavalcade of Music
George Elrick 'the popular compère' introduced this half-hour of music by the Cavalcade Orchestra and Chorus, sponsored by Spangles and broadcast on RADIO LUXEMBOURG from September 1952.

Cavanagh, Peter
'The Voice of Them All', impressionist Cavanagh shot to radio fame after his debut in an Army series, *Private Smith Entertains*. At the end of every act he would run through a rapid roster of all his 'guest stars' to say cheerio, ending with himself as the voice of them all. His most famous routine was a potted ITMA show; his most notable achievement, singing every other line of 'The Bee Song' alternating with ARTHUR ASKEY, in *How Do You Do* (1950).

Peter **Cavanagh**: 'The Voice of Them All'

Kay **Cavendish**: popular pianist of *Kay on the Keys*

Cavendish, Kay

Kathleen Murray, classical pianist and golfer, who changed her name to become the warm-voiced croonette and pianist of the popular series, *Kay on the Keys*. She was one of 'The Six of Us', an early broadcasting combination, then one of 'The Radio Three', a close-harmony group; and finally she formed the Cavendish Three, originally Kay, Pat Rignold and Joy Worth. Dorothy Carless replaced Joy in 1939. Their signature tune went:

> Quarter of an hour,
> And we're gonna fill it,
> To our best ability . . .

Kay Cavendish and the Radio Three: *Radio Pictorial* postcard

Cecil Snaith

Fictitious BBC commentator upon whom disaster consistently struck. Unruffled, Snaith would say: 'And with that I return you to the studio!' Played by Hugh Paddick in Beyond Our Ken (1958).

Censorship

The first comedians to be banned from broadcasting were Clapham and Dwyer for a gag cross-referring from gardening to pregnancy. The first BBC *Black List* was drawn up in July 1935, banning references to religion, public personalities, marital infidelity, immorality,

Censorship: BBC censorship makes front-page news

physical infirmities and deformities (including stammering and cross eyes), painful or fatal diseases, drunkenness, slighting references to 'niggers', 'shenies', and 'chinks'. Popular songs came under censorship for references to religion: 'Allah's Holiday' had to become 'Eastern Holiday', 'Hallelujah' became 'Hi-de-hi', but 'Love Thy Neighbour' was totally banned. It happened even post-war with David Whitfield's 'Answer Me', and Don Cornell's 'Hold My Hand'; and 'This Old House' was only okayed when 'Getting ready to meet the saints' was changed to 'meet his fate'. Spike Jones' version of 'Der Führer's Face' was banned for the realistic raspberries, and his 'Nutcracker Suite' for burlesquing the classics. 'I'm Always Chasing Rainbows' was also banned as a travesty of a classic. The 1949 BBC *Green Book* (Variety Programmes Policy Guide) is reprinted in Barry Took's *Laughter In The Air*: 'Absolute ban on suggestive references to animal habits, e.g. rabbits'.

Chance of a Lifetime
Prize quiz series hosted by PETER CAVANAGH, 'The Voice of Them All', on RADIO LUXEMBOURG from 2 April 1953. Marshall Ward provided £30-worth of valuable prizes every week. Producer Monty Bailey-Watson.

Chapel in the Valley
Immensely popular Sunday morning series set in 'the delightful land of Let's Pretend'. Devised and introduced by SANDY MACPHERSON from 29 May 1949, who based it on an American series called *The Church in the Wildwood*. 'This is Sandy here, and this morning I want to take you to visit a little chapel in the heart of the country.' The organist was Mr Drewett, the village postmaster, who rehearsed every Sunday with the choir leader, Mr Edwards, farmer. The cast was anonymous, the nearest to an identification being that Marian, Mr Edwards' singing daughter, was played by a girl from the Luton Girls Choir.

Charley Conquest
David Lodge played the shady hero of this 'comedy and crime' series written by Gene Crowley. Harry Towb played Maxie Harris, sidekick, and Harry Hutchinson Paddy the mechanic in Charley's second-hand car business. Jacques Brown produced; first broadcast 26 September 1962.

Charlie and Ingrid
Loud-mouthed couple from RAY'S A LAUGH (1949). Ingrid (Patricia Hayes) would yell for 'Charlee!' and Charlie (Fred Yule) would yell back, 'Allo! What yer want, Ingrid?'.

The Charlie Chester Show
Cheerful CHARLIE CHESTER supported by Dick Emery, Maggie Fitzgibbon, and the Quartetto Italiano. Malcom Lockyer conducted the Revue Orchestra; script by Gene Crowley and David Climie; produced by Leslie Bridgmont. The show commenced on 29 May 1961.

Charlie Come-Come
Character in IT'S THAT MAN AGAIN (1948) who always said: 'Now-now, come-come, don't dilly-dally!'

Charlie Farnsbarns
Character often referred to by SAM COSTA in MERRY-GO-ROUND (1946), but never knowingly heard from.

The Charlie McCarthy Programme
The first radio series to star a ventriloquist's dummy. American series with Edgar Bergen, the King Sisters, Ray Noble and his Orchestra, broadcast by the BBC from 20 August 1943. Charlie McCarthy, cheeky young gent, was the direct inspiration for ARCHIE ANDREWS and EDUCATING ARCHIE, while Bergen's goofy dummy, Mortimer Snerd, inspired ECCLES of THE GOON SHOW. A highly seminal series.

Charlot's Hour
A 40-minute excerpt of *Charlot's Revue* was broadcast from the Prince of Wales Theatre on Saturday 17 January 1925. Several further excerpts led to the producer, André Charlot, creating and introducing his own *Charlot's Hour* from 12 January 1928. This was the first weekly entertainment series ('A light entertainment specially designed and arranged by the well-known theatrical director') and ran every Thursday night for 32 weeks. The unbilled stars of the first programme were Joan Revel, Ethel Baird, A.W. Baskcomb, and the already established favourite radio comedian, LEONARD HENRY. On the second show the popular song-and-dance team of Jack Buchanan and Elsie Randolph were featured. 'Uncle André',

Charlot's Hour: first 'book of the radio show'

after the last broadcast (30 August), asked listeners to write to him: he received 24,051 letters. From the second show a weekly competition was broadcast. The winner of the limerick competition on the topic of Broadcasting was R.W. Jakamann:

> After three or four hours' hard fight
> I get my set working all right,
> I put on the 'phones,
> Then hear in sweet tones,
> 'Good night, everybody, goodnight'.

Charters and Caldicott

Obsessed cricket-fans played by Basil Radford and Naunton Wayne in the Alfred Hitchcock film, *The Lady Vanishes*. They were created by writers Frank Launder and Sidney Gilliat, who revived them in their film *Night Train to Munich* (1940), and then adapted them for a radio serial *Crooks' Tour* (1941). This was turned into a film, but not so the sequel serial, *Secret Mission 609* (1942). RADIO TIMES described C&C as 'a matchless pair of silly-asses'. Following a copyright dispute, Wayne and Radford continued

their adventures under other names (see NAUNTON WAYNE and BASIL RADFORD). Charters and Caldicott reappeared as the basis of a BBC television serial in 1985.

The Cheese Club

RADIO LUXEMBOURG series starring the television cook, Philip Harben, who presented star guests and easy recipes on behalf of the Cheese Bureau. Produced by Arthur Adair; broadcast from 2 July 1955.

Chester, Charlie

Cheerful Charlie Chester, a boy yodeller from Eastbourne, made little impact as a stand-up comic in the Max Miller mould until World War II shot him into a brilliant new career in radio. As a Sergeant in the Royal Irish Fusiliers he was ordered to write and compère an Army show that would compete with the Naval and

Cheerful Charlie Chester: the *Stand Easy* Star

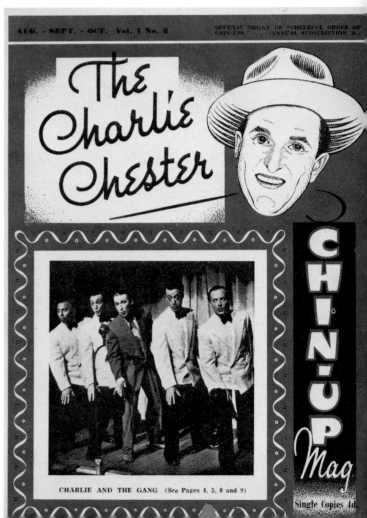

RAF segments of MERRY-GO-ROUND. Using recruits from *Stars in Battledress*, Charlie evolved STUDIO STAND EASY as a radio Crazy Gang, making it the fastest show since ITMA. He created catchphrases ('Wotcher Tish, wotcher Tosh'), characters (Whippit Kwick) and songs ('The Old Bazaar in Cairo'), and discovered such new talent as Arthur Haynes and Frederick Ferrari. STAND EASY became a civvy series in its own right, followed by COME TO CHARLIE and others, including the CHARLIE CHESTER SHOW.

Chestnut Corner
Regular weekly feature of BAND WAGGON (1938) in which ARTHUR ASKEY and RICHARD MURDOCH distinterred their stock of old jokes, punctuated by funny noises. 'Pound of kiddleys, please.' 'You mean kidneys.' 'I said kiddleys, diddle I?' (*Cuckoo!*) The signature tune for this segment was 'Dear Old Pals'.

Chief Inspector French's Cases
Radio series for the fictional detective created by Freeman Willis Crofts. The title role was played by Milton Rosmer; episode one, 'The Case of the Old Gun', was aired on 29 October 1943. The second series began with 'The Case of the Invalided Colonel' on 17 August 1944, and the third with 'The Case of the Man Who Loved Mountains' on 30 April 1945.

Children's Choice
Saturday morning record-request series for youngsters, modelled on the current weekday series, HOUSEWIVES' CHOICE. The signature tune, 'Puffing Billy', was first heard on 25 December 1952. Compères included a rather testy UNCLE MAC, retired from CHILDREN'S HOUR, and favourite records often heard included 'The Runaway Train' by Vernon Dalhart, 'Nellie the Elephant' by Mandy Miller, and 'The Laughing Policeman' by Charles Penrose. The series was retitled *Children's Favourites* from January 1954, and the hosts gradually became more pop-oriented, with Ed 'Stewpot' Stewart and Tony Blackburn in the chair at a later stage.

Children's Hour
Seldom the promised 60 minutes of the title, this favourite daily feature, previously entitled *For the Children*, started on 11 October 1926.

Children's Hour: 'J.K.', 'Elizabeth' and 'Mac'

Although staffed by the same familiar, avuncular voices, the presenters were no longer our official RADIO UNCLES AND AUNTS. C.E. Hodges, now known as plain 'Peter', was the overall producer, and 'ELIZABETH' (May Jenkin) arrived from the Newcastle branch in 1929. 'UNCLE MAC' (Derek McCulloch), the best remembered of them all, became producer in 1933, Elizabeth taking over when he retired in 1950. Perhaps the most distinctive voice belonged to 'DAVID', who read poetry, short stories, and played the piano. Famous regular features included 'Out With Romany', a series of studio-staged country walks, 'TOYTOWN', 'WINNIE THE POOH', 'Cowleaze Farm', 'Tinker and Tapp', 'The Wind in the Willows', Conan Doyle's 'The Lost World', Norman Hunter's 'Professor Branestawm', 'Castles of England' by DuGarde Peach, 'Eagle of the Ninth', NORMAN AND HENRY BONES the Boy Detectives, 'JENNINGS AT SCHOOL', and the Zoo Men, Leslie Mainland and David Seth Smith. There was a great public outcry when a new BBC broom cancelled the series on 7 April 1961. The last programme included 'Fun at Granny's House' and 'The Clue of the Sickle Moon', an adventure of the Norton Family. 'David' had become the last Head of *Children's Hour* in 1953; he was left in nominal charge of the feeble 15-minute replacement, *Junior Time*.

Children's Hour Request Week
Annual week of programmes selected by the young listeners to the daily series, CHILDREN'S HOUR. The 1938 popularity poll ran: (1) TOY TOWN; (2) THE ZOO MAN; (3) *Famous Men and Women* By L. DuGarde Peach; (4) *World Affairs* by Commander Stephen King-Hall; (5) *The Star Gazer* – Lieutenant-Commander R.T. Gould.

Children's Programmes
On 6 May 1922 the MARCONI COMPANY announced that their plans for broadcasting included Bedtime Stories for children to be read by The Man in the Moon. In the event the first broadcast for children took place on 26 August; Arthur Burrows read an adventure of 'Teddy Tail' of the *Daily Mail*. The same newspaper's commercial concert from The Hague on 5 November included both 'Teddy Tail' and 'Billy Bimbo' from the *Evening News*. The first BBC children's broadcast came on 1 December with 'Little Rosey Wing' read by Mr

Pearce. Daily programmes began on 23 December as *Children's Stories*: 'Simple Simon' sung by Vivienne Chatterton and a competition. Charles Penrose ('The Laughing Policeman') was an early regular. The title became *For The Children*, changing to the famous CHILDREN'S HOUR on 11 October 1926. An extra series for the school holidays began in 1949, HELLO CHILDREN, and in 1950 the daily LISTEN WITH MOTHER.

The first children's programme in commercial radio came from RADIO NORMANDY on 17 April 1932 and featured 'The Story of Little Black Sambo'. It was created by Uncle Stephen (Williams) in the CHILDREN's Hour image, with Uncle Benjy (Bernard McNabb) and Uncle John (Sullivan) and, at first, fake birthday greetings to non-existent listeners! First called *Children's Corner*, it became *IBC Nursery Corner* in 1934, with the adventures of a naughty girl, Flossie, at Dr Whackem's School. On 23 June 1935 the title was changed to *The Adventures of Flossie*, and the series was sponsored by Cutey Cream Caramels (sold in cellophane packs for twopence and fourpence).

Chiselbury
School for the Sons of Gentlefolk ruled with a rod of iron-brew by Professor JIMMY EDWARDS (MA applied for), Scholar, Sportsman and Gent, assisted by Mr Pettigrew (Arthur Howard) and Aubrey Potter, Science Master (Roddy Maude-Roxby). Created for television by FRANK MUIR AND DENIS NORDEN, and adapted for radio in the series WHACK-O! (1961).

Chit for Chat
Panel game devised and chaired by Lionel Hale in which two contestants try to get a secret sentence into their conversation first, logically and politely. Cedric Cliffe, Dulcie Gray and Sir Gerald Barry opposed Paul Jennings, ERIC BARKER and Crystal Herbert. Produced by Audrey Cameron beginning 30 July 1953.

Chocolate Coloured Harmony
Billed as 'a new blend of Light and Dark Music' this series starred G.H. Elliott the Chocolate Coloured Coon, Adelaide Hall the Singing Blackbird, the Chocolate Choir and Fela Sowande and his Chocolate Coloured Orchestra. The sponsor was Fry's Chocolate Sand-

wich (of course) and the first programme was scheduled by RADIO LUXEMBOURG for 9 September 1939 – six days after war broke out. Records do not show whether it was ever broadcast.

Christmas Programmes

The first radio Christmas, 25 December 1922, was no great shakes: Olive Sturgess, soprano, Cecil Mannering, entertainer, and some dance music. The second radio Christmas, the first to be marked with a Grand Christmas Number of RADIO TIMES, in its first full-colour cover, was more the shape of Christmasses to come. First there was a special CHILDREN'S HOUR (the first time this title was used) with a play, *On Christmas Eve*, by Constance D'Arcy Mackay. UNCLE CARACTACUS played Santa Claus. Main event of the evening was *A Merry Christmas Party* hosted by comedian JOHN HENRY, with guests Helena Millais (OUR LIZZIE), RONALD GOURLEY the blind siffleur, and Jay Kaye. The evening concluded with the Savoy Orpheans and Havana Band relayed from the SAVOY HOTEL.

Christopher Blaze

The hero of *Meet Christopher Blaze* was a Scotland Yard Inspector who resigned when his aged aunt left him a local newspaper, *The Sentinel*. Jack Hulbert played breezy Blaze and James Thomason his hidebound editor, Mr Meek. Created by Edward J. Mason and produced by Martyn C. Webster, episode 1, 'Thanks For The Memory', was broadcast on 5 July 1951. The series returned a decade later, on 13 June 1961, with an episode entitled 'You Too Can Be A Film Star'.

The Cicely Courtneidge Theatre

Semi-dramatic series starring the long-running husband-and-wife team of Jack Hulbert and CICELY COURTNEIDGE, supported by Sir Donald Wolfit and Francis de Wolff. Geoffrey Bond wrote the first story, 'Double Destiny', which was broadcast on 22 January 1965. Producer was Alastair Scott Johnson.

Cilly

First of many secretaries to TOMMY HANDLEY, Cilly was based on Gracie Allen and played by Canadian actress Celia Eddy in the first series of IT's THAT MAN AGAIN (1939).

Cinemagazine

Radio magazine for picturegoers hosted by 'The Film Critic' on behalf of Reckitt's Bath Cubes. Features included 'Portraits of the Stars', in which Beryl Orde did one of her impressions every week, 'Famous Film Duets' sung by Anne Ziegler and Webster Booth, and 'Music from the Films of the Week' by the Film Studio Orchestra. Started on RADIO NORMANDY on 6 April 1939.

The Circus Comes to Town

Comedy series starring MABEL CONSTANDUROS, with JACK TRAIN, George Buck, Philip Wade and the Augmented Circus Band. RADIO LUXEMBOURG broadcast it (1937), sponsored by Bob Martin's.

Cissie the Cow

Bovine pet belonging to Charlie Clapham of the double-act CLAPHAM AND DWYER, frequently referred to in their thirties broadcasts.

Clancy of the Outback

Australian comedian DICK BENTLEY played the hero of this adventure series set in the roaring gold-rush days of 1885. Reg Lye played Clancy's buddy, Swaggy McCool, with June Salter as Kitty Elliott and David Netheim as Sergeant Roper. Written by Michael Noonan, produced by Charles Maxwell; first broadcast 24 April 1963.

Clapham and Dwyer

The first great comedy double-act 'made' by radio. Their billing was 'A Spot of Bother' and their tangled crosstalk occasionally got them into a genuine one: the BBC banned them for a year! Charlie Clapham, the stuttering 'silly-ass' in topper and monocle, was the one who ad-libbed the act into difficulties, while Billy Dwyer, rotund, stolid, was the straight-man who tried to steer a safe course. Many of their acts are classics, including their recorded version of 'A Day's Broadcasting' (Columbia 4745) in which they burlesqued an entire BBC day. They made their first broadcast in 1926, one year after the formation of their amateur act. Radio led to their variety debut at the Shepherd's Bush Empire in 1928, and their feature film debut in *Radio Parade* (1933). Dwyer died suddenly in 1943, and after a misguided attempt at forming a new act with

Clapham and Dwyer: 'a spot of bother'

ventriloquist Johnson Clark, Clapham continued his career as a solo comic.

Claude and Cecil
Ultra-polite handymen of It's That Man Again (1941). They always entered and exited with 'After you, Claude', 'No, after *you*, Cecil!' Claude was Jack Train and Cecil was Horace Percival. All their dialogue had a tendency to rhyme: 'Where shall I put the board, Claude?' 'On the trestle, Cecil!'

Clay's College
Comedy series built around Clay and Gladys Keyes which failed to repeat their success with The Old Town Hall. The 'fun and games academy' was supervized by Clay, and Gladys played Polly the Cook. Richard Goolden, the Old Nightwatchman in their earlier series, returned as the Old Lodgekeeper. Students were Hattie Jacques, Michael Moore, Hugh Morton, Deryck Guyler, and the Song Pedlars. 'New pupils' (i.e. guest stars) were Jack North and Pat Stoyle, with Music Master Frank Cantell conducting the College Orchestra. Syllabus written by Gladys and Clay Keyes; produced by Frederick Piffard. Term commenced 13 June 1949.

The Clitheroe Kid: Jimmy Clitheroe in the variety version of his radio series

The Clitheroe Kid
Tremendously popular situation series starring Jimmy Clitheroe, the pint-size Lancashire comic in his naughty boy characterization. Renée Houston, variety veteran, played his mum, Peter Sinclair, 'The Cock o' the North' from Scottish variety, played his grandpa, and others around were Leonard Williams, Judith Daugherty, Nan Marriott-Watson, Jimmy Leach and his electric organ, and the Northern Dance Orchestra conducted by Alyn Ainsworth. The programme was written and produced by James Casey from 5 May 1958, when the opening episode was entitled 'Seconds Out'.

The second series started with 'What a Pantomime' on 29 December 1958. Patricia Burke replaced Renée Houston as mum, and

Diana Day arrived as 17-year-old sister Susan. Peter Goodwright was also on hand. Tony Melody joined the cast for the next series, which began on 4 April 1960 with 'The Tale of a Cat'. The fourth series introduced Danny Ross as the stuttering Alfie Hall, 20 February 1961.

The hundredth show, aptly titled '100 Not Out', was broadcast on 2 February 1964. Mollie Sugden joined the cast with the new series starting 18 October 1964, and the series rolled merrily on, year after year, finally concluding on 13 August 1972 after 280 episodes.

Close-Up

1940 series of 15-minute interviews by Leslie Mitchell (the voice of *British Movietonews*) with favourite stars of stage, screen and cabaret. The date 22 April brought together Judy Kelly and Leslie Henson, while 17 June combined Florence Desmond and Tod Slaughter.

Club Ebony

'You are invited to join our coloured guests at the opening of their new club of the air'. George Brown introduced Mike McKenzie, Vic Evans, Chester Harriott, Carl Bariteau, Marie Bryant, Cy Grant, Leslie 'Jiver' Hutchinson (not to be confused with Leslie 'Hutch' Hutchinson), and Uriel Porter, with musical accompaniment directed by Fela Sowande. The only white man was producer John Hooper. Began 24 February 1953.

Club Night

Starring series for Northern comic Dave Morris. 'Meet the character with the straw hat, cigar and glasses, at his weekly get-together, the know-all himself.' Frank Bass played Sniffy Hargreaves, Geoffrey Banks Pongo, Joe Gladwin Little Cedric, Kenneth Connor 'Arry 'Awk, and Fred Ferris the Whacker. Music came from George Mitchell's Five-in-a-Bar and Jimmy Leach's Clubnighters. Script by Dave Morris, Frank Roscoe and Cass James; producer John Ammonds. The club opened for business on 1 September 1955, and for a second season on 5 July 1956.

Cochrane, Peggy

Remembered chiefly as a pianist in many a MUSIC HALL broadcast, this London-born lady

Peggy **Cochrane**: popular pianist

was a musician of great prodigy and versatility. She won a scholarship to the Royal Academy of Music at the age of eight, was 14 when she won the open violin and pianoforte championships on the same day, and was awarded the Dove Prize as the most distinguished scholar. Her career literally spanned the range from classics to jazz: she played a violin concerto at the Queen's Hall and an hour later turned up in a West End restaurant cabaret as pianist to the radio act, 'That Certain Trio'! She composed piano music for children and sang syncopated songs to her own keyboard accompaniment.

Cock-a-Doodle-Doo!

Prestigious but pompous variety series devised and hosted by Charles B. Cochran, the impresario; it was first broadcast on 14 September 1940, starring John McCormack, VIC OLIVER, Fred Emney, Cicely Courtneidge, Pat Kirkwood, Jack and Daphne Barker, and George Jackley as the fruity cockney in a sketch by Nat Gubbins adapted from his *Sunday Express* column, 'Sitting on the Fence'. Music came from C.B. Cochran's Concert Orchestra conducted by GERALDO, vocalist was Dorothy Carless. Producers: Harry S. Pepper and Douglas Lawrence.

Cococub Radio News

Saturday-morning children's series sponsored by Cadbury's Cocoa, and featuring the Cadbury Cowboys, Zoo Talks by Keeper Bowman of the London Zoo, and puzzles. It was 'edited' by Jonathan, the youth whose adventures with the Cococubs were charted in newspaper advertising strips and the monthly *Cococub News* magazine. Weekly from 1 October 1938 on RADIO LUXEMBOURG. Big Chief Oske-non-ton of the Mohawk Tribe joined the show in 1939 to tell the adventures of Dick among the Redskins. Producer Howard Thomas.

The Colgate Revellers
Weekly concert party series on RADIO LUXEMBOURG from 1936, sponsored by Colgate Ribbon Dental Cream.

Colonel Britton
England's answer to LORD HAW-HAW, this fictitious character was played by BBC News Editor Douglas Ritchie in a series of broadcasts to Europe beginning June 1940. His talks were introduced by the 'V' sign in Morse Code, played on a drum by James Blades, followed by the first theme of Beethoven's Fifth Symphony.

Colonel Chinstrap
Bottle-scarred veteran of many a canteen encounter – his catchphrase was 'I don't mind if I do!' – Colonel Humphrey Chinstrap, retired, of the Old Kent Rangers ('The Hop Pickers'), the

Colonel Chinstrap: Jack Train's bibulous *Itma* character

7th Bunghole Lancers ('The Soapy Seventh'), and the 1st Foot and Mouth, was played by JACK TRAIN. He made his drunken debut in IT'S THAT MAN AGAIN in October 1942, and stayed until the final programme, 5 January 1949: the longest career of any ITMA character. On one memorable occasion the Colonel visited his junior officer, MAJOR BLOODNOK, in THE GOON SHOW, 24 January 1957. His life was also detailed in a documentary by his creator, Ted Kavanagh, broadcast 1 January 1954: *The True Story of Humphrey Chinstrap, Col. Retd.*

Bobbie **Comber**: cheerful comedian

Comber, Bobbie
Cheerful, fruity-voiced comedian, popular on pre-war radio as a solo turn and as one of 'THOSE FOUR CHAPS'. Born in Bury St Edmunds ('of very nice parents: my father grew a beard and my mother grew geraniums!'), he went to work in the War Office and formed his own concert party in 1912. After war service Comber went into musical comedy and revue. His first broadcast was in excerpts from *Clowns in Clover* and he was one of the stars in the special production of *Radiolympia Revue* (1933). He recorded comedy songs for Broadcast Records, including the BBC-approved version of 'Barnacle Bill the Sailor', and played Thugmorton the shady company promoter in the 1936 series BIG BUSINESS and its sequels.

Come in and Sing
Boisterous community-song series first tried out in Coronation Week, 3 June 1953, with BILLY

COTTON, Max Bygraves, Charles Smart at the organ, Doreen Stephens, Alan Breeze, and producer Glyn Jones taking a leading part in the proceedings. It was broadcast from the People's Palace, Mile End Road. Jean Metcalfe hostessed the series proper, beginning 7 August and starring ELSIE AND DORIS WATERS, David Whitfield, Douglas Maynard, and Louis Voss and his Orchestra.

Come to Char-lee
Situation series for Cheerful CHARLIE CHESTER, set in his flat, with Cardew Robinson as his valet and Michael Bentine as his eccentric neighbour, a crazy historian living in the past. Two ladies supplied love interest, Dora Bryan and Patricia Cutts, with songs from David Hughes and the Radio Revellers. Script by Pat Dunlop and Maurice Drake; produced by Leslie Bridgmont; first broadcast 26 February 1953.

Come to Sunday Afternoon at Diana Clare's
'The makers of Lux Toilet Soap cordially invite you to an absolutely new, sparkling kind of non-stop entertainment. Light music and songs in an exciting, amusing party atmosphere.' Diana Clare was the singing hostess from 16 April 1939, and her regular guests were known only as Claude, Dickie, Maureen and Honey: 'See if you can guess who they really are!' One of them was JACK WARNER. Produced by Win Barron.

Comedians
The first comedian to broadcast was Will Hay in excerpts from the new revue, LISTENING IN (29 July 1922). The first comedian to broadcast solo at the microphone was Wilfred Liddiatt, with 'The Vicar's Presentation' and 'The Country Curate' (22 September). The first comedienne to broadcast was Peggy Rae with 'Really, One Never Knows, Does One?' (28 September). The first music hall comedian to broadcast was Ernie Mayne with a special comedy number, 'Wireless On The Brain' (11 October). The first comedy character created for radio was 'OUR LIZZIE' (Helena Millais) on 20 October. The first comedian to broadcast officially for the BBC from 2LO was Billy Beer with 'The Parish Magazine' (16 November) and the first comedian to be 'made by radio',

NORMAN LONG, first broadcast his 'Song at the Piano' on 28 November. The first 'pure radio' comedian was JOHN HENRY, who made his debut on 31 May 1923. Henry was the forerunner of later radio comedians TOMMY HANDLEY, LEONARD HENRY, GILLIE POTTER, ARTHUR ASKEY, MICHAEL HOWARD, FRANKIE HOWERD, TONY HANCOCK, and others who developed a special microphone technique.

Comical Chris
Hearty laugher who never knew when to stop joking. Played by Bill Stephens in IT'S THAT MAN AGAIN (1943).

Command Performance
The first all-star radio series created for the entertainment of members of the US Forces serving overseas in World War II. The first show, recorded 1 March 1942, starred Eddie Cantor, Merle Oberon, Dinah Shore, Danny Kaye, Bea Wain, Joe Louis, Buddy Baer, Bert Gordon 'The Mad Russian', the Ambassadors Quartet and Cooky Fairchild and his Band. Harry Von Zell was master of ceremonies, and the producer Vick Knight. The series, arranged by the Armed Forces Radio Section of the War Department in Washington, was broadcast over the BBC FORCES PROGRAMME from 27 April 1942 – and eavesdropped on by every kid in the kingdom! From 12 April the show moved to Hollywood, when Paul Douglas introduced Gene Tierney, Betty Hutton, Gary Cooper, the Andrews Sisters, Edgar Bergen and Charlie McCarthy, Ginny Simms, Bob Burns and Ray Noble's Orchestra. Special Requests from serving men included Carole Landis taking a deep breath and sighing! Opening: 'Command Performance USA, the greatest entertainers in America as requested by you, the fighting men and women of America, presented this week and every week until its over, Over There!'

Commander Highprice
Late of the Secret Service, at your service: JON PERTWEE in MERRY-GO-ROUND (1946) with the catchphrase: 'Hush! Keep it dark!'

Commander Wetherby
Spluttering, stuttering character in THE NAVY LARK (1960), played by JON PERTWEE and based on his WETHERBY WETT character in the wartime series MERRY-GO-ROUND.

Commercial radio: Villa Louvigny, headquarters of Radio Luxembourg

Commercial radio

The first sponsored broadcast in England was the concert given by Dame Nellie Melba (15 June 1920) arranged by the *Daily Mail*. The same newspaper, frustrated by bureaucratic delays, instigated weekly concerts broadcast from the Hague, Holland via Nederlandsche Radio Industrie commencing 27 July 1922. Although advertising was outlawed on the BBC right from the start, a series of programmes 'arranged' by newspapers and magazines was broadcast during 1925. The first was on 10 March, the *Evening Standard Programme* starring the soprano Tetrazini. The *News of the World Concert* (21 April) featured Ethel Hook (contralto) and the Gresham Singers. *Answers* (19 May) presented Benno Moisievitch and Sir Johnston Forbes Robertson reciting Shakespeare. *Daily Graphic* (25 June) starred Henry Ainley, Gladys Cooper, Binnie and Sonnie Hale, and George Grossmith. *Weekly Dispatch*

ran a Wireless Ballot and broadcast the winners on 7 July: Helena Millais ('OUR LIZZIE'), JOHN HENRY, Vivian Foster ('The Vicar of Mirth') and THE ROOSTERS. *Tit-Bits* followed with their own Ballot Programme on 29 September: Carmen Hill, Daisy Kennedy, and again John Henry and The Roosters. The last of the year was a truly national two-hours from the *Daily Herald* (27 October): Miles Malleson, plus the London Labour Choral Union, the Celtic Orpheus Glee Party, the CWS Male Voice Choir (Manchester) and the William Morris Choir (Glasgow). In the same year Captain Plugge got Selfridges to sponsor a fashion talk from the Eiffel Tower station. In 1928 Philips Radio began a series of Sunday concerts by DeGroot, broadcast from Radio Hilversum.

The first series of sponsored programmes in the modern sense began on Sunday 25 August 1929 when Revelation Suitcases broadcast the first of their weekly hours of dance music on records, packaged by Philip Dorte's Radio Publicity Ltd: 'We present the first in a series of light musical programmes which come to you every Sunday evening over RADIO PARIS through the kindness of the Revelation Suitcase Company, the manufacturers of the suitcase that adjusts itself.' The signature tune was 'Pack Up Your Troubles', played by William Stanford and his Revelation Symphonic Orchestra. Universal Radio Publicity took over station 2RN in Dublin for one hour a night, beginning 21 October 1930. The first sponsor was Carroll's 'Sweet Afton' cigarettes, followed by *The Savoy Minstrels* (Savoy Chocolates) and *The Rock Musical Comedy Hour*. Plugge's International Broadcasting Company (IBC) began broadcasting sponsored programmes from Fécamp, renamed RADIO NORMANDY, on 11 October 1931, and also from RADIO TOULOUSE, where their first sponsor was Vocalion Records. PHILCO SLUMBER HOUR began on Normandy on 22 November. Sunday programmes started on RADIO LUXEMBOURG with the *Bush Radio Concert* on 3 December 1933. Most early sponsored programmes were gramophone records linked by staff announcers: *The Three Diamonds Pink Salmon Broadcast*, *The Swift's Plate Corned Beef Concert*, etc. More continental stations joined the English-speaking circuit: Poste Parisien, RADIO COTE D'AZUR, RADIO SAN SEBASTIAN, Radio Ljubljana, RADIO LYONS, Radio Valencia, Radio Madrid, Radio Athlone (later EIREANN), and even a short wave IBC Empire Transmission from Radio Aranjeuz. Sponsored programmes boomed from 14 October 1934 when Luxembourg introduced a 12-hour Sunday, and ended with the outbreak of World War II. Radio Luxembourg was the only commercial radio station to return after the war.

Concert parties

Ancestor of all radio variety shows was the Concert Party, at first bringing pre-packed entertainment from the theatrical stage to the microphone, later developing original shows created for broadcasting. The first was heard on 17 April 1923, *The Bristol Concert Party* starring duettists H. and E. Bristol, with Jessie Bristol at the pianoforte, and soprano Marion Browne. More important, historically and entertainingly, was the West End company of THE CO-OPTIMISTS with Laddie Cliff and Davy Burnaby, who made the first of several broadcasts on 26 April 1923. Then came THE ROOSTERS (20 October), *The Crotchets* (27 November) with Mary Robbie, and in 1924 *The London 8* (7 January) in which SUZETTE TARRI made her first broadcast: *The Happy Family* (8 January) with Eddie Hopworth; *The Moonstones* (10 April) with Jack Rickards; and many more. The first concert party created for the microphone was RADIO RADIANCE (6 July 1925), followed by *Radio Follies* (12 May 1926) with Herbert Darnley, Irene North and Olly Oakley and his banjo. See also BBC CONCERT PARTY.

Confidentially They're Off!

'Series of Horse Laughs', starring Reg Dixon, the 'Confidentially' comedian from VARIETY BANDBOX. Episode 1, 'Soapy Cleans Up', was broadcast on 29 September 1957. Reg played a stable lad, Francis de Wolff was Major Hunt the horse trainer and Dilys Laye was Mary, his daughter. Clara the cook was played by Patricia Hayes, and Anthony Green played Ginger. Soapy the horse and other animals played by Percy Edwards. Script by Eddie Maguire and production by Alastair Scott-Johnston.

Constanduros, Mabel

Actress, writer, but above all the comedienne who created 'THE BUGGINS FAMILY' – Grandma, Emily, Emma, Alfie and Baby. Her first broadcast on 23 March 1925 came about through a friend who had seen her perform her own monologues at the Central School of

Mabel **Constanduros**: see her also as Grandma of *The Buggins Family*

Speech Training, Albert Hall, and who persuaded her to give an audition for R.E. Jeffrey at the BBC. The Bugginses quickly became firm favourites and hit their peak by doing the spontaneous commentary for the broadcast of the ROYAL VARIETY PERFORMANCE (1931). Jeffrey contracted her for the first BBC Drama Repertory Company. She also wrote radio plays, including the mystery *The Survivor* (1929), plays for the theatre, short stories, songs, poems, books and her autobiography, *Shreds and Patches* (1946).

The Cookeen Programme

Thirty-minute series starring CARROLL GIBBONS and His Boys with Anne Lenner and George Melachrino to vocalize. Compère Russ Carr introduced such guest stars as Len Young (The Singing Fool), Bobby Farrell (the one-legged Dublin street singer), and infant prodigy impressioniste, Joan Turner, age 14, on 28 February 1938, RADIO LUXEMBOURG. Later reduced to 15 minutes, the retitled *Cookeen Cabaret* starred Helen Clare with singing guests. Vox Productions for Cookeen Cooking Fat.

Cookery Nook

'Your tea-time rendezvous with Phyllis Peck', the cookery expert from McDougall's Self-raising Flour: RADIO NORMANDY, 1937.

The Co-Optimists

Popular stage concert party who brought their 'pierrotic entertainment' to 2LO on 26 April

1923 for a 50-minute selection, complete with their signature song, 'Bow-Wow!'. Comedian Davy Burnaby would become a frequent broadcaster. Rest of cast: Phyllis Monkman, Betty Chester, Elsa Macfarlane, Laddie Cliff, Melville Gideon, Gilbert Childs, H.B. Hedley.

Copthorne Avenue

Street sought for but never found, by Peter Ustinov and Peter Jones in their several series of IN ALL DIRECTIONS (1952).

Corner in Crime

Magazine series which featured adaptations of mystery stories and a monthly Detective Quiz, devised by John Dickson Carr. The first programme, broadcast 2 August 1945, brought together the novelists Dorothy L. Sayers, Anthony Gilbert, E.C. Bentley, Milward Kennedy, E.R. Punshon, and Freeman Wills Crofts, as a kind of criminal brains trust to answer listeners' questions. Chairman was Val Gielgud.

Coronation Programmes: 1937

In addition to broadcasting the actual Coronation of King George VI and Queen Elizabeth (and publishing a special RADIO TIMES with colour supplement), the BBC celebrated with these special programmes. *The BBC Coronation Revue* (11 May) starring CICELY COURTNEIDGE, George Robey, Frank Lawton, Sir Frank Benson, Harry Welchman, the WESTERN BROTHERS, MABEL CONSTANDUROS, Brian Lawrance, WYNNE AJELLO, Leslie 'Hutch' Hutchinson, Wilson Hallett, REVNELL AND WEST, Peter Taunton, REGINALD FOORT at the organ, Harry Pepper and DORIS ARNOLD at two pianos, and the Variety Orchestra and Chorus conducted by Mark Lubbock. Written by Douglas Furber, produced by Pepper and John Watt. *Coronation Party* (12 May) included 'GERT AND DAISY', 'MRS FEATHER', CLAPHAM AND DWYER, the TWO LESLIES, Raymond Newell, Stuart Robertson, Jan Van Der Gucht, LEONARD HENRY and Davy Burnaby. *Dancing Through* (14 May) presented a non-stop pageant of popular music during 36 years, with GERALDO and his Orchestra, Anne Ziegler, Lily Morris, Eve Becke, Monte Rey, Wilfrid Thomas, the Top Hatters and Al Bollington at the organ. *Gala Variety* (15 May) starred Billy Caryll and Hilda Mundy, Florence Desmond,

Flanagan and Allen, Bertha Willmott, Will Fyffe, Ralph Reader, Elsie Carlisle, Matheson Lang, Irene Vanbrugh, Victoria Hopper, REGINALD FOORT and the Variety Orchestra.

Coronation Programmes: 1953

Queen Elizabeth's Coronation was celebrated with several special programmes, beginning with a *Commonwealth Gala* (31 May 1953) hosted by Richard Attenborough. DICK BENTLEY and Robert Helpmann represented Australia: BERNARD BRADEN and CARROLL LEVIS Canada; Erin de Selfa Ceylon; 'Hutch' West Indies; and Eve Boswell Africa; and there was CICELY COURTNEIDGE, Margaret Lockwood, REVNELL AND WEST, ELSIE AND DORIS WATERS, James McKechnie and Gladys Young, with the George Mitchell Choir and Sidney Torch and his Orchestra. Script by Loftus Wigram, producer Tom Ronald. *As Millions Cheer* (1 June) offered some oblique observations on the event, with ERIC BARKER, Peter Ustinov, Alfred Marks, ROY PLOMLEY, Pearl Hackney, Peter Jones, MAURICE DENHAM, Stanley Unwin and F.R. Buckley, and songs from Dick James, Lita Roza, and the STARGAZERS with Malcolm Lockyer's Orchestra. Writers included FRANK MUIR and DENIS NORDEN; producer was Pat Dixon. *Light Up Again* (4 June) was a 2½-hour special featuring memorable shows from the past seven years, hosted by PC49 and DICK BARTON! Included were HI GANG, WATERLOGGED SPA, RIDERS OF THE RANGE, IGNORANCE IS BLISS, MUCH-BINDING-IN-THE-MARSH, and VARIETY BANDBOX with feudists FRANKIE HOWERD and DEREK ROY.

Costa, Sam

Best remembered for his catchphrase, 'Good mornin' sir, was there something?' as LAC Costa in the wartime RAF series, MUCH-BINDING-IN-THE-MARSH. Sam had three distinct careers in radio: crooner, comedian and compère. He first broadcast in 1935 as JACK JACKSON's crooner, and was often teamed with Judy Shirley. He turned funny in 1939, joining the ITMA team as LEMUEL the Office Boy, coining his first catchphrase, 'ooT123 there's a car outside'. Called into the RAF he joined Murdoch and Horne in MERRY-GO-ROUND, ever bemoaning Emily's twinges with a lugubrious 'Well . . .'. His third career found him compering *Record Rendezvous* (1950) with the

Sam **Costa**: the crooner who became a comedian

signature tune 'Sam's Song'. The first great hit he made was Mel Blanc's 'I Taut I Taw a Puddy Tat'. From the start of Radio 2 in the late sixties Sam hosted such series as *Sam On Sunday*, *Melodies for You*, and *Glamorous Nights*. He also starred in his own comedy series, *The Sam Costa Show*, broadcast from RADIO LUXEM-BOURG during 1950. This was written by Michael Bishop and Talbot Rothwell and produced by Gordon Crier.

Cotton, Billy

Cheerful cockney dance-band leader whose hearty cry of 'Wakey-wakey!' is still ingrained on a million eardrums. His rowdy broadcasts were a post-war phenomenon (see BILLY COTTON BAND SHOW, 1949), although comedy numbers were always in his repertoire, thanks to the versatility of his vocalist Alan Breeze. 'Breezy' was with Billy's Boys from 1931 to the end, and one of their records, 'I've Gone and Lost My Little Yoyo', was banned by the BBC. Billy's signature tune was 'Somebody Stole My Gal', and his vocalists included Al Bowlly, Doreen Stephens, SAM COSTA, Kathy Kaye and the Bandits.

Billy **Cotton**: 'Mr Wakey-Wakey Himself'

Country Home Hour

It was only 45 minutes but this 'radio magazine for country dwellers and all who love the country' was an unusual series for RADIO NORMANDY. Wilfrid Thomas and Bob Danvers-Walker co-hosted and Douglas McDonald Hastings edited, while Molly Gee produced. Beginning 13 March 1939, studio visitors included Captain Hogg the champion archer, and Sid Towney, a coach guard complete with post-horn.

Countryside

Simon the Singer starred in this 'musical panorama of our glorious country highways and byways', accompanied by the Carnation Countryside Quintet. Presented by Carnation Milk, the Milk from Contented Cows, on RADIO LUXEMBOURG from 1937.

The Courts of London

Howard Marion Crawford starred in 'the day-to-day stories of a London Magistrate's Court', sponsored by Lloyd's Adrenaline Cream on RADIO LUXEMBOURG (1951). Produced by HARRY ALAN TOWERS.

Courtneidge, Cicely

Celebrated for her famous vitality, and for her professional partnership with husband JACK HULBERT, this Australian-born comedienne made her first broadcast on 14 August 1925 and never looked back. Her extraordinary laugh, showcased in her frequently-heard sketch 'Laughing Gas', her comic songs ('Why Has a Cow Got Four Legs') and her great patriotism, called upon for every possible radio occasion from Coronations to Jubilees to Victories, made a unique combination. From 1956 Cis and Jack were regular broadcasters in the POCKET THEATRE slot of VARIETY PLAYHOUSE.

Cicely **Courtneidge**: radio star with or without husband Jack Hulbert

Cow and Gate Concert

Sponsored by the popular condensed milk and broadcast on RADIO NORMANDY from 22 October 1932. Signature song: 'Smiler Keep Smiling for Me' (Smiler was the name of the baby on the tin).

Cowleaze Farm

Fictional farmstead in Wiltshire, eastward along the Avonchurch Road from Nadderbourne, five miles from the market town of Wilcester, pronounced Wilster. Ralph Whitlock was the real farmer who wrote and played himself in the monthly *Visit to Cowleaze Farm*, a long-running series which began in CHILDREN'S HOUR in May 1945. Mrs Whitlock was played by Vivienne Chatterton and the young visitors were Rosamund Barnes and Jane Barrett. Other characters around were Joe Tagg the shepherd, Dick the ploughman, Bill and Harry the cowmen, Jonas the odd jobber, and Luke Merryweather, not forgetting Towser the dog.

Crazy Café

'A visit to this popular rendezvous when a number of people will drop in to have tea and talk nonsense.' Jacques Browne played Mr Theopolis Neckancropolis, MABEL CONSTANDUROS Grandma Buggins. Also appearing were C. Denier Warren, SAM COSTA, the Three in Harmony, and the Variety Orchestra; 5 April 1940 on the Forces.

Crazy People

Originally trailed as the *Junior Crazy Show* (4 May 1951), this series materialized on 28 May 1951 as starring Radio's Own Crazy Gang 'The Goons' – Harry Secombe, PETER SELLERS, Michael Bentine, SPIKE MILLIGAN. Music by Ray Ellington Quartet, the STARGAZERS, and Max Geldray (harmonica) with the Dance Orchestra conducted by Stanley Black. The script credit read 'material compiled by Spike Milligan'; uncredited script editor was Jimmy Grafton, and shortly Larry Stephens came in, too. The producer, Dennis Main Wilson, wrote: 'The series is based on a crazy type of fun evolved by four of our younger laughter-makers. Their humour is whimsically irreverent, full of irrational logic, or is it illogical rationalism?' Andrew Timothy was the announcer whose dry tones paved the way for a series of sketches involving Professor OSRIC PUREHEART (Bentine) and his invention of the BRM ('so called because it goes brm-brm-brm!'), a burlesque of DICK BARTON and the Quest for Tutankhamun. Characters included ERNIE SPLUTMUSCLE, ECCLES, and PHILIP STRING. After 17 editions, ending 16 September 1951, the series was permitted to be renewed as THE GOON SHOW.

Crazy Quilt

'A Patchwork Miscellany' of song and comedy co-starring Phyllis Robins and Eddie Pola, who introduced his 'TWISTED TUNES' feature at the piano. Also close-harmonists Three of a Kind, Ronnie Hill, Jacques Brown. The series started 11 April 1939, 'sewn together' by Pascoe Thornton. A return engagement from 26 March 1940 teamed Pola with Addie Seamon, Hugh French, Stephane Grappelly and the Arthur Young Swingtette.

Crime Magazine

Weekly magazine programme introducing famous detectives from fact and fiction, presented and produced by Bill MacLurg. 'Barton of the Yard' featured ex-Detective Inspector Jack Henry as Barton (Episode 1: 'The Ration Robbery'); Henry wrote the series with Patrick K. Heale. 'The Knave', a personal tale by Francis Durbridge, was told by Lionel Gamlin. 'Little Things That Count' was a five-minute thriller by P.K. Heale. 'A Case for SEXTON BLAKE' was written for broadcasting by Durbridge from an original story by Edward Holmes, with Arthur Young as the Baker Street detective, Clive Baxter as his youthful assistant Tinker, Ben Wright as Tony Carradine, Jane Grahame as Joan Dixon, John Morley as Benito Marthioly, and Wilfrid Walter as Peter Marthioly. Home Service from 12 March 1940.

Crime Reporter

Norman Shelley played Pixworth Ames, Crime Reporter, in this RADIO NORMANDY series which began on 21 February 1939. Philip Wade and Ivan Samson were also in the cast, and the sponsor was Limestone Phosphate.

The Critics

Popular Sunday-lunchtime series conducted by Lionel Hale, in which five experts and a guest reviewed and discussed the arts events of the week. First broadcast 5 October 1947, with Arthur Vesselo on films, Stephen Williams on theatre, Walter Allen on books, Spike Hughes on radio, Nicholas Bentley on art, and Stanley Rubenstein as the guest. This series was especially popular with impersonators and satirists! In the guise CRITICS' FORUM, the programme continues in the 1980s.

Crowther's Crowd

Starring series for Leslie Crowther assisted by Ronnie Barker, whose comedy partnership had been established in VARIETY PLAYHOUSE (1960 series). June Whitfield completed the 'crowd', with Mickie Most and his Minute Men. Writers George Evans and Derek Collyer; producer, Alastair Scott Johnston. The first show on 21 September 1963 was described as 'an illustrated argument on the futility of human nature as revealed by a study of the Art of Entertainment.'

Crystal Jollibottom

'I'm Crystal Jollibottom, you saucebox!' cried this large lady, ever suspecting, and perhaps hoping for, an improper advance from TED RAY. Played by PETER SELLERS in RAY'S A LAUGH (1950).

Cuckoo Cottage

Second series for Charles Heslop as Professor Umbridge (see TAKE UMBRIDGE) with RICHARD GOOLDEN as his assistant, Henry Horatio Pibberdy. This time Umbridge Radio Services Inc. presented their Happy Half Hour, assisted by Dick Francis, Dorothy Summers and Billy Ternent and the Dance Orchestra. Written by Heslop and Max Kester; producer Reginald Smith. Weekly from 27 October 1941.

Curioser and Curioser

Anthology of Anglo-American offbeat humour compiled and compèred by David Climie, and starring the voices of PETER SELLERS, Beryl Reid, SPIKE MILLIGAN, Pearl Carr, Miriam Karlin, Georgia Brown, Ronan O'Casey and David Jacobs. Music by Malcolm Lockyer and his Offbeats; producer, Roy Speer. Series started 14 August 1956.

Curly Kale

Ship's cook with penchant for retailing hoary stories with culinary variations: 'That was no ladle, that was my knife!' Played by Carleton Hobbs in IT'S THAT MAN AGAIN (1945).

Cuthbert

Office Boy at WATERLOGGED SPA (1948), an early radio role for Terry Scott. Cuthbert's giggly girlfriend was Pansy Poole, played by Pearl Hackney.

RADIO PICTORIAL, AUGUST 25, 1939. No. 293.
REGISTERED AT THE G.P.O. AS A NEWSPAPER

RADIO PICTORIAL
THE ALL-FAMILY RADIO MAGAZINE

Scott & Whaley

Scott and Whaley: 'Cuthbert and Pussyfoot'

Cuthbert and Pussyfoot

Characters portrayed by Scott and Whaley in THE KENTUCKY MINSTRELS (1933). Eddie Whaley, the straight-man, was Cuthbert, and Harry Scott, the comedian, Pussyfoot. Their tangle-talk was often the result of inept script-reading, and they finished on their signature song 'We're just a couple of pals, making the most of each day'. Their routines were written by Con West.

Cwmcaws

Imaginary Welsh village created for CHILDREN'S HOUR by W.P. Thomas. The villagers, including Dai and Mwkyn and the Cwmcaws Gleemen, sang their way through trips to the seaside, a rugby match, the annual Miners' Concert, etc. (1937).

D

Dad
Character in RAY's A LAUGH (1953) played by Charles Leno: 'Dad's lorst all 'is faith in 'uman nature, Dad 'as!'

Daisy May
Pathetic, waif-like dummy operated by ventriloquist Saveen, who won her own radio series, *Mid-Day With Daisy May* commencing 11 April 1950. She provided the comedy continuity between varying guest vocalists: on the first show, Eva Beynon, Enso Toppano and the Malcolm Mitchell Trio. Rae Jenkins and the Variety Orchestra played the theme tune, 'Daisy May – I'm going to marry you some day', which became quite a popular hit.

Dan Dare
The immensely popular hero of the front page of *Eagle* comic was brought to RADIO LUXEMBOURG as their first post-war daily serial star from Monday 2 July 1951. *The Adventures of Dan Dare, Pilot of the Future* was sponsored by Horlicks, scripted by Geoffrey Webb, announced by Bob Danvers-Walker, and produced by John Glyn Jones, but the man who played Dan was kept a dark secret – to anyone who had never heard the BBC's *Dick Barton*. It was Noel Johnson! Serial titles included 'The Monkton Menace' (September 1952), 'Invaders from Space' (November 1952), 'The Lost World on Mars' (January 1953), 'Revolt on Venus' (April 1953), 'Marooned on Mercury' (September 1953), 'Attack on the Space Stations' (January 1954), 'Sabotage on Venus' (February 1954), 'Mystery on the Moon' (August 1954), 'The Automatons' (November 1954), 'The Mekon on Mars' (December 1954), 'Bartley Greenwood' (January 1955), 'Surprise Assassin' (March 1955), and several untitled serials. The last broadcast was 25 May

1956, and the theme music was entitled 'Radiolocation'.

Dan Dungeon
Deryck Guyler played this pun-prone Guide to Castle Weehoose in the 1946 series of IT's THAT MAN AGAIN.

Dance Music
The first truly popular radio programmes (apart from concerts including popular songs and comedians) were those of dance music, bands playing the latest hits. Listeners were instructed to 'roll back their carpets and dance', but generally were content to tap a toe or two. The first programme of dance music was broadcast at 9 pm on Saturday 23 December 1922, and included 'Humming' (foxtrot), 'Limehouse Blues' (onestep), 'Lady of the Rose' (waltz). The dance band was not billed. On 27 February 1923 Marius B. Winter and his Band played ten numbers: eight of them were foxtrots. The famous SAVOY HAVANA BAND

Noel **Johnson**: 'Dick Barton' and 'Dan Dare'

made their radio debut on 13 April playing 'Classique', and the BBC's first house band, the 2LO DANCE BAND, arrived on 19 May with 'Who Dear' (onestep). The Gleneagles Hotel Dance Band (the radio debut of HENRY HALL) broadcast nationally from Glasgow on 26 August, followed three days later by the first broadcast by JACK HYLTON and his Dance Band. JACK PAYNE's Band from the Hotel Cecil made a Boxing Day debut, 26 December. There was a special Dance Band programme to celebrate the BBC TENTH ANNIVERSARY, including Paul Whiteman from New York.

The Dancing Daughters
Tap-dancing troupe who replaced the Step Sisters on MUSIC HALL from 20 October 1934.

Dancing Through
Programmes of continuous dance music featuring 145 tunes in 60 minutes, devised and played by GERALDO with his Orchestra (1934). Singers starring in the 4 October 1937 broadcast were Tessa Deane, Eve Becke, Monte Rey, Wilfrid Thomas, Cyril Grantham, Bill Tringham, and the Top Hatters.

Dandy Lion
'Radio's own cartoon' featuring a young lion who wanted to leave home and go out into the jungle. Devised by John Watt, who had adapted the Walt Disney cartoons for radio, with music by Henry Reed and lyrics by James Dyrenforth; written by C. Denier Warren and Ted Kavanagh; producer Gordon Crier. From 28 October 1940.

Danger – Men at Work
The first radio Crazy Show starring the American crosstalk comedians Van and Allan, and written by Max Kester (with Anthony Hall). Inspired by the Marx Brothers, Van and Allen were con-men out to trick pompous MRS PONSONBY (Doris Nichols) of her property, with the aid of double-talking Greek NIKOLAS RIDIKOULOS (Jacques Brown). From 11 May 1939 on the National. The second series (1 December) introduced George Moon and JACK TRAIN as the tricksters, while the third, expanded from a quarter to half an hour, brought in Haver and Lee as Eggblow and Duckweed: 'Any resemblance to any person living or dead will be a miracle!' (2 April 1940).

The next series, *Danger – Men Still at Work*, moved the Hotel Mimoar to the seaside, and was subtitled 'How to speak with a gag in your mouth!' (5 June 1940). The fourth series reverted to the original title and introduced Hugh Shirreff as 'The Voice of the BBC' (11 October 1940). The show returned in a post-war series beginning 2 July 1946, but was less successful. Lee had died and been replaced by Charlie Irwin as a new character, Colonel Swiveller. The gang returned for a final series from 25 March 1947, produced by Cleland Finn. There were at least two signature tunes: 'Beware, take care, those men are here again', and

Danger Men at Work Danger,
Men at Work Danger Men at,
Work Danger Men at Work Dange,
Er Men at Work Danger Men!

Dangerous Honeymoon
'How Frank and Nancy Rogers, just married, fall victims of a diabolical plot. Kidnapped and taken to an old castle, they suffer terrifying experiences.' RADIO LUXEMBOURG serial sponsored by Kolynos Denture Fixative, starting 3 August 1939.

Daniels, Bebe and Lyon, Ben
Bebe and Ben will always be remembered as the Hollywood stars who made their homes in England and helped us Keep Smiling throughout World War II. With their talkie careers on the wane, they left Hollywood for a tour of British Music Halls and some films at Elstree in the thirties. Their banter was broadcast on MUSIC HALL more than once, and in 1939 they

Bebe **Daniels** and Ben Lyon: as drawn for *Radio Fun* by George Heath

co-starred in a long series from RADIO LUXEM-BOURG, THE RINSO RADIO REVUE. With the war they further developed the three-handed comedy they had been doing with TOMMY HANDLEY, this time with VIC OLIVER, and their HI GANG! show became an instant BBC hit. It ran 52 weeks without interruption, even from the bombs that fell close to their studio 'in the heart of London'. After the war came an even more popular success with their situation series, LIFE WITH THE LYONS (1950), which introduced their real-life children, Barbara and Richard.

Daphne Whitethigh

Fashion and cookery expert in the ROUND THE HORNE Colour Supplement (1965) played by Betty Marsden at her huskiest. A close relative of FANNY HADDOCK.

The Daring Dexters

Daily serial replacing DICK BARTON from 2 June 1947. This thriller serial of the circus featured Granville Eves as Dan Dexter, ex-high-wire performer and boss of Dexter's Grand Circus. Bill, his son, was played by James Viccars, and Sherry, his wire-walking daughter, by Olive Kirby. Beppo, the philosophical white-faced clown, was Franklyn Bellamy, and Tangey, the red-headed he-man, Edward Percival. Comedy relief came from the Augustes, Tony (Charles Lamb) and Gump (John Sharpe). Frederick Allan announced, Raymond Raikes produced, and Geoffrey Webb wrote the script. There was an omnibus

version every Sunday morning until the series ended on 3 October. The signature tune was called 'London Playhouse'.

A Date With Dickie

'Your musical merry-go-round of films/sport/ discoveries', a daily series starring Richard Attenborough with songs from Carole Carr with Sidney Torch and his Music Men. Sponsored by Cadburys and broadcast on RADIO LUXEMBOURG from 16 July 1951.

A Date With Nurse Dugdale

Series of six spun-off from Arthur Marshall's sensational take-over in the original TAKE IT FROM HERE. Started 21 April 1944 on the Home Service, with Marjorie Westbury as Sister Parkinson, and guest star the Chief Announcer, STUART HIBBERD. Also John Slater, JACK JACKSON and his May Fair Hotel Dance Orchestra, singers Josephine Driver, Dorothe Morrow's Aristocrats, and Ivor Pye the Singing Sailor. Script by Marshall and production by David Yates Mason. A sequel series ran from 27 November 1945, *Nurse Dugdale Takes the Air*. Marjorie Westbury returned as 'Parky-dear', and Dorothy Carless arrived as Probationer Muspratt. The music came from Eugene Pini and his Orchestra, and the guest was announcer ALVAR LIDDELL.

Daventry

5XX was the call-sign of the first High Power Station built at Borough Hill, Daventry,

Daventry: BBC's first high-power transmitter

Northamptonshire. With a 25-kilowatt transmitter it was, when opened (27 July 1925), the biggest broadcasting station and the first long-wave station, in the world. The Opening Ceremony programme began with a new poem by Alfred Noyes:

Daventry calling . . . Dark and still.
The tree of memory stands like a sentry,
Over the graves on the silent hill . . .

Lord Gainford, chairman of the BBC, introduced the Postmaster-General, the Mayor of Daventry, and Chief Engineer PETER ECKERSLEY. Then came a concert by the Wireless Military Band, Kate Winter (soprano), Norman Allin (bass), and Daisy Kennedy (violin). Daventry replaced the Chelmsford station and became the alternative programme to 2LO.

David

Always considered the newcomer to CHILDREN's HOUR (he joined the regular staff in 1935), David was the soft-spoken one who read poetry and played the piano. His real name was Eric Davis, and after 'Mac' retired, then 'Elizabeth', he was made Head of the series in 1953. Eight years later the series was cancelled for ever, leaving the devoted David a broken man.

De Courville's Hour

Following the success of CHARLOT's HOUR (1928), rival revue producer Albert de Courville compiled and presented his own regular radio series, beginning with the six-week run of AIR RAIDS (1928). This was followed by De Courville's Hour from 2 April 1929. The first, subtitled 'Gay Sparks', starred Fred Duprez, Ernest Sefton, Billy Holland, Cyril Smith, Aimee Bebb, Paddy Prior, Imito the animal impressionist, and Jack Padbury's Cosmo Club Six.

De Reszke Personalities

'The Ten Minute Smoke for Intelligent Folk' (DeReszke Minors) presented the first of their weekly star interviews on 8 January 1939, RADIO LUXEMBOURG. George Robey and his wife Blanche Littler were featured with composer Nat D. Ayer and Sydney Jerome and his Orchestra. Later in the series Leslie Mitchell interviewed JACK PAYNE, Florence Desmond, Frances Day, Herman Darewski and Jessie Matthews. Pamela Hopkinson produced for London Press Exchange. Singing commercial:

Mine's a Minor,
The best cigarette that you're able to get,
Mine's a Minor,
Why don't you try one of mine?

De Rohan, Ralph

Better known as MR GROWSER of TOYTOWN ('It's disgrrraceful!') and to an earlier radio generation as the Wicked Uncle of CHILDREN's HOUR. Ralph (pronounced Rafe) was a prolific broadcaster in plays, talks, verse and story readings, and gramophone recitals. He also wrote and presented a series of talks under the name of 'Diogenes' (1925).

Dear Me

MICHAEL HOWARD and his wife Peggy Evans the film actress co-starred in this series written by Ted Kavanagh. Supporting cast: Miriam Karlin, Clarence Wright, John Sharp, David Jacobs, Horace Percival, Reginald Purdell and the Dance Orchestra conducted by Stanley Black. Produced by Leslie Bridgmont; commenced 8 August 1951.

Denham, Maurice

One of the great 'funny voice men' of radio, Beckenham-born, Tonbridge-educated Denham was a repertory actor when he came to the BBC and IT's THAT MAN AGAIN to be the first ITMA char, MRS TICKLE ('Ooh, I always do my best for all my gentlemaine!'). After war service in the Buffs, Denham arrived at MUCH-BINDING-IN-THE-MARSH as DUDLEY DAVENPORT 'at your service, sir' with a laugh that sounded like 'choof-choof !'. By 1950 his rollcall of voices numbered 62, including MR BLAKE the Sexton, IVY CLINGBINE, Group Captain Funnybone, Lieutenant-General Sir Harold Tansley Parkinson, Winston the dog, Gregory the sparrow, and Nigel the silkworm.

Dennis, Gene

'The Woman with the Most Amazing Mind in the World' broadcast weekly from RADIO LUXEMBOURG from 13 January 1935 for Wincarnis Wine. To obtain Miss Dennis's free advice, you had to send a pink wrapper from a bottle of Wincarnis and a three-halfpenny stamp. 'Even if you do not wish to consult Miss Dennis yourself, it is well worth your while to listen in and hear the truly amazing way in which she solves the problems of other listeners, people whom she has never seen or spoken to in her life.' Signature tune: 'This Is Romance', played by the Wincarnis Orchestra.

Desert Island Discs

On 29 January 1942 the following appeared in RADIO TIMES: 'VIC OLIVER discusses with Roy Plomley the eight records he would choose if he were condemned to spend the rest of his life on a desert island with a gramophone for his entertainment.' From that modest half-hour grew the longest-running entertainment series in British radio (even including a few breaks). Roy Plomley devised it, and has hosted each show. The phrase 'always supposing you had an unlimited supply of needles' was added shortly to satisfy pedantic listeners, later dropped when technology improved. Later, too, came the book ('excluding the Bible and Shakespeare') and the Luxury Object. Castaway No. 100 was A.E. Matthews, No. 500 Eddie Calvert ('The Man with the Golden Trumpet') and No. 1000, broadcast 20 December 1969, 'Monty': Field Marshal the Viscount Montgomery of Alamein. Plomley himself was the castaway on programme 15 (the last of the first series). The signature tune is 'A Sleepy Lagoon', accompanied by BBC seagulls. Roy died suddenly after presenting programme No. 1791.

The Detection Club

'Death at 6.30' was the title of the first in a series of original plays for radio by members of the Detection Club. It was written by Anthony Gilbert, produced by John Cheatle, and featured D.A. Clarke-Smith, Mary O'Farrell, and Valentine Dyall (not yet the MAN IN BLACK!). Broadcast 11 May 1940. Eight years later a second series of six was broadcast, beginning with 'Butter in a Lordly Dish' by Agatha Christie (13 January 1948). Anthony Gilbert contributed 'A Nice Cup of Tea', and the series wound up with 'Where Do We Go From Here' by Dorothy L. Sayers.

Dial Doris

Doris Hare starred as an inept but willing muddler who always does her best, in this weekly series by Ted Kavanagh, produced by Michael North. Doris was supported by JACK TRAIN, Vera Lennox, Marcel de Haes and Billy Ternent and the Dance Orchestra. Began 29 January 1941.

Dick Barton

Captain Richard Barton of the Commandos made his demobbed debut as *Dick Barton – Special Agent* on the Light Programme at 6.45 pm on Monday, 7 October 1946. The hero of the first daily serial broadcast by the BBC was played by Noel Johnson, and his signature tune was 'The Devil's Galop', composed by Charles Williams. This fast-moving crime serial, loved by children of all ages, deplored by clergy and educationalists, was fathered by Norman Collins and John McMillan, and scripted by Geoffrey Webb and Edward J. Mason. The producer was Neil Tuson. The full cast was not published until the broadcast of the first Omnibus Edition, at 11 am on Saturday 4 January 1947. Dick's comrades-in-arms were revealed as John Mann, who played Snowey White, and Alex McCrindle, who played Jock Anderson.

Dick Barton – Special Agent: the famous signature tune

Dick's girlfriend (all too soon to be written out of the series for ever!) was Jean Hunter, played by Lorna Dermott, and the current villain, Manoel Garcia, was played by Brian Worth. The announcer who rapped out 'Dick Barton . . . Special Agent!' was Hamilton Humphries. The first series ended on 30 May 1947, but Dick was back on 6 October in a new serial. The third, 'The JB Case', started 20 September 1948. The serial beginning 26 September 1949 introduced a new Dick Barton, Duncan Carse, a real-life adventurer and oceanographer. The announcer was changed, too: John Fitchen. Another Dick, Gordon Davies, took over from 3 October 1950, with a new producer, Archie Campbell. The final episode was broadcast on 30 March 1951. There was a two-week, 10-part revival for the BBC's Jubilee, starting 6 November 1972. Noel Johnson and John Mann were back – in stereo!

Digger Dan

Character played by Australian Dick Griffin in MERRY-GO-ROUND (1947).

Dimbleby, Richard

The first radio reporter, a role he created for himself in 1936 by persuading the BBC that their news programmes needed an on-the-spot observer. His smooth, friendly tones and ability to speak in unruffled continuity won him affection as the Voice for every Great Occasion,

Richard **Dimbleby**: radio reporter and panel-game personality

such as Queen Elizabeth's Coronation, for which he provided the television commentary. In 1939 he became the first accredited War Correspondent and made many historic commentaries, from a mass bombing raid on Berlin to the D-Day landings. He was always in the forefront, and the Italians attempted to surrender to him when the British Army entered Bardia! Freelance from 1945, he entered entertainment and became a regular on TWENTY QUESTIONS and the first host of DOWN YOUR WAY. A second career awaited in television, where his immediate success was marked by a double *Daily Mail* Award in 1950, as Voice of the Year, and Outstanding Television Personality.

Dinner at Eight

Weekly series (at 7.45 pm) on RADIO LUXEMBOURG from 1936, a cabaret starring Harry Welchman, June Clyde and the C&B Band conducted by Sidney Lipton. C&B stood for the sponsor, Crosse and Blackwell's Soup.

Disc jockeys

DJ, or lately deejay, is an American term which came into usage via AFN during the war. To the BBC they were Presenters of Gramophone Record Recitals. The first ever was PETER ECKERSLEY, who included the occasional record in his pioneering programmes for the MARCONI Co. The first form of recorded music broadcast on the BBC was the piano roll: daily Pianola Recitals were given from 26 March 1923. These were boosted by the addition of records from 6 June, usually referred to as 'the phonograph'. The gramophone replaced the pianola completely from 8 September, the records being introduced by the day's duty announcer. A weekly recital of new records began on 27 March 1924, and the first guest presenter was Compton Mackenzie, editor of *The Gramophone*, on 12 June. It was Mackenzie's son-in-law, CHRISTOPHER STONE, who became the first professional DJ on 7 July 1927 with a regular Thursday night series (all earlier programmes had been early in the day). ROBERT TREDINNICK, an author and broadcaster of children's stories in Manchester, was the next 'name' DJ in 1933. Then came specialists such as Alistair Cooke with his I HEAR AMERICA CALLING, Edgar Jackson with jazz records, and Victor Hely-Hutchinson on the classics. DORIS ARNOLD was the first woman DJ with her series,

Disc-jockeys: Luxembourg favourites of 1951,
Pete Madren and Pete Murray

THESE YOU HAVE LOVED, and although records were the mainstay of pre-war commercial radio, the first name DJ on Normandy was Oliver Kimball, the RECORD SPINNER. With the war came the vastly popular record request series such as Roy Rich with his RECORD TIME, and FAMILY FAVOURITES with the likes of Jean Metcalfe and Franklin Engelmann. The emergence of the DJ as a personality really began with HOUSEWIVE'S CHOICE (1946), where GEORGE ELRICK's 'Smiling Voice' renewed his pre-war popularity as a singing band-leader. JACK JACKSON completely remade the medium with his complex and wacky RECORD ROUND-UP (1948). Then came SAM COSTA's *Record Rendezvous* (1950), Jonah Barrington's *Record Album* (1951), and even UNCLE MAC's CHILDREN's CHOICE. Other BBC DJs of the fifties: JACK TRAIN, JACK PAYNE, Godfrey Winn, Wilfrid Thomas, the man who made 'Rose Rose I Love You' (a Chinese record) top of the pops, Richard Attenborough, Alan Melville, Steve Race, Michael Brooke, Philip Slessor, Eamonn Andrews, David Jacobs, and Lillian Duff who specialized in Continental records. RADIO LUXEMBOURG's staff DJs began with Geoffrey Everitt and TEDDY JOHNSON, who were followed by PETE MURRAY, Peter Madren, David Gell, Mel Oxley, Keith Fordyce, Barry Aldiss and Don Moss.

Discord in Three Flats

Situation comedies set in 64 Cambridge Square, with JACK HULBERT as Henry Ashford, bachelor solicitor and landlord, CICELY COURTNEIDGE and VIC OLIVER as Mr and Mrs Oscar Hardwick, tenants, and Joan Benham as Amanda Studd, Hulbert's fiancée in the top flat. Written by Bob Block, produced by Alastair Scott Johnston. Weekly from 7 July 1962.

Dishonest to Goodness

Bernard Bresslaw and John Bluthal starred as two confidence-trickster brothers whose elaborate and felonious schemes never seemed to make them any richer. Bob Todd, Len Lowe and Judy Cornwell made up the cast, with music by Jack Emblow. Episode 1, 'It's in the Kit Bag', was broadcast on 22 September 1963, written by Brad Ashton and produced by John Browell.

The Diver

Entered bubbling from watery sources to splutter, 'Don't forget the Diver, sir, don't forget the Diver!' adding on occasion, 'Every penny makes the water warmer!'. Horace Percival played this real-life memory of TOMMY HANDLEY's in IT's THAT MAN AGAIN (1941), departing with the classic exit line, 'I'm going down now, sir!' and more bubbles.

Dixon, Reginald

'I Do Like To Be Beside The Seaside' was his apt signature tune: he was the 'official organist' at the Tower Ballroom, Blackpool. Born in Sheffield in 1904, he started to learn the piano at the age of nine and by the time he was 15 he was a piano teacher. He started to study the organ at 14 and within a year was appointed church organist. He was 22 when he first played a cinema organ, deputizing at a moment's notice, and two years later became full-time organist at the Birmingham cinema. By the thirties Dixon was a radio regular with his popular mid-day request programmes.

Reginald **Dixon**: organist of the Blackpool Tower

Does the Team Think

Spontaneous comedy quiz in which members of the studio audience posed questions to an all-comedian panel, originally composed of David Nixon, David Tomlinson, Jimmy Wheeler and the man who thought it up, Professor JIMMY EDWARDS. Peter Haigh was the first chairman (20 October 1957), replaced by McDonald Hobley, the popular television announcer, from the second series (1 June 1958). This began with the team of Edwards, ARTHUR ASKEY, Tommy Trinder, and Larry Adler. The 100th show, broadcast 4 March 1963, starred Edwards, Trinder, TED RAY and CYRIL FLETCHER. The last show was aired on 19 July 1976, and the format has recently been revived on television.

Doing the Daily Dozen

First daily keep-fit programme of exercises, broadcast from RADIO NORMANDY at 7 am from Monday 10 July 1939. The physical fitness expert was Eric Egan, and the producer Tom Ronald.

Dolly Dove

Kindly and quick-witted flower-seller of Piccadilly Circus, played by Ruth Dunning in 'Dolly Dove of Dover Street', a regular feature in TO TOWN WITH TERRY (1948). Theme song: 'Who'll Buy My Lavender?'

Don't Listen to This

Late-night comedy series described as 'The VARIETY DEPARTMENT Experimental Hour in 15 Minutes'. First programme, 13 February 1942, was called 'Crewe Sonata' by Aubrey Danvers-Walker and producer Henry Reed.

Don't Look Now

An alternative to television, by 5 October 1962 a considerable threat to radio. Basil Boothroyd of *Punch* selected and introduced this collection of wit, music and humour, aided by Piers Stephens, C. Gordon Glover, Charlotte Mitchell, and Ivor Cutler O.M.P. Produced by John Bridges.

Dotty

Scatty secretary to TOMMY HANDLEY in the 1940 series of IT's THAT MAN AGAIN. Played by Vera Lennox, Dotty was Cilly's sister and seemingly sillier, never getting her boss's name right: 'Mr Handmaid', 'Mr Hambone', etc.

Double or Quits Cash Quiz

Regular feature of *Middle East*, later *Mediterranean*, later still just plain MERRY-GO-ROUND, in which members of the services both supplied and answered questions posed in rotation by three question-masters. These were, for the Navy Lieutenant Harold Warrender; for the Army Will Hay; and for the Air Force Roy Rich (later KENNETH HORNE). Competitors could select a subject from this list: Animals, Current Affairs, Films, Food and Drink, Geography, History, Lucky Dip, Music, Radio, Sport, Theatre, and Tune Titles. Prizes were half-a-crown for the first correct answer, doubling to five shillings, then ten shillings, and finally one pound, with all forfeited if a wrong answer was given. Signature tune: 'We're In the Money'.

Double Top

Comedy with music series devised and scripted by Sid Colin around the talents of singer Anne Shelton and comedian Alfred Marks. Music from Stanley Black and the Dance Orchestra and produced from 10 March 1952 by Roy Speer. The series returned on 28 September but still Stanley Black never managed to speak more words than 'May I . . .' The third series started 2 July 1953.

Double Your Money

HUGHIE GREEN acted as 'Mirth Master' on this cash quiz, the high spot of which was 'The £32 Question'. Lucozade sponsored, John Beard produced, and RADIO LUXEMBOURG broadcast from 5 October 1954. The first winners were newlyweds, Mr and Mrs Smith. Hughie Green was later to host the show on commercial television.

Down-Beat

First radio series for Ted Heath and his Music with the Kordites. Heath, trombonist with a number of dance bands, brought all his former bosses onto the series as guest stars: GERALDO, JACK HYLTON, AMBROSE, MAURICE WINNICK, Sydney Lipton. First broadcast on 10 August 1949.

Down Mangel Street

Cockney family comedies written by MABEL CONSTANDUROS in which she starred as Mrs Ogboddy. Her hubby was John Rorke, with Phyllis Morris, Gwen Lewis, Fred Yule, and the Dance Orchestra conducted by Billy Ternent. Producer Eric Fawcett; weekly from 8 October 1942.

Down Our Street

First solo series for cockney comedienne Ethel Revnell, hitherto the funny half of the double act, REVNELL AND WEST. 1 October 1948 was the first of eight visits 'in which she takes you to meet her friends and relations, not forgetting the Kid'. Ethel, of course, played the Kid: she was a specialist in child impersonation. Ivor Barnard was her main support, with Stanley Black and the Dance Orchestra. Script by Rex Diamond and Carey Edwards; production by Tom Ronald.

Down Your Way

This long-running combination of records and interviews began on 29 December 1946 with the now very familiar signature tune, 'Horse Guards', played by the Queens Hall Light Orchestra: 'STEWART MACPHERSON with the BBC Mobile Recording Unit visits Lambeth and invites Mr and Mrs John Citizen to choose their favourite records and say a few words to the listeners.' The original producer was Leslie Perowne. The 200th show, with RICHARD DIMBLEBY in charge, was broadcast on 26

November 1950 as a special studio production. Twenty of the 2000 people heard in the series were invited back to the microphone. Franklin 'Jingle' Engelmann took over from Dimbleby in 1955 and died in harness after presenting 733 programmes. Sports commentator Brian Johnston took over, and is still the link-man in 1985. The series was cancelled in April 1975, but was eventually restored after a public outcry. *The Down Your Way Book* was published in 1981 to celebrate the 1500th programme.

Dr Carteret

Radio detective created by Anthony Gilbert and played by Cecil Trouncer in 'A Corner in Crime', which was a regular feature of the hospital series, HERE'S WISHING YOU WELL AGAIN (1944).

Dr Fu Manchu

The insidious Oriental menace was the central character of the first sponsored serial, broadcast from RADIO LUXEMBOURG every Sunday starting 6 December 1936. Adapted from the novels of Sax Rohmer, 'I am Fu Manchu' was played by Frank Cochrane; 'Nayland Smith, you are my enemy' by D.A. Clarke Smith, and Dr Petrie by Jack Lambert. Karamaneh, daughter of the dragon, was played by Pamela Titherage, and Inspector Weymouth by Arthur Young. 'Other characters' – Mervyn Johns! The sponsor was Milk of Magnesia. The original title of the serial was *Episodes from Dr Fu Manchu*, and the first episode was 'The Painted Kiss'. The final episode, No. 62, was entitled 'The House of Hashish'; broadcast on Sunday 6 February 1938.

Dr Morelle

'Presenting the secret papers of perhaps the strangest personality in the annals of criminal investigation'. Dennis Arundell played the mysterious doctor with Jane Graham as his nervous secretary, Miss Frayle, in a weekly segment of MONDAY NIGHT AT EIGHT, commencing 20 July 1942; created by Ernest Dudley. The series was *Meet Dr Morelle*, and a second series ran from 15 April 1946. Cecil Parker played the part when a full-blown series of half-hour mysteries began on 23 April 1957. Sheila Sim was Miss Frayle, and the producer Leslie Bridgmont. This run was entitled *A Case For Dr Morelle*.

Dr Muffin

Bumbling schoolmaster played by Will Hay in his wartime series, THE WILL HAY PROGRAMME. Pupils included Charles Hawtrey, Billy Nicholls and John Clark.

Dr Oliver Dither

'Rollicking fun!' was the weekly cry of this crazy physician fond of a practical joke. Played by Eric Woodburn in WATERLOGGED SPA (1948).

The Dream Man

Clive Arnum 'tells you what dreams may mean to you' on RADIO LUXEMBOURG from 29 August 1937. Between dreams there was advice from MRS JEAN SCOTT, President of the Brown & Polson Cookery Club.

The Dregs

Dreadful radio family (Myrtle, Alf, Veronica and Monty) featured in CHARLIE CHESTER's 1959 series, THAT MAN CHESTER. Created by Charles Hart and Bernard Botting.

Drive Inn

Comedy series starring pantomime dame George Lacy as Captain George de Courcy Chiseller *and* Lady Georgina Faggot-Trundle. Written by Loftus Wigram and produced by Reginald Smith; supporting cast Jack Melford, Charles Harison, Horace Percival, Gwen Lewis, Joan Young. Began 1 April 1942.

Duckweed and Eggblow

Comical con-men forever out to part the wealthy widow Ponsonby from her overweight birthright. Played by Harry Haver and Frank Lee in DANGER – MEN AT WORK (1940); catchphrase: 'What a woman!'

Dudley Davenport

'Good morning, sir, Dudley Davenport at your service, sir!' was the well-spoken catchphrase of well-mannered MAURICE DENHAM in MUCH-BINDING-IN-THE-MARSH (1947). His characteristic laugh was spelled in the script 'Keogh-keogh-keogh!', and his closing catchphrase was 'Oh, I say, I am a fool!'. Dudley's mum, Lady Davenport, was played by Babs Valerie.

Duffy's Tavern

'Where the elite meet to eat' – another famous and funny American series broadcast in Britain during the war. Archie the Manager, played by writer Ed Gardner, was first heard on 18 August 1944, and grew so popular that his Paramount film version, which would otherwise have been too obscure for the British, played here with great success. An Anglicized version, FINKEL'S CAFE, was written by FRANK MUIR AND DENIS NORDEN.

The Duke's Discs

'His Grace the Duke of Bedford in his new role as disc-jockey will play you records on his Duke-Box, and will be especially pleased to hear from those listeners in hospital.' RADIO LUXEMBOURG series recorded at Woburn Abbey, ancestral home of the Duke; first heard 4 July 1958.

Dunstan, Eric

Announcer, the first to be known as 'the man with the golden voice'. Appointed announcer on his return from India having failed to create an Indian Broadcasting Service for Sir John Reith. One of the personalities featured as themselves in *Death at Broadcasting House* (Phoenix Films, 1934). Later the radio critic for *The Star* newspaper.

ENSA Half Hour

Variety programmes staged for radio by ENSA beginning with *Drury Lane Calling* on 20 May 1940. Film star Robert Montgomery compèred a cast including Jessie Matthews, Sonnie Hale, Stanley Holloway, and GERALDO's Orchestra, with Naomi Jacob as 'The Voice of the BEF'. Series concluded in January 1944.

The Eager Beavers

Boy Scout troop led by Mr Ponsonby (TONY HANCOCK) in the series HAPPY-GO-LUCKY (1951). Members of the troop: Peter Butterworth, Graham Stark and Bill Kerr.

Eccles

Has good claim to being the Original Goon, having first appeared on HIP HIP HOO ROY (1949) before being christened in CRAZY PEOPLE on 9 July 1951. His creator, SPIKE MILLIGAN, claims Eccles ('Mad Dan' as he was later revealed to be named) was Virgin-born of Ethel Cox, but Walt Disney's 'Goofy' and Edgar Bergen's 'Mortimer Snerd' are likelier parents. Tends to enter with 'Hello, dere!', later modified to 'Ar-lo!'. Harmless idiot, fond of BLUEBOTTLE, his high-point was becoming a BBC announcer ('Winds light to variable!').

Eckersley, Peter

The first real broadcaster in Britain, announcing, hosting, singing, joking, and generally being the life and soul of the MARCONI COMPANY's station at Writtle. His opening words, 'Hello CQ, this is Two Emma Toc Writtle calling!', were first heard on 14 February 1922, introducing the first regular 15-minute programme which was broadcast every Tuesday. As Head of Marconi's Experimental Section, Eckersley continued to run the show from Writtle, faking the farewell champagne toast on close-down night (17 January 1923) with a pop-gun! John Reith made Eckersley the BBC's first Chief Engineer in 1923, then forced his resignation in 1929 because of a divorce. Eckersley's book, *The Power Behind the Microphone*, was published in 1941.

Ed and Don

Singing Cowboys who sang and twanged daily on RADIO NORMANDY from 6 February 1939. Their programmes were announced by Canadian Ralph Hurcombe, and they were eventually sponsored by Novopine Bath Cubes.

Eddie Nimbus

Private eye played by TED RAY in 'The Casebook of Eddie Nimbus', a regular feature of VARIETY PLAYHOUSE which Ray compèred from 5 October 1957. Patricia Hayes and Ronnie Barker played the other characters in this spot.

Educating Archie

We'll be Educating Archie,
What a job for anyone.
He's no good at spelling,
He hasn't a clue,
He thinks that three sevens
Make twenty-two.
What a problem child is he,
Educating Archie.

Peter **Eckersley**: first Chief Engineer of the BBC

Educating Archie: radio series on tour (*opposite*)

MOSS **Empire** THEATRE NOTTINGHAM

Proprietors: MOSS' EMPIRES, Ltd.
Chairman: PRINCE LITTLER
Managing Director: VAL PARNELL
TELEPHONE: 40361-2
Manager: T. H. TILLSON

| MONDAY, OCT. 1st | THE STARS OF | 6.15 & 8.30 |

EDUCATING ARCHIE

RADIO'S TOP LINE FAMILY FEATURE

PETER BROUGH
WITH
ARCHIE ANDREWS

RAVIC & RENE ★ HAROLD TAYLOR

JACK CRISP & JILL

RONALD CHESNEY ★ TANNER SISTERS

EDWARD VICTOR
TONY

ARCHIE ANDREWS' NEW TUTOR

HANCOCK

THE SINGING STARS FROM "EDUCATING ARCHIE"

BRITAIN'S GREATEST

TRIBE BROS., Ltd., London and St. Albans

Incredibly popular and important comedy series starring ventriloquist Peter Brough and his dummy, ARCHIE ANDREWS . . . important for the number of new comedy talents who obtained their first radio breaks in the series. Although gags always reemphasized the wooden nature of the hero, Archie was always played as essentially human. Producer Eric Speer wrote: 'We see him as a boy in his middle teens, naughty but loveable, rather too grown-up for his years, especially where the ladies are concerned, and distinctly cheeky!'

Archie's first tutor was Robert Moreton, he of the BUMPER FUN BOOK ('Oh, get in there, Moreton!'). Hattie Jacques played Miss Agatha Dinglebody and Max Bygraves the hearty cockney: 'I've arrived and to prove it I'm here!' Bygraves also made a catchphrase of 'Big-'ead!', which became popular enough to become a song. Teenage soprano Julie Andrews was Archie's little girlfriend, with song spots by the Tanner Sisters and the Hedley Ward Trio. The Music Teachers were conducted by Peter Yorke, and the script written by Eric Sykes and Sid Colin. First broadcast 6 June 1950, announced by Peter Madden, the show was such a runaway success that it won the NATIONAL RADIO AWARD for the Outstanding Variety Series of 1950. The series starting 3 August 1951 introduced TONY HANCOCK as Archie's new tutor, and also as a flummoxed individual with the catchphrase, 'Flippin' kids!'. During this series Alfred Marks replaced Max Bygraves for a while, and John Sharp came in as the Fire Chief of Pudshill. The next series starting 18 August 1952 introduced the singing Goon Harry Secombe as tutor, and Ronald Chesney with his Magic Talking Mouthorgan, accompanied by Robert Busby and the Revue Orchestra. This all helped win the 1953 NATIONAL RADIO AWARD as the Most Entertaining Programme. The series commencing 15 October 1953 began with cockney comedian Ronald Shiner as Archie's educator, replaced by rustic Bernard Miles on 7 January 1954. The sixth series started 26 September 1955 with film star James Robertson Justice as the crusty tutor, Beryl Reid as schoolgirl MONICA, Ken Platt, Graham Stark, the Coronets and the Dennis Wilson Quintet. The script was now by Ronald Wolfe and George Wadmore. The seventh series started 19 September 1956, with Beryl Reid as an occasional guest. Alexander Gauge was the heavyweight tutor, and Dick Emery the new voice-man:

Monica: Beryl Reid in *Educating Archie*

Lampwick, Punchy, Mr Monty, and GRIMBLE. Pat Dunlop was added to the writing team. The eighth series opened on 25 September 1957 with Jerry Desmonde, Warren Mitchell and Pearl Carr supporting Emery, now promoted. The ninth series started on 28 September 1958 with the little Welsh comedienne with the big laugh, Gladys Morgan, as the cook, Bernard Bresslaw the hulking idiot ('Ullo, it's me, Twinkletoes!'), and Marty Feldman added to the writing team. Producer was now Jacques Brown. The tenth series began with show No. 200 and a new tutor, Bruce Forsythe (7 October 1959); Sidney James replaced him on 6 January 1960. See also ARCHIE'S THE BOY, a doomed attempt to break the mould in 1954.

Edward Byegum
E. Byegum, from Yorkshire of course, was a blunt, bluff industrialist as played by Deryck Guyler in IT'S THAT MAN AGAIN (1946).

Edward Wilkinson
Completely mythical and never-heard character referred to by Murdoch and Horne in MUCH-BINDING-IN-THE-MARSH (1948) merely to fill in time. 'By the way, sir, have you seen anything of Edward Wilkinson lately?'

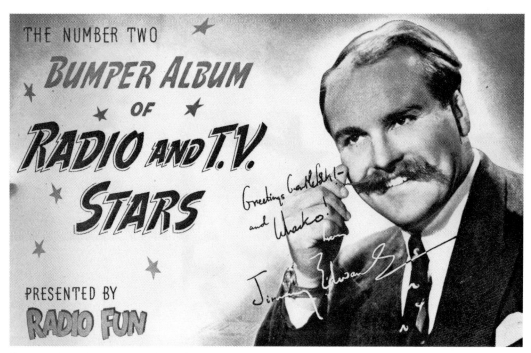

Jimmy **Edwards**: *Radio Fun* free gift

Edwards, Jimmy

'Professor' James Keith O'Neill Edwards, MA, DFC, turned funny after the war by blowing his trombone at the Windmill Theatre. His fruity but educated tones were first heard in the ex-Service series, THEY'RE OUT (1946), from which he developed a light-hearted lecture series, 'You May Take Notes', in NAVY MIXTURE. This led to co-starring with Joy Nichols and Dick Bentley in TAKE IT FROM HERE (1948), his most memorable role being that of the coarse layabout Pa GLUM. Catchphrases include: 'Wake up at the back there!', 'Black mark, Bentley!', 'Clumsy clot!', 'A mauve one!' 'Allo-allo-allo!' His moustache is famous: he helped found the Handlebar Club. He was elected Lord Rector of Aberdeen University in 1951, and published his autobiography, *Take It From Me*, in 1953. Jimmy Edwards also starred in WHACK-O!, and appeared regularly in DOES THE TEAM THINK.

Edwin Carp

Professor Carp, the World's Only Fish Mimic, was first heard in an outside broadcast from a West End revue in the thirties. He reappeared in New York, when he guested on an ENSA presentation, *Broadway Calling* (1941). Finally he returned to his homeland and starred in TAKE IT FROM HERE (1943). And all the time he was really the alter ego of Richard Haydn, who became a film star and director.

Effie Pintable

Cheeky daughter of Percy Pintable (Horace Percival), played by Jean Capra in IT'S THAT MAN AGAIN (1943). Introduced herself as 'seventeen and never been out with an American!'.

Eight Bells

Occasional pre-war series with a Royal Navy setting, written and arranged by Mungo Dewar. ARTHUR ASKEY appeared as A.B. Nobby Clark, with Fred Gwyn as Shorty Sinclair and John Rorke as Lofty Delaney, the comedy element. Fred Yule kept order as Leading Seaman Pincher Martin, and the team of Vine, Moore and Nevard sang under the guise of the Wardroom Wailers. Styx Gibling played Telegraphist Bill Jenkins, the Xylophonic Sparkler, and the Variety Orchestra posed as the Blanco Boys, the ship's band of HMS *St George*, from whose quarter-deck the entertainment was supposedly relayed. Produced by Harry S. Pepper, 'the Old Salt!'. First broadcast 16 April 1935, the series disappeared during the war, only to return on 29 January 1946 as *Eight Bells Home Again*, in which Tommy Brandon and Crew celebrated their return to Pompey.

Eight Step Sisters

Tap-dancing troupe formed specially for radio! They broadcast every Saturday in MUSIC HALL (1933), the intention being to add 'outside broadcast' atmosphere to a studio presentation. The girls were Edith, Eileen, Marjorie, Winnie, Laura, Ida, Queenie and Joan, and they were trained by Mrs Rodney Hudson.

Elevenses With Geraldo and Diploma

'Deep Purple' was the signature tune for this mid-morning music programme, which began on RADIO LUXEMBOURG on 28 March 1937. 'See you take home a box of Diploma, the English Crustless Cheese.'

Elise

Suzette Lamonde played the singing star of this musical thriller serial sponsored by Bourjois 'Evening in Paris' Perfume on RADIO LYONS, weekly from 2 October 1938. With Bernard Clifton (Michael), Inga Andersen (Claire), Scott Harrold (Max Steiner), Neil Arden (Jimmy), James Pirrie (Ricky), Tony Quinn (O'Hara), and Little Maureen Glynne (Sandra), with Richard Crean and his Orchestra. Written by Sheila Fryer; produced by J. Bertram Fryer.

Elizabeth

The former 'Aunt' Elizabeth of CHILDREN'S HOUR was producer May Jenkin, whose entire career was in children's broadcasting. From the Newcastle studio in 1927 she came to SAVOY HILL in 1929, discovering TOYTOWN on a second-hand bookstall, WORZEL GUMMIDGE, and many other C.H. regulars. On 'UNCLE MAC's' retirement in 1950 she became Head of the department, and was awarded an MBE in 1945. She retired in 1953.

Ellinga

African native and occasional Big Chief as played by Ray Ellington with many a 'Cor blimey, man!' in THE GOON SHOW (1955).

Elsie, Winnie and Johnny

HARRY HEMSLEY's 'imaginary family'. Harry played the harassed father of three typical children: Elsie, the prim elder girl, Winnie the giggly little'un, and Johnny, a sometimes surly boy. Later they were joined by baby brother HORACE. Came to fame on MUSIC HALL broadcasts, then travelled to RADIO LUXEMBOURG for a weekly adventure serial in THE OVALTINEY'S CONCERT PARTY (1935).

Elwin, Maurice

Known as the Golden Voiced Singer in the Savoy Orpheans dance band, he also broadcast and recorded with many others, and under a great many pseudonyms. Born in Scotland in 1902, by 1936 he was reckoned to receive the highest salary ever paid to a British dance-band vocalist.

The Embassy Lark

Laurie Wyman, having hit home with the phenomenal NAVY LARK, and muffed with the TV LARK, tried again with this 'chronicle of events in and around Her Britannic Majesty's Embassy in the Kingdom of Tratvia'. Derek Francis played His Excellency Sir Jeremy Crighton-Buller KCMG, with Frank Thornton as his First Secretary Henry Pettyman, Charlotte Mitchell as his wife the Lady Daphne, and Francis de Wolff as the Tratvian Minister of the Interior. Ronald Fletcher was merely the announcer. Produced by Alastair Scott Johnston; first broadcast 26 April 1966.

Emery at Large

Dick Emery, funny voice-man for so many radio series, was promoted to stardom with this show of his own, on 26 March 1964. Supporting cast: Deryck Guyler, Norma Ronald, Julian Orchard, and Paddy Roberts with a weekly ditty. Script by George Wadmore and John Cleese (his first credit); produced by Charles Maxwell. The second series (27 June 1965) credited David Cumming with the script and Charles Chilton with production. Music was by Nat Temple and his Band, and Emery introduced a new character, Emmanuel Finch the Olde English Folk Singer.

Emily

Long-suffering wife of LAC SAM COSTA of MUCH-BINDING-IN-THE-MARSH (1945). Never heard and just as well, as she long-suffered from 'twinges'.

Empire Service

Forerunner of the General Overseas Service, which became today's BBC World Service, it began on 19 December 1932, with five time-zones: Canada, West Africa, South Africa, India and Australasia. Transmissions started at 9.30 am with the announcement, 'This is London calling . . . the Australasian Zone', concluding at 3 am with the Canadian Zone. Studios were at Broadcasting House (later Bush House), and the transmitting aerials at Daventry. Listeners at home heard certain broadcasts preceded with the announcement: 'This programme is also being radiated through GSF – F for Fortune – and GSG – G for Greeting – the Empire broadcasting transmitters at Daventry.'

Empire Soccer Song Time

Teddy Johnson and Kathran Oldfield were the singing stars of this sponsored series, presented on RADIO LUXEMBOURG from November 1951 by Empire Pools of Blackpool. The Empire Music Makers were conducted by Norrie Paramor, and sports columnist Bernie Jay introduced each week's special sporting guest. By the end of the following year, the stars were billed as Teddy Johnson and Pearl Carr, 'Luxembourg's Own Singing Sweethearts'.

England, Paul

Busy, bright talent of early radio combining comedy, singing, and writing. Born in Streatham he sang in the choir of the Inner Temple and ran away from his apprenticeship to a motor engineer to join the Festival of Empire at the Crystal Palace in 1911. Great War service in the Royal Horse Artillery led to a peace-time career in West End musical comedy. By 1936 he had notched up over 500 broadcasts solo, and with such teams as THOSE FOUR CHAPS and 'The Two Pairs'. Co-wrote the *RKO Loud Speakers* revue at the Leicester Square Theatre and the film *Radio Parade* (1933). A pioneer of commercial broadcasting he was a director of Colonial Radio Programmes, which produced and syndicated sponsored shows to far-flung stations of the Empire (1933).

Arthur **English**: 'Prince of the Wide Boys'

English, Arthur

'Prince of the Wide Boys', Arthur's rapid rise to radio fame began when the demobbed decorator from Aldershot auditioned at the Windmill and was on stage an hour later. His broad-shouldered, kipper-tied characterization of the then-prevalent spiv caught on, and in 1950 he was made resident comedian on VARIETY BANDBOX. Catchphrases included 'Watch the boy!', 'Sharpen up there, the quick stuff's coming', and at the end of an incomprehensible gabble, 'Play the music, open the cage!'. His signature tune was 'Powder Your Face With Sunshine'.

The English Family Robinson

First attempt to establish a BBC family serial. Ralph Truman played Charles Robinson, with MABEL CONSTANDUROS as wife Clara, Harold Reese as son Peter, and Elizabeth Gilbert as daughter Joan, and Clive Baxter as John. Megs Jenkins played Shirley the Maid. Written by Mabel and Denis Constanduros, produced by Howard Rose. The first episode of these 'Everyday happenings in an everyday household' took place on 7 October 1938, and was entitled 'Breakfast on Saturday Morning'. A wartime revival from 30 April 1940 found Mr Robinson still travelling from Hawthorn Avenue, Streatham, to the City every day, and Joan desperately keen to marry her soldier boyfriend. The family's adventures were chronicled in Mabel Constanduros' novel, *A Nice Fire in the Drawing Room* (1939).

Enoch

Gormless call-boy of THE HAPPIDROME (1941) with the catchphrase, 'Let me tell you!' Called 'Deadly Nightshade' among other things by his boss, MR LOVEJOY. He did the occasional tap dance. Played by Robbie Vincent on the radio, who was preceded in *The Arcadian Follies* seaside show by Albert Modley.

Entertainment Parade

Fortnightly topical review of the world's entertainment featuring personalities and news of the stage, screen and radio. Introduced by Henry Kendall with the BBC Theatre Orchestra, conductor Mark Lubbock. Devised by Bertram Henson and Bruce Belfrage; producer John Watt. Started 5 October 1936.

Epaminondas

Silly piccaninny star of stories by Constance Egan, read regularly on CHILDREN'S HOUR from 1936. Catchphrase: 'Oh, Epaminondas, yo' ain't got de sense yo' was born wid!', Mammy's eternal rebuke to her simple son as he pulled a leg of lamb home from the butcher's, tied to a piece of string. The stories were told by Dorothy Black.

Ernest the Policeman

Kindly country constable, if a bit slow-witted. Fancy saying to the Mayor of TOYTOWN, 'I shall have to take your name and address!'. Played by Arthur Wynn (among others) in the long-running CHILDREN'S HOUR series.

Ernie Bagwash

The only member of the Bagwash family ever to be heard in BAND WAGGON (1938), he was the adenoidal nephew of ARTHUR ASKEY's charlady. Played at high pitch by RICHARD MURDOCH, Ernie's party piece was 'The Bells' by Edgar Allan Poe, which he concluded with 'Can I have my piece of cake now, Auntie?'.

Ernie Splutmuscle

Squeaky twit and likely ancestor of BLUEBOTTLE. Began life in CRAZY PEOPLE (1951) as portrayed by PETER SELLERS.

Erwin, Wasey

Advertising agency claiming the first sponsored radio programme in English: André Charlot and guests in a broadcast from 'a Continental station' in 1927. The agency opened a Radio Department in 1935 to produce programmes for their clients featuring Gracie Fields, George Formby, Carson Robison and his Pioneers, Morton Downey and JACK JACKSON and his Band. Producers included Charles Maxwell and Harold Jackson.

Eugene Song Parade

Popular Hollywood film star and tenor Tony Martin hosted this musical series for RADIO LUXEMBOURG from 4 May 1954. Produced by Philip Jones; sponsored by Eugene Home Perms.

Europe Confidential

Basil Rathbone acted as host in this, one of the 'World's Greatest Mysteries' series. Lionel Murton played Mike Conroy, an American press correspondent stationed in Paris. Broadcast on RADIO LUXEMBOURG from 6 June 1958; produced by HARRY ALAN TOWERS.

Eustace

The first of PETER SELLERS' horrible kids, Eustace was the awful child who greeted TED RAY with the catchphrase, 'What do you want, soppy?' in RAY'S A LAUGH (1949); he bowed out with another, 'Just like your big red conk!'.

Ex-Corporal Wilf

WILFRED PICKLES as a typical Army Corporal whose demobilization throws him up against problems in making a new start as a civilian. Episode 1, 'Wilf Gets His Ticket', was broadcast on 31 October 1945, and introduced Wilf's wife, still on war work, and his Major, demobbed at the same time. Written by Jack Hargreaves and produced by D.G. Bridson.

False Evidence

Panel game devised and produced by Ian Messiter with GILBERT HARDING as the Judge, and Leslie Mitchell and Franklin Engelmann interrogating the defendants and witnesses. Commenced 17 November 1951.

Family Album (1)

'Weekly record of the home life of a British family in time of war.' The saga of the Harrises began on 4 April 1943, with none of the cast identified.

Family Album (2)

South African singer Eve Boswell (the 'Sugar Bush' girl) starred in this RADIO LUXEMBOURG series sponsored by Marshall Ward. Eve was backed by Philip Green and his Orchestra, and Adrian Foley at the piano. Foley also produced, while the announcer was David Jacobs. There was a £40 cash prize each week, beginning 1 August 1954.

Family Crackers

Comedy series for Harry Tate Junior as patriarch of a weird family: Mother (Doris Nichols), Dahlia (Betty Huntley Wright), Junior (Ronnie Beadle), and Uncle Ned (Clifford Bean), with Fred Leslie as the Odd Man Out. Catchphrases: 'How's your father!' and 'Hullo, I'm coming round!' Written by Tate and Loftus Wigram; producer Eric Fawcett. It started 13 August 1941.

Family Favourites

Most popular of all the record request series, this two-way broadcast between the BBC in London and the British Forces Network in Germany began with the classic signature tune, 'With a Song in My Heart', on 7 October 1945. Created by Maurice Gorham, the original billing read: 'From London, the tunes you asked us to play. From Germany, the tunes that make them think of you. Records played alternately.' The first two presenters were not identified, but the most famous were Jean Metcalfe in London and Cliff Michelmore in Hamburg; they got married. A special *Five Way Family Favourites* was broadcast on 9 December 1956 in the Light Programme's Record Week with Jean Metcalfe in London, Dennis Scuse in Cologne, Alistair McDougal in Hamburg, Kay Donnelly in Cyprus, and Bill Duxbury in Malta.

From 3 January 1960, the programme was known as TWO WAY FAMILY Favourites.

Family Hour

The husband-and-wife crosstalk act Billy Caryll and Hilda Mundy carried the continuity of this magazine programme, with Gabrielle Blunt as their daughter Bunty, and Janet Brown as Jeannie the girl next door. The first show, broadcast 10 October 1949, included baritone Raymond Newell, violinist Campoli, and the STARGAZERS with Stanley Black and the Dance Orchestra. Items were 'Is This You? a nationwide game of Tig in which you might win the prize', Ronnie Waldman's 'PUZZLE CORNER' including the Monday Night Accumulator, and 'Musical News' by Leslie Julian Jones. Written by Sid Colin and Gordon Crier; produced by Harry S. Pepper and Ronnie Waldman.

Family Racket

Wartime comedy series with music featuring the Robinson Family: Edward Cooper (Uncle George), Henry (Fred Gregory), Grace (Doris Nichols), David (Graham Payn), and Paula (Luanne Shaw). Script by Edward Cooper; produced by Reginald Smith. From 4 November 1940.

Famous Music Halls

'A pageant of entertainment at Britain's variety theatres' began on 14 October 1938 with a broadcast from the South London Palace, commemorating '80 years of music and laughter at the Old South'. The story was told by John Watt in the BBC studio with BRYAN MICHIE interviewing at the theatre. Starring in the studio were Dick Francis, Bertha Willmott, John Rorke, and the Variety Orchestra conducted by CHARLES SHADWELL, and, in the theatre, Leon Cortez and his Coster Pals. Producer Roy Speer.

Fan clubs

Radio Fan Clubs flourished in the thirties, so much so that a fan page was instituted in RADIO PICTORIAL from 9 September 1938. It listed 32 clubs included those for AMBROSE (run by Miss Eileen Matthewsman of Maida Vale), Robinson Cleaver (R. Bartlett of East Ham), Gene Crowley (Marie Kendon of Bow), Denny Dennis (Millie Pegras of Bow), Nat Gonella (Miss Ayres of Westminster), RICHARD GOOLDEN (Hilda Kenwright of Chiswick), JACK JACKSON (R. Adams of Bristol), VERA LYNN (Miss Puckey of Wood Green), BRYAN MICHIE (Betty Smith of Ealing) Arthur Riscoe (Marjorie Rogers of Palmers Green), Syd Seymour (Harold Price of Birmingham), Arthur Tracy (Harold Pickard of Blackpool), and Rita Williams (Sally Jarman of Dalston). A badge for the Vera Lynn Club cost a shilling, and the BILLY COTTON Club published a fan mag called *The Cotton Reel*.

Fanny Haddock

Hoarse-voiced cook for BEYOND OUR KEN (1958), played by Betty Marsden in a brilliant burlesque of the real Fanny Cradock.

Farmer Jollop

Crusty rustic in IT'S THAT MAN AGAIN (1939), given to herding cows through the Office of Twirps with cries of 'Git up there, Strawberry, eech oop there, Gladys!'. Played by JACK TRAIN.

Farmer Will Watchet

Radio character who compèred the concerts from WELCOME 'ALL (1942). Played by Hugh Morton; catchphrase: 'You blowsy old faggit!'

Fashions From Paris

Historic radio series: the sponsor was Tampax! Broadcast from Poste Parisien from 3 January 1939, the star was Madame Maya Noel, 'the well-known fashion expert', with 'up-to-the-minute news of the latest lovely creations direct from the fashion centre of the world. Half an hour of Fashion and Gay Music': commère Florence Miller.

Fat Stock Prices

Read out by sombre-toned announcers at the end of the News from 11 March 1929, these quickly became the latest radio joke. They were often burlesqued by CLAPHAM AND DWYER in their 'A Day's Broadcasting' sketches.

Father Brown

Roman Catholic priest/detective created by G.K. Chesterton. Gordon Phillott played him on radio in a series of *Father Brown Stories* adapted by Felix Felton. The first, 'The Blue Cross', was broadcast on 30 December 1946. 'The Blue Cross' was also the first in a second series starting 20 February 1949. This time George Owen played the little detective, but was soon replaced by Arthur Ridley.

Fayne and Evans

Impressionists extraordinary whose specialty was 'placing our radio sets side by side' and giving synchronized impersonations of John Arlott commentating on a Test Match. School friends Tony and David teamed up after war-service and made their radio debut on VARIETY BANDBOX (1949). Many shows followed: STARLIGHT HOUR, FIRST HOUSE, *Golden Slipper Club*, etc.

Feed the Brute

Daily programme: five minutes of fun and recipes from GERT AND DAISY (ELSIE AND DORIS WATERS). 6.15 pm on the Home Service from 9 April 1940.

Feen-a-Mint Fan Fare

'The chewing confection with laxative properties' sponsored this weekly broadcast from Radio Toulouse beginning 17 October 1937. Polly Ward was the commère introducing amateur talent. The gum moved into big-time radio by presenting George Formby as their star, starting on RADIO LUXEMBOURG on 3 April 1938. George ran for over a year, supported in comedy by wife Beryl and voice-man JACK TRAIN. The producer was Charles Maxwell and Harry Bidgood and his Band played the signature tune, which was a parody of Formby's film hit:

> Keep fit, take Feen-a-Mint,
> Keep fit, and take my hint,
> It'll give your eyes a glint
> If you take Feen-a-Mint!

Festival of Britain

Special programmes to celebrate the 1951 Festival of Britain began on 5 May with *Festival Music Hall*, a fortnightly series produced by Bill Worsley and starring RICHARD MURDOCH, KENNETH HORNE, Anne Ziegler and Webster Booth, CHARLIE KUNZ, Charlie Clapham, Bill Kerr and Diana Morrison. Guest stars: ARTHUR ASKEY and the Radio Revellers. Paul Fenoulhet conducted the Variety Orchestra. *Festival of Variety* (6 May) was a two-hour spectacular compèred by WILFRED PICKLES, with Gracie Fields, Danny Kaye, Max Miller, TED RAY, Donald Peers, Anne and Webster (again), ELSIE AND DORIS WATERS, FRANKIE HOWERD, ROBB WILTON, George Robey, Albert Whelan, G.H. Elliott, Bertha Willmott, and BILLY COTTON with his Band. Producer Charles Maxwell. *Festival Parade* (12 May), another fortnightly series, starred BEBE DANIELS AND BEN LYON with Tyrone Power and Linda Christian, Binnie Hale, Jessie Matthews, Lupino Lane, Carol Raye, Peter Graves, AL READ, JON PERTWEE, Freddie Sales and Semprini. Producers, Tom Ronald and Michael North.

Fifi de la Bon-Bon

Mademoiselle Fifi was the Indoor Games Mistress at MUCH-BINDING-IN-THE-MARSH (1949). Barbara Valerie played her with many a coquettish 'Ooh la-la!'.

Fifteen Minute Theatre

'Where comedy, drama and farce each have their crowded moment': unique commercial radio series featuring four brief one-act playlets in 15 minutes. Broadcast from RADIO LYONS beginning 9 January 1937, announced by Adrian Thomas and sponsored by Yorkshire Relish.

Film Time

Series starring JACK PAYNE and his Band and the mysterious 'Man on the Set' who brought interesting gossip direct from the studios. Now it may be told: he was really Philip Slessor! Sponsored by Campbell Soups with the co-operation of Odeon Theatres. RADIO LYONS from 17 January 1937.

A BBC series of the same title began on 21 May 1948, with FREDDY GRISEWOOD as compère. This lunchtime series included 'Film Fan's Forum' (the filmgoer's opinion), 'Flash Back' (can you identify this film?), 'Coming Your Way' (excerpts from the week's releases), scripted by Michael Storm and produced by Denis Monger. The 50th programme (1 July 1949) included 'Ciné Quiz' (circle versus stalls from the Odeon, Bradford) and 'Introduction Please' with guest Alec Guinness. The appropriate theme tune for the series was 'The Way to the Stars'.

Find the Flaws

1939 quiz game from BBC Scotland, devised and produced by Howard M. Lockhart. This 'radio diversion' consisted of two playlets in which a number of mistakes were deliberately planted. Listeners were invited to make a note of the mistakes and check them with the list read after each sketch.

Fine Goings On

First comedy series built around FRANKIE HOWERD after his success in VARIETY BANDBOX. Marjorie Holmes played Miss Medworthy, and assistance came from Bill Fraser and Norman Wisdom. Janet Hamilton-Smith and John Hargreaves contributed romantic duets, and Robert Busby conducted the Revue Orchestra. Written by Eric Sykes and Sid Colin; produced by Bryan Sears. First broadcast 4 January 1951. A new series was broadcast from 2 April 1958, in which Frankie was supported by Dora Bryan, Freddie Mills (the boxer), Hugh Paddick, Moira Charles, Tucker McGuire and John Forde. Written by Terry Nation and John Junkin; produced by Bill Worsley.

Finkel's Cafe

Pronounce it cafe, not café, to get the pun. Comedy series starring PETER SELLERS as Eddie the Irish manager of the cafe where the Elite Meet to Eat. Adapted by FRANK MUIR AND DENIS NORDEN from the American radio series DUFFY's TAVERN by Ed Gardner. Cast: Sidney James, Avril Angers, Kenneth Connor, with guest star David Hughes. Music supplied by the Gypsy Tavern Ninetet; producer Pat Dixon. Opened on 4 July 1956.

Fiona and Charles

'Isn't It Romantic' was the orchestral theme that introduced those ineffable thespians of the

West End Theatre, Dame Celia Molestrangler and Binkie Huckaback, who played the roles of Fiona and Charles in many a romantic excerpt on ROUND THE HORNE (1965). In their turn, Celia and Binkie were played by Betty Marsden and Hugh Paddick.

Fireside Chats

Taking the title from the wartime talks of President Roosevelt, J.B. Priestley presented this series of discursive talks on RADIO LUXEMBOURG from 23 September 1951. Bluff Jack's topics included 'Great Aunts' and he was sponsored by hot Bovril.

Fletcher, Cyril

Originator of the Odd Odes, Cyril was a concert party comic who first broadcast with the FOL-DE-ROLS in 1936. Listeners loved his funny voices, especially the 'Dreamin' of Thee' character who declaimed 'The Lovesick Tommy's Dream of Home' by Edgar Wallace. Then came Mr Parker, 'THE LODGER', with his catchphrase, 'Yerse, thankin' yew!', and many MUSIC HALL appearances introduced by his signature tune, 'Entry of the Gladiators'. He was rewarded with his first series, THANKING YEW, in 1940, and many more followed, including *Thanking Yew Tew* in 1946. His other characterizations included Aggie the Polite Schoolgirl, and he often shared the microphone with his Mrs, the soprano Betty Astell. See also FLETCHER'S FARE.

Fletcher's Fare

Comedy series starring husband-and-wife team, CRYIL FLETCHER and Betty Astell, and the team of scriptwriters, BOB MONKHOUSE AND DENIS GOODWIN. Also Bob Sharples and his Music 'and a few surprises'. Produced by Leslie Bridgmont from 7 August 1952.

Flight-Officer Flannel

Hefty, horse-faced, hoarse-voiced WAAF officer played by her utter opposite, blonde vocalist Dorothy Carless, in MUCH-BINDING-IN-THE-MARSH (1944). At other times she was played by Binnie Hale and Doris Hare.

Flint of the Flying Squad

Detective Sergeant John Flint was played by

Bruce Seton (not yet TV's *Fabian of the Yard*) and created by Alan Stranks as a more serious crime series than his light-hearted PC49. Episode 1, 'Death in Gallows Mews', was heard on 12 June 1951, with Mary Mackenzie as Dinah Martin, Norman Claridge as Chief Inspector Whitelaw, and Sidney Monckton as comical sidekick Hopeless Hopkins. Producer was Vernon Harris. The second series started on 3 April 1952 with 'Undercover Girl', and the third series on 4 November 1952 with 'Sentence of Death'.

Floggit's

Situation series starring ELSIE AND DORIS WATERS in their classic GERT AND DAISY characterizations. The sisters inherited their Uncle Alf's general store in Russett Green where they encountered Emma Smeed (Joan Sims), Old Mother Butler (Iris Vandeleur), Greta of the Red Lion (Joan Sims again), and others including Anthony Newley, Ronnie Barker, Hugh Paddick and, later, Ron Moody. Written by Terry Nation and John Junkin with Dave Freeman, and produced by Alastair Scott-Johnston. Floggit's opened 17 August 1956, and reopened 8 April 1957 with Kenneth Connor to assist.

Flotsam and Jetsam

'Yours very sincerely, Flotsam and Jetsam' was the signing-off song of this favourite double-act. Mr Jetsam ('I sing the low notes – you'd wonder how he gets 'em') was Australian bass Malcolm McEachern; Mr Flotsam ('The songs sung by Jetsam are written by Flotsam') was the creative partner, pianist and composer B.C. Hilliam, born Scarborough 1890. As individual acts they met in New York during the Great War, met again in London in 1926, and made their début as a double-act at the Victoria Palace. Their first broadcast came in November, and so rapid was their rise to fame that they were booked for the ROYAL VARIETY PERFORMANCE in the following February. The blend of their high/low voices was a delight, and their songs witty, especially when dealing with radio: 'Little Betty Bouncer loved an announcer down at the BBC', 'Big Ben Calling' and 'Weather Reports' were among their best-selling records for Columbia. They starred in many radio shows of their own: *Round the World with Flotsam and Jetsam*, *Our Hour*, and *Signs of the Times*; after Jetsam's death (1945) Hilliam continued solo with FLOTSAM'S FOLLIES.

Flotsam and Jetsam: Savage Club menu

Flotsam's Follies

After the death of his deep-voiced partner Jetsam (see FLOTSAM AND JETSAM), B.C. Hilliam (Flotsam) wrote this 'weekly musical, lyrical and topical half-hour' for himself as host, comedians KENWAY AND YOUNG, and Charlie CLAPHAM, and singers Helen Clare, Robert Easton, Charmian Innes and Robert Sydney. Ivor Dennis played a second piano, and production was by Tom Ronald. The series leaped into surprising popularity and ran for six months, commencing 30 July 1945. A second series started on 1 February 1946, a third on 4 July 1947, and a fourth on 3 August 1948. The signature tune was 'Walking Home', which Flotsam had composed for a ballet, *Beau Brummell*, back in 1933. See also FLOTSAM's WHEEL OF FORTUNE.

Flotsam's Wheel of Fortune

B.C. Hilliam (the former Mr Flotsam) at his piano introduced 'stars of today and maybe tomorrow' in this variety series. On the first show (13 July 1955) there were ELSIE AND DORIS WATERS, Gerald Davies, the Londonaires, Patricia Ripley, Dennis Castle, the George Mitchell Choir, and the Variety Orchestra directed by Paul Fenoulhet. Glyn Jones produced.

Flowerdew

Effeminate personage appearing in CRAZY PEOPLE (1951) as portrayed by PETER SELLERS. Favourite phrase: 'Oooh, I could spit!'

The Flying Doctor

James McKechnie starred as Dr Chris Rogers in this adventure series based on the work of the Australian Royal Flying Doctor Service. Bill Kerr, the Aussie comedian, played sidekick Terry O'Donnell, and June Brunell was Jane Hudson. Episode 1, 'The Newchum', was broadcast on 17 July 1958, written by Rex Rienits and produced by Vernon Harris. The second series started on 10 March 1959 with 'Fire Below', and the third series on 8 March 1960 with Rosemary Miller as 'The New Girl'. The fourth series (16 March 1962) had Bettina Dickson as Sally MacAndrew, and the fifth series (4 October 1963) began with 'Man Hunt'.

Flying High

Occasional variety series performed by former members of the RFC, RNAS, and RAF. First broadcast on 25 November 1936 before an audience of the Royal Air Force Association, the stars were G.H. Elliot, Hugh Wakefield, Laddie Cliff, Roy Royston, Will Russell, Ralph

Coram, Sonny Day, and Jack Warman. The producer and deviser of the series was Charles Brewer.

Flying Officer Kyte

Demobbed pilot whose love for Raff slang and his old Adge made it tricky to settle down to civvy life. He was played by Humphrey Lestocq in WATERLOGGED SPA (1946), complete with handlebar moustache (unseen by listeners). Catchphrase: 'I say, I rather care for that, ha-ha-ha-ha-ha!' The last laugh should be brayed.

Flying Officer Kyte: Humphrey Lestocq's radio character

HUMPHREY LESTOCQ

Fogbound Films

Weekly burlesque of a popular film featured in IT'S THAT MAN AGAIN from 1941. JACK TRAIN drawled the regular opening announcement in his best James A. Fitzpatrick tones: 'Fogbound Films Incorporated present an all-coughing, all-sneezing, all-spluttering epic, photographed in Glorious Khakicolor, entitled Tom Marches On!'

The Fol-De-Rols

Popular and long-running seaside concert party whose frequent broadcasts made a radio star of CYRIL FLETCHER ('Thanking yew!'). Many outside broadcasts in the thirties culminated in a special *Round the Fol-de-Rols* hookup

in SHOWS FROM THE SEASIDE on 12 August 1937 linking live excerpts from shows at Eastbourne, Llandudno, Sandown and Hastings. The regular radio series started on 22 March 1939, billed as 'a song and laugh show for highbrows, lowbrows and no-brows'. As well as Fol-de-Rols Fletcher, Ernest Arnley, Irene North, William Stephens, Walter Midgeley and Doris Palmer, the BBC added their Theatre Organ played by SANDY MACPHERSON, and their Variety Orchestra conducted by CHARLES SHADWELL. Produced by Harry Pepper.

Follies of the Air

Concert party show starring George Doonan and Suzette Tarri, with Clarence Wright, Gwen Lewis, Dorothy Summers, and singers Helen Hill and Sydney Burchall, with Billy Ternent and his Follies Orchestra. Written by Dick Pepper and produced by Jacques Brown. Transmitted weekly from 10 November 1942, it was revived from 24 July 1950 by Harry S. Pepper and Gordon Crier, with Ethel REVNELL, Sonnie Hale, Charlie CLAPHAM, Lizbeth Webb, C. Denier Warren, Len Hayes, and Billy Mayerl and Ivor Dennis at two pianos.

Follow On

Fortnightly 'Revue in Miniature' starring Dorothy Summers, Marjorie Westbury, John Bentley and Doris Nichols, with Jack Hill and Jane Minton at two pianos. Produced and compèred from the Midland Region by Martyn C. Webster (1937).

Follow That Man

Unique comedy-drama series in which each episode was written by a different writer. David Jacobs played the hero Rex Anthony, a harrassed BBC radio producer, supported by Diana Olsson, Jeffrey Segal and David Nettheim. The plot concerned the machinations of Professor Lemkin, a radio astrologer. Gale Pedrick devised, Edward Taylor produced, and the writers were Edward J. Mason (the first, broadcast 2 November 1964), John P. Wynn, Lawrie Wyman, Ted Willis, BOB MONKHOUSE AND DENIS GOODWIN, and, for their last-ever script together, FRANK MUIR AND DENIS NORDEN.

Follow the Flag

'A 1940 Song Parade' devised by producer Ernest Longstaffe with additional scenes by Ernest Dudley. Sidney Burchall, Nosmo King and Hubert, Bertha Willmott, Dick Henderson and the Revue Chorus and Variety Orchestra. October 1940.

Follow the Stars

'Radio's shining hour of entertainment': impressionists TONY FAYNE AND DAVID EVANS cohosted this Sunday night series, with Ian Wallace also a regular. Sir Donald Wolfit was their first guest star, with Petula Clark, Peggy Mount, JON PERTWEE and, 'On the Stairway to the Stars', Laura Peterson. Music by Harry Rabinowitz and the Revue Orchestra, script by Gene Crowley; producer John Simmonds. First broadcast 29 December 1957, with a second series from 10 August 1958. The third series, 10 October 1960, featured Fayne without Evans: the act had broken up. David Hughes was the singing compère, pianist James Moody provided 'A Switch in Time', and FRANKIE HOWERD topped the opening bill. Paul Fenoulhet conducted the Variety Orchestra, the Adam Singers sang, and Bill Worsley produced.

Foort, Reginald

Radio's most popular organist, Daventry-born Reggie Foort made his debut as a pianist on 15 January 1923, and as an organist on 12 May 1926 in a relay from the New Gallery Cinema. This was the first of a long series of cinema organ recitals: he reached his thousandth on 9 July 1939. To mark the occasion he returned to the BBC Theatre Organ, for which he had become the BBC's Resident Organist from 20 October 1936. He resigned in 1939 to tour the country with his own mighty Moller Portable Organ. His book, *The Cinema Organ*, became a non-technical standard, and he also edited the monthly magazine, *Cinema Organ Herald*. Foort wrote his original signature tune, 'Regal Chimes', for the organ carillon at the Regal Cinema, Marble Arch.

For Amusement Only (1)

'Pens and pencils ready, please' for this 1939 programme of puzzles broadcast from West Region. There was a Musical Anagram with Ruby Taylor and Frances Keyte (who also

Reginald **Foort**: 1938 song book free with *Family Journal*

provided 'Riddle Rhythm' on two pianos), Jane Carr and a 'Musical Crossword' with the grid printed in RADIO TIMES. Presented and compèred by John Lampson.

For Amusement Only (2)

Wartime topical revue starting 13 September 1939, with LEONARD HENRY 'and a Fool Company of Fellow Mockers' – Vera Lennox, Horace Percival, MAURICE DENHAM, Diana Clare, SAM COSTA, the Three Chimes, and the Rhythm Octet – in 'Gay Gags, Snappy Songs, Laughable Lampoons, Audacious Anecdotes'. Producer Vernon Harris.

For the Love of Mike

Comedy series fashioned around the throwaway humour of MICHAEL HOWARD. Strong supporting cast included Horace Percival the ITMA veteran, Gene Crowley, Ian Sadler, Wilfred Babbage, John Stevens, Patricia Fox and Therese Carroll. Music by Stanley Black with the Variety Orchestra; Tom Ronald produced from 12 October 1946.

For You Madam (1)

'Magazine programme for Every Woman: Topical, Tuneful, Romantic.' Edited by Archie Campbell, items included: Jane Gardener your radio friend talking to you on feminine topics: 'Which Way To Turn?', a human problem in dramatic form; 'Front Page Wife', the private life of celebrities revealed by their wives (No. 1 was Mrs Flanagan and Mrs Allen); 'Echoes Of The Past', love letters of famous men and women; 'Musical Interlude' with the Singing Poet and l'Orchestre directed by Percival Mackey. Commenced 18 October 1938. Programme 15 (2 May 1939) introduced 'The Daily Dodge' with Kathleen Harrison as Mrs Dodge; 'Mrs Jones's Diary, the journal of the average woman' and 'Will You Dance Madam', instruction in the tango.

For You Madam (2)

RADIO LUXEMBOURG wooing the lady listener. Peter West introduced this series of 'programmes for the lady of the family (and something for the menfolk, too)' starting 4 January 1955. Frank Chacksfield and his Orchestra provided lush music and Ruth Drew 'brings experience and a little gaiety to household topics' with hints, recipes and prizes. There was also a serial, SHADOW MAN, and a famous guest. Neil Tuson produced for Stork Margarine.

Forces' All Star Bill

Following on from CALLING ALL FORCES this series 'presents the best of Britain's show business for the Forces serving throughout the world'. TED RAY introduced Betty Driver, Edmund Hockridge, the STARGAZERS, George Mitchell's Glee Club, and Kenny Baker in 'Jazz, Forces for the Use Of', backed by Stanley Black and the Dance Orchestra. Fred Yule and Graham Stark appeared as 'The Fatigue Party', and later Stark played Lieutenant Bowser-Smythe. Dennis Main Wilson produced, beginning 4 August 1952. The second

series which began on 6 January 1953 introduced a resident trio in TONY HANCOCK, Graham Stark and Joan Heal, who was replaced after six weeks by Geraldine McEwen. RAY GALTON AND ALAN SIMPSON wrote the scripts and Alastair Scott-Johnston produced.

Forces' Favourites

Long-running record request series in which music was played at the request of Forces overseas for their relatives at home. It started 24 November 1943 on the FORCES PROGRAMME, as far as British listeners were concerned, but the series had actually begun in 1941 on the General Overseas Service. The last programme went out on 15 April 1946, presented by Joan Griffiths and Barbara McFadyean. See also FAMILY FAVOURITES.

Forces Programme

The first alternative programme of World War II, after the compression of all National and Regional Programmes into a single service. It began on Sunday 7 January 1940 at 6 pm, extending to an 11 am start from 19 February. After a certain nervousness among civilian listeners as to whether they should eavesdrop on a programme originally entitled *For The Forces*, the dominating pattern of entertainment (dance bands, comedy shows, quizzes, etc) soon won the younger listeners away from the heavier HOME SERVICE. The service was retitled the *General Forces Programme* from 27 February 1944, and the day was extended to run from 6.30 am to 11 pm. With the coming of peace, it became the LIGHT PROGRAMME on Sunday 29 July 1945, and the old wavelengths of 296.1 metres (1013 kcs) and 342.1 metres (877 kcs) disappeared.

The Forces Show

Sixty-minute series starting 30 September 1952 and hosted by the MUCH-BINDING-IN-THE-MARSH team of RICHARD MURDOCH, KENNETH HORNE and SAM COSTA. Songs were provided by Eve Boswell, Jimmy Young and the Merrymakers, the Peter Knight Singers and the Dance Orchestra conducted by Stanley Black. The first guest was Cardew Robinson, and Phyllis Calvert and Jack Hawkins appeared in a scene from their film *Mandy*. 'Novelty Corner' featured Sirdani 'the Gully-Gully Man' in conjuring tricks by radio. Script by Bob Monkhouse and Denis Goodwin; produced by Leslie Bridgmont and Frank Hooper. Jewel and Warriss were comedy compères of the second series which started 7 April 1953. 'Can You Beat Pharos and Marina' introduced a new mind-reading act, and Michael Miles conducted 'Forces Quiz'. Also starred were singer Betty Driver, pianist Winifred Attwell, and Woolf Phillips and the Skyrockets. Script by Ronnie Hanbury and George Wadmore; produced by Bill Worsley and Trafford Whitelock.

The third series brought Monkhouse and Goodwin back as writers and a new air of sophistication – Jack Buchanan was hired as host. Geraldo and his Orchestra made most of the music, with the Hedley Ward Trio, Max Jaffa and Lysbeth Webb. Guest stars were Ted Ray and Diana Dors, plus 'Forces Jazz Session' with Humphrey Lyttelton. This began on 15 September 1953. The next series started on 9 May 1954 with Alfred Marks as host, joined by Sally Rogers and Fred Yule. Eve Boswell and Dickie Valentine sang the request numbers, David Berglas presented 'The Ultimate in Magic', Raymond Glendenning 'Sport Corner' and Julian Bream was 'Forces Instrumentalist'. Arthur Askey was the first guest, and the Peter Knight Singers sang to Peter Yorke and his Orchestra. Script by Gene Crowley, Alan Blair, Maurice Rogers and Jimmy Grafton.

The series beginning 3 November 1954 had a new team: Joy Nichols, Kenneth Horne and Derek Roy, whose prime spot was a serial sketch in which 'the Dean of Detectives, Klaxon Horne, finds himself Without A Clue: fantastic adventures to be Continued In Our Next!' Scripts were by Jimmy Grafton, Larry Stephens, Peter Griffiths and Johnny Vyvyan. David Hughes sang Forces' Requests, Leslie Welch the Memory Man returned as did Raymond Glendenning, and Albert and Les Ward were billed as 'The Harmonious Discords'. The Coronets sang to Malcolm Lockyer and the Concert Orchestra, and Trafford Whitelock produced.

Forever Arthur

The title burlesqued *Forever Amber*, a sensational novel and film of the forties. This was a series starring Arthur Askey and Kenneth Horne, with Eve Becke, Tom Henry and the Tomboys, and Stanley Black conducting the Dance Orchestra. Harry S. Pepper produced the series, which was set in a lighthouse! First broadcast 22 April 1946.

Forever Green

Harry Green, the American Jewish comedian, starred in this situation series first broadcast 12 March 1956. Gwen Lewis played Mrs Maintop, Laidman Browne was Lionel Lorimer, Betty Marsden Dulcie Deveaux, and Denis Bryer daughter Betty. Script by Sidney Nelson and Maurice Harrison; producer Jacques Brown.

A Formby Do!

'Come and muck in! George Formy will positively preside, Beryl will probably interrupt, and Harry Leader and his Band will definitely be in attendance!' Series of four fortnightly shows beginning 19 May 1938, written by Vernon Harris.

The Four Kolynos Smiles

'The makers of Kolynos Dental Cream present Sunny, Ready, Bright and Brilliant in a First-Class Nigger Minstrel Entertainment broadcast from Radio Luxembourg every Tuesday and Saturday from 20 April 1937'. Songs in the first show included 'Truckin'' and 'I Wanna Go Back to Honolulu'. Producer Tom Ronald.

Frankau, Ronald

Classy cabaret-style comedian (educated at Eton) who wrote all his own stuff, including his signature song, 'The Preparatory School, the Public School and the Varsity'. He first broadcast on 18 September 1925 in a relay from his own concert party, Cabaret Kittens, from the Summer Pavilion, Sheerness. Frankau developed his Kittens as a radio series, but is best remembered for his solo songs and monologues ('Pity the man who stands alone before the wretched microphone') in which he was accompanied on the piano by Monte Crick (later Dan in The Archers). His friendship with Tommy Handley led to the formation of a double-act for radio, North and South, which in turn led to the wittier pairing, Murgatroyd and Winterbottom. He made records for Parlophone, many of which were too naughty to broadcast ('I'd Like To Have a Honeymoon With Her'), and compiled some of his broadcast material into the book *Crazy Omnibus*.

Ronald **Frankau**: a personal favourite of John Reith

The Frankie Howerd Show

The eccentric and still popular comedian was given big star support in his first 'name' series: Richard Burton, TONY HANCOCK, Eve Boswell, Semprini the pianist, and old faithful Billy Ternent and his Orchestra. Written by Eric Sykes, RAY GALTON AND ALAN SIMPSON; produced by Alistair Scott-Johnston. The first broadcast was 23 November 1953. The second series 'in which Frankie introduces the vitality of the Tanner Sisters, the versatility of the Hedley Ward Trio, the voice of Lee Young, the nimble fingers of Dolores Ventura, and apologizes for Gladys Morgan and Billy Ternent' started on 22 February 1954. The film-star guest was Terence Morgan.

Frankie's Bandbox

FRANKIE HOWERD hosted this variety series from 19 April 1960. Leslie Randall and Joan Reynolds, a married comedy team, supported him, with songs from Petula Clark and music from mouth-organ man Tommy Reilly and the Revue Orchestra conducted by Billy Ternent. Script by Barry Took and Marty Feldman; produced by Bill Worsley.

The Fred Allen Programme

American radio series broadcast by the BBC from 16 May 1943, by arrangement with the Special Services Division of the US War Department. It starred the dry wit Fred Allen, with his wife, Portland Hoffa, and Al Goodman's Orchestra. Favourite feature was the weekly visit to the denizens of Allen's Alley: Mrs Nussbaum, Titus Moody, and Senator Claghorn.

The Fred Emney Show

Rare radio series for the famous fat comedian with the top hat, monocle, and big cigar – stage props of little use on the wireless! Written and produced by Max Kester, the series began on 17 October 1944. Supporting Fred were Maudie Edwards, the Welsh comedienne, Christopher Steel, Hugh French and Cliff Gordon (also from Wales). There was a weekly guest star, and music from Stanley Black and the Dance Orchestra.

Friday at Four

'The Diary of the Week presented by Our Radio Friends, David and Margaret', sponsored by Du Maurier Cigarettes on RADIO NORMANDY from 18 February 1938.

Friday Film Time

'Romantic Rhapsody' was the signature tune of this cinematic series sponsored by the Rank Organization on RADIO LUXEMBOURG from 25 April 1958. Anthony Marriott was the compère who introduced such current Rank favourites as Dirk Bogarde talking about his private life, an interview with Stanley Baker and Philip Leacock, and excerpts from Virginia McKenna's *Carve Her Name With Pride*. The 100th programme was broadcast on 4 March 1960, by which time it had become simply *Film Time*, having moved to Mondays. Produced by Susan Goodfellow.

Friends to Tea

'Vest-pocket Vaudeville' compèred by Walter Hix on the National Programme from Monday 15 November 1937. Players were WYNNE AJELLO, Tommy Brandon, and SUZETTE TARRI; produced by Ernest Longstaffe.

Frisby Dyke

Seeker after knowledge from Liverpool, with a genuinely thick Merseyside accent. Deryck Guyler introduced him into ITMA (1946), asking such questions as 'What's ridiculous rhetoric, wack?', and departing with a regular

'Tara-well!'. His catchphrase was 'They don't tell you nothing these days, do they?'.

From a Seat in the Circle
An experimental outside broadcast of Walt Disney's *Fun and Fancy Free* from the Odeon Cinema, Manchester in January 1948 led to a regular weekly series, beginning 8 December 1948 with *Life With Father*. David Southwood sat in the circle of the Hippodrome, Sheffield, describing the visual bits between the dialogue of William Powell and Irene Dunne. Surprisingly popular, the 100th programme (24 March 1951) visited the première of *The Browning Version* at the Odeon, Manchester, in company with the author, Terence Rattigan.

Front Line Family
The first daily serial produced by the BBC was not heard in Britain, but broadcast only in the Overseas Service. It ran from 21 April 1941 and was designed to give overseas listeners a picture of Home Front life in London during World War II. From 30 July 1945 it transferred to the LIGHT PROGRAMME under a new title, THE ROBINSON FAMILY. The anonymous cast can now be revealed as Ernest Butcher (Dad Robinson), Nell Ballantyne (Mum), Tony Halfpenny (Dick), Cyril Cusack (Andy), and Dulcie Gray. The anonymous scriptwriter was Alan Melville.

Funf
'Dis is Funf speakink!' 'Is that a name or a rude expression?' Immortal words: TOMMY HANDLEY's first telephone encounter with the German spy, 26 September 1939 on IT's THAT MAN AGAIN. Funf's hollow, menacing tones were achieved by JACK TRAIN speaking sideways into a drinking-glass.

Fusspot
Assistant Controller of the Office of Twirps, constantly outraged by the Minister of Aggravation and Mysteries, TOMMY HANDLEY: 'It's most irregular! Most irregular!' IT's THAT MAN AGAIN (1939), played by JACK TRAIN.

Funf: Radio Fun strip by Roy Wilson

Gaffer and Gavotte
Series of West Region programmes of simple humour and unsophisticated dance, broadcast during the thirties. Dialect dialogues between the dances featured Gaffer and his better half, Sairey, set in the bar parlour of the Pheasant Inn at Malgrave. Written by F. Marriott Watson; producer Cyril Ward. The first-ever sketch (27 July 1932) was called 'Gaffer Gets Asthma', and the old chap was played by T. Hannan-Clarke.

Gaiety Stars
Leslie Henson and Fred Emney, comedy stars from the Gaiety Theatre revues, co-starred in this series broadcast from RADIO NORMANDY from 23 January 1938. Henson wrote the scripts with Douglas Furber, and Mary Lawson also appeared, with the Gaiety Singers and Orchestra conducted by Wolseley Charles. Huntley & Palmer's Biscuits were the sponsors.

Gala Night at the Rhubarb Room
Petula Clark starred in this slightly satirical series supposedly broadcast from a slightly sleazy night club. The Master of Ceremonies was ROY PLOMLEY, who also wrote the script with Sid Colin. Musical support came from the Keynotes, the Ray Ellington Quartet, and Sid Phillips and his Band. Produced by Charles Chilton; first broadcast 4 February 1949.

Gamlin, Lionel
Too chucklesome to remain a staid announcer, Birkenhead-born Lionel Gamlin graduated from the BBC's London staff, which he had joined in January 1936, to the new post of Staff Compère of the Variety Department in 1939. He did interviews on IN TOWN TONIGHT, linked the turns in MUSIC HALL, and played straight-man to OLD MOTHER RILEY, quite a long way from his early career as a schoolmaster. During World War II he was seconded to the EMPIRE SERVICE and produced *London Calling Europe*. In 1949 he devised and presented a long-running series, HELLO CHILDREN, designed for the holiday periods. Gamlin wrote the useful book *You're On the Air* (1947).

The Gang Smasher
Detective serial, the first to grip the nation. Episode 1, 'John Martinson Takes a Hand', was broadcast on 4 April 1938, with Ivan Samson in the lead. The gimmick that hooked was not the 'tec, but the crook, TORTONI (Carleton Hobbs), leader of a gang of jewel thieves who not only gave his instructions by wireless, but also had his own fiendish signature-tune! Eileen Erskine played Sylvia Brown and others in the cast were Howard Marion-Crawford, Edwin Ellis, and Norman Shelley. Written by Jack Inglis from Hugh Cleveley's novel; produced by John Cheatle.

Garrison Theatre
Hugely popular wartime radio series, devised by CHARLES SHADWELL upon his experiences in the Great War serving in the West Yorks Regiment as Entertainments Officer. Stars were unbilled at first: 'Famous artists will appear (engagements permitting) to entertain the troops.' Among the troops was 'Private' JACK WARNER, whom the show made a star. He entered ringing a bell and crying 'Mind my bike!', had backchat with Sergeant-Major Filtness, delivered such comedy cockney monologues as 'He Didn't Orter-a-Et It', 'Sealions and Sills', 'Claude and his Sword', 'Frank and his Tank', and 'Walkin' Hup and Dahn the Rollway Laines'. Jack also read aloud letters from 'my bruvver Sid', famous for their 'P.S.' gags. His use of the censor's 'Blue Pencil' where swear-words might have appeared gave a nation at war another catchphrase. Warner also had flirtatious dialogue with uppercrust usherette Joan Winters ('Progems, choclits, cigarettes – mep of the cemp!'). The show was transferred to the stage, an excerpt being broadcast on 6 August 1940. First broadcast 10 November 1939; producer Harry S. Pepper.

Garrison Theatre: free song book with *War Thriller* (1940)

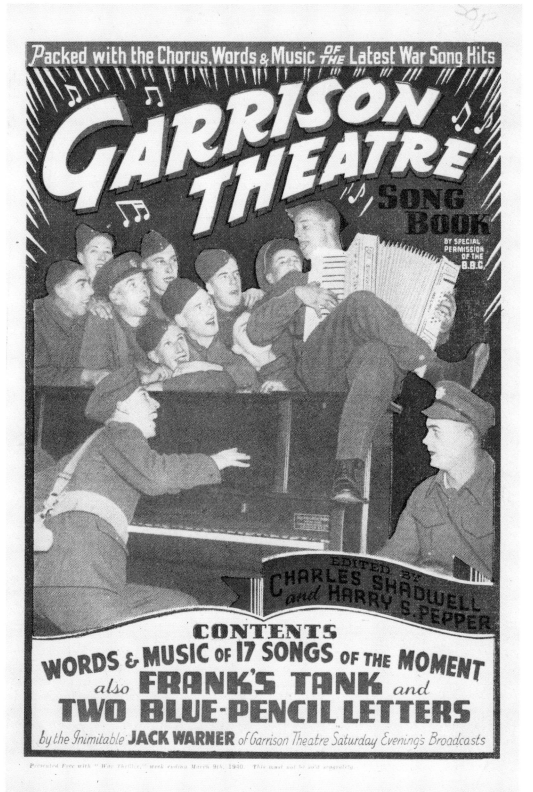

Gaumont British Film Fans' Hour

Early sponsored radio series featuring film stars on gramophone records and extracts from film soundtracks. The first series, broadcast every Sunday on RADIO PARIS from 27 February 1932, was compèred by film publicist Clayton Hutton. Stephen Williams took over and in 1933 live guest artists were featured, the first being comedians Nervo and Knox. From 3 December the programme moved to RADIO LUXEMBOURG, when it featured CICELY COURTNEIDGE and JACK HULBERT in songs from their latest films.

Gay Nineties Revue

'Sparkling entertainment suitable for ladies and gentlemen of all ages', including ballads, humorous and dramatic monologues, and comic songs performed by Beryl Orde, David Davies, Sylvia Roth and Bill Fraser to the accompaniment of the Revue Orchestra, conducted by Frank Cantell. Devised by E.W. Kent; produced by Henry Reed; the first guest star (18 July 1947) was the master of melodrama, Tod Slaughter. In programme three came another old-time monologuist, Bransby Williams.

Gentlemen, You May Smoke

'A Microphone Menu for Men', chaired by TOMMY HANDLEY from 11 September 1939. Guests: John Rorke, Sidney Burchall, Horace Percival, and the BBC Male Voice Chorus. Drinks served by C. Denier Warren.

Gently Bentley

Series for Australian comedian DICK BENTLEY who had attained stardom through TAKE IT FROM HERE, and named by JIMMY EDWARDS' catchphrase in the same programme. Supporting Dick were Josephine Crombie, singer Alma Cogan, and Frank Cordell and his Orchestra. Produced by Roy Speer from 11 August 1952.

George (1)

'The Man With a Conscience' played by TED RAY in RAY'S A LAUGH (1949). George's Conscience was played by Leslie Perrins in an echo chamber. George was a reporter for the *Daily Bugle*, the last Fleet Street newspaper capable of holding vinegar. His editor was Mr (Old Man) Rivers, and his landlady Mrs Dipper.

George (2)

The first dog to broadcast, a fox terrier who howled on cue over 2LO in 1924. George's owner was the singing actress, Vivienne Chatterton.

George Gorge

Chubby Fred Yule played this lip-smacking fat man in IT'S THAT MAN AGAIN (1945). His chuckly catchphrase was 'Lovely grub! Lovely grub!'.

The George Mitchell Glee Club

Leslie Mitchell (no relation) introduced this series of travelling sing-songs starring 40 voices from George Mitchell's sundry vocal combinations: the George Mitchell Choir, the Mitchell Men, and the Mitchell Maids. Not content with 40 voices, the Glee Club Guests on the first show (6 April 1950) were the Swansea Imperial Singers, plus, of course, the entire audience packing the Brangwyn Hall in Wales. Producer Dennis Main Wilson.

Geraldo

Gerald Bright, pianist, returned from Rio to form one of the most successful Gaucho Tango Orchestras ever, changing his name to the more suitable Geraldo. He never changed it back, even after his band became Geraldo and his Sweet Music in 1933. A popular broadcasting band, Geraldo starred in several pre-war series, DANCING THROUGH (1934) in which he played some 150 tunes in 60 minutes, and ROMANCE IN RHYTHM (1935). He also made records in sets: *Geraldoland, Geraldo Nights* (both 1933).

Geraldo's big success as a broadcasting band came during World War II, when his signature tune, 'Hello again, we're on the radio again', and his cockney signoff, 'On behalf of me and the boys, cheerio and thanks for list'nin'!', were part of the fabric. Vocalists included Cyril Grantham, Monte Rey, Eve Becke, Dorothy Carless, Len Camber, Archie Lewis, Sally Douglas, Johnny Green and Three Boys and a Girl. Comedy vocals came from Jackie Hunter, then DEREK ROY.

Geraldo's Guest House

Occasional musical series beginning 23 December 1941, with GERALDO and his Orchestra,

Geraldo: 'Hello again, we're on the radio again!'

Dorothy Carless, Jackie Hunter, and compère Gerry Wilmot. Plus 'any guest stars who may drop in'. Producer, David Miller. Revived 11 August 1949 as *Geraldo's Open House*. After four weeks with George Benson as resident comedian, the show moved to the Jubilee Theatre, Blackpool, with Dave Morris as resident. Produced by Alick Hayes.

Gerry Built

One of the earliest record programmes to be designed in the American manner. Breezy Canadian Gerry Wilmot was the host, and the show went out every Saturday night on the Light from 11.15 pm on 3 August 1946.

Gershom Parkington Quintet

Consistently popular wireless entertainers from 2LO days, led by Gershom Parkington, who first broadcast as a cello soloist on 28 December 1926.

The Gershom Parkington Quintet

Gert and Daisy

Utterly believable cockney women friends invented and performed by ELSIE (Gert) AND DORIS (Daisy) WATERS. Originally created for the B-side of a gramophone record 'Wedding Bells' (Parlophone R789) in 1930, their naturalistic comedy crosstalk was so swiftly popular that the double-sided 'Party at Gert and Daisy's' was released for Christmas. From then

Gert and Daisy: free song book with *Home Companion* (1937)

Thompson, John Blythe and David Jacobs starred with Tommy Whittle and his Orchestra, and songs by Eula Parker. Script by musician Jack Bentley and Dick Vosburgh; produced by Arthur Adair. RADIO LUXEMBOURG from 3 October 1955.

The Ghost Walks on Fridays
Occasional series running through the late thirties and early forties in which stars recalled the incidents which led to their first pay envelope as professionals. Harry S. Pepper produced, with scripts by C. Denier Warren, and the stars heard on 4 March 1944 were Florence Desmond, Naughton and Gold, Sylvia Cecil, Raymond Newell and 'Denny' Warren himself.

Gibbons, Carroll
Remembered as much for his soft American drawl ('Hello, everybahdy' . . . 'G'night, everybahdy') as for his distinctively syncopated piano playing, Massachusetts man Carroll came to London in 1924 and by 4 November 1925 was making his first broadcast as pianist with the Savoy Orpheans Augmented Symphonic Orchestra. On 9 October the following year he made his radio debut as a danceband leader with the Savoy Sylvians. In 1928 he was appointed Director of Light Music for HMV Records, and on 3 December 1933 began a long career in commercial radio by

on Gert and Daisy and Elsie and Doris were inseparable, and many radio appearances in MUSIC HALL followed. The first series built around the cockney couple was *Gert and Daisy's Working Party*, which ran for three months from 23 June 1948, travelling around the country. The first show introduced amateur talent from the London area, and as guest star, their brother, JACK WARNER. There were two pianists, Eric James and George Myddleton, and two producers, Michael North and Bryan Sears. A major variety series, PETTICOAT LANE, followed on 29 July 1949.

Get Wise
Apt title for a comedy series sponsored by Wisdom Toothbrushes. Mirian Karlin, Jimmy

Carroll **Gibbons**: 'On the Air'

broadcasting in the BUSH RADIO CONCERT from LUXEMBOURG. His later sponsors included Palmolive, Colgate, Stork Margarine, Cookeen, Spry, Ovaltine, and again in the post-war revival, Colgate. His many BBC series, both with his band and solo at the piano, included *Carroll Calls the Tunes*. His signature tune was, appropriately enough, 'On The Air'. Carroll's vocalists included George Melachrino and Anne Lenner.

The Gilded Cage

Radio night-club. Sophisticated cabaret compèred by Dick Hurran, and starring Jack and Daphne Barker, Mischa de la Motte, Harry Jacobson, Therese Carroll, and Leonard Whiteley and his Septet. Opened for business on 8 January 1946.

Gillette Sports Parade

Peter West introduced this radio magazine featuring famous personalities from the world of sport, and regular items 'Beat the Panel', 'My Star of Tomorrow', and 'My Closest Shave' (the sponsor was Gillette Razor Blades!). Devised by Allan Blomfield; produced by Monty Bailey-Watson; RADIO LUXEMBOURG from 5 June 1952.

A Gipsy Told Me

'Memoirs of a Traveller in the Land of Romany' featuring the Hungaria Band and sponsored by Bisurated Magnesia. RADIO LUXEMBOURG from 5 March 1939.

Glory Road

American folk-singer Josh White starred in this anthology of Negro music devised and produced by Charles Chilton. First broadcast 7 May 1951 with Edric Connor, Ida Shepley, Benny Lee, Jimmy Dyrenforth, Guy Kingsley Poynter, the George Mitchell Choir and the Freddie Phillips Sextet. The second series, 19 April 1952, featured Josh and his daughter Beverly in charming harmony.

The Glums

Originally presented as a typical English family to comment upon TAKE IT FROM HERE's weekly Talking Point, the characters of Pa (JIMMY EDWARDS), Ron (DICK BENTLEY) and his fiancée Eth (June Whitfield) quickly devel-

oped into a saga of working-class life unequalled in radio. Ron, almost an idiot, would be wooing on the settee ('Just a kiss, Eth!') when in came Pa (''Ullo, 'ullo 'ullo!'). Ma was little more than noises off, provided by Alma Cogan. On 3 March 1960 the Glums emigrated to Australia, never to return – except in repeats and a television series in which only Edwards survived.

The Glymiel Jollities

Glymiel Jelly sponsored this radio concert party which began a weekly series on RADIO LUXEMBOURG in 1937. Billing was Sylvia Cecil, Tessa Deane, Marjorie Stedeford, Gwen Catley, Clarence Wright, Monte Rey, Al Burton and the Glymiel Orchestra. Clarence Wright devised and produced, as he did the second series (1938) which introduced Dorothy Carless, Bettie Bucknelle and Campbell Copelin to the team. Neal Arden read the commercials and the scriptwriter was Joslyn Mainprice.

The Glyndale Star

First post-war daily serial for adults on RADIO LUXEMBOURG, sponsored by Dreft: 'Meet the Kent Family in their exciting adventures' – Ernest Butcher (Arthur Kent), Courtney Hope (Kitty Kent), Anne Cullen (Pamela Kent), Basil Jones (Peter Kent), and Richard Hurndall (Guy Graham). Written by Adrian Thomas and Geoffrey Webb; announced by John Fitchen; produced by Neil Tuson. The theme music was called 'Moon in the Sky'.

Going Places

Starry Sunday series with Jack Buchanan and Elsie Randolph, William Kendall, Vincent Holman, and the Cavendish Three, with Billy Ternent and the Dance Orchestra and Chorus. Written by famous screenwriters John Paddy Carstairs and Val Guest; producer Eric Fawcett. Started 20 July 1941.

Going Places With Godiva

'Meet that amazing, amusing family The Overdews and hear the unique Free Shilling Offer.' Series of programmes for motorists starring Sydney Kyte and his Mobiloilers, starting 30 October 1938 on RADIO NORMANDY. Presented by the Marketers of Mobiloil Arctic.

The Golden Voice of Radio
Morton Downey, the American crooner, who sang in a weekly sponsored radio series for Drene Shampoo: RADIO LUXEMBOURG (1936).

The Good Companions
Star-studded series based on J.B. Priestley's popular novel and sponsored by McDougal's Self-Raising Flour. WILFRED PICKLES played Jess Oakroyd, Petula Clark Susie Dean, Ronald Howard Inigo Jolifant, Grizelda Hervey Miss Trant, Charles Heslop Jimmie Nunn. Music composed by Sidney Torch; produced by HARRY ALAN TOWERS. Weekly on RADIO LUXEMBOURG from 1 December 1952.

Good Evening Each
First starring series for Beryl Reid in her schoolgirl characterization of MONICA, the Brummagem Marleen, and a Mrs Shinbone ('Shake off the shackles with Shinbone!'). Ken Platt played Perkins the Landlord. 'Dig that crazy Beryl who invites all squares and cats to a Palais party to meet Nat Temple, Tony Fayne, and the Variety Orchestra conducted by Paul Fenoulhet.' Script by Ronald Wolfe, David Climie and Frank Roscoe. Producer Roy Speer; began 29 April 1958.

Good Hunting
Comedy series starring Jackie 'Umbrage' Hunter with Lyle Evans, Ian Sadler, Pat Taylor, and Stephane Grappelly and his Quintet. Written by Ray Sonin; producer Roy Speer; began 14 February 1943.

A Good Idea Son
Max Bygraves' catchphrase from EDUCATING ARCHIE made the title for this RADIO LUXEMBOURG series starring Max and a girl called Christine: 'A record programme for children of all ages' sponsored by Primula Cheese. Started 2 December 1953. A similarly titled series, A Good Idea, started on 5 November 1954, with Max and the Blackbirds, a swinging group named for the sponsor, Black & Decker. Produced by Geoffrey Everitt.

Good Morning
'A song, a smile and a story' from Albert Whelan, brought to RADIO LUXEMBOURG listeners three times a week from 1937 by Andrews Liver Salt. Albert sang:

If you sing in your bath
And whistle all day,
It's Andrews that's making you feel that way.

Good Pull-up for Cyclists
Occasional series starring the WOBBLETON WHEELERS: Major Puffin, heavy roadster (Bobbie Comber); Clarry the light sports (Clarence Wright); Helen the featherweight (Helen Clare); Sophie Spoonbrake the two-handled bargain (Gwen Lewis); 'Arry the drop-'andles (John Rorke). Charles Penrose was the guest star in the broadcast of 10 September 1940, in his character of P.C. Evergreen. Producer Ernest Longstaffe.

Goolden, Richard
Radio's own 'little man', the meek-and-mild mousey henpeck who manages to come out on top in the end. He made the role of Mole in *The Wind in the Willows* his own, first on stage in 1930, then on radio in CHILDREN'S HOUR. It was in children's broadcasting that he first made his radio name, playing the 'funny little man' in a long series of plays by L. DuGarde Peach: *The Roads of England, The Waterways of England, The Castles of England*. Adult listeners took him to their hearts when he played the lead in *Goodbye Mr Chips* (1935). Then came the role that really made him, that of MR PENNY (1936). But whatever the name of his character – Mr Meek of MEEK'S ANTIQUES, OLD EBENEEZER the Night Watchman – Dickie Goolden remained for ever delightfully the same.

The Goon Show
This watershed in wireless comedy, the series which extended both humour and radio itself beyond all hitherto horizons, began on 22 January 1952, following on from the first experimental series, CRAZY PEOPLE (1951). 'Featuring those Crazy People': PETER SELLERS, Harry Secombe, Michael Bentine, SPIKE MILLIGAN, with the Ray Ellington Quartet, Max Geldray, and the Stargazers with Stanley Black and the Dance Orchestra. The producer was Dennis Main Wilson, with scripts by Spike Milligan and Larry Stephens, edited by Jimmy Grafton. The announcer, the grave Andrew Timothy, introduced the multi-sketch format which featured OSRIC PUREHEART (Bentine)

The Goon Show: Wallace Greenslade, Peter Sellers, Spike Milligan, Harry Secombe, Wally Stott, Ray Ellington

building everything from the Suez Canal to the Channel Tunnel, and Handsome Harry Seagoon versus such Yellow Perils as Lo Hing Ding. Other characters included Sellers as MAJOR BLOODNOK, HENRY CRUN and ERNIE SPLUTMUSCLE, and Spike as ECCLES and MINNIE BANNISTER.

The second series started 11 November 1952; Bentine had departed for good, Peter Eton produced, and Wally Stott conducted the Orchestra. Spike suffered a breakdown after four shows, and his parts were taken on by Sellers, Dick Emery or Graham Stark. Characters now included arch-criminal MORIARTY, FLOWERDEW, Colonel Slocombe, the Hon. Terence Blatt, and WILLIAM MACGOONAGLE, Scottish poet and tragedian. Secombe played Fred Bogg in 'Fred of the Islands' and other Adapted Classics. There was also a special Coronation Edition on 3 June in which the Goons conquered Everest in 40 minutes. The third series started 2 October 1953, and instead of 26 shows ran 30. Wallace Greenslade arrived as the stolid new announcer, and single-plot shows began to develop revolving around NEDDIE SEAGOON (sometime Ned of Wales). The suave HERCULES GRYTPYPE-THYNNE and the quavery old cock, WILLIAM MATE, arrived,

both being extremes of Sellers. The fourth series opened on 28 September 1954 with show No. 100, 'The Whistling Spy Enigma'. Valentine Dyall guested in 'The Canal' and Charlotte Mitchell in 'Ye Bandit of Sherwood Forest'. The BBC banned Sellers' impersonation of Winston Churchill in this series; and the Goons' burlesque of the George Orwell TV play *1984*, entitled *1985* included JOHN SNAGGE and was so popular it had to be rebroadcast five weeks later. The fifth series began on 20 September 1955, and included one recorded at the National Radio Show, 'China Story'. Pat Dixon came in as producer, and continued the sixth series, starting 4 October 1956. Bernard Miles guested in 'The Rent Collector' (17 January 1957) and JACK TRAIN appeared as his ITMA character, COLONEL CHINSTRAP in 'Shifting Sands' (24 January). LITTLE JIM (Milligan) also made his debut. The seventh series opened with Dick Emery subbing for Secombe in 'Spon' (30 September 1957), and Charles Chilton producing. A.E. Matthews, veteran actor and ad-libber, guested in 'The Evils of Bushey Spon' (24 March 1958). The eighth series, a run of 17, opened on 3 November 1958 with 'The Sahara Desert Statue' produced by John Browell. Sellers missed 'Who Is Pink

Oboe' (12 January 1959 – the only such occasion) and was replaced by Kenneth Connor, Graham Stark, Valentine Dyall, Jack Train and John Snagge. The ninth and last series opened on 24 December 1959 with 'A Christmas Carol' and closed six shows later with 'The Last Smoking Seagoon'.

In addition to the regular series there were several Goon Specials: *Cinderella* (26 December 1951) with Lizbeth Webb; *Archie in Goonland* (11 June 1954) with Peter Brough; *The Starlings* (27 August 1954); *The Reason Why* (22 August 1957); *The GPO Show* (25 December 1964); *The Army Show* (16 June 1965); *The Naughty Navy Show* (25 December 1965). For the BBC Silver Jubilee the cast was reunited for *The Last Goon Show Of All* (5 October 1972), which was also televised (26 December 1972). Theme music for the series varied from 'The Goons Gallop' to 'The Old Comrades March'. Roger Wilmut's *Goon Show Companion* (1976) is essential.

Gordon Grantley KC

Francis De Wolff played this continuing character created by Hans W. Priwin under his new pen-name of John P. Wynn. Episode 1: 'The Perfect Crime', was broadcast on 20 August 1948, with Molly Rankin as Dr Moira Ashfield and Lionel Stevens as Markham the Butler. Produced by Alastair Scott Johnston. The second series opened with 'A Shock for His Lordship' on 18 April 1949.

The Gospel Singer

Roland Robson sang 'sacred melodies that never grow old' on this rare religious series broadcast on RADIO NORMANDY from 4 April 1939, under the sponsorship of Wright's Coal Tar Soap.

Gossip Column

'An indiscreet revue' starring WYNNE AJELLO, Vera Lennox, Guy Verney, Fred Yule, and Patric Curwen. Occasional, from 1 March 1941. Producer Eric Spear.

Gourley, Ronald

Blind from birth, Ronald Gourley was one of the first entertainers to be made by the new medium of radio. Billed as a 'siffleur' he whistled through his first broadcast from 2LO on 28 November 1922. He soon became a

Ronald **Gourley**: blind pianist and siffleur

CHILDREN's HOUR favourite with his signature piece on the piano, 'The Dicky Bird Hop'.

Gracie's Working Party

Not until post-war 1947 did the Lancashire super-star of variety stage, records and films, get a series on BBC radio. But it was worth waiting for, twelve 45-minute OBs (Outside Broadcasts) from halls around the country, singing to and with factory workers. Appropriately the first (23 July 1947) came from Gracie

Gracie's Working Party: belated series for Gracie Fields

Fields' home town of Rochdale, with the local Festival Choir and Richard Varley and his Concert Orchestra backing Our Gracie, a lorry driver tenor, and two worker pianists. The signature song was 'Sally' and the closing song 'Now Is The Hour'. Produced by Bowker Andrews.

Grand Hotel
The first broadcast of Albert Sandler and his Orchestra from the Grand Hotel, Eastbourne, was on 28 July 1925. It remained a popular Sunday series until the 1939 war. Then on 28 March 1943 *Grand Hotel* began as a studio-bound 'programme of the sort of music that you heard in the Palm Court of your favourite hotel in the days before the war'. Albert Sandler continued to play violin, leading the Palm Court Orchestra, and the first guest singer was Frank Titterton. A return series commencing 14 October 1951 introduced Tom Jenkins with the Palm Court Orchestra, and guest baritone Alfred Swain. Jenkins won the NATIONAL RADIO AWARD in 1953 and 1954 as Most Popular Musical Entertainer. The signature tune was 'Roses from the South' by Strauss.

Grand Hotel: Albert Sandler of Palm Court Orchestra fame

Grande Gingold
'Half an hour with Hermione, London's only Lady Witch. Also embroiled in the macabre proceedings' were Alexander Gauge, Kenneth Connor, Bob Harvey, David Jacobs, and Peter Yorke and his Orchestra. The entries in MRS

DOOM'S DIARY continued, with the late Edmund's brother Gregory (Gauge) as the widow's new hubby, and Roland (Connor) her newly acquired stepson. Written by Sid Colin, Myles Rudge, Frederic Raphael and Tony Becker; produced by Roy Speer; weekly from 8 July 1955.

The Great Gilhooley
Eccentric Irish hero, 'a fantastic funster who, much to his own amazement, becomes a colossus of sport', played by Noel Purcell. JACK TRAIN supported as COLONEL CHINSTRAP, ex-ITMA, which was okay as the series was written by Ted Kavanagh, ex-ITMA. Supporting cast: Joe Linnane, Hugh Morton, Jean Capra, John Bushelle, Tony Arpino, and the Four Ramblers. The first of the weekly Sporting Visitors was Jimmy Wilde. Produced by Gordon Crier; first broadcast 2 October 1950.

Green, Hughie
Breezy 13-year-old impersonator who shot to fame with his Gang after a broadcast on IN TOWN TONIGHT (1933). His original signature tune was 'The Wearin' 'o the Green', and among his original Gangsters were Lauri Lupino Lane, Ella Wilson, Jimmy Spence, Mary Kelly and Connie Wood, who later changed her name to Kathie Kaye. Broadcasts included HORLICKS PICTURE HOUSE. After the war Hughie created OPPORTUNITY KNOCKS, and later called his autobiography *Opportunity Knocked* (1965). In it he retails his famous legal battle with the BBC for alleged blacklisting: Hughie lost.

The Greensladers
The Wallace Greenslade Fan Club (39,000 members) as promoted by Wallace Greenslade, announcer of THE GOON SHOW (1954). Their cry: 'Two – four – six – eight – Who do we appreciate? GREENSLADE!'

The Greys Are on the Air
Historic radio series in which the Band of His Majesty's Royal Scots Greys was sponsored by Greys Cigarettes. The first broadcast from RADIO LUXEMBOURG was on Sunday 17 April 1938, conducted by A.W. Crofts, with Raymond Newell singing the signature song:

SENSATIONAL STAGE VISIT | HIPPODROME

SOUTHAMPTON

Lessees: VARIETIES (SOUTHAMPTON) LTD.

WEEK COMMENCING MONDAY
17TH JUNE, 1935
TWICE NIGHTLY

YOU
HEARD
THEM
" ON
THE
AIR "

NOW
SEE
THEM
" IN
THE
FLESH "

HUGHIE GREEN

PRESENTS HIS FAMOUS ALL STAR

B.B.C. GANG

of Child Comedians, Musicians, Singers, Dancers, Mimics and Impressionists

IN A MODERN TELEVISION PROGRAMME

The most Brilliant Entertainment ever offered by Children.

WITH JACK HART & HIS

BROADCASTING BAND

IN THEIR NEW ACT " OUR BIG BROADCAST "

———— SUPPORTED BY ————

JAY GORDON	**DINKS & TRIXIE**
THE NEW STYLE COMEDIAN	TWO BIG LAUGHS

BETTY TURNER

Mezzo-Soprano from the Principal Royal Albert Hall and Queen's Hall Concerts
With LEON STILING at the Piano.

THE DANCING SAUCY SIX	**LES BEAUCAIRES**
THE FAST STEPPING SEXTETTE	COMEDY JUGGLING ENTERTAINERS

THE JOHN SILVER TRIO

THE MEN FROM " TREASURE ISLAND "

FRIDAY NIGHT IS CARNIVAL NIGHT, BOTH HOUSES

Hughie **Green** and his Gang: 1935 poster

Dauntless in the heat of battle,
Heroes all to do and dare,
Ready to defend and serve us,
The Greys! The Greys! The Greys are on the
air!

The compère was Lieutenant-Colonel Graham Seton, author of the popular novel, *The W Plan*, and the producer was Howard Thomas.

Grimble

Funny-voiced character played by Dick Emery in EDUCATING ARCHIE (1958), given to crying 'Livid I was!' and 'I hate yew!'.

Grisewood, Freddy

Freddy's friendly Oxfordshire accent made him one of the most popular BBC staff voices. Beginning as an announcer in 1929, he developed as a commentator, then as a compère of such magazine series as SCRAPBOOK (1933), IN TOWN TONIGHT (1933), THE WORLD GOES BY (1936), and latterly as the Travelling Question Master of ANY QUESTIONS (1950). He also broadcast in CHILDREN'S HOUR and wrote and told the very popular stories of OUR BILL. His book, *My Story of the BBC*, was published in 1949.

Freddy **Grisewood**: from announcer to beloved personality

Grytpype-Thynne

Lance-Brigadier the Hon. Hercules Grytpype-Thynne, British bounder, was modelled by PETER SELLERS upon Hollywood's favourite British cad, George Sanders. After early appearances in THE GOON SHOW he flowered fully from 28 September 1954. His popularity increased with his decline, due entirely to a suspect association with Count Jim 'Thighs' MORIARTY.

Guess the Name

Keith Fordyce provided the clues in this quiz about celebrities from all walks of life. Listeners who solved them correctly won long-playing records. Devised by Geoffrey Everitt; RADIO LUXEMBOURG from 1 March 1957.

Guess the Year

Miniature scrapbook of dramatized accounts of nationally important events and music of the selected year played by the Malcolm Lockyer Sextet, vocalists Bryan Johnson and Marie Bryant. Produced by Monty Bailey-Watson for Marshall Ward, on RADIO LUXEMBOURG from September 1952.

Guilty Party

Or 'You too can be a detective. Listeners are invited to join with a panel of experts in testing their powers of crime detection'. The first dramatized detective story in this series was 'The Witness Vanishes', written by Edward J. Mason and broadcast on 15 March 1954. The panel: John Arlott (cricket commentator), Robert Fabian (of Scotland Yard), and F.R. Buckley. Produced by Tony Shryane. The second series (16 January 1956) introduced a regular detective hero, Joe McCready (Jon Farrell), and Hamilton Dyce as Inspector Galloway. Episode 1: 'Dead Cert'.

Hail Pantomime!

Series tracing the history of Christmas pantomimes and characters, written by Gale Pedrick and produced by Roy Speer. Part 1, 'The Dame', was broadcast on 14 December 1938, and starred G.S. Melvin, Nelson Keys, Dan Leno Jr, Shaun Glenville, Clarkson Rose and George Lacey, with Sylvia Welling as the Fairy Queen and Fred Yule as the Demon King, plus the Variety Orchestra conducted by CHARLES SHADWELL.

Hail Variety!

Series devised and written by Gale Pedrick 'in which he turns the spotlight on various traditional types of Music Hall acts, conjured up by present day exponents of that style'. No. 1, 'The Lion Comique', was broadcast on 6 April 1938, and featured John Rorke, Frith Banbury, Charles Russell, Tom Leamore, and Bert Weston. Producer Roy Speer.

Hair Crow

'Hair Cro-ow!' 'Somebody Ca-all?' was the weekly introduction to this radio character, portrayed by balding George Crow. After demob from MERRY-GO-ROUND and the Blue Mariners Dance Band, he became the Maestro of the Waterlogged Spa Symphony Orchestra.

Hall, Henry

The greatest radio dance-band leader of them all. Henry's hesitant announcement, 'Hello, everyone, this *is* Henry Hall speaking', was a trademark millions looked forward to, either as conductor of the second BBC DANCE ORCHESTRA, which he formed, or as host to HENRY HALL's GUEST NIGHT. Both series were flanked by his two signature tunes, 'It's Just the Time for Dancing' and 'Here's to the Next Time'. Henry, formerly music director for LMS Hotels and in charge of 32 bands, first broadcast on 26 August 1924 with his Gleneagles Hotel Band from Glasgow (signature tune, 'Come Ye Back to Bonnie Scotland'). Completely 'made' by radio, Henry and his Band went freelance from 1937, packing them in wherever he played. Vocalists included Val Rosing, Dan Donovan, Kitty Masters, LES ALLEN, Phyllis Robins, George Elrick, Len Bermon, Bob Mallin, Leslie Douglas, Elizabeth Scott and the Three Sisters.

Hambone Repertory Company

Presented a weekly burlesque of a play in STAND EASY (1948), under the direction of producer Hiram Cheap (Len Marten).

Hancock, Tony

For many, the greatest radio comedian of all, and barely separable from his microphone persona, Anthony Aloysius StJohn Hancock the Third of 23 Railway Cuttings, Cheam. The Birmingham-born character comic made an early broadcast in *A La Carte* (6 June 1941), then the first of several post-war appearances in VARIETY BANDBOX on 9 January 1949. His first mini-series was as Scoutmaster Ponsonby of the EAGER BEAVERS in HAPPY-GO-LUCKY (1951), followed by a term as tutor to ARCHIE ANDREWS in EDUCATING ARCHIE (1951), where he gave the world the catchphrase, 'Flippin' kids!' In 1952 he was made resident compère of CALLING ALL FORCES, which developed into FORCES' ALL STAR BILL (1953). Here Hancock began the situation-type series (with Graham Stark and Joan Heal, scripted by Ray Galton and Alan Simpson) which would develop into HANCOCK's HALF HOUR (1954). Roger Wilmut's companion, *Tony Hancock Artiste* (1978), tells it all, including his highly successful transfer to television (1956) and his sad end in Australia.

Hancock's Half Hour

Or 'H-h-h-Hancock's 'Arf Hour' as the star nervously announced it on 2 November 1954 and for 102 more half-hours before taking it to television. Billed as 'a series of programmes based on the life of the lad himself from the files of the *Police Gazette*, written and adapted from the *Junior Goldfish Keepers Weekly* by Ray Galton and Alan Simpson'. Anthony Aloysius StJohn Hancock the Third, the well-known waif, came on to the well-remembered Hancock Theme composed by Wally Stott and played by Harry Rabinowitz and the Revue Orchestra. He was supported by Moira Lister, his girlfriend from *Star Bill*, Bill Kerr, the misery from Wagga-Wagga, Sidney James, the spiv from so many British B-films, Gerald Campion as Coatsleeve Charlie, and Kenneth Williams as Lord Dockyard. The second series started on 19 April 1955 with Andrée Melly as

Henry **Hall**: souvenir song book free with *Answers* (1937)

Tony **Hancock**: film role for radio star – *Orders Are Orders*

the girlfriend, but without Hancock! Unwell, he was temporarily replaced by Harry Secombe. It was in this series that Hancock first encountered SNIDE (KENNETH WILLIAMS), with his catchphrase, 'No, stop messin' about!' The third series (19 October 1955) found the Hancock menage settled at 23 Railway Cuttings, East Cheam. In the fifth programme of the fourth series (11 November 1956) Miss GRIZELDA PUGH arrived in the shape of Hattie Jacques. Tom Ronald took over production from the fifth series (21 January 1958), which included the most famous Half Hour of them all, 'Sunday Afternoon at Home' (22 April), a tour-de-force of radio at its purest.

The final series began on 29 September 1959, and included another 'pure radio' classic. 'The Poetry Society', which was thirty minutes of 'real time' without the usual incidental music.

The final Half Hour was 'The Impersonator', broadcast 29 December 1959. Curiously it was an attack on TV commercials – in time Hancock would appear in some of the funniest ever, for Eggs!

Handley, Tommy

Star of IT'S THAT MAN AGAIN (ITMA) and considered the greatest radio comedian of all time. Certainly he was of his own time, essentially the War years, when his up-to-the-minute topical cracks showed 'Old Nasty' the British could take it on the grin. His pun-laden Liverpudlian first crackled the ether in RADIO RADIANCE (22 July 1925), a revue in which he met and married Jean Allistone. Together they

The Happidrome

'We're all happy at the Happidrome' was the motto of this series set in an imaginary variety theatre. Doors opened for the first time on 9 February 1941 under the management of Mr Lovejoy (played by Arcadian Follies favourite Harry Korris), his stage-manager Ramsbottom (Cecil Frederick) and gormless callboy Enoch (Robbie Vincent). Enoch's catchphrase. 'Let me tell you!', became a national slogan, far exceeding Lovejoy's riposte, 'Ee, if ever a man suffered!'. Star guests on the first show included Murray and Mooney, Rupert Hazell and Elsie Day, Lily Morris and Tommy Handley. Tessie O'Shea and Billy Russell closed the series 52 weeks later on 8 February 1942. Happidrome returned on 7 March 1943 and celebrated its century on 30 January 1944 (Tessie O'Shea again topped the bill).

A post-war series was launched on 8 October 1945, starring Tessie O'Shea, 'Hutch', Trefor Jones and George Betton ('The Comic You Can Bet On'). Producer Ernest Longstaffe was this time assisted by Peter Duncan. The opening signature song was:

> Come to the Happidrome,
> Come to the show,
> Just take a tip from us,
> That is where to go . . .

and closed with the trio of comedians' plaintive:

> We three in Happidrome,
> Working for the BBC,
> Ramsbottom and Enoch and me.

The last time they 'worked for the BBC' was on Boxing Day 1947.

Happy Days

Series starring Vic Oliver, comedian, and his actress wife, Sarah Churchill, plus a famous 'guess' star. From 3 June 1941; producer Ronald Waldman.

Happy-Go-Lucky

Derek Roy compèred this 'light-hearted blend of comedy and music' which started on 2 August 1951. Husband-and-wife deuttists Jack and Daphne Barker were regulars, with Peggy Cochrane in 'Rhapsody at Random' ('you call the tunes and composer's styles and Peggy gives

Tommy **Handley**: autographed postcard from *Radio Pictorial*

recorded the clucking duet, 'Have You Seen My Chickens'. In the Royal Command Performance of 1924 he broadcast his famous touring sketch, *The Disorderly Room*, Eric Blore's parade of parodies, which became a radio perennial. For the Royal Command of 1927 he did the radio running commentary. Tommy arranged several original revues for radio, including *Inaninn, Handley's Manoeuvres, Tommy's Tours* and *Hot Pot*, and in 1934 formed a broadcasting partnership with fellow comedian Ronald Frankau as Murgatroyd and Winterbottom. Ted Kavanagh, who had been writing for Tommy since the twenties, devised It's That Man Again for him in 1939. After a slow start the war gave it new impetus and topicality and soon the listening audience numbered 30,000,000 and his annual fanmail 40,000 letters. When Tommy died in harness on 9 January 1949 there was national mourning.

you her impromptu interpretation'), and Doreen Harris and the Bar Room Ballad Four in 'The Naughty Nineties'. The most important regular sketch, however, was 'THE EAGER BEAVERS', an improbable series of adventures of a Boy Scout Troop featuring Bill Kerr (Dilberry), TONY HANCOCK (Mr Ponsonby), Peter Butterworth (Botterill) and Graham Stark (Creep). Script by John Law, Bill Craig, Ralph Peterson and John Vyvyan; produced by Roy Speer. Music by Stanley Black and the Dance Orchestra with the Sam Browne Singers; the guest stars on the first show were Suzette Tarri and Benny Hill.

The Happy-Go-Lucky-Hour

Carefree revue devised and compèred by CARROLL LEVIS, the old discoverer himself. The first series began on 10 August 1940, produced by Tom Ronald and written by Aubrey Danvers Walker. Discoveries apart, the series featured Elizabeth Pollock, crooner Dorothy Carless, Hugh Morton and Marjorie Westbury (better known as PAUL TEMPLE and Steve), and Doris Nichols (MRS PONSONBY). Guest star was Dorothy Ward, the famous pantomime principal boy. Hyam Greenbaum conducted the Revue Chorus and Orchestra. A second series started on 29 September 1942, with Billy Ternent conducting the Happy-Go-Lucky Club Orchestra. Johnny Williams was the Club Pageboy, and the Radio Deceivers were Eileen Huckerby and Nick (not yet Nicholas) Parsons. Produced by Michael North.

Happy Hoe-Down

'Calling all square-dancers', this country-style series started on 2 October 1950, with music by Phil Cardew's Cornhuskers and songs from the Maple Leaf Four, the Tanner Sisters, and the Hoedowners. David Miller produced and called the tunes.

Happy Holiday

This 'all star comedy musical' series set in Littleham-On-Sea starred Dennis Price as Major Denzil Pierce, PETER SELLERS as the Mayor and landlady Mrs Larkin, Bill Owen as Charlie Unkers, Jean Brampton as the Mayor's daughter, Elizabeth Larner as Miss Larkin, Dick Emery as Frederick Featherstone Haugh, and Graham Stark as J. Beerbohm Bloggs. Later Harry Secombe made a guest appearance as Bart Underblast, and Emery added Penderby Toop. Songs from the George Mitchell Merrymakers with Stanley Black and the Concert Orchestra. Written by Jimmy Grafton and Jimmy Griffiths; produced by Dennis Main Wilson. First broadcast 15 July 1954.

The Happy Philosopher

One of several dispensers of 'homely philosophy' in thirties commercial radio. This one was the star of *Happy Matinée* (1937), sponsored by Rose's Lime Juice, and was actually none other than BIG BILL CAMPBELL on leave from the Rocky Mountains.

Harding, Gilbert

One of the great radio personalities, famous for his much-loved grumpiness which could lead to unexpected outbursts. A former schoolmaster, he joined the BBC Monitoring Service in 1939, then Outside Broadcasts, before settling down as an erudite quiz-master in TWENTY QUESTIONS, ROUND BRITAIN QUIZ, and other panel games. Served a spell as the dummy's tutor in EDUCATING ARCHIE.

Harmony Hall

Comedy series set in a working-man's club, devised by one of its stars, Leslie Strange. Also featured were Leon Cortez, Beatrice Varley (as Mrs Dropmore the caterer), Peter Sinclair (the Cock o' the North), Arthur E. Owen, Dorothy Darke, John Mann, the Three Imps, and the Revue Chorus and Orchestra conducted by Ernest Longstaffe, who also produced. First broadcast, 7 June 1946, written by one of Charlie Chester's 'Crazy Gang', Len Marten.

Harmony in A Flat

Punning title for a musical series starring the Cavendish Three (Kay Cavendish, Pat Rignold, Dorothy Carless) and their boyfriends. From 26 April 1940, written and produced by Ronnie Hill and Peter Dion Titherage.

Harrison, Beatrice

Lady cellist who made a unique niche in early outside broadcasting by playing mellow tunes on her instrument in order to encourage the song of the nightingale. Location for these nocturnal exploits was her home village of

Gilbert **Harding**: *Speaking of Murder* (1953 film)

Oxted in Surrey. Miss Harrison was born in Roorkee, North West India, where her father was a Colonel in the Royal Engineers. She was a medal-winning cellist at the age of 10.

Harry Hopeful
'The Nation's cheerful wanderer', played by Frank Nichols in a number of North Region programmes from 1935. Created by D.G. Bridson and Crawford McNair, Harry met 'real people' and encouraged them to tell their stories and sing songs in shows like *Harry Hopeful's Party* (15 December 1936). Harry's signature tune, sung to 'Bobby Shafto', was

Harry Hopeful is my name,
I must find work on Monday.

Harry Lime
'The fabulous stories of the world-famous character created in the film *The Third Man*' – by Graham Greene, of course – came to radio in *The Lives of Harry Lime*. This daring and original idea of ex-staff producer HARRY ALAN TOWERS lured Orson Welles to British radio, recreating and occasionally scripting the character he created in the Carol Reed film. He was accompanied, of course, by Anton Karas on the zither. Episode 1, 'See Naples and Live' by Sigmund Miller, was broadcast on 3 August 1951.

Harry's Half Hour
Rare series for Scottish comedian Harry Gordon, 'The Laird of Inversnecky'. Supposedly broadcast from Inversnecky Inn, the series started on 4 December 1944 and featured Jack Holden, Elsie Percival, Janette Sclanders, Ann Downie, Willie Joss, and the Scottish Variety Orchestra conducted by Kemlo Stephens. Produced from Scotland by Howard Lockhart.

The Haunted Ballroom
'Listen with the old caretaker to some ghosts of past tunes': gramophone records presented by Ernest Dudley from 9 July 1942.

Have a Go: Wilfred Pickles on stage

Have a Go!

The most popular quiz show ever broadcast, it travelled England with WILFRED PICKLES in charge and Mabel at the Table. The signature song (musical illustrations by Violet Carson) began:

'Have a Go, Joe, Come on and Have a Go'

and the rest sounded like 'Ransen scransen ransen scransen on your radio . . .' no matter which part of the country it came from. Then Wilf would say: 'People of Land's End (or John o'Groats) – how do! 'Ow are yer?', and one by one both old and young, especially old, would come to the microphone for a long interview and a short quiz. Favourite question: 'What was yer most embarrassin' moment, loov?' The four quiz questions would pay off at 1: half-a-crown, 2: five bob, 3: ten bob, 4: a quid, and answer them right or not, the contestant would invariably walk away with the lot: 'Thirty-seven and six!' as Wilf would proudly proclaim. At the end would come a Jackpot Question ('How mooch on the table, Mabel?' 'Twelve and ninepence and a Yarmouth kipper!'), and a farewell version of the signature song:

'Have a Go, Joe, You've been and 'ad a go, Ransen scransen ransen scransen . . .'

The programme was devised by John Salt, director of BBC Northern Region, and it was first broadcast from Southgate Hall in Yorkshire on 4 March 1946. It was first heard nationally on the Light Programme on 16 September 1946, in a show emanating from Bridlington. The producer was Philip Robinson; and the original 'musical illustrations' were provided by Jack Jordan. The 100th *Have a Go* was broadcast from Rochdale on 2 June 1948, with 'your old friend Wilfred Pickles presenting the people to the people', and at the close of another series on 6 May 1949, celebrated by a special compilation of highlights, the show had travelled 78,000 miles, and Wilfred had asked 3752 questions of 900 competitors. The producer was now Barney Colehan: 'Give 'em the mooney, Barney!' Programme No. 150, broadcast from the Nuffield Centre on 18 January 1950, brought back a selection of past participants including a knocker-upper from Wigan, a disabled Dutchman, and a blind airman. Rather riskily, a live series began on 17 November 1953, when Harry Hudson took over the piano. The 250th programme was broadcast from an old folks' home in Warley on 11 January 1955, and by the start of a new series on 27 September, the show had travelled 125,920 miles and paid out £4000 in prizes. Eric James was the pianist by the time the series reached its 20th year, when there were 350,000 miles on the clock. The last *Have a Go* was broadcast on 10 January 1967, with a Christmas special five years later, on 25 December 1972.

Haver and Lee

Quickfire crosstalk comedians who gained radio fame as residents of HENRY HALL'S GUEST NIGHT when they were billed as 'The Fun Racketeers' and concluded their spot with the catchphrase, 'Play, Henry!'. Later they took over the roles of DUCKWEED AND EGGBLOW in the crazy series, DANGER MEN AT WORK (1940). Supposedly Harry Haver and Frank Lee, they were really CLAY KEYES, a former juggler, and Frank Tully.

Hazel and Edie

Gossiping girlfriends created by Leslie Crowther and Ronnie Barker in VARIETY PLAYHOUSE (1960). The comedians also wrote their own scripts.

Heath, Ted

'Listen to My Music' was the signature tune of Ted Heath and his Music, one of the last great dance bands. Ted played trombone for almost every other band leader in the business – JACK HYLTON, AMBROSE, Sidney Lipton, GERALDO – before the wartime visit of Glenn Miller and his Band of the AEF inspired him to form his own in 1945. Included in Ted's original orchestra were Stanley Black on piano and Woolf Phillips on trombone. The band's name was made by 27 consecutive broadcasts on TOP TEN, and one of his own compositions, 'I'm Gonna Love That Guy', was in the American Hit Parade for 14 weeks. Another of Ted's songs always evokes wartime memories, 'I Haven't Said Thanks for That Lovely Weekend'. Quiet and unassuming, Ted had others announce his programmes, which became a break for Paul Carpenter. It was 1950 before Ted found a suitable girl vocalist, Lita Roza, to join his male singers, Dickie Valentine and Denis Lotis.

Heather Mixture

Miscellany of music and humour from Scotland, originally featuring the Scottish Variety Orchestra and compèred by Alastair MacIntyre. 'Home Sweet Home' introduced a regular family sketch featuring Frank and Doris Droy with Sam Murray as the Man Upstairs (1948). By 1962 the series featured Jimmy Shand and his Band, with songs from Moira Brody and the Joe Gordon Folk Four, introduced by Bill Jack. The programme ran until 7 April 1970.

Heigh Ho!

'As off to work we got with Peter Waring, KENNETH HORNE and Charmain Innes, escorted by Nell Ballantyne, Maurice Denham and the Melody Men.' Written by FRANK MUIR for the conjurer-comedian from the Windmill, Peter Waring. KENNETH HORNE played Uncle Eustace. Produced by Charles Maxwell and first broadcast 11 October 1946.

Heinz Half Hour of Happiness

JACK HULBERT and CICELY COURTNEIDGE starred in this Sunday series on RADIO LUXEMBOURG, starting 14 May 1939. Music was by Lew Stone and his Band, with the Rhythm Brothers and Jack Cooper, and in support, Mercia Swinburne, Lawrence Green, Jevan Brandon-Thomas and Leonard Hayes. Sponsored by Heinz Thick Whip Salad Cream, sixpence a bottle: 'The dressing that has made the nation eat more salad!'

Hello Anybody

Midday comedy series built around the combination of new comedian Gene Crowley and old comedian Charlie CLAPHAM, recently bereft of his straight-man, Dwyer. Support came from the noble Doris Nichols, the confused Horace Percival, the forgotten Marten Tiffen, and Miff Ferrie's Vocaltones who sang with Frank Weir and his Orchestra. Clapham's catchphrase: 'That's where yer trouble is!' Produced by Charles Chilton from 29 April 1948.

Hello Children (Hello There)

Daily series broadcast at noon during school holidays, beginning 4 July 1949 on the Light. LIONEL GAMLIN presented, produced and edited the half-hours, which featured a number of regular items including 'Life's One Big Holiday' (in which RICHARD DIMBLEBY described the joys of his job). 'Autograph Album' (in which Ted Heath recalled a favorite school holiday), 'That's a Good Tune', and CHILDREN'S HOUR favourites such as 'When We Were Very Young' and 'Tammy Troot'. The first serial was *Round the World in Eighty Days*. A Christmas holiday series began on 26 December 1949 with the first science-fiction serial on BBC, *We Went To Mars*, in which three children stowed away aboard Professor McGillivray's rocket ship, 'The Albatross'. This John Kier Cross adaptation of the novel *The Angry Planet* by Stephen MacFarlane, was so popular it was repeated during the Easter run of the programme, commencing 3 April 1950.

To broaden the audience appeal the title was changed to *Hello There* with the run commencing 24 July 1950. Among the features, John Kier Cross's serial *Blackadder*, Robert MacDermott 'At Your Service', 'Holiday Notebook' and 'Saturday Showboat' with Billy Mayerl and his Rhythm Players, Bob Mallin and his guitar, Ronald Chesney and his harmonica, and cockney songs from John Rorke and Joan Young. The Christmas season began on 18 December with 'Trip to Toyland', 'They Shall Have Music', 'Holiday Bookshelf' and the serial, *The Boy From the Forest*. The 1951 series shifted to 1.15 pm and began on 19 March with 'In The Groove' with Marcel

Stellman, 'Meet the Grownups', 'Peacock Pie' with Billy Mayerl and his Rhythmic Piemen, and John Howard Davies in *Saturday Adventures* by John Pudney. The summer series started on 23 July with 'I Haven't a Clue' (Robert Fabian of the Yard), 'Round the Bend' with Wilfred Thomas, 'Peacock Pie' with Julie Andrews and Arthur Marshall, and the serial *The Flying Fortunes* with Barry K. Barnes. The Christmas season started on 27 December with 'Hospital Harmony', 'Friend of the Family', and the serial *What Happens Next?*

When the series returned on 27 April 1952 it was as a weekly programme on Sundays. Items included 'Flying Visit', 'A Girl I Know', 'Curiosity Corner' and 'Let's Have a Story'. Expanded to 45 minutes from 27 September, a serial was added entitled 'Look Before You Leap' with Robin Ray and Patricia Field as the Conway Cousins. *Hello There* said a final 'goodbye there' on 22 March 1953.

Hello Gibraltar

One of the many wartime series aimed at HM Forces serving in specific areas. Joan Gilbert (later the television personality) devised and introduced this one, which was heard by Home listeners from 1944. Eric Winstone and his Orchestra played requests, sung by Julie Dawn and Alan Kane. Features included 'Anniversary Corner' and W.H. Barrington Dalby talking on sport.

Hello Marilyn

Ronnie Hilton sang the songs accompanied by the Jackie Brown Orchestra, in this series sponsored by the Amalgamated Press, publishers of *Marilyn*, the romance comic for girls. Produced by ITMA veteran Clarence Wright, and broadcast on RADIO LUXEMBOURG from 10 September 1956.

Hello Playmates

ARTHUR ASKEY with a new partner, conjurer David Nixon, starred in this comedy series written by BOB MONKHOUSE AND DENIS GOODWIN who also took part. Irene Handl and Pat Coombs made their debuts as MRS PURVIS and Nola, the spinster daughter in search of a husband. Arthur's first guest was soprano Anne Ziegler, who sang with Paul Fenoulhet and the Variety Orchestra. First broadcast 31 May 1954; produced by Leslie Bridgmont. The

second series was the same again save for Bob Sharples and his Music. It began on 16 December 1954 and won the 1955 NATIONAL RADIO AWARD for Most Promising New Programme.

Hello Young Lovers

The 'young lovers' were singing stars Joan Regan and Gary Miller, who sang to Geoff Love and his Orchestra in this RADIO LUXEMBOURG series sponsored by Jays Furnishing Company. Adrian Foley played the piano and produced the series, which started 11 August 1954.

Helter-Shelter

'Show for the Home Front' starring VERA LYNN, with Reginald Purdell and Frederick Burtwell as two cockney odd-job men. LIONEL GAMLIN played the Shelter Marshal, with Eddie Carroll and his Band. Written by Jenny Nicholson; produced by Reginald Purdell. From 19 November 1940.

Hemsley, Harry

Father of his own famous 'radio family', ELSIE, WINNIE, JOHNNY and the baby-talking HORACE. Harry May Hemsley was originally a cartoonist for *Ally Sloper's Half-Holiday* and other comics, then became a singing impressionist with the original WHITE COONS, making his first broadcast in 1923. His child impersonations so fooled listeners that many wrote to the BBC complaining that children should not be allowed to stay up so late! In the thirties he became an integral segment of THE OVALTINEYS Concert Party from LUXEMBOURG, involving his children (now known as the Fortune Family) in adventure serials. His post-war series for the BBC included OLD HEARTY (1947) and HEMSLEY'S HOTEL (1949). PETER CAVANAGH was the only impressionist allowed to impersonate Hemsley and Family.

Hemsley's Hotel

Comedy series for the younger listener starring HARRY HEMSLEY and his imaginary children, ELSIE, WINNIE, JOHNNIE and HORACE the baby. Norman Shelley played Pieface the Chef, Molly Lumley was Miss Pillweed the Receptionist, Martin Benson was Pierre the Head Waiter, and Cecile Chevreau Madame Incognito the mysterious guest. Episode 1, 'The Unexpected Guest', was written by Jill Allgood and

Harry **Hemsley**: father of an 'imaginary family'

Hemsley, produced by Audrey Cameron, and broadcast on 30 October 1949.

Henry Crun

Mr Henry Albert Sebastopol Queen Victoria Crun, of the old firm of Wacklow and Crun. Elderly inventor and boon but never bed companion to Miss Bannister, with whom he holds long, involved, pause-laden conversations. Played with much muttering ('Mnk . . . grnk . . . mnk-mnk . . .'), by Peter Sellers in The Goon Show (1952); he speedily established two catchphrases: 'Morning . . . morning . . .' and 'You can't get the wood, you know!'.

Henry Hall's Guest Night

This famous series, broadcast on and off for some 20 years, started quite casually on Saturday 17 March 1934 in the late night BBC Dance Band slot, 10.45 pm to midnight. Henry Hall, the popular conductor, introduced Anona Winn, soprano and impressionist, Elsie and Doris Waters in their 'Gert and Daisy' characters, Lupino Lane, the musical comedy star, and 'June', the popular songstress. (Legend has it that Flanagan and Allen also appeared.) This new mixture of the latest dance-band hits and surprise stars was immediately popular, and continued in this Saturday night spot for $2\frac{1}{2}$ years. Revived with the 1939 war, *Henry Hall's Guest Night* was broadcast for another run of $3\frac{1}{2}$ years, this time as live shows direct from variety theatres around the country. A further series started on 4 September 1944 with a one hour *Gala Guest Night*, and a weekly half-hour series followed from 1 January 1946. Every show began in the same way: 'Good evening, everyone. This *is* Henry Hall speaking, and tonight is my Guest Night.' They concluded, of course, with the theme song, 'Here's to the Next Time'.

A further long run clocked up its 100th consecutive show on 7 November 1951, and although guests were never billed, a predictable regular was Betty Driver singing 'The Sailor With the Navy Blue Eyes'. The 21st birthday edition 18 March, 1955 broke with tradition by billing Henry's guests: Norman Wisdom, Elsie and Doris Waters, Stanley Holloway, Vanessa Lee, Beryl Reid (whom Henry had made a star as the schoolgirl Monica), Betty Driver, Cyril Stapleton, Albert Marland. Recorded appearances: Gracie Fields, the Mills Brothers, Oliver Wakefield, Harriet Cohen and Richard Tauber. By this time Henry no longer ran a band, and the musical accompaniment was by Harry Rabinowitz and the BBC Revue Orchestra. Producer John Simmonds.

Henry, John

The first comedian to become a national personality through radio. Henry's Yorkshire accent evidently appealed amid the rarified 'Oxford' accents of the BBC. The billing of his first broadcast (31 May 1923) read '9.30: John Henry will try to entertain you', and half an hour later, 'John Henry will try again'. He starred in the 1923 Christmas Day Programme with Helena Millais (Our Lizzie), and on 30 May 1925 expanded his act by introducing his wife, Blossom, into the comedy show, *An Hour in a Restaurant*. It doubled his popularity, too, and the team of John Henry and Blossom, exploiting the eternal situation of the hen-pecked husband, can be considered the start of domestic comedy in radio. He made many records, the first being 'John Henry's Wireless Elephant' on Regal G8059 (1923). He also appeared in a comic strip in the *Daily Sketch*.

Henry, Leonard

Fruity-voiced funny man Leonard Henry is remembered as the first man to blow a raspberry on the radio. He was also the first comedian to be voted top twice in a pre-war

Leonard **Henry**: pictured at the 'meat safe' microphone

newspaper poll of radio favourites. Henry, a concert party comic, was radio's first zany, salting his routines with funny voices, funny noises, and silly songs. He first broadcast on 29 September 1926 compèring variety, and quickly graduated to writing and starring in his own revues, *Humouresque* and *April Foolishness*, and was a regular in CHARLOT's HOUR (1928). He was radio compère of the 1932 ROYAL COMMAND PERFORMANCE, a great favourite on CHILDREN's HOUR, and made many comedy records beginning with 'Let's All Sing the Lard Song' (Lard-i-da-di-da) on Parlophone E5982 (1928). John Watt, introducing Leonard's autobiography, *My Laugh Story* (1937), called him one of the few comedians who invented new jokes.

Herbert Mostyn

Non-person who played all the small parts in TAKE IT FROM HERE (1947). Coined to disguise the acting talents of the two scriptwriters by combining their middle names, Frank Herbert MUIR and Denis Mostyn NORDEN.

Here We Go

Musical variety series starring AMBROSE and his Orchestra with Anne Shelton, Sam Browne, Leslie Carew, and the Greene Sisters, with features 'Truth or Consequences', 'Musical Back Room Boys', 'Film Actor's Scrapbook', 'History Speaks', 'Queer Trades', and the Ambrose Repertory Company. Started 29 April 1942; producer Douglas Lawrence.

Here's George!

'A radio ramble with Robey' starring the Prime Minister of Mirth, George Robey, with Rupert Hazell and Elsie Day, Mario De Pietro, and Ernest Longstaffe conducting the Variety Orchestra. Postponed from 21 January to 13 March 1936 because of the King's death, this series later transferred to RADIO LUXEMBOURG under the sponsorship of Branston Sweet Pickle. Same cast save for Fred Hartley's Orchestra taking over from the BBC's. Commenced 26 April 1936.

Here's Howard

Series starring the casual comedy of MICHAEL HOWARD, originally a one-off in the *Showtime* series. Started 22 September 1949 with Howard 'all alone by a microphone with occasional interruptions from Norman Shelley, Lionel Stevens, Doris Nichols, Pat Coombs and the Revue Orchestra conducted by Frank Cantell'. Script by Laurie Wyman and Bob Monkhouse; produced by Leslie Bridgmont.

Here's Wishing You Well Again

Fortnightly magazine programme for Forces in hospital, broadcast from 10 March 1943. Signature tune:

> Here's wishing you well again,
> Hope to see you soon,
> Here's wishing you all that's good,
> Under the sun and under the moon . . .

– originally sung by hostess BEBE DANIELS, later Paula Green. Marjorie Anderson and Georgie Henschel co-introduced the series, and the New Year edition on 28 December 1944 included guests from past editions: BEBE DANIELS, BEN LYON, VIC OLIVER, Jack Buchanan, the WESTERN BROTHERS, Pat Kirkwood, Florence Desmond, MABEL CONSTANDUROS, CYRIL FLETCHER, 'Hutch', ELSIE AND DORIS WATERS and JACK WARNER. There was also the regular quiz, 'Winner's Luck', plus features 'Out and About' with Donald McCullough, 'A Guest, a Guess and a Guinea', and Cecil Trouncer playing Dr Carteret the Coroner in 'A Corner in Crime' by Anthony Gilbert. Mantovani and his Concert Orchestra provided the music and the producers were Jill Allgood and Howard Agg.

The 1945 (from 7 August) series had Margaret Lockwood as hostess, with quizzes 'Stars and Sterling' and 'Sporting Chance', introduced by JOHN SNAGGE. The 100th show was broadcast on 12 April 1946.

Hi Gang!

Tremendously vigorous and popular wartime series which started on Sunday 26 May 1940, and ran for 52 weeks with the identical opening: Ben Lyon: 'Hi, gang!' Audience: 'Hi, Ben!' Jay Wilbur's Band: 'I'm just wild about Harry...' Ben: 'Welcome to your own Hi Gang show, coming to you from the heart of London, with BEBE DANIELS, VIC OLIVER, and BEN LYON – that's me folks!' Features included Auntie Bebe's Advice Column and Vic Oliver as the Radio Reporter, Peep Keyhole ('Peep-peep!'). Songs were by the Greene Sisters and Sam Browne, who also appeared with Jay Wilbur in the Gainsborough film version in 1942. American film stars often surprise-guested, such as Tyrone Power. Devised and writted by Bebe Daniels and Ben Lyon, with additional dialogue by Dick Pepper. Producers Harry S. Pepper and Douglas Lawrence.

The second series started 9 November 1941 and introduced 'Magic Carpet' and specially recorded greetings from such Hollywood stars as Hedy Lamarr, Cary Grant, Judy Garland, Robert Taylor and Dick Powell. Singers were Jack Cooper and the Henderson Twins, with additional dialogue by Ray Sonin. Ran 26 weeks.

A post-war series slightly retitled *Hi Gang 1949* began on 18 February and ran to 4 August. Supporting the original trio were Benny Lee, George Mitchell's Hi Gangsters, and the Dance Orchestra conducted by Stanley Black. The new writer was Sid Colin and the producer Tom Ronald. The 100th show, broadcast 30 April, had an all-star guest list: announcer Bruce Belfrage, Hebrew comic Max Bacon, film star Valerie Hobson, bandleaders CARROLL GIBBONS and GERALDO, Michael Denison and Dulcie Gray, VERA LYNN, JACK WARNER, veteran disc-jockey CHRISTOPHER STONE, and actress Fay Compton. This final series also introduced Hollywood stars such as Kathryn Grayson and Jane Wyman.

Hi Neighbours!

Comedy series with music written by Ted Kavanagh around Jack Watson's impersonations, plus the Tanner Sisters, Dickie Valentine, Denny Dennis and Sid Phillips and his Orchestra. Started 5 July 1953, produced by John Simmonds.

Hibberd, Stuart

Considered the 'Voice of the BBC', the longest-

Stuart **Hibberd**: a radio French lesson with Monsieur Stephan at Savoy Hill

serving announcer on the staff. Hibberd joined the Company on its second birthday, 13 November 1924, and four years later was made the Chief Announcer. His was the voice that conducted Britain through the great General Strike of 1926 and saddened the world with the phrase 'The King's life is moving peacefully towards its close' in 1935. His other classic phrase, 'This – is London', became the title of his autobiography, which he based on a diligently kept daily diary. He was the first announcer to let his hair down, playing the mouth-organ on CHILDREN'S HOUR, and being a Mystery Voice on MONDAY NIGHT AT EIGHT, singing 'We Mustn't Miss the Last Bus Home'. He celebrated his BBC Jubilee in 1949, and duly retired with his classic close-down, 'Good night, everybody... goodnight'. He explained that the pause was designed to give listeners a chance to say 'good night' back to him!

Highland Barn Dance

'A session of fun and music with a Scottish flavour designed to appeal to all our listeners' claimed RADIO LUXEMBOURG of this unsponsored series commencing 3 May 1956.

'Won't you push back the furniture and join in the fun with us?' 'Us' was Jimmy Shand and his Band, Jim Cameron and his Scottish Dance Orchestra, Seumas MacNeill and his bagpipes, and singer Robert Wilson.

Highlights on Parade

Alfred Van Dam and his Famous Trocadero Broadcasting Orchestra, vocalist Wyn Richmond, starred in this early morning series on RADIO LUXEMBOURG from 7 November 1937. Sponsored by Maclean's whose slogan was sung to the tune of 'On Ilkley Moor Bah't 'At': 'Did you Maclean your teeth today?' Bob Danvers-Walker was the compère.

Hilda Tablet

The gifted composeress and fictitious subject of the Third Programme's burlesque biography *The Private Life of Hilda Tablet*, first broadcast (of many) 24 May 1954. Hilda (Mary O'Farrell) was the daughter of Sir Eric Tablet (Norman Shelley) and her life was researched by Herbert Pearce, scholar (Hugh Burden). This 'parenthesis for radio' was written by Henry Reed, with original music by Donald Swann. Producer Douglas Cleverdon.

Hill-Billy Hoe-Down

American variety act Charles Forsythe and Addie Seamon co-starred in this cowboy musical series as 'the folks of Smoky Mountain'. Also featured were Doris Nichols and singers Johnnie Johnston, Alan Dean, Pearl Carr and Irene King, with Danny Levin and the Smoky Mountaineers. A measure of authenticity was ensured by writer-producer Charles Chilton of RIDERS OF THE RANGE fame. First broadcast 7 October 1949.

Hip-Hip-Hoo-Roy!

DEREK ROY ('Doctor Roy the Melody Boy') former resident comedian with VARIETY BAND-BOX, starred in this comedy series contrived for him by producer Leslie Bridgmont. Support came from Robert Moreton (and his 'Bumper Fun Book'), Alfred Marks, and the goonish newcomer, SPIKE MILLIGAN. Music was provided by Cherry Lind, the Stargazers, and the Dance Orchestra conducted by Stanley Black. First broadcast 5 October 1949, it may be regarded as the first stumbling step towards the

GOON SHOW. Writers included Spike Milligan, Jimmy Grafton, Laurie Wyman, BOB MONKHOUSE AND DENIS GOODWIN.

Hit Parade

The BBC's first attempt to emulate the long-running success of the American radio series *Your Hit Parade* was broadcast on 4 January 1949. Wrote Michael Standing, Director of Variety: 'Its object is to reset the pick of the week's hit tunes in the most favourable setting that can be dressed with star singers, star bands, and star arrangements.' Anne Shelton and Bruce Trent were the star singers, supported by the Song Pedlars, and the star band was the Squadronnaires directed by Jimmy Miller. Six shows later, GERALDO came in with his Concert Orchestra. Sid Colin scripted and John Burnaby produced.

Hit the Road

Comedy and song series built around Lester Ferguson, a former lorry driver turned he-man baritone. Comedy from Ken Platt ('I won't take me coat off, I'm not stopping!'), Bob Pearson as Rudyard the problem child, Bernard Spear as Louie, Miriam Karlin, Eddie Arnold (the impersonator, not the country-western singer), and the Taverners who sang with the Revue Orchestra conducted by Harry Rabinowitz. Script by George Wadmore, George Inns, Ronnie Wolfe; produced by George Inns; first broadcast 26 April 1954.

Hitch Hike

'Road Show' starring SYD WALKER (later Fred Yule) as a lorry driver, Vera Lennox as Ginger, and Joan Young, C. Denier Warren, Dick Francis, and the Four Clubmen, with the Revue Orchestra conducted by the producer, Ernest Longstaffe. Began 21 December 1942, written by Clifford Lewis.

Hogsnorton

Mythical country village created by broadcaster GILLIE POTTER, who regularly reported via radio of the doings theredown. On Wednesday 2 August 1939 it was the wedding of the Hon. Veronica Japonica Harmonica ('Tootles'), daughter of Lord and Lady Marshmallow, to Aubrey Watteau Elijah Twirtle, officiated by Canon Fodder. *Hogsnorton Hob-*

nobbing was an unusual programme broadcast on 1 October 1941, in which Potter was assisted by JOYCE GRENFELL and the Great Boosey Temperance Band under the direction of GERALDO! A series of talks entitled *Heard at Hogsnorton* began on 17 January 1946.

Holiday Music Hall

Summer series hosted by CYRIL FLETCHER; 'To sing for you' David Hughes; 'To bring a smile', Ethel Revnell and the WESTERN BROTHERS. Music came from the Adam Singers with Paul Fenoulhet and the Dance Orchestra. Producer Bill Worsley. Commenced 11 July 1959, it returned on 4 June 1960 with a regular sketch called 'His and Hers', a weekly glimpse into the domestic life of Leslie Randall and Joan Reynolds. There was also 'Country Calendar' featuring the animal impressions of Percy Edwards.

The third season started on 1 April 1961 with Fletcher back in charge, plus 'Calypso Time' with Cy Grant. Hylda Baker topped the bill, which included Chic Murray and Maidie, and Billy Burden. The fourth series began on 26 May 1962 when Fletcher introduced 'Hank 'n' Hannah', featuring Libby Morris and David Kossoff as tourists from America. Resident comedy came from RICHARD MURDOCH and KENNETH HORNE. The fifth series (1 June 1963) introduced Kenneth Connor in 'End of the Pier', Steve Benbow in 'Holiday Folk Club', and Carole Carr and Ian Wallace in 'Ballads Old and New'.

Holiday Playhouse

Summer season of varieties introduced by George Martin 'the Casual Comedian' assisted by Billy Burden and the Visitor of the week at Martin's Inn. Music from Ron Goodwin and his Orchestra with the Adam Singers; script by Eric Merriman, George Martin and Eddie Maguire; producer John Simmonds. Broadcast from 6 July 1957. The programme returned in 1958 hosted by CYRIL FLETCHER, with Tom Mennard as the Roving Reporter, and 'Life with THE BURKES', a family saga by Johnny Speight. Cyril starred as both Albert Burke and his small son, Erbie. Songs from the George Mitchell Glee Club and duets from Tudor Evans and Victoria Campbell. Script by Bill Kelly and Arthur Lay; produced by Alastair Scott-Johnston.

Hollywood Calling

Weekly visit to the film city to talk with the stars and hear some of their favourite songs. Devised and hosted by Desmond Carrington, the first programme, broadcast from RADIO LUXEM-BOURG on 4 October 1954, featured Esther Williams. Carrington-Hale Productions for Christy's Lanoline Face-Packs.

Home and Away

Jack Buchanan and Elsie Randolph, star team of many a stage and screen musical, played Mr and Mrs Fuller, Jack and Daffodil, in this domestic situation comedy series first broadcast 30 March 1954. Their three teenage daughters were played by Josephine Crombie (Billie), Beryl Roques (Janet) and Carole Shelley (Hyacinth). David Jacobs played a boyfriend. Harry Rabinowitz and the Revue Orchestra played the musical links, and the script was by David Climie and Anthony Armstrong. Producer Jacques Brown.

Home at Eight

Richard Attenborough hosted this weekly hour starring Hermione Gingold and Alfred Marks as the gloomy Dooms in the macabre satire, 'MRS DOOM'S DIARY'. Other items were 'On Stage Please', an interlude by students in their last term at the Royal Academy of Dramatic Art; 'Off The Record', a recording celebrity (the first was Billie Worth); 'Thanks for the Melody', hits of yesterday and today by Peter Yorke and his Concert Orchestra and the Ipswich Girls Choir. Began 21 April 1952; produced by Ronnie Hill. The series returned on 26 September with Jerry Desmonde replacing Dickie Attenborough, plus the Stargazers.

The Home Front

The first wartime radio family, the Leversuches, actually started in the July of 1939 with a dramatized programme entitled 'The Air Raid'. The series proper began on 10 October with 'The Leversuch Family at War', an episode mainly explaining how to fill up forms. Created and written by Stephen Potter; the cast was anonymous.

Home Service

The two alternative services, the NATIONAL Programme and the REGIONAL Programme,

The Home Service: Alvar Lidell in the Continuity Suite at Broadcasting House (1962)

were merged into a single all-day service from Friday 1 September 1939, two days before the official Declaration of War. The name 'Home Service' was first used on the following Monday. The first programme on that day, following the 7 am news, was gramophone records of the New Light Symphony Orchestra and the KENTUCKY MINSTRELS. The wavelengths were 391.1 metres and 449.1 metres. Originally a mixture of news and entertainment, the lighter programmes were diverted to the new FORCES' PROGRAMME from 7 January 1940. The famous announcement, 'This is the BBC Home Service' was last heard on 30 September 1967, when the service was renamed Radio 4.

Honey and Almond
'Four Beautiful Hands' at the piano, with Al Bowlly to sing. 'A programme of beauty and romance' presented by Hinds Honey and Almond Cream on RADIO LYONS from 6 February 1938.

Honolulu Beach
Escapist comedy-with-music series with dialogue by the star, Hebrew comic Joe Hayman, who appeared as Jake Rosen. Music was by Peter Bernard, also in the cast, as were Jacques Brown (Plato the Chef), Sydney Keith (Confucious the Waiter), and Robert Wyndham (Spike McGee). Produced by Roy Speer on 20 February 1940 with the CAVENDISH THREE and the Dance Orchestra conducted by Billy Ternent. Later singer Dorothe Morrow joined the cast as Halima.

The Honourable Babs du Croix Fotheringham
Known as Queenie for short. One of the WAAFs stationed at MUCH-BINDING-IN-THE-MARSH (1945), short on dialogue ('Okay, ducks!') but long on song – she was played by Dorothy Carless.

The Honourable Pheeb
LORD WATERLOGGED's unseen daughter in MERRY-GO-ROUND (1946), about whom he was wont to remark: 'Ooh, she sez in the quiet Roedean way of 'er's, yew'll get a slosh in the gob, young man!'

Hoop-La!
'All the Fun of the Fair!' was promised by producer Tom Arnold in this major variety series which opened on 27 November 1944. Veteran comedian ROBB WILTON starred as the Complaints Manager, with Max Wall in strange encounters with Auntie (Doris Nichols) and Guy (Harold Berens). Catchphrases here included Max's mock uppercrust 'Ack – tually!' plus the favourite 'Lashings of toast, simply oooo-zing with butter!'. Polly Ward appeared in 'The Pin-Up Parlour', and GERALDO and his Orchestra in 'The Juke Box', while 'The International Palace of Varieties' brought such guest stars as REVNELL AND WEST and Monsewer Eddie Gray. Characters included Benny Lee as Bert and a coarse voiced female who shouted 'Hup and dahn, hup and dahn!'. Script was by Max Kester and Howard Barnes. Pat Dixon produced the second series, which ran from 9 February 1945, and introduced ITMA regular JACK TRAIN as 'Cheapjack Train from Petticoat Lane'. This time the band belonged to Debroy Somers, and the singer was Beryl Davis.

Hoorah for Hollywood!

Burlesque broadcasts satirizing Hollywood films and personalities, commencing 29 December 1941 with 'Drearitone Follies of 1942'. Devised by and with ROY PLOMLEY, supported by Rosamund Belmore, John Slater, and Sydney Monckton. Producer Frederick Piffard. Later came 'Break for Drearitone', a segment of PICTURE PARADE from 15 January 1947, in which Plomley satirized a current British shocker as 'No Horses for Miss Radish'.

Hooray for What!

Occasional anthology of American humour arranged by M.H. Allen, from the works of Milt Gross, William Saroyan, James Thurber, Robert Benchley, and Hortense Flexner, to name but a few. With the voices of such as Sydney Keith, Macdonald Parke, Leslie Bradley and Peter Haddon, plus records chosen by Leslie Perowne. Began 12 April 1939.

Hopalong Cassidy

Clarence E. Mulford's fictitious cowboy came to RADIO LUXEMBOURG from 3 April 1953, played by William Boyd, the Hoppy of countless B-western films. Andy Clyde played comedy sidekick California, and Topper played himself. Sponsored by Spangles, 'Hoppy's Favourite Sweet'.

Horace

Baby of the family – HARRY HEMSLEY's radio family of 'Imaginary Children'. Introduced in the late thirties, Horace became an immediate favourite with his baby-gabble, only decipherable by little sister Winnie. He appeared in several children's books written and drawn by Hemsley, including *Horace at the BBC* (1947). A typical Horace line in a HEMSLEY's HOTEL script read: 'Oo doe casch she or a orschy asch agay, schnoschi sauscherplay aschoon toscher!' Translated by Winnie: 'You don't catch me on a horse's back again, it's not the sort of place you can doze on!'

Horace Hotplate

Mayor of the North Pole ('Hello, boys!') in *Up the Pole* (1947), played by venerable comedian, Claude Dampier. Later given to turning up in various roles: 'Ooh, you'll never guess!'

Horatio Hornblower

C.S. Forester's fictitious hero of many a naval encounter, Commodore Sir Horatio Hornblower RN, was played by Michael Redgrave in a series produced by HARRY ALAN TOWERS and adapted by Philo Higley. Elizabeth Kentish played Lady Barbara and the music was composed and conducted by Sidney Torch. First broadcast 4 November 1952.

Horlicks Picture House

Sixty-minute series from RADIO LUXEMBOURG, starting 4 April 1937. The first film star featured was Jessie Matthews, supported by Sidney Burchell, Miriam Ferris, Florence Oldham, Helen Raymond, Bert Yarlett, and Debroy Somers and his Band. Maurice Chevalier starred in the second show, followed by Richard Tauber. The compère was Harold Warrender. The 200th *Horlicks Hour* was broadcast on 4 September 1938, starring Charles Laughton, Gertrude Neisen, Oliver Wakefield, Rosalyn Boulter, 'and a dazzling parade of guest stars'. Compère was Edwin Styles. The programmes were recorded at the Scala Theatre, produced by Stanley Maxted and scripted by Irvin Ashkenazy.

Horlicks Tea Time Hour

Sponsored radio show beginning 9 November 1934 on RADIO LUXEMBOURG, featuring Debroy Somers and his Band playing 'Fifty Years of Song', Pat Hyde singing 'Soon', Harry Bentley singing 'I Never Had a Chance', Harry Robbins playing 'Twelfth Street Rag' on the xylophone, and Harry Bidgood playing 'Flapperette' on the piano. The first sponsored programme to run continuously for a year, the Birthday Show broadcast on 3 November 1935 included Sydney Howard, Will Fyffe, FLOTSAM AND JETSAM, Leslie Henson, Florence Desmond, Herman Finck, and Sydney Horler, the mystery novelist. The final show in the series was broadcast on 27 September 1936, when it was replaced by *Sea Time Hour*, a weekly 'cruise' starring Max Miller in his only radio series. *Tea Time Hour* returned on January 1937, retitled *Horlicks Picture House* on 4 April. Signature song:

> You will be healthy,
> Happy and wealthly.
> If you drink your Horlicks today. . . .

Kenneth **Horne**: Round and Beyond

Horne, Kenneth

Jovial, avuncular Sales Director of Triplex Safety Glass who became the jovial, avuncular hub around which many a comedy series revolved. First broadcast in ACK-ACK BEER-BEER, a service series, then joined with fellow Cambridge man RICHARD MURDOCH for a long run writing and performing MUCH-BINDING-IN-THE-MARSH, the RAF wing of MERRY-GO-ROUND. They were both serving officers, Horne the senior being a Wing Commander. As the bland, slightly dim AOC of Laughter Command he worked well with the witty Murdoch, and contributed catchphrases 'Not a word to Bessie' and 'I had the privilege of being shown over a large steelworks'. He also acted as the genial quiz-master of DOUBLE OR QUITS, which stood him in good stead for a later stint chairing TWENTY QUESTIONS. Two other classic comedy series were built around his beamish personality, BEYOND OUR KEN and ROUND THE HORNE, in both of which he remained the sane centre in a whirl of outrageous characters.

Hornerama

The KENNETH HORNE Documentary Feature, 'in which we take a closer look at people and events in the news', was a skit on television's *Panorama*, heard regularly in BEYOND OUR KEN (1958). Horne played the 'Richard Dimbleby' anchorman, and those regularly interviewed included RODNEY AND CHARLES (Williams and

Paddick), a camp couple; Felicity and Ambrose (Marsden and Paddick), an aged but devoted pair; the old geezer who always said 'Thirty Five years!' (Williams); the splashy Stanley Birkenshaw (Bill Pertwee); Ryffe Fobertson, a skit on the *Tonight* Scots commentator, Fyffe Robertson (Pertwee); pop star RIKKI LIVID (Paddick); FANNY HADDOCK (Marsden), the skit on television cook Fancy Cradock; and farmyard philosopher ARTHUR FALLOWFIELD (Williams), for whom the answer always lay in the soil.

Horner's Corners
Imaginary village in Canada, setting and title of a 1938 radio series starring duettists Al and Bob Harvey, with David Miller, Sydney Jerome, and the Village Band. Producer Ernest Longstaffe.

Hospital Mail Bag
Veteran compère CHRISTOPHER STONE introduced this record-request series from 7 June 1945, which included competition results from HERE'S WISHING YOU WELL AGAIN, and a General Knowledge Bee. Producer Audrey Cameron.

Hotel Majestic
Barbara Kelly starred as Sally O'Brien, public relations officer in a famous London Hotel, in this series of adventures which began on 3 October 1957 with 'The Missing Scientist'. Carl Bernard played Inspector Cosgrove and Jack Melford Mr Raud. Producer Tom Ronald.

The House Next Door
Comedy series built around the talents of CICELY COURTNEIDGE: 'The adventures of a family who might live next door to you.' Miss Courtneidge played Cis and Wilfred Babbage was hubby, George, with Brian Roper as their son, Michael. There was always room for a song by Cis: 'Hurdy Gurdy Joe' was the first, broadcast 25 April 1950, accompanied by Frank Cantell and the Revue Orchestra. Producer Tom Ronald; written by David Climie.

Household Hints
Series of six 15-minute comedy sketches starring Yorkshire comedian Sydney Howard,

burlesquing the popular type of broadcast talk. No. 1: 26 May 1936.

Housewives' Choice
'In Party Mood' was the title of the soon-to-be familiar signature tune selected for this daily record-request series – and it was compère George Elrick, the former drummer and comedy singer with HENRY HALL's BBC Dance Orchestra, who overlaid the only words the tune ever had: 'Dum-de-dum-de-dum . . . I'll be with you all again tomorrow morning . . .' The mainly male presenters were given two weeks each, and the first was Robert MacDermott, who opened the long-running

Housewives' Choice: George Elrick

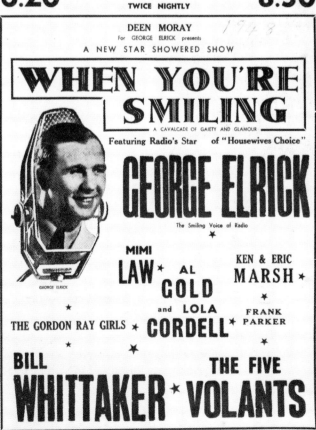

series on Monday morning, 4 March 1946. He was followed by Geoffrey Sumner, Bryan Michie, and many more. A special favourite of housewives was columnist and ex-actor, Godfrey Winn. Within two months the (unbilled) producer, Pat Osborne, was receiving 4000 postcard requests a week. The final programme was broadcast on 25 August 1967.

How

The 'How' series was a rare and sophisticated excursion into radio satire, broadcast intermittently from 1942. The basis was a burlesque of the radio documentary or feature programme, introduced by the deviser/writer, Stephen Potter, with the assistance of Joyce Grenfell and the How Repertory Company with Visiting Specialists. 'How to Blow Your Own Trumpet, including How Not To and How They Used To', was typical (19 April 1945). The Third Programme opened on 29 September 1946 with 'How To Listen' (including How Not To, How They Used To, and How You Want To). This was repeated on 15 November 1947 with the revision of 'How You Ought To'.

How About You?

Comedy with music from pop singer Dickie Valentine, impressionist Janet Brown, Welsh comedian Stan Stennett, and Harry Rabinowitz and the Revue Orchestra. Written by Dick Vosburgh and Brad Ashton; produced by John Hooper. Started 9 February 1960.

How Do You Do?

Unusual comedy series for Arthur Askey in which, in the company of his young daughter Anthea, he visited the home of a selected listener and family and gave a party! The first came from the Camberwell home of Mr and Mrs Miles on 20 January 1949. Mr Miles provided 'family and friends' and Arthur provided singer Barbara Sumner, Delmondi with his accordion, Jimmy Bailey to play the piano, and a Surprise Guest. John Ellison produced.

How to Manage Men

'Light-hearted programme in which four women of experience with vastly different views on how to manage men, give advice to women whose menfolk are sometimes difficult.' Pioneering feminist series featuring Frances

Day, Diana Decker, Charmian Innes and Vanessa Lee, with Jacqueline Mackenzie in the chair. The first male guest was Kenneth Horne on 31 July 1958, and the only other male involved was producer C.F. Meehan.

Howard, Michael

King of the Shaggy Dog story. Howard's laconic Yorkshire tones and dry wit first delighted audiences at the Windmill Theatre in 1942. Soon he was a regular in Music Hall and acquired several series of his own, The Michael Howard Show, For the Love of Mike, Here's Howard, and more. No quickfire gagcracker, Howard called his comedy akin to the old Court Jester: 'My jokes are just a commentary on life in general.'

MICHAEL HOWARD

Michael **Howard**: the 'shaggy dog' tale-teller

Howdy Folks

Satirical revue devised and produced by Leslie Bridgmont, who also appeared as 'The Burgomaster'. Starring Nan Kenway and Douglas Young in several roles, especially Mr Grice of the Startled Hare, to whom everything sounded 'Very tasty – very sweet!' Eric Barker first came to radio popularity as a liftman with the catchphrase 'Olive oil and tinkettytonk, eh, old man?', and as Lord Blockhead: 'Have you no sense of humour, Carstairs?' Others in the series, which started on 7 February 1940: Jacques Brown, Clarence Wright, Helen Clare, and the BBC Revue Chorus and

Orchestra. CYRIL FLETCHER replaced the enlisted Barker from 17 October, and Reginald Purdell replaced Fletcher from 28 November.

The series was revived from 19 January 1943 with Claude Hulbert as the replacement and Eva Beynon to sing. Signature tune:

Howdy folks, how do you do,
We bring a new revue to you,
With satire and humour
And gay syncopation
We're at your Home Service
Whatever your station . . .

Howdy Folks Again, the post-war revival (8 February 1946), teamed Kenway and Young with KENNETH HORNE.

Howerd, Frankie

Quaint comedian whose opening line, 'Now, er, ladies and gentle*men*' was first heard on 1 December 1946, and immediately became his catchphrase. The programme was VARIETY BANDBOX, and Frankie was such a success he was made resident comedian for a run of two-and-a-half years. Extraordinary when you learn that he was four times rejected as a CARROLL LEVIS Discovery and even turned down by *Stars In Battledress*! Frankie's natural nervousness became his trademark, as did other catchphrases: 'Titter ye not!', 'Just make meself comfy!', and, to the ever-present Madam Vera Roper at the piano, 'Poor old girl, she's past it!'. A contrived feud with veteran

Frankie **Howerd**: 'Ladies and gentle-men!'

FRANKIE
HOWERD

comedian DEREK ROY, inspired by the famous American radio feud between Jack Benny and Fred Allen, helped consolidate Frankie's success, leading to his first solo series, FINE GOINGS ON (1950). This included his later catchphrases, 'I was amazed!' and 'And the best of luck!'.

How's Your Father

TED RAY in a family situation comedy. Thora Hird played Mrs Bender, his housekeeper, Eleanor Summerfield his sister Ethel, and Robin Ray, Ted's real-life son, played Robin Ray his radio son. Annette André as Angela Bender completed the family circle, with support from Pat Coombes and Terence Alexander. After a try-out in *Star Parade* (1963), the series started on 10 April 1964. Written by Denis Goodwin, produced by Trafford Whitelock.

Hubert

Straight-man to black-face comedian NOSMO KING. Nosmo was Vernon Watson, and Hubert his son Jack. After his father's death, Jack did a solo act as an impressionist, billed as Jack 'Hubert' Watson.

Hugh Jampton

BBC commentator with a pun-name that fooled his employers (Huge Hampton . . . Hampton Wick . . . prick), played by PETER SELLERS in THE GOON SHOW (1952).

Hulbert, Claude and Trevor, Enid

Unfairly overshadowed by big brother Jack and his chin (Claude's receded), Claude was the better and more popular broadcaster. A classic stage 'silly ass' from 1920, Claude made his radio debut in an Actors' Benevolent Fund Concert on 27 February 1926. His success came in a series of teams formed for radio: THOSE FOUR CHAPS, The Two Pairs, the Hulbert Brothers, and the Family Party. Finally came his most successful teaming, with his wife Enid Trevor in delightful domestic backchat, first broadcast July 1928. Together they made many MUSIC HALL broadcasts, and co-starred in the first weekly domestic situation series, AT HOME WITH THE HULBERTS (Radio Normandy, 1937).

THE JACK HYLTON SONG BOOK

Containing Full Words
and Chorus Music of :

JACK'S BACK
AUF WIEDERSEHEN, MY DEAR
LOVE'S JUST A GAME TO YOU
WHEN THE GUARDS ARE ON PARADE
MARCHING ALONG TOGETHER
SONG OF THE BELLS
SILVER HAIR AND HEART OF GOLD
DANCE OF THE RAINDROPS
WHISTLING WALTZ
ON HER DOORSTEP LAST NIGHT
LET'S ALL SING LIKE THE BIRDIES
SING !
THE GIRL IN THE LITTLE
GREEN HAT
HYDE PARK CORNER
SITTIN' ON A FIVE-
BARRED GATE

This Book is presented FREE with WOMAN'S WORLD, week ending October 27th, 1934, and must not be sold separately

Claude **Hulbert**: with his brother Jack

Hulbert Farm

Musical comedy version of the farm life of Jack Hulbert and his wife, CICELY COURTNEIDGE. It featured Diana Morison, Hugh Morton, Sylvia Marriott, Ewart Scott, and the Variety Orchestra, conductor Charles Shadwell. Writers: Reginald Purdell, C. Denier Warren, Max Kester; producer Harry S. Pepper. Weekly from 14 September 1941.

Hulbert House

Comedy series starring the two Hulbert brothers, Jack and Claude: 'Jack, gay and debonaire, gets himself into various spots of bother, and Claude, in trying hard to follow Jack's example, lands them both in greater difficulties.' Supported by Mary O'Farrell, Jack Melford, Dick Francis, and the George Mitchell Choir with Stanley Black conducting the Dance Orchestra. Written by Jack Hulbert with Max Kester, and produced by Tom Ronald; first broadcast 2 March 1948.

Human Voice Orchestra

Novely act formed for broadcasting by the baritone Tom Burke: a male voice choir impersonating instruments of the orchestra.

Humphrey

Humphrey (Harold Berens) and Mother (Doris Nichols) were frightfully upper-crust and remained haughtily aloof despite weekly encounters with common-as-muck Max Wall in such series as HOOP-LA (1944) and OUR SHED (1946). 'I say, Mother, let's have tea!' cried Humphrey, only to have Max mock: 'With lashings of toast, simply oooo-zing with butter!'

The Hundred Best Tunes in the World

'Played and sung by the greatest artists on record', this popular musical series began on 22 November 1959, and is still running under the amended title of *Your Hundred Best Tunes*. The original presenter was Alan Keith. 'This programme is a challenge, Alan Keith knows what his hundred best are. They range from Bach to Rogers and Hammerstein. Do you agree with him? If not, which would you choose?'

Hylton, Jack

The Singing Mill Boy from Bolton who became one of the great broadcasting bandleaders and subsequently the impresario who reunited the Crazy Gang. With his Dance Band he first broadcast on 29 August 1924, and fronted many hotel bands in the twenties: the Piccadilly Hotel Band, the Kit-Cat Club Band, Kettner's Five, the Ambassadors Club Band. (In 1927 his wife Ennis made her radio debut as Mrs Jack Hylton and her Players, later Boy Friends.) In December 1929 alone his record sales totalled six million. Vocalists over the years included Ennis Parkes (Mrs H), Peggy Dell from Ireland, Dick Murphy, June Malo, and the Henderson Twins. His signature tune was known as 'Oh, Listen to the Band', correct title: 'The Soldiers in the Park'. Hylton also fronted a small jazz group called the Rhythmagicians, with future bandleaders JACK JACKSON (trumpet) and Chappie D'Amato (guitar).

Jack **Hylton**: Free song book in *Woman's World* (1934)

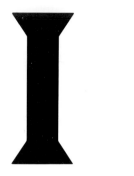

IBC

The International Broadcasting Company was formed by Captain Leonard Plugge in March 1930, to broadcast sponsored radio programmes transmitted to Britain from the Continent. The first 'Special Concert for the Benefit of British Listeners' was broadcast at 8 pm on Sunday 11 October 1931, from RADIO NORMANDY. All gramophone records, the first was 'Moonlight on the Colorado' by the Hawaiian Guitars. Then came Light Orchestral Music, Vaudeville (a record of Gracie Fields), and the IBC Dance Band (later renamed the IBCOLIANS). The second broadcast the same day at 10.40 pm from Radio Toulouse, was their first sponsored show, *The Vocalion Concert of Newly Released Broadcast Records*. The first programme from RADIO PARIS came on 29 November, Rex Palmer introducing a concert of HMV records. RADIO ROME arrived on 24 January 1932 with Mayfair Records presented by Ardath Cigarettes. The first IBC announcers were Commander H.V. McHardy RN, Major J.H.M. Staniforth, and Stephen Williams at Normandy; Alexander R. Wright at Rome; Thomas St A. Ronald and the first lady announcer, Faith Shipway, both at Paris. Programme details were published in the *Sunday Referee* from 11 October 1931, and the weekly *IBC Programme Sheet* from April 1933. By then there were Sunday broadcasts from Normandy (12 hours), Paris ($7\frac{1}{2}$ hours), Toulouse ($1\frac{1}{2}$ hours), Côte d'Azur (1 hour) and Ljubljana. Weekday broadcasts came only from Normandy ($6\frac{1}{2}$ hours a day). RADIO PICTORIAL carried programme information from 31 August 1934.

The headquarters of IBC was at 11 Hallam Street, Portland Place, an address cheekily close to the BBC. After a brief spell as RADIO INTERNATIONAL in the first months of World War II, the company discontinued operations.

IBC's production department was the UNIVERSAL PROGRAMME CO.

IBC Club

The club for dedicated listeners to the International Broadcasting Company's sponsored programmes from the Continent was first announced in the *Sunday Referee* on 12 June 1932. The motto was 'Better and Brighter Radio'. The following Sunday the newspaper announced that 50,000 membership applications had been received.

IBC Empire Transmission

Bob Danvers-Walker was the announcer for this short-wave half-hour, broadcast nightly from EAQ Aranjuez on 30 metres, 10,000 kcs. The programme of records on 2 September 1934 was suitably sponsored by Philco All-Wave Radios.

IBC Yankee Network

Proudly billing itself IBC of London and Radio City, New York, the 'Yankee Network' began a weekly broadcast on Tuesday 11 December 1934 at 12.30 am, via RADIO NORMANDY: 'The first of a series of transcription programmes direct from America.' The same morning at 4.15 am, 15 minutes of dance music was broadcast to England from WNAC in Boston and WEAN Providence. The last Yankee Network programmes were broadcast on 3 September 1935.

The IC Show

Offbeat in style and presentation – a five-day consecutive run of 15 minutes apiece – this one-man series starred Ivor Cutler of Y'Hup, OMP (Oblique Musical Philosopher) 'presenting the kind of thoughts, music and stories that have made him so bitterly misunderstood for years'. Producer John Bridges; daily from 6 January 1964.

I Flew With Bismarck

DICK BENTLEY's 'personal confessions with music' carried a different subtitle each week. The first (1 August 1956) was 'Or Little Women'. Bentley's barmy biography was illustrated by Kitty Bluett, Miriam Karlin, Georgia Brown, Graham Stark, and Harry

Rabinowitz and the Revue Orchestra. Written by David Climie; produced by Roy Speer.

I Hear Music
'A radio panorama featuring melodies of stage and screen' sung by Patricia Clark, Robert Earl, Janie Marden, Bryan Johnson, and the Masqueraders Choir, to music by the Variety Orchestra conducted by Paul Fenoulhet. ROY PLOMLEY hosted the series which began on 25 April 1962, produced by John Hooper.

I Want To Be an Actor
Hilarious audience participation series in which member of the studio audience auditioned for parts in a melodrama. Originally a segment of BAND WAGGON, it graduated to its own spot from 5 May 1939. Devised by Rion Voigt and presented in person by producer Vernon Harris.

I Was Kitchener's Treble
Comedy series inspired by the film *I Was Monty's Double* and built around Dick Bentley (a garrulous Australian) and Richard Wattis (a snobbish Englishman) in a running battle with Patricia Routledge, John Bluthal, and the zither girl Shirley Abicair. Additional music by Paul Fenoulhet and the Khartoum Ensemble; producer Richard Dingley. Commenced 18 April 1966.

The Ibcolians
The IBC Dance Band, who began broadcasting from RADIO NORMANDY on 11 October 1931 with 'I'm An Unemployed Sweetheart'. Changed name to The Ibcolians with their regular midnight broadcasts from 13 June 1932. By 18 November 1934 they were billed as Stanley Barnett and the Ibcolians playing at the Prince's Grill, Piccadilly. Their signature tune: 'The Bells of Normandy'.

If I Had the Chance
Popular spot in HI GANG! (1940) in which a famous guest star was given the chance to achieve a secret ambition. The star on 4 August 1940 was record-player CHRISTOPHER STONE. VIC OLIVER taught him to be a comedian and to sing 'Jeepers Creepers'. The signature tune for the series was 'Just One More Chance'.

Ignorance Is Bliss
The crazy answer to the Quiz Game craze:

> Where Ignorance is Bliss,
> Tis folly to be wise,
> It's better to be ignorant like me . . .

The trial production was transmitted on 1 April 1946, a good choice: 'Tonight of all nights four hand-picked halfwits propose to prove it! Introducing a band of experts who are anxious to get ahead because they think it would be nice to have one! Dr Nitwit and his Philmoronics provide tumult when the shouting dies!' Gordon Crier produced 'by arrangement with Maurice Winnick': it was adapted from a successful American radio series called *It Pays To Be Ignorant*.

The series proper began on 26 July with STEWART MACPHERSON the fast-talking Canadian sports commentator as question-master. Harold Berens was the cockney ignoramus ('What a geezer!'), Michael Moore the monocled upper-class twit ('I have a poem, Mr MacPherson!'), and Gladys Hay the fat lady ('Oh, he's nice, isn't he! What's your first name, ducks?') who provided the regular routine: 'Now we're back to Miss Hay again!' Sid Millward and his Nitwits 'provide the tumult when the shouting dies'. Sid Colin was the scriptwriter. Professor (later Doctor) Crock and his Crackpots replaced the Nitwits from 10 March 1947, founding a successful stage career, and yet another musical ensemble took over from 7 July 1947: the New Foulharmonic Orchestra conducted by Mynheer Hal Evans. When the series returned on 15 March 1948, 'musical indiscretions' were supplied by the Welsh double-act, Albert and Les Ward.

The new series beginning 23 November 1948 replaced the Wards with the Radio Revellers, and another new series beginning 6 May 1949 replaced the Revellers with the Soupstains. A major change occurred in the series starting 27 February 1950: MacPherson, returning to Canada, was replaced by Dublin sports commentator, Eamonn Andrews. The Dixielanders played the music, and the new writer was Ronnie Hanbury. The series commencing 19 August 1953 had another new question-master, Patrick Burns, a sports commentator from Canada. Another nitwit joined the team, Richard Gray as Harold Berens' brother from the audience. The music was back with Sid Millward's Nitwits and George Wadmore helped Hanbury on the scripts.

Ignorance Is Bliss: Sid Millward and his Nitwits

I'm Sorry I'll Read That Again

On 3 April 1964 took place the historic broad-cast of the first of what were described as 'Three Diversions round Cambridge Circus'. The stars of that West-End presentation of the *Cambridge Footlights* (broadcast 30 December 1963) were Tim Brooke-Taylor, Anthony Buffery, John Cleese, David Hatch, Jo Kendall, and Bill Oddie, and together they wrote and contrived this short series. It duly blossomed into the well-loved 'Wonder Show' (4 October 1965). Music for the trial three was by Burt Rhodes and his Quartet, but for the series proper by the Dave Lee Group. The programme, subtitled 'a new kind of laughing', starred a revamped cast: Tim, Graeme Garden, Hatch, Jo, Bill and Jean Hart, with scripts by Cleese, Tony Hendra, Graeme, Johnnie Mortimer, Brian Cooke, Hugh Woodhouse. Humphrey Barclay pro-duced and ANGUS PRUNE sponsored, to the sounds of the Angus Prune Tune. The third series, called 'a radio custard pie', started 28

March 1966, and the fourth on 3 October, introducing a serial, 'The Curse of the Flying Wombat'. This starred Tim Brooke-Taylor as the outrageous LADY CONSTANCE.

ISIRTA (like all successful series the show had reduced itself to unspeakable initials) was the fastest show since ITMA, the craziest show since the GOONS, and the last of the great radio series. It had the most uproarious 'cult' studio audience of any, applauding and howling throughout, booing and groaning at the terri-ble puns with just as much delight. The seventh series (12 January 1969) featured a new serial, 'Professor Prune and the Electric Time Trou-sers' (a skit on *Dr Who*) and Spot the Dog, whom the audience greeted with sighs of 'Aaah!'. The eighth series (15 February 1970) introduced Full Frontal Radio via Radio Prune. Then came a three-year gap before John 'Otto' Clees was able to announce 'It's *I'm Sorry I'll Read That Again* Again!' on 4 Novem-ber 1973. It was a revival, and a finale; the end of radio's Golden Age.

In All Directions

Billed as 'some diversions on a car journey' this milestone in radio comedy starred Peter Ustinov and Peter Jones who improvized their dialogue and sketches into a tape-recorder, whereupon their ramblings were edited into coherent comedy by FRANK MUIR and DENIS NORDEN. The thread was a search for COPTHORNE AVENUE, and on the way they invariably encountered two super-spivs, MAURICE AND DUDLEY GROSVENOR. Produced by Pat Dixon with music by Nat Temple and the Aeolian Players; first broadcast 26 September 1952. The second series was subtitled 'some diversions on a projected transatlantic expedition' and started on 12 May 1953. Rose Hill was added as the occasional female. The third series, 'some further diversions', began on 28 January 1955.

In Town Today

Saturday lunchtime series following on from IN TOWN TONIGHT. Nan Winton and Michael Smee interviewed the celebrities and personalities; Trafford Whitelock produced. Broadcast from 24 September 1960 to 18 December 1965.

In Town Tonight

The strident tones of 'The Knightsbridge March' by Eric Coates blended in with honking taxis and Mrs Baker, a Piccadilly flower-seller, hawking 'Violets, luvly sweet violets'. Then: *Stop!* – and young listeners everywhere longed to be in Piccadilly Circus to see how everything stopped for the BBC at 7.30 on Saturday nights. The stentorian voice of authority continued: 'Once again we silence the mighty roar of London's traffic to bring to the microphone some of the interesting people who are *In Town Tonight!*' LIONEL GAMLIN interviewed them, Michael Standing talked to the Man in the Street (live!) in 'Standing on the Corner', and the programme was edited and produced by C.F. (Mike) Meehan. The famous finale was the return of the stentorian tone to shout: 'Carry On London!' – and the traffic moved again.

The first programme was broadcast on Saturday 18 November 1933, described as 'the first of a series of topical supplements to the week's programmes'. Included were Bette Davis, film star; Annette Mills, composer; Austen Croom-Johnson and Paul England; Robert L. Ripley, cartoonist; George Posford, composer; Tessa Deane, singer; Gwyneth Lloyd, actress; The Stonemasons Dance Band; CHRISTOPHER STONE; and a remarkable dance band consisting of the conductors Howard Jacobs, CARROLL GIBBONS, HARRY ROY, Lew Stone, JACK JACKSON, Ray Noble, GERALDO, AMBROSE, HENRY HALL, and JACK HYLTON! Later presenters included Roy Rich (1947), GILBERT HARDING (1948), and John Ellison, whose 'On the Job' spot (1948) took him into the presenter's seat. Brian Johnston started his live 'LET'S GO SOMEWHERE' spot in 1949, when the last of the current season was a compilation of recorded highlights, including Gracie Fields, Virginia Mayo, Maurice Chevalier, and the night Danny Kaye wrecked the show! Programme no. 500 was broadcast on 26 November 1949 bringing back Annette Mills from programme no. 1, and interviewing Eric Coates, composer of the signature tune. The musical links for the series were written by Bob Farnon, and included 'Portrait of a Flirt', 'Journey Into Melody', 'A Star Is Born', and 'Jumping Bean'.

Programme no. 714 made history by being the first radio show to appear simultaneously on television: 3 April 1954. John Ellison kept his face discreetly turned. The series starting 3 October 1959 changed the format by bringing in Chris Howland and Nan Winton as co-presenters, and regular features 'Talk of the Town', 'Number One Dressing Room', 'Just Touched Down', etc. Show no. 1000 was broadcast on 6 August 1960, reviving 'Standing on the Corner' and 'Let's Go Somewhere' and bringing back BRYAN MICHIE, Joan Miller and Roy Rich. The last programme was broadcast on 17 September 1960, with Nan Winton and Antony Bilbow. There was a revived edition on 26 July 1975 to mark the closure of the BBC's Light Entertainment Department at Aeolian Hall.

In Your Garden

Sunday afternoon series starring MR MIDDLETON, the BBC gardener, who always opened his programme with a warm, slow 'Good afternoon'.

Ingersoll Time Signal

The sponsored time signal, broadcast at 5 pm on RADIO NORMANDY and at closedown on RADIO PARIS (1935). Ingersoll also sponsored the *Ingersoll Slumber Hour* ('Turn down the lights for a programme of sweet music'). The signature tune was 'Close Your Eyes'.

Inspector Brookes of Scotland Yard
Hero of a weekly detective serial sponsored by Milk of Magnesia and broadcast from RADIO LUXEMBOURG from Sunday 13 February 1938. The Inspector was played by G.H. Mulcaster, and his son Dick by Bertie Hare. Jane Welsh played Joan Anderson, girl reporter, and the first episode was entitled 'The Poison Handkerchief Murder': it took three weeks to unravel.

Inspector Cobbe
Radio detective created by Mileson Horton and played by Clifford Cobbe in the series *Inspector Cobbe Remembers*. Episode 1, 'The Oxshott Murder Case', was broadcast on 1 January 1945; producer Leslie Stokes.

Inspector Duncan
Radio detective created by Mileson Horton and played by Scots actor Duncan McIntyre. The first episode, 'The Case of the Staring Eyes', was broadcast on 19 July 1945 as a segment of *Hospital Mail Bag*. Produced by Audrey Cameron.

Inspector Hornleigh Investigates
Series of dramatic sketches in which Detective Inspector Horneleigh interrogated various witnesses to a crime. One of them made a fatal slip: which? 'Are you as astute as Inspector Hornleigh? asked RADIO TIMES. 'The mistake will not be disclosed until later in the programme.' Created by Hans W. Priwin and played by S.J. Warmington, with Ewart Scott as Sergeant Bingham. First broadcast on 31 May 1937 in MONDAY AT SEVEN, Hornleigh's popularity grew so fast that *Leader* magazine

Inspector Hornleigh: S.J. Warmington as the radio sleuth

ran stories from 7 August, John Longden starred in a stage play in 1938, and Gordon Harker starred in three Hornleigh films from 1939.

Inspector Scott
Deryck Guyler portrayed this Scotland Yard man in a series of problems in detection, *Inspector Scott Investigates*, which began on 5 July 1957 with 'The Theft of the Carter Diamonds'. Listeners were invited to spot the fatal error before John Scott solved the mystery. Scott was assisted by Sergeant Bingham (Brian Hayes), whose name is a clue to Scott's own mystery. Sergeant Bingham was assistant to a former radio crime-solver, INSPECTOR HORNLEIGH, and both detectives shared the same creator, although Hans W. Priwin had, by 1957, changed his name to John P. Wynn. Vernon Harris produced, and a second series started on 7 July 1958 with 'A Case of Kidnapping', by which time Scott was a favourite in ten countries, including Holland where he was known as Inspector Vlimscherp. Trafford Whitelock produced, and Scott's music was by Alan Paul. The third series started with 'The Case of the 500 Suspects' on 27 May 1959, and the fourth with 'The Case of the Five Pound Oranges' on 18 May 1960. The fifth series started on 8 March 1961 with 'Death Takes Over' and a new producer, Leslie Bridgmont. 'The Case of the Forged Fivers' began the sixth series on 29 October 1962, produced by Trafford Whitelock. The seventh series started on 22 September 1963 with 'The Case of the French Au Pair Girl'.

Inspector Squirt
Clarence Wright played this Civil Servant who said everything in duplicate: 'Oh, Mr Handley, I said Mr Handley. I've come to look at your factory, I said your factory.' IT'S THAT MAN AGAIN (1942).

Inspector Steele
Radio detective played by Carl Bernard in the series 'Extension 29', broadcast as a regular segment of the hospitals programme, HERE'S WISHING YOU WELL AGAIN from 14 September 1944. Helping to solve Steele's weekly crime problem, written by Charles Hatton, was Sergeant Regan, played by Harry Hutchinson.

Intrigue

Basil Rathbone introduced this 'new dramatic series of amazing adventure stories packed with spine-chilling thrills and tingling suspense'. One of the 'World's Greatest Mysteries' series on RADIO LUXEMBOURG from 7 April 1957. Producer HARRY ALAN TOWERS.

Introducing Anne

'Half an hour of words and music in the Anne Shelton manner' with the AMBROSE Players and presenter David Miller. Weekly from 4 October 1942. After a long hiatus, on 15 March 1948 came *Introducing Anne Again*. David Miller still presented, but the music now came from Frank Cantell and the Revue Orchestra. She returned, 'with a smile and a song', on 13 October 1948.

Irish Film Parade

Folk-singer Seamus Ennis presented this series designed by RADIO LUXEMBOURG for their listeners in Ireland. Soundtracks, songs and music from old and new M-G-M films, together with news of pictures currently on release in Eire. Produced by Desmond Carrington and Spencer Hale.

Irish Half-Hour

Originally designed as a series for Irish men and women in the Forces, this began musically on 15 November 1941 with Count John Mc-Cormack singing to the Revue Chorus and Orchestra conducted by Leslie Woodgate. The compère was L.A.G. Strong. For a while the musical show alternated with a comedy half-hour starring Jimmy O'Dea, and soon the affairs of the Fireman of Ballygobackwards, CARMEL CASSIDY the barmaid ('Dry up, McGinty'), and the most famous O'Dea creation of all, MRS MULLIGAN ('The Pride of the Coombe'), took over entirely. Joe Linnane and Harry O'Donovan (Fixer Finnegan) supported, with songs from Peggy Dell and the Clubmen, and the Strolling Vagabond, Cavan O'Connor. Ted Kavanagh scripted, bringing in ITMA stalwarts Sydney Keith and Horace Percival as two banjo-plucking buskers: 'Take no notice, sing on Sambo!' By 12 April 1943 the show was subtitled 'Monday at Mulligan's' with Linnane as Mickser and Fred O'Donovan as Shamus the Shanaghie. Producer Pat Hillyard.

The Iron Ox Programme

'Fifteen fascinating minutes of music and song' presented by Pharmacol Laboratories, makers of Iron Ox Brand Tablets. RADIO LUXEMBOURG, 1937.

It Goes to Show

Another weekly series for Nan KENWAY and Douglas YOUNG, featuring 'Doug's Diary' and 'Mr Pottle's Prattle', a cetenarian episode written by Robert Rutherford. Produced by Leslie Bridgmont; began 13 August 1942. The title was revived some years later (13 January 1948), still with Kenway and Young, but with the added attraction of another fruity-voiced comedian, Leslie Henson. Gene Crowley, a newish comedian, supported and soprano Helen Hill supplied the songs to Stanley Black and the Dance Orchestra.

It's a Deal

Spivvy Sid James starred in this comedy series, setting up in shady property business with suave Dennis Price. Robin Ray played their office boy, Steve, and June Whitfield their secretary, Susan Corkindale. Wallas Eaton was Benson the general manager. Script by Ronald Wolfe and Ronald Chesney; produced by Tom Ronald. Began 9 March 1961.

It's a Fair Cop

First radio series for Eric Sykes, hitherto a scriptwriter. He played a country policeman at Blossom Hill Station, under Sergeant Deryck Guyler and Superintendent Leonard Williams. The permanent prisoner in Cell No. 1 was Dick Emery, Hattie Jacques was Sykes' unlikely sister. Script by John Junkin and Terry Nation; produced by Herbert Smith. Started 22 May 1960.

It's a Great Life

Comedy series starring the fast-talking Bonar Colleano, then fast-rising as a film star. Bonar was cast as a small-part player with Deadwood Film Studios, who invariably lost out to a major star – in the first show, Dennis Price. Supporting players: Joe Linnane, Benny Lee, Miriam Karlin, with music by Stanley Black and the Dance Orchestra. Script by Sid Colin, producer George Inns; first broadcast 23 June 1948. The series returned on 29 May 1950 with

Benny Lee as the only comic over Bonar was backed up by Canadian Paul Carpenter, plus Daphne Anderson, Deryck Guyler and songs from Johnny Johnston and the Piccolinos. Charles Chilton produced; script by George Wadmore.

It's a Pleasure
The first morning comedy series on the BBC, and a seminal work, influencing the BERNARD BRADEN shows, TAKE IT FROM HERE, and many more 'new wave' comedy series in the post-war period. Produced by Pat Dixon, the series was designed as a showcase for Dick Dudley, a warm-voiced Yank who, as a Sergeant in the US Army, had hosted the popular DUFFLE BAG record shows on AFN. Dudley both wrote and presented the series, which began at 8.25 am on 8 August 1945. Singers Dorothy Carless and Benny Lee also played characters in the show, and announcer Norman Woolland made an admirable straightman. Music came from the Club Royal Orchestra, shortly to be replaced by Nat Temple and his Band. Temple, too, emerged as a considerable comedy character.

It's All Yours (1)
Singer Jane Carr's magazine series for the forces in Iceland, with Olive Groves, Anne Trevor, and the feature 'To Daddy With Love'. Producer Stephen Williams; from 30 May 1942. By 4 March 1944 it had become a programme for the forces in East Africa, introduced by Helen Clare. Music was by Jack Leon and his Orchestra with singers Gloria Kane and Rita Williams, and the feature was called 'Let's Join The Children'.

It's All Yours (2)
Popular Scottish comedy series starring Stanley Baxter and Jimmy Logan, with Willie Joss, Primrose Milligan, Grace McChlery, Margaret MacDonald, the Six in Accord, and the Scottish Variety Orchestra conducted by Kemlo Stephen. Catchphrases included Logan's 'If you want anything, ring me!', Joss's 'Arriverderci!', and Baxter's character Bella who said 'Thingmy-ringmy!'. Show no. 100 was broadcast on 9 November 1952.

It's Fine to be Young
First comedy series specifically designed for what the *Radio Times* cautiously called 'teenagers, Breezy Ralph Reader of Boy Scout *Gang Show* fame was in charge, with a revival of the pre-war favourites, the TWIZZLE SISTERS (Jack Beet and Norman Fellows). The rest of the cast echoed the show's youthful aims, however; Len and Bill Lowe, a double-act from the Palladium, Mary Naylor, a 17-year-old singer, BOB MONKHOUSE, a newly discovered radio comedian from *Showtime*, Douglas Barr, a 16-year-old film actor, and Carol Done, a 21-year-old repertory actress. Sidney Bright, pianist, directed an orchestra of under twenty-fives, and the Four Yeoman, ex-Scouts, sang. Script was by veteran Con West and newish talent, Eddie Maguire; Alick Hayes produced. Began 6 July 1948, as Ralph yelled 'Chicketty-Snitch!'.

It's Follies But It's Fun
CYRIL FLETCHER introduced personalities from the seaside summer shows in this series which started 15 July 1955. CHARLIE CHESTER was the guest star, with Joan Regan as the song star, Dick Emery the fun star, and veteran concert party comic LEONARD HENRY in an item called 'At the End of the Pier' by Patrick Mannock. Also taking part were the Peter Knight Singers with the Jackie Brown Sextet. Script was by Charles Hart and Bernard Botting; produced by Trafford Whitelock.

It's Great To Be Young
Zany comic from Liverpool Ken Dodd starred in this series which started on 2 October 1958 and made a national catchphrase of 'Where's me shirt?'. Peter Goodwright played everyone else except the Barry Sisters and Judith Chalmers. Alyn Ainsworth conducted the Northern Dance Orchestra, with Jimmy Leach at the electronic organ. Script was by Frank Roscoe and James Casey, who also produced. The second series (14 November 1960) brought in more supporting voices than Goodwright could supply: Leonard Williams, Karal Gardner, Jimmy Golden and the Littlewood Songsters. Eddie Braben was added to the writing strength. Features included 'A Journey to Doddyland' in which Uncle Ken read tales from the Doddybook, and Professor Dodd's Mysteries of History. Signature song: 'Oh Boy, It's Great to Be Young'.

It's My Opinion

Pioneering 'vox pop' series in which genial Irishman Joe Linnane invited members of the general public onto the platform to air their views 'for thirty not-so-serious minutes'. Devised and produced by Frederick Piffard; broadcast from 17 November 1946.

It's Only Me

Comedy series with 'the Many Voices of Peter Goodwright, as he presents his observations on life and invites you to "Meet the People" and "The Folks Next Door" in company with Paddy Edwards and Bryan Johnson'. Music from the Northern Variety Orchestra; script by Ronnie Taylor and Jack Bradley; produced by Geoff Lawrence. First broadcast 30 August 1960. The second series starting 16 April 1962 had a less-mundane format, with 'Peter's Playhouse' presenting his many voices in 'The Race Into Space, or, Any More for the Rocket?'. The other feature was 'The Goodwright Spotlight' on Air Travel. Roger Moffat was the announcer, Tommy Reilly blew his mouthorgan, Bernard Herrmann conducted the Northern Dance Orchestra, and Vince Powell wrote the script.

It's That Man Again (ITMA)

The most famous and popular radio comedy series ever, starring TOMMY HANDLEY, written by Ted Kavanagh and produced by Francis Worsley. Titled from the newspaper catchphrase coined to describe Adolf Hitler's latest outburst, it was first broadcast on 12 July 1939 with Handley as Mr Appleby in charge of RADIO FAKENBURG, a shipboard commercial broadcasting studio burlesquing Luxembourg but predicting *Radio Caroline*! Cecilia Eddy, a Canadian, played CILLY his silly secretary and

It's That Man Again: Molly Weir, Tommy Handley, Lind Joyce and Diana Morrison

Eric Eden was VLADIVOSTOOGE, a mad Russian inventor. Built like BAND WAGGON, the show had various features: 'Man Bites Dog', Sam Heppner's topsy-turvy interview, and 'Guess or No', a play-title charade conducted by LIONEL GAMLIN. Radio Fakenburg's motto was 'Defense de cracker!' and an early commercial was 'Mine's a Persico!'. Jack Harris and his Band played Michael North's famous signature tune:

It's that man again,
Yes that man again,
Yes sir, Tommy Handley is here.

The second series started on 19 September 1939, and with the wartime craze for initialese was soon known as *Itma*. Handley was now the Minister of Aggravation and Mysteries at the Office of Twirps and the programme was punctuated by the 'Itma door' as crazy characters came and went, each with their own catchphrase. JACK TRAIN played FARMER JOLLOP, FUSSPOT, and the greatest of all wartime characters, FUNF the Spy. MAURICE DENHAM was VODKIN and the *Itma* char, MRS TICKLE. Crooner SAM COSTA embarked on a comedy career as LEMUEL the office boy, and singing trio the CAVENDISH THREE also contributed with their – 'Well all right, well all right'. Tommy's own catchphrases included 'Wish I had as many shillings!' and 'Friday! Friday!'. Vera Lennox replaced secretary Cilly with Dotty. JACK HYLTON and his Band accompanied the first show, and when the series closed on 6 February 1940, 20 days later Hylton produced a stage version.

When the series finally returned to radio it was as *It's That Sand Again*. This 'seaside showdown' started on 20 June 1941 with Tommy as the Mayor (pronounced 'Mer') of Foaming-at-the-Mouth, assisted by his fast-taking Yankee henchman SAM SCRAM (Sydney Keith), CLAUDE AND CECIL the polite handymen (Jack Train and Horace Percival), the lugubrious DIVER (Percival), LEFTY the gangster (Train), and the snappy Salesman (Clarence Wright), and the saucy seaside postcard seller, ALI OOP (Percival). Kay Cavendish and Paula Green sang to CHARLIE SHADWELL and the Variety Orchestra. Although there were only six shows, the series set the entire *Itma* style, and it reverted to the original title on its return on 26 September 1941. The new funny foreigner was SIGNOR SOSO (Dino Galvani) but the real star of the series was MRS MOPP (Dorothy Summers) with her immortal 'Can I do yer now, sir?',

quite outshining even GEORGE GORGE (Fred Yule) and MR WHATSISNAME (Percival). This series included 'Tom Marches On', produced by FOGBOUND FILMS Incorporated in Glorious Khakicolor.

The next series (18 September 1942) introduced Jack Train's immortal creation, COLONEL CHINSTRAP ('I don't mind if I do!'). The series starting 2 April 1943 ended with the 100th show (5 August). This included newcomer Bill Stephens as COMICAL CHRIS, Fred Yule as Walter Wetwhite the sound effects man and Johann Bull, and Vera Lennox back as a Mayfair Lady. *Itma* returned on 7 October without stalwart Train, seriously ill. Jean Capra made her debut as POPPY POOPAH and the show was set in Tom Pan Alley, an old funfair in Brewery Lane. Soon, though, Handley became Squire of Much Fiddling. During the New Year three special armed service editions were given, including an historic one for the Navy at Scapa Flo. At the end of the series came a special, *Tom Marches Back* (12 June 1944). The next series (21 September) saw Jack Train restored, and with him the Colonel and the ancient MARK TIME. Diana Morrison signed on as Miss Hotchkiss, and VE-Day was celebrated with *V-Itma* on 10 May 1945, which would be repeated exactly ten years later.

The new post-war *Itma* started 20 September 1945 with a new setting, a Utopia called Tomtopia with Tommy as Governor, and a raft of new characters and catchphrases. Carleton Hobbs was MAJOR MUNDAY, an old oppo of the Colonel's; Mary O'Farrell was NURSE RIFF-RAFFERTY; Hugh Morton the irascible SAM FAIRFECHAN; Lind Joyce was BANJULAYO, daugher of chief BIFFA-BANGA (Fred Yule); Jean Capra was NAIEVE; and oldster Clarence Wright was there plus newster Michele de Lys. Handley was in Scotland for the start of the next series (26 September 1946), at Castle Weehoose meeting TATTIE MACKINTOSH (Molly Weir) and Joan Harben as the miserable MONA LOTT. Also new was Deryck Guyler as Dan Dungeon, and when the series returned to Tomtopia again, Guyler created Sir Percy Palaver and Hugh Morton was BASIL BACKWARDS. The new series starting 25 October 1947 began at Radiolympia. Hattie Jacques joined the cast as little SOPHIE TUCKSHOP, the greedy schoolgirl, and Guyler created his memorable Liverpudlian, FRISBY DYKE. The BBC Silver Jubilee Week edition of *Itma* (4

December 1947) was given before the Royal Family, and also simultaneously televised.

The tenth year of *Itma* began on 22 September 1948 and included show no. 300 (28 October) which featured a 'Hall of *Itma*'s Past'; Princess Margaret was in the audience. The last *Itma*, no. 310, was broadcast on 6 January 1949. Tommy Handley died three days later. In place of the advertised *Itma* no. 311 Sir William Haley, the BBC Director General, introduced a Memorial Programme 'Melodies and Memories of *Itma*', compiled by Ted Kavanagh.

Ivor Complaint

Shop steward in STAND EASY (1948) played by Arthur Haynes: 'I represent the Bruvverhood of Badly Browned-off Batter Mixers and Bakery Boys!' (He represented a different trade union every week.) Having won his way with Cheerful CHARLIE CHESTER, he departed with the regular farewell: 'Floggo, chum!'

Ivory and Ebony

Comical cross-talking 'coons' who replaced CUTHBERT AND PUSSYFOOT in THE KENTUCKY MINSTRELS after the demise of Scott and Whaley. Played by C. Denier Warren and Ike 'Yowsah' Hatch.

Ivory Castles

'This is Gibbs Archer calling all good defenders of Ivory Castles to their Daily Dental Drill': Gibbs Dentifrice adapted their famous advertising campaign to RADIO NORMANDY on 27 November 1938. Carl Bernard played the Archer, with Neville and Maureen Gates as the twins, Peter and Mary, and Campbell Copelin as the wicked Giant Decay. Raymond Newell sang the signature song, with a Chorus of Forest Beasties, Fairies, Elves, Imps and the Gibbs Fairy Band.

Ivory Castles: Gibbs' toothpaste programme

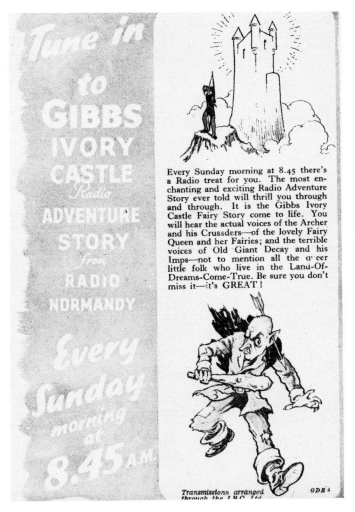

Every Sunday morning at 8.45 there's a Radio treat for you. The most enchanting and exciting Radio Adventure Story ever told will thrill you through and through. It is the Gibbs Ivory Castle Fairy Story come to life. You will hear the actual voices of the Archer and his Crusaders—of the lovely Fairy Queen and her Fairies; and the terrible voices of Old Giant Decay and his Imps—not to mention all the queer little folk who live in the Land-Of-Dreams-Come-True. Be sure you don't miss it—it's GREAT!

Tune in to GIBBS IVORY CASTLE Radio ADVENTURE STORY from RADIO NORMANDY Every Sunday morning at 8.45 AM

Transmissions arranged through the I.B.C. Ltd

J

J. Peasemould Gruntfuttock
Short-winded ancient and moving ruin of ROUND THE HORNE (1965), played at his wheeziest by Kenneth Williams.

J. Walter Thompson
Major advertising agency which drew on its American experience to set up a Radio Department for the production of sponsored programmes before the war. Within a year or so it had developed from two men and a secretary to a staff of 40 producing 44 programmes a week, amounting to 78 hours of air time. Ariel Studio in the basement of Bush House was the first pupose-built studio for commercial broadcasts, using the Philips-Miller system of recording on the soundtrack of 35mm cinema film. Producers included Stanley Maxted, who was in charge of the major productions, HORLICKS PICTURE HOUSE and RINSO RADIO REVUE. Guy Bolam was in charge of the Department, and the staff scriptwriters were American Irvin Ashkenazy and Robert Wilcoxon.

The Jack Benny Half Hour
The famous American radio series starring 'the meanest man in the world' was first broadcast under the above title on the Forces Programme on 15 May 1941. The cast included Mary Livingstone as Jack's long-suffering girlfriend, tenor Dennis Day, the brash bandleader Phil Harris with his orchestra, and genial announcer Don Wilson. Of course, the commercials were cut by the BBC.

The Jack Buchanan Programme
Star-studded Sunday-night series telling the adventures of a theatrical company travelling to Burma to entertain the troops. With the favourite West End star were Moore Marriott the gaffer from the Will Hay films, Vera Pearce the rotund pillar of farce, Jerry Desmonde, Ilene Sylva, and singers Jane Lee and the Modernaires, with Stanley Black and the Dance Orchestra. Written by Jack Davies Jr and Denis Waldock; produced by Henry Reed.

Jack Frost
Frequent broadcaster in the early children's programmes with his regular *Jack Frost's Wireless Yarns*, in which the technicalities of radio were given the whimsical treatment. The first, 'What Wavelength Is', was broadcast on 5 October 1923. Jack was really a Captain Frost.

The Jackdaws
Close-harmony singing group organized by Joe 'Miff' Ferrie: Ranny O'Brien, Fred Latham and Sid Colin. Originally with JACK JACKSON and his Band (1936), they became the regular singers on BAND WAGGON (1938) and changed their spelling to 'Jakdauz'.

Jack's Dive
JACK WARNER ran this radio roadhouse 'opened with money lent by his Auntie Sybil'. Claud Allister, the silly ass from Hollywood films, played the manager, and cabaret on the opening night (12 August 1943) was provided by JOYCE GRENFELL. Dancing was to Ivy Benson and her Girls Band, and the supporting cast included Doris Nichols and Vivienne Chatterton. Warner scripted with Rex Diamond; producer Leslie Bridgmont.

Jackson, Jack
'Public Wisecracker No. 1' was this breezy bandleader's billing when Oxydol sponsored him in a RADIO LUXEMBOURG series starting 1 January 1939. 'The newest, smartest, nuttiest, rhythmest programme you ever heard,' they claimed. It was Jack's first venture into comedy with music, a combination which would spin him into a post-war career as Britain's first radio disc-jockey in the zany Yankee style. Jack blew a cracked trumpet with AMBROSE, JACK PAYNE and JACK HYLTON before fronting his own band at the Dorchester Hotel in 1933. Soon his signature tune, 'Dancing in the Dark',

Jack **Jackson**: from band leader to disc-jockey

began to be heard on the radio. Vocalists included Al Bowlly, Denny Dennis, SAM COSTA, Alberta Hunter, Peggy Cochrane, Marjorie Stedeford, and Freddie Latham. His Oxydol series featured Helen Clare, Jack Cooper, Doris Hare, the Jackdaws, and comedy singer Jackie Hunter. The war broke up the band and Jack began to compère such radio series as *Band Call*, *Salute to Rhythm*, and *Band Parade*, finally finding his forte with RECORD ROUND-UP (BBC 1948; Luxembourg 1954). He was the first DJ to run his own home studio where he used the new tape-recording medium to mix his snippets of speech and music.

Jake and the Kid

BERNARD BRADEN played Jake, inhabitant of a small but typical town in Canada, with Roy Hunter as the Kid, and Bob Keston, Alan Herman, Tucker McGuire, Louis McLean, and Nat Temple and his Orchestra. Episode 1, 'Earn Money at Home', was broadcast 10 May 1957, produced by Pat Dixon and written by W.O. Mitchell.

Jamboree

'Here it is, the newest thing in radio entertainment. 120 minutes of exciting non-stop action-packed fare! Suspense! Surprise! Novelties! Guests! with contributions from all parts of the globe.' Two-hour Saturday night special on RADIO LUXEMBOURG, beginning 30 June 1956. Items included 'Teenage Jury', a panel game, 'Country and Western Music', and Alan Freed presenting the latest craze, 'Rock 'n' roll'. Also featured was Fabian of the Yard. By the time the series concluded on 18 April 1959, items included 'Fantastically Yours' in which Arthur Constance the Encyclopedia Man remembered amazing yarns, 'Hi There' presented by Gus Goodwin the Firecracker discovery of 'Teenage Jury', and 'Murder My Friend' with David Elias. Producer Jack Harris.

Jazz Club

'Greetings, jazz fans', producer Mark White's regular opening phrase, was first heard on Saturday 15 March 1947, when he presented the BBC's first weekly 'half-hour of music in the jazz idiom played by some of Britain's leading jazz instrumentalists, coming to you from the heart of London's West End'. Mark White, who produced, was billed the Club's President,

Billy Munn as Club Secretary, and Harry Parry was 'your host'. By the first anniversary programme, JACK JACKSON had come in as introducer of 'small band jazz and swing by Harry Parry and his Sextet'. At the 18-month milestone, the most featured musician was Freddy Gardner, with 14 appearances on clarinet, alto, tenor and bass saxophones. The 350 tunes played in that period ranged from 'Smokey Mokes', an 1890 cakewalk, to 'Oo-bop-she-bam', the 1948 be-bop hit.

Jennifer

Little girl regularly encountered by TED RAY in RAY's A LAUGH (1949). 'Why, it's a little girl! What's your name?' Back would come a shy giggle: 'Hee-hee-hee! Jenni-ferrr!' The big studio laugh was caused, unknown to listeners, by six-foot-something Bob Pearson, who played the part!

Jennings

Lively, 12-year old schoolboy created by schoolmaster Anthony Buckeridge in his series of plays, *Jennings at School*, first broadcast 16 October 1948 on CHILDREN's HOUR. Episode 1, 'Jennings Loses the Papers', featured David Page in the title role, with Louis Somerville as his best pal, Darbishire. Wilfred Babbage played form-master Mr Wilkins ('Old Wilkie') and Geofrrey Wincott Mr Carter. The school was Linbury Court, Jennings' initials J.C.T., and the producer David Davis. The plays were so popular that they were promoted to adult listening time, 7.30 pm, from 28 September 1954, a unique compliment. The adult actors remained, but Jennings and Darbishire were played by Glyn Dearman and Henry Searle.

The Jewel and Warriss Show

Jimmy and Ben starred in this series supported by Peter Butterworth, Jack Watson, Graham Stark and Barbara Young. Script by Sid Green and Dick Hills; produced by Tom Ronald; weekly from 26 November 1958.

The Jewel and Warris Showboat of the Air

The post-war variation of the wartime series NAVY MIXTURE, which began on 27 July 1946 billed as 'an entertainment designed for the Royal Navy', but obviously designed as a showcase series for the rising crosstalk comedians, Jimmy Jewel and Ben Warriss. Henry Lytton supported as Rappaport the Butler, with singer Benny Lee doubling as MacKay the Caretaker, Betty Paul as Olga, and music from the Radio Three, Charles Smart at the organ, and the BBC Revue Orchestra conducted by Frank Cantell. Written by Eddie Maguire and produced by George Inns.

Jim Spriggs

Minor character in many a GOON SHOW, played by Spike Milligan in musical mood. His greeting was 'Hullo Jim – hullo Jeeem!', this last being perhaps an octave higher. No relation to Little Jim, although he had a brother Adolphus.

Jimmy and Ben

Jimmy was Jewel and Ben was Warriss in this series of comedy thrillers written by Ronnie Hanbury. The first, 'Corn in Egypt', started on 3 November 1950, followed by 'Up and Atom' on 15 December. The comedians were supported by Professor Leon Cortez, Harold Berens, Miriam Karlin. Eric Phillips and Stephen Jack, with the Variety Orchestra conducted by Rae Jenkins. Produced by George Inns.

The Jimmy Durante Programme

The long-nosed American comedian, called 'Schnozzle' by his pals, starred in *Comedy Caravan*, a sponsored series rebroadcast by the BBC (without the commercials) from 13 October 1944. Jimmy's straight-man was Garry Moore and his singer Georgia Gibbs; his characteristic music was provided by Roy Bargy and his Orchestra. His sign-off was 'Good night Mrs Calabash, wherever you are!'

Jock

John 'Jock' Anderson was the stalwart Scots satellite of DICK BARTON (1946). Played by Glaswegian Alex McCrindle.

Johann Bull

Hearty Hun played by Fred Yule in IT'S THAT MAN AGAIN (1942): 'Chust for a liddle choke!'

John Dark

'Adventures in the thrilling career of the man who has a grudge against criminals'. This daily serial, on RADIO LUXEMBOURG from 2 February 1956, was written by Edward J. Mason and John Kier Cross, but the man who played John Dark remains a mystery.

John Quixote

Situation comedy series for WILFRED PICKLES, resting from HAVE A GO, in which he played 'a newly-made and somewhat surprised millionaire' returning to his home in triumph. *The Adventures of John Quixote* began on 25 July 1947, with Antony Holles as Alexander Montgomery Smith, John's 'Sancho Panza'. Written by Cyril Campion and produced by Jacques Brown.

Johnny Canuck's Revue

Variety series presented by members of the Canadian Army and Air Force, with music by Sergeant Stan Shedden and the Canucks, songs by Private Bill Smith, LAC Ted Hockridge and Private Norman Harper, and comedy from Private Wally Brennan. Master of Ceremonies was Gerry Wilmot, producer Jack Kannawin. The series commenced 14 February 1943. By the time of the second series, which began 4 March 1944, Bill Smith was a Corporal and so was Ted Hockridge. There was also a talent contest and a 'Miniature Quiz'.

Johnny Washington

Transatlantic detective created by Francis Durbridge and played by Bernard Braden in *Johnny Washington Esquire*. The first of these 'adventures of a Gentleman of Leisure' was broadcast on 12 August 1949, and entitled 'The Perfect Alibi'. David Kossoff played batman Harry, and Ivan Samson was Inspector Marlow.

Jollyollyday

Summer series of Northern-based comedies starring Albert Modley as Oswald Twistle, Bill Stephens and Marion Dawson and his Mum and Dad, Gwen Lewis, and guest stars Charles Penrose ('The Laughing Policeman'), G.H. Elliott ('The Chocolate Coloured Coon'), and Hetty King. Script by Arthur Mertz, producer Ernest Longstaffe; weekly from 5 July 1942.

Journey Into Space: book of the series (1954)

man, Charles Chilton. 'A tale of the future', it opened in 1965 (on 21 September 1953). Pilot of space-ship 'Luna' was Jet Morgan (Andrew Faulds), accompanied by the Australian designer Stephen 'Mitch' Mitchell (Don Sharp), Lemmy Barnet the cockney radio operator (David Kossoff), and 'Doc' Matthews (Guy Kingsley Poynter). The eerie music was composed and conducted by Van Phillips. The second serial, *The Red Planet*, which took the space explorers to Mars, began on 6 August 1954 and was set in 1971. Bruce Beeby played Mitch, and the echoing announcer was David Jacobs. The third serial, *The World in Peril*, started on 26 September 1955, with Alfie Bass as Lemmy, and Don Sharp back as Mitch. A new production of the original serial *Operation Luna* began on 26 May 1958 with the 'new Lemmy', Alfie Bass, and David Williams as Mitch.

Julia Heron

'Presenting Miss Heron' was the opening episode of *The Adventures of Julia*, a series starring Joy Shelton as Peter Cheyney's lady detective. She was supported by ROY PLOMLEY, Charles Vazey, and Edgar Norfolk who played John Forrester. Commenced 2 August 1945.

Julian and Sandy

Ex-chorus boys, part-time domestics during rest periods, and game for any trendy experience such as the Bona Caterers of Carnaby Street. 'Hello, I'm Julian and this is my friend, Sandy' was how Hugh Paddick introduced himself and KENNETH WILLIAMS to KENNETH HORNE in ROUND THE HORNE (1965), although they were on the more intimate terms of 'Jule' and 'Sand' to one another. They lived in Chelsea with their friend Gordon (Bill Pertwee), a gay gentlemen's gentleman. The characters took their names from Julian Slade and Sandy Wilson.

Just a Minute

Revamped version of ONE MINUTE PLEASE chaired by Nicholas Parsons. Quick-talking personalities must talk for one minute on a surprise topic without hesitation, repetition or deviation. Participants on the first programme (22 December 1967) were Beryl Reid, Derek Nimmo, Clement Freud and Wilma Ewert, but

Journey Into Space

The first truly successful science-fiction serial on radio, written and produced, somewhat surprisingly, by the RIDERS OF THE RANGE later KENNETH WILLIAMS came and virtually took over the show! The first producer was David Hatch; signature tune 'The Minute Waltz' (of course). The show continues as popular as ever.

Just As You Please

Scottish comedy series continuing the teaming of Jimmy Logan and Stanley Baxter begun in IT'S ALL YOURS. Willie Joss also carried over, supported by Madeleine Christie, Sheila Prentice, Betty Pringle, with the Harlequins and the Scottish Variety Orchestra conducted by Kemlo Stephen. Script by John Law, Bill Craig and Mary Mitchell; produced by Eddie Fraser (29 September 1953).

Just Fancy

Soft-pedalled series written by and starring ERIC BARKER who, tired of cracking gags at WATERLOGGED SPA, sought a subtler form of comedy that needed no studio audience. Broadcast fortnightly from 11 January 1951, with Pearl Hackney (Mrs Barker), Desmond Walter-Ellis as Godfrey Clympyng the OB commentator, Patricia Gilbert and John Warrington. Barker and Deryck Guyler created their most-endearing characters as the Two OLD GENTLEMEN, residents of the Cranbourne Towers Hotel, who claimed that it was only by listening to the other fellow, that you get the other fellow's point of view. Charles Maxwell produced. The second series, from 17 April 1952, brought in John Stevens and Freda Bamford and added Elton Hayes 'who sang to a small guitar'. Voices who came and went through the long run included Daphne Anderson, Peter Hawkins, Charlotte Mitchell, Kenneth Connor, Ruth Porcher, and Denise Bryer. Old gents apart, the other regular spot was centred around the romances and jealousies of the LILLIAN FORSDYKE TRIO. The ninth series, which included show no. 100 broadcast 15 December 1961, introduced Mrs Tombs (Hackney) and Mr Thorp (Connor), of the Little Tessingley telephone exchange.

Just Kidd-ing

'Cut-throat show for the piratically minded, broadcast from the Good Shippe Catastrophe' with BOBBIE COMBER as the Chief Cutthroat; Bennett and Williams as the Bottle-washers; Joan Young as the Cook; Helen Hill in the Halyards; Trefor Jones the Joiner; and the Capture of the Week (Jeanne de Casalis in the first show, broadcast 23 September 1941). Also sailing were Sandy Macpherson at the Theatre Organ, Billy Ternent and the Dance Orchestra and 800 Members of the Brotherhood of Boathooks. Produced and written by Loftus Wigram; navigated by Tom Ronald.

Just Sydney

Rare radio series for Sydney Howard, the Yorkshire comedian. In the cast: Betty Warren, Fred Yule, Bill Stephens, Vera Lennox, Philip Wade and the BBC Revue Orchestra conducted by Mansel Thomas. Written by Tommy Thompson; produced by Francis Worsley, weekly from 3 December 1943.

Just William

Richmal Crompton's classic 'bad boy' stories from *Happy Mag*, adapted for broadcasting by the authoress in collaboration with Rex Diamond and producer Alick Hayes. John Clark was the original radio William Brown, with Gordon McLeod and Betty Bowden as his father and mother, Rosamund Barnes as sister Ethel, Tony Stockman as best pal Ginger, Charles Hawtrey as the Cockney nemesis, errand-boy Hubert Lane ('How's yer mother off for drippin'?'), and Olive Kirby as lisping Violet Elizabeth Bott ('I'll thcream and thcream until I'm thick!'). The standard opening ('Will-iam!' 'Alright mother, I'm coming!') was first heard on 30 October 1945. The delightful theme and incidental music were composed and conducted by Leighton Lucas. The second series commenced 20 September 1946, and John Clark made his farewell in an August Bank Holiday special in 1947. Julian Denham took over as William from 14 October 1947, with Maurice Rhodes as Hubert and Valerie Jene as Violet Elizabeth. The next series which started 20 July 1948 introduced yet another child-star in David Spenser, plus a totally new cast: Bruce Belfrage, ex-announcer, played Mr Brown, Enid Trevor (Mrs Claude Hulbert) was Mrs Brown, and Anthea Askey played Violet Elizabeth. The new producer was Audrey Cameron. TED RAY's son Andrew became William in the series commencing 4 October 1952, and his pal Ginger was credited to P. (for Patricia!) Hayes. Ruth Dunning was Mrs Brown and Patricia Fryer Violet Elizabeth.

Just William: Signature tune by Leighton Lucas

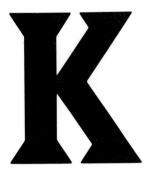

Kaleidoscope

Musical entertainment devised by the Lally Brothers (Arthur and Jimmy), featuring their orchestra and singers Jan Van Der Gucht, Monte Rey and the Langham Four. Commenced 7 July 1937.

Karswood Concert

Karswood Dog Powders sponsored this RADIO LUXEMBOURG series starring Stanley Holloway, who sang such suitable songs as 'Ahr Pincher' and 'Your Dog's Come Home Again'. Started 8 July 1934.

Keating's Calls

Keating's, the famous flea-powder, sponsored this RADIO LUXEMBOURG series, which opened with the appropriate signature tune, 'A-hunting We Will Go'! Brian Lawrance and his Melody Four starred, and on the first show (4 April 1937) played 'Crazy People' and 'Steamboat Bill'.

Keep It Dark

'Torch-light Revue' featuring Joyce Grenfell, Dick Francis, Ronnie Hill, Diana Morrison, Hugh Morton, and the Cavendish Three. Written by James Dyrenforth; producer David Porter.

Keep Smiling

Comedy series for Cheerful CHARLIE CHESTER and his Crazy Gang: Ken Morris, Len Marten, and Frederick Ferrari ('The Voice') from *Stand Easy*, plus Molly Weir, Deryck Guyler, Edna Fryer and the Mitchell Maids. Robert Busby conducted the Revue Orchestra and Leslie Bridgmont produced from Charlie's cheerful script. Began 3 January 1951.

Ken Dodd Show

'Love is Like a Violin' was the sig-tune for Doddy's first name series, which followed the formula of IT'S GREAT TO BE YOUNG. Judith Chalmers added charm to a cast including John Laurie, the crusty Scot from Invercockaleekie, Leonard Williams, Percy Edwards and his animal noises, and Ray Fell, plus Gerry and the Pacemakers and Malcolm Lockyer and the Revue Orchestra. Special feature in the first show (29 September 1963) was 'How to Make Yourself Invisible'. Script by Doddy and Eddie Braben; producer Bill Worsley. The second series (24 May 1964) replaced crusty Scot John Laurie with crusty Scot Duncan Macrae. Newcomers included Patricia Hayes, Wallas Eaton and Val Doonican. Doddy's Diddy Orchestra was introduced in the third series (11 April 1965), by which time Ken had well-established such characters as his Dowager Duchess, his Plummy Parson, and Clint, his Cockeyed Cowboy. The fourth series (12 June 1966) had music by Dave Berry and the Cruisers, while the fifth (18 December 1966) brought in Graham Stark. By now such spots as 'The World's Worst' were well established. 'Doddy Oddities' and 'The Knotty Ash Operatic Society' were featured in the 1967 series, and Professor Chuckabutty arrived in 1970. Later shows were billed as *Doddy's Daft Half Hour* (1972), *Doddy's Comic Cuts* (1973) and *Doddy's World of Whimsy* (1975). Doddy's closing song was 'Happiness' and his farewell cry, 'Tattie-bye!'

Ken Mackintosh Band Show

Major musical series for RADIO LUXEMBOURG starring Ken Mackintosh, his saxophone and his orchestra, with vocalists Patti Forbes, Kenny Bardell and Don Cameron, plus the Mackpies. 'Stay near your telephone and maybe you'll win a big prize.' Produced by Geoffrey Everitt for Lyon's Green Line Mints; first broadcast 26 September 1955.

Kentucky Minstrels

Long-running radio series based on the traditional 'Nigger Minstrel Shows' of an earlier era. The show centred on Mr Interlocutor, the compère and only 'white man', who kept the peace between the 'end men', Bones and Tambo. The leading comedy team was Scott

and Whaley who played 'Cuthbert and Pussy-foot' (they were genuine Negroes), and Ike 'Yowsah' Hatch (also a Negro) sang the jazzier numbers. Musical medleys came from the Kentucky Banjo Team (Joe Morley, Tarrant Bailey Jr, and Dick Pepper) and sentimental spirituals were sung by the Minstrels Choir (arranged by Doris Arnold). C. DENIER WARREN, who played Bones and delivered a regular Stump Speech, usually complaining about his wife, wrote the script, which was always described as 'Book written and remembered by C. Denier Warren'.

Kentucky Minstrels was first broadcast 6 January 1933 with Percy Parsons as Interlocutor. Later replacements: James Carew, Nosmo King, Sydney Burchall, Fred Yule. The original signature tune was 'Rastus On Parade'.

The 100th show was broadcast on 17 December 1948 and featured Jimmy Rich, Sydney Burchall, John Duncan, Alex Henderson, C. Denier Warren and Ike Hatch as 'Ivory and Ebony', Edric Connor, the Banjo Team, the Revue Orchestra and Male Voice Chorus conducted by Leslie Woodgate, and Charles Smart at the organ. As always, the producer was Harry S. Pepper.

Kenway and Young

Classic radio comedy couple, who created some memorable characters and catchphrases beginning with the food-conscious rustic MR GRICE ('Very tasty, very sweet') first heard in *Trolley Bus* in January 1938. Nan Kenway played Mrs Yatton, landlady of the Startled Hare, whose comments led to Grice's other phrase, 'Ar, I dunno mind, but it makes you think!' A long run of HOWDY FOLKS followed, which Douglas wrote with ERIC BARKER, creating the centenarian MR POTTLE. Douglas Young, a clever cartoonist, met Nan (Australian-born Nellie McCartney), a brilliant pianist, when they both appeared in a Weston-Super-Mare concert party called *Bubbles*. They married in 1933, formed their double act and by 1942 were so popular that they appeared in the RADIO COMMAND PERFORMANCE for Princess Elizabeth's birthday.

Kentucky Minstrels: songs and script for a 'do-it-yourself' show

Kerr, Bill

'I don't wanna worry yer . . .' and 'I've only got four minutes' were the catchphrases of this miserable, depressed Aussie. Bill (signature tune, 'The Road to Gundagai') first broadcast on VARIETY BANDBOX in 1948 and was quickly a resident comic with his woes from Wagga Wagga (pronounced Wogga Wogga). In 1952 he got his own weekly *Bill Kerr Show* on RADIO LUXEMBOURG, with Marshall Ward sponsoring. In the cast: Diana Coupland, Chris Webb, Pat Combes, Hector Stewart and the Malcolm Lockyer Quartet. Bill is best known now for his stooging in HANCOCK'S HALF HOUR.

Keyes, Clay

One of the world's worst comedians, this ex-juggler with the Crazy Gang found radio fame twice, first as half of a quickfire crosstalk act, HAVER AND LEE, in DANGER MEN AT WORK, then as the compère, writer, deviser, and genial host of THE OLD TOWN HALL, with its incredibly popular 'Penny On The Drum' quiz. His sister, Gladys Keyes, helped him in the writing and also played the part of Martha in the OLD EBENEZER sketches. Clay's own signature tune was 'Smarty', and although he never broadcast without his transatlantic accent, he was actually a Liverpudlian.

The Keynotes

Close-harmony group formed by Johnny Johnson (later the 'Jingle King') and famous as the singers on TAKE IT FROM HERE (Johnson composed the signature tune). The original group was Johnson, Irene King, Terry Devon and Alan Dean. Miss Devon married band leader Tito Burns, and Pearl Carr came in. Other radio series included GALA NIGHT AT THE RHUBARB ROOM (1949), by which time Cliff Adams had joined the group.

The Kiddies Quarter Hour

Post Toasties Corn Flakes sponsored a pioneering daily children's programme broadcast from RADIO LYONS commencing 8 March 1937. The compère was Uncle Chris (CHRISTOPHER STONE). The show moved to RADIO NORMANDY under the new title of *The Post Toasties Radio Corner*, and on 18 October 1937 introduced the serialized adventures of Tony and Teena the Harvey Twins.

King-Pins of Comedy

Weekly series of interviews by WILFRED PICK-LES commencing 4 September 1940 with Harry Korris of Arcadian Follies fame. Producer Richard North. Star of programme no. 100 was George Robey.

Klaxon Horne

Dean of Detectives played by jovial KENNETH HORNE in THE FORCES SHOW from 3 November 1954. Horne was assisted by his secretary Miss Nicklejoy (JOY NICHOLS) in his pursuit of Shishka Bab the Beautiful Spy (also Joy Nichols). Boy Roy (Derek of that ilk) also lent a hand, and Inspector Pillbody of the Yard (Bob Andrews) did his best. This mini-series was entitled 'Without a Clue'.

Knocking at the Door

Breezy Diana Decker introduced this 'Youth Show' which was first heard on 7 December 1945. Features included 'Magic Carpet' with impersonator PETER CAVANAGH, 'Fools Paradise' with Eric Eden, 'Swing Section' with organist Robin Richmond, and 'Hot Spot' with Billy 'Uke' Scott. Pat Frost, the young xylophonist, was the show's mascot with Anne Chadwick as the Girl Friend. Jimmy Bailey played piano, with songs from George Mitchell and his Royal Army Pay Corps Swing Choir. Production by Cecil Madden and Stephen Williams.

Kolynos Variety of Smiles

The famous toothpaste first brought CYRIL ('Dreamin' of Thee') FLETCHER to the microphone for a weekly series: RADIO LUXEMBOURG from 1936.

The Kraft Show

Sunday series starring BILLY COTTON and his Band, with singers Alan Breeze, Ellis Jackson, Peter Williams and Pat Doyle. Sponsored on RADIO LUXEMBOURG by Kraft Cheese (1936).

Kreema Koons

Sponsored by Needler's Kreema Chocolate ('Creamy, Velvety, Delicious!'), this concert party show began on RADIO LUXEMBOURG on 4 February 1938. LEONARD HENRY was the star, supported by Billy Thorburn, Helen Raymond, Curtis and Ames, and announcer Ronald Fletcher.

Kruschen Family Party on the Air

Mr Kruschen with his son Fred and daughter Anne were the stars of this RADIO LUXEMBOURG series which started on 13 January 1935 with the signature tune, 'I Want to Be Happy'. The required dose of Kruschen Salts was famous: just enough to cover a sixpence!

Kunz, Charlie

Popular pianist from Pennsylvania, where he led his own danceband at the age of 15. Kunz came to England in 1922 and by 1925 began an eight-year stint at the Chez Henri Club. From 1933 he broadcast regularly and recorded on Sterno with the Casani Club Orchestra, establishing his famous signature tune, 'Clap Hands, Here Comes Charlie'. His vocalists were Dawn Davis, Harry Bentley and George Barclay. Through the forties he recorded a regular monthly medley of current hits as a piano soloist for Decca, all churned out in his characteristic if mechanical style.

Charlie **Kunz**: 'Clap hands, here comes Charlie'

Ladies' Man

Rare radio serial starring Henry Ainley as Mark Antoine, 'glamorous film star', in love entanglements with Lady Moira (Lydia Sherwood), Anita (Bessie Love) and Anne (Belle Chrystal). Written by Dale Collins and produced by Hugh Stewart; weekly from 31 August 1942.

Ladies Please

This 'all-woman revue, about women, for women' was the 1950 follow-on from *Ladies' Night*, commencing 22 May. CICELY COURTNEIDGE was the guest star in a company that included Jeanne De Casalis, Doris Hare, Jane Barrett, Cecile Chevreau, Doris Rogers and Margaret Eaves (soprano). Even the producer was a woman, Audrey Cameron, with Diana Morgan writing the script. The only male was the victim of the feature spot, 'Men On Trial': KENNETH HORNE.

Lady Constance de Coverlet

Ageing dowager heroine of I'M SORRY I'LL READ THAT AGAIN (1966) played in finest Dame Edith Evans style by Tim Brooke-Taylor, and always greeted with tumultous audience applause at the sound of her signature tune, 'Happy Days Are Here Again'.

A Lancashire Lad in London

Short series of quarter-hour comedies starring George Formby and his wife, Beryl. Started 7 January 1938; produced by Howard Thomas.

Larger Than Life

'Series of comedy snapshots' starring TONY FAYNE (without his former partner David Evans), Joan Sims, Warren Mitchell, animal impressionist Percy Edwards, the Polka Dots and the Dennis Wilson Sextet. Writers included Johnnie Mortimer and Brian Cooke; producer John Simmonds. Started 8 October 1965.

Larry the Lamb

Leading light in TOYTOWN plays on CHILDREN'S HOUR, where he was played by UNCLE MAC (Derek McCulloch). 'Baa – I'm only a little lamb, sir' was one of his regular sayings. Larry starred in a comic strip in RADIO PICTORIAL (1936), and a different strip in *Okay Comics* (1938), but neither artist used the original wooden-toy design of Larry's creator, S.G. Hulme-Beaman.

Laugh and Grow Fit

The first daily exercise programme, starring Joe Murgatroyd ('The Lad fra' Yorkshire') and broadcast live at 7.45 am from RADIO NORMANDY, every weekday starting 12 July 1937. One sponsor was Freezone Corn Remover, while the piano accompaniment was provided by Poppet (Mrs Murgatroyd).

The Laugh Trail

'Follow the adventures of detectives Cuthbert and Pussyfoot, the human bloodhounds, on the scent from week to week.' Comedy series for Harry Scott and Eddie Whaley, stars of THE KENTUCKY MINSTRELS, written by Con West and produced by Harry S. Pepper, with special music by Hero de Rance. From 12 February 1941.

Laughter in Court

Max Wall played the Judge in this spontaneous comedy series in which couples from the studio audience were put on trial and questioned separately about one another. Frank Berry, a Canadian comedian, acted as Prosecuting Counsel, with Bob Danvers-Walker as Clerk of the Court. Digby Wolfe wrote the script; produced by Monty Bailey-Watson. RADIO LUXEMBOURG from 2 September 1959.

Laughter Incorporated

Eric Morecambe and Ernie Wise 'presided over a company of unlimited laughter-makers' in this series which started 21 July 1958. Peter Goodwright and Judith Chalmers were listed as 'other members of the board', with 'balance sheet' written by Ted Taylor and read by Roger Moffat. Music came from Alyn Ainsworth and the Northern Dance Orchestra, with Sheila Buxton and Rawicz and Landauer, the classical pianists. Produced by Eric Miller.

The Laughtermakers

'Light-hearted survey of comedy illustrated by the modern jesters themselves.' Gale Pedrick wrote this series of appreciations which began on 6 July 1956 with 'The Comic and the Customer' featuring MAURICE DENHAM, Ted Kavanagh, JACK TRAIN, Albert Whelan and others. Having set the scene, the series proceeded to deal with one star comedian each week: TED RAY, TONY HANCOCK, Al Read, ELSIE AND DORIS WATERS, ERIC BARKER, Leslie Henson, Harry Secombe, Beryl Reid, JIMMY EDWARDS, etc.

Law and Disorder

'Legal frolic' starring ERIC BARKER as Mr Trodd, managing clerk at Cheetham and Dabbs. Austin Trevor played Aubrey Cheetham, Terence Alexander was Stephen Cheetham, and Ambrosine Philpotts Angeline Cheetham. Written by Eric Barker and produced by Charles Maxwell. Started 11 October 1960.

Leading a Sheltered Life

'Mr 'Arris entertains a few friends at an alfresco party in his shelter, the 'Ole in the Road.' Series starring and written by C. DENIER WARREN, with Gwen Lewis, Arthur Chesney, Horace Percival, and John Rorke. Produced by Harry S. Pepper, it started 7 August 1940.

Leave It to Me

CICELY COURTNEIDGE starred as the proprietor, manager and principal shareholder of an assistance agency in this situation series. Thorley Walters helped out, with Norman Shelley, Fred Yule, Charles Farrell, Molly Lumley and Rosemary Lomax. Script by Sid Colin and David Climie; producer Audrey Cameron. Commenced 16 August 1952.

Leave It to the Boys

The Boys were a curious combination, comedian MICHAEL HOWARD and singer Monte Rey: 'Willing to undertake or overtake anything!' They were supported by child star Petula Clark, Gwen Lewis, Ann Lancaster, Peter Butterworth, and veteran Dick Francis, with music from the Dore Trio. Talbot Rothwell scripted and Eric Spear produced, commencing 21 November 1947.

The title returned with writer/performers BOB MONKHOUSE AND DENIS GOODWIN starring, supported by the characters they had created for an ARTHUR ASKEY series, MRS PURVIS and Nola (Irene Handl and Pat Coombs). Guests in their first show (13 November 1960) were Max Wall, Dick Bentley and June Whitfield, with songs from the Avons and Paul Fenoulhet and the Variety Orchestra. Producer Geoffrey Owen.

Leave Your Name and Number

This wryly humorous story of two Canadians forever trying to make the grade on the English stage worked because it was based on the real-life experiences of its stars and creators, BERNARD BRADEN and Barbara Kelly. Tried out in the *Show Parade* series on 30 May 1949, it burst into a full-blown series on 28 April 1950. With script by fellow Canadian Eric Nicol, the Bradens were supported by Miriam Karlin and Stephen Jack, with Stanley Black and the Dance Orchestra. Ian Messiter produced.

Lefty

Gangster buddy of SAM SCRAM in ITMA (1941), played by JACK TRAIN. He would let fly wildly with his tommy-gun (*ratatatatatatat!*) only to cry 'Missed 'im! It's me noives, I tell ya, it's me noives!'.

Legionnaires

'Soldats de la Légion – chantez!' was the command from Sergeant Lambkin (Jacques Brown), and the Legionnaires responded despite the dust of the desert! A series of six half-hours from October 1938 was followed by six more in July 1939. Baritone Lance Fairfax played Le Capitaine DuBois (replaced by baritone Fred Yule), with Peter Bernard as Tony Fratelli, Joe Lee as Pieter 'Dutchy' Vanderpump, Denis O'Neil as Mike O'Sullivan, and the deviser of the series, Sonny Miller, as Elmer P. 'Hank' Barton. 'La musique et la choeur de la Légion sous la direction due Chef du Musique, M. Percival

Mackey.' The second series starred JACK WARNER as Albert 'Smiler' Hawkins, a new recruit from London. It was Warner's first regular radio series.

Leisure at Eleven
Jeanne de Casalis starred as the fluff-brained MRS FEATHER in this RADIO NORMANDY series sponsored by Goblin Electric Cleaners (14 December 1937).

Leisure Hour
This 'radio diversion for the whole family informally introduced by Harold Warrender' began 4 October 1951. WILFRED PICKLES read one of his favourite poems, Alan Melville talked about 'A Book By The Fire', Sylvia Welling sang 'Leisure Serenade', John Cameron was 'The Wandering Minstrel', and the guests were GILLIE POTTER, Ethel Revnell and Florence Desmond. Alan Paul supplied incidental music with Max Jaffa and the Leisure Hour Players. There were three producers: Alfred Dunning, Trafford Whitelock and Becky Cocking. Frederick Allen took over as host for the second series (2 July 1952) which featured Jeanne de Casalis in 'The Diary of MRS FEATHER' and ROBB WILTON as 'Councillor Muddlecombe JP'. Colin Gordon read 'A Book in the Sun' and the new Wandering Minstrel was Alfred Orde. The third series (29 July 1953) featured veteran Rex Palmer as the informal introducer, Betty Marsden, and the book choice of Wilson Midgley.

Lemmy Caution
Peter Cheyney's famous fictional G-Man came to the FORCES PROGRAMME from 18 March 1940, in the person of Ben Wright. Peter Madden played Police Captain O'Hagen, Howard Marion Crawford was Sergeant O'Mara, Leo de Porkony was Carlo the Wop, and Robert Beatty Bugs Maloney. Produced by John Cheatle; the title of the series was *Lemmy Caution Calling*.

Lemuel
Adenoidal office boy at the Ministry of Aggravation and Mysteries in the Office of Twirps. Main cry: 'o.o.T.1.2.3. – there's a car outside!' Said his boss TOMMY HANDLEY, 'What a common boy!' This was the first comedy role played by SAM COSTA, hitherto a dance-band vocalist, in IT'S THAT MAN AGAIN (1939).

Let the People Sing
'Songs of the moment – songs of the past – songs of sentiment – songs with a smile – songs with a story – songs of the people' sung by LEONARD HENRY, Bertha Willmott, Helen Hill, the Four Aces, Robert Irwin, and the BBC Revue Chorus. Hugh Morton was the compère and Bennett and Williams played their phonofiddles on the first show, 1 April 1940. Written by Aubrey Danvers-Walker and produced by Tom Ronald.

Let's All Go Round to Norman Long's
And have a jolly good time with Sydney Jerome and his Orchestra, and NORMAN ('A Song, a Smile and a Piano') LONG. Weekly series on RADIO LUXEMBOURG sponsored from 1936 by Kruschen Salts.

Let's Face It
Ronnie Barker's first starring, series, broadcast from 8 January 1965. 'There's no substitute for Barker' claimed the write-up, supporting him with Rex Garner, Gwendolyn Watts, Eira Heath, Donald Spencer and the Burt Rhodes Group. Script by Alastair Foot and Eric Davidson; producer John Fawcett Wilson.

Let's Get Acquainted
Special series to further Anglo-American relations: 'Jimmy Dyrenforth introduces the British and American people to each other.' The first show on 26 June 1942 featured ROBB WILTON, Dorothy Carless, CARROLL GIBBONS and his Savoy Hotel Orpheans, and Helen Kirkpatrick of the *Chicago Daily News*, plus the American Ambassador, John G. Winant.

Let's Go Somewhere
Brian Johnston was the fearless commentator who 'went somewhere' live, and often dangerous, for the weekly magazine programme, IN TOWN TONIGHT, every Saturday from 1949. On 18 February 1955 the spot was promoted to a series in its own right: 'Brian Johnston is out and about with his live microphone, looking for laughter, excitement, and anything else he can find.'

Let's Have the Chorus
LIONEL GAMLIN was the Master of Ceremonies for this occasional musical game, which set two

bands against one another. The 3 March 1941 broadcast was a 'grand challenge match' between the Variety Orchestra conducted by Charles Shadwell, and Herman Darewski and his Band. Devised by Neil Munro and Ernest Dudley.

Let's Meet Again

VERA LYNN, the Sweetheart of the Forces, returned to radio with this song and comedy series which started on 19 May 1952. TONY FAYNE AND DAVID EVANS supplied the comedy with their synchronized impressions, and music came from the George Mitchell Swingsters, and Stanley Black and the Dance Orchestra. Written by Ronald Wolfe.

Let's Play the Mouth Organ

'Join in the fun and incidentally learn to play the mouth organ at Harmonica College, with Ronald Chesney as the master and Roy Rich as the willing pupil.' Forces Programme from 18 June 1940; producer C.F. Meehan.

Letter From America

Longest-running talk series in British radio, this weekly quarter-hour began, under the title *American Letter*, on 24 March 1946, and continues to this day. Alistair Cooke has written and read every one. In fact, the series has roots in an even earlier series, *American Commentary*, which Cooke broadcast on and off from October 1940, and the pre-war talks, *Mainly About Manhattan* (1938). In 1952 the series won the Peabody Award as the outstanding contribution of radio to international understanding.

Levis, Carroll

Genial Canadian radio announcer (CKWX Vancouver) who arrived in England in 1936 and mounted the first amateur talent contest on British radio, *Carroll Levis and His Discoveries* (8 September). Preliminary auditions held at cinemas around the country unearthed such performers as the Singing Apprentices from Lewisham, the Two Laundrymen from Peckham, the Dale Cousins (Olga, Zonie and Helen) – close-harmonists from Birmingham, and Bernard Flynn the Singing Gas Collector from Whitechapel. Amazingly popular, Levis's simple idea became a weekly Luxembourg

show from 17 October 1937. Listeners to his *Quaker Quarter Hour* voted the Crawford Brothers (singing 'Ten Tiny Toes') winners of the Grand Cash Prize (something the BBC could not offer). Carroll and his helpmeet, brother Cyril, starred in a film based on the series, *Discoveries*, in 1939. For his wartime series, THE HAPPY-GO-LUCKY HOUR (1940) and *Carroll Levis Carries On* (1941) the discoveries were boosted by a starry cast, and this became his formula for the lush *Carroll Levis Hour*, which opened on 18 July 1944 with his signature tune, 'Stardust'. Carroll had a ham-fisted crosstalk spot with chirpy Betty Paul and Johnny the cheeky Page Boy, and introduced James Etherington, tenor, and the regular features 'Just the Job', 'Radio Deceivers' and 'Piano Time'. Stanley Black and the Dance Orchestra were replaced by Debroy Somers and his Orchestra when the series was revamped as *The Carroll Levis Show* (5 June 1945). Maudie Edwards and Cliff Gordon did regular impressions.

The series starting 26 February 1946 included a spot called 'Star from the Services', which introduced, among others, Douglas CARDEW THE CAD Robinson. Avril Angers arrived as Levis's scatter-brained secretary, singing a complicated new song every week written by Robert Buckland. Buckland also played her idiotic admirer, Chunky Goon ('You make me so happy!'). The next series, 12 March 1948, was called *Carroll Levis Discoveries* but Carroll himself was not present. He had suffered a breakdown and brother Cyril took charge. Charmian Innis replaced Avril as the scatty lady, and her boyfriend was Dusty McGarry.

When *Carroll Levis and His Discoveries* returned on 25 April 1951, it was with the original title, producer (Tom Ronald), writer (Aubrey Danvers-Walker), and presenter, Carroll himself. There were no guest stars, just 13 new acts, from Alan Breen of Leicester to Rene Rhythm of Salford. There were four series before a last run of *The Carroll Levis Show* in 1954, and a concurrent series for Bird's Custard on RADIO LUXEMBOURG. His last radio series of all was a lunch-time *Carroll Levis Talent Show* from 9 July 1958. Levis was an uninspiring performer, making catchphrases out of clichés. He invariably opened with 'How

Carroll **Levis** and his Discoveries on stage

WINTER GARDENS

TELEPHONE - 8   **MORECAMBE**   CAR PARK

HERE HE IS   **6.15**   MONDAY, SEPT. 24th   **8.30**

TWICE NIGHTLY *1957*

★ **IN PERSON** ★

CARROLL LEVIS

BRITAIN'S STAR-MAKER

PRESENTING HIS STAR-STUDDED RADIO SHOW

FEATURING THE ALL WINNERS FROM **CARROLL LEVIS FAMOUS B.B.C. SERIES**

EVERY DISCOVERY A STAR OF TOMORROW!

THE FAMOUS STAR OF
THE SILVER SCREEN

CHRISTINE NORDEN

FILMLAND'S MOST
GLAMOROUS PERSONALITY

DIRECT FROM PARIS

TWO VENARDS

THE MOST DARING ACT IN THE WORLD

JOE BLACK

CRAZY BUT HARMLESS

2 ANGELLOS

BRITAIN'S YOUNGEST TRAPEZE ACT

DIRECT FROM THE
LONDON PALLADIUM

GALI GALI

"EASTERN MAGIC"

WITH CARROLL LEVIS' LATEST and GREATEST

B.B.C. DISCOVERIES

THE NEW AND UNKNOWN ARTISTS OF TODAY
ARE TRULY THE STARS OF TOMORROW

SPECIAL SATURDAY MATINEE at 2.30

THE WHOLE TWO HOURS SHOW COMPOSED OF LANCASHIRE DISCOVERIES

TRIBE BROS., Ltd. London and St. Albans

do you do, everybody, how *do* you *do*!', continued with 'So let's give him a big hand', and closed with 'The new and unknown artists of today are truly the stars of tomorrow'. A few of the hundreds were: George Meaton, John McHugh, Terry Devon and Barry Took.

Lewis the Goat

'Stinker' Murdoch's pet which he kept in the top flat of Broadcasting House (BAND WAGGON, 1938). 'What about the smell?' asked ARTHUR ASKEY. 'Oh Lewis won't mind that!' The animal was adopted by the RAF who named their World War II mascot A.C. Lewis.

Lidell, Alvar

Best-remembered of the wartime announcers for his 'Here is the news, and this is Alvar Lidell reading it'. Other famous announcements: the abdication of Edward VIII and the Prime Minister's declaration of war. The tallest BBC announcer (6'3"), he joined Birmingham in 1932, coming to London in 1934 and replacing FREDDIE GRISEWOOD as Deputy Chief Announcer in 1937. Appointed to the Third Programme in 1946, he was also a fine baritone and recorded 'I'll Walk Beside You' for HMV.

Lieutenant Keen

'I may not be brilliant but I'm mad keen!' was the catchphrase of this demobbed Lieutenant, who looked for work in MERRY-GO-ROUND (1948). Played, as fresh from Kenya, by Howard Marion Crawford.

Life Begins at Sixty

Situation comedy series ('A Boarding House Saga') written and remembered by, and starring, C. DENIER WARREN as Otis Harbottle ('ex-Gentleman's Gentleman'). Residents at No. 60 Acacia Drive included Colonel Trumper (Bobbie Comber), Miss Lapis the Dumb Blonde (Vera Lennox), Wynne Castleton (Wynne Ajello), Jerry Carew (Graham Payn), and Amelia the Maid (Wynifred Doran). Music was by John Reynders and his Orchestra with the Three in Harmony and the Three Musketeers. Producer Ernest Logstaffe; BBC National (1939).

A Life of Bliss

'Yet another episode in the life story of David Alexander Bliss', a bachelor gay when the term had no sinister implications, began on 29 July 1953 with David Tomlinson in the star role. Tomlinson returned to his film career, allowing George Cole to make the role his own from 9 September. This popular and chucklesome situation comedy quickly caught the listeners' fancy despite other changes in cast.

Originally Nora Swinburne and Esmond Knight played David's sister, Pamela, and husband Robert Batten. From 23 September Phyllis Calvert and James McKechnie took over as David's elder sister Phyllis and husband Christopher Medley. And on the return series, 27 August 1954, Diana Churchill and Colin Gordon came in as yet another sister, Ann, and her husband, Tony Fellows. David's girlfriends included Moira Lister as Shirley Summers, Louise Gainsborough as Jill, Lana Morris as Georgina Jay, and Noelle Middleton as Joy Joel. Regulars included Gladys Henson as Mrs Griffin the char, and Gladys Young and Ernest Jay as David's mother and father. There was also Psyche, 'a comparatively dumb friend' played by animal impressionist Percy Edwards. Godfrey Harrison wrote the scripts and Leslie Bridgmont produced.

The third series started on 19 October 1955 and the fourth on 28 May 1957, by which time Carleton Hobbs played Mr Bliss and girlfriend Penny Gay was Petula Clark. The next series began on Christmas Day 1958 with 'Christmas at Home', and the 100th show was broadcast on 9 March 1959, with Sheila Sweet as the regular girlfriend, Zoe Hunter. After a long interval a new series began on 2 November 1966 with 'The Homecoming'. Brenda Bruce was the new Ann, and Muriel Pavlow played girlfriend Tina. The final episode was broadcast on 3 March 1969; it was called 'The Modest Hero'.

Life With the Lyons

Highly successful situation comedy series starring Hollywood husband and wife, BEBE DANIELS AND BEN LYON, and their real-life children, Barbara and Richard. The support, like the misadventures, was fictional: Horace Percival as the vague Mr Wimple, Molly Weir as the Scots servant Aggie MacDonald, Doris Rogers as nosey neighbour Florrie Wainwright, Ian Sadler as her hen-pecked husband George, and Hugh Morton as Ben's boss, Mr Fox (an in-joke: Ben was an executive with 20th Century-Fox at the time!). Episode 1, 'Thirteen for

Life With the Lyons: Ben Lyon, Richard Lyon, Bebe Daniels Lyon, and Barbara Lyon

Dinner', was broadcast on 5 November 1950, produced by Tom Ronald, with incidental music written by Arthur Wilkinson. The script was by Bebe herself, Bob Block and Bill Harding.

The second series started on 27 September 1951 with 'Home Again', and the third series on 14 November 1952 with 'Home Again' – again! The fourth series (12 November 1953) introduced a new writer, Ray Sonin, who replaced Bill Harding. The fifth series (2 December 1954) opened with 'The Lyons in Hollywood', and the sixth (3 November 1955) with 'It's Great To Be Home'. This time Ronnie Hanbury joined the writing team, replacing Sonin, and the setup continued for the seventh series (11 November 1956) which started with 'Here Comes the Bride', and the eighth series (2 February 1958) which opened with 'Barbara's Dinner Party'.

There was a Christmas special on 25 December 1958, followed by the ninth series on 30 January 1959, starting with 'Voyage Home'. The tenth series started on 24 February 1960 with 'The Meddler', which introduced a new writer in Robert Hounsome. The 11th series started with 'People Who Live in Glass Houses have Happy Neighbours' on 20 January 1961, and the last episode of all was broadcast on 19 May 1961. It was called 'Roaming Scandals'.

Light Listening

Formerly *Midlands Magazine*, a monthly series beginning 14 April 1939. Features: 'In the Midlands Tonight'; the story of the Stratford Theatre; 'Another Tale' by John Brody; 'The Usual Gossip' by John Day; 'Letter from Abroad' (Paris); and 'How to Bake a Hedgehog'.

Late Night Extra

Friday-night/Saturday-morning broadcasting was introduced with this $3\frac{1}{2}$-hour show which started at 10.35 pm on 26 March 1965. Peter Haigh was anchor-man presenting music most of the way, and introducing Don Davis and his Telephone with the first phone-in conversations. Heather Jenner answered listeners' postcard questions on Marriage Bureaux, and Shaun Usher reviewed the night's television. Plus 'news as it happens, where it happens' and competitions with LP records as prizes. Producers John Simmonds and David Carter.

The Light Optimists

Revue designed to present new artists, new writers, new ideas. The new artists were Doreen Duke, Clive Dunn, Charlotte Mitchell, John Forde, Iris Villiers and (not very new) Clarence Wright. The new writers were David Climie, Laurie Wyman, Gordon Crier, Henrik Ege, George Wadmore, Denis Gifford and Tony Hawes. Jack Byfield was at the piano, and the orchestra was directed by Max Jaffa; produced by Michael North. First broadcast 23 July 1953.

Light Programme

The BBC's entertainment alternative to the HOME SERVICE replaced the FORCES' PROGRAMME on Sunday 29 July 1945, on 1500 metres (200 kcs Long wave) or 261.1 metres (1149 kcs Medium wave). The signature tune was 'Oranges and Lemons', taken over from the AEF PROGRAMME. This was followed by Big Ben chiming 9 o'clock, the News, and SANDY MACPHERSON at the Theatre Organ. The Light Programme was turned into Radio 2 on 30 September 1967.

Light Up the Night

Ninety-minute Galaxy of Stars compèred by Don Arrol. Comedy came from Irene Handl and Pat Coombs in their MRS PURVIS and Nola characters (the script was by Denis Goodwin), plus Graham Stark. Songs by Denis Lotis, Anita Harris, the Michael John Singers and Malcolm Lockyer conducting the Galaxy Orchestra. Produced by John Browell and Richard Willcox; first heard 20 March 1965.

Lightfinger and Cook

Local lawyers at Waterlogged Spa, featured in the post-war MERRY-GO-ROUND series (1946).

Lightfinger, played by Bill Stephens, was the forceful member of the firm, while Cook, played by JON PERTWEE, simply agreed with a 'Der-be-der, der-ber-der, that's right, yerse!'.

Lillian Forsdyke

Leader of the Lillian Forsdyke Trio (later Quartette) who played 'Palm Court' teatime music in the Tudor Restaurant of the Cranbourne Towers Hotel, Westbourn-on-Sea. She had a fancy for manager Mr Williams (Deryck Guyler) who had a fancy for cream horns. She was played by Pearl Hackney (assisted by husband ERIC BARKER as Mr Porter) in JUST FANCY (1951). Charlotte Mitchell played Heather, and the late addition was Kenneth Connor as Don Chambers.

Limelight

Jack Buchanan was the sophisticated compère of this series focussing on stars of the entertainment world. The first show, on 31 August 1951, presented Norman Wisdom, Lizbeth Webb, Robert Easton and the George Mitchell Glee Club, with the Revue Orchestra conducted by Robert Busby. John Watt introduced the stars and Glyn Jones produced.

Limelight on Rhythm

'Swung by John Collins' Rhythm Six and Dinah Miller the Personality Girl', a series on RADIO LUXEMBOURG from 18 April 1937, sponsored by Idris Lime Juice.

Listen My Children

'And you shall hear the strangest things' from Robert Beatty, Benny Lee, Jon Pertwee, Harry Secombe, Peter Watson, Patricia Hayes, Carol Carr, and Benny Hill. Musical illustrations were by Vic Lewis and his Orchestra with the Swinging Strings. This experimental series of 'comedy with a gently satirical note' (producer Pat Dixon's description), no identifiable characters, and no studio audience, caused no little controversy when it was aired weekly from 1 June 1948. Among the writers, FRANK MUIR AND DENIS NORDEN.

Listen With Mother: children's book

Listen with Mother

FAVOURITE STORIES FROM THE POPULAR RADIO PROGRAMM

Listen to This Space

First comedy series to be based on the week's news (research by Maxine Crosby) and written on the day of the broadcast (by Anthony Marriott and Alastair Foot). Nicholas Parsons acted the anchor-man, with Denise Bryer, Libby Morris, Bob Todd, and the Tony Osborne Sextet. John Bridges produced the first show on 12 April 1965. Personalities in the news appeared as guests: on 4 June 1965 they were Sir Learie Constantine (who read *Little Black Sambo*!) and SPIKE MILLIGAN.

Listen With Mother

Daily 15 minutes of simple songs and stories for the under-fives. Ann Driver set the nursery rhymes to music and they were sung rather pedestrianly by George Dixon and Eileen Browne. Julia Lang and Daphne Oxenford were the story-tellers: 'Are you sitting comfortably? Then I'll begin.' First broadcast at 1.45 pm on Monday 16 January 1950, produced by an Elizabeth Taylor. A sub-series started in 1954, *Listen On Saturday*, introduced by Franklin Engelmann. The final programme was broadcast on 10 September 1982 – the disappearance of *Listen With Mother* caused a national outcry.

Listeners' Corner

1939 spin-off from LUCKY DIP, presented and compèred by Bill MacLurg. 'Your songs, your anecdotes, your verses' edited by Adrian Thomas, with singers Lorna Stuart and Brian Lawrance.

Listening In

The first stage show based on broadcasting: 'A Musical Burlesque in Fifteen Radio Calls'. A 'forecast' of the revue was broadcast from 6 pm to 6.30 on 29 July 1922, announced by Mr Barnes. Will Hay starred as Professor Broadcaster, in a schoolroom scene and a duet with M'Leta Dolores, 'Boy and Girl'. Also in the company, Miss Clarice Clare and Mr Richard Neller, with Mr Herman Darewski, piano. A review of the show in *Broadcaster* magazine noted that 'a weird and wonderful aerial erected at the top of the stage occasionally emits sparks of fire at least two feet long, for no apparent reason other than to add a jazz touch to the musical selections'.

Little Jim

Small child whose sole purpose in life was to announce 'He's fallen in the wa-ter!' whenever somebody did – which was once a week in THE GOON SHOW (from 17 January 1957). Played by SPIKE MILLIGAN.

Littlewood's Concert

The Liverpudlian football pool was an early sponsor on RADIO LUXEMBOURG, presenting a comedy series from 12 August 1934. CLAUDE DAMPIER, the Professional Idiot, compèred, with CLAPHAM AND DWYER in 'Another Spot of Bother'; Dorothy Glover, and Rita Offenhanden. The signature tune was 'We're In The Money'.

The Lodger

Series of sketches starring CYRIL FLETCHER as Percy Parker, the adenoidally odd-voiced lodger in the dwelling of Mr and Mrs H. First broadcast in the mid-thirties in the radio versions of the seaside concert party, THE FOL-DE-ROLS, and revived in the 1945 series of THANKING YEW. The title came from Mr Parker's persistent catchphrase, 'Yerse, thanking yew!'. Betty Astell (Mrs Fletcher) played Mrs H, and Billy Russell her long-suffering husband.

Lodgers Taken In

'A Guest House Revue' starring Tony Heaton as Mrs Horrocks, with Winnie Collins, Malcolm Graeme, Doris Gamble, WILFRED PICKLES, and Alan Holgate's Swing Trio. Written by Mae Barber; producer Richard North. Weekly from 22 October 1940.

London Lights

Terry-Thomas starred in this big variety series which began on 28 September 1958. Also on hand: George Meaton, the noise-maker, Jimmy Lloyd, Chic Murray and Maidie, a quirky Scots act, Florian Zabach, violinist of 'Hot Canary' fame, Beryl Reid, Jackie Rae and the Adam Singers with Paul Fenoulhet and the Variety Orchestra. Written by Dick Vosburgh and Brad Ashton; produced by Bill Worsley.

Jack Watson introduced the second series which started 14 October 1959, introducing the stars (Ethel Revnell), the music (Teddy Johnson and Pearl Carr) and the discoveries

(Valda Aveling, harpsichord). Script by Gene Crowley; produced by Trafford Whitelock. The host of the third series (19 November 1961) was HUGHIE GREEN, who introduced Professor Stanley Unwin, Peter Goodwright, the Ray Ellington Quartet, and MONKHOUSE AND GOODWIN. Script by Jimmy Coghill and Bill Smith; produced by Bill Worsley. Green was retained for the fourth series (1 April 1962).

Ian Wallace took over the fifth series (23 September 1962) introducing 'The Wallace Collection' in which he sang with Stephanie Voss. Elaine Stritch, Jon Pertwee and Alfredo Campoli were the stars.

London Merry-Go-Round

'Programme of Happy Music from the Shows and Night Clubs with Teddy Randall and his Sensational London Band and the Singing, Smiling Man-About-Town.' RADIO LUXEM-BOURG from 2 October 1938, sponsored by Danderine.

London Mirror

Hour of excerpts from current London entertainments. The first show on 6 January 1962 included Diana Dors in cabaret at the Bal Tabarin, Thomas Round and the D'Oyley Carte Opera Company in *The Mikado* at the Savoy, Donald Sinden and Hugh Sinclair in *Guilty Party* at St Martin's, and the Michael John Singers with the Revue Orchestra conducted by Malcolm Lockyer. Wilfrid Thomas was the introducer and the producer Trafford Whitelock. This was a General Overseas Service production heard on the Light Programme.

London Radio Dance Band

The second regular broadcasting band in Britain, emanating from 2LO. The conductor was violinist Sidney Firman, and the personnel Bert Hargest, F.H. North, Jack Padbury, Jack Pearce, W.C. Whilden, H. Darke, C.H. Knapp and Pasquale Troise, who would later attain

London Radio Dance Band: directed by Sidney Firman

fame with his Mandoliers. The band first broadcast 9 February 1926. Their first record, 'Who Taught You This', was issued by Columbia (1926). They last broadcast 9 March 1928, when they were replaced by the BBC DANCE ORCHESTRA.

London Story

John Mills narrated these half-hour dramas broadcast on RADIO LUXEMBOURG from 5 May 1953. Sponsored by Dreft and Mirro; produced by HARRY ALAN TOWERS.

Long, Norman

Cheery, Chubby comedian, the first 'entertainer' to be 'made' by radio. His home-made songs at the piano were first heard via the 'cat's whisker' on 28 November 1922, and he was back 10 days later to make the first broadcast of conjuring: 'Norman Long will Mystify you with some Magical Card Tricks!.' The BBC changed his billing, 'A Song, a Smile and a Piano' to 'A Song, a Joke and a Piano' on the theory that you can't broadcast a smile! He was proud to have broadcast on the opening night of Savoy Hill, and taken part in the first broadcast ROYAL COMMAND PERFORMANCE (1927). A popular member of STANELLI'S STAG PARTY, where he was affectionately known as 'Old Teeth and Trousers', he recorded several radio burlesques: 'London and Daventry Calling' (1926), 'Luxembourg Calling' (1935) and a song about censorship, 'We Can't Let You Broadcast That' (1933).

Norman **Long**: 'a song, a smile, and a piano'

Look Who's Here

PETER SELLERS made an early solo appearance on the first broadcast of this series, 14 July 1949. Dennis Vance compèred, and also appearing were Sylvia Welling (soprano) and the WESTERN BROTHERS (Kenneth and George). John Hooper produced.

Looking for Trouble

Situation series for crosstalk comedians Jimmy Jewel and Ben Warriss with Betty Paul, their girlfriend from UP THE POLE. Also featuring John Blythe, wide boy in many a British B-picture, Michael Shepley, Jean Anderson and John Gabriel. Script by Len Fincham and Laurie Wyman; produced by Jacques Brown. First broadcast on 2 May 1955, with a second series starting 11 April 1956.

Lootenant Hern-Hern

Burlesque of the typical American Army Officer of many a Hollywood war epic, portrayed by PETER SELLERS in THE GOON SHOW (1958): 'Lootenant Hern-Hern of the Hern Hern, permission to speak, sir?' Apparently on demobilization he became Ed Hern of the Hern Hern, an American radio commentator.

Lord Blockhead

Head of MI5 as played (and written) by ERIC BARKER in HOWDY FOLKS (1940). His adventures invariably ended with being blown sky-high whilst proclaiming to his assistant, 'Have you no sense of humour, Carstairs?'. Sir Alastair Carstairs was played by Douglas Young, while the German menace was Nan Kenway. Their mini-series was entitled 'Wind-up in Whitehall'.

Lord Haw-Haw

Nickname given to the traitorous broadcaster William Joyce, whose sneering tones were heard in nightly propaganda programmes from Germany during World War II. The name was created by *Daily Express* columnist Jonah Barrington, and quickly caught on. The WESTERN BROTHERS recorded two comic songs, 'Lord Haw-Haw of Zeesen' and 'Lord Haw-Haw the Humbug of Hamburg' on Columbia. DB 1883 and DB 1898. Geoffrey Sumner played Haw-Haw in a series of 'Nasty News'

A COMPLETE BIOGRAPHY OF
LORD
HAW-HAW
OF
ZEESEN
BY
JONAH BARRINGTON
AND
FENWICK

Lord Haw-Haw: book jacket by Ian Fenwick
(published by Hutchinson)

Loss, Joe

Last of the great dance-band leaders still
wowing them today with his signature tune, 'In
The Mood'. He began broadcasting in 1933
with his Kit Cat Restaurant Band, making his
record debut simultaneously with 'Mary Rose',
sung by guitarist Jimmy Messini (Winner
5592). Joe's other vocalists included Chick
Henderson, Anne Lenner, Clem Stevens, Marjorie Kingsley, VERA LYNN. Post-war vocalists:
Elizabeth Batey, Pat Macormac, Rose
Brennan and Ross McManus.

Louisiana Hayride

'Jump on the wagon and join in the rural
rhythm, mountain music, rustic romance' with
Al and Bob Harvey, the Canadian singers,
George Moon and DICK BENTLEY (as Halfpint
and Silver), Joan Miller (Lucy), Cecilia Eddy
(Milly), Ike Hatch (Lavender), and the
Hayriders Band and Chorus conducted by
Billy Ternent. Devised by Harry S. Pepper;
dialogue by Max Kester; broadcast from 24
January 1940.

Love Scenes

Coty, the World Famous Parfumeurs, presented 'Love Scenes from your favourite Plays,
Films, Operas and Musical Comedies, played
for you by famous West End Actors and
Actresses', with Dudley Beaven at the Organ of
the Granada Cinema, Clapham. It was transmitted by RADIO NORMANDY from 9 July 1939,
starting with *Private Lives* by Noel Coward,
played by Lilian Harrison and Philip Friend.
Then came Cyril Butcher in *Autumn Crocus*. The
producer was Frank Lee.

items in *Pathe Gazette* newsreels (1939), and a
comic strip by John Jukes ran in *Radio Fun*
(1940).

Lord Waterlogged

Ex-dustman who rose to First Lord of the
Admiralty under the Socialist Government
(MERRY-GO-ROUND, 1947), and was made
Baron Waterlogged of Waterlogged Hall for
the peace-time continuation (WATERLOGGED
SPA, 1946). Never lost touch with his roots, as
can be judged by his genial greeting: ''Ullo
cock, how's yerself!' Heard about but unheard
were Lady Waterlogged, usually busy heating-
up the copper for the family bath, and daughter
the HONOURABLE PHOEB, pronounced 'Feeb'.
The Lord's farewell: 'Reservoir, old dear, and
Bob's yer flippin' uncle!' Played by Richard
Gray.

Luck's Way

Ethel REVNELL, the cockney comedienne,
starred in this series of domestic comedies, with
Wilfred Babbage as her father, Cecile
Chevreau as sister Ruby, Doris Rogers as sister-
in-law Ivy, and Clarice Clare as her neighbour,
Mrs Higginbottom. Hal Stead played the
lodger, and Ethel also played the part of Angela
the awful kid. First broadcast 26 July 1949;
producer Tom Ronald.

Lucky Couple

David Jacobs was the suave host who introduced each week's 'Lucky Couple' to the

LUXEMBOURG
NORMANDY : LYONS
PARIS : EIREANN
PROGRAMMES
Aug. 21 – Aug. 27

RADIO PICTORIAL, August 19, 1938. No. 240
Registered at the G.P.O. as a Newspaper

RADIO PICTORIAL
THE MAGAZINE FOR

3D.

EVERY
FRIDAY

★
SPECIAL
RADIOLYMPIA
NUMBER

ALL ABOUT THE
NEW SEASON'S
SETS AND
EXHIBITION
BROADCASTS

———

HARRY TATE'S
OWN STORY
First Long Instal-
ment by the King
of Radio Comedians

———

THE WEEK'S RADIO
NEWS, GOSSIP, HUMOUR
AND PICTURES

———

B.B.C.
PROGRAMME
GUIDE

Vera LYNN

Radio Luxembourg microphone, produced by Ian Messiter and sponsored by Fyffe's Bananas. Started 6 January 1955.

Lucky Dip

Very popular weekly magazine programme starting January 1939. It made stars of the new comedy team of George Moon and Dick Bentley, two Australians. Features included 'Enter Sexton Blake', a serial with George Curzon as the boys' paper detective; 'The Lucky Melody' (popular song of the week); 'Hands Across the Sea' (this song takes me home); 'Is That The Rule' (expert opinion on sporting topics from Captain Cuttle and his guests); 'Here You Are Then' (selection of melodies chosen by listeners); and 'Mr Medlar Lends a Hand'. Music from Rae Jenkins and his Lucky Dip Orchestra directed by Jack Clarke; produced and presented by William MacLurg. *Lucky Dip* ran 45 shows, ending 18 December 1939.

The Luscombes

West Country village family featured in the serial *At the Luscombes*, created by Denis Constanduros. It began in the West of England Home Service on 24 September 1948, with Michael Holloway as the storyteller; characters included Mr Luscombe (Lewis Gedge), Mrs Luscombe (Phyllis Smale), Ted (John Bradford), Doreen (Peggy Ryalls), Dot (Aileen Mills), Sid (Michael Watson), and June (Pat Roberts). The theme tune was 'Dicken o' Devon', and the producer was Brandon Acton-Bond. By 1964, over 1000 episodes later, Dad Luscombe was being played by William Robinson, June by Mary Hartley, and the storyteller was Robert Pim. Pop's favourite phrase was 'Cor, dash my buttons, Flo!', while she would ask Harry to 'stretch a long arm for the teapot!'.

Lux Radio Theatre

Sponsored by the popular soap, this Sunday show began on Radio Luxembourg in 1938, with Teddy Joyce and his Band and a regular feature, 'School for Stars'. From 13 November, West End maestro Charles B. Cochran took over the show, presenting Beatrice Lillie, Elsie Randolph, Eric Blore, Flanagan and Allen, Jessie Matthews, and others to the music of Eddie Carroll and the Carrolleers.

The Luxembourg Listener

Name of the silver-winged biplane that ferried recorded programmes from Croydon Airport to Radio Luxembourg before World War II.

Lynn, Vera

'Sweetheart of the Forces' of World War II, Vera first broadcast with Joe Loss and his Band, then joined Charlie Kunz, making her first record, 'Sailing Home With the Tide', in 1935. It was with Ambrose that she had her first big hit, 'The Little Boy That Santa Claus Forgot' (1937), a sentimental, slow song that set the style for her wartime career. Sincerely Yours, Vera Lynn began on 9 November 1941, endearing her to servicemen everywhere, especially overseas. After the war her style fell out of favour and she was for a time virtually dropped by the BBC. Her record sales continued to be great and she cheerfully switched to Radio Luxembourg for a long run of Vera Lynn Sings (1951).

Lyons' Red Label Show

Ken Mackintosh, his orchestra and singers starred in this Radio Luxembourg series which started on 5 April 1954. Also featured: Dolores Ventura at the piano, and 'Spot the Tune', a contest in which listeners could win a TV set or '12 exciting food parcels'.

Vera **Lynn**: 'Sweetheart of the Forces'

M

Sandy **Macpherson**: the BBC organist

M-G-M's Movie Magazine

Wilfrid Thomas compèred this glossy weekly series sponsored by the Hollywood studio with 'more stars than there are in heaven'. The first show (RADIO LUXEMBOURG, 2 July 1953) featured soundtrack excerpts from *Remains to be Seen* (Van Johnson and June Allyson) and *Belle of New York* (Fred Astaire, Vera-Ellen). Peter Noble brought the latest news from the studios.

The McFlannels

Glasgow family in situation comedy series written by Helen W. Pryde. Nell Ballantyne, Louise Foulds, John Morton, Mollie Weir and Gordon Jackson were the cast of the series *The McFlannels Rub Along*, which was included in the magazine programme *High Tea*; Scottish Regional, 1939. 'Helen W. Pryde has shown a deft touch in portraying in true-to-life words the sometimes pathetic but mostly humorous adventures of this vigorous family.' In 1941 came *The McFlannels in Wartime*. The producer was W. Farquharson Small.

Macpherson, Sandy

BBC staff organist from 1938, he succeeded REGINALD FOORT. He made his 6000th broadcast on 12 July 1952, still the soft-spoken Canadian 'Sandy' loved by millions who never knew his real names were Roderick Hallowell Macpherson. Originally he was the organist at the Empire Cinema, Leicester Square (1928). His many popular series included *Sandy's Half Hour*, *Twilight Hour*, *From My Postbag*, *At Your Request*, and the long-running, atmospheric series, CHAPEL IN THE VALLEY. In the first four weeks of World War II he was radio's mainstay, making 50 organ broadcasts. His biography, *Sandy Presents*, was published in 1950.

MacPherson, Stewart

Crack Canadian quick-talking commentator well remembered for his comedy career which included acting as question-master in TWENTY QUESTIONS and compèring the crazy quiz, IGNORANCE IS BLISS: his shouted 'Shud-dup!' became quite a catchphrase. Originally a sports commentator in Winnipeg, he came to London in 1936 to broadcast ice hockey. Soon he was covering other sports, especially boxing, and his running commentaries not only ran, they galloped. In 1941 he became a radio War Correspondent and described the Arnhem epic from the air. His secret: 'Talk as if you know what you're talking about and keep your ears sticking out like Japanese fans.' He was voted Voice of the Year for 1949 in the NATIONAL RADIO AWARDS.

Stewart **MacPherson**: commentator and comedian

Magazine Programmes

Running half-an-hour, 45 minutes, and now and then a full hour, Magazine Programmes were the first type of series, bringing a miscellany of regular features at the same time every week. The first was IN TOWN TONIGHT (1933), which in turn became a feature within the first true magazine series, SATURDAY MAGAZINE (1935). This included a detective serial among the factual items. Then came FREDDIE GRISEWOOD'S THE WORLD GOES BY (1936) and the most popular of them all, MONDAY AT SEVEN (1937) with its successors MONDAY NIGHT AT SEVEN (1938) and MONDAY NIGHT AT EIGHT (1939). This entertainment series, with its many popular characters (INSPECTOR HORNLEIGH, DR MORELLE, etc.), ran to 1948, when it was replaced the following year by the more contemporary MONDAY NIGHT AT HOME. Other magazine series were LUCKY DIP (1939) which ran 46 weeks on the trot, and the more specialized CRIME MAGAZINE (1940).

Mail Call

All-star American radio series arranged by the Special Service Division of the War Department in Washington for the entertainment of members of the United States Forces serving overseas. It was broadcast by the BBC from 21 January 1943 in a British edition edited by Norah Neale.

Major and Minor

Another of those double-acts formed specifically for radio. Major and Minor broadcast regularly from 1937, but it was an open secret that they were really Fred Yule and Alec McGill. They starred in a lunchtime series called MELODY AND MIRTH, sponsored by Huntley and Palmer ('They take the biscuit!') on RADIO LUXEMBOURG from 29 August 1937.

Major Bloodnok

Major Denis Bloodnok, Indian Army Rtd, MC (Military Coward) and Bar, made his explosive debut in THE GOON SHOW's predecessor, CRAZY PEOPLE (1951), thanks to PETER SELLERS and curry. He was granted the unusual privilege of his own signature tune which, together with explosions, heralded his opening remark: 'That's better!' Incompetent, ever absconding with the mess funds, the Major remained true to his first love, MINNIE BANNISTER, despite marriage and H. Crun.

Major Munday

Retired English Army officer who married his cook and remained 40 years behind the times. Crony of COLONEL CHINSTRAP in IT'S THAT MAN AGAIN (1945) and father of the naïve NAIEVE, he was played by Carleton Hobbs.

Make a Date

Polly Ward and Gene Gerrard (fading film stars both), made a date with each other, and with Home Service listeners, from 2 January 1945. Features in the series included 'Ukelele Memories', 'Unswinging the Jazz Classics', 'Wives of Famous Men', and 'New Songs for Old'. Produced by Eric Fawcett, with Stanley Black and the Dance Orchestra.

Make a Tape

The national craze for tape-recording inspired this RADIO LUXEMBOURG series, sponsored by Currys Radio and Cycle Shops. McDonald Hobley, the television announcer, compèred listeners' tapes, and Terry Miller, an agent, acted as judge. The first winner was Margaret Ferris of Glasgow singing 'Over the Rainbow' unaccompanied. Producer Monty Bailey-Watson; weekly from 15 January 1961.

Make and Mend

'Magazine programme devised by Peter Cresswell and presented by him to, for, about (and largely by personnel of) the Royal Navy.' Harry Bidgood and his Band punctuated the items, which included 'We Joined the Navy', 'Mrs Wilson's Weekly Letter from her Son, Stoker Tug Wilson', 'HMS Incredible's Ship's Concert', 'The Briny Trust replying to What's the Buzz', and Esmond Knight spinning a yarn. Weekly series beginning 23 December 1941.

Man About Town

Classy show built around ageing entertainer Jack Buchanan who 'entertains you with his friends, the stars of show business'. The first week's friends (10 June 1955) were Fred Emney, the fruity funnyman, Coral Browne, the husky actress, Alan Melville, the witty writer, and a supporting cast made up of

Vanessa Lee, songstress, Pat Coombs, David Jacobs, the Coronets, and Harry Rabinowitz and the Revue Orchestra. In addition, Hubert Gregg sang his own songs of London beginning with 'London In The Rain'. Written by Gale Pedrick; producer Roy Speer.

The Man in Black

'This is your story-teller, the Man in Black, bringing you another . . . APPOINTMENT WITH FEAR!' The sepulchral tones of Valentine Dyall generally sent more chills up wartime listeners' spines than the ensuing play. In 1949 the Man was awarded a series of his own, *The Man in Black*, 'famous tales of mystery and fear' arranged by John Kier Cross. The first, broadcast on 31 January, was 'Markheim' by Robert Louis Stevenson, produced by Martyn C. Webster.

The Man on the Set

Billed as 'the friend of the stars', this mystery man broadcast news of the studios over RADIO LYONS in *Film Time* (1937). He was Philip Slessor, later a popular announcer with VARIETY BANDBOX.

The Mansion of Melody

Mansion Polish sponsored this series of musical shows starring Harold Ramsay at the Organ, with songs from Dorothy Carless and Robert Irwin. Began on RADIO NORMANDY, 16 March 1939.

Many a Slip

Panel-game king Ian C. Messiter devised yet another long-term winner in this series in which ROY PLOMLEY rattled off yards of script riddled with mistakes which required spotting and correcting. The teams were Ladies (armed with a bell) Isobel Barnet and Eleanor Summerfield, versus Gents (armed with a buzzer) RICHARD MURDOCH and Lance Percival. Musical mistakes by Steve Race; producer Charles Maxwell. Started 17 March 1964.

Maple Leaf Matinée

'Sunday diversion presented by the Canadian Forces for all forces both in and out of uniform', starting 17 August 1942. Gerry Wilmot was Master of Ceremonies, introducing 'Service Spotlight', songs by LAC Ted Hockridge, Private Bill Smith and the Smoothies, with music by the Canucks Canadian Army Orchestra conducted by Sergeant Stan Shedden. Broadcast from a Palais de Danse somewhere in the South of England.

March of the Movies

Weekly radio programme for filmgoers devised by HARRY ALAN TOWERS, who later became a film producer himself. Leslie Mitchell (the Voice of *Movietone*) compèred 30 minutes of 'songs, scenes, and personalities from film productions of the past, present, and future.' The programme was broadcast on Sundays on the Forces Programme from 23 August 1942, produced by Charles Maxwell. The second series commencing 4 January 1944 introduced the character of 'Mr Moviegoer', who interviewed Sir Alexander Korda. Another series beginning 26 September 1946 was produced by Lillian Duff, and included the regular features 'This Week's Cartoon', 'The Name is —', 'Newsreel', and 'Film of the Week'. The series signature tune was 'The Voice of London' played by the Queen's Hall Light Orchestra.

Marconi Company

Guglielmo Marconi, 'inventor of wireless' (he took out the first patent for wireless telegraphy on 2 June 1896), founded the Marconi Wireless Telegraph and Signal Company in 1897. The Company built a six-kilowatt transmitter at Chelmsford and began broadcasting twice daily half-hours of news, music and gramophone records from 23 February 1920. G.W. White, an engineer, organized the programmes and Miss W. Sayer, soprano, was the first singer to broadcast in England. The first star to broadcast was Dame Nellie Melba, who sang 'Home Sweet Home' and 'God Save the King' on 15 June. Then the Postmaster General banned broadcasting, until 14 February 1922 when the Marconi Company opened a new transmitter at Writtle, licensed as 2MT ('Two Emma Toc'). The first of a series of fortnightly half-hour concerts was broadcast on 16 May. Isolde O'Farrell, soprano, sang 'Softly Awakes My Heart', accompanied by Emett Adams at the pianoforte, and Mrs Stanley Lupino broadcast an appeal to provide holidays for East End Children. The first broadcast of drama was given on 17 October when Agnes Travers of RADA gave three scenes from *Cyrano de*

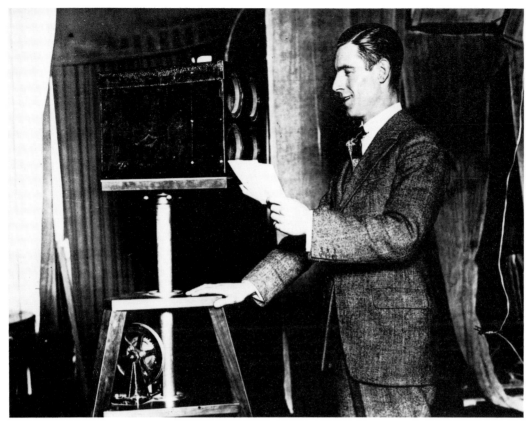

Marconi: Stanton Jefferies broadcasting from Marconi House in 1922

Bergerac. Writtle's last broadcast was made on 17 January 1923. It included a champagne farewell, using the sound effect of a popgun for the cork!

Mark Time

Hal Monty 'the khaki-clad comedian' starred in this series 'on the lighter side of army life' with Bertram Dench, Lauri Lupino Lane, Raymond Newell and the Band of the RAMC. Started 13 August 1943, produced by Max Kester.

Mark Time

Ancient rustic modelled by JACK TRAIN on Moore Marriott's Jeremiah Harbottle (see the Will Hay films). 'I'll have to ask me dad!' was this character's catchphrase: ITMA (1944).

Marmaduke Brown

Hero of a daily serial (the first) of the same name, broadcast on RADIO LUXEMBOURG at 4.45 pm from Monday 8 November 1937. 'The story of an average married couple in an average small town' was sponsored by Milk of Magnesia. 'Marmaduke is an inventor. But what he invents never amounts to very much. So his wife, Matilda, is the breadwinner. The whole town chuckles at Marmaduke, except Matilda. She loves him in spite of everything – so will you!' Among the cast were John Salew and Jon Pertwee.

Master OK the Saucy Boy

Cartoon character featured in press advertising by Mason's OK Sauce came to RADIO LUXEMBOURG from 1 December 1935 in *Adventures of the Saucy Boy*. Master OK, always in trouble with Uncle George, was musically supported by Tommy Kinsman and his Band, with singers Bettie Bucknelle and Johnny Johnston. After World War II the series returned as *What Sauce!* produced by Philip Jones. This time Patricia Hayes played the Saucy Boy, and also sang the signature song to the tune of 'Nuts in May':

Here we come with OK Sauce,
OK Sauce, OK Sauce,
Here we come with OK Sauce,
The Sauce that does you good!

Masterspy

'Basil Rathbone opens the files to bring you a fascinating revelation of the amazing activities of secret agents in the unending battle of spy versus spy, and calls upon Mike, the American roving reporter based in Paris, to disclose another story behind the news.' One of the 'World's Greatest Mysteries' series on RADIO LUXEMBOURG from 5 January 1957; produced by HARRY ALAN TOWERS.

Max Goes West

Max Bygraves 'reminisces on his recent tour of the USA and introduces recordings of famous American stars of entertainment whom he met.' Started on RADIO LUXEMBOURG on 6 May 1953, produced by Barry Barron; this was a Gui de Buire Production for Timex Watches.

The Mayor's Parlour

Occasional 1955 series in *Northern Variety Parade* situated in the borough of Swillit Down Quick. It featured a regular appearance (rare for radio) of the popular variety comedian Jimmy James with his stooges Cass James and Bretton Woods, who as Our Eli ever demanded 'Are you putting it around that I'm barmy?'. Supported by Violet Carson, Jack Watson, Deryck Guyler, Fred Yule, and the young dramatic actress to be, Billie Whitelaw. Written by Cass James (later known as James Casey) and Frank Roscoe; produced by Ronnie Taylor.

The Medicine Chest

'A programme of tunes and tonics devised by Boots the Chemist', compère Stephen Williams. Guest artistes included Olive Groves (RADIO LUXEMBOURG, 6 January 1938).

Mediterranean Merry-Go-Round

Continuation of MIDDLE EAST MERRY-GO-ROUND with virtually the same personnel and pattern. It was during the run of this series that the 'amateur talent' atmosphere developed into something more professional with the gradual introduction of the three service shows which became predominant. The first of these was MUCH-BINDING-IN-THE-MARSH, which had already taken the air in ENSA HALF HOUR on 4 January 1944. Writer/performers were RICHARD MURDOCH and KENNETH HORNE, both serving officers in the RAF. Their *Merry-Go-Round* debut was 31 March 1944. HMS Waterlogged at Sinking-in-the-Ooze, manned by Sub-Lieut. ERIC BARKER and Wren Pearl Hackney, supported by Petty Officer George 'Hair' Crow and the Blue Mariners Dance Band, began on 5 May. The Army shows featured personnel from 'Stars in Battledress'. The title was changed to MERRY-GO-ROUND from 12 January 1945.

Meek's Antiques

Mr Meek of Meek's Antiques, played by mousey RICHARD GOOLDEN, made his radio debut on 13 February 1938, as a segment of MONDAY NIGHT AT SEVEN. Created by Ernest Dudley.

Meet Our Joe

Rare radio series for Northern comedian Norman Evans, with Billy Scott Coomber, WILFRED PICKLES, Billy Pearce, the Singing Grenadiers, the Three Jacks, and Johnny Rose and his Swing Spotters. Written by Clifford Lewis; producer Richard North. The series started 6 June 1942.

Meet the Huggetts

Very popular situation comedies based on the Huggett Family who first appeared in the film *Holiday Camp*. Jack Warner as Joe and Kathleen Harrison as Ethel were the only players brought from the films. Joan Dowling played Jane Huggett and Anthony Green her younger brother Bobby. Episode 1, 'One Extra', was broadcast on 2 July 1953, written by Eddie Maguire and Betty Davies, and produced by Peter Eton. The second series began with 'Beg, Borrow or Steal' on 13 May 1954, with starlet Vera Day as daughter Jane, poor little Joan Dowling having killed herself. The third series began on 9 June 1955 with 'What The Butler Saw' and Valerie Jene as Jane. The fourth series (3 May 1956) began with 'Phoney Business' and introduced Marian Collins as Jane and Christopher Sanders as Bobby. The next series (11 May 1958) opened with 'Food for Thought' and featured Cynthia Bizeray as Jane and George Howell as Bobby. Jacques

Brown produced the next series (22 May 1959) and brought in Alona Royce as Jane and James Langley as Bobby, in 'Ringing the Bell'. Michael Hammond replaced him in the following series (15 June 1960), which began with 'The Driving Force'. The final episode was broadcast on 8 September 1961, with Roger Shepherd as Bobby. It was entitled 'The Rights of Man' and included in the cast a character who had appeared throughout the programme's history, neighbour Fred Stebbings, played by Charles Leno. The signature tune was 'Horse Feathers'.

Melody and Co.

'A new style show' devised for Irish comedian Jimmy O'Dea by Vernon Harris and Eric Spear. It featured Jack Melford (Mike), Patricia Leach (Penny) and SAM COSTA (Rodney) with the BBC Variety Orchestra conducted by Ernest Longstaffe. Written by Aubrey Danvers-Walker and Harry O'Donovan; from 30 May 1940.

Melody and Mirth

Starring MAJOR AND MINOR (Fred Yule and Alec McGill) on RADIO LUXEMBOURG from 29 August 1937. 'They take the biscuit – Huntley and Palmer's of course!'

Melody and Song

'We bring you Melody and Song' sang the '120 favourite artists and musicians' who provided this weekly half-hour of music for grown-up drinkers of Ovaltine (see THE OVALTINEYS for the rest). Norman Shelley was the compère of this pre-war RADIO LUXEMBOURG series.

Melody Fair

Forty-five-minute series of 'music and song for everybody', introduced by LIONEL GAMLIN from 19 August 1946, and including community singing led by veteran Dale Smith, who invited listeners to join in with the audience at the People's Palace, London. Music was provided by the Augmented Variety Orchestra conducted by Rae Jenkins, with songs from Frank Titterton (tenor) and Marjorie Thomas (contralto), and instrumentals by Leon Goossens (oboe). Produced by Henry Reed.

Melody Meeting

'A new programme of quaint negro harmonies, Jungle-beat rhythms, and modern swing tunes' introducing the Head Man, the Four Ink Spots, and Eddie Matthews (finest of Negro baritones), 'sent to you by the makers of Fairy Soap' on RADIO LUXEMBOURG from 31 January 1937.

Melody on Parade

Dorothy Holbrook and her Harmony Hussars starred in this RADIO NORMANDY series sponsored by Do-Do, commencing 27 November 1938.

Meltonian Programme of Dancing Moods

JOE LOSS and his Band starred in this musical series sponsored by Meltonian Shoe Dressings. 'A Dance Romance' was featured every week, beginning on 16 February 1939 with 'The Waltz'. Chick Henderson sang, and DICK BENTLEY compèred. Shorn of its commercials, the series was also broadcast over the wartime station, RADIO INTERNATIONAL.

The Memory Man

Leslie Welch, whose phenomenal memory for sporting results and information won him several series. In 1947 'Ask the Memory Man' was a regular feature in NAVY MIXTURE, and later Welch had a similar spot in CALLING ALL FORCES. Oft-repeated phrase: 'I think I'm right in saying. . . .' In 1952 he featured in a RADIO LUXEMBOURG series, Beat the Memory Man, sponsored by Bovril. Listeners received a guinea for every question correctly answered, or £25 if they stumped him.

The Men From the Ministry

Delightful situation comedy series starring Wilfrid Hyde-White as the ever-unruffled head of the General Assistance Department of the Civil Service, assisted by the confused RICHARD MURDOCH. Their character names were Roland Hamilton-Jones and Richard Lamb, and the first episode, 'The Great Footwear Scandal', was broadcast on 30 October 1962. In their long-running career the Men managed to lumber the War House with 20,000 left-foot boots and provoke the Isle of Wight into declaring war on England. The series was written and produced by Edward Taylor, who later accepted some General Assistance from Johnnie Mortimer and Brian Cooke. Secretary Mildred Murfin was played by Norma Ronald, and Sir Gregory Pitkin by Roy Dotrice. When Hyde-White returned to Hollywood, Murdoch was given a new 'One' in the gruff Mr Lennox-Brown of Deryck Guyler. The series was particularly popular with the World Service, who even produced several of their own, unheard at home. The show ran for 15 years finishing on 22 August 1977.

The Merry Andrews

Sunday musical programme sponsored by Andrews Liver Salts, featuring Andy Mac, Frederick Bayco at the organ and Jay Wilbur and his Band. Broadcast on RADIO LUXEMBOURG from 1936.

Merry-Go-Lucky

'Come and join the happy-go-lucky crowd on the merry-go-round.' CLAY KEYES was the happy-go-lucky compère who introduced such items as 'The Vanity Case' with Magda Kun and Vera Lennox, 'Balcony Scene' with Helen Hill and Eric Stanley, 'The Orchestra At Large' with Billy Ternent and the Dance Orchestra, and a guest star. The first, on 5 March 1941, was Hermione Gingold. Deviser-producer was Eric Spear.

Merry-Go-Round (1)

'The Army, the Navy and the Air Force' whistled by a forces audience opened this show which 'week by week goes round the services bringing music and fun to boys and girls in khaki and two shades of blue.' Originally MEDITERRANEAN MERRY-GO-ROUND, then MIDDLE EAST MERRY-GO-ROUND, the show expanded to all forces 'serving afloat or overseas' w.e.f. 12 January 1945. The Naval Edition was written by its star, Sub-Lieutenant ERIC 'Hearthrob' BARKER, and was set in HMS Waterlogged at Sinking-in-the-Ooze. WREN Pearl Hackney assisted, and Telegraphist Ivor Pye sang with the Blue Mariners Dance Band, directed by Petty Officer George 'Hair' Crow. The DOUBLE OR QUITS CASH QUIZ feature was conducted by Lieutenant Harold Warrender RNVR, and Leading WREN Meg Merryfield introduced the show, produced in collaboration with the Personal Services Department of the Admiralty by David Manderson.

The Air Force edition featured visits to MUCH-BINDING-IN-THE-MARSH, a remote fighter base in Laughter Command, written by its stars, Flight Lieutenant RICHARD MURDOCH (as the CO), and Wing Commander KENNETH HORNE (as the AOC). Flight Sergeant Anne Grisewood compèred and Pilot Officer Roy Rich conducted the 'Double or Quits Cash Quiz'.

The Army edition, STUDIO STAND EASY, was written by its star, Sergeant CHARLIE CHESTER, whose 'happy band of Other Cranks' from Stars in Battledress included Arthur Haynes, Kenny Morris, Raymond St Clair, Joe Giggs and Louise Gainsborough or Corporal Sally 'Click-Click' Rogers. The 'Double or Quits' quiz was conducted by Will Hay.

After 'demobilization' MUCH-BINDING-IN-THE-MARSH and STAND EASY became series under their own titles, while MERRY-GO-ROUND (15 February 1946) remained the name for Eric Barker's naval-based series. HMS *Waterlogged* became WATERLOGGED SPA, still at Sinking-in-the-Ooze. JON PERTWEE, a wartime discovery, was the main character man (COMMANDER HIGHPRICE, ROBIN FLY), and Humphrey Lestocq arrived as FLYING OFFICER KYTE. Thus the 200th programme was broadcast from Waterlogged Spa (via RADIOLYMPIA) on 19 September 1947.

Merry-Go-Round (2)

Not the famous BBC wartime series but a magazine programme 'for children of all ages, full of competitions and exciting events'. Humphrey Lestocq (television's 'H.L.') hosted such items as 'The Magic Carpet', 'Tom Tex', 'How to Win a Camera', and 'The Adventures of Tarna'. Produced by Peter Wilson and sponsored by *Swift*, a Hulton Publication and the first comic to sponsor a RADIO LUXEMBOURG programme. Started 4 October 1954.

The Merrymart

Variety series in a store setting, designed as the first radio show for cockney film comedian Alf Goddard. Unhappily, illness defeated the purpose, and Alf's role of Mr Jolly was taken on by Dick Francis. Audrey Wayne played Miss Fitt, and Alfie Dean (the high-voiced one of Collinson and Dean) was Basil, with Robert Naylor as Emilio. Written by Ernest Longstaffe and Con West, the first show featured Denis

Noble, Billy Shakespeare, Nat Mills and Bobbie, the Vickers twins, and Betty Hobbs' Happy Tappers.

The Michael Howard Show

The laconic comedian became one of the few honoured with a series named after him (others were THE WILL HAY PROGRAMME, THE RICHARD TAUBER PROGRAMME, etc.), from 4 August 1945. He was supported by Phyllis Robins, Eric Woodburn, Pat Rignold, Peter Madden and Philip Green and his Orchestra. Produced by Leslie Bridgmont.

Michie, Bryan

As fat and fruity as his voice, Michie (pronounced Mickey) quickly rose from running the BBC Sound Effects Department to compèring and producing. By 1938 he was running a comedy quiz show on RADIO LUXEMBOURG as Professor Bryan Michie *The Riddle Master*, on behalf of Brown and Polson's Custard.

Mid-Day Music Hall

Lunchtime variety show starting 2 January 1953, compèred by Michael Miles. The first bill: the Four-in-a-Chord. Gladys Hay from IGNORANCE IS BLISS, Ronald Jackson as this week's Professional Protégé, Mischa de la Motte, Sylvia Marriott and Douglas Taylor in 'Your Favourite Musical Comedy', and CYRIL FLETCHER. Producer Trafford Whitelock. The series went twice-weekly from 6 May, with Bill Gates compèring the Wednesday edition. From 10 April 1961 the programme was extended to a full hour, when Bill Gates introduced Max Miller, Jacqueline Delman, Bob Andrews, the Lana Sisters, the Peter Crawford Trio, and Irene Handl and Pat Coombs in their characters of MRS PURVIS and Nola. Malcolm Lockyer conducted the Revue Orchestra. Although the time-slot remained mid-day, the title was changed to merely *Music Hall* from 7 January 1963, the show's tenth birthday.

Brian **Michie**: from sound effects man (right) to star

Middle East Merry-Go-Round
Weekly variety show for services overseas, first broadcast to home listeners on the General Forces Programme on 3 March 1944. It was unique in that the series was devised and presented by the services themselves, with the Army, Navy and RAF each taking turns. BBC production was by David Manderson, and common to each show was the DOUBLE OR QUITS CASH QUIZ in which members of the audience answered questions for half-a-crown, five shillings, ten bob, and a pound. Each service had its own question-master: Will Hay for the Army, Lieutenant Harold Warrender for the Navy, and Pilot Officer Roy Rich for the RAF. There were individual introducers, too: Corporal Sally Rogers (Army), Leading Wren Meg Merryfield (Navy) and Flight Sergeant Anne Grisewood (RAF). The show changed its name to MEDITERRANEAN MERRY-GO-ROUND from 17 March 1944.

Midnight in Munich
Charlie Barnet's 'Skyliner' was the roaring sig-tune of this great late-night record show from AFN Munich (1946). Ralph 'Muff-it' Moffatt was the amiable and influential disc-jockey. He was the first continually to replay favourite records, such as 'Heartbreaker', and Francis Craig's 'Near You'.

Milligan, Spike
Once billed as 'The Performing Man', Spike (Terence) is the writing genius behind THE GOON SHOW, the great post-war breakthrough in comedy writing for radio. He extended the use of the medium itself, employing music, sound effects, and silence as never heard before. His main character is ECCLES, the original Goon, but he also played the wretched MORIARTY, the quivery MINNIE BANNISTER, and the limited LITTLE JIM. Spike made his first broadcast in HUGHIE GREEN's OPPORTUNITY KNOCKS (1949), and was voted Comedy Writer of the Year in 1957.

Millward, Sid, and His Nitwits
Comedy band that grew crazier with the passing years. Sid Colin was billed as Muddler of Ceremonies on their first solo show, 12 April 1939, which included Pat Taylor (Our Leading Lady), Peter Barrie (A Backward Gent) and Jack Shields. From 26 July 1946 they were resident roustabouts on IGNORANCE IS BLISS, and were finally presented with their own series, Nitwit Serenade, on 23 March 1950. The lineup was then Wally Stewart, Cyril Lagey, Roger Smith and his Talking Guitar, and 'probably somebody else'. Credits read: 'Scripted (invisible ink) by Sid Colin, produced (reluctantly) by John Freeman'.

The Milton Sisters
Played by Dinah Miller and Pat Hyde, 'Two girls with a sense of humour and a new way of singing new songs'. The Milton Sisters, 'with their entertaining announcer, Bob Danvers-Walker', were sponsored by Milton Proprietory of John Milton House, makers of Milton. RADIO NORMANDY from 8 November 1937.

The Mind of Mr Reeder
Series adapted from Edgar Wallace's stories with Leslie French as the fusty investigator. It commenced 27 February 1942 with 'Sheer Melodrama' narrated by Ronald Simpson. Belle Chrystal played his secretary Margaret Bellman; producer was Fred O'Donovan. A further series started on 5 August 1946. This time Eliot Makeham played Reeder, and Preston Lockwood narrated. The first episode was 'The Poetical Policeman', adapted by Hugh Stewart and produced by David Godfrey.

Minnie Bannister
Formery Miss Bannister, spinster of the parish, known as 'Modern Min' to her constant companion, HENRY ('Hen-reee!') CRUN. This elderly Darling of Roper's Light Horse (MAJOR BLOODNOK was once her beau) was played by SPIKE MILLIGAN, who wobbled his under-chin skin to obtain the required tremolo for her frantic cry: 'We'll all be murdered in our beds!' Minnie made her début in THE GOON SHOW on 1 April 1952.

Mint Julep
Serial story of the Old South starring the American variety act Forsythe, Seamon and Farrell. They played Mr Carter, Mrs Clinton and the Conjure Woman. It was written by James Dyrenforth (who also appeared as Mizzy the Halfwit) with new music by Kenneth Leslie-Smith, plus interpolated spiri-

tuals played by the Revue Orchestra conducted by Hyam Greenbaum. Episode 1, 'The Dangerfield Place', was broadcast on 25 February 1941; producer Eric Fawcett.

Miss Dangerfield

'Danger, they called her. Some said she was a detective, some a psychologist, others that she was an angel and left it at that.' *The Fabulous Miss Dangerfield* was played by Rita Vale in Edward J. Mason's series which started 4 September 1947. Sidney James was Bill Stewart, her cynical assistant. Episode 1, 'Money For Danger', was produced by Cleland Finn. A second serial, *Miss Dangerfield and the League of Sound Sleepers*, started on 20 July 1948 with Episode 1, 'The Master Hypnotist'. The third serial followed on 19 January 1951, *Miss Dangerfield and the Irresistible Nightingale*, chapter 1, 'The Vanishing Lady with Incidental Music'. This was specially composed by Basil Hempseed. June Tobin took over the role of Irene Dangerfield in a new production of the third serial broadcast from 17 June 1963.

Miss Dinglebody

Over-amorous Agatha Dinglebody, ever making simpering play for tutor TONY HANCOCK in EDUCATING ARCHIE (1951). Portrayed by Hattie Jacques.

Miss Goodbody

Louisa Goodbody, as played by Vivienne Chatterton, was the frail old spinster who was nonetheless ready 'to have a bash' in MUCH-BINDING-IN-THE-MARSH (1948).

Miss Hotchkiss

TOMMY HANDLEY's fire-breathing snapdragon of a secretary, introduced into IT'S THAT MAN AGAIN (1944) by Diana Morrison. 'Mister Hand-lay!' was her battlecry, and her exit-word an irate 'Doh!'.

Miss Pugh

Grizelda Pugh came to Railway Cuttings as TONY HANCOCK's secretary but moved in to become an aggressively domineering housekeeper. Hattie Jacques in HANCOCK'S HALF HOUR from 11 November 1956.

Miss Throat

Hoarse-voiced assistant in THE GOON SHOW played by SPIKE MILLIGAN in a series of monosyllabic belches: 'What?' . . . 'Right!'

Miss Tidball

Spinster of Shepton Mallet and late music mistress to ERIC BARKER in MERRY-GO-ROUND (1946), about whom he would reminisce to the lovelorn Miss Hackney (Pearl), his secretary.

Mixed Doubles

Domestic comedy series centred on neighbouring couples, Michael Denison and Dulcie Gray, and CYRIL FLETCHER and Anne Crawford. The writers BOB MONKHOUSE AND DENIS GOODWIN originally intended the show to be based on two real-life partnerships, but Mrs Fletcher (Betty Astell) fell ill and was replaced by film star Anne Crawford. First broadcast was 18 June 1956; shortly thereafter Miss Crawford died and was replaced by another film star, Jean Kent. The second series (14 June 1957) was happier thanks to Betty Astell's recovery. Also featured were Pat Coombs and Anthea Askey. Producer Leslie Bridgmont.

Mona Lott

Lugubrious laundress created by Joan Harben in IT'S THAT MAN AGAIN (1946). 'It's being so cheerful as keeps me going!' ended her weekly moan, which often had to do with her unappreciative hubby, Little.

Monday at Seven

Fore-runner of the well-remembered weekly series MONDAY NIGHT AT SEVEN, this radio magazine began on 5 April 1937 as an hour containing a number of set segments separated by the Bow Bells interval signal. This formality was shortly replaced with the informality of a 'singing commère', Judy Shirley, to introduce the items and the programme itself:

> It's Monday Night at Seven,
> Oh can't you hear the chimes,
> They're telling you to take an easy chair,
> To settle by the fireside,
> Look at your *Radio Times*,
> For Monday Night at Seven's on the air . . .

The first line-up: Charles Heslop and Friends in a big-game hunter sketch; Greta Keller;

Leslie Henson and Norma Howard as 'Thompson and Johnson', butler and cook to Lord and Lady Crackenleigh, written by Nat Gubbins of the *Sunday Express*; CARROLL GIBBONS at the piano; Interlude by CHARLES SHADWELL and the Variety Orchestra; 'The Strange Adventures of MR PENNY' with RICHARD GOOLDEN, written by Maurice Moisiewitch. The soon-to-be-famous 'INSPECTOR HORNLEIGH' arrived on 31 May, and the programme went weekly from October. The first series concluded at No. 43 on 6 June 1938.

Monday Night at Eight

Successor to MONDAY NIGHT AT SEVEN commencing 27 November 1939 with the regular singing commères, The Three Chimes, harmonizing the variant signature song: 'It's Monday Night at Eight O'clock, Oh can't you hear the chimes . . .', accompanied by CHARLES SHADWELL and the Variety Orchestra. Regulars 'INSPECTOR HORNLEIGH Investigates' and 'PUZZLE CORNER' were joined by 'The Services Sing', 'OUR ADA' by Robert Rutherford featuring Suzette Tarri, and 'Youth Takes a Bow' presented by JACK HYLTON and compèred by BRYAN MICHIE. SYD WALKER came from BAND WAGGON for a series of 'Mr Walker Wants to Know' starting 29 January 1940. The second series began 24 March 1941 with Jack Melford as a British secret agent in 'CALLING X2', 'Something Old Something New', 'SOS Sally' ('a little showgirl whose quiet spirit and grave blue eyes attract people who are in trouble'), Leonard Urry's 'May We Introduce' and, of course, 'Puzzle Corner'.

The third series began 20 July 1942 with 'Meet DR MORELLE' by Ernest Dudley, with Dennis Arundell as the mysterious doctor, 'Radio Rendezvous', a weekly meeting of factory workers and famous personalities, arranged by Leonard Urry, 'Musical Alphabet' and 'Puzzle Corner'.

The next series started 18 October 1943 with 'Crime Chasers Ltd' by Ernest Dudley, with Jane Grahame, 'Many Happy Returns of the Day', 'The Lodger' by Dick Pepper, starring CYRIL FLETCHER and Betty Astell, 'Take The Stand' with Frederick Burtwell examining Jack Buchanan and Frances Day in the Case of the People Versus Boredom, presented by Leonard Urry, and 'Puzzle Corner'. Singing commères: the Bachelor Girls, with Charles Shadwell and the Variety Orchestra. On 14 February 1944 'Michael Starr Investigates' began, by Francis Durbridge and featuring Henry Oscar. On 27 March 'The Lodger' left to be replaced by 'Things in General', written by Henrik Ege and starring BASIL RADFORD AND NAUNTON WAYNE. This series concluded on 8 July 1944.

The fifth series began 9 October 1944, and introduced Keneth Kent as a French detective in 'The Memoirs of André d'Arnell', written by Francis Durbridge. Kent's assistant was film star Linden Travers. RICHARD MURDOCH presented 'Puzzle Corner', and features included 'With a Star and a Song' and 'The Hall of Fame', to which famous personalities are summoned by Dick Francis as the Major Domo, by arrangement with Leonard Urry. This was changed from 18 December to 'May We Introduce', with Ronald Waldman as the Interviewer. Leonard Urry continued to arrange. A new detective was introduced on 16 April 1945, played by Edgar Norfolk: 'Inspector Wise Hurries' was written by Mileson Horton.

The sixth series began 15 April 1946 by reviving 'Meet Dr Morelle' and introducing a new series, 'The Young Sullivans' (Sarah Churchill and David Hutcheson), by Gordon Duncalfe. KENNETH HORNE hosted 'Monday Birthday Party' in which the first personality to be given 'The Freedom of the Air' was playwright Ian Hay. Another feature was 'Something Old, Something New', and the 'Singing Introducers' were Doreen Lundy and Cyril Grantham.

The seventh series (28 October 1946) introduced Norman Shelley as a wheezy old bruiser employed by detective Richard Wattis in 'The Old One-Two'. Listeners were invited to solve the weekly problem by phoning the BBC in 'Telephone Challenge'. Gordon Duncalfe wrote a new series for Mackenzie Ward and Maxine Audley as 'John and Annabella', and there was also 'Musical Alphabet'.

The final series (13 October 1947) revived 'Meet Dr Morelle' with Heron Carvic as the detective, and 'Monday Birthday Party' with Kenneth Horne. 'Puzzle Corner' included the 'Monday Night Accumulator' and the Singing Introducers were changed to Dick James and Bette Roberts. 'Songs of the Stars' were sung by the Andrews family, Ted, Barbara and their daughter Julie. The last programme went out on 29 March 1948.

Monday Night at Home

René Cutforth hosted this 60-minute series which started 11 May 1959. Among the items: 'Drama at the Piano' with the Gaunt Brothers; 'Speaking of Speeches' with Lord Birkett, 'Countryside Column' with Walter Flesher, 'Courts Day by Day' with Edward Chapman, 'Mainly for Men' by J.B. Boothroyd, and 'Radio Echoes' with veteran broadcaster PETER ECKERSLEY. Edited and produced by John Bridges.

The second series started 21 September 1959 and was hosted by singer Ian Wallace, who introduced regular wits Piers Stephens and Paul McDowell, C. Gordon Glover, and Ivor Cutler of Y'Hup, OMP, a grave Scot given to dire tales like 'Gruts for Tea'. The 100th edition, broadcast 4 December 1961, was hosted by J.B. Boothroyd and featured Alan Melville in 'Melvilliany', Stephens and McDowell in 'Buzzard Fancier', and Michael Flanders and Donald Swann, at the drop of their well-known hat.

Monday Night at Seven

This follow-up to MONDAY AT SEVEN retained the successful formula and signature tune sung by the Singing Commère, and started 17 October 1938. INSPECTOR HORNLEIGH investigated again, and there were new characters 'Mrs H and Mrs C' in 'Over the Garden Wall'. Guests: Beryl Orde, impressioniste, SYD MILLWARD AND HIS NITWITS, and Beatrice Lillie. 'Meek's Antiques' began 13 February 1939, with RICHARD GOOLDEN as Mr Meek; created by Ernest Dudley. Series ended 29 May 1939.

Monday Spectacular

Shaw Taylor and Muriel Young brought you the Best in Entertainment in this 60-minute series broadcast on RADIO LUXEMBOURG from 26 June 1961. Cliff Richard and Helen Shapiro featured on the opening show, produced by Arthur Muxlow and sponsored by EMI Records.

Monkhouse, Bob, and Goodwin, Denis

Bob, who drew comics, and Denis, who sold radio sets, were schoolmates from Dulwich College who teamed up as scriptwriters, then as a double act in the style of their heroes, MURGATROYD AND WINTERBOTTOM. Bob had begun broadcasting as a solo comic whilst still in the RAF (resident on SHOW TIME 1948), and was the first comedian to be signed to a 12-month contract by the BBC (1949). As writers the team turned out HERE'S HOWARD, HIP HIP HOO ROY, IT'S A GREAT LIFE, and a two-and-a-half year run of CALLING ALL FORCES and THE FORCES SHOW. Their series for ARTHUR ASKEY, HELLO PLAYMATES, won the NATIONAL RADIO AWARD for 1954. They also appeared as characters in this show, Denis having become a professional if nervous performer in OPPORTUNITY KNOCKS (1950). Characters they created for others include MRS PURVIS and Nola (Irene Handl and Pat Coombs). After successful television appearances the team broke up to pursue separate careers.

Monsieur Stephan

Famous as the man who taught listeners French by wireless, he was born in Brittany. He came to England to learn the language, married an English girl, and stayed on as a staff member of the University of London. Made his first broadcast in 1927 and appeared in the British Instructional Film *The King's English* in 1932.

More Monkey Business

Weeky series on RADIO LUXEMBOURG from 1936, starring Billy Reid and his Accordion Band, with singers Ivor Davies and Dorothy Squires. Sponsored by Monkey Brand Soap.

The Morecambe and Wise Show

Eric and Ernie in 'a radio romp' by Eric Merriman, with Elaine Taylor, Anita Harris, the Mike Sammes Singers, and Burt Rhodes and his Orchestra. Produced by John Browell, starting 24 July 1966. A later series (1974) featured their full names in the title, *The Eric Morecambe and Ernie Wise Show*. Their signature song was 'Two of a Kind'.

Moriarty

Count (Comte) Jim 'Thighs' (or 'Knees') Moriarty (pronounced 'Mor-*i*-arty'), ex-master criminal reduced to toadying for HERCULES GRYTPYPE-THYNNE. Unsavoury swine played by SPIKE MILLIGAN in THE GOON SHOW from 18 November 1952, and has a tendency towards uttering oaths such as 'Sapristi Knockoles!'. Also gave forth with so many cries of 'Owww!' that he recorded the song, 'You Gotta Go Owww!' in 1956.

Morning, Noon and Night

Major sponsored radio series starring AMBROSE and his Orchestra, with Evelyn Dall (America's Blonde Bombshell), and comedian Max Bacon. 'Gay new entertainment in Lifebuoy Toilet Soap's Radio Show' began on RADIO LUXEMBOURG on Sunday 31 May 1936. A regular feature of the series was the 'Roving Microphone' – 'a new radio technique which brings to the audience real-life situations'.

Morris and Dudley Grosvenor

Likably inept spivs, Jewish brothers from the East End who tried very hard to con their way through IN ALL DIRECTIONS (1952) but invariably concluded with the cry: 'Run for it, Dudley!' Played by Peter Ustinov and Peter Jones, the latter reviving Dudley for a further series, WE'RE IN BUSINESS (1959), in harness with Harry Worth.

The Motor Way

Comedy series subtitled 'The log-book of a garage owner'. JACK WARNER returned to radio to star as Jack Turner, sole prop. of Turner's Garage (established 1922, licensed to sell nuts and bolts on or off the premises), with Deryck Guyler as his foreman, Crocker, Peter Byrne as his son Peter, and Heather Chasen as Jill. Graham Stark was also around. Script by Laurie Wyman; produced by Geoffrey Owen. First broadcast 25 June 1962.

Movie-Go-Round

Peter Haigh introduced this 'Sound approach to the cinema', edited and produced by Trafford Whitelock as a major Sunday series from 16 September 1956. Features: 'Music from a New Release' (Dan Dailey in *Viva Las Vegas*), 'Picturegoers' Quiz' (test your ears and your memory); 'Around the British Studios' (Peter Noble); 'Our Hollywood Correspondent' (Donovan Pedelty, last heard of previously as a Quota Quickie producer in 1937!); 'New Musical' (*The King and I*); 'Stargazing' (Jack Hawkins); 'Pocket Edition' (*The Solid Gold Cadillac*); 'Soundtrack Memories'. The series returned on 29 September 1957 with a pocket edition of Charles Chaplin's *A King in New York*, adapted by Roy Bradford. The 150th show was broadcast on 20 December 1959 and featured a preview of *Ben Hur* and a few words from Mitzi Gaynor; while the 150th show (26 November

1961) had a special interview with Bob Hope. The series went into a unique 'double feature' format on 25 September 1966. At 5.30 pm came 'First House' which concentrated on films past and present, followed at 9 pm by the 'Second House', future films with the emphasis on the offbeat. The writer was now Lyn Fairhurst and the producer John Dyas. The last programme was on 14 September 1969.

Movie Magazine

Daily series presented on RADIO LUXEMBOURG from 16 July 1951 by Wilfrid Thomas on behalf of Silvikrin Shampoo. 'Bringing you music and scenes from your favourite films and introducing the stars of M-G-M, Warner Bros, and ABC.' From 1952 Peter Noble came on every Friday with news and views of the week in 'Around and About Movieland'.

Movie Matinée

'Weekly half-hour for cinemagoers containing news and views of film-land, excerpts from films to come, records of films you would like to see again, and interviews with the stars and those who made them.' Compèred by Lilian Duff and Leslie Mitchell, produced by Peter Eton, commencing 1 November 1942.

Movie Time

This 'morning performance of films' began on 3 January 1961, hosted by Brian Reece of PC49 fame. The first programme was a double bill: soundtrack adaptations of *The Crowded Sky* (Dana Andrews) and *Anything Goes* (Bing Crosby). Show No. 288 on 22 July 1966 featured *The Moving Target* (Paul Newman), adapted by Gordon Gow, who did most of the radio versions. Alfred Dunning was the first producer, and the series was a product of the Film Unit at Maida Vale.

Mr and Mrs Music

Apt title for a series starring former bandleader JACK PAYNE and his pianist wife Peggy Cochrane in 'a musical conversation piece with piano and some records'. Started 3 July 1955.

Mr and Mrs Neemo

Billy Caryll and Hilda Mundy, a real life husband-and-wife double act, played the argumentative pair in this comedy series which began 5 September 1938. Their son, Little Reggie, also known as 'His Nibs', was played by MAURICE DENHAM. Written by Vernon Harris, produced by Gordon Crier and Ronald Waldman, the comedy spots were punctuated by singers SAM COSTA, the Cavendish Three, and Jay Wilbur and his Band, with street musicians 'From the London Streets'.

Mr and Mrs North

American husband-and-wife detective team created by husband-and-wife novelists Frances and Richard Lockridge, and brought to radio by husband-and-wife comedy actors, BERNARD BRADEN AND BARBARA KELLY. Episode 1, 'Murder With a Will', was broadcast 4 August 1950, produced by Ian Messiter.

Mr Battersburn

North-country Clerk of the Court of Nothing Common Please, Nether Backwash, presided over by MR MUDDLECOMBE, JP (ROBB WILTON). Played by Ernest Sefton with the catchphrase: 'Ee, what a to-do!'

Mr Bentley and Mr Braden

Dick and Bernard to their listening friends used the old 'Mr Gallagher and Mr Shean' song in this comedy series which began on 20 October 1957. Eleanor Summerfield, Lorrae Desmond, and Bernard Cribbins as 'nearly everybody else' completed the cast, with music from the Variety Orchestra conducted by Paul Fenoulhet. Script by David Climie and Pat Dunlop; producer Leslie Bridgmont. The second series (28 August 1958) changed very little, other than the music which was now by Harry Rabinowitz and the Revue Orchestra.

Mr Blake

Mr Blake the Sexton (Sexton Blake, see?) was the ruminative rustic of MUCH-BINDING-IN-THE-MARSH (1948). He was played by MAURICE DENHAM in incomprehensible dialect: 'Oh-er-um-er-ee . . .' (etc. etc.), ending up with 'Muck spreadin'!'.

Mr Bones

Black-faced comedy man in THE KENTUCKY MINSTRELS (1933), always in trouble with 'the wife' and 'the mother-in-law'. Played by C. Denier Warren, who not only wrote Mr Bones' regular spot in the programme, 'The Stump Speech', but also the entire series.

Mr Cropper's Conscience

Wartime fairy stories with lots of morals written by Henrik Ege. Mr Cropper was Frederick Burtwell, and Wynne Ajello his Conscience. Also appearing were the Cavendish Three. Episode 1, 'Stormy Petrol', was broadcast on 7 November 1941. A sequel series, Mr Cropper Looks at Life, ran during 1943. Produced by Gordon Crier.

Mr Dove

Antique dealer much addicted to cocoa, played by Eliot Makeham in Mr Dove Lends a Hand, a series of studies in unorthodox detection written by Lester Powell. Episode 1, 'The Gaspard Sampler', was broadcast on 23 May 1947, produced by Martyn C. Webster. Peregrine Dove's lady assistant, Pamela Wingate, was played by Marjorie Westbury, and Detective Sergeant Bill Somerset by Charles Leno.

Mr Grice

Ancient rustic with nothing on his mind but food, as evidenced by his every conversation with London visitor Nan Kenway. 'My brother is in the Navy. He's a carpenter. They say he is a very efficient "chips".' 'Ah, I likes that.' 'Likes what?' 'Fish and chips. Very tasty, very sweet.' Douglas Young played him in HOWDY FOLKS (1940) and many more shows.

Mr Growser

Bad-tempered inhabitant of TOYTOWN given to complaining 'It's disgrrrraceful!' which, with his other favourite remarks, 'It ought not to be allowed!' and 'I wonder you are not ashamed to look me in the face!', can be numbered among radio's earliest catchphrases. Played by Ralph de Rohan, who earlier had been known as the CHILDREN's HOUR Wicked Uncle.

Mr Interlocutor

Host, compère, and baritone, the only 'white man' in the black-face revue, THE KENTUCKY MINSTRELS (1933). Originally played by the American actor Percy Parsons; later Interlocutors included James Carew, Nosmo King, Sydney Burchall, and Fred Yule.

Mr Keen, Tracer of Lost Persons

Played by Milton Rosmer in the daily serial sponsored by Lavona Hair Tonic, and broadcast from RADIO LUXEMBOURG from 24 October 1938. 'Mr Keen could have been a great detective, but rather than fight crime he fights human heartbreak and misery. He's out to help, not to punish – to help anyone who's lost someone they love.' In the cast: Lawrence Anderson, Yolande Terrell and Valentine Dunn; producer Bertram Fryer.

Mr Lovejoy

Guv'nor of THE HAPPIDROME, imaginary theatre of varieties featured in the popular series of the same name (1941). Played by Lancashire comedian Harry Korris of the long-running seaside show, *The Arcadian Follies*. Catchphrase: 'Ee, if ever a man suffered!'

Mr Middleton

The Radio Gardener, C.H. Middleton, who virtually became his own 'character' complete with catchphrase, 'Good afternoon'. Recommended by the Royal Horticultural Society when the BBC requested somebody to give a talk on gardening, Mr Middleton became a 'wireless natural', broadcasting regularly from 1931. He became the first Television Gardener in 1936. There is a gate dedicated to him at the entrance of the garden at 10 Cavendish Place, London.

Mr Mosseltoff

Hebrew character in OUR SHED (1946) played by Harold Berens.

Mr Muddle, Private Detective

Not Mr Muddlecombe, but clearly a close relative: the part was played by ROBB WILTON! He also wrote the scripts, which were described as 'dramatized episodes from his casebook'. Phoebe Hodgson played Mrs Muddle, Reginald Purdell was Charlie Evans (a name made famous in Robb's wartime monologues), and Michael North produced. First broadcast 22 April 1946.

Mr Muddlecombe JP

Thoroughly disorganized Justice of the Peace played by ROBB WILTON, created by Barry Bernard and scripted by Adrian Turner (later by Max Kester). The first sitting of the Court of Nothing Common Place sat on 9 January 1937. By 26 January 1939 John Muddlecombe was Chairman of the Nether Backwash Rural District Council in *Public Futilities*, and by 14 March 1940 was *Mr Muddlecombe JP, ARP*, assisted by those pillars of the Bench, Major Todd and MR BATTERSBURN. On 25 April 1942 Mrs Agnes Muddlecombe entered the scene, played by Marion Dawson, in *Mr Muddlecombe at Home*, 'episodes from the eminent magistrate's domestic life'. However, even this appears to have been muddled, for when he starred in a regular spot in HOOP-LA (1945), Mrs Muddlecombe was named Dora and played by Doris Nichols! The final Muddlecombe series commenced 11 October 1948.

Mr Penny

Described as 'a sort of Little Man' this meek and mild gent, played by RICHARD GOOLDEN at his meekest and mildest, found himself up to the neck in trouble every Saturday from 21 November 1936. Maurice Moiseiwitsch created *The Strange Adventures of Mr Penny*, the first of which was entitled 'Mr Penny on Government Service'. It was later released as a 12" 78 by Columbia Records. Henry Penny's wife Annie was played by Doris Gilmore. Mr Penny moved to RADIO LUXEMBOURG from 11 December 1937 when Cadbury's Bourneville Cocoa presented 'Mr Penny, Superman' as Episode 1 of *The Exploits of Mr Penny*. There was also a film, *Meet Mr Penny* (1938).

Mr Philpott

Chairman of the forties series of PALACE OF VARIETIES, a boozy old buffer played by Nosmo King.

Mr Pottle

Centenarian played by Douglas Young in 'Mr Pottle's Prattle', segment of the Kenway and Young radio series, IT GOES TO SHOW (1942). The quavery old boy's signature song: 'He knows, he's a hundred years old.'

Mr Reeder

Mr J.G. Reeder, quaint little investigator in the Office of the Public Prosecutor, first came to radio on 30 April 1939. *Mr J.G. Reeder* was

Mr Penny: book of the series

sponsored by Milk of Magnesia and broadcast on RADIO LUXEMBOURG. Eliot Makeham, meek little man of many British films, played Reeder in Hugh Stewart's adaptations, *The Mind of Mr Reeder*, which was featured in *Time for Crime* from 13 August 1940. Leslie French took over in a new series from 27 February 1942, and Makeham returned for a further run from 5 August 1956. Mr Reeder was created by Edgar Wallace.

Mr T. Pott

'Mr T. Pott's Time Signal' was a regular punctuation of the RADIO NORMANDY programmes in 1938.

Mr Trumble

TED RAY's irascible boss in RAY'S A LAUGH (1949), played by character actor Laidman Browne.

Mr Walker Wants to Know

Fruity-voiced cockney comedian SYD WALKER played the radio junk-man in this series of mini-dramas posing the catchphrase question: 'What would you do, chums?' Began in BAND WAGGON 5 October 1938 and continued in MONDAY NIGHT AT EIGHT from 26 May 1940. Listeners were asked to solve Syd's weekly problem: 'Lummy, I do bump into some queer how-d'ye-do's, don't I, chums?' Signature song: 'Day after day, I'm on me way, any rags, bottles or bones . . .' Adapted as a feature film, *What Would You Do Chums* (British National 1939). The series was written by Ernest Dudley and Gordon Crier. Fred Yule played Mr Walker in the Jubilee revival of *Band Waggon* (1947), the real one having wandered on.

Mr Whatsisname

Unforgettable character who forgot what he was saying and departed with a muttered 'I'll forget my own name in a minute!' Created by Horace Percival in IT'S THAT MAN AGAIN (1943).

Mrs 'Arris

Cockney character created in short sketches by C.B. Poultney and performed by the pantomime dame, Fred Spencer. First broadcast of many, 19 May 1923; typical title: 'Mrs 'Arris in the Toob' (24 November 1923).

Mrs Bagwash

'Who's she?' 'The woman's who's come to do the spring cleaning.' 'She's very quiet, isn't she?' 'Ah, it isn't the people who make the most noise who do the most work!' Charlady who gave rise to the longest catchphrase in radio history, yet never spoke on the air. Created by ARTHUR ASKEY and DICKIE MURDOCH in BAND WAGGON (1938), Mrs B. was also the mother of NAUSEA and aunt of ERNIE.

Mrs Borrett

First woman announcer on BBC radio was Mrs Giles Borrett. Much publicity surrounded her appointment; she made her first broadcast on 28 July 1933, and actually read the news on 21 August! She departed to sing to her own ukelele accompaniment in nightclubs, when she was revealed as Sheila Stewart. Many years later she returned to radio to introduce LADIES' NIGHT (1949).

Mrs Cruikshank

'My friend Mrs Cruikshank', often referred to but seldom heard, during the TWO OLD GENTLEMEN sketches in JUST FANCY (1951). The other old friend's old friend was Miss Foster-Brown.

Mrs Dale's Diary

The most famous daily serial of them all, 'in which Mrs Dale the doctor's wife reads the daily happenings in the life of her family'. Ellis Powell, the first Mrs Mary Dale, opened her Diary (to the pluckings of a harp improvized by Sidonie Goossens) on Monday 5 January 1948 at 4 pm in the Light Programme. The first scriptwriter was John Bishop, who may or may not have created Mrs Dale's classic cliché, 'I'm a little worried about Jim'.

The Dales lived in a cosy house in Kenton, Middlesex, where Dr Dale (Douglas Burbidge) had been a GP for 25 years. Son Bob (Hugh Latimer), age 22, was just demobilized from the Army, while daughter Gwen (Virginia Hewitt), three years younger than Bob, worked in an office in London. Frequent visitors to the Dale domicile were her sister Sally Lane (Thelma Hughes), a completely contrasting character, Mrs Freeman (Courtney Hope), whom Dr Dale insisted on addressing as 'mother-in-law', and her cat, Captain. The domestic help was the garrulous Mrs Morgan (Grace Allardyce). The first producer was Cleland Finn. The 1000th episode was broadcast on 4 December 1951, by which time the Dales had moved to Virginia Lodge, Parkwood Hill. The 2000th episode was broadcast 14 November 1955, by which time James Dale was played, incredibly enough, by James Dale, Leslie Heritage was Bob, and the producer was Betty Davies (the former Betty Ann Davies, film star). The tenth anniversary week was celebrated by *Mrs Dale Looks Back* (6 January 1958), a review of her many diaries by Jonquil Anthony. The 3000th episode was broadcast on 19 October 1959. The title was changed to *The Dales* on 26 February 1962, and a signature tune and an announcer replaced the harp and the diary readings.

Jessie Matthews, faded film star, found a new career by becoming Mrs Dale on 18 March 1963, a traumatic event for Ellis Powell. There was a new Dr Dale, too – Charles Simon, plus a move to Exton New Town, and a signature tune by Ron Grainer. The script was now by Robert Turley and production by Molly Rankin and Eileen Cullen. Ruth Dunning subbed for Jessie Matthews during her 1966 illness, and the final entry was broadcast on 26 April 1969. *The Dales* was also the title of a book version by Rex Edwards.

Mrs Dodge

The BBC charwoman, portrayed by Kathleen Harrison long before she became Mrs Huggett. Cheerful cockney philosopher who solved the problems of the Clayton family in FOR YOU, MADAME (1939); created by Francis Durbridge.

Mrs Doom's Diary

Parody of MRS DALE'S DIARY in which Hermione Gingold, at her most macabre, served her weekly witch's brew to her doom-laden husband, Alfred Marks: 'Tea, Edmond?' 'Yes, Drusilla.' 'Millock?' Their nasty son was played by Richard Attenborough in the first series of *Home at Eight* (1952), while butler Trog was heard only as heavy footfalls.

Mrs Doom's Diary: Hermione Gingold

Mrs Feather

Feather-brained, fluttery housewife forever suffering verbal confusions on the telephone. Created and written by actress Jeanne de Casalis and first broadcast (with husband Colin Clive) on 20 April 1931. Mrs Feather went commercial on 14 December 1937, ap-

Mrs Feather: created for radio by Jeanne de Casalis

pearing on the weekly *Leisure at Eleven* sponsored on RADIO NORMANDY by Goblin Electric Cleaners.

Mrs Gibson

The unseen, unheard friend of comedian Claude Dampier, 'The Professional Idiot'. Invented on the spur of the moment when he dried-up during a performance in Dunedin, New Zealand ('Why there's Mrs Gibson . . . hello, Mrs Gibson . . . I don't think its Mrs Gibson after all!'), Claude kept her in the act. She became so popular that in 1936 he named his boat after her, and in 1944 broadcast a series called *Mrs Gibson's Guest House*.

The first show went out on 5 December, and co-starred Billie Carlisle, Dampier's long-standing partner. Guests in the Guest House included Sydney Howard, Muriel George, Dick Francis, Carl Carlisle the impersonator, Michele de Lys and the BBC Revue Orchestra, conductor Alan Crooks. Written by Rex Diamond, James Bunting and the producer, Alfred Dunning.

Mrs Ginochie

Next-door neighbour to OLD MOTHER RILEY (Arthur Lucan), who knew her intimately as 'Ivy'. Played in the Riley radio series by Joan Young (1942).

Mrs Goodsort

The lady who gave household hints in the form of commercials for Rinso, beginning with THE RINSOPTIMISTS in 1935, and continuing as Woman's Editor of the RINSO SIX-THIRTY SPECIAL. She also turned up every week in RINSO MUSIC HALL: 'She is as popular with the listening public as any other star of the air.'

Mrs Higgins

Cockney woman played by Fred Beck in sundry broadcast sketches such as 'Mrs Higgins and the Plumber' (10 March 1936), written by Robert Rutherford, and 'Mrs Higgins Calling', which was in *Palace of Varieties* for 5 March 1933. Her cockney oppo was played by George Buck.

Mrs Hoskin and Ivy

Fat lady, ever ailing, and her sympathetically squeaky friend, played by Bob Pearson and TED RAY in RAY'S A LAUGH (1949). 'Ee, it was agony, Ivy' Mrs Hoskin would bewail. 'What happened, Mrs Hoskin?' Ivy would enquire, and a lengthy account of illness would ensue, ending with the sending for Dr Hardcastle. 'Young Dr Hardcastle?' Ivy would exclaim. 'He's luvly, Mrs Hoskin, he's *luvly*!'

Mrs Jean Scott

Head of the Brown and Polson Cookery Service who read out recipés on RADIO LUXEMBOURG in *Music and Sweets* from 11 August 1935. Whether the recipes were for Creamed Carrots or Custard, they always seemed to call for half-an-ounce of Brown and Polson's Patent Corn Flour. The title of the programme was later changed to *Musical Menu*, while Mrs Scott's motto became 'Happy Cooking'.

Mrs Mopp

Celebrated ITMA char, coarse-voiced but good-hearted, played by Dorothy Summers from 10 October 1941. Her entry line was 'Can I do yer now, sir?' and her exit 'T.T.F.N.' – ta-ta for now. In between, an only slightly lesser catchphrase, 'I've brought this for you, sir!' This was a home-made delight changed weekly according to topicalities. When ITMA visited the Home Fleet she brought a Bosun's Blancmange! She was awarded her own 15-minute series, *The Private Life of Mrs Mopp*, from 25 November 1946: 'Mrs Mopp does it again! A new series of interludes in the life of radio's most-famous charwoman.' Ted Kavanagh scripted and Jacques Brown produced.

Mrs Mulligan

Irish dame fond of her tipple, played by stage comedian Jimmy O'Dea. She made her radio début on 22 November 1941 in IRISH HALF HOUR, and soon took over the entire series. Her signature song was 'Biddy Mulligan the Pride of the Coombe' and her husband, Mick, was played by Joe Linnane. *Over To Mulligan's* started on 21 August 1944, written by Harry O'Donovan, O'Dea's old stage partner who also played the Sergeant. David Curry and his Irish Rhythms provided the music, with the Colenso Quartet, and James Mageean produced. Josie Day played Liz, and Jim Johnson was Pat Mulligan. The 1945 series began on 22 May, with 'Murder at Mulligan's'; in this cast was Cyril Cusack. Local guest stars included Billy Branff and his Tin Whistle, Thomas Turkington and his Fiddle, and the Antlers (five men and a piano). The 1946 series was entitled *At the Mulligan Inn* and started 7 July. Maureen Potter played Maureen Mulligan, and Tom Ronald produced. Her role was somewhat subsidiary in *Merry Ireland*, a weekly revue from the Calamity Theatre, Ballymescara (20 May 1947), but she was back in charge at *The Mulligan Menage* from 16 November 1948.

Mrs Murgatroyd and Mrs Winterbottom

The wives of radio comedians Ronald Frankau and TOMMY HANDLEY who, when their husbands appeared as MURGATROYD AND WINTERBOTTOM, teamed up as their missuses. Renee Roberts was Mrs Murgatroyd and Jean Allistone Mrs Winterbottom. Their broadcast on 8 January 1937 was subtitled: 'The female of the species is more deadly than the male.'

Mrs Placket

Proprietress of the Everything Shop in Little Binding, down apiece from MUCH-BINDING-IN-THE-MARSH (1948). Her name was Ivy, she had a daughter, Ethel, and her catchphrase was 'Ooh, what have I sayed!'. Played by MAURICE DENHAM.

Mrs Ponsonby

Proprietress of the Hotel Mimoar, and heavyweight lovelight in the eyes of rival wooers DUCKWEED AND EGGBLOW (Haver and Lee) and NICKOLAS RIDIKOULAS (Jacques Brown). 'Ah Mrs Ponsonby – Neuralgia – I want to take off my shoes and run barefoot through your hair!' Mrs Ponsonby was played by stalwart Doris Nichols in DANGER MEN AT WORK (1939) and was given to protesting: 'This is too much! Much too much too much!'

Mrs Pullpleasure

Eccentric entertainer in early radio revues, played by Hermione Gingold. Her son Barrymore was played by young George Inns, age 16, and light-years away from producing UP THE POLE to name but one.

Mrs Purvis

Irene Handl embarked on a radio career with this comedy character, forever trying to palm off her ugly-duckling daughter Nola, pronounced 'Noley', on any male in the offing. Created by BOB MONKHOUSE AND DENIS GOODWIN for HELLO PLAYMATES (1954), the Purvis pair were too good to lose and have appeared many times since. Pat Coombs played Nola with the Catchphrase: 'Speak as you find, that's my motto!

Mrs Shufflewick

Tipsy old biddy with a touch of pathos who made her début in VARIETY BANDBOX in 1950, and turned up in many an act show thereafter. Rex Jameson, who always played in character and never revealed his name or sex, was the man behind the roseate makeup. Signed off with his own monologue, 'I'm Just a Simple Mother'.

Mrs Tickle

First name Lola, she was the first ITMA char, addressing TOMMY HANDLEY as 'Mister Itma, and claiming that she 'always did her best for all her gentle-maine!' Given to malapropisms ('Don't cast excursions at me!') and lapses into chortles of 'Oo-hoo-hoo!'. Played in the 1939 series by MAURICE DENHAM.

Much-Binding-in-the-Marsh

This famous RAF station in Laughter Command (for whose wartime history see MEDITERRANEAN MERRY-GO-ROUND and MERRY-GO-ROUND) began its peacetime career on 2 January 1947, when RICHARD MURDOCH (ex-CO) and KENNETH HORNE (ex-AOC) converted the aerodrome into a roadhouse. SAM COSTA was retained, as were Emily's Twinges, with

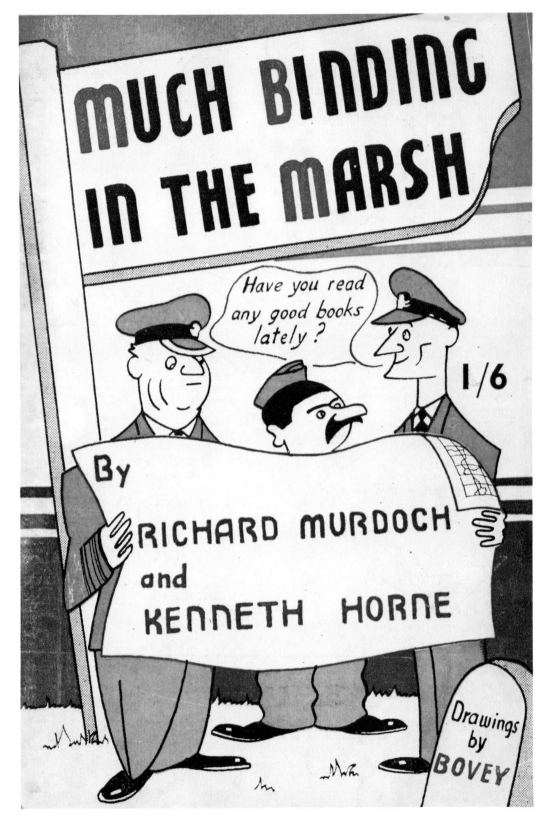

Much-Binding-in-the-Marsh: book of the show

Marilyn Williams to sing with Stanley Black and the Augmented Dance Orchestra. The next series began on 26 November 1947, with Janet Davis as singer. She was replaced by Gwen Catley. Soprano Helen Hill came in for the third series, starting 21 September 1948. MAURICE DENHAM played Dudley Davenport ('Oh, I say, I am a fool!'), with Maureen Riscoe as Hyacinth Meadows. The 100th show in the series was broadcast on 12 April 1949, when characters included MR BLAKE the Sexton (Denham). The new series starting 15 March 1950 introduced Diana Morrison, formerly of ITMA, as Denham's partner in funny voices: 'Fraid!' 'Yaice?' (*i.e.* 'Fred!' 'yes?'), and Barbara Leigh as vocalist. Then came a move to RADIO LUXEMBOURG, with Woolf Phillips and the Skyrockets as highly appropriate accompanists, and Bob Danvers-Walker to announce that the sponsor was Mars Bars. The final BBC series, called simply *Much Binding*, began on 31 July 1953 and was bound around 'The Weekly Bind', the local newspaper. Dora Bryan joined the team as Miss Plum, and Leslie Woodgate conducted the BBC Men's Chorus.

The highspot came during a supposedly secret visit from Royalty on 28 December 1948, when Murdoch was prevailed upon to let rip with his catchphrase, 'Good old Char-lee!'. It brought the house down: a reference to the baby Prince Charles, of course. The signature song, which changed every week, was 'a little thing that goes something like this' (tiddle-im-pom-pom):

At Much-Binding-in-the-Marsh,
Our aeroplane is something we're quite keen on,
At Much-Binding-in-the-Marsh,
It's used for WAAFS and bicycles to lean on,
Although the undercarriage isn't what it used to be,
And though the rudder blew away in 1893.
The radiator still provides hot water for our tea,
At Much-Binding-in-the-Marsh.

'The Chronicles of Much-Binding' written by Murdoch were published monthly in *The Strand Magazine* (1948).

Muir, Frank and Norden, Denis

Tall team of writer-performers who brought a new style to post-war radio comedy. Frank began with 'You May Take Notes', a weekly lecture which JIMMY EDWARDS gave in NAVY MIXTURE. Producer Charles Maxwell teamed him with Norden and TAKE IT FROM HERE (1948) ensued to win the NATIONAL RADIO AWARD for 1951. Their many other series include THIRD DIVISION, LISTEN MY CHILDREN, BREAKFAST, BEDTIME and BETWEEN TIMES WITH BRADEN, GENTLY BENTLEY, IN ALL DIRECTIONS, FINKEL'S CAFE, and more. They first broadcast under the joint mike-name of HERBERT MOSTYN, then blossomed out as popular panellists on ONE MINUTE PLEASE, THE NAME'S THE SAME, MY WORD and MY MUSIC.

Murdoch, Richard

Forever saddled with the nickname Stinker, from an ad-libbed 'Cavey, Stinker!' in an early BAND WAGGON, Dickie Murdoch is a classic of radio comedy, both as writer and performer. Formerly a chorus boy in musicals, he came to radio as the straight-man to bubbly ARTHUR ASKEY and soon proved he was more than a feed. As well as co-scripting the series, he contributed memorable characters like the adenoidal ERNIE BAGWASH reciting 'The Bells' by E.A. Poe. When World War II called him into the RAF it was not long before Dickie became half of a new team, sharing with KENNETH HORNE the writing and performing of the Air Force edition of MERRY-GO-ROUND dealing with doings at MUCH-BINDING-IN-THE-MARSH. In this series he used 'Put On Your Old Gray Bonnet' as his signature tune, and signed off with 'A little thing that goes something like this . . .', the Much-Binding Song. His catchphrases included 'Have you read any

Richard **Murdoch**: creative comedian, with Kenneth Horne

good books lately?', 'Good morning sir, it is good to see you!' and 'It takes a long time to warm up!' Dickie began writing and singing rapid parodies to 'Sabre Dance', 'Nola', and other fast tunes, including 'My Aunt's name is Ella Wheeler Waterbutt'. Later he had another long run as Mr Lamb in THE MEN FROM THE MINISTRY.

Murdoch in Mayfair

Starring series for RICHARD MURDOCH as manager of a new nightspot owned by Michael Trubshawe (David Niven's old chum turned professional). Howard Marion-Crawford assisted, Tonia Bern was the receptionist, and Ron Moody played sundry others. Music by Bob Sharples; script by George Wadmore, Ian Grant and Dickie Murdoch; producer Leslie Bridgmont. The club opened on 22 August 1955.

Murgatroyd and Winterbottom

Remarkable quick-fire double-act formed for radio in 1934 by solo comedians TOMMY HANDLEY (Winterbottom) and Ronald Frankau (Murgatroyd). Both clever wordsmiths and fast talkers, they specialized in pun-laden topical commentaries on current events, such as the Boat Race and the Derby, usually given the same night on MUSIC HALL. Their wives formed a double-act, too: MRS MURGATROYD AND MRS WINTERBOTTOM.

Music for Always

'A glossy magazine of music with illustrations of yesterday, today and tomorrow, played in the style of the BBC SHOW BAND directed by Cyril Stapleton.' Songs by Lee Lawrence; 'These Were Hits'; 'News and Views'; 'Talking Points' in which Stapleton discussed various topics with the week's guests. In the first show (11 January 1957) these were Majorie Proops and Roy Fox. Producer John Browell.

Music From the Movies

Long-running series starting 31 January 1946, starring Louis Levy and his Gaumont British Studio Orchestra, introduced by film critic Moore Raymond. Singers included Beryl Davis, Benny Lee, Jack Cooper and the Georgettes, and the feature item 'The Screen Presents', in which famous film stars were brought to the microphone. Star compères

were occasionally used: BEN LYON introduced the February 21 show.

The Music Goes Round and Round

Series of afternoon cabarets commencing 21 February 1940, compèred by soft-spoken James Dyrenforth and starring Adelaide Hall, Clarence Wright, Robert Ashley, the Three in Harmony, and Billy Ternent and the BBC Dance Orchestra. Guests of the week on the first show were the WESTERN BROTHERS.

Music Hall

'Ladies and gentlemen – *Music Hall*!' was the standard opening announcement – usually by Lionel Marson, in the war years by Norman Woolland. Then the Variety Orchestra, conducted by CHARLES SHADWELL, crashed in with the signature tune, 'The Spice of Life'. John Sharman devised and produced with John Watt, and the first show was broadcast on Saturday 26 March 1932 from the No. 10 Studio underneath Waterloo Arches. It was the first radio programme to be given before a large invited, live audience. The first stars were Max and Harry Nesbitt (Songs with Ukelele), Mona Gray (Vari-voiced Entertainer), Flanagan and Allen (Comedians: 'Oi!'), Randolph Sutton (Light Comedian), Scott and Whaley (Darkie Patter), Winnie Melville and Derek Oldham (Musical Comedy Artistes), and top of the bill, the real Music Hall veteran, Gus Elen (Coster Comedian). The show, the peak programme of the listening week, ran for 20 years, with breaks, and the retiring Sharman produced his farewell show on 29 January 1949, with Randolph Sutton and the Nesbitt brothers making a return engagement from show no. 1. Also in the bill: Peter Cavanagh ('The Voice of Them All'), Suzette Tarri, Janet Hamilton-Smith and John Hargreaves, Sandy Powell ('Can you hear me mother?'), and Harry Lester and his Hayseeds. Lionel Marson announced, and Rae Jenkins conducted the Variety Orchestra. Michael North took over as producer, and in the series commencing 24 September 1949 introduced the first regular comedian-compère, TED RAY. Ted was replaced from 7 October 1950 by the comedy double-act, Jewel and Warriss, an idea of new producer Bill Worsley. The last *Music Hall* was broadcast on 20 July 1952, produced by C.F. Meehan and starring Troise and his Banjoliers, CYRIL FLETCHER, Percy Edwards, Rawicz and Landauer, VIC

HIPPODROME
SOUTHAMPTON

Managing Director : A. E. STORY. Box Office Open 10 a.m. to 10 p.m. Telephone : 2978

| 6-30 | MONDAY, APRIL 12th | 8-40 |

MUSIC HALL

WITH YOUR

SATURDAY NIGHT BROADCAST FAVOURITES
INCLUDING

BERTHA
WILMOTT
RADIO'S BRIGHT STAR

MARIO
DE PIETRO
The Banjo and Mandoline Wizard of
the "air."
with JACK HOPSON
at the piano

NAVARRE
Radio's Prince of Mimics

DUNCAN GREY
Comedian without a smile

STAN GILPIN
A New Comedian

# LEONA	**RISDON** **and VEDALE**	**THE** # ANDREWS
A Versatile Young Lady	Unusual Singing Unique Dancing	Just to Entertain

Music Hall: from stage to radio and back again

OLIVER, and Sir George Robey celebrating his 83rd birthday. Bill Gates compèred, with Paul Fenoulhet and the Variety Orchestra and the Peter Knight Singers.

Music Hall Memories

'Back to Those Happy Days' was the signature tune of this 15-minute evocation of old-time music hall. Fred Douglas impersonated the likes of George Lashwood, R.G. Knowles and Hamilton Hill, while Muriel Farquhar took off Marie Lloyd and Kate Carney. The sponsor was Maclean's Stomach Powder ('Look for the signature, Alex C. Maclean') and the music came from Charles Star's Old Time Variety Orchestra. Packaged by Universal Programmes and broadcast over RADIO LUXEMBOURG from 7 February 1937.

Music of the Stars

RADIO LUXEMBOURG series sponsored by Empire Pools (1951). The first Hector Ross Radio Production, produced by Monty Bailey-Watson. The new company made a clear profit of £1 a programme!

The Music Society of Lower Basin Street

'British Branch' of the famous American radio series, with Helen Clare, Ike Hatch, Lew 'Styx' Freeman, and Phil Green's Basin Street Band and Rhythm on Reeds Orchestra. 'Discussions under the misguidance of Joe Linnane; the meeting inspired by Jimmy Dyrenforth'. Opening night: 16 March 1943.

Music Through the Window

Series 'sent specially for housewives by the makers of Phospherine Tonic Wine' and presented by Gordon Little, a baritone who sang the signature song: 'Throw Open Wide Your Window, Do.' Produced by Universal Programmes Corp. and broadcast on RADIO NORMANDY from 25 August 1937.

Music While You Work

Famous wartime series broadcast twice daily (10.30 am, and 10.30 pm for the night shift) on the FORCES PROGRAMME, designed to keep factory hands busy to rhythm. Specialist bands producing the uninterrupted music included Primo Scala's Accordion Band, TROISE and his

Banjoliers, Harry Davidson and his Band, although the music for the first-ever broadcast on 23 June 1940 was provided by Dudley Beaven at the BBC THEATRE ORGAN. By the third anniversary broadcast on 23 June 1943, (programme no. 255) four million workers in 7000 factories listened regularly. By the fifth anniversary show in 1945 (programme no. 4700), the total number of factories tuning in was 9000. The final broadcast was given on 29 September 1967 by Jimmy Leach and his Organolians. The strident sig-tune was 'Calling All Workers'.

Musical Menu

Sunday-morning series on RADIO LUXEMBOURG starring MRS JEAN SCOTT, head of the Brown and Polson Cookery Service, and featuring a 'special recipe each week', which always featured Brown and Polson's Patent Corn Flour, of course. Started as MUSIC AND SWEETS on 11 August 1935.

Musical Round-Up

Peter Haigh 'invites you to drop in at the Ranch House and meet that loveable old cowboy, Texas Jim Lewis, and his Lone Star Rangers, for a real hootie-toot round-up'. Produced by Monty Bailey-Watson for Empire Pools; RADIO LUXEMBOURG from 8 October 1953.

Musical Tour of Your Garden

Sunday morning series on RADIO LUXEMBOURG, with music by Alfredo Campoli and his Orchestra and helpful advice from H.T. Wilkin. Presented by Carter's Tested Seeds from 1936.

Musical Voyage

'A Health Cruise Round the World' starring BOBBIE COMBER as Walter and Reginald Purdell as Hubert. Sponsored by Hall's Wine and broadcast on RADIO LUXEMBOURG from 14 April 1935. Music was provided by Nat Ayer and his Band.

Muspratt

Squeaky waiter who did his best to serve the Two OLD GENTLEMEN residing at the Cranbourne Towers Hotel, Westbourn-on-Sea. Played by Kenneth Connor in JUST FANCY (1959).

The Mustard Club

Famous advertising campaign to promote Colman's Mustard which was brought to life on RADIO LUXEMBOURG beginning 1 September 1936. The founder of the Club, Baron de Beef, was played by Dick Francis, Miss Di Gester by Diana Morrison, and Lord Bacon by Gordon Little. The full title was *Guest Nights at the Mustard Club*.

M'Wamba M'Boojah

Native of Tomtopia whose Oxford accent was acquired when he was an announcer on the BBC Overseas Service! Played by Hugh Morton in IT'S THAT MAN AGAIN (1945): 'I say, Handley old man, this is really a bit thick!'

My Music

This panel-game follow-up to MY WORD, also devised by Edward J. Mason and Tony Shryane, started on 3 January 1967. Steve Race set the questions to two teams, David Franklin and FRANK MUIR, and Ian Wallace and DENIS NORDEN. Graham Dally gave forth with appropriate illustrations on the Mellotron. The game and teams, little changed (John Amis has replaced David Franklin), continue on television and radio to this day, but the final singing round no longer pretends to be spontaneous. For Christmas 1972 a special combined show was broadcast called *My Word, It's My Music*, in which Dilys Powell, David Franklin and Frank Muir competed against Anne Scott-James, Ian Wallace and Denis Norden.

My Patricia

Pat Kirkwood and Hubert Gregg were real-life husband and wife when they co-starred in this series as Pat and Hubert Jerome. Episode 1, 'Stargazing', was broadcast on 21 May 1956, with script and songs by Hubert. David Jacobs supported with Peter Akister directing the Piccadilly Players. Producer Roy Speer.

My Wildest Dream

Off-the-cuff comedy series in which a panel of comedians, TED RAY, Tommy Trinder, JIMMY EDWARDS and HARRY SECOMBE, attempted to discover the secret ambitions of members of the studio audience. Peter Haigh did his best as chairman, and Peter Eton produced. Began 3 October 1955.

My Word

This 'word game played by people whose business is words' was first broadcast on 8 January 1957 and was still running in 1985. It was devised by Tony Shryane and Edward J. Mason, creators of THE ARCHERS. John Arlott was the original umpire, and the teams were (Miss) E. Arnot Robertson and FRANK MUIR versus Nancy Spain and DENIS NORDEN. The comedy writers relied on puns for their definitions: 'Kittiwake', the end of a catnap; 'Lettish', food for a drunken rabbit. They also concluded each programme with a supposedly spontaneous explanation of a well-known phrase or saying, thus: 'A nod is as good as a wink to a blind horse' produces a lengthy yarn ending with 'A prod is as good as a blink to a shined Morse'. One famous story gives the title to the first of several books based on the programme: *You Can't Have Your Kayak And Eat It*. Michael O'Donnel is the present Chairman, following Jack Longland and John Julius Norwich, and Muir and Norden are accompanied by Dilys Powell and Lady Antonia Frazer respectively.

Myrtle and Bertie

Played by Claude Hulbert and Enid Trevor, a real-life husband-and-wife comedy team, in *The Adventures of Myrtle and Bertie*. This pioneering weekly series was first broadcast from RADIO LUXEMBOURG on 9 June 1935, sponsored by Monkey Brand Soap. Their in-laws were played by the stage and screen stars, Wylie Watson and Bertha Belmore.

Mystery and Imagination

Half-hour drama series designed to follow on the success of JOURNEY INTO FEAR. Described as 'new and revived radio plays on fantastic and imaginative themes', the first play, 'Golden Organ City', was broadcast on 1 November 1945. Written by Lord Dunsany, it concerned a mysterious window with magic properties. Producer Felix Felton.

Mystery Voice

The famous low-toned voice which announced 'And the next object is . . .' on TWENTY QUESTIONS belonged to Noel Coward's pianist Norman Hackforth. Later he became a panellist on the programme.

Naieve

Teenage daughter of Major Munday given to asking embarrassing questions of Governor TOMMY HANDLEY on IT's THAT MAN AGAIN (1945), played by Jean Capra.

The Name's the Same

Panel game adapted from an American series (by arrangement with MAURICE WINNICK) in which a team of experts (originally Frances Day, Phyllis Cradock, FRANK MUIR AND DENIS NORDEN) try to discover the names of contestants who bear the same name as famous people. The chairman was Raymond Glendenning; first broadcast was 9 June 1953. A typical programme (6 July 1954) included the name doubles of Ernest Hemingway, Pat Smythe, John Bull, Harriet Cohen, Miss Muffet and Percy Edwards (the real one being the surprise guest). The series won the NATIONAL RADIO AWARD for 1954 as the Most Promising New Programme.

National Programme

'This is the National Programme' was first heard on Sunday 9 March 1930 on 261 metres. Explained RADIO TIMES: 'The National Programme is so called because it is to be the most far-reaching British programme, part of which will be relayed to stations outside London.' The first item to be heard on the National was the Bach Cantata No. 8 played by the Guildhall School of Music. On 1 September 1939 the National became the only programme on the air, and from 3 September it disappeared forever, renamed the HOME SERVICE.

National Radio Awards

The first annual awards for broadcasters were sponsored by the *Daily Mail* at the suggestion of HARRY ALAN TOWERS, who produced the prize-givings. The first awards (5 December 1950) were presented by Lady Rothermere to:

> James McKechnie: Outstanding Actor
> Gladys Young: Outstanding Actress
> RICHARD DIMBLEBY: Voice of the Year
> EDUCATING ARCHIE: Outstanding Variety Series

Leslie Mitchell was MC and Sidney Torch conducted his orchestra.

The second awards (2 March 1952) were broadcast live from the Coliseum. Silver Microphones went to

> WILFRED PICKLES: Personality of the Year
> TAKE IT FROM HERE: Outstanding Radio Programme

The remaining awards went to television.

The third awards (1 February 1953) came from the Scala Theatre, compèred by Franklin Engelmann:

> GILBERT HARDING: Personality of the year
> Howard Marion Crawford: Outstanding Actor
> Gladys Young: Outstanding Actress
> Tom Jenkins: Most Popular Musical Entertainer
> EDUCATING ARCHIE: Most Entertaining Programme
> THE AL READ SHOW: Most Promising New Programme

The fourth awards (31 January 1954), again with Englemann at the Scala, were:

> Gilbert Harding: Personality of the Year
> James McKechnie: Outstanding Actor
> Marjorie Westbury: Outstanding Actress
> Tom Jenkins: Most Popular Musical Entertainer
> THE ARCHERS/TAKE IT FROM HERE: Most Entertaining Programme
> THE NAME'S THE SAME: Most Promising New Programme

The fifth awards (30 January 1955):

> Jean Metcalfe: Personality of the Year
> Richard Williams: Outstanding Actor
> Marjorie Westbury: Outstanding Actress
> Cyril Stapleton: Most Popular Musical Entertainer
> THE ARCHERS: Most Entertaining Programme
> HELLO PLAYMATES: Most Promising New Programme

National Radio Celebrity Gala

All-star concert sponsored by the *Daily Herald* for the Wireless for the Blind Fund, and broadcast from the London Palladium on Sunday 2 October 1949. John Ellison compèred special editions of TWENTY QUESTIONS, PETTICOAT LANE, TAKE IT FROM HERE, OPPORTUNITY KNOCKS, GRAND HOTEL and the KENTUCKY MINSTRELS. Also appearing: Anne Shelton, the Radio Revellers, FRANKIE HOWERD, the Black Dyke Mills Band conducted by Harry Mortimer, Freddy Randall and his Jazz Club Band, and Jimmy Miller and the Squadronnaires. Producer Gordon Crier.

Nausea Bagwash

Daughter of ARTHUR ASKEY's silent charlady in BAND WAGGON (1938), and equally unheard on the air. Arthur wooed her in the classic sketch 'The Proposal'.

The Navy Lark

Hugely successful series frankly inspired by Granada TV's *The Army Game*: 'a surely fictitious account of events in a Naval detachment only loosely connected with the Senior Service'. Dennis Price played 'No. 1' in charge of HMS *Troutbridge*, with Sub-Lieutenant Leslie Phillips, CPO John Pertwee, Wren Heather Chasen, and Richard Caldecot as Commander Povey. Ronnie Barker played A.B. (Fatso) Johnson and Tenniel Evans A.B. (Taffy) Goldstein, with Michael Bates as A.B. Ginger.

The show was written by Laurie Wyman and produced by Alastair Scott-Johnston, first broadcast 29 March 1959, with a second series from 16 October when Stephen Murray replaced Dennis Price. The third series (2 November 1960) included the 50th show which was given as a special performance before the Queen and Queen Mother on the 21st birthday of the WRNS. The fourth series (15 September 1961) introduced a new Wren in the shape of Judy Cornwell. After an unpopular decision to demob the team into *The TV Lark* on 25 January 1963, they were all recalled to the service by 5 April. The next series, starting 11 July 1965, introduced Jan Waters as Wren Heather, and Robin Boyle as the regular announcer. A special show for the Queen's Jubilee was broadcast on 26 June 1977.

Leslie Phillips' catchphrase, heard immediately preceding a disastrous crash, was 'Everybody down!'. The signature tune was 'Trade Wind Hornpipe', and by the time the series was discontinued after $18\frac{1}{2}$ years, it had become the longest-running comedy series of all time.

Navy Mixture

Wartime series broadcast from 4 February 1943 on the General Forces Programme: 'Blended to suit the taste of the Royal Navy'. Compère was 'Hubert' (Petty Officer Jack Watson), and Telegraphist Ivor Pye sang songs. Regular features included 'Turn Back The Clock' (musical memories revived by Judy Shirley and Sam Browne); 'Sing a Song Sailor' (join in the chorus with Joan Young); and 'Archie Takes the Helm' (with Peter Brough and ARCHIE ANDREWS). Music was by CHARLES SHADWELL and the Variety Orchestra, producer Michael North. 1945 features included Sirdani in 'Knot-ical Magic', 'Million Airs' sung by Robert Easton, and 'Naval Intelligence', a Quiz Bee for All Ranks; producer Charles Maxwell. Introduced in 1946 were the comedy characters Stripey and Bunts, played by John Slater and Ronald Shiner. A new series started on 10 May 1947 starring fast-talking Bonar Colleano Jr, with Benny Lee, Betty Paul, Maurice Denham, the Song Pedlars, and Gaby Rogers' Serenaders. Script by Ronnie Hanbury and Sid Colin; producer George Inns.

The last series began on 12 July 1947 and proved to be the most seminal of all. It starred a young Australian newcomer, JOY NICHOLS, supported by 'Professor' JIMMY EDWARDS, fresh from the Windmill Theatre, in a light-hearted lecture entitled 'You May Take Notes'. Leslie Welch the MEMORY MAN tackled questions on sport, Jack Cooper presented 'A Picture in Song', and the Revue Orchestra was conducted by Frank Cantell. Guest on the first show was Suzette Tarri, and the producer was Charles Maxwell. The final show was broadcast from the Royal Naval Barracks at Plymouth on 22 November 1947, with ex-PO Jack Watson making a sentimental comeback. From the ashes rose TAKE IT FROM HERE!

Neddie Seagoon

Stolid Welsh hero of THE GOON SHOW, known on occasion as Hairy Seagoon, and portrayed with many a quacking 'What-what-what-what' by Harry Secombe, with a tendency to open programmes by shouting 'Hello, folks!

Calling folks!' through a leather megaphone, and bursting into 'Be my love!' at the drop of a trouser. Proudly patriotic, he can be duped into anything, especially by H. GRYTPYPE-THYNNE ('You silly twisted boy, you!').

Nellie of the NAAFI

Character played by Doris Hare in the wartime series ACK-ACK BEER-BEER. Nellie was supported by Rookie Gee at the Canteen Counter.

Nelson

TED RAY's brother-in-law in RAY's A LAUGH (1949), played by fat Fred Yule. Ted had a name for him – Rumbletummy! He tended to enter with the line, 'I heard you say that, Teddy boy!'.

Nether Backwash

Mythical radio village created by Max Kester for ROBB WILTON's MR MUDDLECOMBE JP series, and spun-off into *Nether Backwash Does Its Bit* (25 September 1939). This 'topical slice of village life' featured Dick Francis, Doris Hare, JACK TRAIN, MAURICE DENHAM, and the Nether Backwash Silver Tuba Band.

New Voices

Regular segment of BAND WAGGON (1938) inspired by *New Faces*, the stage show which introduced aspiring talent. Miff Ferrie's Jakdauz sang the signature song:

> New voices now appearing,
> New voices for your hearing,
> Each trying to make a reputation,
> Each seeking your approbation.

Nichols, Joy

The Joy in 'Joy, Dick and Jimmy', the star trio of TAKE IT FROM HERE. A broadcaster almost from birth, she played Tiny Tim on Australian radio at the age of seven. She compèred *The Youth Show* for Palmolive Soap, then came to England in 1946 as hostess on NAVY MIXTURE. This led to *TIFH*, where she sang as well as played such characters as Miss Arundel ('My boy friend Gilbert . . .'). By 1949 she was starring at the London Palladium, billed as 'The First Lady of Radio'. When she left *TIFH* it took two to replace her, June Whitfield for the comedy and Alma Cogan for the songs.

Joy **Nichols**: star of *Take It From Here*

A Night at the Varieties

First regular old-time music-hall series to displace PALACE OF VARIETIES. It was broadcast from the stage of the City Varieties, Leeds, with Mr Terry Wilson as Master of Ceremonies and Mr Norman George as Fred the Fiddler. On the first night (28 September 1959) the stars were Mr Billy Danvers ('Always Merry and Bright') and Miss Margery Manners, plus members of the Leeds City Police Choir accompanied by the Gentlemen of the Pit Orchestra. Produced by Mr Bill Scott Coomber.

Nightingale

The Song of the Nightingale and attempts to broadcast same, live, was a late-night sensation of early radio. The first attempt was made at 10.30 pm on 19 May 1924, during dance music by the SAVOY BANDS. E. Kay Robinson was billed as 'The Expositor', deep in the Surrey Woods, where Miss BEATRICE HARRISON sawed away on her cello in an attempt to lure the bird into song. This quaint BBC fixation was burlesqued in *The Punch Bowl Revue* by Robert Hale as the Expositor and Gwen Farrar as the cellist.

Nightride

'An invitation to meet the beat' introduced by pop singer Gary Miller, with 'Top Tunes' by Glen Mason and Toni Eden, 'Jazz Corner'

The Nightingale: *Punch* cartoon by L. Raven-Hill (1922)

"BROADCAST" WIRELESS.

First Clubman. "AH! THE NIGHTINGALE!"
Second Clubman. "THAT SOUNDS LIKE A KNOCK-OUT."

with Christ Barber and Ottillie Patterson, 'Hum Along' with the Mike Sammes Singers, and 'McGuffie at the May Fair'. Malcolm Lockyer directed the Swinging Strings and the Top Ten Men; produced by Johnnie Stewart. Began 7 January 1959, and not to be confused with *Night Ride* which came with the revamped radio networks on 30 September 1967.

Nikolas Ridikoulas

Goofy Greek played by Jacques Brown in DANGER – MEN AT WORK (1939). He entered with 'Hello, Mrs Promsonby, how is getting?' and exited with 'Ree-diculous!'.

Nimrod Nark

Town Clerk of Foaming-at-the-Mouth, played by JACK TRAIN in IT's THAT SAND AGAIN (1941). He referred to TOMMY HANDLEY as 'Mister Mer' and had a tendency to rhyme: 'Have a cer, Mr Mer!'

No. 7 Happiness Lane

RADIO LUXEMBOURG series sponsored by Instant Postum, commencing Sunday 19 June,

No. 7 Happiness Lane: advertised in *Radio Pictorial* (1938)

GLADYS BRINGS THE HOUSE DOWN

... and Fame comes to **No. 7 Happiness Lane**

Amateur Night at the Larminster Hippodrome—and what a night! The Gibbons Family present in force, with Gladys Gibbons the star of the show! It's Gladys' big chance—and does she make the most of it! Switch on to Radio Luxembourg *next* Sunday morning and hear this thrilling instalment of "No. 7 Happiness Lane"—the fascinating real-life programme

brought to you on Radio Luxembourg every Sunday morning at 10.15, by the proprietors of Instant Postum.

No. 7 Happiness Lane
Radio Luxembourg, Sundays
10.15 a.m.

ON THE AIR ON FRIDAYS, TOO
Switch on to Radio Luxembourg every Friday at 5.00 p.m. and hear other episodes of "No. 7 Happiness Lane."

1938. 'The romantic adventures of a musical family' featured landlady Mrs Gibbons (Betty Warren) and her lodgers, Tom Warner (Eric Anderson) saxophonist, and Spencer Doughty Holmes, actor, not to mention her husband Jim, violinist, and daughter Gladys (Eileen Bennett), pianist. Producer Charles Maxwell.

No. 17 Sauchie Street

Andy Stewart and Margo Henderson played Jamie and Jessie, residents of this Scottish series which ran from 1958. Other members of the Guthrie Family included Aileen Wilson, Nan Scott, Willie Joss, with songs from Betty Pringle and Alistair McHarg accompanied by Jack Leon and the Scottish Variety Orchestra. Written by Kenneth Little; producer Eddie Fraser.

Noel Whitcomb's Party

The famous columnist of the *Daily Mirror* invited RADIO LUXEMBOURG listeners to 'meet his friends, the celebrities, at Grosvenor House'. This pioneering chat-show started on 4 April 1955 with Freddie Mills, Jerry Wayne, Laurence Harvey, Tessie O'Shea, Sandra Dorne and Jill Adams as Noel's guests. Sponsored by Nestlé's Milk.

Nor'-East Sidelights

Enterprising entertainment from BBC Scotland: 'a sound magazine' devised and produced by Howard M. Lockhart (1939). Items included: 'Radio Revuesreel', 'Passing Through', 'This Might Be You', and 'Aunt Aggie's Glamour Corner'.

Norman and Henry Bones

Schoolboy detectives, sons of the Reverend George Bones, who featured in a long-running series of CHILDREN's HOUR plays written by a schoolmaster, Anthony C. Wilson. The boys were played by Charles Hawtrey, as the older Norman, and Peter Mullins, who was later replaced as Henry by Patricia Hayes. The first play, 'Mystery at Ditchmoor', was broadcast on 17 July 1943, produced by Josephine Plummer.

Norman the Doorman

Usher of the Handleydrome, played by Fred Yule in IT's THAT MAN AGAIN (1942). Pronounced 'vice versa' as 'Vicky verky!'.

Nosmo King

Impersonator Vernon Watson took the name from a 'No Smoking' sign. He performed in black-face and an admiral's hat, always ending on a straight, sometimes heart-breaking, monologue. His stooge, HUBERT, was played by his son, Jack Watson. Played the Chairman in many editions of PALACE OF VARIETIES.

Not to Worry

CYRIL 'Odd Ode' FLETCHER was the star of this series which began on 31 July 1964. Support came from Ronnie Barker, Joan Heal, Eira Heath, David Kernan, and the Max Harris Group. John Fawcett Wilson was producer, and the script was by Alistair Foot and John Cleese.

A Note With Music

Nice programme of words and music taking the form of 'a weekly letter to a friend overseas written by' Joyce Grenfell and George Benson, with Nat Temple and his Orchestra. Producer Ronnie Waldman; first broadcast 22 February 1949.

Now Listen

FRANKIE HOWERD in a series named after one of his many catchphrases. In this one he was supported by veteran farceur Robertson Hare ('Oh Calamity'), Kenneth Connor and Carole Allen. The sketch format introduced Frankie as a dithery disc-jockey, a new student in an art class, and causing chaos in a supermarket – and that was just the first show. Script by Charles Hart and Peter Bishop; producer Bill Worsley. First broadcast 15 April 1965. The series returned under the title *Frankie Howerd* on 24 July 1966, with June Whitfield and Wallas Eaton supporting 'Bunny' Hare, and Hart writing the script with his former partner, Bernard Botting.

Nurse Dugdale

Superb female characterization created, written and portrayed by Arthur Marshall in the 1944 series, A DATE WITH NURSE DUGDALE. Hurried on with the commanding catchphrase, 'Out of my way, deahs, out of my way *instantly*!'. Sequel series: *Nurse Dugdale Takes the Air* (1945), and an 'international spy episode' entitled *Nurse Dugdale Has a Clue* (1946). 'Duggie-dear' was ever ready to oblige with a chunk of favourite fiction, such as '*Life's Treadmill* by Mercy Staunch'.

Nurse Johnson Off Duty

'A special programme for mothers' broadcast on RADIO LUXEMBOURG from 1935, sponsored by California Syrup of Figs. By 1937 her 'interesting talks' were to be heard between light musical items by Alfredo Campoli and his Orchestra.

Nurse McKay

'Mothercraft' was her topic, and she talked about it twice a week on RADIO LUXEMBOURG from 6 October 1937, on behalf of Price's Night Lights in *Night Light Time*.

Nurse Riff-Rafferty

Hearty Irish nanny who had nursed the young TOMMY HANDLEY in his cradle, leading to much embarrassment in IT'S THAT MAN AGAIN (1945). Played, with many a 'begob!', by Mary O'Farrell.

Nurse Vincent

She gave a weekly talk on the *Cow and Gate Concert* (signature tune 'His Majesty the Baby') sponsored by the baby food on RADIO LUXEMBOURG from 3 September 1935.

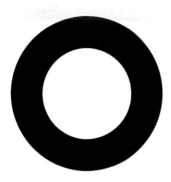

Odes and Ends

Starring series for CYRIL FLETCHER and his Odd Odes, featuring his wife, singer Betty Astell, with Frederick Burtwell and Billy Ternent's Dance Orchestra. Producer Ronald Waldman; began 30 December 1941.

Off the Cuff

Weekly musical quiz in which questions, serious and not so serious, set by Spike Hughes, were posed by chairman Antony Hopkins to the panel consisting of DICK BENTLEY, Carole Carr, Gerald Moore and KENNETH HORNE. The former FLOTSAM, B.C. Hilliam, played illustrative bits at the piano. Producer Roy Speer; first broadcast 17 July 1957.

Off the Reel

Magazine programme which began as *Set to Music* on 26 October 1939, changing its title from 23 November. DICK BENTLEY compèred this 'Mixture with a Difference', which included such items as 'Please Mr Aesop', fables retold in words and music by Henry Reed; 'The Song and the Story' (No. 1: Brother Can You Spare a Dime); 'Old and Mild', a Mellow Supplement; and 'Scored for Crime' (No. 1: The Cadenza Club), an Unusual Thriller by Gale Pedrick. Billy Ternent conducted the Revue Chorus and Dance Band, while production was by Francis Worsley and David Porter.

Office Hours

Weekly series of confusing quarter-hours with MR MUDDLECOMBE JP (ROBB WILTON) trying to run a solicitor's office with the help of ADOLPHUS the Office Boy (Lauri Lupino Lane). Written by Wilton with Max Kester; from 13 August 1941.

Oh!

Michael Scott introduced this 'novelty record programme full of deliberate mistakes and unexpected incidents, designed to keep you on your mettle and test your wits'. Produced by Peter Pritchett-Brown for RADIO LUXEMBOURG, commencing 4 May 1956.

Oi!

Bud Flanagan and Chesney Allen in their only weekly radio series, billed as 'A variety of stars in star variety'. First broadcast 5 April 1941, compèred by Sonny Miller, with dialogue by Max Kester; producer Harry S. Pepper. Music was by GERALDO and his Band. A regular character was Nettlerash, who sang such complex songs as 'The songs of today don't last no time compared with the songs of a bygone age'.

Old Acquaintance

John Witty 'presents a programme specially designed for those listeners who, in the spirit of Auld Lang Syne, have long wanted to renew their friendship with an Old Acquaintance'. Sponsored on RADIO LUXEMBOURG from 1 May 1953 by Do-Do Asthma Tablets; producer Philip Jones.

Old Ebenezer

Night Watchman at the OLD TOWN HALL in which he told a tale, always beginning with 'One night as I was sitting by my old fire bucket . . .' and ending with 'Well, I'll be jiggered!'. Played by RICHARD GOOLDEN, while his daughter Martha, who brought him his nice cup of cocoa, was played by co-writer of the playlets, Gladys Keyes.

Old Hearty

Character played by Fred Yule in the 1947 series *Old Hearty the Longshoreman*, written by and also starring HARRY HEMSLEY and his 'Radio Family'.

The Old Maestro's Music Room

Millicent Phillips, billed as 'Radio's Fifteen Year Old Wonder Soprano', starred in this RADIO NORMANDY series, which began on 15 June 1939 under the sponsorship of George Payne & Co.

Old Mother Riley Takes the Air

First radio series for Arthur Lucan and Kitty MacShane; 'introducing a loveable character of stage and screen', Old Mother Riley and her daughter Kitty. Started 21 June 1941: 'Good evening Mr and Mrs Wavelength, long, short and medium, Home and Forces and the catswhisker! It's me! I'm here! Old Mother Riley, and I'm taking the air. Where's me daughter?' And on came Kitty to the tune of 'When Irish Eyes Are Smilin''. Norman Shelly compèred, and the cast included Doris Nichols, Vera Lennox, Rex Ramer and Sid Buckman. Devised by Harry Alan Towers, written by Arthur Lucan, producer Tom Ronald.

Their second series, entitled *Old Mother Riley and her Daughter Kitty*, ran for ten weeks beginning 6 June 1942. Joan Young played Mrs Ginochie, the compère was Michael Lynd, and music came from Billy Ternent and the Dance Orchestra with the Bachelor Girls. This title was retained for the dame's third series, starting 20 September 1948, but the supporting cast was now Willer Neal, Alvin Burleigh, Rhoderick Walker, plus Frank Cantell and the Revue Orchestra. The producer remained Tom Ronald but the scriptwriter was now Kitty McShane! The old girl's signature tune was 'The Kerry Dancers' and her catchphrase 'As long as we know it'll be quite all right!'.

Old Salty

'The kiddies love his fantastic yarns of weird adventures, and the grownups enjoy his humour and songs.' And we all enjoy Rowntree's Cocoa. This sponsored series began on RADIO LUXEMBOURG on 5 January 1936, with the yarn 'How the Monkeys Saved Old Salty from the Wild Cannibals'. The signature tune, played on the hero's accordion, was 'Salty Sam the Sailor Man'. Salty was played by Ernest Butcher.

The Old Town Hall

Amazingly popular variety series beginning 16 January 1941 on the Forces Programme, 'weekly meetings organized by Gladys and Clay Keyes and presented by Eric Spear'. CLAY KEYES was the breezy Master of Ceremonies (signature tune: 'Smarty'), and Gladys Keyes played Martha, daughter of OLD EBENEZER the Nightwatchman, played by RICHARD GOOLDEN. Features included 'The Court of Melody' (where tunes are on trial and the ear is the evidence) and 'CAN YOU BEAT THE BAND' with Billy Ternent and the Town Hall Orchestra and its catchphrase, 'Penny on the drum!'. Signature song:

> The Old Town Hall,
> Extending you a greeting to
> The Old Town Hall,
> We hold our weekly meeting,
> It's so jolly and gay,
> There's nothing to pay,
> So come right in and let us drive
> Your troubles away . . .

The first series ran an incredible 64 weeks. There was a further series from 29 June to 28 September 1943, which included a 'Musical Newspaper' feature. The next series (27 April 1944) introduced 'Clay's Canteen', while the fourth (1 October 1945) featured Gladys Keyes as Martha the gossipy carrier.

Olga Meine Zeitung

Beautiful German spy played by Nan Kenway in the 'Wind-up in Whitehall' sketches featured in HOWDY FOLKS (1940).

Oliver, Vic

'The Old Vic', as his sparring partner Ben Lyon branded him, was both a comedian and musician of high order, although his fiddle scraping was an agonizing interlude between gags. The son of Baron Viktor von Samek of

Vic **Oliver**: 'the Old Vic himself'

Austria, he toured America as a concert pianist, adding jokes to the act in 1927. He came to London for a Cochran revue and was soon being billed as 'England's Favourite American Comedian', making his first MUSIC HALL broadcast in 1930. He is best remembered for his long wartime partnership with BEBE DANIELS AND BEN LYON in HI GANG, the first series of which ran for a year non-stop. Vic played PEEP KEYHOLE, the radio reporter with the low down on the *Hi Gang* stars. After the war he formed the British Concert Orchestra and combined comedy and classical music as Master of Ceremonies of VARIETY PLAYHOUSE (1953). With characteristic immodesty he called his autobiography *Mr Showbusiness* (1954). Catchphrase: 'I'm colossal!'

Oliver Again
Comedy series for comedian VIC OLIVER, supported by Deryck Guyler, Steve Conway, Doris Rogers, Daphne Anderson and Wilfred Babbage. Music by the Variety Orchestra conducted by Paul Fenoulhet, and produced by Bill Worsley. Began 25 September 1951.

Oliver's Twists
Solo series for VIC OLIVER, the comedian from HI GANG, with songs and support from Pat Kirkwood, Billy Milton and the Song Pedlars, accompanied by Stanley Black and the Dance Orchestra. Written by Veteran Dick Pepper and newcomer FRANK MUIR, produced by Jacques Brown. First broadcast 26 March 1948.

The Omar Khayam Show
SPIKE MILLIGAN's first solo series as star and writer, following the demise of THE GOON SHOW. Adapted from *Idiot's Weekly* which he had written and performed for Australian radio, there was a definite down-under flavour about both titles and cast. Bill Kerr, John Bluthal, Brian Wilde, Barry Humphries and Bob Todd supplied voices for 'Ned Kelly' (19 December 1963), 'The Ashes', 'The Prime Minister's Trousers', 'The Flying Dustman' and 'The America Cup'. Music was by George Chisholm and his Jolly Jazzers.

On Our Way
'Radio review for the Under Twenties' was the BBC's coy way with teenagers starting 19

November 1949. Joan Webster introduced three segments: 'In The News', an outside broadcast 'to meet interesting young people on their own ground'; 'Question Time' from Staines, with Majorie Tait, Jack Longland and Rex Alston answering questions; 'You're Only Young Once' – everyday episodes with the Caldicott Family, written by Edward J. Mason.

On Stage Everybody
'A Spectacular in Sound' starting 3 April 1960 and starring Evelyn Laye, 'who recalls a famous musical in which she has starred', Anne Rogers, 'musical star from a star musical', Cyril Ornadel 'behind the scenes', plus Ivor Emmanuel the Welsh singer, Roberta Leigh, the Rita Williams Singers, and Harry Rabinowitz and the Revue Orchestra. Script by Robert Bishop; producer Ronnie Hill.

On the Good Ship Symington
Symington's Table Creams and Jelly Crystals invited you to 'come aboard with this cheery, tuneful crew' every Sunday from 19 May 1935, on RADIO NORMANDY. STANELLI of *Stag Party* fame was the Captain, and the TWO LESLIES were the Mates, with Elsie Carlisle as the Midshipmite, and ALEXANDER AND MOSE as Bosun and Bozo; Mrs Stanelli acted as the Cook, the Symington Twins were the Able Bodied Pianists, and Billy Bennett was 'Almost a Cabin Boy'! Produced by Mather and Crowther's Radio Department.

On Your Marks
'Alfred Marks invites you to get *On Your Marks* for half an hour's entertainment featuring his wife, Paddie O'Neil, his friends Glyn Houston and Maxine Daniels, his guest Dennis Price, his music played by Sid Phillips and his Band, with the help of his scriptwriters Dick Vosburgh and Brad Ashton, and his producer Alastair Scott-Johnston.' He started on 8 May 1957.

Once Over Lightly
Curious comedy series starring TED RAY and DICK BENTLEY as proprietors of the *Weekly Once-over*, a crazy newspaper reflecting current events. Joan Heal and Sheila Buxton were the girls involved, with music from Malcolm

Lockyer and the Revue Orchestra. Written by Maurice Wiltshire and David Climie, and produced by Leslie Bridgmont, who said, 'It is unintelligble, which saves us a lot of money in libel actions'. First broadcast 4 October 1961.

Once Upon a Time

'A programme of dreams come true' in which famous stars were granted seven wishes. Margaret Lockwood was in the first show, broadcast 15 March 1941, and requested to hear Greta Garbo and Melvyn Douglas. Devised by HARRY ALAN TOWERS; producer Charles Maxwell.

One Man's Meat

The search for situation comedies came up with an unlikely entry here: Brian Rix as Brian Singleton was the brother-in-law of Terry Scott as Terry Binks, who is left half shares in a cooked-meat factory with his wife, Joyce, played by Elspet Gray. To confuse things further, the supporting cast consisted of Richard Baddiley and John Baddeley. Written by Eddie Maguire; produced by Alastair Scott Johnston. First broadcast 6 June 1964.

One Minute Please

Very popular, amusing and long-running radio game, devised and produced by Ian Messiter, in which personalities talked on different subjects for 60 seconds without pausing, repeating or deviating. In addition extra points were scored by the chance use of hidden 'passwords'. ROY PLOMLEY was the chairman, with Ladies (Yvonne Arnaud, Valerie Hobson, Nan KENWAY) versus Gents (Sonnie Hale, Charles Heslop, Reginald Purdell). The appeal jury on the first show (26 August 1951) consisted of three nurses from Charing Cross Hospital. Favourite of the early panellists was musical cartoonist Gerard Hoffnung, who held the highest score of 17 points (the average score was 4!). Fastest talker was Jack Sherry with 286 words per minute. Revamped years later as JUST A MINUTE.

The Open Road

Sunday morning series from RADIO LUXEMBOURG sponsored by Carter's Little Liver Pills from 26 May 1935. 'Well-known songs from all the best musical shows, catchy tunes, and a

The Open Road: advertised in *Radio Pictorial* (1938)

quick-fire one-minute Drama of Everyday Life, the kind of thing that will really entertain you.' The Drama of Everyday Life was solved, of course, by the use of a Carter's Little Liver Pill. Signature tune:

Take Carter's Little Liver Pills,
Don't wait, help your ills,
Get out of bed, be happy and so,
Make yourself a nice person to know.
Healthy folk are happy folk,
They sing, they laugh, they joke,
So if you don't feel good
I'll bet you that you would,
If you took Carter's Little Liver Pills.

Harry Karr directed the Carter Cavaliers, the announcer was Alan Keith, and the producer for J. Walter Thompson was Bill Sansom.

Opportunity Knocks

HUGHIE GREEN, former boy wonder, devised
and presented this talent-spotting series which
made its radio debut on 18 February 1949.
Hughie was billed as the Master of Opportuni-
ties, assisted by small-part film player, Pat
McGrath, and the first show presented Jean
Bayless (soprano), Archie Biggs (vocalist),
Louise Traill (soprano), Billy Martin (comedi-
an), Bosenka Duglosz (pianist), Les Chester
(comedian), and a star talent-spotter, Sheila
Sim. Scriptwriter was James Coghill, producer
Dennis Main Wilson. By the final of the series,
Green and Wilson had travelled 20,000 miles,
auditioned 4000 acts, and broadcast 165 of
them. From 1950 the show was broadcast from
RADIO LUXEMBOURG, produced by Gordon
Crier and sponsored by Horlicks. The discover-
ies were backed by Cyril Stapleton and his
Orchestra, changed in 1951 to Roberto Inglez.
Winners received their first professional book-
ing in *A Date With Steve Race*, sponsored by
Airwick.

Opportunity Knocks: Hughie Green discovers Denny
Miller

The Organ, the Dance Band, and Me

Long-running series of half-hour programmes
of uninterrupted music, beginning in the mid-
thirties. Billy Thorburn and his Music with
H. Robinson Cleaver at the BBC THEATRE
ORGAN were featured on 14 July 1939, and
were still at it on 2 August 1945. The only
difference was that Robinson Cleaver had
dropped his H.!

Organola

Half an hour of rhythm and romance presented
by Jimmy Leach (piano), Bettie Bucknelle
(singer), Henry Farmer (Organ), Jack Ross
(drums), and the compère, soft-spoken James
Dyrenforth. From 4 April 1940, produced by
Martyn C. Webster.

Orlando the Marmalade Cat

Famous feline featured in stories written by Kathleen Hall, whose adventures were retailed in CHILDREN'S HOUR by 'DAVID' with special music by Henry Reed. Began on 8 October 1946.

Chief Os-ke-non-ton

Real life Red Indian who told tales on the CADBURY'S COCOCUBS programmes on RADIO LUXEMBOURG (1938).

Osric Pureheart

Adventurer/inventor, and therefore either Captain or Professor accordingly; designer of the Brabagoon, the Merseygoon Tunnel, and the Goonitania, to name but a few. Portrayed by Michael Bentine in the early Goon series, CRAZY PEOPLE, beginning 28 May 1951. Prof. Pureheart made one final guest appearance in THE GOON SHOW on 26 December 1953, as inventor of the Giant Bombardon.

Our Bill

Cotswold countryman created by FREDDY GRISEWOOD in a series of short stories written and read by himself. First heard in a CHILDREN'S HOUR broadcast for Guy Fawkes Day, Bill's most famous and popular appearance was in 'The Celestial Gardener', in which the deceased rustic makes the Pearly Gates a homelier sight with familiar flowers. *Our Bill* in book form was published by Harrap in 1934.

Our Eli

Stuttering stooge to Jimmy James, played by Bretton Woods. Catchphrase: 'Are you putting it around that I'm barmy?'

Our Elizabeth

Cockney character played by Hermione Baddeley in a series of sketches by Florence A. Kilpatrick broadcast weekly from 26 August 1940. Also in cast: Fred Yule, Hugh Morton, John Rorke and Ernest Jay. Producer Tom Ronald.

Our Lizzie

The first comedy character popularized by radio. Helena Millais, actress and comedienne, created her and wrote the 'Fragments from Life' which Lizzie narrated. Her cockney greeting was ''Ello, me ducks, here I am with me old string bag', and she first broadcast from 2LO on 20 October 1922.

Our Shed

'Ahhh – but things are different there!' Max Wall would cry, dramatically. 'Where?' he would be asked. 'Our Shed!' he would reply, in a soppy kid's voice. ''Ere, it's everso nice in there . . .' and a somewhat weird reminiscence of the delights of the edifice would ensue. Such as: 'I've got a little green apple in there, and when I tap it a little worm pops its 'ead out of the 'ole! Coo, it ain't 'arf good!' First featured in the series HOOP-LA (1944), *Our Shed* was promoted to its own full-blown series from 17 July 1946. Billed as Max Wall's Trained Troupe of Performing Zombies were Doris Nichols (who played Ma, a lady with a weakness for milk stout, and the Duchess), Harold Berens (as Mr Mosseltoff, chiefly concerned with the black market, and Humphrey), and Arthur Rigby (as 'The Voice'). Who played Guppy and Fogg the Handymen is not clear, but the cast included Kenneth Blain, Marian Pola, Patricia Hayes, Hamish Menzies (the Maestro of the Joanna), and Reg Leopold's Our Shed Salon Orchestra. The show was written by Max Wall, 'shuffled and cut' by Pat Dixon.

Out of the Blue

Ruth Dunning appeared as the Reckitt's Reporter on this RADIO LUXEMBOURG series (1938) sponsored by Reckitt's Bluebags.

Ovaltineys' Concert Party

The first radio series sponsored by Ovaltine was broadcast from RADIO LUXEMBOURG on 21 December 1934. The show starred JACK PAYNE and his Band, who played 'Sing Holly Go Whistle Hey Hey', and HARRY HEMSLEY, the child impersonator. Hemsley's spot, described as 'The first of the series of Children's Programmes', was entitled *The Adventures of the Fortune Family*.

Hemsley's radio family, ELSIE, WINNIE AND JOHNNY, formed the nucleus of the new series of *Ovaltiney's Concert Party* which began on Sunday 3 February 1935. Hemsley himself was the director, and the opening chorus, soon to be sung by almost every child, was:

OVALTINEYS are among the brightest and happiest of children. They know that 'Ovaltine' is a delicious, appetizing drink and make it a golden rule to drink this nourishing beverage every day. It is delightful with any meal and is a favourite bedtime drink with thousands of Ovaltineys. It helps to keep them strong and full of energy.

Every Girl and Boy should join the League of Ovaltineys.

Members of the League of Ovaltineys have great fun with the secret high-signs, signals and code. You can join the League and obtain your badge and the Official Rule Book (which also contains the words and music of the Ovaltiney songs), by sending a label from a tin of 'Ovaltine' with your full name, address and age to: THE CHIEF OVALTINEY (Dept. Q.1), 42 Upper Grosvenor Street, London W.1.

The Ovaltineys: 'Happy Girls and Boys!'

We are the Ovaltineys, little girls and boys,
Make your request, we'll not refuse you,
We are here just to amuse you.
Would you like a song or story,
Will you share our joys?
At games or sports we're more than keen,
No merrier children could be seen,
Because we all drink Ovaltine,
We're happy girls and boys.

Listeners were invited to join the Ovaltineys club, with badge and rule-book, and each week the Chief Ovaltiney gave out a message in Secret Code. Children took part in the show, led in the songs by Clarence Wright. The children from Italia Conti's School were only identified by the letters in Ovaltine: Ivy Woodward was known as 'V'.

In 1937 cast included Auntie Mary (Tessa Deane), Uncle Jack (Jack Miranda), Uncle Monty (Monte Rey), Uncle George, Noel Dainton (villain in the serials) and Uncle Phil (Philip Green) and his Ovaltiney Orchestra. Producer Alan Stranks. The series ran until closed down by World War II, and was among the first to return to Luxembourg, with Clarence Wright singing and producing. The songs on 31 October 1950 were 'Tzena Tzena', 'Strawberry Fair', 'Give a Little Whistle', 'Hey Neighbour', and, of course, 'We are the Ovaltineys'.

Over and Up
Cyril Ritchard and Madge Elliott in a series 'featuring some of our best-known friends who are popular both down under and over and up', devised and written by HARRY ALAN TOWERS; producer Tom Ronald. From 27 December 1940; the second show featured Claude Dampier and Billie Carlisle, with Malcolm MacEachern (Mr Jetsam).

Over the Garden Wall
Norman Evans, the Lancastrian comedian who had established his character of Fanny the garrulous gossip on the variety stage, brought his creation to radio in this series which began on 10 February 1948. Ethel Manners (of the music-hall act Hatton and Manners) played Mrs Higginbottom, with Percy Garside as Grandpa and Peter Broadbent as Little Willie. Mary Naylor sang to the music of Richard Valery and his Concert Orchestra. The programmes were produced in the Naafi Club,

Manchester, by Bowker Andrews, and scripted by Ronnie Taylor. The series returned on 7 October 1948 and again on 4 November 1949. Now Herbert Smith played Grandpa, and Betty Jumel played Betty Butterworth. Songs were by Lee Lawrence and Norma Evans (Norman's daughter), with the Maple Leaf Four and Ray Martin's Orchestra.

Over to You
A new series for the cast of MUCH-BINDING-IN-THE-MARSH, but apart from the title it was much the same. RICHARD MURDOCH and KENNETH HORNE co-starred and co-scripted (with help from Anthony Armstrong and Talbot Rothwell), supported by SAM COSTA, MAURICE DENHAM, Diana Morrison, and Stanley Black and the Dance Orchestra. Started 30 September 1951, produced by Leslie Bridgmont.

Owt Abaht Owt
Monthly magazine programme produced in the Northern Region of the BBC, devised by E.A.G. Harding and Alfred Dunning. 1935 programmes included moustrap collectors, the Henpecked Husbands Club, and a treasure hunt to the Cocos Islands.

Oxydol Minstrel
His signature tune was 'Stay As Sweet as You Are', and he started broadcasting from RADIO LUXEMBOURG on 18 March 1935. Jack O'Day starred with the Oxydol Orchestra directed by Jack Harris. Compère was John Wood. Oxydol ('For a Bigger Tub of Richer Suds') cost $3\frac{1}{2}$d a packet, 6d for the Giant Size.

Oxydol Pioneers
Cowboy singer/composer Carson Robison and his Oxydol Pioneers, featuring Pearl Pickens, started on RADIO LUXEMBOURG on 6 October 1935. 'The stories of stirring romance and adventure they tell, the plaintive and beautiful songs they sing, are threaded with the folklore of their fathers who conquered that country.' The shows reputedly came from the 'C.R. Prairie Ranch', and in 1938 you could obtain the Famous Carson Robison Song Book (value 2/-) for only one Oxydol boxtop. Harold Jackson produced for the Erwin, Wasey company.

CARSON ROBISON
AND HIS PIONEERS
IN A RODEO OF RHYTHM

All the rhythm and drama of the prairies is captured in this grand Fairy Soap programme. From the haunting melodies of the camp fireside to the rollicking tunes of the saddle, Carson Robison gives a show which grips you all the time. Listen in to the C.R. Ranch and get the genuine lure of the West.

Tune in next Sunday and listen for details of a grand offer made to Carson Robison admirers. Note the times and be sure you don't miss it.

★

NORMANDY (274 m.)
Sundays 10.15—10.30 a.m.

LUXEMBOURG (1293 m.)
Sundays 3.0 — 3.15 p.m.
Wednes. 5.0 — 5.15 p.m.

PARIS (312.8 m.)
Sundays 6.30 — 6.45 p.m.

★

MAKE SURE OF BEING IN ON THIS !

Transmissions from Radio Normandy arranged through International Broadcasting Co., Ltd.

The Oxydol Pioneers: advertised in *Radio Pictorial* (1939)

PC49

'Incidents in the career of Police Constable Archibald Berkeley-Willoughby' were first heard in *The Adventures of PC49*, Episode 1 'The Case of the Drunken Sailor', on 24 October 1947. Upper-class Archie was played by Brian Reece, with Leslie Perrins as Divisional Detective Inspector Wilson, and Eric Phillips as Detective Sergeant Wright: 'Out yer go, Fortynine!' Archie's catchphrase was 'Oh, my Sunday helmet!' and his girlfriend, Joan Carr, was played by Joy Shelton. Written by Alan Stranks, produced by Vernon Harris, the series was promoted to a full half-hour, peak-time slot from 8 June 1948 with 'The Case of the Frightened Flowergirl'. The third series opened with 'The Case of the Burning Passion' on 11 November 1948, and 'The Case of the Falling Star' started the fourth series on 14 April 1949. Series Five began with 'The Case of the Nimble Shilling' on 10 October 1949, and the sixth series started appropriately with the 49th adventure, 'The Case of the Black Diamonds', on 27 July 1950. The seventh series began on 31 December 1950 with 'The Case of the Heavenly Murder', and the eighth on 25 September 1951 with 'The Case of the First Cuckoo'. The ninth started on 5 May 1952 with 'The Case of the Clean Sweep' and the 100th episode commenced the tenth series on 3 March 1953: 'The Case of the Blue Booties'. The final episode was broadcast on 26 May 1953: 'The Case of the Small Boy'. PC49's signature tune was 'Changing Moods'.

Palace of Varieties

Series devised by Ernest Longstaffe, 'licensee', who also conducted the music, recapturing the atmosphere of old-time Music Halls. A doorman set the scene, announcing 'Early Doors this way' as a barrel-organ ground out 'Let's All Go Down the Strand', and bidding us to enter, 'Straight through the plate-glass doors!'. The band struck up with 'Let's All Go to the Music Hall', and we met the Chairman ('For He's a Jolly Good Fellow'), who might be Nosmo King, or later, Rob Currie. First broadcast on 5 January 1937 with unannounced personalities, the show soon developed a pattern of old-time guest stars mixed with lesser-known chorus singers. Jack Hylton produced a stage version of the show in 1938, with Herman Darewski as Chairman, and starring Bertha Wilmott and Nosmo King. The first post-war series started on 8 October 1947, with Nosmo King as Mr Philpott, the chairman. Bunny Doyle topped the bill. Tod Slaughter, the famous 'Sweeney Todd' star, took over as chairman from 2 February 1951, followed by George Street on 16 March.

Palmer, Rex

'Uncle Rex' to the young listeners to the early Children's Hour, where in common with many of the BBC officials, he took his turn with a song or two. Palmer was the first London Station Director of 2LO, and his announcing style led to journalists dubbing him the Golden Voice of Wireless. Resigning in 1929 to join HMV Records led to his compèring the first sponsored programme on Radio Paris, *A Concert of HMV Records* on 29 November 1931. After retiring he returned to the BBC in the fifties as a disc-jockey and host of the nostalgic These Radio Times.

Palmolive Programme

The longest-running series in pre-war commercial radio, first broadcast on 8 April 1934; its last scheduled appearance was 10 September 1939. The cast remained nominally the same throughout: Olive Palmer, Paul Oliver and the Palmolivers, but the pseudonymous performers changed. The first song in the series was 'You've got to give a little, take a little'. Comedy was added in 1938 with Yankee-style crosstalk between Eddie Pola and Goofy Sal. Producer John Kirkby.

Papers! Papers!

Weekly series with Harry Fowler and Leslie Adams as two cockney newspaper-boys, written by Cyril Campion and produced by Jacques Brown. Started 5 April 1942.

PC 49: book of the series

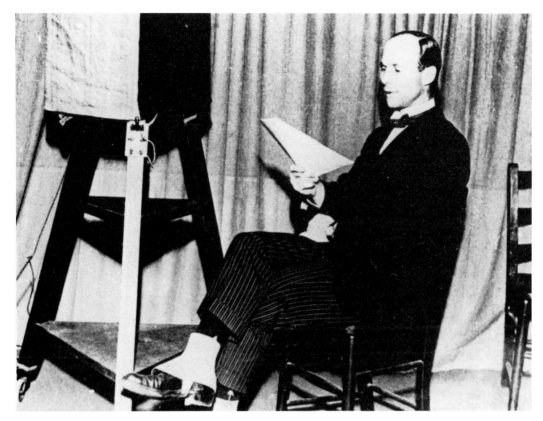

Rex **Palmer**: first London station director at the 'meat-safe' microphone

Paradise Isle

'A musical picture of the South Seas' featuring Sonny Miller and the Paradise Islanders, with the Three Admirals and the Three Dots. From 3 March 1937, produced by Max Kester.

Paradise Street

Max Bygraves took a weekly stroll down this East End thoroughfare in the company of Adele Dixon, SPIKE MILLIGAN, Hattie Jacques and the Paradise Street Kids. Musical backing from Harry Rabinowitz and the Revue Orchestra; script by Eric Sykes; producer Roy Speer. First broadcast 20 April 1954, with catchphrases 'A good idea – son!' and 'She's only eight!'.

Passing Parade

BILL KERR, the Australian comedian, starred in this weekly magazine programme which began on 15 April 1957. Features included 'Music Page' (Alan Loveday, violinist); 'Chance in a Million' (with Larry Forrester); 'Men of the Moment' (Michael Flanders and Donald Swann); 'Carry On' (ERIC BARKER and Pearl Hackney); and the Bill Shepherd Singers, with Harry Rabinowitz and the Revue Orchestra. Producer Pat Dixon.

Pat Raymond's Party

Saturday night series starring Pat Raymond, a fashion-and-beauty expert, with advice for teenage girls, interviews, record releases, and guest stars Diana Decker, Ron Moody and Stephanie Voss. RADIO LUXEMBOURG from 1 October 1960; producer Tig Roe.

Paul and Virginia

Couple whose escapades were featured in the 1938 series MONDAY NIGHT AT SEVEN; played by Derrick de Marney and Phyllis Konstam.

Paul Temple

Amateur detective created by Francis Durbridge for an eight-part Midland Region serial, he continued to crack crimes for 30 years. *Send For Paul Temple* started on 8 April 1938

"NOW I'M SCHOOLGIRL
COMPLEXION ALL OVER!"
TUNE IN TO THE
PALMOLIVE
HALF HOUR
of LIGHT
MUSIC
SUNDAYS at 8 p.m. FRIDAYS at 3.30 p.m.
Radio Luxembourg
(1293 metres)
TUESDAYS at 5.30 p.m. Radio Normandy
Transmission through I.B.C. Ltd.
(212.6 metres)
with OLIVE PALMER·PAUL OLIVER
and the PALMOLIVERS
PALMOLIVE
3d
per tablet

(Episode 1, 'The Green Finger') and concerned a series of daring jewel robberies at various Midlands mansions. To add realism the names of the actors were not revealed until the final episode: Hugh Morton played Paul and the mysterious Steve Trent, whom he married, was Bernadette Hodgson. In the second serial, *Paul Temple and the Front Page Men* (2 November 1938) she was replaced by Marjorie Westbury, who played her to the final serial in 1968, despite several changes of Paul. The original signature tune was 'Scheherazade', later changed to the well-remembered 'Coronation Scot', played by the Queens Hall Light Orchestra.

The first wartime serial, *News of Paul Temple*, began 13 November 1939. Carl Bernard became Paul in *Paul Temple Intervenes* (30 October 1942). The first post-war serial, *Send for Paul Temple Again* (13 September 1945) introduced Barry Morse as Paul. *A Case for Paul Temple* (7 February 1946) had Howard Marion Crawford as Paul, and Kim Peacock took over for *Paul Temple and the Gregory Affair* (17 October 1946). *Paul Temple and Steve* (30 March 1947) introduced a narrator played by Preston Lockwood. Another variation was *Mr and Mrs Paul Temple* (23 November 1947), a 45-minute one-off. This was quickly followed by a new serial, *Paul Temple and the Sullivan Mystery* (1 December 1947). A year later came *Paul Temple and the Curzon Case* (7 December 1948), with *Paul Temple and the Madison Mystery* (12 October 1949), *Paul Temple and the Vandyke Affair* (30 October 1950), and *Paul Temple and the Jonathan Mystery* (10 May 1951), which concluded Peacock's run. The next serial was not broadcast until 29 March 1954, *Paul Temple and the Gilbert Case*, which introduced Peter Coke as the detective. He played Paul in the first old serial to be revived, *Paul Temple and the Madison Mystery* (20 June 1955). *Paul Temple and the Lawrence Affair* (11 January 1956) and *Paul Temple and the Spencer Affair* (13 November 1957) were both new stories, followed by another revival, *Paul Temple and the Vandyke Affair* (1 January 1959). *Paul Temple and the Conrad Case* (3 July 1959) was new, while *Paul Temple and the Gilbert Case* (22 November 1959) was a revival. *Paul Temple and the Margo Mystery* (1 January 1961) was followed by a Silver Anniversary revival of *Paul Temple and the*

Jonathan Mystery (14 October 1963). *Paul Temple and the Geneva Mystery* (11 April 1965) led to the final case, *Paul Temple and the Alex Affair* (26 February 1968). Then he started all over again on television!

Paul Tremble

'Send for Paul Tremble!' was this character's entry-line. And as he was played by Hugh Morton, the original PAUL TEMPLE, the satire had more to it than met the ear. One of the last characters introduced into IT'S THAT MAN AGAIN (1948).

Payne, Jack

Dance-band leader who formed the first BBC DANCE ORCHESTRA. Legend says he conducted the band in Jefferson Gardens, Leamington Spa, in 1900, with a rolled-up newspaper – age one! As conductor of the Hotel Cecil Dance Band he made his first broadcast on Boxing Day, 1925, playing 'Yes Sir, That's My Baby', and became so popular that he was invited to form the BBC Dance Orchestra. This made its debut on 12 March 1928. Four years later Jack resigned to take his band on the Music Halls, where they were an enormous success. He married pianist Peggy Cochrane, and his vocalists included Leslie Sarony, Billy Scott Coomber, Val Rosing, Elsie Carlisle, Ronnie Genarder and most frequently, Jack himself. After the post-war collapse of the big bands, Jack hosted a music series which used his signature tune as its title: SAY IT WITH MUSIC. He called his autobiography *Signature Tune*.

Peep Keyhole

VIC OLIVER played this gossip columnist of the air in HI GANG! (1940): 'This is Peep Keyhole, your radio reporter, bringing you the lowdown on the personalities in the *Hi Gang* programme.' Each gag was punctuated by a 'peep-peep' on his whistle.

The Peers Parade

Sumptuous series starring the Cavalier of Song, Donald Peers, 'in which he greets personalities from the entertainment world and welcomes his regular friends'. These latter were pianist Semprini, Ann Lancaster, Harold Smart at the electronic organ, the Show Band Singers, and Paul Fenoulhet with the Variety Orchestra.

The Palmolive Programme: Luxembourg's longest run

208

The first show (5 May 1957) included 'Picture Puzzle', a four-round contest of movie knowledge refereed by John Blythe, who was later replaced by MICHAEL HOWARD. There was also 'On Stage', featuring drama students on the threshold of their professional careers, and 'Memories Are Made Of This', a musical flashback to the tuneful twenties. Script by George Wadmore and Dennis Castle; producer Roy Speer.

Penguin Parade
Barbara MacFadyean and Garry Marsh with tunes and stories from the young to all the family, a daily series sponsored by Macdonald's Chocolate Penguin Biscuits on RADIO LUXEMBOURG from 9 July 1951. The series returned on 7 August 1954, still with Garry Marsh, but as 'Luxembourg's first Quiz Show for Children'. Young listeners were asked to send in questions for King Penguin Solomon, a wise bird in the Arctic Sea-Circle, to answer. There were prizes for every question broadcast. Producer Eric Goldschmidt.

People Are Funny
'Would you prove your love for your sweetheart by climbing the highest mountain and swimming the deepest river?' The classic American comedy participation show, Anglicized by Ross Radio Productions for Pye Radio, came to RADIO LUXEMBOURG on 3 November 1953 and ran for 72 weeks. Peter Martyn was the original host who proved that 'People *Are* Funny', assisted by Laurie Main and announcer Bob Danvers-Walker. The show came from a different theatre each week, its most prestigious date being the Royal Albert Hall on 15 September 1954. Martyn died in harness and was replaced by overweight cabaret pickpocket, Vic Perry. The stunt devisers included Denis Gifford and Lionel Hinton; director was Hugh Rennie. The second series started 24 August 1955 with Larry Cross, directed by John Whitney.

Percy Pintable
Character with the catchphrase, 'Lo and be'old!', played by Horace Percival in ITMA (1943).

Jack **Payne**: *Radio Dance Band Song Book* free with *Ideas*

Perry Mason
Erle Stanley Gardner's fictional detective came to RADIO LUXEMBOURG in a daily serial broadcast from 1 October 1951, sponsored by Tide. The first 'exciting adventure of the lawyer-detective and his faithful secretary, Della Street' was entitled 'The Case of the Martyred Mother', which was finally followed in September 1952 by 'The Case of the Invisible Empire'. Three months later came 'The Case of the Prodigal Daughter', then in February 1953 'The Case of the Frightened Flirt'. 'The Case of the Sinister Sister' started in September 1953, and 'The Case of the Hungry Hearts' in October 1954. The signature tune for the series was 'Changing Scenes'.

Persil Personalities
'Intimate broadcasts by the great stars of our time' introduced by the Irish singer, Denis O'Neil. In between presenting Binnie Hale and her ilk, he had the odd word about washday. Peter Yorke and his Music provided the accompaniment, and the signature tune, 'With a Smile and a Song'. RADIO LUXEMBOURG, 1938.

Pertwee, Jon
One of the great funny-voice men of radio who rose to fame through bringing to life ERIC BARKER's creations in MERRY-GO-ROUND (Naval Edition). His characters and catchphrases are legion: SVENSON the Svede ('Nyeden nyaden nyeden neggidy crop de bombit'), COMMANDER HIGHPRICE ('Hush, keep it dark'), the POSTMAN from Puffney ('What does it matter what you do, me dear, as long as you tear 'em up') who spun off into his own series, Viscount Pugh of Plumstead, ROBIN FLY, Mr Cook ('Dabbera dabbera that's right, yerse'), all from WATERLOGGED SPA. Later came Mr Burp of UP THE POLE. Born in Devon (hence the delightfully authentic postman), son of Roland Pertwee the actor-playwright, Jon joined the Navy in 1939 and was in the studio audience when Eric Barker called for a volunteer to read the line, 'You leave 'im alone, you're always pickin' on the poor perisher!'. Jon jumped in and a comedy career was born, culminating in a long run as the Chief Petty Officer in THE NAVY LARK (not to mention a stint as television's Doctor Who!). See also PERTWEE'S PROGRESS.

People Are Funny: book of the show

Pertwee's Progress

JON PERTWEE was the multi-voiced star of this series, supported by Dick Emery, Kirk Stevens, 'MRS SHUFFLEWICK', Mercy Haystead, Fenella Fielding, and Denis Wilson and his Orchestra of Pianos. Harry Rabinowitz and the Revue Orchestra provided the music and the producer was Dennis Main Wilson (who inserted the Main to avoid confusion with the pianist). First broadcast 6 April 1955.

Pet's Song Party

Each week Petula Clark visited the Dr Barnardo's Village Homes at Barkingside for a sing-song with the children there. Broadcast on RADIO LUXEMBOURG from 11 February 1955 and produced by Geoffrey Everitt.

Pet's Song Party: Petula Clark as drawn for *Radio Fun* comic by Bertie Brown

Pete's Party

'A Sunday night get-together around the gramophone' introducing Pete Murray, staff disc-jockey from RADIO LUXEMBOURG, to BBC Light Programme listeners. Twenty weeks of 70-minute pop-record programmes, starting 17 August 1958.

Peter Geekie

Mysterious Scots character who 'appeared' in ITMA (1943) without ever appearing; he was only referred to. As in 'Who did that?' – 'Peter Geekie!'. Later, his uncle Andrew (pronounced Andra) began to phone in threats from Glas-

gow: 'Is that yon sleekit creepit gowk, TOMMY HANDLEY?'

Peter Goodwright Show

Situation comedy series for the Northern impressionist in which he shared a flat in Cemetary Road, Chorlton-cum-Hardy, with Anton Rogers. Episode 1, 'Last of the Big Time Spenders', was broadcast on 18 March 1963, with Joe Gladwin as their neighbour, Arnold Potter, and Tina Mullinger as Angela Forsyth-Smith. The second series began on 29 March 1964 with 'The Cheap Day Excursion', Tony Melody and Brian Trueman in the cast. Scripts by Vince Powell and Harry Driver; producer Geoff Lawrence.

Peter the Planter

Solar-topee'd star of *Peter the Planter*, a musical series sponsored by Lyons Green Label Tea. He made his debut on RADIO LUXEMBOURG, 29 August 1937, when the music was provided by Fred Harley and his Sextette. Peter was played by Michael Moore, who became a professional impressionist. In 1938 the series switched to a somewhat different plantation, featuring the Plantation Minstrels, the Plantation Singers, the Plantation Players and the Plantation Banjo Team.

Petticoat Lane

'You want it – they've got it! An imaginary tour of London's famous market to join ELSIE AND DORIS WATERS as they make their way from stall to stall to meet unexpected people in the most unexpected places.' Elsie and Doris played the expected people, GERT AND DAISY, and the stars they met were MICHAEL HOWARD, Max Wall (continuing his reminiscences of OUR SHED), Benny Hill, Joan Young, Albert and Les Ward, Benny Lee, Doris Nichols (as Auntie), Ian Sadler and Kenneth Blain. Rae Jenkins conducted the Variety Orchestra, and Pat Dixon produced. First broadcast 29 July 1949.

> Petticoat Lane,
> There's not another street like
> Petticoat Lane, Petticoat Lane,
> It may be poor and tumble down,
> It's the Sunday morning rendezvous of
> London Town.

Petticoat Line

ANONA WINN, perennial panellist, thought up this feminist affair, with a little help from Ian Messiter. She was chairwoman of a panel consisting of Scots comedienne Renee Houston, *Daily Mirror* sob-sister Marjorie Proops, film star Jill Adams and film starlet Jane Asher, and their purport was to answer lady listeners' letters and air their points of difference on the grievances women have against men. Bobby Jaye was the beset producer. First broadcast 6 January 1965. A series in which men answered back, BE REASONABLE, was instituted in 1968.

Gipsy Petulengro

Musical fortune-teller who starred in *Sky High With Skol*, a Friday radio series from RADIO NORMANDY. 'His romantic Romany Melodies are as soothing as the product which brings him into your home.' This was Skol, an antiseptic, costing 1/6d per bottle, but you could get a free sample if you wrote in for Petulengro's Luck Chart. On the variety stage he had a thought-reading act called 'The Talking Fiddle', and in 1934 formed an all-girl orchestra called Gipsy Petulengro and his Lady Hussars.

Philco Slumber Hour

This early commercial radio series formed part two of the Philco Hour, the first half being *Philco Dance Music*. It was first broadcast from 11 pm to midnight on RADIO NORMANDY on Sunday 22 November 1931 with five items of classical music beginning with Dvorak's 'Humoresque', played by the Philco Symphony Orchestra under the direction of Harold Barlow. The announcer was Commander H.V. McHardy RN, and the series concluded on 31 January 1932.

Philip Odell

Irish detective created for radio by Lester Powell, played by Robert Beatty in the original radio serial, *Lady in a Fog* (6 October 1947), and by Cesar Romero in the 1952 film version. Brenda Bruce played his lady assistant, Heather McMara, and the producer was Martyn C. Webster. Odell returned on 7 June 1948 in *The Odd Story of Simon Ode*; this time Joy Shelton played Heather. The third serial, *Spot the Lady*, started 25 April 1949, followed by the fourth, *Love From Leighton Buzzard*, on 4 April

1950. Heather was now played by Joyce Heron; and she stayed on for the fifth serial, *The Lady On the Screen*, which began 9 February 1952. Odell returned in a new production of the first serial on 29 April 1958, and a brand-new serial, *Test Room Eight*, on 22 December 1958. Heather was played by Sheila Monahan and the producer was David H. Godfrey. The next serial, *Tea on the Island*, introduced Diana Olsson as Heather. It started on 19 June 1961.

Philip String

Hero of 'The Adventures of Philip String' serialized in CRAZY PEOPLE (1951), and played by SPIKE MILLIGAN.

Phoney Island

Starring Dicky ('Large Lumps') Hassett as the cockney boss of an amusement park, with Arthur Chesney, Frederick Burtwell, VERA LYNN, Dick Francis, Dudley Rolph and the Phoney Islanders directed by Billy Ternent. Contrived by the ITMA production team of Ted Kavanagh and Francis Worsley, from 14 May 1940.

Piccadixie

'From Piccadilly to Dixie and back again in the space of half an hour' with Adelaide Hall, Oliver Wakefield, and Gerry Fitzgerald as passengers, conducted by James Dyrenforth. From November 1940.

Piccalilli

Contrived around the fast-rising talents of homely Yorkshire comedian WILFRID PICKLES: 'A comedy concoction of ingredients calculated (with great relish) by various authors, designed to achieve a unique blend of mixed pickles.' Cast included Avril Angers, Gene Crowley, Dick Francis and C. Denier Warren, with the Revue Orchestra conducted by Alan Crookes, and special music and production by Henry Reed. Started 11 October 1944.

Pick a Tune for £200

You could win £50 each and every week by putting eight songs in your order of merit. Roy Rich was the Competition Master, and Lou

Wilfred **Pickles**: 'Have a Go'

Praeger and his Hammersmith Palais Band played the week's top eight. On 3 February 1952 they were 'Jezebel', 'While You Danced', 'The Slippery Samba', 'Autumn Leaves', 'Kissing Bug Boogie', 'I Found You Out' and 'American Patrol'. Sponsored by Airwick on RADIO LUXEMBOURG.

Pick of the Pops

Franklin Engelmann was the original disc-jockey on this long-running series, beginning 4 October 1955. It was described as 'Jingle assisted by Belle make a selection from the top shelf of current popular gramophone records'. It was not until 7 January 1962 that Alan Freeman arrived with his 'Greetings, Pop Pickers!' Then the show divided into three parts: new releases; Freeman's personal choice of possible hits; and a Top Ten countdown in reverse as compiled by Derek Chinnery of the BBC Gramophone Department.

Pickles, Wilfred

Possibly the most popular radio personality of all time, his long-running HAVE A GO made history as the first live, ad lib series to bring the voice of the people to the microphone, under the thin guise of a quiz. Our Wilf was a Halifax builder who began in regional radio in 1931. A born broadcaster, he 'had a go' at everything, singing, story telling, poetry reading, compèring, stand-up comedy, straight acting, pantomime, and in 1941, with his Yorkshire accent, was the first news reader to break the standard 'BBC English' rule. At the end of the midnight news his sign-off shocked many: 'Goodnight everybody, and to all Northerners wherever you are – good neet!' He also played the radio characters BILLY WELCOME and EX-CORPORAL WILF before *Have A Go* shot him to permanent fame. There were two autobiographies, *Between You and Me*, and *Sometime Never*.

Picture Book

Series of soundtrack adaptations of currently popular movies, adapted and presented by Desmond Carrington and Spencer Hale. The first, broadcast 12 August 1957, was *Let's Be Happy* starring Tony Martin and Vera-Ellen.

Picture Parade

'Fortnightly film programme on every aspect of picture production and film gossip, with views of the stars and those who make them, and pictures of the past, present and future.' Edited by Gale Pedrick and produced by Peter Eton, the first show (17 April 1946) featured a rare conversation between veteran star Mary Pickford and Rank starlet Peggy Evans. Other items: 'Review' (Rita Hayworth's latest hit, *Gilda*); 'Criticizing the Critic' with Matthew Norgate; 'Round the Studios with Roy Rich' (No. 1 – Gainsborough); 'Spotlight on Hollywood' (Greer Garson): 'Pictures from the Past' (*Laura*); and Roy Plomley's weekly burlesque, 'How Not To Make a Picture', began with 'The Happy Ending' by the Boulting Brothers. Programme No. 50 (5 November 1948) introduced 'What a Business', a satirical look at cinema by Noel Langley, and 'Difference of Opinion', critic Milton Shulman versus the producer of *Noose*, Edward Dryhurst. John Hollingsworth was billed as conductor of the Picture Parade Orchestra.

Picture Reporter

'A radio filmagazine introducing filmland gossip and news of favourite movie stars', presented by Douglas Moodie from 28 March 1941. Features: 'Films in the Making (*49th Parallel*), 'General Releases', 'M.O.I. Presents' (a radio version of the latest propaganda film), 'They Also Serve' (David Lean), 'Music From the Movies' by Louis Levy and his Orchestra.

The Piddingtons

Sensational and unique mind-reading series starring an act from Australia, Sydney Piddington and his wife Lesley Pope, who came to radio from 14 July 1949 to 'entertain you with their own kind of mystery'. For example, Sydney transmitted the title of the show *Oklahoma* to Lesley, while he was in the studio and she was touring the West End in a taxi with Lionel Hale. Colin Wills was the commentator, and Frederick Piffard produced. The Piddingtons returned for a second series on 16 January 1950. This time Stephen Grenfell commented while Ian Messiter produced.

The Pig and Whistle

'Truly Rural Episodes' set in an imaginary village pub where the atmosphere was so strong

---

Picture Parade: theme music for the radio series

PICTURE PARADE

PIANO SOLO BY JACK BEAVER

THEME MUSIC FROM THE POPULAR B.B.C FEATURE 'PICTURE PARADE'

The Identity of the stars is on the back page.

CHAPPELL

2/-

1904

MADE IN ENGLAND

that listeners believed it really existed. Charles Penrose ('The Laughing Policeman') scripted and played Police Sergeant Bob Evergreen, with Miriam Ferris as Rosie Jones the Landlady, Charles Wreford as Old Granfer, baritone Sidney Burchall as Jimmy Larkin, Peter Penrose as Egbert Ullage, John Rorke as 'Erb the Cockney Cousin, and Dick Francis as the Squire. Music by Rae Jenkins and his Buskers, and production by Ernest Longstaffe. First broadcast 17 January 1938; last broadcast 19 October 1944.

Pixworth Ames
Played by Norman Shelley in the 1939 RADIO NORMANDY series *Crime Reporter*, sponsored by Limestone Phosphate.

Plain Jane
'The story of Plain Jane Wilson and her struggle for those things that every woman longs for – love and happiness.' Daily soap opera presented by Rinso on RADIO LUXEMBOURG, commencing 5 September 1938, with Jane Welsh as Plain Jane. Written and produced by Irving Ashkenazy.

Plantation Love Song
Starring Edith Day and Thorpe Bates, with 'Down South' as the signature tune, this weekly series began on RADIO LUXEMBOURG on 15 September 1935, sponsored by Carreras Virginia Cigarettes.

Play It Cool
'A sort of summer show' starring Ian Carmichael, Joan Sims, Hugh Paddick, Roy Dotrice, Elvira Heath, Rosemary Squires and the Mike Sammes Singers, with the Gordon Franks Decktette. Written by Eric Merriman; produced by John Simmonds; first broadcast 5 August 1963 and turned into a series from 26 July 1964.

Play My Way
Ronald Chesney, the mouth-organ king, 'invites both young and old to learn the simple art of playing the harmonica' on this RADIO LUXEMBOURG series commencing 1 October 1954. Produced by Geoffrey Everitt, the sponsor was Hohner, the Harmonica of the Stars: 'It's fun to own a Hohner!'

Play the Game
Medley of games and puzzles devised by John P. Wynn and chaired by Wynford Vaughan Thomas. KENNETH HORNE, Iris Ashley, Charmian Innes, and Robin Richmond at the electronic organ played panel games, musical contests, met mystery guests, and set a prize sound quiz for listeners at home. Started on 4 January 1960, produced by Joan Clark.

Plays
The first stage play to be broadcast was an extract from Brandon Thomas's famous farce, *Charley's Aunt*, coupled with an extract from *The Private Secretary* (13 January 1923). The first Shakespearean broadcast was an excerpt from *Julius Caesar*, acted by Shayle Gardner and Hubert Carter (16 February). The first play to be broadcast live from a theatre was Act 1 of *Battling Butler*, from the Adelphi Theatre (21 March). The first complete play broadcast from a studio was Shakespeare's *Twelfth Night*, with Cathleen Nesbitt (Viola), Nigel Playfair (Sir Andrew Aguecheek), and Henry Caine (Toby Belch) (28 May). The first complete modern play broadcast from a studio was *Five Birds in a Cage* by Gertrude Jennings, produced by Milton Rosmer, with Athene Seyler, Fred Groves and Hugh Wakefield (29 November).

The first original play written for radio was *The Truth About Father Christmas*, by ARTHUR BURROWS, Christmas Eve 1922. The first dramatic play for radio was *A Comedy of Danger* (later rebroadcast as *Danger*) by Richard Hughes. This 'wireless melodrama' was produced by Nigel Playfair, with Joyce Kennedy, Keneth Kent and H.R. Hignett (15 January 1924).

The Playtime Programme
Uncle Coughdrop starred in this children's series sponsored by Pineate Honey Syrup on RADIO NORMANDY from 1936. He told tales of Brer Rabbit to Auntie Clara and ten-year-old Betty.

Pleasure Beach
'Radio's New Luxury Holiday Camp' held its Gala Opening on 4 July 1946, with Fred Emney and Claude Hulbert co-starred. 'Permanent staff and holiday-makers' included Hugh Morton, Lyle Evans, Sally Browne, Brian Reece and Arthur Young, with the

Pleasure Beach Dance Orchestra conducted by Stanley Black. Produced by Roy Speer and written by Rodney Hobson.

Pleasure Boat

Norman Shelley played the Skipper in this star-studded series which set sail on 15 March 1953. He was 'in charge of a talented crew whose adventures at sea always culminate in a shipboard concert' – not perhaps surprising when the crew consisted of Anne Shelton, Bob and Alf Pearson, Freddie Sales, Lee Lawrence, George ('I'm not well!') Cameron, Julie Andrews, Bernard Spear, the George Mitchell Mariners, and Ray Terry's Crewmen conducted by Phil Cardew. Not to mention a guest traveller, the first being VIC OLIVER. Script by George Wadmore, Sidney Nelson and Maurice Harrison; produced by Dennis Main Wilson.

The Pleasure's Mine

WILFRED PICKLES, 'assisted by some friends, reads a selection of his favourite poems'. The friends included Binnie Hale, Betty Hardy, Colin Wills and Arthur Marshall. This was the first popular poetry series, broadcast from 21 November 1949, with a second series from 15 February 1951. This time Wilfred's friends were Peggy Ashcroft, Barbara Jefford, Michael Redgrave and Duncan McIntyre. Producer Joe Burroughs.

Plomley, Roy

Failed film extra who became a familiar voice to commercial radio listeners hosting RADIO NORMANDY CALLING and many other pre-war series. His wartime work for the BBC included the satirical series about Drearitone Studios, HURRAH FOR HOLLYWOOD, a tongue-in-cheek style that later gave us THE RHUBARB ROOM ('the tattiest nightclub in town'). His main contribution is, of course, the creation and continued hosting of DESERT ISLAND DISCS, on the air regularly since 1942. He was also the unruffled chairman of such games as WE BEG TO DIFFER and ONE MINUTE PLEASE. His autobiography, *The Days Seemed Longer* (1980), is a good account of pre-war commercial broadcasting.

The Plums

First radio family to appear in a regular series, *The Plums* made their début on 4 October 1937, with the trumpet-blowing Augustus Plum singing their signature tune in broad Lancastrian:

> Come, come, come, says Jolly Mr Plum,
> Never start a-worrying if things look glum,
> For no matter what the weather,
> The Plums will always hang together,
> Come, come, come, remember you're a
> Plum.

Written by Max Kester from Sonny Miller's devising, *The Plums* were originally anonymous, but public demand led to the revelation that Mr Augustus Plum was played by Foster Carlin, Mrs Aggie Plum by Minnie Rayner, daughter Victoria Plum by Audrey Cameron, and grumpy old Uncle Ed by Clifford Bean. In the revival from 1 January 1942, the new cast was Wylie Watson, Beatrice Varley, Paula Green; only Clifford Bean remained unchanged.

Pocket Theatre

Jack Hulbert and CICELY COURTNEIDGE, the well-known but ageing theatrical husband and wife, co-starred in this regular segment of VARIETY PLAYHOUSE from 1956. These dramatic sketches, written by Jeremy Bullmore, Gary Blakeley and others, might be set in Mayfair, Old Austria, or the French Revolution, but the stars remained obstinately Jack and Cis.

Polly Put the Kettle On

– 'And we'll all have fun! A light tea-time show' starring Polly Ward with 'Wives of Famous Husbands'. 'Think of a Number', 'New Songs for Old', and guests Stanelli, Horace Percival, Jack Cooper and the Debonairs, with Billy Ternent and the BBC DANCE ORCHESTRA. Written by Ray Sonin and Rex Diamond; producer C.F. Meehan. Weekly from 27 November 1943.

Pompeiian Star Programme

Sponsored by Pompeiian Beauty Preparations, the hostess was Lady Charles Cavendish, better known as Adele Astaire (Fred's dancing sister), supported by Fred Hartley and his Orchestra. On the first show, broadcast on RADIO LUXEMBOURG, 7 October 1934, Lady Cavendish's guest was film star Jane Carr. Listed for the following weeks: Enid Stamp Taylor, Nancy Burne, Jeanne de Casalis, Greta Keller and

ANONA WINN. The signature tune was 'Sweet and Lovely'.

Pond's Serenade to Beauty

This 1936 series on RADIO LUXEMBOURG – 'A Programme for Lovers' – was presented by Pond's Extract Company. Van Phillips led his Dance Orchestra, and Stella Wayne 'discussed human problems'. Singers were Helen Clare and Bill Clayton, announcer Michael Riley, producer Tony Marr.

Poppy Poopah

Frightfully upper-class young lady introduced into IT'S THAT MAN AGAIN (1943) by Jean Capra.

Portrait of a Star

David Jacobs introduced this series of musical biographies which began with Ray Ellington on 1 October 1954. Philip Jones produced for RADIO LUXEMBOURG and the sponsor was Harris's Harella.

Post Toasties Radio Corner

Daily programme for children broadcast on RADIO NORMANDY from 8 March 1937. 'Uncle Chris' was BBC renegade CHRISTOPHER STONE, and his call-sign was 'Hi-de-hi!'. There were prizes of half-a-crown to be won by young listeners, and a serial story of 'Tony and Teena the Harvey Twins' started on 18 October.

The Postman

JON PERTWEE in WATERLOGGED SPA (1946) who was always 'blowin' me bugle in Plymouth Barracks. It was buglin', buglin', the whole time buglin'!' He wound up his weekly appearance with the catchphrase: 'What does it matter what you do as long as you tear 'em up!' He was such a success that the Postman was awarded his own series, *Puffney Post Office* (1950).

The Potted Show

'Potted Facts, Potted Puzzles, Potted Fun' presented by Seniors, purveyors of potted meat. The first programme, broadcast over RADIO NORMANDY on 6 April 1939, featured DICK BENTLEY and Peggy Desmond.

Gillie **Potter**: 'Hogsnorton calling'

Potter, Gillie

Stage comedian and eccentric dancer who became a classic humorous broadcaster from 1931, with his monologues concerning the bucolic affairs of HOGSNORTON. Although he was a familiar figure on the Music Halls with his broad-brimmed Harrovian boater, his striped blazer and Oxford bags, his erudite wit was better suited to his many series of 15-minute talks given without a studio audience. His famous opening catchphrase mocked the pomposity of early radio: 'Good evening, England, this is Gillie Potter speaking to you in English!' He recorded *Heard At Hogsnorton – The Truth About the BBC* on Decca K650 in 1932.

The Preservene Minstrels

Series presented on RADIO LYONS from 20 June 1937 by the makers of Preservene Soap. The star was Johnny Schofield, a familiar face from British B-pictures, with Kent Stevenson, described as 'that wise-cracking interlocutor'. Advertisements commented: 'We don't know how the Preservene Nigger Minstrels get the black off, but we can tell you how millions of clever housewives get the dirt out. They use Preservene, the all-purpose soap, now only $5\frac{1}{2}$d a bar!'

Press Gang

Musical-stage favourite Stanley Lupino starred in this 'amusepaper story' devised by

Jacques Brown with dialogue by producer Max Kester. Also heard: BOBBIE COMBER, Teddie St Denis and Helen Clare. Weekly from 26 March 1941.

Princess for a Day
Film star Richard Attenborough escorted some lucky young lady through this programme which had music by the Dorchester Hotel Orchestra. Produced by Peter Wilson for Phensic, and broadcast on RADIO LUXEMBOURG from 1 October 1955.

Private Bar
Atmospheric series for Stanley Holloway, 'who invites you to join him in the company of the regulars, Gordon Crier and ROY PLOMLEY. Behind the bar, Rosamond Barnes, at the piano, Eric James.' Monologues and ballads by Marriott Edgar and Wolseley Charles. First broadcast 5 May 1948, producer Eric Speer.

The Private Life of Renee Houston
Weekly series for the Scots comedienne, her family, and 'her friends the stars'. Sponsored by McDougall's Self-Raising Flour, RADIO LUXEMBOURG from 17 January 1937.

Prize Puzzle Corner
The first cash-prize contest broadcast by the BBC. £100 prize competition in aid of the Red Cross Penny-a-Week Fund, with Ronald Waldman as Master of Ceremonies presenting twelve puzzles in sound compiled by Neil Munro. Ellen Wilkinson, MP, introduced the first show on 7 December 1940. For later series the title was changed to *Radio Red Cross Contest*.

Professor Branestawm
Eccentric and thoroughly absent-minded inventor created by Norman Hunter in a long-running series of stories for CHILDREN's HOUR. These were first gathered into a book, *The Incredible Adventures of Professor Branestawm*, in 1933, dedicated to 'Ajax' (T.C.L. Farrar), the man who read them aloud.

Professor Burnside
Radio detective created by Mileson Horton and played by Frederick Leister in the series *Professor Burnside Investigates*. Episode 1, 'The Case of the Fifteen Coppers', was broadcast on 19 March 1945, with John Witty as Inspector Frost. Producer Victor Watts.

Professor El-Tanah
'The World Famous Eastern Astrologer' (based in Jersey) who offered personal predictions from the stars on Business, Love, Courtship, Marriage Ties, Travel, Speculation, and Knowing Friends from Enemies. Free, but 'you may enclose threepence to cover postal and clerical expenses'. *Professor El-Tanah's Concert* was broadcast from RADIO LUXEMBOURG at noon every Sunday (1935).

Professor Schtopundschtart
Hailing from Europe in the Middle, the Professor delivered a series of talks on 'British Schports and Pass-der-times' in many a pre-war variety programme. He was created by JACK WARNER, who dropped the character when war was declared against Germany.

Professor Umbridge
'Phoney teacher of music and voice production' played by Charles Heslop in two radio series, TAKE UMBRIDGE and CUCKOO COTTAGE (1941).

Professor Whup
Eccentric character played by Hugh Morton in various Variety programmes featured in CHILDREN's HOUR (1937).

Programme Parade
Daily trailer for HOME SERVICE and FORCES PROGRAMME, compiled initially by Peter Bax and broadcast from January 1941 at 8.15 am.

A Proper Charlie
Comedy series starring Cheerful CHARLIE CHESTER (originally billed as *Good Old Charlie*), with Edna Fryer and Len Lowe from his old Crazy Gang, plus Deryck Guyler, Marian Miller and the Radio Revellers, with Harry Rabinowitz and the Revue Orchestra. Script by Charles Hart and Bernard Botting; produced by Leslie Bridgmont. First broadcast 17 April 1956, with a new series on 6 April 1958, introducing Bill Pertwee.

Putting on the Donegan: skiffle story

Public Ear

Alan Scott introduced this fortnightly magazine programme of news, reviews, music and opinions. Erudite entertainment with Pauline Boty (pop painter), Tony Hall (disc-jockey), Dick Vosburgh (script writer), and the Max Harris Group. Producer John Fawcett Wilson. First heard 6 October 1963.

Puffney Post Office

Situation series for comedian JON PERTWEE, deliberately toned down from the verbal slapsticks of his previous radio characteriza-tions, although based on his popular Postman from WATERLOGGED SPA. As postmaster of Puffney, Pertwee also presided over the general store in 'the village where nothing happens, but if it does he knows all about it'. Norman Shelley played the village constable, Susan Richards the middle-aged spinster assistant, Franklyn Bellamy the local hedger-and-ditcher, with the rest of the village supplied by Courtney Hope, Janet Brown, and David Jacobs. Incidental music by Frank Chaksfield and his Orchestra; devised and produced by George Inns; written by notable non-humorists, Neil Tuson and Geoffrey Webb. First broadcast 21 April 1950.

Putting on the Dog

Comedy series starring Magda Kun, Joe King, BRYAN MICHIE, Bettie Bucknelle, and the Re-vue Orchestra conducted by Mansel Thomas – not forgetting Mr Wilks the Talking Dog! Written by cartoonist St-John Cooper and Loftus Wigram; producer Eric Spear; started 23 April 1942.

Putting on the Donegan

Lonnie Donegan the Skiffle King starred in this RADIO LUXEMBOURG series, singing his record hits 'Cumberland Gap', 'Putting On The Style', etc. Weekly from 14 March 1960.

'Puzzle Corner'

Popular feature of MONDAY NIGHT AT SEVEN/ EIGHT (1937) which spun off into a half-hour series of its own from 30 July 1939. Chief Puzzler (i.e. compère) was LIONEL GAMLIN. It was devised by Harry S. Pepper and produced by Ronald Waldman, who would later present the series on radio and, post-war, on television. Waldman's 'Hello Puzzlers' and 'Deliberate Mistake' became catchphrases. Later present-ers included RICHARD MURDOCH, but Waldman returned to present his puzzles as a feature of FAMILY HOUR (1949).

One popular spot was the weekly Musical Medley arranged by Wally Wallond. The series' signature song, sung by various singing commères, went:

Get your pencils and your paper out,
You're the winner if you know about,
Who the what the where and why and when,
Which and wherefore and how, now.

Query Programme

The first radio contest for listeners was broadcast on 7 May 1926. Unbilled artistes had to be listed in correct RADIO TIMES billing, the three listeners with closest entries being invited to 2LO for the evening. The performers were Kate Winter, Ashmoor Burch, James and Partner and W. Todd. There were eight *Query Programmes* in all.

Question Mark

Robert MacDermott introduced this series which 'posed intriguing questions of the day'. Sponsored by *Picture Post*, a Hulton magazine, and produced by Peter Wilson. On RADIO LUXEMBOURG from 2 November 1954.

A Question of Taste

Weekly series starring the WESTERN BROTHERS (Kenneth and George), the wireless cads. Sponsored by Quaker Oats on RADIO LUXEMBOURG from 16 May 1937, the show took the form of a musical debate: 'Hot music or swing? Romantic tunes or jazz?'

Queue for Song

'Almost a Revue' starring Edward Cooper, Dorothy Carless, Gwen Lewis, Hugh Morton, and Ronnie Hill who also wrote the script with Peter Dion Titherage. Producer Reginald Smith; April 1940.

Quiet Please!

'Almost a riot' starring Forsythe, Seamon and Farrell (still in a tangle) and Rupert Hazell and Elsie Day (in the land where good gags go). The series began 27 February 1941 with a great hubbub, over which a voice shouted 'Quiet Please!'. Written by HARRY ALAN TOWERS;

producer Tom Ronald. The first guest star was TOMMY HANDLEY. A second series (7 May 1941) continued the misadventures of Addie's boyfriend Wilbur, and Rupert Hazell's parrot Hilarius.

Quiz League

Weekly quiz game featuring 'your favourite football stars' and refereed by Roy Rich. Presented by Reckitt's, makers of Bathjoys, over RADIO LUXEMBOURG from 1950.

Quiz Party

MICHAEL MILES the cheerful 'Quiz Inquisitor' hosted this jolly affair which included such favourite audience-participation sequences as 'I Want to Be an Actor', 'I Want to Be a Conductor', and 'The Yes-No Interlude' from previous programmes. New was a musical quiz, 'Turn Back the Clock'. Sheila Buxton sang songs and the producer was Bill Worsley. Started 11 March 1962.

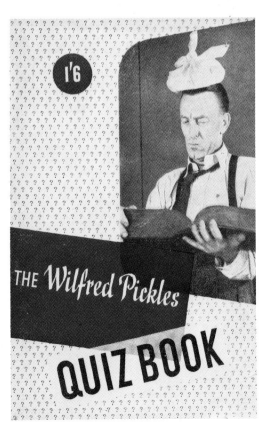

Quizzes: *Wilfred Pickles Quiz Book*

Quiz Team

Roy Rich was the urbane question-master of this post-war quiz series, which began on 14 December 1945. The Residents were CHRISTOPHER STONE, Margaret Stewart, ANONA WINN, and Daniel George, and they played the Visitors – Joyce Barbour, Cliff Gordon, Rose Macaulay, and Ted Hockridge. The programme for 14 August 1946 was interesting in that the Visitors were all cartoonists: J.F. Horrabin, Joe Lee, Norman Pett and Carl Giles. Questions were set by Elkan Allan and the producer was Joan Clark.

Quizzes

The grandfather of all quiz shows was THE QUERY PROGRAMME (1926), but the idea was not developed further until PUZZLE CORNER became part of MONDAY NIGHT AT SEVEN eleven years later. This ran for many years, part of the time as a series in its own right. The first quiz game to be battled out on the air between contestants was the SPELLING BEE (1938) with Freddy Grisewood as Spelling Master. Once again commercial radio was the pace-maker, introducing the weekly TEASER TIME on RADIO NORMANDY from 4 December 1938. World War II brought a boom in quizzes, with the first money prize to be won: 'DOUBLE OR QUITS CASH QUIZ' in MERRY-GO-ROUND (1944) had a different quiz-master for each service. More erudite was TRANSATLANTIC QUIZ (1945) devised by Alastair Cooke, followed by ROUND BRITAIN QUIZ (1947). The most popular of all radio quizzes was undoubtedly HAVE A GO (1946), although nobody ever lost ('Give 'er the money, Barney!'). The first fun quiz was RADIO FORFEITS (1946), where it was more fun to lose than to win. For other classic quizzes, see individual entries.

Rab the Rhymer

'The Bard of Breembraes', a popular broadcaster in Scottish Children's Hour before World War II. The BBC kept his real name a secret, referring to him only as 'the man who makes them up and sings them as he toddles doon the road'.

Radcliffe's Revels

Rare series for Scots comedian Jack Radcliffe, supported by Max Kirby, Ian Sadler, Robert Wilson, Billy Bowers and the Three Quavers, with the Scottish Variety Orchestra conducted by Ronnie Munro. Produced by Eric Fawcett from 27 May 1942.

Radio Boost

'Your favourite commercial radio station by courtesy of Nightingale's Natty Nightshirts.' BBC series burlesquing RADIO LUXEMBOURG programmes, beginning 1 January 1941. Arthur Riscoe starred as Plug Murphy, advertising agent, with Dick Francis as Sir Sam Nightingale, John Morris as Cyril his infant prodigy son, Hugh French as the Dream Lover, Betty Driver as Birdie, and Phyllis Stanley as Polly Poppet. The Radio Boost Mighty Orchestra was conducted by Billy Cotton, with production by Bill McLurg and Howard Thomas.

Radio Charades

Parlour games featuring the resident team of Raymond Glendenning, Doris Hare and Peter Watson, competing against a team of three selected from the studio audience. Both sides were piloted by sports commentator, Wynford Vaughan Thomas, and the game was rather given away by the credit, 'script by Henrik Ege'. First broadcast 24 March 1948, produced by Michael North.

Radio Circle

Children's club organized by the BBC in October 1923 for the young listeners to their daily CHILDREN'S HOUR. There were two sections, Juniors (up to 15 years of age) and Seniors (over 15), and an annual subscription of ninepence due every first of January. This brought members an enamelled badge with a pendant for the Regional branch, and a new coloured Membership Card each year. Proceeds beyond costs went to charity: by June 1930 the London and Daventry branch had reached a total of £3152. Only members of the club were entitled to birthday greetings broadcast over the radio. By the end of 1928 there were 19,000 badge-wearing members. Incidentally, the Newcastle Station had its own organization called 'The Fairy Flower League'. The Circle was disbanded in the autumn of 1933, causing a great deal of distress.

Radio Command Performance (1)

The first royal variety programme mounted by the BBC was given before the Prince of Wales on 15 November 1932. A star-studded broadcasting cast included HENRY HALL and the BBC DANCE ORCHESTRA, Jeanne de Casalis as 'MRS FEATHER', GILLIE POTTER, CLAPHAM AND DWYER, CECILY COURTNEIDGE in 'Laughing Gas', Leslie 'Hutch' Hutchinson, Florence Desmond, Jack and CLAUDE HULBERT, and Marion Harris (American Cabaret Artiste). Sir Gerald Du Maurier made an appeal on behalf of stage charities. The programme was called *Birthday Week Variety* and celebrated the tenth birthday of the BBC.

Radio Command Performance (2)

This historic show was never broadcast but exists on discs in the BBC Archives. It was presented at Windsor Castle to celebrate the 16th birthday of Princess Elizabeth, on 21 April 1942. John Snagge announced KENWAY AND YOUNG in 'VERY TASTY VERY SWEET', Max Geldray and his harmonica, JACK WARNER doing 'You Can't Help Laughing' and 'Frank and his Tank', accompanied by Bobby Alderson, VERA LYNN singing 'Yours' and 'Christopher Robin Is Saying His Prayers', ROBB WILTON as MR MUDDLECOMBE JP in the Home Guard, and a complete special ITMA with TOMMY HANDLEY, JACK TRAIN, Sydney Keith, Horace Percival, Clarence Wright, Fred

Yule, Dorothy Summers, Deryck Guyler, Kay Cavendish and Paula Green. The whole was accompanied by CHARLES SHADWELL and the BBC Variety Orchestra, and ran 88 minutes.

Radio Côte d'Azur

The Juan-les-Pins station which broadcast sponsored programmes in English from 10.30 pm on Sunday nights under the auspices of IBC. The first programme listed in RADIO PICTORIAL for 2 September 1934 was *Strang's Football Pools Broadcast*. The announcer was Miss L. Baillet.

Radio critics

Reviews of radio programmes date from the earliest years of broadcasting. *The Daily News* ran 'Listening In' by Preston Benson on 22 March 1922, followed by many unsigned reviews once broadcasts regularized. The same year Walter Fuller began reviewing for the *Westminster Gazette*. In 1926 L. Marsland Gander was appointed radio correspondent of the *Daily Telegraph*. Famous radio critics include Collie Knox of the *Daily Mail* (1934), Bernard Buckham of the *Daily Mirror*, Jonah Barrington of the *Daily Express* (1935), Leslie Baily of the *Sunday Referee* (1933), Dick Richards of the *Sunday Pictorial* (1946), and Leslie Ayre of the *Evening News* (1946).

Radio Doctor

'The doctor with the greatest number of patients in the world' was Charles Hill, M.D., whose plummy bedside manner brought early morning comfort in THE KITCHEN FRONT from 1941. He was also the first and only man to become chairman of both the BBC and ITA (as Lord Hill of Luton).

Radio Eireann

'Tune in to Radio Eireann for Luck' was the motto of this commercial station which broadcast on 531 metres 565 kcs. It changed its name from Radio Athlone on Sunday 27 February 1938. The first programme was *Glare, Glow and Glimmer*, 'an hour of illuminations and their significance'. Only one hour a day was broadcast (9.30 to 10.30 pm), mostly by 'electrical transcriptions' (*i.e.* gramophone records).

Radio Fakenburg

Cod commercial broadcasting station set aboard ship and run by TOMMY HANDLEY in the early series of IT's THAT MAN AGAIN (1939). Opening announcement ('Ici Radio Fakenburg. Defense de cracher!') and closer ('Mesdames et messieurs, vous pouvez cracher!') delivered by announcer VLADOVO-STOOGE. Singing commercials by SAM COSTA.

Radio Follies

Radio version of *Television Follies*, discontinued from the outbreak of World War II. Vera Lennox, Helen Clare, Clarence Wright, Hugh Morton, Dick Francis: 'Television viewers, listen to all your old favourites wired for sound.' Produced by Michael North and Gordon Crier, from 20 April 1940.

Radio Forfeits

Billed as 'the new comedy quiz in which victors win a prize and victims pay a penalty', this series made its Light Programme debut on 22 August 1946 and swiftly shot to the top. Breezy MICHAEL MILES was the cheerful 'Quiz Inquisitor', and he devised the show along the lines of the American success, *Truth or Consequences*. Prizes were pittances compared with the USA show, but this did not seem to worry the audiences or the contestants, who were only too happy to suffer good-humoured humiliation. Favourite spot was the 'Yes-No Interlude' wherein victims had to answer rapid-fire questions without using the forbidden words, 'yes' and 'no'. Miles originally ran the series under the title of *Army Forfeits* on South African services radio from March 1943. Billy Ternent and his Orchestra provided musical backing, and the producer was Jacques Brown.

Radio Fun

Children's comic featuring popular broadcasting personalities in strip cartoons and stories, its enormous and instant popularity marking radio's importance as the major pre-war entertainment medium. Significantly, although aimed at children aged 9–14, the comic never included a single personality from the BBC's CHILDREN'S HOUR! Published every Thursday

---

Radio Fun comic

from 15 October 1938, price twopence, the first issue featured ARTHUR ASKEY, Flanagan and Allen, REVNELL AND WEST, SANDY POWELL and, curiously, Clark Gable. In 1939 came Duggie Wakefield, in 1940 Harry Gordon, DICKIE HASSETT, and LORD HAW-HAW, and in 1941 JACK WARNER, TOMMY HANDLEY, the WESTERN BROTHERS, BEBE DANIELS AND BEN LYON, VIC OLIVER, and HAVER AND LEE. 1945 introduced Petula Clark as 'Radio's Merry Mimic' and Tommy Trinder. 1946 brought Jewel and Warriss, CHARLIE CHESTER, and a serial story starring Felix Mendelssohn and his Hawaiian Serenaders! WILFRED PICKLES arrived in 1947, with GEORGE ELRICK, STEWART MACPHERSON, Jimmy O'Dea and Issy Bonn's Finkelfeffer Family. 1948 introduced Gracie Fields, DEREK ROY, Avril Angers and Max Bacon. Anne Shelton led off 1949, supported by the TAKE IT FROM HERE trio, ARCHIE ANDREWS, and CARDEW Robinson. 1950 brought in Reg Dixon and Arthur English, from VARIETY BANDBOX. Norman Wisdom was the newcomer for 1952, and the Beverley Sisters and Robert Moreton arrived in 1953. Stan Stennett appeared in 1954, and Benny Hill in 1955. Hylda Baker in 1956 was the last true radio star, later additions being drawn from television shows. The last issue, renamed *Radio Fun and Adventures* and desperately trying to hang on by reprinting American *Superman* strips, appeared on 18 February 1961. After 1167 editions *Radio Fun* was merged with *Buster*, in its own way marking the decline and fall of radio.

The first *Radio Fun Annual*, dated 1940, was published in September 1939. All 21 issues are now collectors' items. The season of films based on radio shows at the National Film Theatre to mark the 60th Anniversary of the BBC was called *Radio Fun* in honour of the comic.

Radio Gang Show

'We're riding along on the crest of a wave' was the signature song of this breathless half-hour of comedy and song, broadcast weekly on RADIO LUXEMBOURG from 29 May 1938. Lifebuoy Soap sponsored, and Ralph Reader was the star, supported by Nan Kennedy, Veronica Brady, Eric Christmas, Gwen Lewis, Dick Francis, Jack Orpwood, Ted Smith, Syd Palmer, Bill Bannister, and the Three in Harmony. Favourite funsters were the TWIZZLE SISTERS (Jack Beet and Norman Fellowes), 'doing our party piece', and a little pest who wanted to 'say 'ullo to my mum!'. A Lintas production.

Radio International

'The Station Behind the Lines' which broadcast all-day (7 am to 8 pm) entertainment to the British Expeditionary Forces in France in the early months of World War II. Using the transmitter and resources of RADIO NORMANDY, ROY PLOMLEY, Bob Danvers-Walker, Ralph Hurcombe (a Canadian) and Philip Slessor compèred recorded programmes shorn of their sponsors, and built records into series such as *Merry Morning Music, Sunday Serenade, Bandbox Revue, Top of the Morning* and *Crooners' Corner*. The only 'new' series was *Dancing Moods* with JOE LOSS telling 'The Story of the Tango' (3 December 1939). The one big show was *Christmas Cavalcade* (25 December) with messages from Tommy Trinder, Frances Day, Sir Seymour Hicks, Alice Delysia, Douglas Byng, sports personalities Bunny Austin, Patsy Hendren and Jimmy Wilde, plus CHRISTOPHER STONE and Sabu the Elephant Boy. The programme journal achieved two issues and was called *Happy Listening*. The station closed down on Wednesday 3 January 1940.

Radio Luxembourg

'Ici Radio Luxembourg!' and a bong on the gong: the station identification that was so familiar to pre-war listeners, heralding programmes that were so different from the homegrown BBC – they were bright, lively, friendly, and sponsored! Test transmissions began on 15 March 1933 on 1190 metres, 200 kilowatts, and became a regular Sunday service from 29 October. By 3 December programmes ran from 3.30 pm with Concerts (i.e. gramophone records) presented by Bush Radio, R.W. Inductors, New Ideal Homesteads, Sharps Toffee, Cow and Gate Milk, Rap Radios, Tungsram and Milton. The first proper show was the *Gaumont British Studio Concert* with Jack Hulbert, CICELY COURTNEIDGE, and Roy Fox and his Band. Next week Bush Radio presented Flanagan and Allen, CARROLL GIBBONS and his Boys, and Hugh E. Wright to compère. In 1934 came Claude Hulbert and Enid Trevor in the weekly BEECHAM'S CONCERT (4 March), Ford Motors presenting Sir Henry Lytton on Gilbert and Sullivan (18 March), Finlay Currie and Percy Parsons in comedy crosstalk in FILM FANS' HOUR (8 April), and the first of the

Radio Luxembourg: promotion picture

longest series in British commercial radio, THE PALMOLIVE PROGRAMME (8 April).

Success was swift and from Sunday 14 October sponsored programmes in English were broadcast from noon to midnight, beginning with the station signature tune by JACK PAYNE and his Band, 'Tune In', and closing down with Al Bowlly's 'It's Time to Say Goodnight'. By 1935 (now on 1204 metres) the Luxembourg Sunday was so popular that NORMAN LONG was able to record a double-sided burlesque, *Luxembourg Calling* (Columbia FB1208), and commercial jingles had entered the national memory: 'Hurrah for Betox!', 'We Are The OVALTINEYS'. From 1 August 1936 the station ousted IBC and formed its own pro-gramme-packaging company, Wireless Public-ity Ltd. The outbreak of World War II closed the station on 21 September 1939, the last item broadcast being 'For Liberty', composed by a local Luxembourger.

The station reopened its English transmis-sions on 1 July 1946, with Stephen Williams in charge and Geoffrey Everitt as his assistant. All programmes were built out of records until WILLIAM HILL the Bookmaker led the return of sponsorship. Then came Horlicks, Curry's Cy-cle and Radio Shops, until by 21 May 1950 the Luxembourg Sunday (now 1293 metres) be-gan at 2.30 with *The Stanley Holloway Show* (Oxydol), and ended with TOP TWENTY (Out-door Girl) at midnight. Between came Gracie Fields in THE WISK HALF HOUR, Hughie Green's OPPORTUNITY KNOCKS, Jo Stafford's *Time For A Song*, and the good old Ovaltineys. The first staff announcer/presenter (apart from Geoffrey Everitt) was Teddy Johnson (20 May 1948) who broke into the Top Twenty himself with 'Beloved Be Faithful'. He was replaced by Pete Murray (September 1950), and later presenters were Peter Madren, David Gell, Mel Oxley, Keith Fordyce, Barry Aldiss and Don Moss. Long Wave was switched to medium, the famous 208 metres, on 2 July 1951. *208 Magazine* became the monthly pro-gramme guide, then the weekly *Tit-Bits*. The traditional sponsored programmes began to die out during 1956 and by 1961, when the daily schedule ran from 7 pm to 1 am, Sundays included, out of 91 programmes broadcast, 84 were pop-record shows.

Radio Lyons

Last of the major Continental stations to broadcast commercial programmes in English. Transmissions began on Sunday 1 November 1936 on 215 metres, arranged by Broadcast Advertising Ltd of 50 Pall Mall, London SW1. The first staff announcer was Tony Melrose. Sunday shows included YOUR OLD FRIEND DAN (Johnson's Wax Polish), Carson Robison and his OXYDOL PIONEERS, CARROLL GIBBONS and the Savoy Orpheans (Dolcis Shoes), and Carroll Gibbons and his Rhythm Boys (Stork Margarine). By 1937 Morton Downey was singing for Drene Shampoo, Alfredo Campoli was playing the violin for Syrup of Figs, and Gerald Carnes was announcing records for Zam-Buk, Bile Beans, and Dinneford's Magnesia. Programmes were punctuated by the H. Samuel Everite Time Signal, and were produced by Lyons' London arm, Vox Productions of 10a Soho Square. Staff scriptwriters were Ethel Levy and Nora Blackburne.

Radio Newsreel

The longest-running series of all time began in July 1940 and is still going. Described as 'a microphone feature page of news and views, recording and actuality' it was originally a daily programme for North America only. A Pacific edition was added in October 1940, and an African edition in October 1941. It was last heard at home on 3 April 1970, but carries on in the World Service.

Radio Normandy

Originally spelled Radio-Normandie and transmitting on 246 metres from Fécamp, this was the first of many Continental commercial radio stations to broadcast daily sponsored programmes for British listeners. The brainchild of Captain Leonard Plugge and his IBC, programmes started on Sunday 11 October 1931 with recordings of the IBC Dance Band (the IBCOLIANS). The first sponsored programme was the PHILCO SLUMBER HOUR on 22 November, and the first staff announcer was Major Max Staniforth. Early sponsors were record companies Vocalion, Filmophone, HMV and Piccadilly, and the first programme schedule to exceed an hour or two was on 31 January 1932: 6 pm to 3 am. Stephen Williams joined as announcer from 3 April 1932, introducing the first CHILDREN'S PROGRAMME on 17 April. Weekday programmes were from 11 pm

Radio Normandy advertisement, 1938

to 1 am, and like the Sunday programmes always concluded with the 'IBC Goodnight Melody' – Ted Lewis crooning 'Goodnight, Sweetheart, Goodnight'. By 1934 when Bob Danvers-Walker became Chief Announcer, Sunday transmissions ran from 10 am to noon, 2 to 6.30, and 9.30 to 1 pm. Weekday programmes were from 11.30 am to noon, 4.30 pm to 6 pm, and 11 pm to 1 am. Reception in Britain improved considerably following a change of wavelength in 1935 to 1304 metres.

Although RADIO LUXEMBOURG came to dominate the commercial wavelengths, many listeners preferred Normandy and recall it with affection, although World War II silenced their English-speaking programmes for good.

Radio Normandy Calling

ROY PLOMLEY compèred this half-hour show presented by Maclean's Peroxide Toothpaste and Stomach Powder from 20 March 1938. The first show, recorded in a cinema, included Alfredo and his Gipsy Band, Joe Young, Ward and Draper, Maisie Weldon, and the finalists in an Amateur Talent Spotting Competition. The signature Song was sung by the Belles of Normandy;

> Radio Normandy calling you,
> Bringing you music from out the blue,
> Laughter and rhythm so when you hear . . .
> (bells ring)

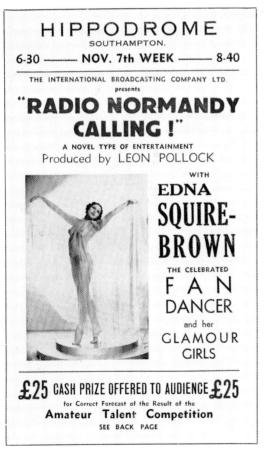

Radio Normandy Calling: unbroadcastable version for the stage

You know it stands for
Radio Normandy coming through,
With lots of enjoyment for all,
So be sure to listen in to
Radio Normandy Calling!

Radio Parade

Elstree's answer to Hollywood's *Big Broadcast* series. *Radio Parade* (1933), a British International Picture, introduced virtually every BBC favourite: CLAPHAM AND DWYER, ELSIE AND DORIS WATERS, Florence Desmond, MABEL CONSTANDUROS, CLAUDE HULBERT (who wrote the film with Paul England), Jeanne De Casalis, the Houston Sisters, CHRISTOPHER STONE, FLOTSAM AND JETSAM, Elsie Carlisle, LEONARD HENRY, STAINLESS STEPHEN, STANELLI and Edgar, Harry S. Pepper and Doris Arnold, Reginald Gardiner, the CARLYLE COUSINS, Mario 'Harp' Lorenzi, and Roy Fox and his Band. Unfortunately only the trailer still exists. The following year BIP produced *Radio Parade of 1935*, an even more sumptuous revue complete with a dufaycolor sequence predicting colour television. Arthur Woods directed a huge cast including WILL HAY, DAVY BURNABY, Billy Bennett, Lily Morris, Nellie Wallace, the WESTERN BROTHERS, Clapham and Dwyer, HAVER AND LEE, the Carlyle Cousins, Gerry Fitzgerald, Claude Dampier, Eve Becke, PEGGY COCHRANE, RONALD FRANKAU, Alberta Hunter, TED RAY, Beryl Orde, STANELLI and his Hornchestra, and Teddy Joyce and his Band. A restored print was shown during the 'Radio Fun' season at the National Film Theatre.

Radio Paris

Also known as 'Poste Parisien the Paris Broadcasting Station', began transmitting commercial programmes in English on Sunday 29 November 1931 with *A Concert of HMV Records* announced by REX PALMER, a former BBC official. The first record played was Noel Coward's 'Cavalcade Suite'. The first staff announcers, supplied by the contractors, IBC, were Mr Townsend and Miss Shipway, who made their joint début on 24 January 1932. Then came Tom Ronald (later a top BBC producer) and the long-serving John Sullivan. Studios were in the Avenue des Champs-Elysées, and English programmes were limited to an hour or two from 10.30 pm. Sponsors

Radio Normandy: the studio

listed from 2 September 1934 in RADIO PICTO-
RIAL included William S. Murphy's Staunch
Pools, Gordon Mackay's Pools, Ballito Fishnet
Stockings, and Bile Beans. IBC lost their
contract from October 1937 when the station's
own subsidiary, Anglo-Continental Publicity,
took over with offices in Cavendish Mansions,
Langham Street. Al Burton, a Canadian was
put in charge of programmes, and Allan Rose
became resident announcer. The IBC
'Goodnight Melody' was replaced with
'Lullabye Land', and a 60-minute record-
request series was introduced on Sunday morn-
ings, *Listeners' Command Performance*.

Radio Pictorial
'The New Weekly Pictorial Magazine for
Every Radio Listener', 40 pages of sepia and
two-tone photogravure for twopence, was published every Friday from 19 January 1934. No.
1, with its free Crayon Portrait of HENRY HALL,
featured 'Variety at ST GEORGE's HALL' by
John Trent, 'If I Were Governor of the BBC' by
Oliver Baldwin, 'I Want More Radio Plays'

by Val Gielgud, 'Records I Like to Broadcast'
by CHRISTOPHER STONE, and 'A Joy Ride' by
story-teller A.J. ALAN. But the magazine really
took off with No. 33, dated 31 August 1934,
when full English programmes from the Continental commercial stations began to be listed.
Although some token BBC information remained, *Radio Pictorial* virtually became the
official programme magazine for NORMANDY,
LUXEMBOURG and the rest, and is today the
prime source of pre-war information on their
stars and shows. The sudden collapse of commercial radio with the declaration of World
War II saw *Radio Pictorial*'s equally sudden
disappearance. No. 295 was the last, dated 8
September 1939, and from the following week
it turned into *War Pictorial*.

Radio Pie
Occasional comedy series broadcast from 5
November 1936, devised by Leslie Sarony, and
starring him and his partner, Leslie Holmes
(THE TWO LESLIES), with TOMMY HANDLEY,

Mario de Pietro, and Anne Ziegler. It was so popular that a stage production was toured in 1939, starring the Two Leslies, Suzette Tarri, Tubby Turner, Robin Richmond and his £2000 Hammond Organ, and 'Hugo'.

Radio Post

Variety magazine for Forces overseas introduced by J.B. Priestley assisted by his secretary, Angela Wyndham-Lewis. Features: 'Riddles' with Commander Gould; 'What Can We Do About It'; 'Once Upon a Time' with Margaret Lockwood; 'The Sporting Life' with Sydney Howard and Bill Stephens; and guests René Ray, Naunton Wayne and Cherry Lind. Producer Corporal Gordon Crier; began 13 February 1944.

Radio Radiance

The first regular CONCERT PARTY entertainment created for broadcasting started on 6 July

1925. Comedian Arthur Chesney starred with Eveline Drewe, Violet Parry, Bertha Russell, and a Dancing Chorus! R.E. Jeffrey and J. Lester produced, from a 'book' (script) by Jackie Hellier. The third edition (22 July) introduced TOMMY HANDLEY, a new comedian who would make radio his own. The broadcast of 20 August introduced soubrette Jean Allistone to the cast, and to Handley, who married her! The eighth edition (7 November) was the first comedy show to boast all-original material written for radio. The sketches were by Roland Leigh and the music by Dick (later Richard) Addinsell.

Radio Revels (1)

'The World's Biggest Dance', a nationwide radio event first staged on the night of 15 December 1925, running from 9 pm to 4 am (but only broadcast until 2 am!). Dance music by Sidney Firman's Cavour Band, the Savoy Havana Band, the Olympia Band, and JACK

Radio Post: obscure series for broadcaster J.B. Priestley

HYLTON's Band was broadcast to 20 *palais de danses*, from Olympia in London where tickets cost a guinea, to the Cricklewood Palais where tickets were 3/6d, to distant dance-halls in Aberdeen and Belfast.

Radio Revels (2)

Game-show follow-up to RADIO FORFEITS devised by Quiz Inquisitor MICHAEL MILES. Winners became Singer or Conductor of the Week, taking over Stanley Black's baton with the Dance Orchestra. First broadcast 20 June 1948; produced by Frederick Piffard.

Radio Review

Weekly fan magazine devoted to broadcasting and published by D.C. Thomson from 9 November 1935, price twopence. Features included 'Between Ourselves – Longwave's Gossip', 'The Stars as I Know Them' by Flotsam, Rex King's Radio Criticism ('The Snappiest Thing in Broadcasting'), 'Talks and Talkers', 'Down Rhythm Row' by One of the Boys, and 'Laugh with LEONARD HENRY'. Despite Grand Free Gifts of Silvertone Photos of Radio Stars (HENRY HALL, Bertha Willmott, Mantovani), it ran only 28 issues.

After World War II another *Radio Review* became familiar to British listeners. This one was published in Dublin but besides Radio Eireann and BBC programmes it carried RADIO LUXEMBOURG, AFN and a selection of Continental stations.

Radio Rhythm Club

Long-running series which did much to educate and entertain the hitherto jazz-starved British. It began on the FORCES PROGRAMME on 13 July 1940, with Charles Chilton presenting rare records in 'Collectors' Corner'. The first live jam session featuring the St Regis Quintet was broadcast on 23 July. Featured on clarinet was Harry Parry, whose Radio Rhythm Club Sextet would grow to dominate the series.

Radio Roadhouse

'Situated on the Roundabout By-Pass under the direction of VIC OLIVER. He offers you unrestricted fun in a built-up area.' CHARLES SHADWELL conducted the Roadhouse Orchestra in a 50-minute series on Regional from 7 July 1938, devised by Leonard M. Barry; produced by John Sharman. The 1939 series starred NAUNTON WAYNE.

Radio Rodeo

Monthly variety shows broadcast from cinemas and featuring three organists: Robinson Cleaver, Phil Park and Harold Ramsay. Ramsay also presented the programme, which on 20 October 1937 included Harry Richman, Scott and Whaley, Jeanne De Casalis (MRS FEATHER), Issy Bonn, Bennett and Williams, and the Eight Step Sisters. Writer Phil Park; producer Leon Pollock.

Radio Rome

First broadcast a sponsored programme in English on 24 January 1932, a *Concert of Mayfair Records* presented by Ardath Cigarettes. The announcer for IBC was Alexander Wright. Broadcasts continued spasmodically to 1934.

Radio Roundabout

Comedy series starring Max Wall, sponsored by Rinso, broadcast from Luxembourg during 1950. Max was supported by ERIC BARKER, Max Geldray and his harmonica, Saveen the ventriloquist with Daisy May, Eric Whitley, and an orchestra conducted by Miff Ferrie.

Radio San Sebastian

One of the several Continental stations broadcasting the odd hour of English programmes in the early hours of the morning. H. Gordon Box announced the records on behalf of IBC, back in 1934.

Radio Sports Club

Sports enthusiasts were invited to 'let the experts improve your game' in this series which came from the Pioneer Health Centre in Peckham, commencing 4 January 1949. The experts were Joe Davis on the correct stance at snooker, W. Barrington Dalby on footwork in boxing, Walter Winterbottom on kicking with both feet, and Rex Alston answering listeners' queries.

Radio Star of the Year

Nationwide contest sponsored by *Tit-Bits* magazine, which by 1957 had become the Official RADIO LUXEMBOURG programme guide. Anne

Radio Review: free Album of Silvered Stars (1935)

Shelton and Tommy Trinder were among the judges and the first winner, announced 23 June 1958, was Billy Raymond, who won £250.

Radio Telebunken

Burlesque of German radio propaganda broadcasts, with ERIC BARKER as the LORD HAW-HAW character. Featured in HOWDY FOLKS (1940).

Radio Times

'Journal of the British Broadcasting Corporation', this was the BBC bible in weekly instalments of 106 pages for twopence every Friday. Apart from planning the week's listening (the radio week ran from Sunday to Saturday in those days, as if building up from Religious Services to Music Hall) on the several alternatives (the NATIONAL PROGRAMME and seven REGIONAL PROGRAMMES), there were the magazine's regular features to peruse. 'Both Sides of the Microphone' by The Broadcasters; 'What the Other Listener Thinks', a letter page; 'Strolling Commentaries' by humorist A.A. Thomas; 'Tempo di Jazz' by Leonard Feather; 'Samuel Pepys, Listener' by R.M. Freeman; 'I Saw Yesterday' by Irene Veal. Another delight was the line drawings by such excellent illustrators as Eric Fraser, Mervyn Wilson, Sherriffs, Reinganum (the surrealistic one), Nicolas Bentley, and others, all of whom really went to town in the Grand Christmas Numbers and other special issues, such as the Variety Number, the Woman's Number, and the Coronation Number. The first issue was dated 28 September 1923.

Radio Toulouse

This Continental station began broadcasting commercial programmes in English in 1929. On Sunday 11 October 1931 it broadcast the first IBC programme, *The Vocalion Concert of Newly Released Broadcast Records*. The last programme in English, *Old Favourites*, presented by Gordon Mackay's Football Pools, was broadcast 2 September 1934.

Radio Uncles and Aunts

The first Radio Uncle was the earliest 'voice of radio', ARTHUR BURROWS, who read the first bedtime story on the air on 26 August 1922 (see CHILDREN'S PROGRAMMES). Most early broadcasters took turns in the avuncular hosting of the daily children's slot: Rex Palmer became 'Uncle Rex', L. Stanton Jeffries 'Uncle Jeff', Cecil Lewis 'Uncle Caractacus' (he wrote an article called 'The Fun of Uncling' in a 1923 issue of *The Broadcaster*); later came the programme chiefs 'Uncle Peter' (C.E. Hodges), and 'UNCLE MAC' (Derek McCulloch), the latter most popular of them all. Aunties included 'Sophie' (pianist, Cecil Dixon), 'Geraldine' (Geraldine Elliott) and 'ELIZABETH' (May Jenkin). There was even a 'Wicked Uncle' (Ralph de Rohan)! Regions had their own radio relations, including 'Uncle Humpty Dumpty' (Kenneth Wright), 'Uncle Dan' (Godfrey), 'Uncle Willie (Cochrane) in Manchester; 'Uncle Percy' (Edgar) in Birmingham; 'Uncle Sandy' in Aberdeen; 'Uncle Donald' in Cardiff; 'Uncle Jumbo' in Newcastle; 'Uncle Mungo' and 'Auntie Cyclone' (Kathleen Garscadden) in Glasgow. Duties included the reading out of birthday greetings to members of the RADIO CIRCLE: 'Hello, twins!' They ceased to be Uncles and Aunts by BBC edict with effect from 11 October 1926 – but not to their young listeners.

IBC revived the idea in their RADIO NORMANDY *Children's Corner* (1932), which was introduced by 'Uncle Stephen' (Williams), 'Uncle Benjy' (Bernard McNabb) and 'Uncle John' (Sullivan).

Radio Week

The BBC in co-operation with the Radio Manufacturers' Association and the British Valve Manufacturers' Association promoted a national Radio Week from 12 to 18 January 1930. Special posters proclaimed the slogan, 'Go Home and Listen!' and special programmes included *Vaudeville* (14 January) with TOMMY HANDLEY, Will Hay, FLOTSAM AND JETSAM, MABEL CONSTANDUROS, the BBC DANCE ORCHESTRA and a relay from the Coliseum; *The Wrecker* (15 January), 'A Mystery of the Sea' by Robert Louis Stevenson and Lloyd Osbourne; *All Star Vaudeville* (16 January) with Jack Hulbert and CICELY COURTNEIDGE, Bransby Williams, RONALD FRANKAU, Wish Wynne, Muriel George and Ernest Butcher; and a 75-minute relay of Francis Laidler's pantomime from the Theatre Royal, Leeds, *Mother Goose* (18 January) staring George Lacy and Norah Blaney.

Radio Times: number one, volume one

Radio Times, September 28, 1923.

THE Radio Times

ABERDEEN
GLASGOW
NEWCASTLE
MANCHESTER
CARDIFF
BIRMINGHAM
BOURNEMOUTH
LONDON
BBC

THE OFFICIAL ORGAN OF THE B.B.C.

Vol. 1. No. 1. [Registered at the G.P.O. as a Newspaper.] **EVERY FRIDAY.** **Two Pence.**

WHAT'S IN THE AIR?

By ARTHUR R. BURROWS, Director of Programmes.

HULLO, EVERYONE !
We will now give you *The Radio Times.* The good *new* times. The Bradshaw of Broadcasting.

May you never be late for your favourite wave-train.

Speed 186,000 miles per second ; five-hour non-stops.

Family season ticket : First Class, 10s. per year.

* * *

[*All this, presumably, is "by the way" ; not "In the Air."*—EDITOR.]

* * *

So I am instructed to write about programmes and not "talk like an Uncle " !

* * *

Let me tell you all about our plans.

Wait, though ! I—I'm just a little bit uneasy. My predecessor in the broadcasting business made a mistake of this character with painful consequences.

You probably remember the incident.

A Company, with distinguished Directors, having lofty ambitions, established a power-station at Westminster. Despite quite a stirring programme there were no oscillations, owing to Government intervention. The Director (Guido Fawkes) and his colleagues somehow lost their heads, and the long-anticipated report failed to materialize.

When WE broadcast Parliament—and it's bound to happen this century or next—the process will be a more dignified one than that planned in 1605. The fate of the culprits may be another matter.

* * *

Perhaps, after all, it is by stepping clear of the pitfalls of ancient and modern history that British broadcasting has got so far without any serious mishap. (Touch wood !)

* * *

Do you know that from November 14th last year until now, with only six out of eight projected stations in operation, and despite oppo-

[Photo] [Foulsham & Banfield.
Mr. ARTHUR R. BURROWS.

sition from some of the "Big Noises" in the entertainment industry, we have shaken the ether of Great Britain for approximately 8,000 hours and have transmitted roughly 1,700 distinct evening programmes. How this ether-shaking process has been carried through so uninterruptedly is for my unrepentant colleague, Captain Eckersley, to tell (possibly with Morse and reactive obligato). The fact remains that if our plans for the next twelve months go through, even in their present basic form, we shall add to this record 2,500 other distinct programmes, consisting of 16,500 hours of ever-changing musical, dramatic, and instructive entertainment.

* * *

Two thousand five hundred distinct programmes !

[*Perhaps it IS as well that your comments are inaudible.*]

And some folk pressing for a six-hour day !

* * * *

Have you ever played jigsaw ?

At 2, Savoy Hill, London, W.C.2, is the biggest jigsaw puzzle yet invented, railway time-tables *not* excepted. It goes by the name of simultaneous broadcasting, a process which comes into existence so far as our musical programmes are concerned on Monday next, October 1st. For some weeks now the writer and others of the same Department, all in varying states of mental distress, have pored over this latest brain-teaser, trying to coax a refractory twiddly-bit into some time-space for which it was never intended.

(Continued in column 3, page 2)

Radio Weekly Diana Coupland, cover girl

Radio Weekly

Post-war paper which failed to recapture the glamour of pre-war commercial radio, so well presented in the photogravure RADIO PICTORIAL. *Radio Weekly*, a 12-page paper, started 1 June 1951, and for fourpence listed the week's programmes of RADIO LUXEMBOURG, AFN and RADIO EIREANN.

Radioddities

George Hendy devised this 'weekly magazine of queer, unusual and amusing incidents in real life, bringing you the actual people concerned'. Features included 'Twice in a Lifetime', 'Advice Corner' with Jeanne de Casalis, 'What You Never Had You Never Miss', 'Claim to Fame', and 'Like to Change Places' in which comedian JACK TRAIN switched roles with footballer Tommy Lawton. The compère was Bob Danvers-Walker of *Pathé Gazette* fame, and Bill Worsley produced, from 3 November 1946.

Radiolympia

Annual radio show staged at the Empire Hall, Olympia, London, by the Radio Manufacturers' Association, beginning 4 September 1926.

The first programme broadcast from the Exhibition was the opening ceremony by Sir Alfred Chatfield with music from the Wireless Orchestra, WYNNE AJELLO, soprano, and Winifred Small, violin. More fun was *The Awful Revue* at 8 pm, with TOMMY HANDLEY, Peter Haddon, Lilian Lane, Iris May, Alan Howland, and the Radio Chorus and Orchestra directed by Sidney Firman. By 1934 major shows were being staged: *Variety from Olympia* starred HENRY HALL and the BBC DANCE ORCHESTRA (vocalists Kitty Masters and LES ALLEN), Tommy Handley, CLAPHAM AND DWYER, CLAUDE DAMPIER and Billie Carlyle, Collinson and Breen, Hermione Gingold, Phyllis Robins and Rosalind Wade and her Sixteen Radiolympia Girls. There was also a special edition of IN TOWN TONIGHT. The 1937 Radiolympia had a special signature tune composed by Damerell and Evans, 'Listen In Your Radio' sung by Paula Green. The first post-war Radiolympia was in 1947, and special programmes staged there included Tommy Handley in ITMA, RICHARD MURDOCH and KENNETH HORNE in MUCH-BINDING-IN-THE-MARSH, and Geraldo's *Café On The Corner*.

Radio's Cavalier of Song

Bill-matter of Donald Peers, popular vocalist, as heard on RADIO NORMANDY (1938) sponsored by DDD Prescription. Mr Peers was accompanied by Arthur Young and the DDD Melody Makers. It was not until the post-war boom in crooners that Peers suddenly found himself the idol of screaming teenagers and swooning mums, and a whole new career hit the slightly bemused Welshman. His signature tune, 'In a shady nook, by a babbling brook', became a best-selling record. His 1949 BBC series was interrupted when he had to have his tonsils out, but he was back from 8 February 1950, with Joe 'Mr Piano' Henderson and Rae Jenkins conducting the Variety Orchestra.

Raffles

A.J. Raffles, the gentleman cracksman and cricketer of fiction, was created by E.W. Hornung. Frank Allenby played him in the radio adaptations, which began with 'The Ides of March' on 3 December 1945. Eric Micklewood played the faithful manservant,

---

Radiolympia programme

Bunny. Adapted for radio by Beatrice Gilbert and produced by Leslie Stokes.

Rainbow Room

'Radio's new Saturday-evening musical rendezvous where you can listen to the music of the orchestra directed by Reg Leopold'. The signature tune was 'Melody on the Move' by Clive Richardson, and Franklin Engelmann introduced the first 'visiting artists', Isador Goodman (piano) and Frederick Harvey (baritone) on 7 December 1946. The series returned on 13 February 1950, with Alan Skempton as host to the piano duettists, Rawicz and Landauer, and baritone Peter Dawson. Lou Whiteson conducted the orchestra.

Ralph Reader Parade

The old Rover returned in a RADIO LUXEMBOURG series sponsored by Tide ('You get the world's cleanest washing when you turn to Tide'). The signature song was, of course, 'On the Crest of the Wave'. Ralph and his songs were supported by the Four-in-a-Chord and Jackie Brown and his Orchestra. Started 4 November 1955.

Ralph Reader's Revue

'Gang Show' series arranged for radio: 'Rolling along at sixty miles a second, by and with the *Gang Show* star himself!' Also featuring Betty Driver, Eric Christmas, Veronica Brady, Gwen Lewis, George Cameron, and the TWIZZLE SISTERS (Jack Beet and Norman Fellowes). Started 4 February 1937; producer Harry S. Pepper.

Rambling Syd Rumpo

Wandering minstrel of ROUND THE HORNE (1965) with many a ditty in his ganderbag, such as 'The Ballad of the Woggler's Moulie' sung to the tune of 'Clementine' by Kenneth Williams;

> Joe he was a young cordwangler,
> Monging greebles did he go,
> And he loved a bogler's daughter
> By the name of Chiswick Flo.

Ramsbottom

Stage manager of THE HAPPIDROME (1941), an imaginary variety theatre owned by MR LOVEJOY. Functioned principally as a straight-man between Lovejoy and ENOCH, the callboy, whom he was ever beseeched to 'Tak' him away, Ramsbottom!'. Played by Cecil Frederick.

Ray, Ted

Wireless wisecracker who, like TOMMY HANDLEY, whose ITMA his RAY'S A LAUGH would replace, was born in Liverpool. After years on the Music Halls with his 'Fiddling and Fooling' act (wisecracks accompanied on the violin), and many broadcasts beginning in 1939, Ted was rewarded with his own half-hour series ten years later. It ran for so long that listeners believed he was married to Kitty Bluett, who played his radio wife. Ted wrote much of the script, and also played the plaintive Ivy ('Ee, he's loovely Mrs Hoskin'). As compère of CALLING ALL FORCES he had the catchphrase 'You should use stronger elastic!', and his signature tune was 'You Are My Sunshine'. Among many series, outstanding was his off-the-cuff gagging in DOES THE TEAM THINK, which used his ability as a instant jokester to the full.

Ray of Sunshine

Sunday afternoon series on RADIO LUXEMBOURG from 1936, compèred by CHRISTOPHER STONE and sponsored by Betox. Signature song (composed by Annette Mills):

> Hurrah for Betox!
> What a delightful smell!
> The stuff that every self-respecting
> Grocer ought to sell!

The 1938 series was sponsored by a different product, whose jingle ran:

> Phillips Tonic Yeast gives you life,
> It's Nature's gift to man and wife,
> Life will be a feast,
> With Phillips Tonic Yeast.

Ray's a Laugh

Highly popular comedy series starring TED RAY in domestic situations with Kitty Bluett, an Australian comedienne who played his wife, followed by conversation with his conscience (Leslie Perrins), an office scene, and various encounters with curious characters and catchphrases. There was JENNIFER, a little girl played by towering Bob Pearson; SOPPY, a

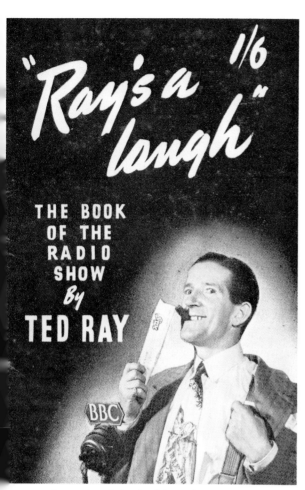

Ray's a Laugh: book of the series

small boy who got ticked off by the nation's watchdogs for his catchphrase, 'Just like your big red conk!': and a fruity old girl with the giggles: 'My name's CRYSTAL JOLLIBOTTOM, you saucebox!' Both were played by young PETER SELLERS. Then there was the glamour girl who would do anything, but 'Not until after six o'clock!'. Songs came from the Beaux and the Belles, and the variety act Bob and Alf Pearson: 'We bring you melody from out of the sky – My brother and I.' Fred Yule and Patricia Hayes were also around: 'Char-lee!' 'Whatcher want, Ingrid?', but the two best and funniest characters were MRS HOSKIN AND IVY, the two old dears played by Ted and Bob Pearson.

The opening signature tune was:

Ray's a Laugh! Ray's a Laugh!
When you're feeling sad and blue just Ray's a Laugh!

and the closing song, written by Ted, was 'My good friends and I are saying goodbye now'. First broadcast 4 April 1949: written by Ronnie Hanbury and George Wadmore; produced by George Inns.

The first series ran for 65 weeks. The third series began with show No. 111 on 1 November 1951 and by this time Ted had left the Cannon Enquiry Agency for a job as reporter on the *Daily Bugle*. Jack Watson and Charles Leno joined the cast, and new characters included Mrs Dipper and Roger Curfew the paying guest, with songs by John Hanson and the Kings Men. Scripts by Ted and Eddie Maguire. The series starting 1 October 1953 brought quaint Charles Hawtrey into the cast, plus Kenneth Connor as the awful SIDNEY MINCING, telling the longest jokes in radio. The next series began 13 October 1955 with a new domestic situation theme. Diane Hart played Ted's wife, Mary, and Kenneth Connor his brother-in-law, Harold. Alexander Gauge, a fat menace from B-pictures, was Ted's boss Mr Faraday, and Patricia Hayes Mrs Chatsworth, with Pamela Manson as Jane Foster. Music by the Peter Akister Players; script by Sid Colin, Talbot Rothwell and George Wadmore; and production by Roy Speer. The series starting 25 October 1956 brought back Kitty Bluett as Mrs Ray, and Connor played Herbert Toil the Odd Job Man. Ted's new boss, Mr Trumble, was Laidman Browne. Charles Hart and Bernard Botting took over the script, and Leslie Bridgmont the production. Further series started 4 October 1957, 26 September 1958, and 4 September 1959. That beginning 2 September 1960 introduced Pat Coombs as Miss Ursula Prune. PERCY EDWARDS was also around with his animal impressions. The last show was broadcast on 13 January 1961 and played off, as always, with 'You Are My Sunshine'.

Read, Al

Meat-pie manufacturer from St Anne's-on-Sea who became one of the greatest natural broadcasters in comedy history. Discovered by Bowker Andrews, who put him into a Manchester variety programme, Read became resident comedian of VARIETY FANFARE in 1951, and starred the same year in his own summer show, named *Right Monkey* from his catchphrase. Read's was the comedy of observation, multi-voiced 'pages from life' humorously re-creating everyday situations: in the

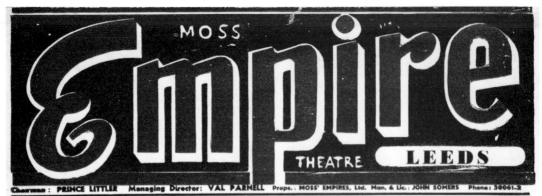

MOSS Empire

THEATRE · LEEDS

Chairman: PRINCE LITTLER   Managing Director: VAL PARNELL   Props.: MOSS' EMPIRES, Ltd. Man. & Lic.: JOHN SOMERS   Phone: 30061-2

6.0 ★ **MONDAY, DEC. 3rd**
TWICE NIGHTLY ★ **8.15**

FIRST LEEDS PERSONAL APPEARANCE OF
THE RADIO STAR
AL READ
RIGHT MONKEY!

TEX & PEGGY SHAMVA

THREE 20th CENTURY FUNSTERS **JOKERS**

TERRY HALL THE ENGLISH VENTRILOQUIST
WITH **MICKY FLYNN** THE IRISH DUMMY

IRIS SAUCY — BUT NICE **SADLER**

THE DARING ROSINAS
FLIRTING WITH DANGER

JOAN VOCAL IMPRESSIONS **TURNER**

MACKENZIE ACE ACCORDIONISTS **REID & DOROTHY**

THE TRIO CROSSETTO
EUROPE'S FINEST JUGGLERS

bus, in the pub, in the cinema queue, in the dentist's waiting room, in the football crowd. His signature song was 'Such Is Life', and his catchphrases included 'That's the wife from the kitchen' and 'You'll be lucky!'.

Record Round-Up

JACK JACKSON, the former dance-band leader, embarked on a new career that would last him the rest of his life, when he launched *Record Round-Up* on Saturday 10 January 1948. Originally broadcast at 4 pm, it became the first late-night disc-jockey series when it was moved to 11 pm on 26 June. This 60-minute slot set the seal on the whole pattern of modern record presentation, a fast-moving mixture of gags, new releases, chart-toppers, old favourites, and dialogue contrived with phrases snipped from recordings. Jackson virtually created a new form of pure radio, paving the way for Terry Wogan and Kenny Everett today. On 9 July 1950 his programme moved to Sundays at 6.30, and on 25 December 1954 crossed to RADIO LUXEMBOURG sponsored by Decca Records; Bunny Lewis was named as producer.

The Record Spinner

The first compère of record programmes to use this familiar term was Oliver Kimball, whose series with this title began on RADIO NORMANDY on 4 May 1937. His sponsor was Bismag Bisurated Magnesia.

Record Time

Pace-making record request series beginning 4 June 1940: 'Soldiers, sailors, airmen – what's your favourite record? Send along the title and as many as can be played in half an hour will be played to you by Roy Rich.' The third series, which started on 24 September 1942, was aimed at the men in the Middle East.

The Red Bladder

Dreaded desert enemy of MAJOR BLOODNOK, inspired by The Red Shadow in *The Desert Song*. Played with dramatic authority by Ray Ellington in THE GOON SHOW (1956).

Al **Read**: 'Right Monkey!' on stage

The Red Label Show

The title came from Lyons' Red Label Tea, sponsor of this 1954 RADIO LUXEMBOURG series built around Ken Mackintosh and his Orchestra with singers Kenny Bardell, Gordon Langhorn, Patti Forbes and the Mackpies. Dolores Ventura played the piano, and the producer was Geoffrey Everitt. 'This is your opportunity to win many valuable prizes including a brand new car!'

Reflections

Daily programme of quiet music featuring the singing of Canadian Larry Cross ('Boulevard of Broken Dreams'), brought to you by Carter's Little Liver Pills on RADIO LUXEMBOURG from 2 July 1951.

Reg Raspberry

Sound effects boy in IT'S THAT MAN AGAIN (1946). All noises made by Tony Francis.

Regional Programme

The BBC's Regional Scheme was conceived by PETER ECKERSLEY, the Chief Engineer, in 1924, and began on 21 October 1929 when 2LO moved to Brookman's Park with the new name of London Regional. Midland Regional (Daventry) opened on 9 March 1931, Scottish Regional (Westerglen) in September 1932, West and Welsh Regional (Washford Cross) in

Regional Programme *Pot-Pourri*, the first Midland Region variety show: starring Vivien Lambelet

August 1933, and Northern Ireland in 1934. These stations provided alternative local programmes to the NATIONAL PROGRAMME (1930).

The first programme on London Regional, broadcast at 3.30 pm on Sunday 9 March 1930, the official start of the scheme, was *Military Band Concert* by the City of Birmingham Police Band, with Walter Glynne, tenor. Weekday programming ran from noon to midnight, winding up with dance music in a link-up with the National. The first Midland Regional variety show, broadcast at 7 pm on 13 March 1930, was *Pot-Pourri* with Vivien and Napoleon Lambelet.

London Regional became simply the Regional Programme from 4 January 1935, a national alternative service drawing on material from all the regions. On 1 September 1939 Regional was suddenly discontinued, merging with the National to become the HOME SERVICE. While the provincial Regional

Programmes were restored after World War II, from 29 July 1945, the Regional Programme itself did not return.

The Rev

Sporting padré and star of *Meet The Rev*, a series within the hospital show, HERE'S WISHING YOU WELL AGAIN, first featured on 4 June 1946. Hugh Morton played the 'Rev' (real name Simon Cherry). The Rev's sparring-partner, Charlie Banks, landlord of the Lovers' Knot, was played by Roy Plomley, and the series written by Gale Pedrick. *Meet the Rev* returned as an independent series of playlets on 8 July 1947.

Revnell and West

Variety act which shot to fame after a MUSIC HALL broadcast in 1934. They played two

Revnell and West: radio's cockney kids

cockney kids, Ethel tall and skinny with the up-and-down voice, and Gracie, the titch with the squeak:

> Long and short, short and long,
> But if names are best,
> The long one's Ethel Revnell
> And the short one's Gracie West!

Their radio career together was short, Gracie retiring through sickness. But Ethel, undaunted, went solo from 1945, and in 1949 starred in the first of her one-woman radio revues, SOLITAIRE. Ethel's other trick was to impersonate a baby, which she did in DOWN OUR STREET (1948).

Rhyme With Reason
'Keep Young and Healthy' was the signature tune of this 'musical programme in a new style' sponsored by Bile Beans. The 'new style' was Bob Danvers-Walker compèring in rhyme. Marius B. Winter and his Seven Swingers provided the music for the Three Heron Sisters and the Two Black Notes. RADIO LUXEMBOURG 1937.

The Richard Tauber Programme
Sunday-night series in which the world-famous tenor sang with the British Band of the AEF, conducted by Regimental Sergeant-Major George Melachrino. Percy Kahn was at the piano, and Tauber's first guest artiste was Ida Haendel. The series began on 26 April 1945,

Richard Tauber Programme

and the programme returned on 20 July 1947. This time Tauber had the George Melachrino Orchestra as backing, and Isador Goodman as guest artiste. Ronald Waldman presented and produced.

Riders of the Range
Radio's first attempt at a serious horse opera beyond BIG BILL CAMPBELL. Described as a 'musical drama of the West', this weekly serial 'drew upon the highly coloured background of the Wild West of the Twenties, from material assembled by Charles Chilton from documents and diaries of contemporary Americans to present an authentic picture in song and story of the best of all real-life settings for pioneer work and adventure'. The original cast was Cal McCord (a rancher), Carole Carr (Mary, his daughter), Paul Carpenter (Jeff Arnold), Charles Irwin (Luke, an old cowhand), Bob Mallin (Bob, a singing cowhand), with music by the Four Ramblers and the Sons of the Saddle, led by Jack Fallon, guitarist Freddie Phillips ... 'Arf! Arf!' ... 'Oh, yes – and RUSTLER!'

The first series told of the opening up of the Chisholm Trail, and was broadcast from 13 January to 28 April 1949. The second series was written around the building of the Atcheson, Topeka and Santa Fe Railroad (2 October 1949) and the third featured Billy the Kid, played by Alan Keith (21 April 1950). The fourth series, set in Tombstone, dropped Cal McCord and brought in Macdonald Parke as rancher J.C. Macdonald. Carole Carr became his niece, Mary. The fifth series started 17 April 1952 and was written around Jesse James, while the sixth series, 15 June 1953, described the building of the Union Pacific Railway. The boys of the 6T6 outfit rode into the final sunset on 14 September 1953.

The Ridgeway Parade
Early entertainment series blending revue, concert-party, and variety, devised and produced by Philip Ridgeway. The first *Parade* was broadcast on 10 September 1930 and featured Philip Ridgeway, of course, Hermione Gingold, A.E. Nickolds, Doris Yorke, Jack Hodges (later known as 'The Raspberry King'), Gerald Osborne, Babs Valerie, Mavis Bennett, Bernard Clifton and Albert Chevalier Junior. Music from the Revue Chorus and

MOSS'
Empire
THEATRE NEWCASTLE

Proprietors: MOSS' EMPIRES, Ltd.
Chairman: PRINCE LITTLER   Managing Director: VAL PARNELL   Telephone: 24444 (3 lines)
Manager: STANLEY C. MAYO

6.15   MONDAY, OCTOBER 5th   8.30

TEXAS PRODUCTIONS present
A HAPPY RIP-ROARING TRAIL OF THRILLS, MUSIC, LAUGHTER AND SPECTACLE

YIPP-E-EE
SPECTACULAR NEW MUSICAL REVUE
BASED ON THE FAMOUS RADIO SERIES

"RIDERS of the RANGE"
BY PERMISSION OF THE B·B·C· & CHAS. CHILTON, MARSHALL OF TOMBSTONE, ARIZONA.

CHARLES IRWIN THE HILARIOUS DUDE RANCHER **LUKE**

DOLORE WHITEMAN THE COWBOYS' SWEETHEART **MARY**

NORMAN HARPER THE SINGING COWBOY **JEFF ARNOLD**

DON CAMERON H.M.V. RECORDING STAR   **12 TOTEM INDIAN DANCERS**   THE TOOTIN' SHOOTIN' **BIG BILL HICKOCK**

BIG CHIEF EAGLE EYE
AND HIS HUMAN TARGET "PRAIRIE FLOWER"

THE HILL-BILLY RANCHERS SONGS OF THE SADDLE

THE WONDER HORSE **STARLIGHT**
THE FAMOUS RADIO DOG **RUSTLER**

FIVE MIGHTY MOHAWKS
WHIRLWIND INDIAN TUMBLERS

DAVID KEAN ★ TINY ROSS

MORTON FRASER'S HARMONICA GANG

SHERIFFS' BADGES and CERTIFICATES GIVEN AWAY AT EACH PERFORMANCE to BOYS and GIRLS COWBOY OUT-

TWELVE TEXAN BELLES

SPECIAL MATINEE SATURDAY AT 2.30

Ridgeway Parade: Philip Ridgeway and his young Ladies

Orchestra was conducted by Gershom Parkington. Scripts were by Ridgeway, G.M. Holloway, and Holt Marvell (a pseudonym for Eric Maschwitz). Casts varied from show to show. The series became very popular and a stage version was mounted in 1934, while several double-sided records were also made.

Right Away!

Successor to *Ralph Reader's Revue*, 'racing along at sixty miles a second', by and with Ralph himself and produced by Harry S. Pepper. With Dick Francis, Veronica Brady, Gwen Lewis, Eric Christmas, Winifred Izard, MAURICE DENHAM and the Three in Harmony. The TWIZZLE SISTERS and Dimmock (Ted Smith) also appeared. Started 14 April 1939.

Rikki Livid

Teenage pop idol played by Hugh Paddick in BEYOND OUR KEN (1958). Greeted listeners to 'Hornerama' with his catchphrase, 'Hello an' that!'.

Riders of the Range: from radio to the stage

Ring-a-Ding-Ding

'Have a late-night fling!' with Danny Williams, Rose Brennan, Russell Sainty, the Four Kestrels, Judd Heath and the Plainsmen, and your host, Pat Campbell. Produced by Jimmy Grant from 3 April 1962.

Ring That Bell

Cheerful CHARLIE CHESTER and his Gang (Len Marten, Arthur Haynes, Ken Morris and Edna Fryer) starred in this occasional series heard in *Northern Variety Parade* during 1955. There were also 'Moments of Charm' from Marion Miller, the Littlewoods Girls Choir, and the Northern Variety Orchestra conducted by Alyn Ainsworth. Alan Clarke introduced and Eric Miller produced.

Rinso Music Hall

'The Biggest, Brightest, Most Brilliant Medley of High-Powered Talent ever Broadcast' made its debut on RADIO LUXEMBOURG at 6.30 pm on Sunday 12 July 1936. Stars heard in the first show were Albert Whelan, Freddie Dosh, Nina Devitt, G.H. Elliott and Nellie Wallace. The Music Hall band was conducted by Jock McDermot, and the compère was Edwin Styles. The series concluded on 29 August 1937. See also RINSO RADIO REVUE.

Rinso Radio Revue

'To entertain you with the most thrilling music, the funniest back-chat on radio', this weekly half-hour started on 5 September 1937, RADIO LUXEMBOURG, starring JACK HYLTON and his Band, with Dick Murphy (the Singing Star), Alice Mann (the Personality Girl), the Swingtette (the Harmony Team), and Johnnie Weekes (Compère Extraordinary). Guest stars on the first show were visiting Hollywood film stars, BEBE DANIELS AND BEN LYON. A week or so later a comedy character called Baron Schnitzel appeared, together with the Mightly All Star Art Players, compère Eddie Pola. From 11 September 1938 the series was revamped to star Bebe and Ben, with TOMMY HANDLEY (the Jester with the Quick Quips), and singers Peggy Dell, Sam Browne, and the Henderson Twins. Producer Stanley Maxted; written by Robert Wilcoxon.

Rinso Six-Thirty Special

Billed as 'The First Newspaper of the Air', this half-hour sponsored programme débuted 24 November 1935 on RADIO LUXEMBOURG. Featured were such items as Gossip Column, Film Page, Star Reporter, the Week's Best Story, Stop Press, Latest Hits, Comic Strip, and Household Hints by 'Mrs Goodsort', Woman's Editor. A novel idea, it failed to enlist listeners and changed its format to 'A Musical Weekly' in 1936.

The Rinsoptimists

Concert Party sponsored by Rinso. Their inspiration was 'THE CO-OPTIMISTS', of course, strengthened by sharing the star of that show, Davy Burnaby. Broadcast from RADIO LUXEMBOURG starting 6 January 1935. 'Mrs Goodsort', Rinso's advertising character, also appeared in the show, billed above Alice Lillie, Fred Yule, Hale Gordon and Harry Wolseley Charles.

Rise and Shine

Record-request programme, the first to be broadcast over the AEF PROGRAMME on D-Day plus 1 (7 June 1944). The series was co-hosted by Sergeant Dick Dudley of the US Army, and AC Ronald Waldman of the RAF: 'Hi, fellers!' . . . 'Morning, blokes!' The first record to be played was Artie Shaw and his Orchestra with 'Begin the Beguine'.

Rizla Fun Fair

'Roll up! Roll up! All the fun of the fair!' with Fred Douglas as the Fun Fair Barker, Wyn Richmond, Michael Moore, Wilfred Thomas, and Special Barrel Organ Arrangements by Signor Pesaresi. RADIO NORMANDY from 17 April 1938.

Rizla Sports Review

Bob Danvers-Walker announced this Sunday morning sporting series on RADIO NORMANDY, beginning 19 March 1939. Harold Palmer acted as host to the sporting guest of the week (the first was Big Bill Tilden), and the sponsor of this package of 'Interviews, Forecasts, Gossip and Guidance' was Rizla Cigarette Papers.

Robbialac Concert

CLAPHAM AND DWYER starred in this early comedy series sponsored by Robbialac Paints and broadcast on RADIO LUXEMBOURG from 29 April 1934. Also featured were Leslie Weston and Paddy Prior in comedy duologues, and Joan Pounds, piano.

Robin Fly

Board of Trade Efficiency Expert ('Efficiency's the ticket – did I say ticket?') played by JON PERTWEE in MERRY-GO-ROUND (1946). A schizophrenic when it came to music, the strains of which switched him from super-brisk ('Mr Fly to you, Barker!') to a melting romantic ('Call me Robin!'). And, of course, back again.

Robin Hood

His life, his adventures, his death, retold by Max Kester with Guy Verney as Robin, Fred Yule as Little John, Clarence Wright as Will Scarlet, Malcolm MacEachern as Friar Tuck, Trefor Jones as Alan-a-Dale, and Horace Kenney as Much the Miller's Son, with Mansel Thomas conducting the Revue Orchestra and Chorus. Six episodes beginning 5 February 1943.

The Robinson Family

The first daily serial on the BBC, this 'Day-to-day history of an Ordinary Family' began at 2.45 pm on Monday 30 July 1945. The cast was anonymous, perhaps as an aid to realism. Mr Robinson was described as a North Country-man who had worked in London for 30 years as a smallholder. His wife was a Scotswoman, and their three children were all grown up and married. The serial, produced by David Godfrey and John Richmond, had begun life four years earlier as *Front Line Family*, in the Overseas Service. One of the three anonymous scriptwriters was Jonquil Anthony, and the producer was Archie Campbell. By the time the series concluded on Christmas Eve 1947, the subtitle read 'An Everyday Story of Everyday People'.

Rocky Mountain Rhythm

Longest running of several series starring BIG BILL CAMPBELL and his Home Town Mountain Band (originally his Hilly Billy Band). Big Bill would open with his 'Howdy, friends and neighbours', and generally host the show, which over the years featured such pseudo-hilly billies as Old Buck (Fred Douglas), who passed the apple jack, Peggy Bailey ('The Sweet Voice of the West'), Jack Curtis ('The Cowboy Songster'), Chief White Eagle ('The Red Indian Tenor'), Norman Harper ('The Yodelling Buckaroo'), Jack Trafford ('The Mountain Boy'), Little Jakie Connolly, Mervyn Saunders ('The Sergeant of the Mounties'), and Ronnie Brohn and his Old Squeeze Box. First broadcast: 31 May 1940. The series which started on 4 January 1944 featured the serial play 'Death in the Canyon' with Leslie Bradley as Lucky Leamon. The 16 October 1947 series introduced Norman Harper, yodeller, and Sergeant O'Doherty of the Mounties. A little dramatic continuity was introduced into the series which began 23 July 1948. Doris Nichols played Annie, the money-loving missus of Buck Douglas, and Lionel Stevens played Black Jack McGrew, owner of the Lucky Horseshoe saloon. The final series, commencing 14 August 1949, was back to music, with Jimmy Hawthorne as the Yodelling Buckaroo and Wally Brennan as the Hired Hand, plus the Royal Canadian Mounties Chorus. The last show, produced by Hugh Middlemass, went out on 23 October 1949, and was, in Big Bill's famous catchphrase, 'Mighty fine!'.

The Rocky Mountaineers
Series of cowboy musical dramas written and presented by BIG BILL CAMPBELL and his Hilly-Billy Band from June 1935. Bill, a genial Canadian, played Old Zeke Winters, with Gerry Fitzgerald as Colonel Cook of the Royal Mounted, Sidney Keith as Tony the Camp Cook, and the Three Canadian Bachelors as Hy, Si and Old John. Fiddles and guitars by Rae Jenkins and the Bunkhouse Boys; production by Archie Campbell. Big Bill and his Boys joined RADIO LUXEMBOURG in 1939, first at No. 7 HAPPINESS LANE for Instant Postum, then in their own series for Grape Nuts (18 June). The company included Larry Adamson the Yodelling Buckaroo, Buck Douglas the Singing Cowboy, Jack Trafford the Mountain Boy, and the Three Top Hands.

Rodney and Charles
Effeminate pair who met every week ('Hello, Rodney!' 'Hello Charles!') in BEYOND OUR KEN (1958). Played in gay mood by Kenneth Williams (Rodney) and Hugh Paddick (Charles), but not so gay as JULIAN AND SANDY, their undoubted offspring.

Romance in Rhythm
Dance-music series starring GERALDO and his Orchestra with the Romantic Young Ladies, the Top Hatters, Webster Booth and Angela Paselles (1935).

Romany
Popular broadcaster in the Northern Region edition of CHILDREN's HOUR, where his series, *Out With Romany*, began on 7 October 1932 and went national from 1938. Romany's real name was George Bramwell Evens; he was a Methodist minister of gipsy descent. A natural broadcaster, he reconstructed country walks in the studio in the company of two children, Muriel (Levy) and Doris (Gambell), and Raq the dog. *A Romany in the Country* was the first (1932) of his many books.

Romeos of the Radio
Singer Denny Dennis was the first Romeo of the Radio to be introduced by Dinah the Outdoor Girl on her RADIO LUXEMBOURG series: 9 November 1937.

The Roosters
Army concert party formed by Private Percy Merriman in Salonica, 1916, and one of the first professional teams to broadcast. The date was 20 October 1923 and the cast was William Mack, Arthur Mackness, Percy Merriman and George Western (one of the WESTERN BROTHERS). Their humorous and musical reminiscences of trench comradeship was very popular with listeners, and they made several descriptive gramophone records: 'A Camp Concert', etc. From 10 October 1937 they broadcast weekly from RADIO NORMANDY on behalf of Fynnon Salt.

Ros, Edmundo
Leader of the most popular Latin American dance band since GERALDO gave up the maraccas, Ros, a Venezuelan, came to London in 1937 and formed his Rumba with Ros band in 1941. Records and broadcasts followed, with his signature tune, 'Cuban Love Song'. Series included THE GOLDEN SLIPPER CLUB and *Mr Ros and Mr Ray*, the latter being Ray Ellington.

Round Britain Quiz

Weekly contest of wit and knowledge in which teams from the BBC regions take turns in challenging the permanent team in London. This successor to TRANSATLANTIC QUIZ began on 2 November 1947, with Professor D.W. Brogan and Christopher Morley (soon replaced by Hubert Phillips) as the regular London Team under their Question-Master, Lionel Hale. The first challenge came from Scotland (James Fergusson and Jack House) under the Travelling Question Master, GILBERT HARDING. Then came teams from Wales (Ernest Hughes, Wyn Griffith), West (Jack Longland, C.F. Carr), the North (Professor Pear, Douglas Pringle), Northern Ireland (Magdalen King-Hall, James Boyce), Birmingham (Sir Barry Jackson, Professor Bodkin). The final score of the first series was London 203, Challengers 195. ROUND BRITAIN QUIZ continues to this day.

Round the Bend

Michael Bentine, one of the original GOON SHOW team, starred in this 'Radio Digest Show', a crazy series which began on 13 October 1957. Benny Lee, David Nettheim, Martin Benson, and announcer Ronald Fletcher supported Bentine, who co-wrote with Nettheim. Nat Temple and his Orchestra supplied music, and production was by Pat Dixon. The second series started on 26 December 1958, and this time Dick Lester (later Richard Lester, film director) joined the team as supporting voice and co-author. Peter Hawkins, Jean Campbell, Judith Chalmers and announcer Tim Gudgin completed the cast, and the new producer was Charles Chilton, John Law also helped on the script. The third series started on 27 May 1960 with newcomers Ron Moody and Clive Dunn.

Round the Horne

The HORNE was, of course, KENNETH of that ilk, and the series a follow-on to the highly successful but discontinued BEYOND OUR KEN. Billed as 'Five characters in search of the authors' (who were Barry Took and Marty Feldman), Horne was supported by KENNETH WILLIAMS, Hugh Paddick, Betty Marsden, Bill Pertwee, the Fraser Hayes Four, and Paul Fenoulhet and the Hornblowers. Douglas Smith announced and John Simmonds produced. The first broadcast was 7 March 1965. Ken continued to be the avuncular rock around which a gaggle of crazed characters revolved, but these extended the permissiveness that had begun to creep in the earlier series, until Took and Feldman's script was virtually one string of *double*, and often single, *entendres*. JULIAN AND SANDY, the camp couple from Carnaby Street (Paddick and Williams) were the most outrageous with their 'bona omipalone' chat, although RAMBLING SYD RUMPO (Williams) the folk singer was not far behind with his 'Cheerio my dearios!'. Marsden and Paddick played Dame Celia Molestrangler and Binkie Huckaback, who in turn played FIONA AND CHARLES. Marsden was also DAPHNE WHITETHIGH, a fashion-plate variant on FANNY HADDOCK, whilst Williams was also the tattered J. PEASEMOULD GRUNTFUTTOCK. Pertwee's best was SEAMUS ANDROID, a wicked skit on Eamonn Andrews. The series was topped and tailed by announcer Douglas Smith and his commercials for Dobbiroids. The last show was broadcast on 9 June 1968.

Roundabout (1)

'An entertainment circuit' with live contributions from all BBC Regions: Idris Lewis sang from Wales; 'Family Foibles' featured the Legpenny's Bridge Party by E.M. Delafield, from Western; Ian Sadler's 'One Man Revue' from Scotland; 'Indoor Sports' brought shoveha'penny from Midlands; 'News Narks' were the WESTERN BROTHERS with headlines from London; 'Please Mr Aesop' was fables retold in music by Henry Reed, from the North. Link-man was LIONEL GAMLIN; commenced 3 May 1939.

Roundabout (2)

Nigel Patrick, 'your columist of the air' assisted by Gwenda Wilson 'as his plain-speaking secretary, Miss Prendergast', broadcast this RADIO LUXEMBOURG series on behalf of Cadburys during 1952. Script by Robert Buckland; produced by Desmond Carrington.

Roundabout (3)

Daily series for homing car-drivers (5.30 to 6.45 pm) beginning 13 October 1958. A different host each day: Peter King, David Jacobs, Alan Dell, Ken Sykora, RICHARD MURDOCH, and a policy decreeing 'no item longer than four minutes'. Items included 'Can I Help You' with Dudley Perkins, 'Spotlight on a Star' (Antony Hopkins talks to Maria Callas), 'The 6.15 Spin', 'The (Tony) Bilbow Spot', 'Tonight's Topic', plus News, Views and Interviews. Dennis Wilson at the piano; producers Roy Speer and John Simmonds. The 500th edition was broadcast on 5 December 1963, hosted by Tim Brinton. By now the show ran 90 minutes, scripted by Anthony Marriott and produced by Peter Duncan. The 1000th programme was broadcast on 10 August 1965, with Don Davis as host. The signature tune was 'The Windows in Paris'.

The Rowntree Aerodrome
'A Programme of Flying and Music' which took the air from RADIO NORMANDY on 17 January 1937. Sponsored by Aero Chocolate, the first show included 'Sailing Along On a Carpet of Clouds'.

Rowntree's Rendezvous
RADIO LUXEMBOURG listeners were invited to 'Meet at the Rowntree Rendezvous' every Sunday morning from 28 July 1935, for a light orchestral concert by Alfredo Campoli and his Rendezvous Orchestra. The compère was Garry Marsh, and the sponsor Rowntree's Table Jellies.

Roxy Time
Romantic songs sponsored by the girls' comic, *Roxy*, and sung by Jim Dale with Mike Sammes, his Band and Voices. Compèred by smooth David Jacobs; RADIO LUXEMBOURG from 10 March 1958.

Roy, Derek
'I'm Doctor Roy the Melody Boy' was Derek's signature song, first heard when he became resident comedian on VARIETY BANDBOX in 1945. This was a record run of $3\frac{1}{2}$ years, boosted by a fabricated feud with FRANKIE HOWERD. Previously, Derek was comedy singer with GERALDO and his Band, replacing Jackie Hunter in 1942. His catchphrase, 'Ah, yes!', was also heard in such starring series as VARIETY FANFARE, HIP HIP HOO ROY, and HAPPY GO LUCKY.

Derek **Roy**: 'Dr Roy the Melody Boy'

Roy, Harry
'Are ya listenin'?' was Harry Roy's opener as his Boys blasted into his signature tune, 'Bugle Call Rag'. He was originally clarinet blower in his brother's band (Sid Roy and his Lyricals). Harry's first band, the Bat Club Boys, blossomed into the RKO-lians at the Leicester Square Theatre in 1930. Broadcasting and variety tours followed with Harry the hyperactive little showman out front, calling himself 'Your little ha-cha-ma-cha-cha' and singing scat songs à la Cab Calloway. Other vocalists: Bill Currie, Elizabeth Brooke, Dinah Miller, Wendy Clare, Carol Dexter, Renée Lester and Edna Kaye. Out of the band came Ivor Moreton and Dave Kaye on two pianos, as the Tiger Ragamuffins. From 13 July 1949 he had his own comedy band series, *Harry Roy and Co.*, with Eve Lombard, Johnny Green, and the faithful Bill Currie. There was a serialized

Harry **Roy**: 'my little hot-cha-ma-cha-cha!'

operetta featuring Gertie Goldfish. Harry wrote a number of tunes, including 'Sarawakee', for his wife Princess Pearl the Ranee of Sarawak, and 'Leicester Square Rag'.

Royal Arcade
'The shops are lovely and the band is great': musical series with plot starring Bobby Howes as Jack Robbins, and CHARLES SHADWELL

conducting the Variety Orchestra. Special music, Billy Mayerl. Written by Lauri Wylie; producer Eric Spear. Began 10 September 1941.

Royal Command Performance
Radio must take much of the blame for this perennial misnomer for the Royal Variety Show, as it continually used the label from the first-ever transmission, a 30-minute extract relayed from the Alhambra Theatre on 27 May 1926. Those heard were Bransby Williams in Dickens characterizations, comedy songs from the Houston Sisters, and Billy Bennett, 'Almost a Gentleman'. The 1931 show was specially compèred by the BUGGINS FAMILY (MABLE CONSTANDUROS and Michael Hogan), and the 1932 show, running 2 hours 20 minutes, by LEONARD HENRY.

Ruby Rockcake
Irish tea-lady whose previous appointment in a Railway Refreshment Room led her to shout 'No cups outsoide!' in IT's THAT MAN AGAIN (1945). Played by Mary O'Farrell.

Running commentaries
Name given by the BBC to their live broadcasts

Running Commentaries: outside broadcast from Brooklands Race Track (1922)

covering public events such as the Derby, the Boat Race, and Royal occasions. The first Derby commentary was given by Geoffrey Gilbey, after which Captain R.C. Lyle took over. The Boat Race commentary was always given by John Snagge, while Wimbledon tennis was described by Captain H.B.T. Wakelam. The first football commentator (1927) was GEORGE ALLISON; Charlie Garner described darts matches; and STEWART McPHERSON came from Canada to cover ice hockey.

Rustler

Dog star of RIDERS OF THE RANGE, an Alsatian named 'Romulus of Welham' trained to bark on cue by H.P. Colbourne of Uckfield.

Rusty and Dusty

Rusty Brown, red-headed urchin with patches where he sits down, and his mongrel dog, Dusty, were featured in a weekly adventure set to song, a radio comic strip. Written by Jimmy Kennedy and Michael Carr and broadcast as a 'children's corner' in HENRY HALL's Wednesday Dance Orchestra programmes during 1936–7.

Radiolympia souvenir programme 1935

SOS Messages

'Here is an SOS message' was always a dramatic announcement at the end of a radio news bulletin. 'Will Mr So-and-so who is on holiday at such-and-such return home at once as his daughter is dangerously ill' was typical. FREDDIE GRISEWOOD recalled his most dramatic message broadcast during a Chamber Music Concert from Savoy Hill: 'Here is an SOS message for Miss So-and-so, who is urgently requested not to take the white powder which was given to her in error by her doctor.' In 1936 a total of 1120 SOS messages were broadcast, of which 53.75 per cent were successful. The first SOS message was broadcast on 23 March 1923, and by the end of 1948 a total of 11,747 messages had been broadcast. The service was suspended from May 1940 to October 1945, because of war conditions.

Said the Cat to the Dog

Popular CHILDREN'S HOUR play series in the forties, with Betty Hardy as Mumpty the Cat and Stephen Jack as Peckham the Dog. Wilfred Babbage and Mary O'Farrell played Dad and Mum Jackson, and the narrator was Lionel Gamlin.

The Saint

Leslie Charteris' famous fictional detective was portrayed by Terence De Marney from 18 October 1940, in a series of stories adapted by James Parish and produced by Peter Creswell.

Sale This Day

Comedy series starring Murray and Mooney as George Grabbit and Dan Droppit the Auction Touts, with Dick Francis as Mr Bidgood the Auctioneer. Also heard were Emilio the accordionist, Donald Peers, radio's Cavalier of Song, and CHARLES SHADWELL with the Revue Chorus and Variety Orchestra. Script by Dick Pepper; producer Ernest Longstaffe. Weekly from 5 November 1941.

Sam and Janet

David Kossoff and Joan Sims played the title roles in this situation comedy series. Sam was a manufacturer of plastic table mats, and Janet had been his wife for 19 years. Alan Curtis and Kim Grant played their children. Script by David Cumming; producer Bill Worsley. Started 12 January 1966.

Sam Fairfechan

Contradictory Welshman played by Hugh Morton in IT's THAT MAN AGAIN (1945): 'How are you today – as if I cared!' Sam's equally contradictory daughter, Pam Fairfechan, was introduced in 1946, as played by Lind Joyce.

Sam Scram

Nervous, fast-talking, Yankee crony of TOMMY HANDLEY in IT's THAT MAN AGAIN (1941), played by Sydney Keith. Opening line was always: 'Boss, boss, sumpin' terrible's happened!', and he departed with 'Well, for ever more!' Sam turned out to have a brother, Butch (Bryan Herbert), who entered the series in 1943. Less verbose than Sam, his dialogue was limited to 'Uh-huh!'.

Sample Simon

Otherwise known simply as The Salesman. Played by cheerful Clarence Wright in IT's THAT MAN AGAIN (1941), he entered with 'Good morning! Nice day!' and after failing to sell his wares, exited with the same line, leaving TOMMY HANDLEY to add the gag ('That was Dan Druff, the Demon Barber!', etc.).

Sanders of the River

Mr Commissioner Sanders, the famous fictional hero created by Edgar Wallace, first came to radio in a serial entitled *The Palaver Is Finished*, commencing 10 October 1936. The adapter was Anthony Hall and the cast anonymous. Howard Marion Crawford played Sanders in a series beginning 25 September 1946. Geoffrey Wincott narrated the episodes which began with 'The Leopard that Ate Ivory'. Laidman Browne played the native chief Bosambo, and the producer was John Richmond.

Saturday Club

From 10 am to noon every Saturday morning, starting 4 October 1958, Brian Matthew introduced 'the best of today's pop entertainment' to the young-in-spirit. On the first show: Terry Dene and the Dene Aces, Humphrey Lyttelton's Jazz Cellar, Johnny Duncan and the Blue Grass Boys, Gary Miller, Folk and Spasm from Russell Quaye's City Ramblers with Hylda Sims, Scots folk-singer Jimmy Macgregor, and 'First Time Round', spinning the new releases. Produced by Jimmy Grant. An experimental stereo sequence was broadcast via Network Three on 18 May 1963, featuring Helen Shapiro. The programme's fifth birthday was celebrated on 5 October 1963 by the Beatles, the Everley Brothers, Frank Ifield, Joe Brown and the Bruvvers, Clinton Ford, Kathy Kirby and Arthur Greenslade and the Gee Men. The last show was broadcast on 18 January 1969.

Saturday Diversion

Weekly magazine programme on the Home Service from 15 March 1941. William Gates compèred CARROLL GIBBONS and his Savoy Orpheans, Jack and Daphne Barker (cabaret stars), and several features including 'Gertie the Girl on the Spot' (a modern melodrama in one act), 'Across the Table' (topical discussion), 'Transatlantic Tease Time', and 'Accent on Love' with Anne Lenner.

Saturday Magazine

'The Old Comrades March' was the signature tune for this replacement for IN TOWN TONIGHT from 5 October 1935. FREDDIE GRISEWOOD compèred, and his 'Let's turn over' between items became something of a catchphrase. Items included a capsule version of the parent programme, a comedian commenting on the week's event, 'Radio Gazette', and 'The Scarlet Orchid', a thriller serial by Renaud. Ran 35 weeks; produced by A.W. Hanson.

Saturday Merry-Go-Round

RADIO LUXEMBOURG's big bid for the Saturday-night audience, a two-hour 'cavalcade of songs, melodies and laughter designed to bring the world of entertainment to you at home'. Mel Oxley was the host, and Derek Johnson the deviser of such items as 'The Screen Presents' (songs from *Deep In My Heart*), 'Memory Corner', 'Everybody Dance' (with Russ Morgan), 'From the Footlights' (Joyce Grenfell), and Surprise Items. First broadcast 7 January 1956.

Saturday Night on the Light

Unpleasantly acronymed SNOL, this vast, three-hour 'kaleidoscope of live and recorded music, stars, features, news and personalities' took over the LIGHT PROGRAMME from 7.30 pm on the night of 26 October 1957. Roger Moffat and Charles Richardson hosted a string of features: 'Meet the Melodys' (Marjorie Mars and Ewen Solon), 'I Hit the Headlines' (Brian Johnston), 'Hysterical Histories' (Jonathan Miller), 'Pros and Cons' (George Villers and Alastair Dunnett), 'Nature Notes' (Walter Flesher), 'Short Story' (Derek Birch), 'The Man from Missilly' (Stanley Unwin), 'Well I Declare' (Jon Farrell), 'Cockney on the Farm' (Frank Marchant), 'Topical Talk' (Sam Pollock), plus Max Jaffa and his Music, Jimmy Leach at the electronic organ, and the Montmartre Players directed by Henry Krein. Producer John Bridges. The second series arrived on 12 July 1958, slightly shortened to $2\frac{1}{2}$ hours, and 'introduced from the piano' by Phil Park. 'Brainies' was a new quiz calling for the identification of 20 sound effects; 'Talking Music' was an interview between Maria Eitler and Maria Callas; 'Stump the Storyteller' was a tour-de-force by BOB MONKHOUSE; Brian Johnston presented 'Headliner'; plus guests ELSIE AND DORIS WATERS, the Gaunt Brothers, Kitty Bluett and singer Joan Small with the Jack Douglas Quartet.

Saturday Night Out

Major BBC LIGHT PROGRAMME series commencing 15 September 1945, and mounted by the OB (Outside Broadcasts) Department 'In which the microphone will follow the crowds to entertainments old and new, all over the country. Listeners are invited to join tonight's crowds at the Victoria Palace for *Me and My Girl*, the Royal Albert Hall for the Last Night of the Proms, Central Pier Morecambe for *Starlight of 1945*, and Lewisham Hippodrome for the Top of the Bill.'

Saturday Night Theatre

This long-running sequence of plays for late

(9.35 pm) weekend listening began on 3 April 1943 with an adaptation of a Lord Peter Wimsey story by Dorothy L. Sayers, *The Man With No Face*. Robert Holmes played the detective.

Saturday Radiogram

Series taking you 'behind the scenes with records and those who make them', with scriptwriter ROY PLOMLEY as Mr Bell, proprietor of the High Street Record Emporium, Eliot Makeham as Mr Goodbury, the regular customer, and Paddy Browne as assistant Miss Wimple. Musical director Jay Wilbur. Producers Leslie Perowne and Frederick Piffard; from 26 April 1941.

Saturday Roundabout

Jimmy Young presented 'a relaxing weekend survey of this and that' from 24 August 1963. Assisting him were Bernard Levin, Barry Bucknell with tips for Do It Yourselfers, Alex Welsh and his Band and the Don Riddell Four. Script by David Carter: producer John Fenton.

The Saturday Show

Pop-music and comedy series starring the BBC SHOW BAND directed by Cyril Stapleton with Rikki Fulton as the Scots compère, later assisted by BOB MONKHOUSE (co-writer with Denis Goodwin). Started 26 September 1953 with such features as 'The Stargazers' Music Shop', 'the Barnstormers invite you to the Old Log Cabin', and 'Children's Corner' with Pip and Pop. A timeshift from afternoon to lunch brought in 'Piano Playtime' with Bill McGuffie, 'Can I Forget You', the memory of an evergreen, 'The Vocal Touch' with Julie Dawn, and 'Banjo On My Knee', minstrel melodies from the Show Band Singers. Harold Smart played the electric organ and Johnnie Stewart produced.

Saturday Skiffle Club

Trend-setting Saturday-morning series, the first to reflect young people's own popular music. Brian Matthew introduced the Chas McDevitt Skiffle Group with singer Nancy Whiskey (their great hit was 'Freight Train') in the first show, broadcast 1 June 1957, and in the succeeding weeks came Bob Cort's Skiffle Group, the Cotton Pickers, Russell Quaye's City Ramblers, the Vipers, the Black Diamonds, Dickie Bishop, and Johnny Duncan. Producer Jimmy Grant. RADIO LUXEMBOURG introduced their *Amateur Skiffle Club* on 23 April 1958. Patrick Allen compèred and presented a £50 prize to the winners.

Saturday Social

Comedy series set in a working man's club run by Billy Russell, with Jeanne De Casalis in charge of the canteen and Phyllis Robins as JACK WARNER's ATS girlfriend. Opened for business 28 February 1942, scripted by Max Kester and produced by Harry S. Pepper.

Saturday Spotlight

Will Hay's first regular series, in which he and his film partner CLAUDE HULBERT appeared in 'You Take My Tip'. Other items in this magazine programme: Edward Cooper in a Piece of Rhymed Nonsense, 'Novelty Corner', and 'What Will They Think Of Next'. Began 20 July 1940, CYRIL FLETCHER replacing Hay and Hulbert from 31 August, with 'Dere Mother', (a very raw recruit writes home). Introduced by Hugh Morton; devised and produced by Harry S. Pepper and Ronald Waldman.

Savoy Hill

First permanent studios and headquarters of the BBC, No. 2 Savoy Hill on the Thames Embankment, next door to the Savoy Hotel, which was handy for broadcasting dance bands. The BBC (2LO) moved in on 2 February 1923 and the first day's programme was broadcast on 1 May: an hour's orchestral music from 11.30 am, Children's Stories at 5.30, the evening's items beginning at 7 pm with the General News. Then came the Band of the Grenadier Guards; Daisy Kennedy on the violin; a talk by Lord Gainford, Chairman of the BBC; NORMAN LONG, entertainer at the piano; and the first regular *Talk For Men* given by the Earl of Birkenhead. Originally there were two studios, heavily draped: No. 1 on the ground floor for orchestras, and No. 3 on the second for 'general purposes'. New studios were added in 1925 when alternative programmes were introduced: No. 6 was for gramophone record recitals. The last broadcast was made on 14 May 1932, on the move to BROADCASTING HOUSE: *The End of Savoy Hill*, written and

Savoy Hill: Studio No. 1 in 1928

produced by Lance Sieveking. This panorama of ten years of British broadcasting included the Postmaster-General, Robert Speaight, Harman Grisewood, Geoffrey Wincott, Peggie Robb-Smith and recordings on the BLATTNERPHONE. Last to leave was STUART HIBBERD, whose live goodnight to Oliver the night-watchman, brought tears to old-timers' eyes and marked the end of the 'good old days of wireless'.

Savoy Hotel Dance Bands

The several dance bands employed by the Savoy Hotel were regular late-night broadcasters once the BBC had moved to its neighbouring premises at SAVOY HILL. First to broadcast from the studio was the Savoy Havana Band, from 10 to 10.30 pm on 13 April 1923. First of their 12 tunes was 'Classique'. Bert Ralton

conducted and Ramon Newton sang the vocals. The first direct relay from the Hotel was on 11 October, with Debroy Somers conducting the Savoy Orpheans. His famous 'Symphonic Dance Arrangements' were specially billed on 28 June 1924. The Selma Four, a specialty group, were featured with the Bands from 3 May 1924, and Veraldi's Tango Band added a popular new dance rhythm on 1 October 1925. Later the Orpheans were taken over by pianist CARROLL GIBBONS and continued to broadcast with him in the lead.

Say It With Music

The signature tune of the former dance-band leader JACK PAYNE made a good title for this 'weekly parade of the stars of show business' which he hosted from 28 October 1954. On the

Savoy Hotel Orpheans: filmed for *Pathétone Weekly*

first programme Jack's guests were VERA LYNN, BOB MONKHOUSE, the Three Monarchs and Edmund Hockridge, and the Band of the Week was Jack Parnell's Orchestra. The George Mitchell Choristers sang with the Variety Orchestra, and the producer was Glyn Jones. A second series started on 5 November 1955 with Johnny Dankworth leading the Band of the Week. Also featured: Vanessa Lee, Bruce Trent, Albert and Les Ward, Ruby Murray. The third series (11 April 1957) was different again, with items such as 'Songs from the Theatre' and 'The Popular Song', and singers Pearl Carr, Bruce Trent and David Hughes.

The Scandal Mongers
Comedy crosstalk double-act often heard in the early 2LO days: Jack Rickards and Violet Stevens, first broadcast 7 March 1923.

The Scarlet Pimpernel
Baroness Orczy's fictional hero, Sir Percy Blakeney, the Regency fop who snatched victims of the French Revolution from the guillotine, was played by Marius Goring in *The New Adventures of the Scarlet Pimpernel*. A 'Gibbs Radio Playhouse' presentation on RADIO LUXEMBOURG beginning 1 December 1952, produced by Harry Alan Towers.

Scoop
Leslie Banks played a press photographer in this series of adventures adapted by Cyril Campion from the short stories of Patrick Brand. It started 22 May 1947 with Jacques Brown as producer.

Scrapbook
The first and most popular series of documentary programmes ever broadcast. Devised and arranged by radio journalist Leslie Baily, produced by Charles Brewer, the first, *Scrapbook for 1913* ('A Microphone Medley of Twenty Years Ago') was broadcast on 11 December 1933. An excellent blend of archive recording, old gramophone records, impersonations of deceased personalities, and survivors, the famous narrative link was 'The page of *Scrapbook* turns', spoken by narrator Freddie Grisewood. In the first programme: Ernest Shannon, Robert Hale, Matthew Boulton, Carleton Hobbs, Nancy Brown and Ida Crispi. A special production of *Scrapbook for 1910* was made as a 12″ record for the 1935 Silver Jubilee (Columbia DX679). The Silver Jubilee of the series was celebrated on 19 December 1957 with *The Story of Scrapbook*, produced by Vernon Harris.

Scrapbook of Song
Lee Lawrence brings you popular melodies of

the present, evergreen ballads, and a touch of nostalgia in 'Memory Corner'. Brought to you by Rennies Indigestion tablets; RADIO LUXEMBOURG series from 6 August 1956.

Seamus Android

Thick Oirish host of the ill-starred *Seamus Android Show*, a cruel caricature of Eamonn Andrews, host of the equally ill-starred *Eamonn Andrews Show*. Played by Bill Pertwee with many an 'all roight' in ROUND THE HORNE (1965).

Seaside Sing-Song

Summer series starring WILFRED PICKLES and holidaymakers, beginning with those at Hove on 11 June 1959. Eric James played the piano and a weekly feature was 'Mabel and her Mailbag'. Produced by Stephen Williams.

Second House

Major variety series in which Professor Leon Cortez attempted to put on a special show for the h'uplift and h'eddification of the masses, despite continual h'interruptions from Collinson and Breen. Fruity-voiced Will Collinson and high-pitched Bobby Breen were a popular and singularly hilarious double-act with the unlikely catchphrase, 'Somebody's pinched me puddin'!'. Star guests on the first show were George Doonan ('Whatsa matter wit'chew?'), Clive Richardson and Tony Lowry at two pianos, Maria Perilli and Audrey Brice, and Peter Cavanagh ('The Voice of Them All'). Rae Jenkins conducted the Variety Orchestra, Dick Pepper devised and scripted, and Jacques Brown produced. Début, 2 July 1948

Secret Mission 609

Serial starring BASIL RADFORD AND NAUNTON WAYNE in their film characters of Charters and Caldicott, beginning 9 February 1942 with 'There Goes the Bridegroom'. Written by Frank Launder and Sydney Gilliat, produced by Vernon Harris, with music by Kenneth Leslie-Smith played by GERALDO and his Orchestra.

Secrets of Scotland Yard

Clive Brook, 'star of stage and screen', assisted by Percy Hoskins, Fleet Street's top crime reporter, appeared in this 'weekly visit behind the scenes at Scotland Yard where Britain's ace detectives match their wits against the underworld'. Sponsored by *208 Magazine*, the official organ of RADIO LUXEMBOURG, from 22 October 1951.

Sellers, Peter

Creator of the most incredible cast of comic characters ever broadcast: Wilberforce the Detective ('Hist! Never fear, Hugo's here!'), Guiseppe the Chef, Luigi the Waiter, Wilf the Tough, CRYSTAL JOLLIBOTTOM ('You saucebox!'), the Dowager Duchess of Dillwater, EUSTACE ('What do you want, soppy?'), PHILLIP STRING, ERNIE SPLUTMUSCLE, HENRY CRUN, WILLIUM MATE, HERCULES GRYTPYPE-THYNNE, MAJOR DENIS BLOODNOK, BLUEBOTTLE, WILLIAM McGOONAGLE, and many more. Discovered doing film-star impressions at the Windmill, he first broadcast in SHOW TIME in July 1948. VARIETY BANDBOX, RAY'S A LAUGH and THE GOON SHOW followed.

Semprini Serenade

'Old ones, new ones, loved ones, neglected ones' was the formula for this successful series starring pianist Semprini with the Revue Orchestra conducted by Harry Rabinowitz, first broadcast 29 September 1957. The 100th show was 19 November 1959.

Send for Doctor Dick

Series of seven weekly shows starring fruity Dick Francis as 'the happy-go-lucky kill-em or cure-em quack doctor' with Sonnie Hale as his nimble-witted assistant, Helen Clare, and the Variety Orchestra conducted by CHARLES SHADWELL. Script by Ted Kavanagh and Michael North, produced by Vernon Harris, from 23 October 1940. Features within the show: 'Show Piece', 'Dr Dick's Recoveries', 'Melody Special' and 'The Clubmen'.

Send for Shiner

Ronald Shiner, chirpy cockney of so many supporting roles in British films, starred in this series from 21 September 1948. He played a news-agency reporter, ever wheedling excessive expenses out of his mean boss, editor Macintosh, played by Ian Sadler. Episode 1:

'Lost, the Emperor of China', was written by Eddie Maguire and produced by Charles Maxwell.

Serials

The first serial to be broadcast was a reading of Herbert Strang's adventure novel for boys, *Jack Hardy*, which ran in the daily *Children's Stories* programme from 17 September 1923 to 1 February 1924. The first serial for adults was *The Mayfair Mystery* ('Every Listener a Detective!'), which offered a £100 reward for the correct solution. It began on 7 December 1925, ran three episodes, and gave out the correct solution on 22 December. The first serial story for adults was A.E.W. Mason's novel, *At the Villa Rose*, introduced by the author on 23 July 1926. Campbell Gullan read the five episodes, concluding 31 July. The first dramatized serial was the mystery, *Ghostly Fingers* by Hilda Chamberlain. Percy Rhodes, Ian Fleming, Carleton Hobbs and Gwendoline Evans took part in this production by R.E. Jeffrey. Parts 1 and 2 were broadcast on 23 August 1926, with part 3, 'The Mystery Solved', on 28 August. The first radio serial in the modern sense was *The Mystery of the Seven Cafés*, specially written by novelist Sydney Horler and featuring Norman Shelley as his popular hero, the Hon. Timothy 'Tiger' Standish of Q.1. Episode 1 of this 'Secret Service Serial with Music' was broadcast on 20 June 1935. A.W. Hanson produced, and the special music was by Walford Hyden.

Series

The simple concept of a radio series (the same title, the same stars, the same day, the same time) eluded the BBC for many years, although 'See you next week, same time, same spot on the dial' had been the staple of American radio from the start. Several series were launched but despite their success with listeners, tended to be monthly or even more spasmodic. The first popular music series was WINNERS (1925), and the first comedy series RADIO RADIANCE (1925) with TOMMY HANDLEY. Then came RADIO FOLLIES (1926), CHARLOT'S HOUR (1929), and THE RIDGEWAY PARADE (1930), all arranged by outside producers. With the establishment of the VARIETY DEPARTMENT, homegrown series began to appear: MUSIC HALL (1932), THE KENTUCKY MINSTRELS (1933), AMERICA CALLING (1933), EIGHT BELLS (1935), RADIO PIE

(1936), and WIRELESS PUPPETS (1936). Meanwhile commercial radio raced ahead with regular weekly series, such as MUSICAL VOYAGE (1935), ADVENTURES OF MYRTLE AND BERTIE (1935), THE RINSOPTIMISTS (1935), RINSO MUSIC HALL (1936), STORK RADIO PARADE (1937), and AT HOME WITH THE HULBERTS (1937). The comedy series format began on the BBC with BAND WAGGON (1938), followed by BUNGALOW CLUB (1938), DANGER MEN AT WORK (1939) and IT'S THAT MAN AGAIN (1939). By the start of World War II the formula was set.

Service With a Smile

Ken Platt ('I won't take me coat off, I'm not stoppin'!') played the junior porter under head-porter Dick Emery in this series set in a hotel. Emery was also Humphrey Sycamore, Dozy Dan and Otto Rubenstein, while Herbert Smith played Hoo Flung Soo the Chinese Laundry Man. Resident cabaret artistes were the Coronets. Script by Frank Roscoe and Ken Platt; produced by John Ammonds. Opened 8 July 1957.

Sexton Blake

George Curzon starred as the famous boys' paper detective in *Enter Sexton Blake*, a serial broadcast from 26 January 1939 as part of the magazine programme LUCKY DIP. Brian Lawrance the crooner played his young assistant, Tinker. Adapted by Ernest Dudley from the story by Berkeley Grey, episode 1 (of 12) was entitled 'The Quitter'. Blake returned, impersonated by Arthur Young, in *A Case for Sexton Blake*, a serial by Francis Durbridge adapted from the story by Edward Holmes. This featured in CRIME MAGAZINE from 12 March 1940, and Clive Baxter played Tinker.

'Shadow Man'

Thriller serial broadcast as a segment of *For You Madame* on RADIO LUXEMBOURG from 4 January 1955. Robert Beatty starred, with Anne Cullen (as Anne Delaney), Petula Clark, Felix Felton and Basil Jones. Script by Edward J. Mason; produced by Neil Tuson; sponsored by Stork Margarine.

Shadwell, Charles

Conductor of the BBC Variety Orchestra who became radio's Number One Stooge. Used as a

Charles **Shadwell**: 'new' signature tune of the BBC Variety Orchestra

butt or a feed by comedians broadcasting in MUSIC HALL, Charlie's name, voice, and infectious chuckle brought him national fame. As conductor in the pit at Coventry Hippodrome he became used to back-chatting the comics, and when old acquaintances began to receive radio bookings, they naturally revived the old relationships. The first act to use him thoroughly on radio were the American film stars, BEBE DANIELS AND BEN LYON, who adapted the tradition of American radio comedians' banter with their band-leaders. VIC OLIVER made his radio debut by rushing on stage shouting, 'Telegram for Charlie Shadwell. His wife's just given birth to a bouncing baby!'. Charlie gasped in shock, then brayed with laughter at Vic's payoff: 'They don't know if it's a boy or a girl – it's still bouncing!' Charlie gave himself a larger role to play in GARRISON THEATRE (1939), a show he devised out of his own Great War experiences. But he is best remembered for his long run in IT'S THAT MAN AGAIN, where he virtually became one of the cast of characters. TOMMY HANDLEY, the star, had a weekly insult for him: 'the Human Hairpin', etc.

She Knows Y'Know

Series starring Hylda Baker and named for her catchphrase. The gossipy northerner was supported by Robert Moreton (of *Bumper Fun Book* fame), the Beverley Sisters, and Albert and Les Ward. Produced by James Casey from 10 July 1956.

Sherlock Holmes

Sir Arthur Conan Doyle's fabulous fictional detective has been a frequent broadcaster. Sir Cedric Hardwicke impersonated him in *The Adventure of the Speckled Band* (17 May 1945), adapted by John Dickson Carr from the writings of Dr John Watson (Finlay Currie). Later the same year (9 August) Laidman Browne and Norman Shelley took on sleuth and assistant in *Silver Blaze*, adapted by C. Gordon Glover in 'Corner in Crime'. Shelley, the definitive radio Watson, first encountered the definitive radio Holmes, Carleton Hobbs, in CHILDREN'S HOUR, of all places, on 13 October 1952. *The Naval Treaty* was the first of a series adapted by Felix Felton and produced by David Davis. Hobbs also starred in William Gillette's play, *Sherlock Holmes*, adapted for *Saturday Night Theatre* (3 January 1953) by Raymond Raikes. A curious situation arose

during October 1954: while Hobbs and Shelley were solving six more cases on CHILDREN'S HOUR, commencing on 1 October with *The Norwood Builder*, over on the LIGHT PROGRAMME John Gielgud and Ralph Richardson commenced their *Adventures of Sherlock Holmes* on 5 October. This series, adapted by John Kier Cross, was produced by HARRY ALAN TOWERS. Wonderful as they were, it was to be Hobbs and Shelley who remained the BBC's perfect pair. They solved a six-part serial of *The Hound of the Baskervilles*, scripted by Felton, commencing 6 April 1958, and followed with a six-part series when Michael Hardwick adapted *The Man With the Twisted Lip*, from 12 May 1959. However, more confusion arose when, five days later, Richard Hurndall and Bryan Coleman took on the roles in Felton's serial of *The Sign of Four*. The originals were back in harness for Hardwick's SATURDAY NIGHT THEATRE production of *The Valley of Fear* (31 December 1960), followed by a run of seven short stories starting with *The Empty House* on 27 November 1961. *A Study in Scarlet* was SATURDAY NIGHT THEATRE on 22 December 1962. A series of eight started on 7 August 1964 with *The Abbey Grange*, and nine more followed from 2 November 1966, beginning with *A Scandal in Bohemia*. Martyn C. Webster produced and Mrs Hudson the housekeeper was played by Barbara Mitchell.

Shilling a Second

'A new series in which contestants win a shilling for every second they remain on the stage.' Sponsored by CWS Silver Seal Margarine, Ross Radio Productions adapted their format from the American show, *Dollar a Second*. Paul Carpenter hosted, assisted by Patrick Allen, and the announcer was Lloyd Lamble. Produced by Monty Bailey-Watson, directed by Tig Roe, and broadcast from RADIO LUXEMBOURG from 8 October 1954. Tony Hawes scripted and the show toured the country, starting at the Camberwell Palace. The second series began on 4 November 1955 with Jack Watson as host, shortly replaced by Gerry Wilmot. Philip Waddilove directed.

Shipmates Ashore

Weekly wartime series commencing Saturday 10 January 1942, recorded at the Merchant Navy Club. 'A meeting place in the heart of London for men of the Merchant Service. Call in or tune in for music, dancing, refreshments, and a friendly welcome from your Chief Stewardess, Doris Hare.' Features included 'Ship's Newspaper' with George Ralston, the Ship's Reporter; 'In the Club Room'; 'Home Port'; 'Hello Shipmates'; 'Good Old London', and music by Debroy Somers and his Band. 'Love from Doris' was Miss Hare's famous sign-off, with a chorus of 'Sailor who are you dreaming of tonight'. Produced by Howard Thomas.

Shorty
London taxi-driver played by Jerry Verno in the long-running radio series TAXI! Created in 1942 by Cyril Campion.

Shout for Joy
Starring series for JOY NICHOLS, formerly the feminine leg of the TAKE IT FROM HERE triangle. From 5 July 1955 she was escorted by John Cazabon, Alan Keith, the Nicholodeons, and Harry Rabinowitz and the Revue Orchestra. Written by Sid Colin, Eddie Maguire and Ronald Wolfe; produced by Charles Maxwell.

Show Band Show
Long running music and comedy series 'spotlighting the world of popular music' and showcasing the new BBC SHOW BAND directed by Cyril Stapleton. Rikki Fulton was the Scots compère on the first broadcast, 2 April 1953, introducing the Stargazers, Julie Dawn and the Show Band Singers with Harold Smart at the organ. Features included 'Melody-go-round', 'Hit Parade', 'Down South' with Freddy Randall and the Dixielanders, 'Happy Birthday', 'I Hear a Violin' with Louis Stevens, 'Melodies and Memories' with Bill McGuffie at the piano, and 'South American Way' with the Show Band Strings in Tango Time. Producer Johnnie Stewart. Special guest on 16 July 1953 was Frank Sinatra. By 1955 the comedy compère was Alfred Marks reading scripts by Dick Vosburgh and Brad Ashton. The new series beginning 27 August 1956 was written and introduced by BOB MONKHOUSE AND DENIS GOODWIN, and introduced new singing star Dawn Lake.

Show Business
Weekly miscellany of music, song, reports and gossip on what's new in the world of entertainment, brought to you by the three RADIO LUXEMBOURG presenters, Keith Fordyce, Barry

Alldis and Don Moss. The first show on 30 December 1957 included Shirley Bassey, Dickie Valentine, the Four Jones Boys, and Ted Heath and his Music.

The Show Must Go On
Comedy series co-starring the two impressionists, Carl Carlisle and Maisie Weldon (she was the daughter of old-time Music Hall comedian, Harry Weldon). There was also a weekly 'Guess Star', and singers The Radio Three provided songs with Stanley Black and the Dance Orchestra. Written by Sid Colin and produced by Charles Maxwell.

Show Parade
Umbrella title for a series of self-contained programmes designed to give broadcasting experience to promising new writers and artists, and develop possible formulas for future series. It started 14 March 1949 with *It's In The Bag* starring Kitty Bluett (who became Ted Ray's radio wife), BOB MONKHOUSE, and Terry Scott. SOLITAIRE, a one-woman revue by Leslie Julian Jones starred Ethel Revnell, and later became a series, *Cottage On The Corner* starring melancholy BILL KERR, Desmond Walter Ellis and Charles Hawtrey. *Flowers for Friday* introduced Hugh Latimer and Violet Loxley. TALK YOURSELF OUT OF THIS was a successful panel game chaired by Harold Warrender, with Hermione Gingold and Patricia Laffan. *Meet the Band* teamed Bill Kerr, Robert 'Bumper Fun Book' Moreton, and Bob Monkhouse. HERE'S HOWARD by Laurie Wyman became a series for comic MICHAEL HOWARD, as did LEAVE YOUR NAME AND NUMBER, written by the stars, BERNARD BRADEN AND BARBARA KELLY.

Show Time
A weekly parade of variety's up-and-coming attractions, introduced by DICK BENTLEY. Newcomers on the first show (8 April 1948) included Terry Scott, April May and June, Leo Massey and Leslie Adams. Musical support from the Showtimers, with Frank Cantell and the Revue Orchestra. Script by DENIS NORDEN; producer Roy Speer.

Show Time From the London Palladium
RADIO LUXEMBOURG's biggest series of 60-minute shows, 'a full hour of top-line entertain-

ment from the world's most-famous variety house' sponsored by Phensic, Lucozade, and Amami Wave Set. Wilfrid Thomas compèred, and the first show (1 December 1952) starred the Keynotes, Jimmy Wheeler, Robin Richmond, John Rorke, Marian Saunders, Peter Brough and ARCHIE ANDREWS, and the Skyrockets. Produced by HARRY ALAN TOWERS.

Showland Memories
'A Musical Cavalcade of Theatreland Past and Present' with Webster Booth, Olive Groves, and the Showlanders. Presented by California Syrup of Figs on RADIO NORMANDY from 28 November 1937.

Shows From the Seaside
Series of broadcasts from summer seaside concert parties, commencing 8 July 1937 with *Gay Parade* from the Pier Pavilion, Worthing. Introduced by Harry S. Pepper and Davy Burnaby.

Showtime 63
Peter Brough, for the first time appearing without ARCHIE ANDREWS, compèred this series starring 'the year's favourite artists'. The first show (31 March 1963) featured Erich Shilling in *Iolanthe*, Lance Percival and Patsy Rowlands, Millicent Martin and Ronnie Carroll, Joe 'Mr Piano' Henderson, Hy Hazell and Tony Fayne 'With a Tongue in Cheek', Johnny Lockwood, the Ray Ellington Quartet and the Michael John Singers, with Paul Fenoulet and the Variety Orchestra. Written by Ray Taylor; produced by Trafford Whitelock.

Sidney Mincing
Character in RAY's a LAUGH played by Kenneth Connor, given to saying 'Do you mind?' and 'My name is Sidney Mincing and I am the proprietor of this emporium'. Also given to telling long-winded stories with awful punning payoffs.

Signature Tunes
Signature tunes and theme tunes foredate radio, of course. Albert Whelan always claimed to be the first with his use of 'The Jolly Brothers', but music-hall stars were always played on with their most popular hits. The first radio signature tune was 'The Dance of the Goblins' used by Birmingham to introduce their children's programmes (5 December 1922). THE CO-OPTIMISTS always opened with their stage signature song, 'Bow Wow' (1923) and the whistling pianist Ronald Gourley signed off with his own 'Dicky Bird Hop' (1923). The first broadcasting dance band to use a signature tune, 'Whispering', was Marius B. Winter's (1923), while HENRY HALL and his Gleneagles Hotel Band introduced their relays with 'Come Ye Back to Bonnie Scotland' (1924). When JACK PAYNE formed the BBC DANCE BAND in 1928 he opened and closed with 'Say It With Music'. FLOTSAM AND JETSAM composed their own signature song (1926), as later did MURGATROYD AND WINTERBOTTOM, REVNELL AND WEST, and other broadcasting comedy acts. Eric Coates' 'Knightsbridge' was used to introduce IN TOWN TONIGHT (1933), one of the first radio series with a regular theme tune. Soon original tunes were being composed: 'It's Monday Night at Seven' (1937), 'Band Waggon' (1938), 'It's That Man Again' (1939).

Commercial radio used signature tunes from the start: 'Pack Up Your Troubles' by the Revelation Suitcase programme (1929) and 'Smiler Keep Smiling for Me' by Cow & Gate (1932). RADIO NORMANDY itself had sig-tunes, opening each day with 'The Bells of Normandy' and closing with its so-called 'Goodnight Melody' (Ted Lewis singing 'Goodnight Sweetheart') (1932). RADIO LUXEMBOURG followed with the specially composed and recorded 'Tune In' by JACK PAYNE's band (1934). By the end of the thirties it was obligatory for almost every programme to have its own signature tune.

Signor So-So
TOMMY HANDLEY's 'foreign secretary' whose mangled English made him an IT'S THAT MAN AGAIN favourite (1941). 'Ah, Mister Handlebar, I am delightful!' he would cry on entering, whilst wooing MRS MOPP with such phrases as 'You attract me like a maggot!'. Played by Dino Galvani who made a national catchphrase of 'Nutting at all, nutting at all!', and only just missed with 'I love *all* the ladies!'.

Signature Tunes: song book

SIGNATURE TUNES
OF FAMOUS RADIO ARTISTES
SELECTION

"WHEN DAY IS DONE"

AMBROSE

"TORCH SONG"

SIDNEY TORCH

"MY SONG GOES ROUND the WORLD"

DONALD THORNE

"PAINTING THE CLOUDS WITH SUNSHINE"

LESLIE SIMPSON

"FOR YOU"

ALBERT SANDLER

"SONS OF THE SEA"

HARRY DAVIDSON

"A LITTLE BIT OF HEAVEN"

TERENCE CASEY

"WHEN YOU'RE SMILING"

GEORGE ELRICK

"LET THE GREAT BIG WORLD KEEP TURNING"

LLOYD THOMAS

"I DO LIKE TO BE BESIDE the SEASIDE"

REG. DIXON

SEE BACK PAGE FOR PERSONAL SIGNATURES

Silver Jubilee Programmes
Radio celebrated the Silver Jubilee of King
George V and Queen Mary with *All-Star
Variety* (6 May) from the New Corn Exchange,
Brighton: NORMAN LONG, the DANCING
DAUGHTERS, Jane Carr, ELSIE AND DORIS WA-
TERS, Nosmo King, Anona Winn, and LEON-
ARD HENRY compèring with JACK PAYNE and
his Band. The first radio production of *The
Desert Song* (8 May) offered original stars Edith
Day, Harry Welchman and Dennis Hoey.
Variety of the Empire (9 May) had Al and Bob
Harvey (Canada), Afrique the impressionist
(Africa), Albert Whelan (Australia), Keith
Wilbur (New Zealand), 'Hutch' (West Indies)
and Denis O'Neil (Irish Free State). *Songs From
The Shows* (10 May) was compiled from shows
seen by Their Majesties: Huntley Wright,
Adele Astaire, Derek Oldham, Jose Collins and
W.H. Berry. *Jubilee Gala* (11 May) was an
Anglo-American entertainment with Anna
May Wong, Larry Adler, the Mills Brothers,
CARROLL GIBBONS and the Savoy Hotel
Orpheans, Peter Dawson and CICELY
COURTNEIDGE. For radio's own 25th anniver-
sary programmes see BBC SILVER JUBILEE.

Silvester, Victor
Maestro of Strict Tempo and famous as host of
the BBC DANCING CLUB, where his oft-repeated
'Slow, slow, quick-quick, slow' became almost
a catchphrase. Victor won the title of World's
Professional Dancing Champion in 1929 and
formed his band in 1934 to make records of
strict-tempo dance music. Broadcasting followed in 1937, and within ten years he was
voted the most popular broadcasting band in
polls conducted by the *Daily Express* and *Sunday
Pictorial*. His signature tune was 'You're Dancing On My Heart'.

Simon and Laura
Series adapted from the stage play by Alan
Melville, with Hugh Burden as Simon Foster
and Moira Lister as Laura. James Hayter
played Wilson the Butler, Ian Harrison the
Producer, and Brian Oulton the writer,
Wilfred Higgins. Script by Ted Taylor; first
broadcast 9 July 1956.

Sincerely Yours, Vera Lynn
'To the men of the forces, a letter in words and
music from VERA LYNN, accompanied by Fred
Hartley and his Music'. The series which
consolidated Our Vera as 'Sweetheart of the
Forces' began on 9 November 1941 and included 'News from Home' (messages from
munition-girls to their husbands) and 'Con-
gratulations' to some new fathers in the forces.
Presented by Howard Thomas.

Sing It Again
It was the Kordites who originally sang:

> Sing it again,
> Let's sing that song again,
> That lovely tune that makes you want to
> Sing it again!

on 26 March 1950. This 'song-a-minute selec-
tion of popular melodies old and new' featured
Carole Carr, Terry Devon, Josephine
Crombie, Benny Lee, Alan Dean and Harry
Dawson. Producer was Johnnie Stewart. By the
series starting 24 June 1956 the Keynotes were
the main group, supported by Patti Lewis,
Franklyn Boyd, Jean Campbell, the Johnston
Brothers, the Steve Race Quintet and Harold
Smart at the organ. Oh yes, and Benny Lee!
The last programme was broadcast on 4 May
1971.

Sing It Through
'And Don't Forget the Chorus! A popular get-
together with a cheerful cast': LEONARD
HENRY, Al & Bob Harvey, MABEL CONSTAN-
DUROS, and the Revue Chorus and Orchestra.
This sing-song with comedy started on 3
October 1939, and changed its name to THE
SMILERS' LEAGUE from 3 December.

Sing Something Simple
'Songs simply sung for song-lovers' was the
subtitle for this half-hour of non-stop pop songs,
first heard on 3 July 1959 and every week since.
Devised and compiled by ex-Stargazer Cliff
Adams for his group, the Adam Singers (12
men, 3 women), accompanied by accordionist
Jack Emblow and his Quartet; the original
producer was John Browell. The 25th anniversary of the series was celebrated by an hour-
long special, *Sing Something Silver*, on 11 August
1984.

Victor **Silvester**: 'Dance Time' for sixpence

ROLAND'S PIANOFORTE TUTOR · THE BEST IN THE WORLD
ENGLISH FINGERING   CONTINENTAL FINGERING
No 2879.

Feldman's 6d *Edition*

Dance Time

(No 1. *The Waltz*)

Described by VICTOR SILVESTER

A WALTZ MEDLEY SELECTED AND EDITED BY
VICTOR SILVESTER
and Arranged Specially for Dancing

GUITAR &
PIANO-ACCORDION ACC.

MR. & MRS. VICTOR SILVESTER

PHOTO: YVONNE

Contents

BEAUTIFUL OHIO
TO-NIGHT YOU BELONG TO ME
I'M FOREVER BLOWING BUBBLES
THREE O'CLOCK IN THE MORNING
TING-A-LING (The Waltz of the Bells)
TILL WE MEET AGAIN
I'LL BE YOUR SWEETHEART
LET ME CALL YOU SWEETHEART
SWEET ROSIE O'GRADY
OH! WHAT A PAL WAS MARY

RECORDED, BROADCAST & FEATURED BY
VICTOR SILVESTER & HIS BALLROOM ORCHESTRA

RECORDED ON
PARLOPHONE
RECORD
No F942

London · England: B. FELDMAN & Co. *125-9 Shaftesbury A^v W.C.2.*

6D·
NET.

COPYRIGHT.

Sing Song
Saturday Night on the National was the slot for this occasional one-hour show, starting 16 July 1938. Rupert Hazell and Elsie Day were the cheery host and hostess of this mixture of variety acts and community singing. 'Do join in the choruses if you feel like it, and even if you don't!' was the advice of producer/conductor Ernest Longstaffe. Show no. 16, broadcast on 22 July 1939, also featured Dan Young (the Dude Comedian), Dorothy Brett and Reg Powell (Comedy Bits and Pieces), Emilio (the Wonder Boy Accordionist), Harold Berens (Something New), and ETHEL REVNELL AND GRACIE WEST (the Two Oddments); also SANDY MACPHERSON at the BBC THEATRE ORGAN, and Percival Mackey's Orchestra. The 19 August 1939 show starred a very special guest, cowboy singer Gene Autry!

Singing Joe the Sanpic Man
'Will he sing your song?' Singing Joe the Sanpic Man sang listeners' request songs every week on the *Sanpic Quarter Hour*, sponsored by Reckitts from RADIO LUXEMBOURG starting 21 August 1936. Sanpic described itself as: 'The new non-poisonous disinfectant that smells good!'

Sir Percy Palaver
Deryck Guyler played this almost inarticulate Governor of Tomtopia, who had taken office in TOMMY HANDLEY's absence and peppered his mumbles with 'Hrrrumphs'. IT's THAT MAN AGAIN (1946).

Sir Short Supply
Strangulated civil servant in IT's THAT MAN AGAIN (1946), played by Deryck Guyler.

Sirdani
The Radio Magician – he taught conjuring tricks in his 'Knot-ical Magic' spot in NAVY MIXTURE (1944). His catchphrase was 'Don't be fright!'.

Sister Parkinson
Nurse Dugdale's 'Parky dear', played by Marjorie Westbury in A DATE WITH NURSE DUGDALE (1944).

Sitting on the Fence
Nat Gubbins' famous humorous column in the *Sunday Express* was adapted for radio from 13 June 1944. 'A full anonymous cast' was billed, with music by Alan Rawsthorne played by the BBC Revue Orchestra conducted by Charles Groves. Produced by John Watt and Michael North.

The Six Pips
The first broadcast time signal was at 10 pm on 4 August 1923. This was later developed by F. Hope Jones, who suggested 'six dots', the last of which should mark the exact hour. This was adopted and the first broadcast, introduced by the Astronomer Royal, Sir Frank Dyson, was transmitted from the Greenwich Observatory at 9.30 pm on 5 February 1924. In recent years the sixth pip has been elongated for emphasis, and for those who cannot count up to six. ARTHUR ASKEY played the Keeper of the Pips in his film, *Back Room Boy* (1942).

Sky High With Skol
'The makers of Skol Healing Antiseptic present the Famous Petulengro reading the Stars for You, and a programme of Gipsy Music.' RADIO NORMANDY from 5 March 1937.

A Slight Delay
Comedy situation series for film stars Moore Marriott and Graham Moffatt, written by their screenwriters, Val Guest and Marriott Edgar. Cast: Hugh Morton, Anne Lenner, Joan Young, 'and whoever is in the waiting-room'. Produced by Tom Ronald from 7 January 1942.

Slim Callaghan
Tough private detective created by Peter Cheyney (who had been an early 2LO broadcaster of his own monologues). Slim first appeared in *The Callaghan Touch*, a series broadcast from 3 April 1941. Jack Livesey was the tec, with Betty Hardy as Effie Thompson, secretary, and Macdonald Parke as Windermere 'Windy' Nicholls, assistant. The second series, *Again Callaghan*, started on 10 July 1942, with Ralph Truman as Slim in 'The Insurance Case'. The third series, entitled *The Callaghan Comeback*, started 9 April 1943. This time Freda Falconer was Effie, and Harry Lane was Windy.

Smart Work With Gumption

Music for the family played by the Harold Smart Quartet, introduced by Robert Marsden, and sponsored by Gumption Smooth Paste Cleanser. Produced by Philip Jones; RADIO LUXEMBOURG from 6 April 1954.

Smash Hits

RADIO LUXEMBOURG's highly popular record show in which 'records of your favourite hates are played before being broken on the spot'. Comments from listeners' letters were read by all three Luxembourg disc-jockeys of the time, Geoffrey Everitt, Pete Murray and Peter Madren. Shows compiled by Philip Jones; first broadcast 1 December 1952. A new series sponsored by Aspro started on 5 February 1956, with Charmian Innes and Harold Berens doing the smashing. Cash prizes were a new fringe benefit, and the producer was Peter Pritchett-Browne.

The Smilers' League

Formerly SING SONG. President LEONARD HENRY ran the League from Headquarters, Cheeryble House, Sunshine Street, Giggleborough. Ernest Longstaffe produced and the 1 January 1940 show featured NOSMO KING and Hubert, Sidney Burchall, Rupert Hazell and Elsie Day, and Jean Melville at the piano.

Smokey Mountain Jubilee

Canadian singing group the Maple Leaf Four 'invite you to a get-together western style in the old barn' from 31 May 1956. The Four played Gabby, Zeke, Ezra and Happy Pappy. Appearing as themselves were Louise Howard, Jim Hawthorne, Slim Weston and his Smokey Mountain Boys. Producer Jacques Brown.

Smoking Concert

'A Convivial Congregation with a Cigarette and a Song on their lips' – not to mention smoke in their eyes and something else in their lungs? Weekly series on RADIO NORMANDY from 28 March 1937, starring Charlie the Chairman and sponsored by Rizla Cigarette Papers.

Snack Bar

'Mixed menu of light fare' conducted by Muriel Levy and served up by Doris Hare. Produced by Leslie Bridgmont from 1942.

John **Snagge**: cover star of the *Leader*

Snagge, John

Snagge usurped STUART HIBBERD's title as 'the Voice of the BBC'. He joined the Company only four weeks after the famous Chief Announcer. After training Snagge was dispatched to Stoke-on-Trent, returning to London in 1928 having been, among other things, the local Radio Uncle. In 1931 he gave the first of what would become his annual 'special', the Running Commentary on the Boat Race. His 'In . . . out . . . in . . . out . . .' became a virtual catchphrase, and his 'I can't quite see who's winning, it's either Oxford or Cambridge' a classic microphone fluff. From 1933 the Outside Broadcast department made him a full-time commentator, and from 1935 he did a long series of stunt commentaries in which he rode bareback in a circus, went deep-sea diving, etc. His famous commentaries include the Royal Jubilee, Funeral and Coronation, and with the onset of World War II he became Presentation

Director. He was the voice that announced D-Day, V-Day and VJ-Day. Like others of his ilk, he was not averse to letting his hair down: he appeared on occasion in THE GOON SHOW.

Snibson's Choice

Series starring Lupino Lane as his stage character Bill Snibson, with Margery Wynn as Polly. Written by Cyril Campion and Max Kester, with music by Noel Gay played by Mantovani and his Orchestra. Began 27 May 1942.

Snide

Ingratiatingly unpleasant character created by KENNETH WILLIAMS for HANCOCK'S HALF HOUR. Snide said his first 'Good evenin'' on 7 June 1955, and soon won applause with his catchphrase, 'Stop messin' about!' (which was, some two decades later, to become the title of a show starring Williams – this was a short-lived successor to the immortal ROUND THE HORNE).

Snowy

George 'Snowy' White, the Captain's former Sergeant in the Commandos, was the cheery cockney companion of DICK BARTON (1946). Played by John Mann.

Soccer Songtime

Kathran Oldfield sang songs such as 'Silver Dollar' on this series presented by Empire Pools of Blackpool; RADIO LUXEMBOURG 1950.

Soft Lights and Sweet Music

Romantic series of music and song devised and produced by Austen Croom-Johnson, who also played the piano. The first programme featured Eve Becke's voice and Len Fillis's guitar. Later came Elisabeth Welch, George Melachrino and Rudy Starita. The title was used for a 1936 dance-band film starring AMBROSE and his Orchestra. From 30 May 1937 the show made history by being the first BBC series to transfer to commercial radio. Pepsodent Toothpaste presented the series on RADIO LUXEMBOURG, with CARROLL GIBBONS and his Orchestra. Singers were George Melachrino and Dorea Charles, and the soft-voiced compère James Dyrenforth.

Solitaire

One-woman radio revue series starring comedienne Ethel REVNELL after her double-act with Gracie West had been discontinued. Originally tried out in SHOW PARADE on 21 March 1949, it became a series from 20 June 1950, with book, music and lyrics by Leslie Julian Jones and Hal Stead at the piano. Frank Cantell conducted the Revue Orchestra, and Tom Ronald produced.

Something to Shout About

This 'light-hearted look at the advertising world' starred Michael Medwin as Michael Lightfoot, account executive with Apsley, Addis, Cone, Barbican, Blythe, Giddy and Partners. Fenella Fielding played his secretary, Janet, and Eleanor Summerfield was Maggie Tufnell, the TV advertising exec. Nicholas Phipps played Adrian Beales, copywriter ('A Fridge in Every Igloo'), and Joan Sims was Mavis Wilks, floating typist. Warren Mitchell played Mr Pimslow, and the singing commercials ('Niblo's Food') were by the Jingle Belles accompanied by the Bernie Fenton Quartet. Satirically written by Myles Rudge and Ronald Wolfe; produced by John Simmonds. Started 5 July 1960, with a second series on 2 January 1961. Show no. 50 was broadcast on 29 January 1962.

Somewhere in England

Wartime variant of IN TOWN TONIGHT, as its subtitle, 'In the Canteen Tonight', suggests. It started Saturday 14 October 1939 with 'such familiar figures as Canteen Kate, Sergeant Atkins, to say nothing of Smithy, the embodiment of every old sweat that ever was'. Produced by C.F. Meehan.

Songs From the Shows

Immensely popular series of musical programmes devised and compèred by John Watt. The first edition was broadcast on 3 November 1931, with just two singers, Tessa Deane and William Stephens, plus the BBC Theatre Orchestra conducted by Leslie Woodgate. The 21st Birthday programme on 5 November 1952 featured Barbara Leigh, John Hanson, Eve Becke, Jack Cooper, ANONA WINN, C. DENIER WARREN, Olive Groves, George Baker, WYNNE AJELLO, and the Grosvenor Singers, with the Variety Orchestra conducted by Paul Fenoulhet.

Songs You Might Never Have Heard

Fortnightly programmes of new songs 'selected by a Committee of Listeners, for whose probable popularity you are invited to vote'. BRYAN MICHIE compèred, and singers included Morgan Davies, Eve Becke, Gerry Fitzgerald, Bertha Willmott and the Tin Pan Alley Trio. Music by the Variety Orchestra and REGINALD FOORT at the Theatre Organ. (1937).

Sophie Tuckshop

Little girl with a little voice, played by oversized Hattie Jacques, much to the delight of the studio audience for IT'S THAT MAN AGAIN (1947). Sophie was a schoolgirl with a penchant for midnight feasts in the dorm . . . 'But I'm all right now!'.

Sound Idea

Panel game 'in which Peter West encourages RICHARD MURDOCH and KENNETH HORNE to vie with Johnny Morris and John Slater in giving fairly reasonable explanations of varied noises'. Edward J. Mason devised the show in several sections, with sequences of unrelated sounds, one-sided telephone conversations, and one where the panellists were required to make noises representing popular phrases. Produced by John Farrington; started 28 July 1958.

South of the Border

Exotic musical series devised by Dorothe Morrow, with music arranged by Don Felipe. Featuring the Three in Harmony and the Rancheros; producer Norah Neale. Occasional broadcasts from 1941.

Spare a Copper

The old George Formby film inspired the title of this comedy series built around Kenneth Connor as PC Albert Hereward Lamp. Graham Stark, Deryck Guyler and Roy Dotrice supported in scripts by John Esmonde and Bob Larbey. Producer Ronnie Taylor; first broadcast 27 August 1965.

Spelling Bees

The first form of radio quiz shows, based on the Victorian kindergarten game. The first BBC Spelling Bee was broadcast in CHILDREN's HOUR in 1937, and the first adult Spelling Bee, a Transatlantic operation with Oxford University versus the Americans, was broadcast on 30 January 1938. The Americans won (they had the edge; Spelling Bees had been a popular American radio entertainment for some years). Question-masters were Tommy Woodrooffe (England), Paul Wing (America). The first All-British Spelling Bee followed on 20 March 1938: the Over-Forties versus the Under-Twenties. The spelling-master was FREDDY GRISEWOOD.

Spencer and Woolcott

Howard Spencer and Bentley Woolcott were BBC clones of Charters and Caldicott, the cricket-loving adventurers created by Frank Launder and Sidney Gilliat for the films. Unable to continue their radio adventures for contractual reasons, scriptwriter John Jowett was commissioned to create doppelgangers for comedy actors BASIL RADFORD AND NAUNTON WAYNE. Spencer and Woolcott made their serial debut in *Fool's Paradise*, chapter 1, 'A Sticky Wicket', broadcast 11 June 1945. Vernon Harris produced with such success that a second serial, *Double Bedlam* followed on 8 May 1946.

The Spice of Life (1)

Story of the British Music Hall from 1820 to 1942, written and introduced by W. McQueen Pope with music by Kenneth Leslie-Smith. Eight episodes beginning 2 October 1942, with Vernon Watson, Ernest Shannon, Joan Young, Harold Scott, the Revue Chorus and Orchestra conducted by Mansell Thomas, and narration by Dick Francis.

The Spice of Life (2)

'A Carefree Mixture of Comedy and Music' starring TED RAY with June Whitfield, Deryck Guyler, Gene Crowley, Therese Burton, and Harry Rabinowitz with the Revue Orchestra. Items: 'At the Launderette' (a radio strip cartoon); 'The Voice of Romance' (Hutch); 'For the Record' (a singing discovery); 'The Ted Ray Repertory Co.'; 'Do You Know Your Music' (pit your knowledge against the Magic Music Man, Sid Phillips); 'Many Questions' (topics of the day aggravated by a panel of experts). Script by Gene Crowley; producer Roy Speer. Weekly from 8 October 1956.

Spike Harrigan

Live-wire private investigator whose cases involved him with some of the toughest characters in America. 'Tonight we invite you to follow him behind the glittering façade into the New York Underworld.' One of the 'World's Greatest Mysteries' series presented by Basil Rathbone on RADIO LUXEMBOURG from 3 September 1957.

Spoken in Jest

VIC OLIVER and Yvonne Arnaud starred as Charles and Margot Marlow in this domestic series of comedies bringing to life famous quotations: 'There's Many a Slip twixt the Cup and the Lip', etc. Script by Carey Edwards; producer Tom Ronald; broadcast from June 1957. A second series started 6 June 1958 with 'Truth is Stranger than Fiction'.

Sporting Challenge

Godfrey Evans, the England team wicket-keeper, put sporting questions from listeners to Leslie Welch the MEMORY MAN. 'Stump him and win a cash prize.' RADIO LUXEMBOURG from 10 January 1958.

Sportsman's Choice

Freddie Mills, the former world champion boxer, was host on this series broadcast on RADIO LUXEMBOURG from 4 March 1955. As well as favourite singing stars of the day, there was 'this week's sporting celebrity who will tell you some of the secrets of his line'. Sponsored by Turf Cigarettes who offered four prizes of £10.

Spot the Mistakes

Alan Freeman presented this record programme which included five deliberate mistakes designed to test listeners' general knowledge. 'Listen carefully, for an all-correct entry could win you an attractive cash prize.' Devised by Geoffrey Everitt; RADIO LUXEMBOURG from 8 April 1957.

Spot the Winner

Amateur talent contest introduced by amiable KENNETH HORNE, accompanied by CHARLES SHADWELL and his Orchestra, and arranged by the CARROLL LEVIS Organization. First broadcast 24 November 1949; produced by Alfred Dunning. An early winner was comedian Charlie Drake.

Spread Your Wings

Robert MacDermot hosted this weekly 'programme for children of all ages, full of competitions and exciting events' based on, and sponsored by, *Eagle* and *Girl* comics. Items included 'Sing-Song' accompanied by Steve Race and Our Own Orchestra, 'Competition Corner', and the dramatized strip cartoon, 'Luck of the Legion'. This alternated with 'Storm Nelson'. Produced by Peter Wilson and broadcast on RADIO LUXEMBOURG from 15 November 1954.

Spry Broadcasting Theatre

Weekly half-hour from RADIO NORMANDY starring Dick Francis (the Comic Compère with a Thousand Crazy Quips), Byrl Walkley (singing Memorable Melodies), Sandra Shayne (the Clever Crooner with the Captivating Voice), the Radio Revellers, and the Spry Syncopators. Plus a weekly instalment of 'Sweet Henrietta', a skit on old-time melodramas. CARROL GIBBONS the dance-band leader produced this 1938 series for Spry, a cooking fat with 'Lookie, Lookie, Lookie, Here Comes Cookie' as its signature tune.

The Squadronnaires

'There's Something in the Air' was the apt signature tune of the No. 1 Dance Orchestra of the Royal Air Force, organized in March 1940 and soon to become known as the Squadronnaires. Originally led by the singing Sergeant Jimmy Miller, from 1950 the band was taken over by pianist Ronnie Aldrich. Other vocalists: George Chisholm, Sid Colin and Roy Edwards.

St Fanny's

Educational establishment attended by CARDEW THE CAD, Fatty Gilbert and other young limbs, ruled over by Dr Jankers. Featured in countless broadcasts by CARROLL LEVIS's 'Star from the Services', Douglas Robinson.

St George's Hall

Former home of Maskelyne's Magical Entertainments, this building (1867) became the home of the BBC VARIETY DEPARTMENT from April 1934. Under director Eric Maschwitz, producers and productions flourished away from the rarified atmosphere of BROADCASTING

House. The staff was enlarged by Bryan Michie, who rose from Sound Effects to producer/compère, and Max Kester, the first staff comedy scriptwriter. The BBC Variety Orchestra was also formed, under conductor Charles Shadwell. The BBC Theatre Organ was installed in 1936, with Reginald Foort as staff organist. The first comedy series of note, Band Waggon, came from St George's Hall, which was finally closed by incendiary bombs in the autumn of 1940.

Stabu the Elephant Boy

Regular character in Charlie Chester's Stand Easy (1946) serial, 'Tarzan of the Tapes'. Played by Len Marten in broad Cockney, Stabu addressed his elephant thus: 'Git up there, Forsythe, yer perisher!' The elephant's name was an in-joke directed at Charlie Forsythe, heavyweight comedian in the Forsythe, Seamon and Farrell trio.

Stage Door

Major comedy series for Dave and Joe O'Gorman, famous Music Hall comedians, in 'Fun behind the Footlights'. Ernest Sefton played the bullying manager, and unlikely acts on the bill included Tyhiminaknotto the only Radio Contortionist! Real acts in the first show (8 May 1940): Vera Wootton (the Sparkling Soubrette), Emilio (Maestro of the Accordion), the Four Aces and the Six Snappy Flappers. Script by Dick Pepper; producer Ernest Longstaffe.

The Stage Presents

'Theatreland's tribute to the Forces everywhere, sponsored by every branch of the entertainment world and offered to you by the Theatre's War Service Council, produced by John Watt and Ronald Waldman from a theatre in the heart of London.' It started 2 May 1943 with an all-star cast: Vic Oliver, Binnie Hale, Vivien Leigh, Laurence Olivier, Vera Lynn and the chorus of the London production of *The Merry Widow* with Jay Wilbur and his Orchestra.

Stainless Stephen

Arthur Clifford, who took his broadcasting alias from his home town of Sheffield, famous for stainless steel, and to prove it wore a steel band around his bowler and a waistcoat to

Stainless Stephen: semi-conscious comedian

match. He gave up schoolmastering for a comedy career after making a hit in local radio (January 1923). His first national broadcast was in *An Hour In a Restaurant* (30 May 1925), and he created several early radio characters including Oscillating Oscar. Fame came with his audible punctuation: 'This is Stainless Stephen comma comedian question-mark.' His first record, *The Punctuating Punchinello*, was issued on Decca F1530 in 1929.

Stand At Ease!

Rare series starring Jessie Matthews and Sonnie Hale in a burlesque of army life by Edward J. Mason. With Alan Robinson (Major Bagley-Poonah), Dorothy Summers (Mrs Pomeroy-Fielding), and Godfrey Baseley (Sergeant Bunk). Producer Martyn C. Webster; began 22 February 1941.

Stand Easy

Ring that bell! (Ding! Dong!)
Bang that drum! (Bang! Bang!)
Sound that horn! (Honk! Honk!)
Shoot that gun! (Bang!)
The boys are back in the studio,
So roll back the carpet and let yourself go!

The signature song for Charlie Chester's Civvy Street Rag, the Merry-Go-Round Army Show demobbed and crazier than ever, broadcast from 11 February 1946. 'It's look out

SUNDERLAND
EMPIRE
HIGH STREET WEST

BOOKED BY MOSS' EMPIRES, LTD.

Proprietors - THE EMPIRE PALACE LTD.   Managing Director - RICHARD REED   Manager - JESSE J. S. CHALLONS

TELEPHONE 3274-5

6.15   FOR ONE WEEK
MONDAY, FEBRUARY 27th   **8.30**

GEORGE & ALFRED BLACK *present*

CHEERFUL
CHARLIE
CHESTER

AND HIS FAMOUS RADIO CRAZY GANG—IN

STAND EASY

FRED THE VOICE **KEN** MURDERING A SONG
FERRARI ★ **MORRIS**

ARTHUR ★ **EDWINA** ★ **LEN**
HAYNES **CAROL** **MARTEN**

THE **GRIP** SENSATIONAL PARISIAN ADAGIO TEAM

QUARTETTE

MARRIOTT & WENMAN DANCE STYLISTS

5 BRAHIMS ARAB ACROBATS

GENE ANDERTON | HARRY RICHARDS

12 JOHN TILLER GIRLS 12

THE COAST TO COAST LAUGHTER RIOT!

for laughs in the next half hour with Cheerful Charlie Chester and his Crazy Gang – Arthur Haynes, Ken Morris, Len Marten, Louise Gainsborough, Ramon St Clair and the Blue Rockets Dance Orchestra directed by Eric Robinson.' The hysterical studio laughter during that standard opening announcement was caused by Charlie and Co debagging the announcer! Top spot in the show was the Amazing Adventures of WHIPPIT KWICK the cat Burglar, whose mysterious appearances were always heralded by a musical call-sign, a tune best known as 'Half a Pint of Mild-and-bitter'. Kwik was played by Ken Morris, who as your *Stand Easy* crime reporter murdered songs at the piano. Haynes was a spiv ('Wotcher, Tish – Wotcher, Tosh!'), and the song spot was taken over by 'The Voice', Frederick Ferrari, a tenor who came on belting 'When love descended like an angel'. Henry Lytton joined the Gang in 1947, and Edwina Carroll became the girl in 1948. Terry Scott and a group, the Singing Silhouettes, joined in 1949, and all wartime echoes were wiped away when the title was changed to KEEP SMILING in 1951. Cheerful Charlie wrote all the scripts, and the producer was Leslie Bridgmont.

Standing on the Corner
Michael Standing was the first BBC commentator to broadcast live interviews with 'The Man in the Street'. First broadcast on 8 October 1938 as a segment of the magazine programme, IN TOWN TONIGHT, it developed into a wartime feature in its own right. There was also a 1940 variation called *Standing in the Shelter*.

Stanelli's Crazy Cruise
Subtitled 'Ship A-hooey!', this 1939 follow-up to STANELLI's STAG PARTY found the fiddle-playing comedian as captain of the SS *Freeneasy*. Crew included Horace Kenney as Jitters the Mess Waiter, Ted Andrews as Sliggs the Bar Steward, and Sydney Jerome as the First Officer. Passengers: Mamie Soutter ('That Woman Again!'), the Three Ginx, and Judy Shirley, with the Variety Orchestra conducted by CHARLES SHADWELL. Script by Stanelli and Max Kester; producer John Sharman.

Stand Easy: on stage!

Stanelli: fiddle fanatic

Stanelli's Stag Party
Stanelli, former 'Fiddle Fanatic' of the comedy team Stanelli and Edgar, devised the idea of a radio stag party during a genuine one in his own flat, recorded it privately, and played it to Director of Variety Eric Maschwitz. It went on the air on 4 July 1935, and the successful recreation of a party atmosphere at once caught on with listeners. Unfortunately the title ran into trouble with the Reithian administration, but as *Stanelli's Bachelor Party* it continued for years. Stan was host, assisted by his cockney batman, Jim Emery (played by Jack Wynne): 'More sandwiches, Mister Stanelli sir?' Regular partygoers were NORMAN LONG, Al and Bob Harvey, Russell and Marconi, Sydney Jerome, and even the Revue Orchestra conducted by Hyam Greenbaum. Signature song: 'We're nobody's husbands now', signing off with 'Goodnight goodnight goodnight goodnight goodni-i-ight . . . (etc)'. Columbia issued a two-record set of the Stag Party on FB 1309-10 (1936).

Star Bill
TONY HANCOCK, Geraldine McEwen and Graham Stark formed the resident trio of funmakers in this series which began on 7 June 1953. Actual stars on the bill were TED RAY, Lizbeth Webb, David Hughes, Semprini, the George Mitchell Glee Club, and Stanley Black and his Concert Orchestra. Written by RAY

ENTIRELY NEW VERSION OF
STANELLI'S
Stag Party
RADIO'S GREATEST COMEDY SUCCESS

Introducing
ALL THOSE JOLLY OLD PALS OF THE AIR
Including

STANELLI
NORMAN LONG
RUSSELL & MARCONI
THE THREE MUSKETEERS
JIM EMERY
TEX SHAMVA   THE GREAT HERMAN
ETC., ETC.

STANELLI

NORMAN LONG

HIPPODROME
SOUTHAMPTON
6.30 Twice Nightly 8.40
MON., AUGUST 29TH & ALL WEEK

THE LONDON COLISEUM COMPANY
COMES
TO THE SOUTHAMPTON HIPPODROME

GALTON AND ALAN SIMPSON; produced by Alistair Scott-Johnson.

The second series began on 28 February 1954 with Moira Lister replacing Geraldine McEwen, plus Joan Turner ('The Girl of a Thousand Voices'), Eddie Calvert ('The Man With the Golden Trumpet'), and the George Mitchell Millionaires with Tony Mercer. The first guest star was James Robertson Justice, and Dennis Main Wilson produced. The third series (6 March 1955) replaced Hancock with Nicholas Parsons, and added TONY FAYNE AND DAVID EVANS the simultaneous impressionists, Petula Clark, Kenny Baker and his trumpet, Bob and Alf Pearson ('My Brother and I'), the George Mitchell Glee Club in 'Songs of Britain' and GERALDO and his Concert Orchestra. Script by Lionel Harris, Richard Waring and Nicholas Parsons.

Star Gazing

They coined a new word for this series: 'A Radiobiography'. The first subject was Robert Hale, who was backed up by his talented offspring, Binnie and Sonnie. Also featured: John Rorke, Ida Crispi, Belle Baker, Foster Carlin, and the Revue Orchestra and Chorus, conductor CHARLES SHADWELL. The series was compèred by 'The Playgoer' and presented by Leslie Baily and Charles Brewer; it began 22 October 1936.

The Star Show

Saturday-night 75-minute series starting 27 September 1952 and hosted by genial Joe Linnane. Googie Withers and John McCallum (married film stars) and DEREK ROY starred, supported by Jack Watson, Max Jaffa, Teddy Johnson, Beryl Reid, Lizbeth Webb, the George Mitchell Choir and the Variety Orchestra conducted by Paul Fenoulhet. Produced by Tom Ronald and Michael North.

The Stargazers' Music Shop

'Step inside the Music Shop and meet radio's foremost vocal group' sponsored by RADIO REVIEW, the Irish answer to RADIO TIMES. On RADIO LUXEMBOURG from September 1952. The series crossed to the BBC on 3 March 1957; the Stargazers (Bob Brown, June Marlow, Cliff

Stanelli's Stag Party: censored for radio, okay for stage

Adams, Fred Datcheler, Dave Carey) were backed by Harold Smart and his Rhythm Shopwalkers. Michael Brooke manned the Information Desk and the producer was Frank Hooper.

Starlight Hour

GERALDO with his Concert Orchestra and Singers (Doreen Lundy, Archie Lewis and George Evans) were the solid musical base for this prestigious series which started on 11 October 1948. Edwin Styles was the sophisticated compère, Alfred Marks and Benny Hill were the newcomers who provided the comedy, and there were 'visiting stars from home and abroad'. Written by FRANK MUIR, DENIS NORDEN and Sid Colin; produced by Roy Speer. The second series, starting 23 July 1949, was introduced by Brian (PC49) Reece, and written by Peter Myers and Lionel Harris. The stars were BERNARD BRADEN AND BARBARA KELLY, Daphne Anderson, Marcia Owen, the Men About Town, and Peter Yorke and his Concert Orchestra. The only link with the first series was Alfred Marks, continuing the comedy. The third series (23 January 1950) retained Reece and Marks, adding Joan Greenwood and NAUNTON WAYNE, with the Radio Revellers, Lee Lawrence and Paddie O'Neil. Marks was held over for the fourth series commencing 7 May 1951, with Beryl Reid, TONY FAYNE AND DAVID EVANS, and Harry Dawson.

The series was revived from 19 September 1964 with KENNETH HORNE as compère. He introduced 'Singing Star' Kenneth MacDonald, 'Radio Début' Maureen Keetch, 'Celebrity Pianist' Valerie Tryon, 'World of Comedy' with Kenneth Connor, June Whitfield and Ronnie Barker, and 'Special Guest' Moira Lister. Malcolm Lockyer conducted the Revue Orchestra, the script was by Carey Edwards and Bob Block, and the producer was Bill Gates.

Starlight Roof

Hector Stewart 'requests the pleasure of your company to meet celebrities from the world of entertainment at the fabulous rendezvous of the stars. Your table is reserved, the floor show is international, and the Teddy Wilson Trio will play in the intermission.' Produced by John Powell, from 31 March 1962.

Starline Show

'Starring your singing host, Bryan Johnson, and the Starline Handyman who answers listeners' problems.' Starline was a Chinese Lacquer. Produced by Monty Bailey-Watson and broadcast on RADIO LUXEMBOURG from 3 November 1953.

Stars of Tomorrow

Not a talent show, but a series designed to showcase newcomers in the profession. Jerry Desmonde, Sid Field's stage straight-man, acted as compère, and in the first show (11 July 1949) introduced Jerry Turpin, Philippe and his Cockney Cubans, and Pat Stoyle and Jack North. Produced by Eric Spear.

Starstruck

Variety series starring the writers, BOB MONKHOUSE AND DENIS GOODWIN. In the first show, broadcast 7 June 1955, they were starstruck by TED RAY, DICK BENTLEY, Alfred Marks, Patti Lewis, and Johnny Dankworth and his Orchestra. Produced by Pat Dixon.

Steamboat

'A programme of variety, music and drama from our floating playhouse reviving for you some of the glories of the old steamboat days.' Dick Francis played the Showman, with songs from Lorna Stuart and Robert Ashley, with the Variety Orchestra and Chorus. Producer William MacLurg; commenced 20 July 1938.

Stella Dallas

'A continuation on the air of the world-famous story of a mother whose love for her daughter was the uppermost thought in her life.' Daily serial on RADIO LUXEMBOURG commencing 3 October 1939; sponsored by California Syrup of Figs.

Step This Way

'Entertainment in an Emporium of Fun' starring Sandy Powell and Johnny Lockwood. Among the assistants: Cecilia Eddy, Cliff Gordon, Helen Clare, Ivor Dennis, and Stanley Black with the Dance Orchestra and Revue Chorus. Written by Ray Sonin and produced by C.F. Meehan from 28 February 1945.

Steve Larrabee

'Adventures of Steve Larrabee the Lone Star Rider' began on RADIO LUXEMBOURG on 1 November 1952. Steve was the cowboy hero of *Lone Star* comic magazine, and featured on several western toys for boys. The first serial was 'The King of the Gamblers', followed by 'The Greedy Vulture' in January 1953. Producer Stanley Maxted; sponsor Rowntrees Cocoa. Steve returned as the singing star of a later series, supported by Danny Levan and his Rodeo Rhythm. This ran from 1 November 1955 under the sponsorship of Empire Pools of Blackpool.

Stone, Christopher

'Daddy of the DISC-JOCKEYS', Christopher Stone was the first personality to present Gramophone Record Recitals (as the BBC called them) on the radio and make a profession of it. His Thursday-night series began on 7 July 1927, and his avuncular, relaxed tones shot him to such fame that he was booked to top the bill at the London Palladium – playing records! He was also the first broadcaster to be given a three-hour programme of his own, on a Christmas Day. His taste was catholic, cheerfully mixing Mendelssohn with Fats Waller, and he was equally cheerful about broadcasting for the pre-war RADIO LUXEMBOURG, even when he became the first personality to be blacklisted by the BBC for so doing. 'His engagements for us need not continue after 29 August 1934', runs a memo. However, World War II changed all that, although his cheery catchphrase for children, 'Hi-de-hi! Ho-de-ho!', achieved national notoriety when a CO ordered his troops to use it. He returned to the BBC and in 1950 RADIO TIMES called him 'The man with a million friends'.

Stork Radio Parade

Weekly series from RADIO NORMANDY, recorded in cinemas of the Union Circuit, who were the original sponsors. Beginning as *Radio Parade* on 22 August 1937, with Harold Ramsay at the organ of the Union Cinema, Kingston-on-Thames, it was taken over by Stork Margarine from 7 November, with the addition of three more organists, H. Robinson Cleaver, Jack Dowle and Phil Park, and guest stars NORMAN LONG, Bertha Willmott and Rudy Starita. By 1938 the show had moved to the Granada circuit, with Bobby Howell and his band to

Christopher **Stone**: grand-daddy of the DJs

play the signature song:

> Fall in for Radio Parade,
> On Parade, On Parade again,
> Join in the merry cavalcade,
> Lead the way with a gay refrain.

The New Stork Radio Parade started on 15 January 1939, compèred by DICK BENTLEY. Peter Yorke and his Concert Orchestra made music with Sam Browne and Dorothy Carless to sing. Also featured was 'Radio's lovable new character, The Man in the Street'. Producer David Miller recorded the series at the Scala Theatre.

Strange to Relate

'In which radio brings to life curious tales of the past and present.' First broadcast 22 April 1936, an occasional series devised and compèred by Charles Brewer.

Stork Radio Parade advertisement in *Radio Pictorial*

The Street Singer

Arthur Tracy, romantic balladeer from America, starred in this weekly RADIO LUXEMBOURG series for Poudre Tokalon, from 4 December 1936. His signature song: 'Marta, Rambling Rose of the Wildwood'.

Streeter, Fred

Pulborough-born radio gardener who brightened the Saturday edition of TODAY for nine years before dying quite suddenly at the grand age of 98, in 1975, as his last (recorded) words were being broadcast: 'Old Fred Streeter will keep pegging away.' His spot was almost a comedy cross-talk, with straight-man Frank Hennig feeding him the questions and the cue for his closing catchphrase: 'Just time for me to say cheers for now, Fred.' A hearty ho-ho-ho, and Fred would respond with 'Cheerio, Frank, and cheerio, everybody!'.

Strictly Off the Record

JACK JACKSON took his personal style of record playing to RADIO LUXEMBOURG in 1950, where he was sponsored by Mars Bars.

Strike It Rich

Eamonn Andrews introduced this 'show with a heart'. Listeners were invited to tell their personal stories on the air and win £100. Research by Larry and Pauline Forrester; produced by Henry Caldwell for Palmolive. Began on RADIO LUXEMBOURG, 1 November 1954.

Strike Up the Band

'A Comedy Musical Presentation' from BBC Scotland (1939), with Wullie Peebles, Johnny Niven, Pat Wilson, Madeleine Christie, The Jokers, and the BBC Scottish Orchestra conducted by Kemlo Stephens. Devised by Andrew P. Wilson.

Stripey and Bunts

John Slater and Ronald Shiner played this pair of below-decks conversationalists in NAVY MIXTURE (1946), the first radio scriptwork of Eddie (RAY's A LAUGH) Maguire.

The Strolling Vagabond

Cavan O'Connor, the Irish tenor, whose signature song was 'I'm only a Strolling Vagabond, so goodnight, pretty maiden, goodnight'. He strolled through many a musical series, including one commencing 28 October 1946, in which he was accompanied by Rae Jenkins and the Variety Orchestra, and another commencing 30 November 1949, with Frank Cantell and the Revue Orchestra. An inspiration to many, not the least the GOONS.

Students' Song

'Gaudeamus Igitur' was the signature song for this long-running programme by the BBC Male Voice Chorus, conductor Leslie Woodgate with Ernest Lush at the Pianoforte. Other songs heard almost as regularly included 'Upidee-i-dah', 'Down in Demerara' ('Here we sits like birds in the wilderness'). 'Riding Down to Bangor', 'One More River to Cross', 'Vilikins and his Dinah'. The series ran from the thirties to the fifties.

Studio Audiences

Audiences in broadcasting studios were a bone of contention from the start. Originally added as atmosphere to MUSIC HALL, the Saturday-night variety show broadcast from ST GEORGE'S HALL, the laughter irritated many listeners, who wrote to the RADIO TIMES about it. Comedians, of course, loved them and soon played up by silently mugging or wearing funny clothes to boost the laughs even more. Most producers frowned upon this, but loosened-up during World War II when DEREK ROY was allowed to change funny hats during his impressions, and Arthur Lucan to appear in his full OLD MOTHER RILEY drag. Other producers, like Jacques Brown, thought comedy purer without laughter of any kind (DANGER MEN AT WORK), while other shows simply encouraged the band to laugh (BREAKFAST WITH BRADEN). In 1950 the BBC handed the following printed notice to all 1500 members of the VARIETY BANDBOX audience:

> We welcome your laughter at any time. We hope for your applause, but in appropriate places only, that is, at the end of a scene or a musical number, or on the entrance or exit of an artist who you think deserves it. But we do NOT want: (1) Clapping for individual gags or jokes during an act or scene. It holds up the programme and often spoils the show for listeners. (2) Catcalls, whistles and cheers. They make a horrible noise on the air.

Strolling Vagabond: Cavan O'Connor

The legend of cue cards marked 'Laugh' and 'Applaud' came from American films about radio shows.

Studio Stand Easy

The Army segment of the all-forces entertainment series, MERRY-GO-ROUND, devised and written by CHARLIE CHESTER as a fast-moving crazy show. 'You are invited to Studio Stand Easy to meet Sergeant Cheerful Charlie Chester and the happy band of Other Cranks from

Stars in Battledress: Sergeant Arthur Haynes, Corporal Ken Morris, Driver Joe Giggs, Ramon St Clair, Corporal Sally ('Click-click') Rogers, and the Blue Rockets Band conducted by Sergeant Eric Robinson.' Started 12 September 1945 with the signature song:

Shoot – the khaki to me,
Does something to me,
I'm funny that way!

Regular spots included the serial TARZAN OF

THE TAPES, with the topical chant of the natives; a song murdered at the piano by Professor Ken Morris, who also provided 'The Riddle of the Middle', and a comedy song written by Charlie, such as 'The Old Bazaar in Cairo'. Demobbed into the Civvy Street Rag, STAND EASY.

Study in A Flat
Situation series with songs for teenager Petula Clark, with Neville Williams, perky Canadian Diana Decker, Clive Baxter, and Frank Cordell with his Orchestra. Written by Spike Hughes; produced by Douglas Moodie; first broadcast 7 June 1950.

The Stuff to Give the Troops
One of the ENSA HALF HOUR series devised and presented by newspaper columnist Jonah Barrington 'featuring Guest Stars, Resident Stars, Touring Stars and Stars in the Making' with Cyril James the Roving Reporter and GERALDO and the ENSA Variety Orchestra. Guests in the first show (7 October 1942) were Mr Jetsam and Leslie Howard.

Sunday Cinema
Series of radio adaptations of successful British and American films shown during recent years, adapted by Desmond Carrington. The first film to receive radio treatment was Noel Coward's *Blithe Spirit*, 24 July 1949.

Sunday Matinée
Gerry Wilmot compèred this series of broadcasts from dance-halls which began on 2 February 1941, with Lew Stone and his Band and the Albert Sandler Trio.

Sunday Night Excursion
Symington's Soups sponsored this series on RADIO LUXEMBOURG (1938), starring CLAUDE DAMPIER and Billie Carlisle. But the show really took off when the stars of BBC's BAND WAGGON were booked: ARTHUR ASKEY and RICHARD MURDOCH. Backing the comedians were crooner Al Bowlly, Marjorie Stedeford, the Southern Airs, and Harry Karr and his Club Royal Orchestra. To cope, the programme expanded from 15 to 30 minutes from 21 May 1939. The setting was switched from the famous BBC Top Flat at Broadcasting House to a bungalow called 'Seaview' in Kennington! Also featured: the Askey Mighty Art Players and the Askitini Corps de Ballet from the Royal Opera House, Hoxton, and a weekly recipé by Helen Burke, Principal of Symington's Cookery Advice Bureau. The announcer was Kent Stevenson, and the producer Pat Dixon.

The Sunday Nighters
Variety series for the Forces broadcast from local dance-halls and compèred by Canadian Gerry Wilmott from 22 August 1940. The first programme featured Oscar Rabin and his Romany Dance Orchestra with Phyllis Robins.

Sunday Sing-Song
Dick James led the community singing in this RADIO LUXEMBOURG series, backed by Harold Smart at the organ. It started 5 August 1954, produced by Philip Jones, sponsored by Neodex Skin Treatment.

Sunny Jim
Famous character from the Force packet who hosted *Sunny Jim's Programme of Force and Melody* at breakfast time on RADIO LUXEMBOURG from 1 January 1936. His signature song is still remembered:

> High o'er the fence,
> O'er the fence leaps Sunny Jim,
> Force is the food,
> Is the food that raises him.
> Health such as his
> Can be yours, it is at your call,
> Force is wheat, the staff of life,
> In Force there's energy for all!

Sunny Side Up
First starring series for Max Bygraves, who had shot into popularity through EDUCATING ARCHIE. Stanley Black and the Dance Orchestra accompanied his many songs, and Norman Wisdom helped provide comedy. First broadcast 25 July 1951; produced by Ronnie Hill.

Superintendent Pepper Remembers
Hamilton Dyce played this different radio detective, Tom Pepper, who, retired from Scotland Yard, browsed over his scrapbook of cuttings. Wife Mildred was played by Ella

Milne, and his policeman son Len by Cavan Malone. Written by Michael Kendrick and Jeffrey Segal; produced by Audrey Cameron; weekly from 29 July 1958.

Surprise Item

Billed only as 'Surprise Item' in RADIO TIMES, these short spots became tremendously popular in the thirties. The first was broadcast on 13 July 1928, and we hope it won't spoil the surprise to reveal that the artistes were 'The Co-Optimist Trio': Davy Burnaby, Wolseley Charles, and Stanley Holloway. The deviser/producer was John MacDonell.

Suspense

Sixty-minute series of 'true stories of heroism and adventure in dramatic form', beginning on 8 January 1953 with film star Richard Todd in 'You'll Die In Singapore', adapted from Paul Brickhill's book *Escape to Die* by Felix Felton and produced by Alan Burgess.

Svenson

Norwegian stoker stationed at HMS *Waterlogged* in MERRY-GO-ROUND (1945). Played by JON PERTWEE at his most guttrally incomprehensible: 'N'yeden n'yaden n'yeden, neggidicrop de bombit!' Wren Hackney acted as translator.

Swinging in the Bathtub

'This bright-and-early programme (9 am on RADIO LUXEMBOURG from 8 April 1938) brings to your bedroom, your bathroom, and your breakfast-table all the latest song-hits, tangoes, and Roy Foxtrots, with Denny Dennis and Mary Lee to add an extra splash!' Roy Fox and his band, sponsored by Reckitt's Bath Cubes.

Swinging Out of School

Celia Lipton and John Singer, supported by Phil Cardew and his Schoolmates in Swing. Written by Spike Hughes; producer Douglas Moodie; weekly from 1 January 1941.

Sylvan Sweethearts of the Air

'Radio's New Golden-Voiced Couple', Sylvia White and Jerry Brooks: 'You'll be fascinated when they sing their golden-voiced songs of love and romance.' RADIO LUXEMBOURG series which started on 14 April 1935, featuring Jack Harris and the Sylvan Orchestra, and sponsored by Sylvan Flakes, 'The Biggest and Finest Box of Soap Flakes a Shilling Ever Bought'. The opening show included 'Love Is Just Around the Corner' and 'One Night of Love'.

Symington's Soups Film Star Competition Programme

Sponsored radio series beginning on RADIO LUXEMBOURG on 14 October 1934. Stanelli compèred a sequence of soundtrack excerpts from films featuring Gracie Fields, Jack Buchanan, Sophie Tucker, Elsie Randolph, Irene Dunne, G.H. Elliott, Winifred Shotter and Noah Beery with Wheeler and Woolsey singing 'The Big Bad Wolf Is Dead'. Entry forms were obtainable from grocers and 12 names were to be listed in order of popular appeal, from a list of 15. A packet of 15 photographic postcards of the stars was available at Smiths Bookstalls for a shilling. Entries had to be accompanied by three empty twopenny cartons of Symington's Soups, and prizes ranged from the first prize of £1000 to 10,000 vouchers for soup.

The TV Lark

The demobilized characters of THE NAVY LARK set themselves up as a commercial TV station, Troutbridge Television, opening on 25 January 1963. Stephen Murray was the producer, Leslie Phillips the director, Jon Pertwee the floor manager, Janet Brown the production secretary, Michael Bates the design department, and Ronnie Barker and Tenniel Evans manned cameras One and Two as Fatso Johnson and Taffy Goldstein. Robin Boyle was the announcer, Laurie Wyman scripted and Alastair Scott Johnston produced. After one short series the stars were all called back into the Navy, much to the relief of their faithful audience.

Take a Note

Robb Wilton starred in this series subtitled 'Leaves from a Loose Agent's Ledger'. The first episode, 'Entrance of the Dwarfs', was broadcast on 3 December 1942, with C. DENIER WARREN, Sydney Keith and Bettie Bucknelle, and music by the Novachord Hornswogglers. Script by Loftus Wigram; producer Henry Reed.

Take It From Here (1)

Starring Richard Haydn as Professor EDWIN CARP, with Cliff Gordon (who also wrote the series), John Slater, Josephine Driver, the Four Star Girls, and JACK JACKSON's May Fair Hotel Orchestra. Weekly from 7 December 1943, with Arthur Marshall as NURSE DUGDALE replacing Haydn who returned to Hollywood, 25 January 1944. Producer Vernon Harris.

Take It From Here (2)

The title was the only old thing about this new comedy series which made its debut on 12

Take It From Here: book of the series

March 1948. Producer Charles Maxwell created it out of elements of his NAVY MIXTURE series: the attractive young Australian comedienne, JOY NICHOLS, the ebullient 'Professor' JIMMY EDWARDS, and 'Master' DICK BENTLEY, another Australian and veteran of a pre-war double-act with George Moon. Wilfred Babbage provided character voices, and Frank Cantell and the Revue Orchestra played the signature tune, sung by the Keynotes (Johnny Johnson, Alan Dean, Terry Devon and Renee (Irene) King):

Take It From Here!
Don't go away when you can
Take It From Here,
Why don't you stay and maybe
Join in the fun now,
The show has begun.
Half an hour of laughter beckons,
Every minute packed with seconds!

The show, quickly shortened to TIFH, pronounced 'Tife', was introduced by David Dunhill ('Forward, Dunners'). Early catchphrases were Jimmy Edwards shouting 'Wake up at the back, there!', 'A mauve one!', 'Clumsy clot!' and 'Black mark, Bentley!'

The writers were the new team of FRANK MUIR AND DENIS NORDEN, who occasionally played odd voices in the show under the mutual pseudonym of 'HERBERT MOSTYN', a combination of their middle names. Babbage was soon replaced by Clarence Wright as Henpecked Harry Hickory, always on the run from the wife: 'Sh!' 'What?' 'Thought it was 'er for a minute!' Bentley had a spot as an adenoidal lovelorn sighing 'Oh, Mavis – how ravishing you look in your nee-glige with its tantalizing glimpses of vest!'. He also did a regular 'man-in-the-street' interview spot, invariably encountering a Miss Arundel (Joy) who saw the sexy side of every question, answering with a throaty giggle and a reference to her boyfriend, Gilbert. There was also the regular 'TIFH Film Award': on the famous broadcast from HMS *Indefatigable* at Spithead (15 June 1953) it was 'The Cruel B.B. Sea'.

Wallas Eaton arrived with the second series (4 January 1949) beseeching the Professor to return to his East End roots: 'Come 'ome, Jim Edwards!' In the third series (11 October 1949) 'Save the Buildings!' became Wal's rallying-cry, and in the next he called upon Jim to 'Take the plunge!'. In April 1952 Sally Rogers took over while Joy Nichols had a baby, but when Joy decided to leave permanently she was replaced by two girls, June Whitfield for the funny voices and Alma Cogan for the songs (12 November 1953).

It was with this series that the Glums arrived, originally as a Typical British Family to comment upon 'This Week's TIFH Talking Point', but ultimately to dominate the programme, with Ron's long-standing engagement to Eth, ever-interrupted by hearty Pa. Writers Eric Merriman and Barry Took took over for the unluckily numbered 13th series (22 October 1959): it was the last.

Take Umbridge

Comedy series written by Charles Heslop, who appeared as Professor Umbridge, 'phoney teacher of music and voice production', with RICHARD GOOLDEN as his assistant, Henry Pibberdy. Also appearing were Doris Nichols

(Mrs Termigan), Guy Verney (John), Marjorie Westbury (Marjorie), and John Singer (Victor), with Billy Ternent and the Dance Orchestra; produced by Gordon Crier (15 April 1941).

Take Your Choice

Weekly magazine programme modelled on the successful MONDAY AT EIGHT, but broadcast in the afternoons. Items: 'The New Sleuth – Percy the Pickpocket' (by and with Billy Bury and Frank Atkinson); 'School for Song' (some musical nonsense); 'Front Page Story: The Stolen Star' (by Aubrey Danvers-Walker); and The Three Cheers. Started 6 April 1938, presented by William MacLurg.

Take Your Pick

Listeners could win a television set (black-and-white, of course), a Wedgewood dinner service, a movie camera and projector (16mm) – or a turnip, on this RADIO LUXEMBOURG comedy quiz show which started 20 September 1953. Cheery host was MICHAEL MILES and the sponsor Beecham's Pills. Produced for Star Sound Studios by John Beard. The second series started 26 December 1954, advertised as

Michael **Miles**: 'Your Quiz Inquisitor'

'Britain's newest radio quiz game packed with fun and games'. The 1957 series introduced 'the added thrill of Air Partners' and the Mystery of Box 13. The 1959 series clocked up a listening figure of 2,000,000, and the 1960 series, the eighth, was the last. Producer Peter Aldersley. The show had a further career on commercial television.

Take Your Turn Please!

Shakespeare W. Ackermiraculous (Jacques Brown) and his secretary (Gladys Merredew) interviewed sundry stars, aided and abetted by Billy Ternent and the Dance Orchestra. Written by Dick Pepper; produced by Tom Ronald; from 4 April 1940 on the Forces Programme.

Taking the Waters

The WATERS were Elsie and Doris in this 'weekly beaker' by Marjorie and Anthony Bilbow. Elsie and Doris, for the first time not playing GERT AND DAISY, lived at Arcadia Grove, Putney, with their nephew Michael (David Spenser) and his Australian fellow-student, Ronnie (Ronald Wilson). Produced by Alastair Scott Johnston, first broadcast 5 July 1962.

Talk About Jones

Peter Jones, having made a hit IN ALL DIRECTIONS with Peter Ustinov, went solo with this series first broadcast 19 February 1954. Written by himself with John Jowett, who also took a part, the cast included Lind Joyce from IT'S THAT MAN AGAIN, Mary Mackenzie, Sydney Tafler, Geoffrey Sumner and Peter Akister and his Orchestra. Produced by Vernon Harris. The second series (11 February 1955) was the same again save for Richard Pearson, who replaced Geoffrey Sumner.

Talk Yourself Out of This

One of the many popular panel games broadcast in the forties, this was devised by the son of strict-tempo bandleader VICTOR SILVESTER. Harold Warrender was the Referee, and three Guest Victims had to explain away awkward situations posed in dramatized sketches, in answer to questions asked by three Guest Inquisitors. On the first of the series, broadcast 2 August 1949, the teams were Thora Hird, Commander Campbell and playwright R.F. Delderfield versus Patricia Laffan, Humphrey Lestocq and Alec Campbell. Frederick Piffard produced and the sketches were written by Godfrey and Alec Harrison.

Talks

The BBC was very fond of fifteen-minute talks, and opened a Department especially to produce them. Typical of the many regular 'talkers' heard from the thirties were Commander Stephen King-Hall on current events, Sir Oliver Lodge and his 'Inquiry into the Unknown' series, Oliver Baldwin the wireless film critic, Sir Walford Davies and his 'Keyboard Talks', Vernon Bartlett on 'Foreign Affairs', and the Marchioness of Reading on 'Life as I See It'.

Tammy Troot

Scottish fish (real name, Tommy Trout) played by Willie Joss in CHILDREN'S HOUR adaptations of the underwater fantasies by Lavinia Derwent. First broadcast 2 October 1942.

Tantalizing Tunes

'You've hummed it, you've sung it, you've tapped your toes to it – but what is it called?' Tune in to the new Lacto-Calomine Programme on RADIO NORMANDY and guess the titles. Compèred by 'radio's newest personality', Steven Miller, from 9 June 1937.

Tarri, Suzette

Quavery cockney gossip who always opened with 'Good evenin', it's me, Suzie, Suzette Tarri', and closed with 'Red Sails In The Sunset', her signature tune, which later segued into 'If You Knew Susie'. Originally a child impersonator (stage debut 1911) she made her first broadcast on 7 January 1924. It was not until 1937 that she found fame as 'the BBC char' and played the character OUR ADA in MONDAY NIGHT AT EIGHT. A very popular turn in any act show, she was unusually hot on topical gags, especially during World War II: rationing was her meat. See also TARRI AWHILE.

Tarri Awhile

Starring series for SUZETTE TARRI, the former 'BBC char'. Here she ran Suzette's Social Club, with Horace Percival as the Chairman, John Rorke as the Barman, Alma Vane as the

Suzette **Tarri**: BBC charlady

supported by John Rorke and the Boys of the Town, with Alan Paul and Ivor Dennis at the pianos. Presented by Roy Speer from 13 September 1939: 'You are welcome to join in the repeat choruses.'

Taxi!
'Taxi . . . I say, Taxi!' was the cry that started this long-running series by Cyril Campion, telling the adventures of Shorty, a London cab-driver, played by Jerry Verno. First broadcast on 3 January 1942; producer Jacques Brown. Shorty always carried a mystery passenger whose identity was duly revealed at the end of the programme.

Teaser Time
The first regular weekly quiz game on radio came from RADIO NORMANDY, starting Sunday 4 December 1938. Described as 'an entirely unrehearsed Battle of Knowledge between two teams of Listeners', this 15-minute show was compèred by Wilfrid Thomas and sponsored by Genozo Brand Toothpaste. Chappie D'Amato, the band leader, acted as score-keeper, Jack Phillips played the piano, and Tom Ronald produced. Star players were introduced on 13 August 1939 when Tucker McGuire and a team from the play *The Women* challenged George Benson and a team from *The Little Revue*.

Waitress, and the Four Clubmen to sing. CHARLES SHADWELL conducted the Variety Orchestra, with script by David Jenkins and Dick Pepper, and production by Ernest Longstaffe. Weekly from 10 December 1941.

Tarzan of the Tapes
Serial burlesquing Edgar Rice Burroughs' *Tarzan of the Apes*, featured weekly in the Army segment of MERRY-GO-ROUND (1964). Written and narrated by Cheerful CHARLIE CHESTER, the regular opening ran: 'In the heart of the dreaded jungle of Janzibullah which is situated in the African province of Japonica . . .' The crazy adventures were punctuated by the chanting of the natives:

Down in the jungle, chanting every day,
You will hear the natives, all say . . .

The most famous of all the topical couplets was:

Down in the jungle, living in a tent,
Better than a prefab – No rent!

Tattie Mackintosh
Clever name for Molly Weir's first venture into comedy characterization. Wee Glaswegian lassie in IT's THAT MAN AGAIN (1946).

The Tavern in the Town
C. DENIER WARREN played Chairman in this half-hour series of 'the songs that father sang',

The Ted Kavanagh Show
The famous comedy writer's follow-up to IT's THAT MAN AGAIN, after the death of TOMMY HANDLEY, was this series sponsored by Horlicks. It started on RADIO LUXEMBOURG on 5 June 1949, starring Deryck Guyler as crotchety Lord Pikestaff, penniless owner of Handmedown Hall. ITMA stalwarts included singer Lind Joyce as his daughter Prue, Bill Stephens as Bunn the Butler, Horace Percival, Sydney Keith, Wilfred Babbage, Joan Young, plus ROY PLOMLEY as Hank B. Honk, Yank. Bob Danvers-Walker announced and the George Melachrino Masqueraders were conducted by Eric Robinson; produced by Gordon Crier.

Ted Ray and the Tuba
First in a new-style comedy series starring TED RAY in a weekly 'unlikely adventure' by

Lawrie Wyman. Vocal comment came from the Polka Dots with music from the Ken Moule Septet. The tuba in the story was played by Jim Powell. Produced by Trafford Whitelock; broadcast 4 October 1962. The second show was entitled *Ted Ray and the Elephant*.

Ted Ray Time

'The old maestro presents a new series' was the billing, but TED RAY failed to make the impact of his former RAY'S A LAUGH. Ted was supported by Harold Berens, Kenneth Connor, Audrey Jeans, Don Peters (an Irish tenor), and a weekly guest star. The first, heard on 25 October 1954, was fruity FRED EMNEY. The Beaux and the Belles sang with Paul Fenoulhet and the Variety Orchestra; script by Ted with George Wadmore and Sid Colin; producer George Inns.

Tess and Bill

'All the Fun of the Air' with Tessie O'Shea ('Two Ton Tessie') and Billy Cotton, plus, of course, Alan Breeze and the Cotton Band. Script by Ray Sonin; produced by Eric Spear. First broadcast 8 August 1949.

Thank Your Lucky Stars

Barbara Kelly from Canada was hostess on this variety series, so perhaps it was not surprising that her first 'Lucky Star' should be her husband, BERNARD BRADEN. Music from Al Martino, Semprini, the George Mitchell Choir and Ray Martin and the Concert Orchestra. Producer Dennis Main Wilson; first broadcast 8 July 1954.

Thanking Yew!

Starring series for CYRIL FLETCHER, the 'Odd Ode' comedian, and named after his radio catchphrase. First broadcast 1 October 1940, with Pat Rignold, Bettie Bucknelle, Cavan O'Reilly, Billy Ternent and the Dance Orchestra, 'and not forgetting Mr Mahoney'. Producers Harry S. Pepper and Ronald Waldman. A post-war series began on 7 October 1945, in which Cyril co-starred with Billy Russell as two rustics, Bob Under and Ben Tupp. Betty Astell (Mrs Fletcher) also appeared, with Jack Cooper, Morton Fraser, and Peter Fettes as the compère. Cyril also played 'Aggie the Polite Schoolgirl' and Percy Parker was the LODGER. Written by Dick Pepper, and produced by

Harry S. Pepper. The 1946 series, beginning 24 February, was entitled *Thanking Yew Tew!* Veteran Davy Burnaby joined the cast.

Thanks for the Memories

Veteran comedy star Leslie Henson told the story of his 25 years of West End stardom in this RADIO LUXEMBOURG series sponsored by Huntley and Palmer's Biscuits (1938).

That Certain Trio

Popular singing combination of 1938: Anne De Nys, Patrick Waddington and John Ridley.

That Child

Awful girl, heroine of the first regular domestic situation comedy series on radio. *That Child* was written by Florence Kilpatrick and played by Lorna Hubbard, with MABEL CONSTANDUROS as Netta and Michael Hogan as Henry. There were six episodes, the first of which was broadcast on 12 April 1926.

That Man Chester

Cheerful CHARLIE CHESTER in a new series in which he was supported by Deryck Guyler, Pat Coombs, Jimmy Lavall, Bill Pertwee and the Maple Leaf Four, with Bob Sharples and his Orchestra. Featured were an awful radio family called 'The Dregs' (Myrtle, Alf, Veronica and Monty) and a serial entitled 'The Quite-a-mess Saga' burlesquing the TV success, *The Quatermass Experiment*. Guyler played Professor Quite-a-mess trying to cope with a malignant plant bent on strangling London! Produced by Leslie Bridgmont; script by Charles Hart and Bernard Botting. Started 12 June 1959.

Thats Telling 'Em

'A crazy ramble into transatlantic radio', the forerunner of IT's THAT MAN AGAIN. Starring TOMMY HANDLEY, Cecilia Eddy, Joan Miller, David Miller, Sydney Keith and Billy Bissett and his Canadians. Written by Lee Bevis and produced by Archie Campbell: 13 May 1939.

Theatre of the Air

Sunday morning series subtitled 'Showland Memories' and starring Elena Danielli and Robert Irwin, singing with Percival Mackey and his Orchestra. Sponsored by California Syrup of Figs on RADIO LUXEMBOURG from 1938.

There's One Born Every Minute
A switch of the old saying made it into an apt title for this series about a District Nurse. Thora Hird played Lizzie Oldshaw, supported by Bill Owen as Sam Gudgeon, poacher. Also in the cast were Patsy Rowlands and Barbara Mitchell. Written by Dick Sharples; produced by Trafford Whitelock: Lizzie started her rounds on 26 August 1966.

Theresa Blades
Sharp secretary to TOMMY HANDLEY – she deputized during the absence of MISS HOTCHKISS (Diana Morrison was having a baby!). Played by Joan Harben in IT'S THAT MAN AGAIN (1946).

These Foolish Things
Remind you of what? Panel game based on the association of sounds and events, chaired by Roy Plomley who played the sounds to Nancy Spain, René Cutforth, Joyce Grenfell, Michael Pertwee, Alan Melville and A.G. Street. Devised by Nancy Spain; produced by Pat Dixon. First broadcast 6 July 1956.

These Radio Times
'A Happy History of Everyman's Entertainment' written and researched by Gale Pedrick and produced by Thurston Holland. The first series based on the history of radio, it commenced 29 September 1951, with Anthony Armstrong as 'Everyman with a Wireless Set'. Heard in the first programme: ARTHUR ASKEY, STUART HIBBERD, L. Stanton Jeffries, WYNNE AJELLO, John Rorke, and the recorded voices of JOHN HENRY and Blossom, Lily Morris, NORMAN LONG and TOMMY HANDLEY. Unexpectedly popular, the series was renewed from 18 April 1952, and again from 29 September 1953, when Tommy Woodroofe introduced DORIS ARNOLD, Harry Pepper and Ralph Reader. A fourth series began on 19 September 1954 with veteran REX PALMER as narrator. Leslie Henson, Gladys Hay and George Melachrino appeared in the first programme. Palmer introduced the fifth series on 3 July 1955, with SPIKE MILLIGAN, Peter Eton, Pat Kirkwood and Billy

Mayerl among the guests. Palmer also hosted the series starting 9 September 1956, introducing veteran Vivienne Chatterton, Kenneth Connor and Eric Winstone.

These You Have Loved
Extremely popular series of middle-brow gramophone record programmes, originally devised and introduced by DORIS ARNOLD. She took the title from Rupert Brooke's poem, 'The Great Lover'. First broadcast was 6 November 1938, when the records included 'The Blue Danube', 'Roses of Picardy', 'The Londonderry Air', 'The Floral Dance', and, of course, the signature tune, Handel's 'Largo'. By the launch of a new series in February 1947 she had played 2500 records, and the 300th programme was broadcast on 12 March 1951. The last programme under this title was broadcast on 11 November 1978, introduced by Richard Baker.

They're Out!
Variety series in which artistes from the Forces back in Civvy Street were ordered to report to ex-Corporal Sally Rogers of the Radio Release Centre. In charge of the party, Gordon Crier and John Burnaby, with the Skyrockets Dance Orchestra conducted by Paul Fenhoulet. The first programme (12th February 1946) featured Jack François, Charles Dorning, Michael Moore (impressionist), and Oliver Wakefield, the pre-war favourite ('The Voice of Inexperience'). Peter Waring, a new comedian, debuted on Show 2, Gerry Fitzgerald the crooner returned on Show 3, and Sid Millward and his Nitwits wreaked havoc on Show 4. The last show, broadcast 2 July, was historic: it featured the first broadcast of young Max Bygraves.

Third Division
Experimental comedy series mounted by the highbrow THIRD PROGRAMME, subtitled 'Some Vulgar Fractions' and starring Robert Beatty, Benny Lee, Bruce Belfrage, Patricia Hayes, Harry Secombe, PETER SELLERS, Michael Bentine, Benny Hill, Carole Carr, Margaret Lindsay and Robert Moreton. Music and song by the George Mitchell Choir, Vic Lewis and his Orchestra and Reg Leopold's Strings. Written by FRANK MUIR, DENIS NORDEN and Paul Dehn; produced by Pat Dixon, who said: 'We shall try above all to avoid the whimsy-

whamsy, and the whole thing will be made as radiogenic as possible.' First broadcast 26 January 1949.

Third Programme
The first completely new radio network after World War II began on Sunday 29 September 1946 at 6 pm. Although as the 'intellectual's music channel' it is not central to the theme of this book, it included a few comedy shows and series in its early years. Opening night began with a How programme, '*How to Listen, including How Not To, How They Used To, and How You Want To*', by Stephen Potter and Joyce Greenfell plus 'especially selected members of the How Repertory Company'. There was also the seminal comedy series THIRD DIVISION (1949). For a time, daytime broadcasts in the same wavelength were known as Network Three. The Third Programme became Radio 3 on 30 September 1967.

Thirty Minutes Worth
Harry Worth, ex-ventriloquist who had become television's bespectacled, bewildered blunderer, starred in this series commencing 23 September 1963. Confused by the proceedings: Deryck Guyler, Anthony Sharp, and Doris Rogers as Mrs Williams the Daily. Script by Vince Powell and Harry Driver; produced by James Casey.

This and That
Famous series of weekly chats given by John Hilton to unemployed listeners during 1936. 'He is always cheering, and his talks brim with sympathy, information, and kindly advice.'

This I Believe
'The programme which brings you human drama and tells the story of people where courage and belief form an integral part of their life.' Adapted from an American series, the very British host was Sir Basil Bartlett. Script by James Carhartt and Nicholas Winter; produced by Monty Bailey-Watson; sponsored by the CWS. On RADIO LUXEMBOURG from 16 September 1956.

James McKechnie hosted the second series (6 October 1957), which was researched by Susan Franks and written by James Eastwood. The third series (5 October 1958) was hosted by Richard Hurndall and scripted by Paul Tabori. This one concentrated on showbusiness personalities such as Shirley Bassey, Vanessa Lee and T.E.B. Clarke.

This Is Your Jim
JIMMY EDWARDS starred in this series of burlesques, beginning on 27 May 1965 with 'The Wimpoles of Barrett Street', in which he protected his delicate son from the wiles of Miss Roberta Browning. She was played by Miss June Whitfield, while Ronnie Barker supported. During the intermission Steve Benbow entertained with his guitar. Scripts, which included 'Jim and Juliet' and 'Man in a Dressing Gown', were by George Evans and Derek Collyer; production was by Charles Maxwell.

This'll Be a Lesson to You
Ronald Frankau's Universal University opened for business on 10 December 1943, with Anne Lenner, John Rorke, Kenneth Blain, Monte Crick and Billy Ternent with the Dance Orchestra. Written by Frankau; produced by Max Kester.

Those Four Chaps
Four comedians who broadcast and recorded as a comedy team in the early thirties: Claude Hulbert, BOBBIE COMBER, Paul England and Charles Collins (replaced by Eddie Childs).

Those Four Chaps: Paul England, Eddie Childs, Claude Hulbert, Bobbie Comber

Those Were the Days

Popular series of old-time dance music ('The Gay Gordons', 'The Dinky One-Step') played by Harry Davidson and his Orchestra with introductions by Raymond Glendenning and A.J. Latimer as the Master of Ceremonies. There were also ballad interludes by such sopranos as Margaret Eaves ('Waltz from *Merrie England*'). The programme commenced its stately way on 21 December 1943 and duly reached its 500th edition on 27 February 1954. Other notable introducers included FREDDY GRISEWOOD, and Patric Curwen, the playwright. The signature tune, 'Those Were The Days', was written by Meyer Lutz, and the original producer was veteran Stanton Jeffries. The last dance was broadcast on 12 December 1974.

The Three Chimes

Singing commères of MONDAY NIGHT AT SEVEN, who sang in close harmony:

It's Monday Night at Seven,
Oh can't you hear the chimes . . .

The Three D's

Doris Day, Dean Martin and Dickie Valentine (four D's, surely?) 'sing songs and bring personal messages from both sides of the Atlantic'. RADIO LUXEMBOURG from 3 July 1957.

The Three Mincemeateers

Rob, Bert and Son, in RADIO LUXEMBOURG adventures sponsored by Robertson's Mincemeat (or had you guessed?) from 1936.

Thrilling Dramas of Newspapermen's Adventures

First dramatized series of sponsored broadcasts commencing on RADIO NORMANDY on 7 October 1934. Programme 1, 'The Kidnapper's Mistake', was described as 'Fifteen minutes of excitement from the country of gangsters and gold'. Sponsored by Cystex, 'the guaranteed cure for all kidney trouble that starts its work in fifteen minutes'.

Ticking Clock

BBC interval signal introduced in December 1930. 'This ticking (which represents exact seconds) will be employed only during non-advertised intervals of over a minute or two, but of not long enough duration to warrant a pianoforte interlude.' Popularly known as 'The Death Watch Beetle'!

Time for Crime

Magazine series including dramatized sketches: 'G-Men at Work' (Dick O'Connor's experiences as a newspaper reporter); 'I Remember' (interviews with Ex-Superintendent Cornish of Scotland Yard); and Edgar Wallace's 'The Mind of MR REEDER' with Eliot Makeham as the amateur sleuth. Weekly from 13 August 1940.

Time to Laugh (1)

'Sixty per cent script and forty per cent music' with Van Phillips and his Two Orchestras and singers Cyril Grantham and the Men About Town. Comedy came from James Hayter as Uncle Jim, George Arden the Gloucestershire Yokel, Vera Lennox and Gee Gee the Dog. Started 4 April 1939; producer Vernon Harris.

Time to Laugh (2)

Rare radio series for ETHEL REVNELL and GRACIE WEST, 'The Long and Short of It', with Bert Platt, Bertram Dench and Margaret Eaves, with CHARLES SHADWELL and the Variety Orchestra. Started 5 October 1943.

Tip Top Tunes

GERALDO introduced and conducted his Orchestra in this major music series, commencing 19 April 1956. Items included 'Top of the Hits', 'Meet the Band', 'The Geraldo Glee Club', 'Composers' Corner' (No. 1, George Gershwin), 'From the Song Shop' with Rosemary Squires, 'Songs with Strings' with Roy Edwards, and a potted version of Gerry's famous series, 'DANCING THROUGH', a cavalcade of non-stop music. Producer David Miller. The new series starting 24 September 1956 introduced new vocalists Doreen Hume, Eric Whitley and David Winnard.

Tish and Tosh

'Wotcher, Tish!' 'Wotcher, Tosh!' Weekly duologue between CHARLIE CHESTER and Len Marten as a pair of spivs in STAND EASY (1948). Catchphrase: 'Four-an'-a-narf, Tish!'

To Be Continued

'The Listeners' Own Serial Thriller', devised by Gale Patrick and written (from listeners' contributions) by Max Kester. 'Listen tonight and send your suggestion for next week's instalment on a postcard. The writer of the one used will receive one guinea.' Characters included Sally Seldom (air hostess), Christopher Cripps (newsreel cameraman), Hildebrand Hurst (world-famous tenor), Ferguson (the man from a Soho Café), and The Lady in Grey (Baronees van Suidenthal). The mysterious 'Joker' was unmasked in the final episode: 19 August 1939.

To Brighten the Break

Lunchtime entertainments for Women War Workers devised by Ellaline Terriss (Lady Hicks) and produced by Douglas Moodie. The first show (10 July 1940) starred Binnie Hale, with Carroll Gibbons and his Band, Anne Lenner and Eric Whitley.

To Town With Terry

First series to star Terry-Thomas, a gentlemanly comedian: 'How do you do – are you frightfully well? Good show!' Ruth Dunning played DOLLY DOVE of Dover Street, the flower-seller. Guest stars came in pairs: Anne Shelton and VERA LYNN; RICHARD DIMBLEBY and LIONEL GAMLIN. A most original spot was 'Imaginary Music Hall' in which Terry and a guest star combined. One classic broadcast had Terry and 'Hutch' impersonating the WESTERN BROTHERS! April May and June were the singing trio, backed by Rae Jenkins and the Variety Orchestra. Terry-Thomas wrote the shows with Talbot Rothwell, and the producer was Audrey Cameron. First broadcast 12 October 1948.

Toad of Toad Hall

Delightful serialized adaptation of Kenneth Grahame's fantasy novel, *The Wind in the Willows*, by David Davis via A.A. Milne's stage-play version. Norman Shelley played Toad, RICHARD GOOLDEN Mole, Leslie French Rat, and Stephen Jack Badger. First broadcast in CHILDREN's HOUR on 30 April 1948, narrated by Mary O'Farrell, with music by H. Fraser Simson.

Toast of the Town

Eamonn Andrews was Toastmaster in this Saturday-night series of 'sparkling tributes to well-known personalities, outstanding newcomers, and successes in London's world of entertainment'. The first show (5 April 1958) starred Norman Wisdom, currently in *Where's Charley*, Larry Adler, harmonica virtuoso, Kay Hammond and husband John Clements in *Rape of the Belt*, Yvonne Mitchell from *Woman in a Dressing Gown*, Jill Day, 'glamorous singing star', and Cliff Adams and the Town Criers. Harry Rabinowitz conducted the Revue Orchestra (theme music by Ron Goodwin), and Trafford Whitelock produced.

Today

This still-running daily breakfast-time magazine 'bringing you News, Views and Interviews' began on the HOME SERVICE on Monday 28 October 1957. For some years it was split into two editions, the first at 7.15, the second at 8.15, separated by five minutes of *Morning Music* from the Light, *Lift Up Your Hearts* at 7.50, the weather at 7.55, the Greenwich Time Signal and the News at 8, and PROGRAMME PARADE at 8.10. The first *Today*, introduced by Alan Skempton, featured 'Briefing a Pilot at London Airport', 'First Night at Liverpool', 'The Sale of Napoleon's Letters', and 'Out Today: New Gramophone Records'. As RADIO TIMES announced, 'the accent is on pace, variety, and informality.' Later presenters included Joy Worth and, best remembered of all, Jack de Manio, who attained national fame by his total inability to give the correct time.

Tom, Dick and Harry

'Tom, Dick and Harry – we're the boys to stick together, oo-ha-ha!' Serial with music being the off-duty adventures of Private Tom Entwhistle, Able-Seaman Dick Rooney, and Aircraftman Harry Hardwell. Devised by Henry Reed; lyrics by Max Kester; written by Tommy Thompson; produced by Francis Worsley. Weekly from 22 October 1941.

Tom Patch

The Wandering Philosopher who, with his doggy pal Raffles, starred in 'programmes to interest all dog lovers'. The sponsor, naturally enough, was Bob Martin's Dog Powders, and Tom's wanderings started on RADIO LUXEMBOURG on 21 August 1937.

Tommy Get Your Fun

Half-hour of comedy for 'You Lucky People' starring Tommy Trinder and CLAUDE HULBERT, with Dorothy Carless singing to Billy Mayerl and his Orchestra. Produced and scripted by Max Kester and the visiting American radio writer, Hal Block.

Tommy Handley's Half Hour

Weekly wartime series featuring the star of IT's THAT MAN AGAIN in a completely different show designed to be heard by British and US forces in the Middle East and India. Only one show of the series was ever broadcast to home listeners, on 28 November 1942. In the cast: JACK TRAIN, an ITMA stalwart, Dorothy Carless and Beryl Davis, glamorous singers, and the GERALDO Orchestra and Ensemble. John Snagge compèred; script by Ray Sonin and Rex Diamond; producer Pat Dixon. The special guest star that week was Edward G. Robinson, the Hollywood tough-guy. The signature song was 'You're here and I'm here'.

Tommy Takes a Chance

Early live series marking RADIO LUXEMBOURG's post-war return in 1946. Geoffrey Everitt compèred this musical challenge in which listeners sent in requests for any dance tune to be played, without music or rehearsal, by Tommy Dallimore and his Band. If Tommy failed, the prize was one guinea. A more sumptuous series began on 3 January 1953, with Harold Berens as the comedy compère. This was retitled *Harry Takes a Chance* and the

Tommy Takes a Chance: Tommy Dallimore's Band with Geoffrey Everitt

band was now Harry Gold's. The sponsor shelling out the guineas was Horace Batchelor of the famous Infra-Draw Method. Then came *Norrie Takes a Chance* in September, with Berens and Norrie Paramor's Orchestra, produced by Philip Jones. The August 1954 series was called *Beat The Band*, again with Berens, but the 1955 series changed to YOU LUCKY PEOPLE in deference to the new compère, Tommy Trinder.

Tommy Trinder Goes Job Hunting

First weekly series for the cockney comedian, sponsored by Symington's Table Creams on RADIO LUXEMBOURG from 15 May 1938. Helping Tommy in his quest for work were Judy Shirley, Walter Williams, and the Symington Serenaders.

Tommy Trouble

Lyn Joshua played the Welsh hero of 'The Adventures of Tommy Trouble', broadcast as part of the long-running series, WELSH RAREBIT. His best pal, Jimmy Jones, was played by the author of the series, E. Eynon Evans, and others in the cast were Rachel Thomas as Mrs Rees, Tom Jones as Llewellyn, and Philip Phillips as Willie the Whip.

The Toni Twins

'Which twin has the Toni?' was the famous advertising slogan posed by the Home Perm people. The Toni Twins came to RADIO LUXEMBOURG on 13 September 1953 to present Ted Heath and his Orchestra, with Lita Roza, Dickie Valentine, and Denis Lotis on the vocals. Script by Jonquil Anthony (later David Climie); produced by Godfrey Howard.

Tonight

Saturday-night series presented by Peter Haigh, 'bringing you music, laughter and celebrities from a leading London night club' – actually the Embassy Club – on behalf of the *News of the World*. Produced by Geoffrey Bellman; a Ross Radio Production for LUXEMBOURG starting 6 October 1956.

Tonight at Six

Daily record show on the LIGHT PROGRAMME designed for car-radio listeners. Jimmy Kingsbury introduced such spots as 'First Rungs', the debut record of a new artist, 'Star of the Week', the first being Peggy Lee, 'Old Wine in New Bottles', a tune of yesterday in the style of today, and 'Over My Shoulder' in which veteran comic Albert Whelan recalled a memory of the stars of the past. Produced by Teddy Warwick; broadcast nightly from 8 September 1958.

Top of the Bill

Long-running series in which 'Top Notch Stars of the entertainment world beguile you with their acts'. Tom Arnold produced, and the first show starred George Formby, broadcasting from the Empire Theatre, Leeds, on 20 February 1940.

Top of the Form

A long run was in store for this quiz contest for children that appealed to adults, when it made its début on 1 May 1948, originally as 'a battle of wits between teams representing boys' schools in London', chaired by Question Master Wynford Vaughan Thomas. Producer Joan Clark finally succumbed to feminist pressure and brought in a girls' school with the new series commencing 3 October 1949. For the record, the first was the Church High School for Girls, Newcastle upon Tyne, who competed with Taunton's School for Boys, Southampton. By this time there were two question-masters, LIONEL GAMLIN and Robert MacDermott. The questions were originally set by a Mr W.T. Williams, who, by the start of the 3 October 1950 series, had compiled 2000 of them! *Top of the Form* continues in the 1980s.

Top of the Town

Terry-Thomas starred in this major series which began on 1 November 1953. Joan Sims and Leslie Mitchell were the regulars, and the first star to be 'top of his town this week' was TONY HANCOCK of Birmingham. 'Musical highlights' came from Victoria Sladen, Patrick O'Hagen and the George Mitchell Town Criers, with Stanley Black and his Concert Orchestra. Script by Jimmy Grafton; produced by Dennis Main Wilson. The second series started 31 October 1954 and Terry-Thomas brought ancient Herbert C. Walton over from his television series as Moulting the valet. Anne Shelton sang, Elton Hayes sang to his small guitar, and 'top of his town' was Benny Hill of Southampton. Woolf Phillips conducted the

Concert Orchestra, and the producer was Bill Gates.

Top Ten

The first radio series to feature best-selling popular music started on 18 December 1944, billed as 'a weekly review of the music popular in Great Britain, the United States, and Canada'. Music and song by the Brass Hats, the Singing Strings, the RAF Dance Orchestra, Beryl Davis, and the US Navy Dance Band. Producer Pat Dixon.

Top Town

Each week the top amateur talent of two towns competed for points awarded by three judges: Jonah Barrington the radio critic, DORIS ARNOLD the pianist and broadcaster, and John Beaumont. The series began in the summer of 1950 on the North Regional, then went national from 12 June 1951, when Round 1 featured Belfast versus Darlington. Ray Martin and his Orchestra provided musical backing, and the producer was Barney Colehan.

Top Twenty

The first programme to present the week's hit parade on gramophone records, devised by Geoffrey Everitt and originally hosted on RADIO LUXEMBOURG by Teddy Johnson (1949). The 20 best-sellers were presented in reverse order and based on sheet music sales: 'Selected recordings of last week's best-selling songs in accordance with the Music Publishers' Association'. Sponsored by Outdoor Girl from 1950.

Topps With Ros

Popular music programmes starring Edmundo Ros and his Latin-American Orchestra, 'brought to you by Topps, the amazing silicone furniture cream'. Produced by Philip Jones; RADIO LUXEMBOURG from 1 January 1954.

Tortoni

'Thees ees Tortoni!', a phrase that sent a chill up young spines. The villain of *The Gang Smasher* crime serial which began on 4 April 1938, starring Ivan Samson and Eileen Erskine. Tortoni was played by Carleton Hobbs.

Towers, Harry Alan

Italia Conti kid who joined RADIO LUXEMBOURG at 15 as a putter-on of records and rose to become the biggest producer of commercial radio shows in Britain, as Towers of London. With the 1939 closure of LUXEMBOURG he began writing for BBC as 'Peter Welbeck' (a name he still uses in his film productions), and soon had eight shows a week to his credit including a CHILDREN'S HOUR serial, TOMMY HANDLEY'S HALF HOUR (overseas series), *Accordion Club*, and OLD MOTHER RILEY TAKES THE AIR. By 1944 he had scripted 2000 programmes as an AC2 in the RAF heading the RAF Radio Production Unit. He created MUCH-BINDING-IN-THE-MARSH, bringing to radio Wing Commander KENNETH HORNE, and the long-running MARCH OF THE MOVIES. In 1943 Towers became Controller of the Overseas Recorded Broadcast Service supervizing Services radio entertainment. After joining M-G-M as their radio adviser, he started a transcription service, producing recorded programmes for RADIO LUXEMBOURG and the world. By 1951 he had 30 shows a week running on LUXEMBOURG including Gracie Fields, THE THIRD MAN, A DATE WITH DICKIE, MOVIE MAGAZINE, TWENTY QUESTIONS, DAN DARE, Edmundo Ros, THE BLACK MUSEUM, SHERLOCK HOLMES, and SHOW TIME FROM THE LONDON PALLADIUM. Towers created the NATIONAL RADIO AWARDS.

Toytown

The most popular of all CHILDREN'S HOUR series. The first *Toytown* play, 'Proud Punch' was broadcast on 19 July 1929, the last on 4 February 1963, well after the closure of its parent programme. 'ELIZABETH' (May Jenkin) found S.G. Hulme Beaman's book, *Tales of Toytown*, by chance, and the stories were adapted and narrated by 'UNCLE MAC' (Derek McCulloch), who also played the main mischief-maker, LARRY THE LAMB ('I'm only a little la-a-a-mb, sir!'). Larry's partner-in-crime was Dennis the Dachshund (Ernest Jay), and their bitter enemy was MR GROWSER (Ralph De Rohan): 'It's disgr-r-r-raceful!' Arthur Winn played the slow-witted ERNEST THE POLICEMAN ('I shall have to take your name and address!'), and the Mayor was Felix Felton (earlier C.E. Hodges). There was also the Magician (Reginald Purdell), CAPTAIN HIGGINS (Frederick Burtwell), Mrs Goose (Mary O'Farrell) of the tuckshop, Letitia Lamb (Sheila Moloney), and the slightly shabby Mayor of Arkville (Lawrence Baskcomb). Signature tune: 'Parade of the Tin Soldiers'.

Trad Tavern

The hostelry where the Chamber Music Society of Lower Bond Street met every Saturday night for a swinging soirée of all kinds of jazz. Mine host Diz Disley welcomed such combos as Chris Barber and his Band with Ottillie Patterson, Dick Charlesworth and his City Gents with Jackie Lynn, and Lennie Felix at the piano. Producer Eric Miller; started 19 September 1961.

Train, Jack

One of radio's greatest comedy voice creators, Train's own Plymouth accent was not heard until he became a long-term member of the TWENTY QUESTIONS team. His 'Can you eat it?' became yet another catchphrase to add to a long string beginning on IT'S THAT MAN AGAIN (1939) with 'Dis is FUNF speaking'. Among Jack's characters were FUSSPOT ('Most irregular! Most irregular!'), FARMER JOLLOP, LEFTY ('It's me noives!'), CLAUDE ('After you, Cecil'), COLONEL CHINSTRAP ('I don't mind if I do'), and MARK TIME ('I'll have to ask me dad'). He also played Cheapjack Train from PETTICOAT LANE, and became a disc-jockey with *Record Express*. His autobiography, *Up and Down the Line* (1956), talked frankly about his battle with tuberculosis.

Jack **Train**: character creator

JACK TRAIN

Transatlantic Quiz

Popular and erudite, this long-running series of two-way broadcasts between London and New York began on 29 July 1945, described as 'a contest to find out who knows more about the other's country'. The London team was D.W. Brogan, Professor of Political Sciences at Cambridge University, and David Niven, film star, under question-master Lionel Hale. The team in New York was Christopher Morley, author of the best-seller *Kitty Foyle*, and John Mason Brown, dramatic critic of the *New York Times*, under question-master Alastair Cooke. A co-production between the BBC and the ABC, the series concluded in 1947, then returned on 6 May 1951 for a 13-week run during the Festival of Britain. Hale and Cooke continued as QMs, and the teams were Denis Brogan and Jack Morpurgo versus Christopher Morley and John Mason Brown.

Transatlantic Spotlight

'Flashes between Britain and America, a joint venture of the BBC and NBC heard simultaneously in both countries.' Two-way variety show produced in New York by Joe Mansfield and in London by James Dyrenforth and Tom Ronald. The debut show, 1 January 1944, starred Anna Neagle, Flanagan and Allen, and the National Fire Service Dance Orchestra from London, and the American Air Force Band directed by Captain Glenn Miller. The title was changed to *Atlantic Spotlight* from 8 January, and the regular compère was Leslie Mitchell (courtesy *British Movietonews*).

Treble Chance

Comedy series built around three newish radio stars, Avril Angers, Jimmy Young and Stan Stennett. Script by Len Fincham and Laurie Wyman; produced by Roy Speer; first broadcast 23 July 1953.

The title returned in 1962 as a tripartite quiz game on music, sounds and general knowledge. Brian Johnston was quizmaster with Nan Winton and Charles Gardner as residents versus teams from the radio regions.

Tredinnick, Robert

Popular disc-jockey in the days of 'presenters of gramophone record recitals'. Prolific freelance writer for the *Daily Sketch* and other journals, he first broadcast from Birmingham in 1934, reading his own stories in the Midland Regional CHILDREN'S HOUR, where he was billed as 'Robert the Teller of Stories'. By 1936 *Radio Pie* called him 'one of the most masterly gramophone impresarios'.

The Trinder Box

'Or the Gift of the Gag!' starring Tommy Trinder and involving Louise Howard, Muriel Cooke, Chappie d'Amato, Paul Fenoulhet and the Variety Orchestra, and a number of unsuspecting visitors. 'The box is packed and posted by Tommy Trinder, Monja Danischewsky and Ronnie Hanbury.' Producer Johnnie Stewart; first broadcast 1 October 1951.

Troise

Troise, who never used his Christian name (Pasquale), was an Italian mandolinist who led two celebrated string dance bands: the Mandoliers and the Banjoliers. Their relentless twanging and plucking was a popular ingredient of the BBC's series, MUSIC WHILE YOU WORK.

The Trouble With Toby

Solo series for Richard Lyon, son of Bebe and Ben, as Tobias T. Trodd, teenager. Regulars in this domestic series: Elizabeth Allan, Claude Hulbert, Andrée Melly, Hugh Paddick, and Nan Marriott-Watson. Written by Ted Taylor and produced by Bill Gates. Weekly from 18 July 1957.

Tuesday Radiogram

The BBC Gramophone Department entertains with 'Record of the Week', 'Birthday Tribute' and 'Brain Twisters' introduced by Robert Shafto and produced by Anna Instone. Began 2 February 1943.

Tune In

Signature tune of RADIO LUXEMBOURG from 1934, played by JACK PAYNE and his Band:

> Tune in, Tune in,
> Just sit in your easy chair
> And through the air to anywhere
> Tune in, Keep tuning in.

Despite its delightfully dated thirties sound, the original record was used again when LUXEMBOURG returned after the war.

Tune-Pools

Popular music contest in which RADIO LUXEMBOURG listeners chose the best of competing song-hits. Lou Praeger and his Hammersmith

Palais Orchestra (vocalists Rusty Hurren, Paul Rich and the Sunspots) played these pairs on 2 September 1952: 'Any Time' v. 'Cry', 'Kiss of Fire' v. 'La Cumparsita', 'Slow Coach' v. 'Be My Life's Companion'.

Twenty Questions

Simply subtitled 'a radio parlour game' this quiz series based on the ancient pastime called 'Animal, Vegetable or Mineral' (to which was added 'Abstract') shot to the heights of popularity following its first broadcast on 14 March 1947. Fast-talking Canadian sports commentator STEWART MACPHERSON was the chairman who knew all the answers, and the original panel was RICHARD DIMBLEBY, famous for his commentaries, ANONA WINN, singer and actress about to embark on a whole new career as a 'talking personality', JACK TRAIN, hitherto a funny-voice man in ITMA, and Olga Collett. Miss Collett soon became unwell and was replaced by another 'unknown', Daphne Padel. The MYSTERY VOICE ('And the next object is . . .') also sparked-off a new career for pianist Norman Hackforth. The producer was Cleland Finn. The 200th show was broadcast on 20 September 1951, by which time the team was Winn, Train, Dimbleby and Joy Adamson, with GILBERT HARDING in the chair. Actually the total was much more because from 8 December 1950 the series had also been running on RADIO LUXEMBOURG, where the original Stewart MacPherson chaired a new panel: Frances Day, RICHARD MURDOCH, Daphne Padel and Ex-Detective Superintendent Fabian of Scotland Yard. The sponsor was Craven A Cork Tips.

The 500th BBC show was broadcast on 1 August 1962, with KENNETH HORNE as chairman. After 18 years Dimbleby left the series, to be replaced by veteran 2LO broadcaster, Cecil Lewis (28 April 1965). Then Mystery Voice Norman Hackforth came out of his closet to become a panellist. He was replaced by a new celebrity Mystery Voice, making a fresh subject for the team to guess each week from 29 July 1965. The last edition was broadcast on 28 July 1976: Isobel Barnett, Penelope Keith, Richard Briers, James Burke, and chairman Cliff Michelmore; producer Bobby Jaye.

Twisted Tunes

'The Confoundation of Popular Songs': clever series devised by the star, Eddie Pola, illustrating how popular tunes borrow from one another, and from classical music. Jimmy Bailey was at the piano. First broadcast on 2 January 1937, and transferred to RADIO LUXEMBOURG from 25 July by courtesy of Monkey Brand Soap.

The Twizzle Sisters

They did their Party Piece – which was a song called 'Doing Our Party Piece' – in Ralph Reader's *Radio Gang Show* (1938). 'Oh, Mister Reee-der!' was their catchphrase cry. The Twizzlers were Jack Beet from the Stock Exchange, and Norman Fellowes who worked at Boy Scout Headquarters. Perhaps they were the parental predecessors of Hinge and Bracket, but in those innocent days we found nothing dubious in such goings on. The girls were still at it ten years later in Reader's *It's Fine To Be Young.*

2LO

Famous call-sign of the first London radio station, which made its first broadcast on Thursday 11 May 1922: ARTHUR BURROWS gave news of the boxing match between Kid Lewis and Georges Carpentier. Originally known as MARCONI's London Wireless Telephone Station, 2LO broadcast on 360 metres with a power of 100 watts. The studio was in a small cinema on the top floor of Marconi House, in the Strand, and the transmitter was in a former furniture warehouse renamed 'Radio House', in Wilson Square, E.C.

The first proper programme was a concert broadcast at 6 pm on 20 July 1922: songs from musical-comedy star Marjorie Gordon, impersonations of famous comedians by Arthur Margetson, and songs at the piano from Morland Hay. Piano accompaniment was by L. Stanton Jeffries. This preceded the first programme listed in BBC records, which is for 26 July: Charles Winter Coppin, baritone, Dorothy Clark, contralto, Edward Reach, tenor, and John Pennington. The first popular song, 'Limehouse Blues', was sung by Velma Deane on 29 July. Will Hay was the first comedy star to broadcast, in excerpts from the revue *Listening In* (29 July). The first children's programme was a 'Teddy Tail' story read by Arthur Burrows on 26 August. The first item of drama was Robert Atkins in a speech from *The Merchant of Venice* (2 September). The first comedian was Wilfrid Liddiatt in 'The Vicar's

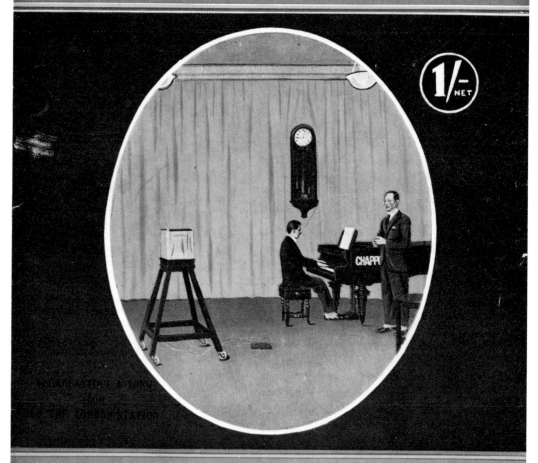

2LO: *Radio Favourites* (1925)

Presentation' (22 September). In the same programme W. Pett Ridge the novelist read the first broadcast short story, *The Principal Speaker*. The first comedienne was Peggy Rae in 'Really, One Never Knows, Does One?' (28 September). The first music-hall comic to broadcast was Ernie Mayne in 'Wireless On The Brain' (11 October). The first radio character, 'Our Lizzie' (Helena Millais) broadcast on 20 October.

2LO became the London Station of the British Broadcasting Company from 14 November. Arthur Burrows read the first news bulletin – twice – once at normal speed and once slowly. Items were punctuated with a chiming clock, later revealed to be Mr Burrows at the tubular bells. Daily concerts now ensued, introducing NORMAN LONG's songs at the piano (28 November), Vivian Foster the Vicar of Mirth (7 December), Charles Penrose the Laughing Policeman and G.H. Elliott the Chocolate Coloured Coon (9 December), the first CHILDREN'S STORIES programme (23 December), the first talk (Captain E.B. Towse, VC) and the first Dance Music (23 December). In 1923 came the first OB (Outside Broadcast), Mozart's *The Magic Flute* by the British National Opera Company from the Royal Opera House, Covent Garden (8 January); the first play excerpt, *Charley's Aunt* (23 January); and the first variety show, VETERANS OF VARIETY (30 January).

Broadcasting hours and scope expanded with the move to new studios at SAVOY HILL (1 May 1923). A more powerful transmitter was introduced on 6 April 1925: it was on the roof of Selfridges store in Oxford Street. 2LO officially ceased to exist from 9 March 1930, when the alternative programme services, NATIONAL and London REGIONAL, began.

2LO Dance Band
The first 'house dance band' of the BBC, which made its first broadcast at 7.30 pm on Saturday 19 May 1923. The programme opened with 'Who Dear', a one-step. The band consisted of nine members of the Wireless Orchestra plus a saxophonist.

2LO Dancestra
BBC 'house dance orchestra' playing more formal music for dancing than the foxtrots beloved of the 2LO DANCE BAND. First broadcast, 10 November 1923.

The Two Leslies
Comedy double-act formed in 1933 by comedian/singer/composer Leslie Sarony and song-plugger/pianist Leslie Holmes, 'The Man with the Smiling Voice'. Their hits included 'I'm a Little Prairie Flower', 'Teas, Light Refreshments and Minerals', and 'Let's Have a Jolly Old Game of Darts'. See RADIO PIE.

The Two Leslies: Leslie Sarony and Leslie Holmes

Two Old Gentlemen
Unnamed (perhaps because they forgot them) pair of ancients who sat on a park bench in JUST FANCY (1951), and discovered that it was only by listening to the other fellow, that you got the other fellow's point of view. Later retiring to the Cranbourne Towers Hotel at Westbourn on Sea, they were the bane of waiter Muspratt (Kenneth Connor) and a problem to Mrs Cruikshank. Played by Eric Barker (who scripted) and Deryck Guyler at their most brilliant. Guyler was the testier of the two: 'Oh, Glory!'

Two Way Family Favourites
Change of title for the popular FAMILY FAVOURITES record-request series, effective from 3 January 1960. Presenters included Jean Metcalfe in London and Bill Crozier in Cologne for the British Forces Network.

Two's a Crowd
The first comedy series to star a ventriloquist's dummy, ARCHIE ANDREWS. Archie was supported by Peter Brough, while all the other voices came from impersonator Peter Cavanagh ('The Voice of Them All'). Written by Gene Crowley and produced by Charles Maxwell. First broadcast 19 February 1948.

U

Ukridge

Series of episodes in the life of Stanley Featherstone Ukridge, P.G. Wodehouse's untidy giant, always on the verge of making a fortune and counting his thousands before they are made. Adapted for radio by Helmar Fenbach, commencing 20 January 1940, with 'our hero' played by Malcolm Graeme. Michael Shepley took over the role years later, in a series of six produced by H.B. Fortuin, starting 25 May 1956.

Uncle Caractacus

Guiding spirit of the early children's programmes. In reality Cecil Lewis, pioneer of wireless telephony in aircraft and original programme director of the Metrovick-GEC broadcasting company, set up to rival MARCONI. With the formation of the BBC he became Deputy Director of Programmes under ARTHUR BURROWS, taking over as director on Burrows' departure. Lewis was responsible for most early programming, writing and adapting over 40 plays for the microphone, reading the 'Philemon' talks series, and conducting the children's page in RADIO TIMES. Finding the bureaucracy of the BBC stifling to creativity he resigned, became radio critic of *The Observer*, and wrote *Broadcasting From Within*.

Uncle Caractacus: Cecil Lewis in *Children's Hour*

Uncle Coughdrop

Star of *The Playtime Programme*, broadcast on RADIO NORMANDY and sponsored by Pineate Honey Syrup, the Cough Remedy for Children, 1s 6d a bottle (1936). Also in the show, Auntie Clara and ten-year-old Betty, who enjoyed Coughdrop's Brer Rabbit stories.

Uncle Gabby

'Well, hellooo there!' was this garrulous old-timer's greeting to his niece, Barbara Kelly. Played by her real-life husband, BERNARD BRADEN, in BEDTIME WITH BRADEN (1950) and similar series.

Uncle Mac

Derek McCulloch, a former announcer (1926), whose regular broadcasts on CHILDREN'S HOUR led to his taking over production of that series in 1933. He eventually dropped the 'Uncle' title, and as 'Mac' narrated the popular TOYTOWN comedies, also playing the leading role of LARRY THE LAMB. After retiring in July 1950 he became the slightly testy compère of CHILDREN'S CHOICE, a request record series. His famous farewell, 'Goodnight children . . . everywhere' became the title of a heart-rending song about evacuees in the first months of World War II.

Uncle Jim

Not one of your regular CHILDREN'S HOUR 'uncles', Uncle Jim was the one and only exciting personality to emerge from BBC Schools Programmes. He was Jim Smith, who explored prehistoric Britain in the series *How Things Began*, first broadcast on 24 September 1941: 'This is the BBC Service from the Past. Today our observer, Jim Smith, will speak to us from a forest of the carboniferous period, 200 million years ago.' Uncle Jim was memorable because he had his faults: 'I think I'll sit down on this treetrunk – why, it's a huge amphibian and it's after me!'

Uncle Mac: Derek McCulloch

Uncle Oscar

Ancient relation of Crun and Bannister, usually heard joining in their 'Morning . . . morning . . .' chorus. Played by Harry Secombe in THE GOON SHOW (1952).

Uncle Remus

The famous stories by Joel Chandler Harris were adapted for radio by James Dyrenforth, to music by Henry Reed; producer David Porter, Negro actor Robert Adams played Uncle Remus, with C. DENIER WARREN as Brer Rabbit, supported by WYNNE AJELLO, Dick Francis, Elsie Otley and others all trying to sound like deep-south Americans. Series started 22 February 1940.

Under One Roof

Series which sowed the seed of the half-hour 'sitcom'. Hollywood star Roland Young returned to his native England to appear as George Banter, architect, with Sophie Stewart as his wife. These domestic comedies were written by Mabbie Poole and produced by Douglas Moodie. Also in the cast were Roger Braban, Patsy Smart, Stephen Jack, John Warrington and Cecile Chevreau. First broadcast 31 July 1947.

Under (S)Tate Control

Crazy comedy series in 15-minute episodes starring Harry Tate Junior, with Reginald Purdell, Thea Wells, Clarence Wright, and Vera Lennox. Written by Loftus Wigram and produced by Charles Maxwell; from 28 October 1946.

Under Your Tin Hat

Weekly wartime radio magazine programme for ARP, AFS, WVS, Fire-watchers, and Civil Defence Workers. 'Entertainment by and for the men and women who are guarding the homes of Britain.' First broadcast 2 April 1941; features included 'Salute to Heroes', 'What Did You Do', 'Stars in Civil Defence', and music by the ARP Dance Band. Producers Bill MacLurg and Howard Thomas.

Universal Programmes Company

Production unit of IBC, packaging sponsored programmes broadcast from the Continent in the thirties. Earliest printed credits (RADIO PICTORIAL from 10 February 1935): The *Kruschen Family Party On The Air*, *L'Orle Tango Time*, *Gene Dennis* with the Wincarnis Orchestra, *Ingersoll Slumber Hour*, *Going Places* with Dermot O'Neil, *Sylvan Sweethearts*, and *The Odeon Theatre Broadcast* with Bernard G. McNabb. In charge of production was Jack Hargreaves. Producers included Tom Ronald, Canadian David Miller and Australian Bruce Anderson. Scriptwriters were Aubrey Danvers-Walker, Canadian Cal Haggitt, New Zealander Don Taska, and Australian Ann Shead. Britain's 'other Broadcasting House' was 100 yards away from the original, at 37 Portland Place.

Universal Radio Publicity

Pioneering production company making programmes for sponsors under the direction of Philip Dorté. They were formerly known as Radio Publicity Ltd. Their first programme was an hour of dance music by William Stanford and his Revelation Symphonic Orchestra, broadcast from *Radio Paris* on 25 August 1929. The sponsor was Revelation Suitcases. By October they had 15 advertisers and were also broadcasting from the Eiffel Tower. From 21 October 1930 under their new name they broadcast a nightly hour of sponsored shows from Radio Dublin, beginning with Sweet Afton Cigarettes.

Up and Coming

Wallas Eaton acted as host for this series designed to introduce some of the newer voices in radio. The first show, broadcast 13 January 1950, included Doreen Stephens, Peter Valerio, and Martin and Chester, with the Revue Orchestra conducted by Frank Cantell.

Up and Doing

Magazine programme described as 'an entertainment for everyone'. Began on 2 January 1947 with musical comedy star Elsie Randolph as the commère. Features: 'Home Town', songs and tunes of the counties and towns of Britain; 'In the Barber's Chair', a serial story by Rex Diamond; 'Your Hobby Horse' with C. DENIER WARREN on toy soldiers; 'Comedy Spot' with impressionist Peter Cavanagh. Frank Cantell conducted the Revue Orchestra, and the producer was Audrey Cameron.

Up in the Morning Early

Early-morning (7.45 am) programme of exercises performed and described by Florence

Bracken (younger women and older men: Tuesday, Thursday and Saturday) and J. Coleman Smith (younger men and older women: Monday, Wednesday and Friday), daily from November 1939. Signature tune: 'Up in the morning's no for me, up in the morning early.' Improvized piano accompaniment by Andrew Bryson and Barbara Lang. From 1 May 1940 the ration was doubled to 7.30 and 7.40 daily, and the participating audience had enlarged to 1,250,000. The series was devised by the director of the BBC Scottish Region, Melville Dinwiddie.

Up The Pole

Long-running comedy series starring Jimmy Jewel and Ben Warriss as the cross-talking proprietors of a trading post in the Arctic, with CLAUDE DAMPIER as HORACE HOTPLATE, the Mayor of the North Pole. The Frozen North setting soon melted away. Supporting cast: Valerie Tandy, JON PERTWEE as Mr Burp, and the Five Smith Brothers ('Hello, hello, hello, hello, hello-ho!'). Guest star on the first show (27 October 1947) was Tod Slaughter in his classic stage role of Sweeney Todd. Written by Ronnie Hanbury with Brian and Richard Rowland; producer George Inns. Betty Paul (a name-change from Percheron) arrived to become the permanent girlfriend on 1 November 1948, the start of the second series. Bertie Hare (Doris's brother) joined the cast of the third series, beginning 21 November 1949, which was set in a rural police station with Hotplate as Superintendent ('Oh, you'll never guess!').

The fourth series started 20 June 1952 with Josephine Crombie as the new girlfriend, and Fred Yule as the new character man. Songs were now supplied by the Taverners with Frank Chacksfield and his Orchestra.

Up the Pole: Jewel and Warriss in *Radio Fun*, drawn by Alex Akerbladh

Up With the Curtain

Tommy Trinder's first BBC series, commencing 8 July 1939 on the National. Tommy and straight-man Peter Vokes fought over the favours of Jasmine Dee, in a mini-series, 'He Was a Handsome Territorial'. Another feature was 'Star of the Week', in which a guest was interviewed by producer Vernon Harris. Also in the cast: singers Gwen Catley, Monte Rey, Cyril Grantham and the Top Hatters, with GERALDO and his Concert Orchestra. The show, which ran 60 minutes, had an unusual broadcast pattern: every ten days, with the Saturday editions being transmitted to the USA.

Vagabond Lover

The original Vagabond Lover was Rudy Vallee, the American singing band-leader, but the BBC adopted the title in 1935 for a series of romantic broadcasts by an unnamed mystery singer. The signature song was 'Just a Vagabond Lover' and the programmes were narrated by an unnamed 'inspiration girl'; the Lover never spoke. Perhaps we may now reveal the secret: he was Cavan O'Connor. Even more, the inspiration girl was Lorna Hubbard.

The Vaguelys

Domestic situation comedies based by writer Max Kester on the tribulations of himself and his wife during a two-year search for a house in the country. Mary Jerrold and Christopher Steele played Mr and Mrs Vaguely, with Joan White as Babs. First broadcast 1 September 1947, produced by Vernon Harris.

Valentine's Night

Vocalist Dickie Valentine in 'his own programme of songs you all want him to sing for you'. Dickie was accompanied by the Don Phillips Quartet and sponsored by Tress Wave Set. The 1955 series changed sponsor to Cosmedin Beauty Lotion. Produced by Philip Jones; RADIO LUXEMBOURG from 5 May 1954.

Variety

Although there were frequent variety entertainers and entertainments on early radio, the first programme to be labelled *Variety* was broadcast on 25 July 1924. Stars of this two-hour bill: Marjorie Booth (contralto), George Pizzey (baritone), Ray Wallace (impersonator), Helena Millais (OUR LIZZIE), RONALD GOURLEY (siffleur), Radio Rufus (entertainer), and the Amboyna Banjo Quartet. Variety programmes were renamed VAUDEVILLE from January 1928.

Variety Bandbox

Weekly series of Sunday-night hour-long shows originally designed for a service audience. Began 27 December 1942 in the Overseas Programme and attained huge home listening popularity when it moved to the new General FORCES PROGRAMME on 27 February 1944. Devised by Cecil Madden as *Bandbox Variety* and renamed when his secretary accidently mistyped the title. Produced by Madden and Stephen Williams from the stage of the Queensbury All Services Club at the London Casino, the first show starred Issy Bonn, Ted and Barbara Andrews, Mario 'Harp' Lorenzi, ANONA WINN, Jack Simpson, and Edmundo Ros and his Orchestra. The first Resident Comedian of many was Hal Monty ('Larf and be 'appy!'), followed by DEREK ROY, FRANKIE HOWERD, Reg 'Proper Poorly' Dixon, Arthur 'Open the Cage!' English, Albert 'Ninety-two!' Modley, and others. The opening signature tune was 'I Love To Sing', followed by Billy Ternent's 'She's My Lovely'. The show always closed with the audience singing 'Let's Have Another One'. Film stars compèred during 1944 (Margaret Lockwood did the first on the Forces Programme), but later announcer Philip Slessor made the show his own with: 'Welcome to *Variety Bandbox* presenting the people of variety to a variety of people.'

The Sixth Birthday Show, broadcast 17 December 1948, starred Frankie Howerd, Charlie Kunz at the piano, Suzette Tarri, Janet Hamilton Smith and John Hargreaves (duettists), Peter Cavanagh ('The Voice of Them All'), and Billy Ternent. A return run commencing 8 October 1951 marked a move to Mondays with AL READ as Resident and Cyril Stapleton and his Orchestra. The final show was broadcast on 28 September 1952. Bernard Miles was the last resident comedian, and the final act was fittingly, Frankie Howerd.

Variety Cavalcade

Stupendous series saluting the BBC VARIETY DEPARTMENT's activities during World War II, broadcast in seven weekly instalments of one hour apiece. The background story was told by Kenneth Adam and John Watt, the Director of Variety (1937–43), and the series written and compiled by Loftus Wigram. Tom Ronald was the producer, and Jack Beaver's incidental music was played by the Variety Orchestra and Revue Chorus, conducted by Charles Shadwell. The series started on 11 February 1946 with 'London to Bristol' and extracts from BAND WAGGON, GARRISON THEATRE, and IT's THAT MAN AGAIN. Part 2, 'Bristol to Weston Super Mare' featured HI GANG, THE OLD TOWN HALL, VERY TASTY VERY SWEET, and ACK-ACK BEER-BEER. The last episode was entitled 'London Full Circle'. Unbelievably this historic survey was not deemed worthy of preservation in the BBC Archives!

Variety Department

The BBC removed Variety from the responsibility of Val Gielgud, Head of Drama and Variety, in the autumn of 1933, and created the Variety Department. The first Director of Variety was Eric Maschwitz, editor of RADIO TIMES, and his responsibility was to fill $17\frac{1}{2}$ hours a week with vaudeville, musical comedy, operetta, cabaret, dance music, and Surprise Items. He was assisted by Charles Brewer and Stanford Robinson (music), and the programme producers were John Watt (SONGS FROM THE SHOWS), Harry S. Pepper (KENTUCKY MINSTRELS), John Sharman (MUSIC HALL), Gordon McConnell, Ernest Longstaffe, and Denis Freeman. First series created by the Department were IN TOWN TONIGHT and CAFÉ COLETTE. Studios used were BA, which admitted an audience of 60, 8A, borrowed from the Military Band, the Concert Hall, and No. 10, an ex-warehouse by Waterloo Bridge. The Department grew quickly and moved from BROADCASTING HOUSE to ST GEORGE's HALL in April 1934. Its final home was Aeolian Hall, Bond Street.

Variety Fanfare

Series 'heralding variety in the North', first broadcast as simply *Fanfare* from 11 April 1949, changing title on 18 July. The original resident comedian was MICHAEL HOWARD, replaced by Douglas (CARDEW) Robinson on 9 May. The first show starred CYRIL FLETCHER, Betty Driver, Tommy Reilly (harmonica), and the Kordites, with the Northern Variety Orchestra conducted by 'Toni'. The first *Variety Fanfare* also starred Betty Driver, supported by ROBB WILTON, Albert and Les Ward (comedy musicians), and new comedians Gene Crowley and Robert Moreton (with his Bumper Fun Book). Bowker Andrews produced.

Variety Mansions

Edwin Lawrence played the porter and Jane Worth the charlady in this comedy series first broadcast on 22 January 1936. Also heard: Harry Chapman and his Broadcasting Buskers, Foster Richardson, and the Three Herons. Ernest Longstaffe produced and revived the series from 27 October 1938 with Charles Penrose and SUZETTE TARRI as porter and char. This time Winsor and Lever lived on the top floor, Paulo on the second, HARRY HEMSLEY and his imaginary children on the first, and CLAUDE DAMPIER and Billie Carlisle occupied the ground floor. Writer Robert Rutherford.

Variety on Tour

A new name for the old WORKER's PLAYTIME, beginning on 13 October 1964 with Roger Moffat introducing Ken Dodd from a factory canteen in Hebden Bridge.

Variety Playhouse

VIC OLIVER was Master of Ceremonies of this prestigious Saturday night series: 'each week he invites stars of all branches of the entertainment world'. The first show (2 May 1953) included Ann Todd, Jean Sablon, Elizabeth Welch, Benny Hill, Ronald Chesney and his harmonica, ARTHUR ASKEY, the George Mitchell Choir and the Revue Orchestra conducted by Harry Rabinowitz. Script by Carey Edwards, producer Tom Ronald. On 9 July 1955 RICHARD MURDOCH rang up the curtain on a new summer season starring Billy Eckstine, Derek Roy, Campoli, the Ray Ellington Quartet, the Peter Knight Singers; producer John Simmonds. Vic Oliver returned to take charge on 1 October 1955, including the conducting of the British Concert Orchestra. The 1956 summer season starting 30 June had Jack Buchanan as host, with Jack Hulbert and CICELY COURTNEIDGE as permanent guests in sketches by Eric Merriman and Louis Schwartz. TED RAY hosted the next series, which started on 5 October 1957. Hulbert and Courtneidge continued as stars of 'POCKET THEATRE' and Ronnie Barker and Patricia Hayes provided voices. Music came from the George Mitchell Choir and Harry Rabinowitz and the Revue Orchestra. Scripts by Terry Nation and John Junkin; producer Alastair Scott-Johnston.

Ray, Hulbert and Courtneidge continued with the next series (27 September 1958), this time with Ted as 'Nidge of the News', and a spot by Leslie Randall and Joan Reynolds. Vic Oliver returned for the new series commencing 27 December 1958, with a number of series sketches: 'Jobs I Have Held' (No. 1: Father Christmas) written by Johnny Speight; 'Vic in a Spot', a mystery puzzle by Ernest Dudley; Oliver also conducted the BBC Revue Orchestra. Guests were ELSIE AND DORIS WATERS, Cardew Robinson, and June Bronhill.

The old format returned with the 3 October 1959 series – Vic with Jack and Cis in their 'Pocket Theatre' spot and this was repeated in the 24 September 1960 series. However, a new team was added in the shape of Ronnie Barker and Leslie Crowther, who wrote their own scripts. The new series starting 21 September 1961 replaced Jack and Cis with another theatrical personality, Sir Donald Wolfit as 'The Storyteller'.

Suave film star Dennis Price became the host of the next series, 24 March 1962, but Vic Oliver was back for 6 October 1962, as were Wolfit and his wife, Rosalind Iden, for 'Playhouse Theatre'. Vic continued to compère and conduct the next series, 28 September 1963, with Margaret Lockwood and John Stone in the drama spot, and songs from Victoria Elliott and the George Mitchell Choir. Tom Ronald returned as producer.

Vaudeville

Entertainment programmes previously labelled 'Variety' changed their title to *Vaudeville* from 10 January 1928. The first bill starred Gracie Fields, supported by Rex Evans and Cicely Debenham (entertainers), Neil Kenyon (Scots comedian) and D. Wise (violinist).

Vaudeville of 1944

Saturday-night variety shows featuring stars of music hall, music and drama, beginning 1 January 1944 with JACK WARNER, Harriet Cohen, Binnie Hale, Dennis Noble and Ann Todd, with the Revue Orchestra conducted by Charles Groves. Producers John Sharman and Harry S. Pepper.

Vera Lynn Sings

'Songs for forces everywhere, their wives and sweethearts, their families and friends.' VERA LYNN was supported by Roberto Inglez and his Orchestra, and recorded each week before a different services audience. On 13 April 1951 she was at RAF Stanmore, sponsored by Horlicks and broadcast from RADIO LUXEMBOURG. The series returned on 27 September 1953 under the sponsorship of Kraft Cheese. Vera was backed by Stanley Black and his Orchestra, and squired by Donald Gray. Gordon Crier produced for Star Sound Studios, and there was a recipe competition. Vera's opening signature tune was 'Yours' and she closed with 'Auf Wiedersehen'.

The Veri-Neats

Cod camp concert-party series devised by Lieutenant CHARLES SHADWELL, late West Yorks Regt, conducting the Camp Chorus and the Veri-Neats Orchestra. With JACK TRAIN, Sylvia Welling, Donald Peers, Doris Hare, Alec Pleon, and Arthur Sandford at the piano. Irregular during 1941.

Very Tasty – Very Sweet

Catchphrase of Nan Kenway and Douglas Young in their characters of Mrs Yatton, landlady of the Startled Hare, and MR GRICE, the food-conscious veteran. Frequent use in HOWDY FOLKS brought about their own show with this title on 24 May 1940, and a series followed on 30 June. Music by the Three in Harmony, and Billy Ternent and the BBC Dance Orchestra.

A later series commencing 25 February 1942 added Hugh Morton and Bettie Bucknelle to the cast. Producer Leslie Bridgmont. Surprisingly, the series was revived on RADIO LUXEMBOURG from December 1950, sponsored by Currys Radio and Cycle Shops. Kenway and Young were supported by Geoffrey Sumner.

Veterans of Variety

The first 'old-time music-hall' shows on radio were these occasional gatherings of veteran performers singing their famous successes. The first was broadcast on 30 January 1923 and included Tom Costello, H.V. Henson, Margaret Cornille, Lily Burnand, Marie Collins and Sable Fern. The second show, 31 July 1924, featured Willie Rouse (WIRELESS WILLIE) as Chairman and starred Charles Coburn ('The Man Who Broke the Bank at Monte Carlo'), Frank Leo, Leo Dryden, Arthur Roberts and Jake Friedman. These irregular broadcasts led to the eventual creation of radio's own old-time music hall, PALACE OF VARIETIES.

Vic Oliver Introduces

This prestigious programme of comedy and music began under the title of *The Vic Oliver Show* on 12 September 1945, and was changed to the above on 24 October. Designed to showcase the serious side of the well-loved Austrian comedian, it featured his Concert Orchestra in popular classics, as well as a weekly guest personality. The supporting cast, in sketches written by Ray Sonin, included Slim Allan, Stephen Jack, Margaret McGrath, Betty Hamilton and Kenneth Newte. Henry Reed produced. The second series began on 25 September 1946, under producer Eric Spear. The musicians were now called the British Concert Orchestra, and comedy content reduced to sophisticated backchat with Sally Rogers. Guests were singers Kyra Vane and Walter Midgeley, plus Dame Lilian Braithwaite.

Vic Samson, Special Investigator

The first daily adventure serial for children, broadcast on RADIO LUXEMBOURG from 21 August 1939, sponsored by Quaker Puffed Wheat. Vic Samson of Scotland Yard was assisted by Mike and his young schoolboy brother, Bobby Samson. 'How a remarkable man pits his keenness and trigger-fast energy against the united efforts of a gang of ruthless crooks.' In his first adventure Vic was hired by the Ivory Dealers' Association to catch smugglers on the African Gold Coast. Unhappily the outbreak of World War II cut short Samson's career.

Vicar of Mirth

Vivian Foster, an early broadcasting favourite, who had already appeared on the music halls in the guise of a parson some 10,000 times. First broadcast on 7 December 1922, complete with his catchphrase: 'Yerse, I think so. . . .'

Victory Programmes

The end of World War II in Europe was celebrated on radio with several special programmes. *Victory Party*, a variety show produced by John Watt, was on 9 May 1945, with *V-Itma* and *Victory Sing-Song* on the 10th. The latter was a Grand Gala at the Palace of Varieties, with Harry Duke, Eve Lynd, Andy Payne, Sylvia Kellaway, Alec Pleon, George Betton, Connor and Drake, and Hetty King.

The Chairman was Bill Stephens. 11 May presented *Victory at St Michael's* with Will Hay and Co., and *Cap and Victory Bells*, a celebration edition of the regular revue starring BASIL RADFORD AND NAUNTON WAYNE, with Carole Lynne, Hubert Gregg and Zoe Gail to sing her famous wartime song, 'I'm Going to Get Lit Up When the Lights Go On In London'. Also two Gordons, Cliff and Noele.

On 12 May came *In Town Tonight Victory Edition* edited by C.F. Meehan, and *Victory Music Hall* with Josephine Baker, the Western Brothers, Evelyn Laye, Suzette Tarri, Issy Bonn, TED RAY and CHARLES SHADWELL with the Variety Orchestra. 13 May brought *Victory Music Parade* with the combined Stoll Theatres Orchestra and Monia Liter, and the 14th a special *Monday Night at Eight* with ARTHUR ASKEY, RICHARD MURDOCH, KENNETH HORNE, CYRIL FLETCHER, Ann Todd and Joyce Grenfell.

Programmes to celebrate the end of World War II began on 8 June 1946 with *Victory Day Music Hall*. John Sharman produced this special edition starring Johnnie Riscoe and Violet Terry, NOSMO KING, Peter Waring, Vincent Tildsley's Master Singers, Murgatroyd & Winterbottom, Anne Ziegler and Webster Booth, Jewel and Warriss, and CICELEY COURTNEIDGE. Lionel Marson compèred. *Victory Star Show* was on the Light, a forces occasion. The Navy was represented by Michael Redgrave, ERIC BARKER and Pearl Hackney, and Esmond Knight; the Army by CHARLIE CHESTER and his Gang, Terry-Thomas, and Robert Flemyng; the RAF by Max Wall, KENNETH HORNE, Cyril Raymond, and the Squadronnaires; and 'Favourite of All the Forces' was Anne Shelton. *Victory Variety Bandbox*, broadcast on the 9th, was introduced by Margaretta Scott. Stars included Marie Burke, Ronald Chesney and his harmonica, Monia Liter, Avril Angers, and STAINLESS STEPHEN. Joy Russell Smith produced from the Camberwell Palace.

Vladivostooge

Russian announcer of RADIO FAKENBERG ('Ici Radio Fakenberg – defense de cracher!') in the first series of IT'S THAT MAN AGAIN (1939). Played by Eric Egan.

Vocalion Concert

First commercial radio series to be advertised

(*Sunday Referee* 11 October 1931), consisting of newly released records on the Broadcast label. This half-hour programme of seven records went on the air with 'Blaze Away' (vocal march) at 10.40 pm on RADIO TOULOUSE, transferring to RADIO PARIS on 13 December at 11.30 am, and concluding its weekly run on 3 January 1932.

Vodkin
Eccentric inventor in IT'S THAT MAN AGAIN (1939) with a line of broken English that pre-echoed SIGNOR SOSO: 'Ah Mister Handme-down, my egg factory has eggceded all my cackle-ations!' Played by MAURICE DENHAM from the Ministry of Misconstruction.

The Voice of Experience
'Your Guide, Philosopher and Friend' presented by Pepsodent Tooth Paste on Radio Normandy from 17 April 1930. The Voice answered listeners' problems between such appropriate melodies as 'It's a Sin to Tell a Lie' and 'Let's Face the Music'.

Voice of Philco
'With the playing of *The Song Ethereal* the world's largest makers of radio receivers greet you once again. Across the ether we send greetings, good wishes, and a little music to cheer you on your way.' Musical series on RADIO LUXEMBOURG, 1937.

The Voice of Romance
'Music and the words of love blended by the Mystery Voice to set the mood for romance.' The Mystery Voice is still a mystery, but Ellis Powell (MRS DALE) gave household hints between the words of love. Produced by Monty Bailey-Watson for L.G. Hawkins & Co.; broadcast on RADIO LUXEMBOURG from 6 March 1953.

Wait for It

'A Break for Barker' starring ERIC BARKER with his wife, Pearl Hackney, masquerading as Wendy Kaye. They played Hon. Godfrey Crumpett, private detective, and Lady Ethel. Also in cast: Eric Woodburn and Eileen Vaughan. 'An inexpensive production in the basement of the BBC to exploit the genius of Eric Barker', beginning 14 June 1940. On 27 July 1944 it was revived as a series of topical revues also starring KENWAY AND YOUNG, with Cherry Lind, Wilfred Babbage, and Melville Christie and his Dance Orchestra.

Waiting for Jane

Series starring singing pianist Billy Milton, who whiled away 15 minutes a week with his manservant, Fred Yule. Signature song:

> Waiting for Jane,
> She's bound to be late,
> So that's why I'm waiting for Jane. . . .

First broadcast 7 April 1941; producer Eric Spear, written by Ernest Dudley.

Wallace

Usher at the Court of Nothing Common Place, Nether Backwash, presided over by MR MUDDLECOMBE, JP (ROBB WILTON). He punctuated the proceedings with the words, 'Argey-bargey, argey-bargey!', in fruity tones provided by Ernest Sefton.

Ward Sister

Margaret Lockwood played Sister Fairchild in this 'weekly serial of hospital life: drama, comedy, pathos, suspense, romance. A human story with human interest.' Written by Felicity Douglas; 28 episodes on RADIO LUXEMBOURG from 14 September 1958.

Warner, Jack

Wartime radio shot Jack to stardom when he played the cockney private in GARRISON THEATRE. His many catchphrases became national language: 'Mind my bike!', 'de-da-de-da!', 'Littel gel', and particularly 'Blue pencil!', the censored bits from his weekly letter from 'my bruvver Sid . . . P.S.'. Jack wrote all his own stuff, including the monologues 'Frank and his Tank', 'Claude and his Sword', 'Sea-lions and Sills', 'Walking Hup and Dahn the Rollway Laines', 'Funny Occupations' (the proper title of 'Bunger Upper Rat'oles'), 'My Bruvver in the Life Guards', and 'E Didn't Ortera Et It'. Earlier he had been half of the song-at-the-piano act, Warner and Darnell, later creating the comic character PROFESSOR SCHTOPUNDSCHTART. A completely different peacetime radio career followed from his playing of Joe Huggett in *Holiday Camp* and other films. As Joe in MEET THE HUGGETTS he had a nine-year run.

Jack **Warner**: the *Garrison Theatre* star

Warren, C. Denier

Comedy writer and performer forever typecast as a Yankee, thanks to his Chicago accent. He came to England with his parents, a double-act called Fish and Warren, in 1897, and an early concert party association with Harry S. Pepper led to a long radio partnership when 'Pep' brought his father's WHITE COONS to the microphone. This series, and the later KENTUCKY MINSTRELS, made 'Denny' a radio name through his byline, 'Book written and remembered by C. Denier Warren'. He played Mr, sometimes Professor, Bones, and gave a regular 'Stump Speech'. He was also Otis Harbottle in LIFE BEGINS AT SIXTY, another series he 'wrote and remembered'. The 'C' stood for Charles.

Was There Something?

SAM COSTA's catchphrase from MUCH-BINDING-IN-THE-MARSH served as the title for his RADIO LUXEMBOURG series, in which he visited listeners in their homes and played their choice of records. Sponsored by Bile Beans on Radio Luxembourg from 6 June 1954; produced by John Whitney; directed by Hugh Rennie.

Waterlogged Spa

This 'laughter resort for all' situated at Sinking-in-the-Ooze, was the demob version of MERRY-GO-ROUND which spun off into its own series from 17 September 1948. ERIC BARKER was the hesitant manager (and scriptwriter) assisted by secretary Pearl Hackney. JON PERTWEE played the POSTMAN and Wetherby Wett, Eric Woodburn was DR OLIVER DITHER and FLYING OFFICER KEEN ('I'm Mad Keen!'), and both played Du and Dai of the Secret Police. Richard Gray continued as LORD WATERLOGGED, and Sylvia Robin was the songbird, accompanied by George 'Hair' Crow and the Blue Mariners. Leslie Bridgmont continued to produce.

Waters, Elsie and Doris

Sister act who became better known as their radio characters, cockneys GERT AND DAISY. After studying piano, violin and elocution at the Guildhall School, they joined the family orchestra with brother JACK (WARNER). Elsie and Doris made their Concert Party début at Southwold in Will Pepper's WHITE COONS, and later joined the radio version of the show. Their radio début came in March 1927, and they

Elsie and Doris **Waters**: 'Gert and Daisy'

brought Gert and Daisy to radio in 1930. One of their great claims was that they never broadcast the same act or song twice. Main radio series: GERT AND DAISY'S WORKING PARTY (1948), PETTICOAT LANE (1949) and FLOGGIT'S (1956).

Way Out West

Johnny Denis and his Ranchers starred in this music-and-comedy series designed for the early morning entertainment of youngsters. Fred Yule was Panhandle, Graham Bailey was Willie, Gunsmoke was the pony and Judy the terrier. Also around were Netta Rogers and the Cactus Kids. Script by David Climie; produced by Glyn Jones; first broadcast 13 November 1949.

Wayne, Naunton, and Radford, Basil

Whilst their film billing was Basil Radford and Naunton Wayne, radio reversed the order, perhaps because Wayne was a regular solo broadcaster in his capacity as compère: CAP AND BELLS, etc. After a couple of serials in their cinematic characters of CHARTERS AND CALDICOTT, the writer-creators Frank Launder and Sidney Gilliat claimed their copyright, causing the BBC to devise new personas for this popular team. John Jowett wrote and Vernon Harris produced the serial *Double Bedlam* (1946) in which Wayne and Radford played Bentley Woolcott and Howard Spencer. This was followed in 1947 by *Traveller's Joy*, in which former film star Judy Kelly played Woolcott's wife, Sally. They changed names again for *Crime Gentlemen Please* (1948), an eight-part serial by Max Kester: Berkeley and Bulstrode. And they were Hargreaves and Hunter in Kester's *Having a Wonderful Crime* (1949). *That's My Baby* (1950), another Kester serial, identified them as Fanshawe and Fothergill, but the next year's serial, *May I Have the Treasure*, found them back as Woolcott and Spencer, perhaps because Jowett was once again the writer. Jowett not only wrote, he narrated their 1952 adventure, *Rogues' Gallery*. It was their last: Radford's terminal illness meant Wayne ended the adventure alone.

Wayne, Women and Song
NAUNTON WAYNE ('Nonchalent Nonsense') in a cabaret entertainment devised by Henry Sherek; dialogue by Max Kester; producer Eric Spear. The 2 January 1941 edition also starred Magda Kun, Inga Anderson, and Flotsam and Jetsam.

We Beg to Differ
One of the many popular panel games of the period, this set women against men in 'a lively discussion on subjects upon which the sexes may disagree'. The original teams (23 September 1949) were Kay Hammond (of the deliciously plummy voice), Joyce Grenfell, Charmian Innes, an acid comedienne, and Gladys Young ('the First Lady of Radio Drama'), versus John Clements (Miss Hammond's hubby) and his guest of the week, the Radio Doctor (Charles Hill). Roy Plomley was in the chair, and the deviser-producer was Pat Dixon. Another popular husband-and-wife team featured in the 1966 series, BERNARD BRADEN AND BARBARA KELLY. The chairman by then was Michael Smee.

We Bring You a Love Song
Denny Dennis and Esther Coleman sang, with Jack Wilson and his Versatile Five. Neal Arden compèred this series broadcast from 7 February 1939 on RADIO LUXEMBOURG, courtesy of Turog Bread.

We're in Business
Peter Jones returned as his IN ALL DIRECTIONS character, DUDLEY GROSVENOR, this time in harness with Harry Worth. Also involved were Paddy Edwards, Betty Marsden and Harry Locke. Script by Jones with George Wadmore; producer Charles Maxwell. Started 3 April 1959 and returned on 19 February 1960 with Irene Handl as the landlady, Jubilee Boot, and Dick Emery, with Marty Feldman helping Jones on the script.

Weatherby Wett
Chapel Organist at Sinking-in-the-Ooze and determined wooer of LORD WATERLOGGED's daughter, the Honourable Pheeb. Made a weekly presentation of a blood red pe-o-ny nurtured in his window-box! Played by JON PERTWEE in MERRY-GO-ROUND (1946).

Wedding Bells
Mervyn Johns, Welsh character actor in many a British film, compèred this series of listeners' real life stories, romantic memories, and the tunes associated with them, as well as a full-length dramatized story – again a true romance, of course. Every story read out on the programme won a guinea, with five guineas for the week's best. What's more, every letter received was guaranteed a personal reply from Mervyn Johns! Presented by Kolynos Denture Fixative on RADIO LUXEMBOURG from 1 April 1952. Announced by Ric Hutton, written by Tommy Twigge, and produced by Eric Goldschmidt.

The Weekly Bind
Newspaper published at MUCH-BINDING-IN-THE-MARSH. Prudence Gush, the radio critic, was SAM COSTA while Dora Bryan played Gladys Plumb, fashion editress.

Welcome 'All
'Oh we're going to Welcome 'All, welcome all . . .' sang the audience at this weekly concert from an imaginary village hall. Master of Ceremonies was Farmer Will Watchet (Hugh Morton), interrupted by Dan Young and Dorothy Summers ('You blowsy old faggot!'). Music by CHARLES SHADWELL and the Variety Orchestra; producer Harry S. Pepper. Weekly from 1 October 1941, with a second series of 26 shows from 31 April 1942.

Welsh Rarebit
Long-running magazine programme emanating from Wales in wartime. 'A unique programme of variety and topicalities', it was first broadcast on 29 February 1940. Wynford Vaughan-Thomas compered such items as 'Gossip Corner', 'The Young Idea', 'This Week's Visitor', and 'A New Welsh Song'. As the war wore on this show proved a valuable link with home for Welsh servicemen, and

features included 'They Can't Stop Us Singing' with Tudor Davies; 'Dai's Letter to the Forces'; and 'The Adventures of TOMMY TROUBLE' by and with E. Eynon Evans. Mai Jones produced and wrote the signature song, which is still sung:

> We'll keep a welcome in the hillsides,
> We'll keep a welcome in the vales,
> This land you know will still be singing,
> When you come home again to Wales . . .

In peacetime the series changed to become a 60-minute variety show, beginning 8 April 1949. 'Tommy Trouble' was still at it, and stars included David Lloyd, Maudie Edwards, Albert and Les Ward, the Harmoniacs, the Girls in Harmony, and the Lyrian Singers.

Wendy Warren and the News
Adventures of a girl reporter (plus a novel competition with valuable prizes) presented by Bird's Custard on RADIO LUXEMBOURG from September 1952. The cast was anonymous but the signature tune was called 'Leading Lady'.

The Western Brothers
'Good evening, cads, your better selves are with you once again!' was the traditional greeting drawled by Kenneth while brother George (actually cousin George) tinkled the jolly old joanna. They closed with 'Cheerio, cads, and happy landings!' during Word War II, and after with 'Do look after yourselves, there are very few of us left, you know!'. George was the pianist for THE ROOSTERS and thus broadcast early, not encountering cousin Ken until 1925, when the latter's writing talent encouraged the two to team up. Immaculate monocled cabaret stars they first broadcast in 1930, their topical lyrics making an immediate appeal. Songs included 'The Old School Tie' (colours Egg, Green and Egg), 'Play the Game You Cads', and the delightful BBC burlesques, 'We're Frightfully BBC' and 'Oh Dear What Can the Matter Be, No-one to Read Out the News'. Motto: 'Pro Bono Public-houso'.

The Western Trail
'The Texas Tiger' was one of the episodes in this 'thrill-packed half-hour bringing you true stories of men and women of the Wild West.' Producer, Joy Sharpen; RADIO LUXEMBOURG from 2 April 1959.

Whack-O
The first sign of radio's decline, an adaptation for sound of a successful television series. JIMMY EDWARDS repeated his performance as headmaster of Chislebury School, supported by Arthur Howard as Mr Pettigrew. Joan Young was the Matron and Deryck Guyler the Inspector. Adapted by David Climie from the television scripts of FRANK MUIR AND DENIS NORDEN. Producer Edward Taylor; first broadcast 23 May 1961. The second series introduced Roddy Maude-Roxby as Aubrey Potter and Frederick Treves as Mr J. St.L. Dimwiddie.

What a Life!
Ken Dodd starred in this 'story of the Nut from Knotty Ash', with Eddie Leslie, Irene Handl, Herbert Smith, Fred Fairclough, and the Northern Dance Orchestra conducted by Alyn Ainsworth. Written by Frank Roscoe and James Casey. First broadcast 16 April 1957.

What Do You Know
'A programme of problems and brain-teasers devised for your entertainment' by John P. Wynn, originally in two parts: 'Beat the Experts' and 'Ask Me Another'. Franklin Engelmann chaired both, and Dilys Powell, Ivor Brown and Christopher Cummings formed the panel; first broadcast 2 August 1953. Producer Joan Clark gradually turned this into the 'BRAIN OF BRITAIN' (prize, a diploma). The 300th show was broadcast on 2 May 1963, by when Wynn had set 25,000 questions. It included a feature called 'Ten Years Back' with ANONA WINN and Lionel Hale. The series ran to 16 July 1967, whereafter it was known as *Brain of Britain*.

There was an earlier series called *What Do You Know* which started on 27 January 1951. This was a transatlantic quiz between American and British Universities, and began with those of Boston and London. LIONEL GAMLIN was question-master.

What Ho There!
Revue following on from HOWDY FOLKS, starring NAN KENWAY AND DOUGLAS YOUNG, Frederick Burtwell, Reginald Purdell, Bruce Winston, Clarence Wright and Helen Clare, with the Revue Orchestra conducted by CHARLES SHADWELL. Written by Douglas Young and ERIC BARKER; producer Leslie Bridgmont. Weekly from 18 November 1941.

What's My Line?

The first radio version of a television panel game, sponsored on RADIO LUXEMBOURG by Beecham's Pills. 'Question and Quip Master' was BERNARD BRADEN, and the panel attempting to identify the strange occupations of the contestants were Elizabeth Allan, Jerry Desmonde, Margot Holden and Robert Beatty. It started 1 December 1952 and returned on 6 June 1954 with a new chairman, Peter Martyn, a new panel – Barbara Kelly, Isobel Barnett, David Nixon and Richard Attenborough – and a new sponsor, Kellogg's Corn Flakes. Peter Wilson produced. The 1955 series had Roy Rich as chairman, and on the panel ANONA WINN, Frank Owen, Barnett and Nixon. The sponsor was Aspro and the producer Biddy Martin.

What's Yours?

'A lightning programme of artists' devised and written by Ernest Longstaffe and introduced by Janet Lind. Al and Bob Harvey (Our Two Canadian Pals), Arthur Sandford (solo pianoforte), Bruce Green (The Essence of a Lady), Alf Lewis and Leslie Urrell (Trumpet Duettists), Sidney Burchall (baritone), John Warren (comedian), and the Variety Orchestra. From 23 February 1940 on the FORCES PROGRAMME.

When You and I Were Dancing

'A series of musical recollections': famous husbands and wives dance through the years to Dave Frost and his Band, with singers Helen Clare and Len Arthur. BBC NATIONAL, presented by Dave Frost during 1939.

When You're Smiling

Larry Cross was the Canadian host of this amateur talent show which toured the Butlin's Holiday Camps for RADIO LUXEMBOURG, commencing 10 June 1956 at the Butlin's Camp in Clacton. Pye Radio sponsored, and Geoffrey Bellman produced for Ross Radio Productions.

Where Are You Now

'Have you lost touch with old friends, neighbours, workmates or comrades in the forces? WILFRED PICKLES would like to help you bring about a reunion by telling your story and playing a record.' Weekly from 2 October 1958.

Whippit Kwick

Cat burglar, whose Amazing Adventures were retailed weekly in STAND EASY (1946). Created by Cheerful CHARLIE CHESTER and played by Ken Morris with a musical call-sign: 'Who said that?' (whistle) 'Whippit Kwick!' His partner-in-crime was Ray Ling the Chinese fence, played by Arthur Haynes. Louise Gainsborough was Ann Cuff the burglar's moll, and others in the cast included Humpty Gocart the gangster, Carrie Oka the native lovely, and Cutta Lumpoff the head-hunter!

The White Coons

'Come on and listen to the Gay White Coons' was the rather dated signature song of this series. Originally a seaside concert party founded by Will C. Pepper, it was adapted and produced for radio by his son, Harry S. Pepper. The first broadcast (31 August 1932) introduced ELSIE AND DORIS WATERS ('Gert and Daisy'), Jane Carr (soubrette), WYNNE AJELLO (soprano), Paul England and C. DENIER WARREN (comedians), Joe Morley (banjo), and 'Pep' himself with his wife, DORIS ARNOLD, at the pianos. Later broadcasts featured TOMMY HANDLEY, Stanley Holloway, and others. A junior version appeared in CHILDREN'S HOUR with Handley as the headmaster of St Basil's and England with his catchphrase: 'Yes sir, no sir, please sir!'

The White Coons: produced by Harry Pepper

Who's Who

Another panel game: 'A guessing game of wit and knowledge between the Gentlemen and the Players.' Lionel Hale was question-master, and the panellists were Paul Dehn, GILBERT HARDING, Robert MacDermot, Denis Brogan and Diana Morgan. First broadcast 12 February 1950.

The Whoopee Club

'Radio jollificasion' with a different dance band every week. The first show, broadcast 3 January 1942, featured BILLY COTTON and his Band, with Alan Breeze, Dolly Elsie, and the Greene Sisters. Also included was 'Jazz Novelette' (a serial story in song) with singers Helen Clare and Bernard Hunter. Produced and compèred by Philip Brown.

Whose Baby Are You?

Panel game in which the children of well-known people challenge the panel to find out who their father and mother is. The original panel was Ethel REVNELL, Bill Jupe, Sheila Van Damm the racing-driver, and singer Betty Driver. Jimmy Hanley was the chairman and Lewis Flander the Mystery Voice. Devised by Keith Fell and Phil Tate; producer Alastair Scott Johnston; first broadcast 15 June 1965 (and still a popular series on television).

Will Hay Programme

After a pilot programme, *The Diary of a Dominie*, broadcast on 21 July 1944, the

Will Hay Programme: cigarette card

popular stage and film comedian Will Hay began a regular radio series from 18 August 1944, under the subtitle 'The Diary of a Schoolmaster'. Unable through ill-health to pursue his cinema career, Hay quickly shot to the top as a radio favourite, in the role of bumbling DR MUFFIN. The series, devised by Hay and scripted by Max Kester and Con West with Alick Hayes as producer, fell into two halves. The first dealt with Dr Muffin's relationships with his housekeeper Mrs Potts (Beryl Riggs) and her son Alfie (Clarence Wright). The second half of each show was a school scene, inspired by Hay's famous stage and screen characterizations. Charles Hawtrey was the rude, smart-alecky Smart; John Clark was D'Arcy, the know-all, and Billy Nicholls was Beckett, the ancient youth cast in the Moore Marriott mould. Signature tune, 'Boys and Girls Come Out to Play', played by Stanley Black and the Dance Orchestra. A second series ran from 20 December 1944, and a special, *Victory at St Michael's*, on 11 May 1945.

William MacGoonigall

Long-winded Scots poet and tragedian based on the long-winded Scots poet, William McGonagall. Opened many a GOON SHOW from his first appearance on 2 December 1952, setting the scene with his moans of 'Ohhhhh . . .'. Played by both PETER SELLERS and SPIKE MILLIGAN, according to fancy.

The William Hill Show

William Hill was not the star, but the sponsor (a bookmaker). This was the first major series of sponsored programmes broadcast on RADIO LUXEMBOURG after its wartime closure. Stars included ARTHUR ASKEY, Max Miller, Tommy Trinder, and Billy Ternent and his Orchestra. Derek Faraday, who would shortly launch Star Sound Studios, recorded the programmes in the Rudolf Steiner Hall.

Williams, Kenneth

Creative 'funny voice' man, latterly the outrageously uninhibited panellist of JUST A MINUTE. Williams came out of revue to radio; his ingratiating SNIDE on HANCOCK'S HALF HOUR (1955) remains immortal, from his 'Good evenin'' to his 'No, stop messin' about!'. Equally immortal are Kenneth's creations for BEYOND OUR KEN (1958), the gay Rodney, the earthy ARTHUR FALLOWFIELD, and the nameless dotard given to reminiscing 'Thirty-five years!' ROUND THE HORNE (1965) continued the gay parade with Sandy, as well as J. PEASEMOLD GRUNTFUTTOCK, and RAMBLING SYD RUMPO with his 'Cheerio, my dearios!'.

Willium

Constabule Willium 'Mate' Cobblers, elderly Londoner and ex-tea boy (unpaid), as likely to turn up as a rag-and-bone man as a policeman, although everyone is a 'mate' to him. Played by PETER SELLERS in THE GOON SHOW from 2 October 1953.

Winifred Atwell Show

Trinidad's Queen of the Keyboard hammered out the hits supported by Geoff Love and his Music, with Teddy Johnson and Pearl Carr to sing the words. Recorded with a live audience in various venues (the Town Hall, Wembley, was the first on 16 September 1956), with 'wonderful prizes given away each week'. Produced by Peter Pritchett-Brown for Curry's Cycle and Radio Stores; announcer Gordon Davies.

Winifred Atwell Show: 'the Black and White Rag'

Wilton, Robb

One of the masters of radio comedy, hilarious but human as the befuddled MR MUDDLE-COMBE JP in many series. On the stage from an unbelievable 1899, he turned funny in 1903, presenting a long series of sketches with his distraught wife, Florence Palmer. These included 'The Police Station', 'The Fire Station' and the one which led to Muddlecombe, 'The Magistrate'. A lugubrious Liverpudlian, he contributed to the National phrasebook when he coined 'The day war broke out . . .'.

Anona **Winn**: singer, dance-band leader, impressionist, panellist

Winn, Anona

Versatile vocalist, expert impressionist, and Queen of the Panel Games. Born in Australia, Anona gave up the law for studying singing at Dame Nellie Melba's Conservatoire, coming to England for *The Blue Mazurka* at Daly's. She first broadcast in June 1928 in *Fancy Meeting You*, and 16 SONGS FROM THE SHOWS. By 1934 she had clocked up 300 broadcasts, written songs ('What More Can I Ask'), and fronted her own dance band, Anona Winn and her Winners. Her post-war triumphs stemmed from TWENTY QUESTIONS (1947): she devised and chaired PETTICOAT LINE (1965).

Winners

One of the first radio series, *Winners* was an hour and a half of best-selling songs and melodies, produced by R.E. Jeffrey and first heard on 29 May 1925. The Wireless Orchestra

Maurice **Winnick** and his orchestra

and Chorus accompanied such singers as George Pizzey, Rita Page, Patrick Ludlow, Raymond Trafford and Joan Hay. Later shows followed themes, such as Music Hall and Musical Comedy Memories.

Winnick, Maurice

Saxophonist and violinist who began broadcasting with his Piccadilly Hotel Band in 1931. His signature tune changed from 'Lend Me Your Ear' to 'The Sweetest Music This Side of Heaven'. Similarly, his career changed, too. After World War II he became the leading packager of programmes for radio, and the phrase 'By arrangement with Maurice Winnick' was heard in connection with TWENTY QUESTIONS, IGNORANCE IS BLISS, THE NAME'S THE SAME, and on TV, WHAT'S MY LINE. His dance-band vocalists included Al Bowlly, Harry Bentley, SAM COSTA, Judy Shirley, VERA LYNN, Hughie Diamond, and Ronnie Odell.

Winnie the Pooh

A.A. Milne's famous teddy bear of little brain, played by Norman Shelley in many CHILDREN's HOUR series. In *The House at Pooh Corner*, beginning 22 April 1940, John Rorke played Piglet, Geoffrey Wincott Eeyore the donkey, and Robert Holland Christopher Robin, the human hero. The special music was by H. Fraser-Simson, and UNCLE MAC (Derek McCulloch) narrated the adaptations by DAVID (W.E. Davis), who also played the piano. In later series, casts varied: in 1949 Christopher Robin was played by Sheila Maloney, and David became the Narrator. Lionel Stevens played Piglet. The signature tune was Pooh singing 'How Sweet to be a Cloud'.

Winter Sunshine

'A few ultra-violet rays supplied by' gravel voiced cockney SYD WALKER and velvet-voiced singer Adelaide Hall, with the Revue Chorus and Dance Orchestra, conductor Billy Ternent. First broadcast 23 November 1943, produced and introduced by Jimmy Dyrenforth.

Wireless Licence

Nobody was supposed to listen to the radio until they had bought a Wireless Licence from the local Post Office, price ten shillings. The first went on sale on 1 November 1922, and by the end of the year 35,777 had been sold. The rise of radio was rapid: 595,496 licences by 31 December 1923, 1,129,578 by 1924, 2,178,259 by 1926. The three-million mark was reached in 1930, four million by 1931, five million by 1932, and nine million by 1939. There were ten million licenced listeners in 1946 and eleven million by 1947. The low cost of listening was celebrated by NORMAN LONG in his song, 'All For Ten Shillings a Year'.

Wireless Publicity

Production company set up by RADIO LUXEM-BOURG in 1936 to make sponsored programmes for broadcasting to Britain. General manager was Montague Skitt, operating from Electra House on the Victoria Embankment, and the company's first announcer was Ogden Smith. Their first rate card quoted £75 per 200-word commercial. The company became Radio Luxembourg London in 1954.

The Wireless Puppets

Periodical radio revue commencing 16 October 1936, written and devised by the theatrical producer, Lauri Wylie. No. 1 starred Caryll and Mundy, ARTHUR ASKEY, Fred Yule, Dick Francis, Marjorie Lotinga (later Sandford), Clarence Wright, and the Variety Orchestra conducted by CHARLES SHADWELL. Producer Max Kester.

Wireless Willie

One of the first comedy characters created for radio: William Rouse (Entertainer) who broadcast frequently from 24 January 1924. He also chaired the VETERANS OF VARIETY shows from 31 July.

The Wisk Half Hour

Gracie Fields starred in this Sunday series sponsored by Lever Bros, makers of Wisk, broadcast from Luxembourg from 1950. BER-NARD BRADEN compèred, and the Keynotes also sang, backed by Billy Ternent and his Orchestra. Braden was later replaced by Gerry Wilmot, another Canadian, and the regular announcer was Russell Napier. Producer, John Watt. In 1952 the title was changed to The Gracie Fields Show and on February 3 it was presented before a service audience 'some-where in Germany'. Produced by Gordon Crier.

With a Smile and a Song (1)

Title of one of the songs in Snow White and the Seven Dwarfs, used as the title for a bi-weekly broadcast starring Anne Ziegler and Webster Booth. James Dyrenforth linked favourite songs with 'a charming story of young love', on behalf of Persil the Amazing Oxygen Washer (29 August 1938).

With a Smile and a Song (2)

The BBC used this same title for Anne Shelton's series starting 30 October 1946. Anne sang, while Neal Arden acted as her escort. Stanley Black conducted the Augmented Dance Orchestra, and Peter Duncan produced.

The Wobbleton Wheelers

'A Reveucycle Show' written by producer Ernest Longstaffe, with MABEL CONSTAN-DUROS. The first programme was called The Wednesday Wheelers and was broadcast on 12 September 1945. John Rorke played 'Arry, Tommy Brandon Tommy, Clarence Wright Clarry, Bettie Bucknelle Betty, Dick Francis Major Puffin, and MABEL CONSTANDUROS Miss Spoonbrake. 'Guests on a tandem' were Nat Mills and Bobbie, with 'standard equipment' by the Four Clubmen and the Revue Orchestra. See also GOOD PULL-UP FOR CYCLISTS.

Woman's Hour

Billed as 'a daily programme of music, advice and entertainment for the home', this long-running (still-running) series started on the LIGHT PROGRAMME on 7 October 1946. The first presenter was a man, Alan Ivimey, described as a London-born journalist and ex-RAF Intelligence Officer who specialized in writing and talking to women. First-day features included 'Mother's Mid-Day Meal' by Mary Marton, 'Putting Your Best Foot For-ward' by Kay Beattie, 'Housewife's Choice' of gramophone records, and Part 1 of a serial reading, Stanley Weyman's Under the Red Robe. The first programme was listened to by a special review panel consisting of Margaret Bondfreed, MP, Deborah Kerr, film star, and Mrs Elsie May Crump, housewife, of Chorlton-cum-Hardy. They reported their reactions on the second programme. The first regular female introducer was Joan Griffiths, who took over the programme from 1 January 1946. By the 1000th programme, celebrated on 28 April 1950, the presenter was Olive Shapley. The signature tune was the Overture to 'The Merry Wives of Windsor' by Nicolai.

Women at War

Weekly magazine programme for the WRNS, the ATS and the WAAF, including 'Wartime Confessions' of stage and screen stars; 'Beauty in Battledress' from Civvy Street to Barrack Square; 'The Editors' Own Column' of news and gossip; 'Many Questions', a weekly meeting of the Brainstormer Trust, chairman Roy Rich; CARROLL GIBBONS and his Band with commère, Elizabeth Cowell. Contributors: Audrey Lucas, Jenny Nichols and Robert MacDermot; editors: Archie Campbell and Janet Anstey. From 1 December, also featured was Arthur Ferrier's radio strip cartoon: 'Jill of All Trades', played by Kay Hammond.

The Wonder Hour

2.30 to 3.30 every weekday afternoon from Monday 3 October 1938 was designated RADIO LUXEMBOURG's Wonder Hour. Four quarter-hour programmes, three of them soap operas.

> BACKSTAGE WIFE (Dr Lyons' Tooth Powder)
> YOUNG WIDOW JONES (Milk of Magnesia)
> SWEETEST LOVE SONGS EVER SUNG (Dental Magnesia)
> STELLA DALLAS (California Syrup of Figs)

'Four great shows in succession, with all the pathos, drama, love and excitement of life itself. It is your chance to enjoy the wonderful entertainment wireless offers you. Don't miss it!'

Woodbine Quiz Time

The small cigarettes sponsored this RADIO LUXEMBOURG series of 'a new and different quiz game' compèred by Gerry Wilmot. The Stargazers starred; started 4 January 1959.

Workers' Playtime

Wartime series of lunch-time entertainments for factory workers, broadcast direct from factories 'somewhere in England'. Beginning as a Saturday show on 24 May 1941, it moved up to thrice-weekly from 28 October, when the first of the new series was introduced by the Minister of Labour, Ernest Bevin. Regular compère was Bill Gates, and Jack Clarke and George Myddleton were at the pianos. Favourite and most frequent stars: ELSIE AND DORIS WATERS as 'Gert and Daisy'. Producers Michael North and Glyn Jones. The Fifth Birthday Show broadcast 6 June 1946 starred Elsie and Doris of course, but for the occasion their brother, comedian JACK WARNER, shared the spotlight. The special one-hour edition came from a canteen in Coventry and included Harry Lester and his Hayseeds. Producers John Inglis and Bryan Sears. The 21st birthday

Workers' Playtime: Bill Gates the long-standing compère

show (broadcast from a telephone-cable factory at Dagenham on 23 October 1962) still top-billed Elsie and Doris, supported by Peter Goodwright, Eve Boswell, and James Moody at the piano.

The last show came from a corrugated-case manufacturers at Hatfield Heath on 6 October 1964. Bill Gates introduced Anne Shelton, CYRIL FLETCHER, Val Doonican, the Four Pickles, and Harold Smart at the Organ. But it was only a title change to suit the times: see VARIETY ON TOUR.

Works Wonders

Wartime series of mid-day programmes staged in factory canteens, broadcast from November 1940. Described as 'A lunch-time concert presented to their fellow workers by members of the staff of a large munition works "somewhere in England". Arranged by Victor Smythe.'

The World and His Wife

Peter Watson introduced this series of weekly magazine programmes with features on Hobbies, Fashion, True Stories of Adventure, Popular Science, Queer Characters, Sport, Flying and Behind the Names. No. 1 included

'Filming Radar for the RAF' by J.R.F. Stewart; 'Bats I Have Known' by Brian Vesey-Fitzgerald; 'Dangerous Dressing' by a French fashion commentator; 'The True Ghost Story of a Strange House' by Walter Palmer; and MacDonald Hastings in 'Low Company' (21 January 1946).

The World Goes By
A mid-week variation of IN TOWN TONIGHT in which FREDERICK GRISEWOOD 'brings to the microphone people in the news, people talking about the news, and interesting visitors to Britain'. Devised by John Pringle in 1936.

Worzel Gummidge
Almost human scarecrow featured in many CHILDREN'S HOUR adaptations of the stories by Barbara Euphan Todd. The first story, 'The Scarecrow of Scatterbrooke', was broadcast in 1935, and revived on 7 October 1950. Philip Wade played Worzel, although others also took the part, including Norman Shelley (1947). Earthy Mangold was played by MABEL CONSTANDUROS, and Aunt Sally by Gladys Young.

Wot Cheor Geordie!
Lively, local variety series: 'Music and Mirth in the Tyneside Manner'. Cecil McGivern's early production on 21 August 1940 featured Charlton and Batey, Jack Dalziel, and Joseph Q. Atkinson and his Quintet, introduced by playwright Esther McCracken. Richard Kelly produced the post-war series, with Esther McCracken introducing Owen Brannigan, Frank Burns and the Northumbrian Serenaders who sang the signature song, 'Wherever Ye Gang Ye're Sure to Find a Geordie' accompanied by Willie Walker and his Band. By 1955 Lilian Chalmers was the hostess, Bobby Thompson a regular comedian, and Lisle Willis scripted the weekly crosstalk between Septimus and the Squire (Gilbert Scott and Chislett Ging). Tom Coyne compèred the 1956 series, with the Newcastle Ladies' Choir and the close-harmony of the Barry Sisters. Broadcast from various venues via the North of England Home Service.

Write a Tune for £2000
Hugely successful competition for would-be composers, with £1000 (a vast sum for the period) as top prize, and £1000 divided among the runner-ups. The money was provided by the Hammersmith Palais de Danse (despite all BBC strictures against sponsored radio!), and the tunes played by Lou Preager and his Orchestra. Singers were Paul Rich, Lynne Shaw and Rita Carr. The series was broadcast direct from the famous Palais, and ran for 17 weeks, from 30 July 1945. Listeners at home were the judges, and the winner, picked from 73,852 entries was the old-fashioned waltz, 'Cruisin' Down the River', written by two elderly ladies, Nelly Tollerton and Eily Beadell. A second contest ran from 4 January 1947, hosted by Roy Rich within the series *Saturday Night at the Palais*. Signature song:

> Write a tune for a thousand pounds,
> That's all you have to do,
> Write a tune for a thousand pounds
> And the prize may come to you . . .

Write a Tune for £2000: the winner!

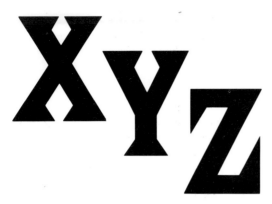

Yankee Doodle Doo!

Anglo-American variety series starring VIC OLIVER with Slim Allen, Leslie Mitchell and Billy Ternent conducting the Dance Orchestra. Features: 'Brothers in Arms', 'Salute with Music', and guest stars from both sides of the Atlantic. Script by American writer Hal Block; produced by Gordon Crier. Started 29 May 1943.

The Yes-No Interlude

Sequence in the popular RADIO FORFEITS quiz show in which compère MICHAEL MILES would fire rapid questions at his victims, who tried not to use the words 'yes' or 'no' in their answers – and invariably failed.

Yorky and Scotty

Double-act formed for radio and broadcast in MUSIC HALL from 1939. Yorky was Hal Jones, formerly of the *Splinters* concert party, and Scotty was Jock MacKay, also well known as a solo comedian.

You and I

Series starring a popular pair of performers, Petula Clark and Joe 'Mr Piano' Henderson with his Quintet. Introduced by Stephen Miller on behalf of the Cooperative Permanent Building Society. Script by Hector Stewart and Nat Lamont; producer John Whitney. On RADIO LUXEMBOURG from 6 October 1955.

You Lucky Customers

Tommy Trinder called on lucky listeners, cracking gags and awarding prizes, in this RADIO LUXEMBOURG series broadcast from 11 April 1960.

You Lucky People

Tommy Trinder's popular catchphrase formed the title of this series in which the comedian invited the studio audience to 'Beat the Band'. If Norrie Paramor and his Orchestra failed to play the requested tune, there was a prize in store. Produced by Geoffrey Everitt and broadcast from RADIO LUXEMBOURG from 1 September 1955. See also TOMMY TAKES A CHANCE.

You're Only Young Once

First radio series for Eric Morecambe and Ernie Wise, 'who invite you to make the best of things' with Pearl Carr (as their scatty secretary), Deryck Guyler (as their office-boy) and Robert Beatty (their first guest star). Each week a star guest brought another baffling case to the Morecambe and Wise Detective Agency. Alyn Ainsworth conducted the Northern Variety Orchestra, the Three Imps sang, and John Ammonds produced the scripts by Frank Roscoe, Eric and Ernie. First broadcast 6 May 1954.

The Young Idea

Popular (in Ireland) Irish series starring Irish comedian James Young, with Patricia Stewart, Bridie Warde, Patricia McAlinney, tenor Frank Lloyd, and the Kordites, with the BBC Northern Ireland Light Orchestra, conductor David Curry. Script by Michael Bishop and Jack Hudson, producer Sam Denton (1951).

Young Lady at Large

Musical adventure serial created for Jessie Matthews by Jenny Nicholson, with music by Kenneth Leslie-Smith. Miss Matthews bowed out at the last moment, and her role of Carol was taken over by Gabrielle Brune. Betty Astell played Topsy, Billy Milton was Danny, and Frederick Burtwell Felix. Producer Gordon Crier. Weekly from 19 November 1940.

Young Widow Jones

'The moving human story of a woman's heart and woman's love. Living in the small town of Appleton, Peggy Jones, in her twenties, with two children to support, ponders long on the question of what she owes to her children and what she owes to herself. A story of joy and despair, life and love as we all know it.' Presented by Milk of Magnesia on RADIO LUXEMBOURG, daily 3 October 1938.

Your Mother's Birthday

Godfrey Winn, a favourite columnist in women's magazines, presented this series of records chosen for mothers whose birthdays fell during the week, which was 'offered by the makers of Knight's Family Health Soap' over RADIO LUXEMBOURG from 1951. Each week Stephen Grenfell interviewed a housewife to talk about her daily life, and the mothers featured on the show received a birthday card and 'a lovely bouquet of roses'.

Your Music Shop

JACK JACKSON was 'at your service behind the counter of your favourite record shop' in this RADIO LUXEMBOURG series produced by Geoffrey Everitt and broadcast from 7 June 1954. As the sponsors were Decca Records the selection was somewhat limited.

Your Old Friend Dan

'Rise and shine, life's what you make it' was the signature song of Your Old Friend Dan, who brought you songs, music and philosophy on behalf of Johnson's Wax Polish. Dan's real name was Lyle Evans; he was a Canadian who began broadcasting from RADIO NORMANDY on 4 September 1936.

Your Picture Show

Diana Coupland and Robert Earl sang songs from the films, accompanied by the Jackie Brown Orchestra, in this RADIO LUXEMBOURG series sponsored by the Amalgamated Press, publishers of *Picture Show* magazine. Weekly from 3 March 1956.

Your Sunday Valentine

Romantic songs from Denis Lotis, plus country-western from Johnny Duncan and his Blue Grass Boys, and music by Jackie Brown and his Orchestra. Sponsored by *Valentine*, a comic for girls; RADIO LUXEMBOURG from 8 September 1957.

Youth Takes a Bow

JACK HYLTON devised this series-within-a-series to bring new talent to the MONDAY NIGHT AT SEVEN microphone in 1938. BRYAN MICHIE compèred, and did the same when the show was elaborated into a variety tour in 1939. Notable for the discovery of the young Master Ernie Wise, who sang 'Let's Have a Tiddley at the Milk Bar'.

The Zoo Man

David Seth-Smith, Curator of Birds and Mammals at the Regent's Park Zoo, who broadcast regularly in CHILDREN'S HOUR from 19 January 1934. The first Zoo Man had been Leslie Mainland (L.G.M. of the *Daily Mail*), who started his radio talks as early as 1924.

RADIO PICTORIAL

ABERDEEN 233·5

SCOTTISH 391·1
SCOTTISH NATIONAL 285·7

BELFAST 307

NEWCASTLE 267·4

ATHLONE 531

DUBLIN 222·6

NORTH 449·
NORTH NATIONA

NATIONAL (DROITWICH) 1500

MIDLAND 29

REGIONAL 342·1
LONDON NAT: 261·1

WEST 373·1 NAT: 261·1

PLYMOUTH 203·5   BOURNEMOUTH 2

NORMANDY 206

RADIO PARIS 1648
POSTE PARISIEN 312
PARIS P·T·T·431
EIFFEL TOWER 139

THIS Station Chart is a rapid wavelength guide to British and European transmitters as well as a simple index to the English programmes from leading Continental stations. Details of the British, Irish and Continental programmes are given every week in the "Radio Pictorial," Fridays, 3d.—full of pictures and stories of your radio favourites.